THE INVESTOR'S DICTIONARY

OTHER BOOKS BY THE AUTHOR

Automation, Manpower and Education

The Computer Prophets

The Death of Privacy: Do Industrial and Government Computers Threaten Our Personal Freedom?

Dictionary of Business and Management, 2nd edition

Dictionary of Banking and Financial Services, 2nd edition

Inside The Wall Street Journal: The History and Power of Dow Jones & Company and America's Most Influential Newspaper

Dictionary of Computers, Data Processing, and Telecommunications

THE INVESTOR'S DICTIONARY

Jerry M. Rosenberg, Ph.D.

Professor, Graduate School of Management
Chairman, Department of Business Administration
Faculty of Arts and Sciences
Rutgers University
Newark, New Jersey

JOHN WILEY & SONS

New York • Chichester • Brisbane • Toronto • Singapore

Library of Congress Cataloging-in-Publication Data:

Rosenberg, Jerry Martin.
The investor's dictionary.

1. Investments—Dictionaries. I. Title.

HG4513.R67 1986 332.6'03'21 86-4089
ISBN 0-471-83678-8
ISBN 0-471-84567-1 (pbk.)

Printed in the United States of America

10 9 8 7 6 5 4 3 2 1

To Ellen with love
an enchanting partner for 25 years,
5 dictionaries, 2500 pages, and 50,000 terms

To Ellen with love
an enchanting partner for 25 years,
5 dictionaries, 2500 pages, and 50,000 terms

PREFACE

The last decade has witnessed more significant changes in investment than any similar period in the past 50 years. Deregulation, tax law revisions, internationalization of markets, corporate mergers, and—most challenging—the widespread use of computers and sophisticated communications technology, have all altered the world of investing. Not only have these incredible advances led to an avalanche of new terminology, but, in a major way, they have encouraged redefinitions of standard words and phrases.

The elimination of fixed commission rates on security exchanges occurred on May 1, 1975 and the 1980 Depository Institutions Deregulation and Monetary Control Act introduced a period of deregulation and diversification that led the way for a host of new investment facilities and services. Federal tax acts between 1976 and 1985 have significantly altered the way we all have in the past, and will in the future, manage our money. These acts have introduced new opportunities for tax shelters and clamped down on past loopholes along with new techniques of investing for capital gains, income and retirement, and providing for heirs.

For the 42 million U.S. investors, old-line exchanges are facing new challenges. Worldwide, with 24-hour investment services utilizing computer and telecommunication systems, we will witness a growing range of investment alternatives by institutions competing for debt and equity capital in the international markets.

The *Investor's Dictionary* incorporates traditional terms used by the 190-year-old securities exchange system and the 140-year-old commodity and futures exchange system, and the more recent development in our financial markets. Innovations center on adaptations of standard instruments and markets in areas such as government securities and foreign exchange accompanied by a virtual explosion of essentially new investment instruments. Intense competition, by its very nature, will encourage further innovation, resulting in the ever-growing need to be aware of investment terminology.

This work of approximately 8000 entries has been prepared with the hope that awareness of the accepted meanings of terms may enhance the process of sharing information and ideas. Though it cannot eliminate the need for the user to determine how a writer or speaker treats a word, such a dictionary shows what usages exist. It should reduce arguments about words and assist in stabilizing terminology. Most important, it should aid people in saying and writing exactly what they intend with greater clarity.

A word can take on different meanings in different contexts. There may be as many meanings as there are areas of specialty. A goal of this dictionary is to be broad and to establish core definitions that represent the variety of individual meanings. My purpose is to enhance parsimony and clearness in the communication process.

Many terms are used in different ways. I have tried to unite them without bias of giving one advantage or dominance over another. Whenever possible (without creating a controversy), I have stated the connection among multiple usages.

Commonly used symbols, acronyms, and abbreviations are given. Foreign words and phrases are included only if they have become an integral part of our English vocabulary.

Other dictionaries that deal with a similar subject tend to define their task rather narrowly, whereas this work purports to reach throughout all departments within investment organizations, both private and public, by acknowledging that the sum of an organization is greater than any of its individual parts—the result, an all-inclusive dictionary of investing terms.

Among the numerous investing areas included in this dictionary are antiques, art, bank depositories and securities, bonds, collectibles, commodity markets, currency trading, debentures, diamonds, exchanges, futures, government issues, insurance, investment trusts, legislation, metals, mortgage-backed bonds, mutual funds, oil investments, pass-through securities, pension plans, real estate/property ownership, stocks, tax-exempt bonds, tax shelters, and venture capital.

ORGANIZATION

This is a defining work rather than a compilation of facts. The line is not easy to draw because in the final analysis meanings are based on facts. Consequently, factual information is used where necessary to make a term more easily understood.

All terms are presented in the language of those who use them. Obviously the level of complexity needed for a definition will vary with the user; one person's complexity is another's precise and parsimonious statement. Several meanings are sometimes given—relatively simple for the layperson, more developed and technical for the specialist.

I have organized the dictionary to provide information easily and rapidly. Keeping in mind two categories of user—the experienced person who demands precise information about a particular word, and the newcomer, support member, teacher, or student who seeks general explanations. I have in most cases supplied both general and specialized entries. This combination of "umbrella" entries and specialized definitions should make this dictionary an unusually useful reference source.

FORMAT

Alphabetization. Words are presented alphabetically. Compound terms are placed where the reader is most likely to look for them. They are entered under their most distinctive component, usually nouns, which tend to be more distinctive than are adjectives. Should you fail to locate a word where you initially look for it, turn to a variant spelling, a synonym, or another different word of the compound term.

Entries containing mutual concepts are usually grouped for comparison. They are then given in inverted order; that is, the expected order of word is reversed to allow the major word of the phrase to appear at the beginning of the term. These entries precede those that are given in the expected order. The terms are alphabetized up to the first comma and then by words following the comma, thus establishing clusters of related terms.

Headings. The current popular term is usually given as the principal entry, with other terms cross-referenced to it. Some terms have been included for historical significance, even though they are no longer in common use.

Cross-References. The rule followed for cross-references calls for going from the general to the specific. Occasionally, "see" references from the specific to the general are used to inform the user of words related to particular entries. "See" and "see also" references to currently accepted terminology are made wherever possible. The use of "cf." suggests words to be compared with the original entry.

Synonyms. The phrase "synonymous with" following a definition does not imply that the term is exactly equivalent to the principal entry under which it appears. Frequently the term only approximates the primary sense of the original entry.

Disciplines. Many words are given multiple definitions based on their utilization in various fields of activity. The definition with the widest application is then given first, with the remaining definitions listed by areas of specialty. Since the areas may overlap, the reader should examine all multiple definitions of a term.

JERRY M. ROSENBERG, Ph.D.

New York, New York
January 1986

ACKNOWLEDGMENTS

No dictionary can be the exclusive product of one person's effort. Even when written by one individual, such a work requires the tapping of many sources, which is especially true of this book. By the very nature of the fields included, I have had to rely on the able and extensive efforts of others.

As best I can discern, I have not deliberately quoted definitions from any copyrighted source. Any apparent similarity to existing, unreleased definitions in these cases is purely accidental and the result of the limitations of language.

Much assistance has come indirectly from authors of books, journal articles, and reference materials. They are too numerous to be named here. Various organizations have aided me directly by providing informative source materials. Some government agencies and not-for-profit associations have provided a considerable amount of usable information.

Stephen Kippur, executive publisher, and Nettie Bleich, my editor, both of John Wiley & Sons, have been enlightened professional supporters for this lexicon.

Ellen, my wife, and Lauren and Elizabeth, my daughters, continue to be my inspiration. Time away from them, whether spent researching an article or struggling with a complex term, is more than compensated by their affection.

Finally, to my reader—the ultimate jurist—I continue to seek your critical comments and urge you to bring errors and suggestions to my attention.

J. M. R.

THE INVESTOR'S DICTIONARY

A

A

(1) see *account.*

(2) includes Extra (or Extras) (in stock listings of newspapers.

(3) the quality rating for a municipal or corporate bond, lower than AA and higher than BBB.

(4) the total average dollar inventory.

A1: the highest class rating.

AA

(1) see *active account.*

(2) see *active assets.*

(3) the quality rating for a municipal or corporate bond, lower than AAA and higher than A.

AAA: the Standard & Poor's bond rating, given "only to bonds of the highest quality." Moody's grants a parallel Aaa rating.

AAA (Triple A) tenant: a well-known tenant, usually with a net worth in excess of a million dollars. If large and important, synonymous with *anchor.*

Aaa: see *AAA.*

AAD: see *at a discount.*

AAII: American Association of Individual Investors.

ABC Agreement: when buying a New York Stock Exchange seat, the applicant's membership can be bought by a member firm for his or her use with monies advanced by the member firm.

ability to pay

(1) ***general:*** the ability of a bank or financial organization's management to meet principal and interest payments on long-term obligations out of earnings. synonymous with *ability to service.*

(2) ***general:*** a borrower's capacity to pay back.

(3) ***taxation:*** a criterion used to ascertain who shall bear the cost of government programs; the rational for taxing individuals in the form of a progressive income tax.

(4) ***bonds:*** an issuer's present and future ability to generate sufficient tax revenue to meet its contractual

obligations, accounting for factors concerned with municipal income and property values.

ability to service: synonymous with *ability to pay* (1).

above par (value): the price of a stock or bond, higher than its face amount.

absolute priority rule: the concept that creditors' rights must be satisfied prior to stockholders' equities following liquidations or corporate reorganizations.

absolute title: a title without any conditions. An absolute title is usually critical to the granting of a mortgage by a bank.

absorb

(1) ***general:*** to merge by transfer all or portions of an account with another account, resulting in the loss of identity of the first account.

(2) ***general:*** to include pertinent actual costs in determining a price or standard cost.

(3) ***investments:*** to assimilate sell orders of stock with offsetting requests to buy.

absorbed: designates a security, no longer in the hands of an underwriter, and now with a shareholder.

absorption point: the point at which the securities market rejects further offerings unaccompanied by price concessions. see *digested securities, undigested securities.*

ABT: see *American Board of Trade.*

abusive tax shelter: a limited partnership that the IRS claims to be an illegal deduction as it inflates property values beyond their fair market value. Should such writeoffs be denied by the IRS, investors often pay significant penalties and interest charges, in addition to back taxes.

A/C: see *account.*

accelerated cost recovery system: see *ACRS.*

accelerated depreciation: depreciation at a larger than expected rate; makes the depreciation allowance, therefore the tax allowance, available sooner, resulting in a benefit to the owner.

acceptance house: an organization that specializes in lending funds on the security of bills of exchange or offers its name as an endorser to a bill drawn on another party.

account (A/C)

(1) ***general:*** an agreement between a buyer and seller under which payment is to be made at a future time.

(2) ***general:*** a record of all transactions and date of each, affecting a particular phase of a bank or financial institution, expressed in debits and credits, evaluated in money, and showing the current balance, if any. see *bank account.*

(3) ***investment banking:*** a financial and written arrangement between parties to an underwriting syndicate, or the status of stocks owned and sold.

(4) ***securities:*** an arrangement between a broker-dealer house and its client wherein the firm, through its registered representatives, serves as agent in purchasing and selling

stocks and sees to related administrative matters.

accountant: an individual engaged in accounting work. cf. *certified public accountant.*

accountant's certificate: see *accountant's opinion.*

accountant's opinion: a signed statement by an independent public accounting firm describing the scope of the examination of an organization's books and records. synonymous with *auditor's certificate.*

account balance: the net debit or net credit amount in a specific account in the ledger. An excess of total debits over total credits results in a debit balance, whereas an excess of total credits over total debits results in a credit balance.

account day: the day identified by stock and commodity exchanges for the settlement of accounts between members. synonymous with *settlement day.*

account executive: synonymous with *registered representative.*

accounting cycle: the series of accounting activities that occur from the commencement of an accounting period to the end of that period. The cycle begins with the determination of the account balance at the beginning of the period; then the effects of transactions occurring during the period are recorded, the records are closed, and financial statements for the period are prepared.

accounting period: the 12-month period used for keeping a taxpayer's records. When the accounting period ends other than in the month of December, a fiscal year is established. For income tax purposes a special 52–53-week accounting period is also acknowledged. cf. *fiscal year.*

accounting processes: the classification of accounts, accounting records, forms, procedures and controls through which changes in assets, liability, reserves, capital, income, and expense account transactions are generally recorded and controlled.

accounting rate of return: income for a period divided by the average investment that has occurred during that period.

accounting system: the total structure of records and procedures that discover, record, classify, and report information on the financial position and operations of a governmental unit or any of its funds, balanced account groups, and organizational components.

account sales: a record prepared by a broker, consignee, or other agent, indicating the proceeds of goods or securities purchased for the account of the owner.

account statement

(1) a summary statement of all transactions that shows the status of an account with a broker-dealer house, including long and short positions. These statements are issued quarterly, but when accounts are active more are usually issued monthly. (2) the option agreement required when an option account is opened.

accredited investor: a wealthy investor who does not count as one of the maximum of 35 people permitted to put funds into a private limited partnership. The SECs Regulation D states that in order to be accredited, an investor must have a net worth of at least $1 million, an annual income of at least $200,000, or must put at least $150,000 into the deal, and the investment cannot account for more than 20 percent of the investor's worth.

accreted value: the theoretical price of a bond if market interest rates were to remain unchanged.

accretion: a monthly increase in value for tax and accounting needs for adjusting the purchase price of an original-issue discounted bond so that the acquisition price will equal par value at maturity. cf. *amortization.*

accretion account: a record of the increase between the acquisition value and the face value of bonds purchased at a discount.

accrual basis: the basis of accounting under which revenues are recorded when earned and expenditures are recorded as soon as they result in liabilities for benefits received, notwithstanding that the receipt of the revenue or the payment of the expenditure may take place, in whole or in part, in another accounting period.

accrual of discount: the yearly addition to book value of bonds that have been bought below par. see *amortization.*

accrued dividend: the customary regular dividend considered to be earned but not declared or payable on legally issued stock or other instruments of part ownership of a legally organized business or financial institution.

accrued expenses: expenses that are recognized by a firm prior to that firm's disbursement of cash. Accrued expenses arise when a company has used goods or services before it has paid for them.

accrued income: income earned (e.g., commissions or interest on notes receivable) but not received.

accured income receivable: income earned but not yet received.

accrued interest (AI): a bond's accumulated interest made since the last interest payment. The purchaser of the bond pays the market price plus accrued interest. Bonds that are in default and income bonds are exceptions. see *flat.*

accrued interest payable: interest accumulated on an indebtedness (e.g., time deposits or borrowed money) but not yet paid.

accrued interest receivable: interest earned by a bank but not yet collected.

accrued liabilities: liabilities arising from expenses that have been incurred but have not yet been paid. Accrued liabilities are the counterpart of prepaid expenses.

accrued taxes and interest: money set aside to pay taxes and interest incurred but not yet paid.

accumulate: a purchase by traders who hope to retain the contracts for a more or less extended period.

accumulated distribution: the income received by a trust for later distribution. The income is taxed to the beneficiaries in the year when the trust receives the income rather than when it is distributed.

accumulated dividend: a dividend not paid when due. The dividend is expected to be paid at a later time, but it becomes a business liability until payment.

accumulated profit tax: a tax penalty directed at corporations that avoid announcing dividends to reduce stockholders' declarations of additional income.

accumulated surplus: a corporation's excess of profits that are either reinvested or held.

accumulation

(1) ***general:*** adding income from dividends, interest, and other sources to the principal amount of a fund, and the treatment of such additions as capital.

(2) ***investments:*** the deliberate, well-controlled assembling of blocks of stock without necessarily bidding up prices.

(3) ***investments:*** profits that are not distributed to stockholders as dividends but are instead transferred to a capital account.

(4) ***mutual funds:*** an investment of a fixed dollar amount regularly and reinvestment of dividends and capital gains.

accumulation area: the price range within which investors accumulate shares of an issue. Analysts identify accumulation areas when a security does not fall below a specified price.

accumulation bond: see *bond, accumulation.*

accumulation plan: a schedule that permits an investor to buy mutual fund shares on a regular basis in differing amounts, with provisions for the investment of income dividends and the acceptance of capital gains distribution in additional shares. Such plans can be either voluntary or contractual.

accumulation unit: in annuities, when an individual purchases an annuity, either fixed or variable, through a lump-sum purchase for future payout or with periodic purchases. Should the buyer chose a payout method, these units are then converted to annuity units. see also *annuity unit.*

accumulative dividend: see *cumulative dividends.*

ACE: see *AMEX Commodities Exchange.*

ACH: see *automated clearinghouse.*

acid test ratio: a credit barometer used by lending institutions; indicates the ability of a business enterprise to meet its current obligations. The formula used to determine the ratio is

$$\frac{\text{cash} + \text{receivables} + \text{marketable securities}}{\text{current liabilities}}$$

Usually a 1:1 ratio is considered to be satisfactory.

Ack.
(1) acknowledge.
(2) see *acknowledgement.*

acknowledgement
(1) on a document, a signature that has received certification from an authorized person.
(2) a written notification that an item, now received, is available for its immediate payment.
(3) a statement that a proper document has been submitted.

Acq.: see *exchange acquisition.*

acquired surplus
(1) the surplus of an enterprise existing at the date of its acquisition by another enterprise.
(2) the initial surplus of a successor enterprise where there has been a pooling of interests and no full capitalization of surplus. The initial surplus may be paid-in surplus or retained earnings or both, depending on the nature of the predecessor.

acquisition: a general term for the taking over of one company by another. see *amalgamation, merger.*

acquisition cost
(1) monies paid in order to obtain property title prior to the granting of a mortgage.
(2) the cost to a company of securing business; primarily commissions to agents and brokers.

across the board
(1) ***general:*** applying to all, in a uniform fashion.
(2) ***investments:*** the unified price activity of the daily securities market, as when described as being weak, slow, strong, or active across the board.

ACRS: accelerated cost recovery system. A provision in the Economic Recovery and Tax Act of 1981 permitting investors in a limited partnership to depreciate an asset, such as oil, gas equipment, real estate, faster in the first few years, then slower in the final years of a typical 10 to 15 years life of the partnership.

acting in concert: the coordination of securities transactions among people in a way that might influence the price of a particular security.

action
(1) the performance by a stock with respect to trading volume and price trend.
(2) in France, a share of stock.

active account: an account handled by one broker who makes frequent purchases and sales.

active assets: company assets that are used for daily operations of the firm.

active bond crowd: members of the bond department of the NYSE responsible for the heaviest volume of bond trading. cf. *cabinet crowd.*

active box: collateral used for arranging brokers' loans or customers' margin position in the place (or box) where stocks are held in safekeeping for customers of broker-dealer or for the broker-dealer itself.

active crowd: see *active bond crowd.*

active management: a style of investment management that seeks to attain above average risk-adjusted performance.

active market (AM): characterized by numerous transactions in securities trading. see *New York Stock Exchange.*

active securities: stocks and bonds that are actively traded each day and where quotations on these transactions are available to the public.

active stock: see *active securities.*

activity
(1) the trading volume of a specific stock or group of stocks.
(2) the trading volume on an exchange for a given time period.

actual cash value (ACV): the value of a contract on redemption.

actually outstanding: securities that have actually been issued and not reacquired by or for the issuing corporation.

actual market: synonymous with *spot market.*

actuals: an actual physical commodity; as distinguished from *futures.*

actuary: an individual, often holding a professional degree, whose primary functions include determining rates and rating systems, determining reserves against future liabilities for corporate and rate-making purposes, and designing and interpreting experience systems. see *insurance.*

ACV: see *actual cash value.*

AD
(1) see *accrued dividend.*
(2) anno Domini (in the year of our Lord).
(3) ante diem (before the day).

A-D: see *advance-decline ratio.*

ADB: see *adjusted debit balance.*

add-on interest: a method of calculating interest payments where a percentage of the desired principal is used to calculate the interest cost. Interest cost is then added to the principal to calculate the total amount to be repaid by the borrower.

adequate consideration
(1) the price of the security prevailing on a national securities exchange.
(2) when the security is not traded on a national securities exchange, a price not less favorable to the plan then the offering price for the security as established by current bid and asked prices quoted by persons independent of the issuer and of any party in interest.
(3) any asset other than a security, the fair market value of the asset as determined in good faith by the trustee or named fiduciary.

adjustable life insurance: insurance that allows the insured to switch the type of protection, raise or lower the face amount of the policy, increase or decrease the premium, and lengthen or shorten the protection period.

adjustable mortgage rate: see *variable-rate mortgage.*

adjustable-rate preferred stocks (ARPs): corporations that qualify with these stocks to be largely exempt from taxes on the dividends, whose floating rate lessens the risk of price plunges that often ravage fixed-income investments. With APRs the corporation receives a tax break by allowing them to set their yields far below those of prevailing bond rates. ARPs dividends are pegged at a fixed relationship to the highest of three interest rates—those on three-month Treasury bills, 10-year Treasury bonds, and 20-year Treasury bonds—and reset quarterly. ARPs are issued with a collar. see *collar.*

adjusted basis: a base price for judging capital gains or losses on the sale of an asset, such as a stock or bond.

adjusted debit balance (ADB): a formula for determining the position of a margin account, as required by the Federal Reserve Board's Regulation T. Calculated by netting the balance owing a broker with any balance in a special miscellaneous account, and any paper profits on short accounts. see also *special miscellaneous account (SMA).*

adjusted exercise price: in put and call options for Ginnie Mae contracts, protects investors and the public by ensuring that all contracts are traded fairly, and that the final exercise price of the option is adjusted taking into account the coupon rates carried on all Ginnie Mae mortgages.

adjusted gross income: an individual's gross income minus business expenses, deductions for income producing property, some property losses, self-employment expenses, and moving expenses. Used primarily in federal income tax returns.

adjustment: the Options Clearing Corporation procedure for adjusting an option contract following stock splits or stock dividends to maintain, as equitably as possible, the original amount of the contract. Adjustments are not made on option contracts when cash dividend distributions are made.

adjustment bond: see *bond, reorganization.*

adjustment mortgage: any mortgage that has been released out of a reorganization.

adjustment preferred securities: preferred stock that has resulted from an adjustment of claims in a restructuring of the company.

adjustments: deductions made to charge off losses, as with bad debts or the sale of commodities.

administrator: in securities, the individual responsible for supervision of state securities regulations.

admission by investment: the addition to a partnership of a new partner who contributes more cash to the business, thus increasing the assets and the number of owners of the firm.

admitted to dealings: following approval by the SEC, a security can be officially listed and traded on an exchange.

ADR

(1) see *American Depository Receipt.*

(2) see *depreciation range system.*

ad referendum: indicating that even though a contract has been signed, specific issues remain to be considered.

ad valorem: according to value. Rates or duty on a percentage of the invoice value, not on weight or quantity.

ad valorem taxes: synonymous with *land tax.*

advance
(1) ***general:*** a price increase.
(2) ***general:*** a loan.
(3) ***general:*** a payment on account made prior to due date.
(4) ***general:*** a rise in value or cost.
(5) ***investments:*** an increase in the price of stocks.

advance commitment
(1) ***investments:*** an agreement by a private buyer to take up a bond issue at some future date.
(2) ***real estate:*** a written contract calling for the sale of a specified amount of mortgages (or mortgage-backed securities) at a given price or yield within a specified time.

advance-decline ratio: a barometer of the market's condition. Following an upward sweep, speculative interest is concentrated on the small number of stocks that struggle forward while, masked by the performance of those few, the rest of the market fades. For example, while the Dow Jones approaches a peak, the number of securities going up becomes fewer. By plotting the number of stocks that advanced minus those that declined, a line will normally turn down months before the Dow does.

advance refunding
(1) ***public debt refinancing:*** possessors of a government security maturing soon are able to exchange their securities ahead of the due date for others that mature at a later time. By this process, the national debt is extended.
(2) ***bonds:*** the sale of new municipal bonds in advance, usually by several years, of the first call date of the old bonds. The refunding issue has a lower rate than the issue to be refunded, and proceeds are invested, traditionally in government securities, until the higher-rate bonds become callable.

advances versus declines: the number of stocks that closed higher versus those which closer lower than the previous trading day. Intraday figures are also available.

advancing market: the state of a market where stock prices are generally rising.

advantage: favorable state or circumstances; superiority over a competitor.

adventure
(1) ***general:*** a speculative undertaking involving the sale of goods overseas at the best available price.
(2) ***investments:*** a security flotation by a syndicate; a joint venture.
(3) see *venture.*

advertisement: in securities, any material for use in the media.

adviser: the organization employed by a mutual fund to give professional advice on its investments and management of its assets.

advisory funds: funds placed with a bank to invest at its own discretion on the customer's behalf.

advisory service: a service offered for a fee that provides market information and/or particular buy or sell recommendations to its subscribers.

AE: account executive. see *registered representative.*

A&F: August and February (semiannual interest payments).

affairs, statement of: a declaration indicating the estimated results of liquidating a financially depressed firm, frequently prepared for creditors or for a receiver or court of bankruptcy.

affiant: one who makes an affidavit.

affidavit: a written, notarized, dated, and sworn statement of the facts pertaining to a financial transaction or civil event. Such a statement must show the name and address of the affiant, be signed by that person, and bear the signature of the attesting official (e.g., a notary).

affiliate

(1) ***government:*** in the Banking Act of 1933, pertaining to any organization which a bank owns or controls by stock holdings, or which the bank's shareholders possess, or whose officers are also directors of the bank.

(2) ***taxes:*** for consolidated tax returns, composed of firms whose parent or other inclusive corporation owns at least 80 percent of nonvoting stock, except preferred stock.

(3) ***investing:*** according to the Investment Company Act, any firm in which there is any direct or indirect ownership of 5 percent or more of the outstanding voting stocks.

affiliated group: see *consolidated tax return.*

affiliated person: an individual in a position to exert direct influence on the future activities of a corporation. Usually these persons include directors, senior corporate officers, members of the immediate family and owners of 10 percent or more of the voting shares of stock. synonymous with *control person.*

after-acquired clause: a section of the mortgage stating that any additional property which the mortgagor acquires after the mortgage is drawn will also be used as security for the loan.

after-acquired property: property acquired by a corporation subsequent to the execution of a mortgage or by a testator subsequent to the making of his or her will.

after market (AM): the market that automatically exists once a corporation's securities have been offered for sale to the public. see *go public.*

aftertax: the profit or loss received from a business operation or investment after allowing for state and federal taxes.

aftertax basis: a basis for comparing returns on a corporate taxable bond and a municipal tax-free bond.

aftertax real rate of return: adjusted for the rate of inflation, the amount of funds that an investor keeps, out of the income and capital gains earned from investments.

AG: Aktiengesellschaft (West German stock company).

against actuals: see *exchange of spot.*

against the box: in a short sale of stock, a person selling against the box actually owns the security sold short but prefers not to or cannot deliver the stock to the buyer. The result is that, through a broker, he or she borrows the stock in order to make delivery. see *short sale.*

age change: the date halfway between natural birthdays when the age of an individual, for the purpose of life insurance rating, changes to the next higher age.

aged fail: a contract between two broker-dealers that is not settled 30 days following the settlement date. At that time the open balance will no longer count as an asset, and the receiving firm is required to adjust its capital accordingly.

agency (Agy.)
(1) ***general:*** certain types of accounts in trust institutions. The main distinguishing characteristic of an agency is that the title of the property does not pass to the trust institution but remains in the name of the owner of the property, who is known as the principal.
(2) ***investments:*** purchasing or selling for the account and risk of a client. Traditionally, a broker or agent serves as intermediary between buyer and seller, having no financial risk personally or as a firm, and charging a commission for its service.

agency bond: see *bond, agency.*

agency issues: debt issued by a government agency.

agency securities: see *government agency stock.*

agent (Agt.): an individual who acts on behalf of another. The agent initiates transactions in the name of the principal and charges a commission for services rendered. see *broker.* cf. *dealer.*

agent de change: a member of the Paris Bourse (stock exchange).

aggregate: any total (e.g., the gross national product; the sum of monthly sales).

aggregate balance: the calculated accumulation of account balances during the statement period.

aggregate corporation: an incorporated venture having more than one stockholder.

aggregate demand: the total of personal consumption expenditures, business investments, and government spending.

aggregate exercise price
(1) in stock options trading, the number of shares in a put or call contract multiplied by the exercise price.
(2) options traded on debt instruments; the aggregate exercise price determined by multiplying the face value of the underlying stock by the exercise price.

aggregate indebtedness: used in broker-dealer compliance with SEC net capital requirements, the total of a broker-dealer's indebtedness to clients.

aggressive growth: the emphasis of maximum growth and capital gains over quality, security, and income.

aggressive growth fund: a mutual fund whose investment objective is capital appreciation. Most investments are in common stocks of higher growth potential and risk.

aggressive portfolio: a securities portfolio held for appreciation rather than defensive quality or yield opportunity.

aggrieved party
(1) an individual who accuses a firm or individual associated with an exchange member of a trade practice complaint under the NASD Rules of Fair Practice.
(2) an individual requesting arbitration of a controversy with a member of NASD with NASD, a rulemaking board, or an exchange.

aging: synonymous with *aging schedule.*

aging schedule: the categorizing of trade accounts receivable by date of sale; used primarily by grantors of credit. synonymous with *aging.*

agreement among underwriters: a contract between members of an investment banking syndicate including who appoints the originating investment bankers as syndicate manager and agent, identifies members' proportionate liability and agrees to pay each member's share on settlement date, and so on. In Great Britain and in Eurobond markets, it is usually confined to an agreement among managing underwriters, and the latter proceeds to make a subunderwriting agreement with other underwriters.

Agt.: see *agent.*

Agy.: see *agency.*

AI: see *accrued interest.*

AIBD: see *Association of International Bond Dealers.*

AICPA: American Institute of Certified Public Accountants.

air pocket: noticeably extreme weakness in a specific stock.

all rights: the right to use open space above a property, or conversely, the right to control the air space by not constructing to ensure that light and air will not be blocked out.

AJOJ: April, July, October, January, (quarterly interest payments or dividends).

alienate: the transfer of title to property.

alienation: the transfer of interest and property title to another person or organization. see *involuntary alienation, voluntary alienation.*

alienation clause: a form of acceleration clause that requires full payment of the mortgage note upon the transfer of title of the mortgaged property either through sale or some other means.

alien company: an incorporated company formed and operating under the regulations of a foreign nation.

allied members: voting shareholders or partners in a stock exchange member organization who are permitted to carry out business on the trading floor of the exchange.

alligator spread: a spread option where the potential for profiting is negated by commissions involved in trading that result in more gain for a brokerage firm than for its clients.

allocation: a standard procedure for the issuance of stock option exercise notices by exchange member firms. These procedures purport to ensure fair and nondiscriminatory practices through an approved random-selection method.

all or any part: used in discretionary accounts by brokers when representing their clients. It authorizes the securities broker to execute all or any part of an order as he or she deems appropriate, but only at the customer's specified price limit.

all or none order (AON)
(1) a stipulation that a request to purchase or sell a security must be achieved in total or not at all.
(2) all securities sold by a broker or underwriter of a new issue become final only when the entire issue is purchased within a stated time period.

allotment
(1) ***general:*** an assignment of pay for the benefit of dependents.
(2) ***general:*** the separation of anticipated revenues among specific classes of expenditures.
(3) ***investments:*** the part of a stock issue apportioned or assigned by an investment firm to a purchaser or subscriber.

allotment ledger: a subsidiary ledger that contains an account for each allotment, showing the amount allotted, expenditures, encumbrances, the net balance, and other related information.

allotment notice: a document completed by an investment banker or syndicate manager which states the amount and related information or price and time of payments for securities and which is transmitted to the subscriber. It can be for the full amount of securities asked for by the subscriber, or less.

allottee: the firm or person that has subscribed to buy securities and has been assigned a share or allotment.

allowable depreciation: the amount of depreciation that could have been claimed on a capital asset, but which was not claimed during a particular reporting period. This amount is added to the value of the asset.

allowance: a reserve, or money set aside, for bad debts or for depreciation.

allowance for bad debts: an account showing the estimated loss on uncollectable debts as an offset against the value shown for accounting receivables. synonymous with *reserve for bad debts*.

All-Savers certificates: a tax break under the Economic Recovery Tax Act of 1981 to encourage savings, the law created this instrument designed basically to benefit savings and loan associations rather than investors. Under the act, thrift institutions were able to offer a new, one-year Treasury note yield for a little more than 10 percent at current interest rates. What made the new certificate attractive was that interest income up to $1000 ($2000 on a joint return) was exempt from federal income tax. Now defunct.

all your market: in the over-the-counter market, indicating a limited interest in a particular security, usually by geographic area.

alpha: the premium a fund would be expected to earn if the market rate of return were equal to the Treasury bill rate—that is, a premium of zero for the market rate of return. A positive alpha indicates that the investor has earned on the average a premium above that expected for the level of market variability. A negative alpha indicates that the investor's fund received on the average a premium lower than that expected for the level of market variability. see *beta.*

alpha-beta: an approach to portfolio analysis purporting to monitor what risk a manager takes to achieve his or her gains. see also *alpha.*

alternate account: an account in the name of two or more persons, any of whom may draw against the account without further authority from the others. see *joint account.*

alternate depositors: holders of a joint account; a deposit account made out in the names of husband and wife or of two partners which is payable to either or to the survivor is a joint account.

alternative minimum tax (AMT): requires some payments from every taxpayer with substantial income, even if part or all of such income would not ordinarily be taxable, as in the case of long-term capital gains. AMT was established by the 1978 tax act as one of two additional taxes designed to raise more revenue for the federal government. The other was a 15 percent surtax known as an *add-on minimum tax,* which affected certain tax preferences, such as those for accelerated depreciation of real estate or oil-depletion allowances. The 1982 tax law eliminated the add-on tax for individuals, placed most of its preferences under the alternative minimum tax, and changed some other elements of the AMT.

alternative mortgage instruments (AMIs): one of three alternatives to the traditional fixed-rate mortgage. see *graduated-payment mortgage, reverse-annuity mortgage, variable-rate mortgage.*

alternative mortgages: see *flexible loan insurance plan, graduated-payment mortgage, shared-appreciation mortgage.*

alternative order: an order giving the broker the choice between two alternatives: either to buy or sell, but never both. synonymous with *either-or order, one cancels the other order.*

AM

(1) see *active market.*
(2) see *after market.*
(3) ante meridiem (before noon).

AMA: see *Asset Management Account.*

amalgamation

(1) the joining together of businesses for the mutual advantage of all.

(2) a combination under a single title of all or a portion of the assets and liabilities of two or more business units by either merger or consolidation. It may take the form of a merger, where one company absorbs another, or a consolidation, in which the original companies form a new one. see *consolidation, merger.*

AMBAC: see *American Municipal Bond Assurance Corporation.*

amendment: an addition, deletion, or change in a legal document.

American Board of Trade (ABT): since 1969, providing the nation's only spot and deferred markets. Its ABT National Market System offers investors the same access to market information and market activity previously available only to large investors and institutions.

American Depository Receipt (ADR): a form similar to a stock certificate which is registered in the holder's name. The certificate represents a certain number of shares in an alien corporation. Such shares are held by an alien bank that serves as the agent for a domestic commercial bank which has released the depository receipt.

American Municipal Bond Assurance Corporation (AMBAC): a corporation that offers insurance policies on new municipal offerings covering payment of both principal and interest. Bonds covered by AMBAC automatically carry the highest bond rating.

American option: an option that can be exercised any time up to maturity.

American parity: in foreign exchange, showing the equivalent in U.S. funds of the foreign price of securities traded overseas.

Americans: the expression used on the London Stock Exchange for U.S. securities.

American Stock Exchange (Amex): the second largest securities exchange in the country; called the Little Board or the Curb Exchange, from the market's origin on a street in downtown Manhattan. Amex began listing stock options in 1975. see *commodity exchange.* cf. *Big Board.*

American Stock Exchange market value index: the average value of all the common shares listed on the AMEX in addition to rights and warrants. This average contains a larger number of growth firms and natural resource companies than the NYSE Index or the Dow Jones Industrial Average.

Amex: see *American Stock Exchange.*

Amex Commodities Exchange (ACE): a commodity exchange launched by the American Stock Exchange in 1977 to offer its member firms a broader range of products. ACE functions as an independent exchange, sharing facilities and services with the Amex by contract. Merged in 1980 with the New York Futures Exchange. see *New York Futures Exchange.*

Amex Options Switching System (AMOS): a computerized options order-routing system for transmitting incoming options orders to appropriate trading posts. Should the orders be executed, AMOS in turn reports the executions to the exchange member who has entered the order.

AMIs: see *alternative mortgage instruments.*

amortisement: synonymous with *amortization.*

amortization
(1) the gradual reduction of a debt by means of equal periodic payments sufficient to meet current interest and to liquidate the debt at maturity. When the debt involves real property, the periodic payments often include a sum sufficient to pay taxes and insurance on the property.
(2) an attempt to liquidate a future obligation slowly by making charges against a capital account or by adding monies to cover the debt.
(3) synonymous with *amortisement.*

amortization of debt discount: noncash expenditures charged on a company's income statement to offset, over the life of a bond issue, the difference between the proceeds of bonds sold at a discount and the par value payable at maturity.

amortization of discount on funded debt: a charge to income each fiscal period for a proportion of the discount and expense on funded debt obligations applicable to that period. The proportion is determined according to a rule, the uniform application of which through the interval between the date of sale and date of maturity will extinguish the discount and expense on funded debt. However, the accounting company may, at its option, charge to profit and loss all or any portion of discount and expense remaining unextinguished at any time.

amortization of premium: charges made against the interest received on bonds in order to offset any premium paid for the bonds above their par value or call price. The premium may be gradually amortized over the life of the bond issue or paid off at one time.

amortization reserve: a balance sheet account in which are recorded the net accumulated provisions for the extinguishment of an asset at the end of a predetermined period.

amortization schedule: a table showing the amounts of principal and interest due at regular intervals and the unpaid principal balance of the loan after each payment is made.

amortize
(1) to write off a portion or all of the cost of an asset; to retire debt over a period of time.
(2) to discharge a debt in periodic payments until the total, including the interest, has been paid.

amortized mortgage loan: a mortgage loan that provides for repayment within a specified time by means of regular payments at stated intervals (usually monthly, quarterly, or semi-annually) to reduce the principal amount of the loan and to cover interest as it is due.

amortized value: the investment value of a security determined by the process of amortization. This value is appropriate for use in connection with bonds that are fully secured, and are not in default as to either principal or interest. see *amortization.*

AMOS: see *Amex Options Switching System.*

amount: the value or quantity of a transaction.

amount at interest: principal sum deposited for the purpose of earning interest.

amount financed: the amount lent or financed exclusive of finance charges; total of payments less the finance charge.

AMT: see *alternative minimum tax.*

Amt.: see *amount.*

analyst: a specialist in a brokerage firm or other investment organization who is primarily responsible for determining the assets and liabilities of a new or existing corporation for purposes of making a recommendation to the sales representatives of his or her organization. Analysts are also found in banks. see also *technical analyst.*

analyze: to study and interpret past, present, and projected corporate, economic, and market information so as to make forecasts.

anchor: see *AAA (Triple A) tenant.*

and interest: a bond quotation term to show that accrued interest is to be added to the price; that is, the price quoted is exclusive of interest. see *accrued interest.*

ANFM: August, November, February, May (quarterly interest payments or dividends).

Ann.
(1) annual.
(2) see *annuity.*

announcement date: the date a firm announces that a dividend will be paid. Provides the record date, payment date, and amount of the dividend. synonymous with *declaration date.*

annual basis: statistical shifting of data that are for a period of less than 12 months in order to estimate the full results for an entire year. To be accurate, the processing should consider the effect of the seasonal variation.

annual earnings: the total of all monies received during a year; income less expenses during a year.

annual financial statement: an accounting statement indicating income or loss or the financial position of a corporation at the end of the last day of its fiscal year and bearing that date.

annual investment accumulation tables: see *tables, annual investment accumulation.*

annualize: translation of statistics that apply to a short period of time into the statistics that would apply for a full year.

annualized linked-median return: rates of return determined by compounding the annual median returns and annualizing the result.

annualized return: an assumed calculated return on an investment over one year. This return is based on dividends, interest, and possible appreciation.

annual meeting: a yearly gathering where all shareholders can elect the firm's board of directors and vote on corporate matters. synonymous with *stockholder's meeting.*

annual renewable term insurance: see *term life insurance.*

annual report: a report of financial and organizational conditions prepared by corporate management at yearly intervals. In most cases, the Securities Exchange Commission requires an annual report for publicly held firms. see *annual statement.*

annual return: see *yield.*

annual statement: the annual report made by a company at the close of the fiscal year, stating the company's receipts and disbursements, assets and liabilities. Such a statement usually includes an account of the progress made by the company during the year.

annual yield: the percentage of return or income in dividends or interest that an investment yields each year.

annuitant: an individual to whom an annuity is payable, the person usually to receive the annuity during his or her lifetime. see *variable annuity.*

annuitize: commencing a series of payments from an annuity. see also *annuity.*

annuity (Ann.)

(1) a scheduled payment to a retired person.

(2) a series of equal payments at fixed intervals.

annuity, installment refund: a life annuity with an agreement that the insurer will, on the death of the annuitant, continue payments to a beneficiary until the total of the payments to annuitant and beneficiary equals the consideration paid to the insurer.

annuity, joint and survivor: an annuity payable as long as any one of two or more persons survive.

annuity, life: an annuity payable as long as the annuitant or annuitants live.

annuity, retirement: a deferred annuity for which the premiums, less loading, are accumulated at interest and are used to purchase an annuity at a specified age. Prior to that age, the annuitant is entitled to a cash surrender value. In case of death, the surrender value is paid to his or her beneficiary.

annuity, survivorship: an annuity payable to the annuitant for the period during which he or she survives the insured.

annuity bond: see *bond, perpetual.*

annuity certain: an annuity payable for a particular period of time, regardless of the time of the death of the annuitant.

annuity certain and life: an annuity payable for a specified time period and for as long thereafter as the annuitant lives.

annuity deferred: an annuity, beginning more than one year from the payment of a lump sum, or from the beginning of periodic payments, to the insurer.

annuity due: an annuity where the initial payment is made at the beginning of each period (i.e., month, quarter) rather than at the end.

annuity insurance: an insurance contract providing for payment of a stipulated sum annually or periodically to a party called the annuitant for life or for a stated period.

annunity method of depreciation: taking the initial cost of a capital asset, deducting the expected salvage value at the time it is discarded, and assuming a rate of interest, the straight-line portion of cost plus interest in the undepreciated balance is charged to each period.

annunity plan: a type of retirement insurance whereby, after having made payment for a specified number of years, a person receives income for a given period (or for life).

annuity reserve: a monetary sum equal to the actuarial value of future payments to be made on account of an annuity.

annunity reserve fund: an amount or sum set aside in a reserve to provide for the payment of annuities. Usually derived from the members' accumulated contributions, or contributions by the members and the employer.

annuity table: a listing of the present values of $1 per year or month payable for life, or for a term of years at specified ages for each sex, computed on the basis of assumed rates or mortality and interest.

annuity unit: an accounting method for converting accumulation units of an annuity into units for which payments to an annuitant is determined. see also *accumulation unit.*

annunciator boards: large boards on a stock exchange wall were a telephone clerk seeks the attention of the firm's floor broker. Each broker is assigned a number that is flashed on the board to call the broker or a messenger to the firm's booth on the rim of the trading floor.

antecedents: used in making credit inquiries to determine if the corporation has been controlled by the existing employer(s) for a short or long time period and how often the firm has changed ownership.

anticipated holding period: the time when a limited partnership anticipates holding on to an asset.

anticipation
(1) ***general:*** the payment of an account before the actual due date, thus permitting a discount.
(2) ***general:*** assigning or making charges against income or profit before such gain is actually realized.
(3) ***trade:*** a bill that is paid prior to its due date.

anticipation notes: short-term municipal debt instruments issued to secure funds in anticipation of revenues or permanent financing. see *bond anticipation notes, revenue-anticipation notes, Tax Anticipation Note.*

antique: an investment collectible, usually 100 years old or more, deriving its value from age, condition, and current market demand.

antitrust: describing an action of the courts taken to curb monopolistic tendencies or to limit power stemming from monopolies.

antitrust acts: see *Celler Antimerger Act, Robinson-Patman Act of 1936.*

any-quantity rate: a transportation rate applicable to any quantity of a commodity shipped.

A&O: April and October (semiannual interest payments).

AON: see *all or none order.*

APB: Accounting Principles Board.

application of funds statement: constructed from balance sheets to two periods, the statement allows an analysis of the changes that have evolved during the period that was chosen.

applied proceeds swap: the sale of a block of bonds, the proceeds of which are applied to purchasing another block of bonds.

appraisal: the setting of a value or evaluation of a specific piece of personal or real property, or the property of another as a whole.

appraisal fee: a charge for estimating the value of collateral being offered as security.

appraisal of business: an examination to decide how much a business is worth.

appraisal report: a written report of the factors considered in arriving at a valuation of a particular piece of property.

appraisal rights of minority stockholders: the statutory rights for the protection of dissenting minority stockholders during a shift in shares at the time of a merger or consolidation.

appraisal surplus: the excess of appraised values over book values.

appraise: to determine the cost, quality, or value of an item (e.g., to appraise the value of one's house). Also used to appraise the adequacy and effectiveness of systems and procedures.

appraised value: an estimate of property value reached by an appraiser.

appraiser: a person who makes appraisals.

appraising: synonymous with *valuation.*

appreciation: the increase in the value of an asset in excess of its depreciable cost which is due to economic and other conditions; the increase of present value over the listed book value. see *capital gain.*

appreciation potential: the forecasted increase in market value that is projected for an investment. The quote includes a market price and percentage of increase.

appreciation rate: the index figure used against the actual or estimated cost of property in computing its cost of reproduction, new as of a different date or under different conditions of a higher price level.

appreciation surplus: the addition to net worth appearing in surplus as the result of a revaluation upward of the value at which assets are shown on the books of an enterprise.

appropriated retained earnings: see *retained earnings, appropriated.*

appropriate surplus: that part of the surplus of a corporation which has been set aside by the board of directors for a specific purpose other than to recognize an existing liability. The appropriation can be reversed by the board.

appropriation: an authorized sum of money set aside to pay certain known or anticipated costs of a given item or service.

appropriation ledger: a subsidiary ledger containing an account with each appropriation. Each account usually shows the amount originally appropriated, transfers to or from the appropriation charged against the appropriation, the net balance, and other related information. If allotments are made and a separate ledger is maintained for them, each account in the appropriation ledger usually shows the amount appropriated, transfers to or from the appropriation, the amount allotted, and the unalloted balance.

appropriation of income or surplus: action taken by a board of directors, setting aside amounts for specific use, such as payment of dividends, allotments to sinking funds, and additional investment.

approved bond: see *bond, approved.*

approved depository: an exchange-approved bank or trust company where exchange clearing members deposit cash, Treasury bills, letters of credit, or shares of underlying stock to fulfill exchange margin requirements.

approved individual: a person, not an employee of a member firm who serves in a control capacity, for example, a member of the board of directors of a member firm who is not an employee of the corporation. Such people are required to accept the rules as stated by the exchange.

approved list: a list, statutory or otherwise, which contains the authorized investments that a fiduciary may acquire.

AR: see *annual report.*

Arb: see *arbitrager.*

arbitrage
(1) simultaneous purchasing and selling of the identical item in different markets in order to yield profits. The result is that the price of an item becomes equal in all markets.
(2) the purchase of foreign exchange, stocks, bonds, silver, gold, or other commodities in one market for sale in another market at a profit.
(3) the simultaneous purchase and sale of mortgages, future contracts, or mortgage-backed securities in different markets to profit from price differences.

arbitrage bond: see *bond, arbitrage.*

arbitrage house: a financial institution, such as a foreign exchange dealer or private banker, conducting business in arbitrage. see *arbitrage.*

arbitrager (arbitrageur): an individual who engages in the activity of arbitrage. see *arbitrage.*

arbitragist: synonymous with *arbitrager.*

arbitration: see *board of arbitration.*

arbs: short for *arbitrager.*

ARIEL: Automated Real-time Investments Exchange. Established in 1974, ARIEL is a computerized system for dealing in large blocks of securities. cf. *NASDAQ.*

arithmetic investing: a statistical analysis intending to reduce the investor's speculative risk by calculating rates of return with reasonable accuracy for a specific time period. The objective is to invest in stocks for a relatively short period with the expectation of achieving an annualized return of anywhere from 20 to 35 percent. Often used in averaged buyouts and takeover situations.

arithmetic mean: the sum of all items divided by the number of items added.

ARMs: see *adjustable-rate mortgages.*

arm's length system: a method of figuring state taxes on corporate income. For example, ABC, an in-state subsidiary of a foreign parent with worldwide earnings of $100 million, pays state income taxes only on the $20 million in income that it claims was generated within the state. The $80 million that the parent firm says was earned abroad escapes state taxation.

arm's length transactions: a transaction where the involved parties are completely independent of each other, for example, in a securities transaction taking place through an exchange, the purchaser and seller are independent from each other.

around: used in quoting forward premium/discount (e.g., five-five around means five points on either side of pan.)

ARP: see *adjustable-rate preferred stocks.*

arrearages on preferred securities: the accumulation of unpaid dividends. A statement that such dividends of cumulative preferred stock must be paid prior to payment on the firm's common stock.

arrears
(1) a real or contingent obligation remaining unpaid at the date of maturity. Frequently used in connection with installment notes, mortages, rent, and other obligations due and payable on a certain specified date.
(2) monies due but unpaid.

articles of agreement: any contract between two or more people that is reduced to a written instrument.

articles of association: any instrument that is similar to a corporate certificate; usually used with nonstock corporations (e.g., charitable organizations).

articles of copartnership: the written agreement by which a partnership is formed.

articles of incorporation: a document filed with an appropriate state agency by persons establishing a corporation. Upon return accompanied by a certificate of incorporation, the document becomes the firm's charter.

articles of partnership: a written agreement between business partners that outlines the provisions of their business arrangement.

AS:
(1) see *accumulated surplus.*
(2) see *active securities.*
(3) see *assented securities.*
(4) see *assessable stock.*

as agent: an individual acting as a broker in a transaction and assumes no financial risk.

ASAP: as soon as possible.

ascending tops: a chart trend showing a stock's price over a given time period indicating that each peak in a stock's price is higher than a preceding peak. An upward trend is considered bullish and likely to continue. cf. *descending tops.*

Asd.: assented.

ASE: see *American Stock Exchange.*

ASE index: see *stock indexes and averages.*

ask: an offer to sell at a designated price.

asked: see *bid and asked.*

asked (asking) price
(1) ***general:*** the price that is officially offered in a sale.
(2) ***investments:*** the price at which a stock is offered for sale. In open-end shares, the price at which the purchaser may buy stock from the investment firm. In closed-end shares, the lowest price at which the stock is then offered for sale in the public market. synonymous with *offering price.*

assay: a test of content, composition, and purity, often carried out in an assayer's office, on metals, usually gold and silver.

assay office: a location designated for the testing of ore, commodities, and bullion in addition to foreign coin.

assay office bar: assayed by an assay office and made at a mint, a bar of pure or near pure gold or silver.

assemblage: the act of bringing two or more individuals or things to form an aggregate whole; specifically, the cost or estimated cost of assembling two or more parcels of land under a single ownership and unit of utility over the normal cost or current market prices of the parcels held individually.

Asian CD: any certificate of deposit issued by a bank located in Asia; usually denominated in U.S. currency.

assented securities: securities whose owners agree to some change in status, usually in case of corporate restructuring, when an assessment is made or the amount of securities is reduced according the some logical plan.

assess: to determine the value of something, or to fix its value for tax purposes.

assessable insurance: an insurance contract in which the policyholder is liable for an additional premium payment if losses are unexpectedly large.

assessable stock: security that is subject to an assessment order resulting from a corporation's reorganization or insolvency.

assessed valuation: the dollar value assigned to property by a municipality for the purpose of assessing taxes. Assessed valuation is important not only to homeowners, but also to investors in municipal bonds that are backed by property taxes.

assessed value: see *assessed valuation.*

assessment
(1) a charge made against property for the purpose of levying a tax. see *nonassessable stock.*
(2) any levy on members of a corporation for purposes of raising capital.

assessment bond: see *bond, assessment.*

assessment insurance: a form of mutual insurance where the policyholders are assessed whenever there is a loss.

assessment ratio: the ratio of the assessed value of property to the full or true property value. Full value may be defined as fair market value at the bid side of the market, less a reasonable allowance for sales and other expenses.

assessment roll
(1) in the case of real property the official list containing the legal description of each parcel of property and its assessed valuation. The name and address of the last known owner are also usually shown.
(2) in the case of personal property, the assessment roll is the official list containing the name and address of the owner, a description of the personal property, and its assessed value.

assessor: a designated public official who makes the official estimate of value.

asset:
(1) anything owned by an individual or business that has commercial or exchange value. Assets may consist of specific property or claims against others, in contract to obligations due

others. see *balance sheet, current assets to current debt, fixed assets, intangible asset, tangible assets.*
(2) uses of bank funds—cash, security investments, loans, and fixed assets.

asset, capital: see *capital assets.*

asset, current: see *current assets to current debt.*

asset, deferred: see *deferred asset.*

asset, fixed: see *fixed assets.*

asset, floating: see *floating assets.*

asset, fluid: see *current assets.*

asset, hypothecated: see *hypothecated asset.*

asset, inactive: see *inactive asset.*

asset, intangible: see *intangible asset.*

asset, liquid: see *liquid assets.*

asset, net: see *net assets.*

asset, net value: see *net asset value.*

asset, nominal: see *nominal asset.*

asset, nonledger: see *nonledger asset.*

asset, ordinary: see *ordinary asset.*

asset, original: see *original asset.*

asset, permanent: see *permanent asset.*

asset, physical: see *tangible assets.*

asset, pledged: see *pledged assets.*

asset, quick: see *quick assets.*

asset, tangible: see *tangible assets.*

asset, value: see *value asset.*

asset, wasting: see *wasting assets.*

asset, working: see *working asset.*

asset allocation decision: the means for determining the optimal distribution of funds among various types of assets that offer the highest probability of consistently achieving investment objectives within the confines of a predetermined level of risk.

asset and liability statement: a balance sheet.

asset coverage: *direct*—the extent to which net assets (after all prior claims) cover a specific senior obligation, whether bank loans, debentures, or preferred stock. It may be expressed in either dollar, percentage, or ratio terms. *Overall*—the ratio of total assets to the sum of all prior obligations including that of the specific issue under consideration taken at liquidating value.

asset depreciation range system (ADR): the range of depreciable lives permitted by the IRS for specific depreciable assets. The Economic Recovery Tax Act of 1981 allows the costs of assets acquired after 1980 to be recoverable faster under an accelerated cost recovery system.

asset financing: financing to convert specific assets into working cash in exchange for a stock interest in those assets.

asset-liability management: matching a person's level of debt and amount of assets.

Asset Management Account (AMA): an account at a financial institution, brokerage firm, or bank that combines banking services, such as checking account writing, and credit cards, with brokerage services, such as purchasing stocks, making loans on margin, and the convenience of having all financial transactions listed on one monthly statement.

asset play: a security that is appealing because its current price fails to truely reflect the value of the firm's assets.

assign: to transfer to another. A person to whom property is assigned.

assignability: the capacity of property to be transferred to another person or organization.

assignee
(1) ***general:*** one to whom an assignment is granted.
(2) ***law:*** an individual to whom property or rights have been transferred for the benefit of self or others. see *assignment, assignor.*

assignment
(1) the endorsement of a stock certificate by an owner of record rendering it negotiable.
(2) the notification to a put or call option contract writer that the contract has been exercised by the buyer of that contract. see *exercise.*

assignment of leases: additional security often taken in connection with mortgages of commercial properties.

assignment of mortgage: the written instrument evidencing an association's transfer of a loan obligation from the original borrower to a third person.

assignment of rents: a written document that transfers to a mortgagee on default the owner's right to collect rents.

assignment separate from certificate: a detached assignment or stock (bond) power. The certificate is the same as the rear portion of the security and includes a complete description of the security. This permits the holder to transfer the certificate safely by sending the unsigned certificate and properly filled out stock power under separate cover. One without the other has no value, so little damage would result if it is lost or stolen.

assignment to creditors: the transfer of property in trust or for the benefit of creditors.

assignor: an individual who assigns or transfers a claim, right, or property.

assimilation: the completed distribution of new shares of securities to the public by the issue's underwriters and syndicate members.

associated person: an individual associated with a broker-dealer as a proprietor, partner, director, manager, investment banker, or sales agent.

associate member: a stock exchange membership classification. Such members have certain privileges but do not have seats as do full members.

associate specialist: any exchange member serving as an assistant to a regular specialist. As trainees, they will often execute orders, but only under proper supervision.

Association of International Bond Dealers (AIBD): headquarters in Zurich; dealers' professional organization that recommends procedures and policies.

assumable mortgage: a home mortgage where the buyer takes over the seller's original, below-market-rate mortgage. synonymous with *used mortgage.*

assumed bond: see *bond, assumed.*

assumed liability: an obligation for payment accepted by another person.

assumption: loan payments accepted by a party other than the original maker.

assumption of debt: taking on another's debt.

assumption of mortgage: accepting a property title that has an existing mortgage with personal liability for all payments by another.

AT: see *absolute title.*

at a discount (AAD): a security selling in the marketplace below its par value.

at a premium: a security selling in the marketplace above its par value.

ATB: see *across the board.*

ATBE: see *tenants by the entireties.*

at best: an instruction given to a dealer to buy at the best rate that he or she can obtain.

at call: any transaction occuring in the call money market. see *call money, call money market.*

ATM: see *at the market.*

at market: see *at the market.*

at or better: when placing a purchase order for securities, to buy at the price specified or under; in a selling request, to sell at the price given or above.

at par: designating a bond or share of preferred stock issued or selling at its face amount.

at risk: possessing the possibility of loss.

at seller's option: see *seller's option.*

at sight: in the body of negotiable instruments indicating that payment is due upon presentation or demand.

attest: to bear witness to; as, to attest a will or other document.

attestation: the act of bearing witness or giving authenticity to a document by signing as a witness to the signature of another. see *notary public.*

attestation clause: the clause of a document containing the formal declaration of the act of witnessing; in the case of a will, the clause immediately following the signature of the testator and usually beginning "Signed, sealed, published, and declared by the said. . . ."

attesting witness: one who testifies to the authenticity of a document, as the attesting witness to a will.

at the close (CLO): an order to be executed at the best price attainable at the close of the market on the day it is entered. Rule 130 of the American Stock Exchange does not permit this arrangement.

at the market: an order that the broker has executed at the best price available after it was received by the broker on the floor of the exchange. synonymous with *market order.* see *limited order.*

auction: a unique trading market in which there is one seller and many potential buyers. see also *Dutch auction.*

auction fee: see *fee.*

auction market: the system of trading securities through brokers or agents on an exchange such as the New York Stock Exchange. Buyers compete with other sellers for the most advantageous price. Most transactions are executed with public customers on both sides since the specialist buys or sells for his own account primarily to offset imbalances in public supply and demand. see *dealer, quotation, specialist.*

Aud.
(1) see *audit.*
(2) see *auditor.*

audit
(1) inspection of a firm's books; a final statement of account.
(2) periodic or continuous verification of the stated assets and liabilities of a company or other organization.

audit function: periodic or continuous verification of the bank's assets and liabilities. This function is performed by the auditor. The auditor is appointed by the board of directors and is responsible for the carrying out of this verification. Among the assets and liabilities more regularly verified are cash, loans, collateral for loans, and savings and checking accounts. Verification may consist of a physical count of the assets as reflected by the general ledger or a listing of the balances, as shown on each savings or checking account, with a proof of the total as shown on the general ledger. Direct verification may also be made with borrowers or depositors.

auditor: a person qualified to conduct an audit. Qualification is defined by each state. see *audit, certified public accountant.*

auditor's certificate: synonymous with *accountants opinion.*

audit report: the report prepared by an auditor covering the audit or investigation made by him or her. As a rule, the report should include a statement of the scope of the audit, a summary of findings, recommendations, a certificate, financial statements, and, sometimes, statistical tables.

audit trail: a printed record of transaction listings created as a by-product of data-processing runs or manual or mechanized accounting operations.

audit trail number: a 10-digit number recorded on the top right-hand corner of a payment for tracing purposes.

autex system: an electronic system to alert brokers that other brokers wish to purchase or sell large blocks of stock. At the time a match is identified, the actual transaction occurs over the counter or on the floor of an exchange.

authenticated copy: a copy of an instrument on which an attestation is made in the manner required by law by an official authorized to make such certification, as by the certification and seal of a specified public official.

authentication
(1) ***investments:*** the signing of a certificate on a bond by a trustee in order to identify it as having been issued under a specific indenture, thereby validating the bond.
(2) ***law:*** the verification of a document as truthful, genuine, or valid. authority bond: see *bond, authority.*

authority bond: see *bond, authority.*

authorized capital stock: the full amount of stock that a corporation is permitted by its charter to issue.

authorized depositary: in Great Britain, people authorized by an order of H.M. Treasury to receive securities into deposit in accordance with the terms of the Exchange Control Act of 1947.

authorized investment: an investment that is authorized by the trust instrument; to be distinguished from *legal investments.*

authorized issue
(1) the total number of shares of capital stock that a charter permits a corporation to sell.
(2) the total number of bonds that may be sold under a given mortgage.

authorized stock: the maximum number of all classes of securities that can be issued by a corporation. see *capital stock.*

Automated Bond System: the NYSE computerized system that matches all orders of listed nonconvertible bonds.

automated clearinghouse (ACH): a computerized facility used by member depository institutions to process (i.e., combine, sort, and distribute) payment orders in machine-readable form (computer tapes or punched cards).

Automated Pricing and Reporting System: the NYSE computer system for processing and assigning a price to qualified odd-lot orders based on the following round-lot sale of the same security. The transaction information is forwarded to a specialist and the firm presenting the order.

automatic dividend reinvestment: see *automatic reinvestment.*

automatic reinvestment: a service, often associated with mutual funds, enabling the investor to automatically put income dividends or capital gains distributions back into the fund to buy new shares and thereby build up new holdings.

automatic withdrawal: a mutual fund program entitling stockholders to a fixed payment every month or each quarter. Payment comes from dividends and income on stocks held by the particular fund.

autonomous investment: new investment caused by events independent of changes in the interest rate or the level of consumption or national income.

AV: see *ad valorem.*

Av.: see *average.*

avail: the amount remaining following a discount or expense deduction.

available assets: a person's or firm's assets that may be readily sold to meet a need. Such assets would usually not be mortgaged or pledged.

available balance: the book balance less any hold, uncollected funds, and restrictions against an account.

average
(1) ***general:*** a measure of central tendency.
(2) ***investments:*** to buy or sell more shares, items, or whatever with the goal of receiving a better average price. see also *averages.*

average bond: see *bond, average.*

average down: reducing the average cost basis of a stock by purchasing more shares of that same stock at a lower price.

average equity: the average daily balance in a trading account.

average life: the number of years needed for one half of a debt to be retired through a sinking fund, serial maturity, or amortizing payments.

average price: the mean, or average, price of a security obtained in the purchase or sale of a security by a process of averaging.

average revenue: the amount received from all sales divided by the number of items that have been sold.

averages: various ways of measuring the trend of securities prices; one of the most popular is the Dow Jones average of 30 industrial stocks listed on the New York Stock Exchange. Formulas—some very elaborate—have been devised to compensate for stock splits and stock dividends and thus given continuity to the average. In the case of the Dow Jones industrial average, the prices of the 30 stocks are totaled and then divided by a divisor which is intended to compensate for past stock splits and stock dividends and which is changed from time to time. As a result, point changes in the average have only the vaguest relationship to dollar price changes in stocks included in the average. see NYSE *Common Stock Index, point, split.*

average up: see *averaging up.*

average yield: in Great Britain, the average of all the yields implied by the prices bid for U.S. Treasury bills at the Bank of England tender.

averaging
(1) ***federal income taxes:*** a benefit allowing individuals to average taxable income for four preceding years over a five-year period.
(2) ***investments:*** the methods used in an attempt to improve the average price paid or received for securities.

averaging the dollar: see *dollar (cost) averaging.*

averaging up: in the stock market, the practice of selling short the same dollar amount of shares as the market price is rising so that prices can fall only partway back toward the original starting price and there will be a net profit if the shares are brought to cover before the original prices are reached again.

Avg.: see *average.*

award
(1) ***general:*** the acceptance of a bid or the assigning of a project on the basis of a made offer. see *competitive bid.*
(2) ***investments:*** the acceptance by a borrower of a competitive bid for a security issue in the form of notification to the high-bidder investment banker or syndicate.

away from me: a quote, transaction, or market in an issue made by a market maker that originated with another individual.

away from the blue: any municipal securities offering by a dealer who has not already advertised it in the Blue List book.

away from the market: when a bid on a limit order is lower, or the offer price is higher than the current market price for the stock. Such orders are held by the broker for later execution unless fill or kill is placed on the order entry.

AY: see *annual yield.*

B

B
(1) see *bid.*
(2) the annual rate plus stock dividend (in stock listing of newspapers).
(3) the monetary base.
(4) the quality rating for a municipal or corporate bond, lower than BB and higher than CCC.

B & A: see *bid and asked.*

baby bond: see *bond, baby.*

back: see *backwardation.*

backdating
(1) ***general:*** placing a date on a statement that is prior to the date on which it was drawn up.
(2) ***mutual funds:*** the practice allowing fundholders to use an earlier date on a promise to invest a given sum of money over a stated time period in exchange for a reduced sales charge.

back door: another name for the U.S. Treasury.

backdoor financing: the practice enabling a government agency to borrow from the U.S. Treasury insteadof relying on congressional appropriations. synonymous with *public debt transaction.*

backdoor listing: a company's practice of making itself eligible for listing on an exchange by acquiring a listed firm and merging itself into acquisition, after failing to fulfill the listing requirements of an exchange on its own.

back-end load: designed to discourage withdrawals; a redemption charge to an investor for withdrawing money from an investment.

backing away: a broker-dealer's failure to make good on a bid for the minimum quantity. A practice considered unethical by National Association of Securities Dealers.

backlog: the existence and accumulation of unfilled requests on a firm's books.

back office: a brokerage house's operations department, handling record keeping, statements, margin account requirements, and so forth.

back office crunch (crush)

(1) ***general:*** a delay in daily operations, often resulting from a pileup of unprocessed work.

(2) ***investments:*** an operational failure, where brokerage houses are deficient in processing a heavier than normal volume of transactions.

back spread: exists when the price for identical items in two markets is less than the normal difference (e.g., a stock is selling for $50 on a New York stock exchange and for the equivalent of $55 on the London Stock Exchange, the difference being due to shipping costs, insurance, and other factors).

back up: the reversal of a stock market trend; a turn around. When prices move in one direction, investors speak of a sudden reversal caused by the market backing up.

backup line: a bank line of credit in the name of an issuer of commercial paper, covering maturing notes in case the new notes fail to be marketed to replace them.

backwardation

(1) a basic pricing system in commodity futures trading. A price structure in which the nearer deliveries of a commodity cost more than contracts that are due to mature many months in the future. A backwardation price pattern occurs mainly because the demand for supplies in the near future is greater than the demand for supplies at some more distant time.

(2) a London Stock Exchange term for fees and interest due on short sales of delayed delivery securities.

bad debt: the amount due on an open account that has been proved to be uncollectible; any uncollectible receivable.

bad debt expense: the cost of uncollectible accounts receivable. In most companies, bad debt expense is debited for the estimated amount uncollectible, and allowance for uncollectible accounts is credited.

bad debt recovery: money collected on a bad debt account.

bad debts collected: amounts earlier written off as uncollectible that are subsequently collected.

bad delivery

(1) ***general:*** a delivered item not conforming to the original terms of agreement.

(2) ***investments:*** an improperly prepared or transferred security or certificate.

bad faith: the intent to mislead or deceive (mala fides). It does not include misleading by an honest, inadvertent, or uncalled-for misstatement.

balance

(1) the net difference between all debits and credits of an account.

(2) an equality of debits and credits in an account.

balanced budget: a budget in which forward expenditures for a set period are matched by expected revenues for the same period.

balanced fund: a mutual fund which has an investment policy of *balancing* its portfolio, generally by including bonds, preferred stocks, and common stocks.

balanced manager: an investment manager whose expertise includes the supervision of portfolios containing a variety of classes of investments, that is, bonds, stocks, cash reserves, and so on.

balanced mutual fund: see *balanced fund.*

balance due: the total amount needed to equalize the debit and credit sum of an account; the amount you owe.

balance of account: the net amount of the total debits and total credits posted to a given account. Balances are of three types: *zero balance,* indicating that total debits and total credits are equal; *debit balance,* indicating an excess of total debits over total credits; and *credit balance,* indicating an excess of total credits over debits, at a given time.

balance owing: the amount outstanding.

balance sheet: an itemized statement listing the total assets and the total liabilities of a given business to portray its net worth at a given moment in time.

balance sheet audit: an examination of a statement of financial condition as of a given date, usually at the end of the normal accounting period.

balance sheet equation: the equation stating that the total of assets equals the total of liabilities plus net worth (ownership).

balloon
(1) ***general:*** the final payment on a debt that is considerably larger than the preceding payments.
(2) ***mortgages:*** the lump-sum payment a home borrower owes after expiration of a home loan payable to the loaning bank.

ballooning: price manipulation used to send prices beyond safe or real values.

balloon interest: in serial bond issues, a higher coupon rate on bonds with later maturities.

balloon loan: a loan on which small payments are made during the term of the obligation.

balloon maturity: a bond issue having a substantially larger dollar amount of bonds falling due in the later maturity dates.

balloon mortgage: a mortgage that allows for payments that do not completely amortize the loan at the time of termination. As a result, the final payment is larger than any single payment made previously.

balloon note: a promissory note requiring only a small payment during the initial loan period, which is then offset by larger payments made before the date of maturity.

balloon payment: a large extra payment that may be charged at the end of a loan or lease.

Baltimore Stock Exchange: see *Philadelphia Stock Exchange.*

bank: an organization, normally a corporation, chartered by the state or federal government, the principal functions of which are: (a) to receive demand and time deposits, honor instruments drawn against them, and pay interest on them as permitted by law; (b) to discount notes, make loans, and invest in government or other securities; (c) to collect checks, drafts, notes, and so on; (d) to issue drafts and cashier's checks; (e) to certify depositor's checks; and (f) when authorized by a chartering government, to act in a fiduciary capacity.

bank accommodation: a short-term bank loan to a customer, either on the individual's own note or on the endorsement of another's note owed to him or her.

bank account: a financial relationship created in the name of a business or individual. There are a variety of such accounts, including time accounts; demand accounts; and single name, mutiname, joint, or trustee accounts. Minimum balance and payment of interest will vary. see specific types of accounts.

banked costs: where dealers who charge less than regulations allowed in the past can add those past undercharges to present margins.

bank-eligible issues: issues of U.S. Treasury obligations eligible for immediate purchase by commercial banks—mainly those due or callable within 10 years.

banker's acceptance: a bill of exchange drawn on or accepted by a bank to pay specific bills for one of its customers when the bills become due.

banker's blanket bond: see *bond, banker's blanket.*

banker's shares: shares issued to an investment banker which frequently in the past could control or manipulate the firm because of voting features which the banker's shares had compared to the lack of vote or fractional vote of other share, such as Class A stock.

bank-guaranteed bond funds: a portfolio of bonds unconditionally guaranteed against default by a major bank because the bank has agreed to buy any of the underlying securities in the portfolio at face value on six days' notice.

bank guarantee letter: a document issued by an exchange-approved bank certifying that the bank retains sufficient funds to cover the writing of a put option or that shares are on deposit covering the writing of a call option.

bank holding company: in general usage, any company that owns or controls one or more banks. However, a bank holding company as defined in the Bank Holding Company Act of 1956 is one that controls two or more banks. Such companies must register with the Board of Governors of the Federal Reserve System and are commonly referred to as registered bank holding companies. see *Bank Holding Company Act.*

Bank Holding Company Act of 1956: applied to any corporation controlling 25 percent or more of the voting shares of at least two banks, or otherwise controlling the election of a majority of the directors of two or more banks. The law formulated standards for the formation of bank holding companies. These companies were strictly limited to the business of banking, managing banks, and providing services to affiliated banks.

Bank Holding Company Act Amendments of 1966: established uniform standards for bank agencies and the court in evaluating the legality of bank holding company acquisitions. see *Bank Holding Company Act of 1956, Bank Holding Company Act Amendments of 1970.*

Bank Holding Company Act Amendments of 1970: ended the exemption from the Bank Holding Company Act that one-bank holding companies had enjoyed since 1956. This last amendment clearly regulated the ownership of bank shares and limited bank holding company entries into activities related only to the business of banking. see *Bank Holding Company Act of 1956, Bank Holding Company Act Amendments of 1966.*

Banking and Securities Industry Committee (BASIC): a group responsible for setting standards of securities operations and certificate processing systems.

banking syndicate: a group of banks created for the purpose of underwriting and selling of an issue of securities.

bank line: a moral obligation of a bank to make loans to a known borrower up to a given maximum during a specified period, usually one year. Not a legal commitment, it is the practice to charge a commitment fee.

bank loan: any money borrowed from a bank for the purposes of business investment.

bank note: a promissory note released by an authorized bank that is payable on demand to the bearer and can be used as cash. Such notes, as established by law, are redeemable as money and are considered to be full legal tender.

bank quality: see *investment grade.*

bankrupt: a person, corporation, or other legal entity which, being unable to meet its financial obligations, has been declared by a decree of the court to be insolvent, and whose property becomes liable to administration under the Bankruptcy Reform Act of 1978. see *insolvent.*

bankruptcy: the conditions under which the financial position of an individual, corporation, or other legal entity are such as to cause actual or legal insolvency. Two types are: (a) *involuntary bankruptcy*—one or more creditors of an insolvent debtor file a petition having the debtor declared a bankrupt; and (b) *voluntary bankruptcy*—the debtor files a petition claiming inability to meet debts and willingness to be declared a bankrupt. A court adjudges and declares a debtor a bankrupt. see *Bankruptcy Reform Act of 1978, insolvency.*

Bankruptcy Reform Act of 1978: taking effect on October 1, 1978, the first complete overhaul of bankruptcy statutes in 75 years. Some major provisions are: (a) a consolidation of the three sections of the old law that dealt with business reorganizations—in effect, a restructuring to permit a company to return to fiscal soundness—into a new, streamlined Chapter 11; (b) various new tactical weapons for business creditors, one of which may allow them, in certain instances, to file their own reorganization plans for a company; (c) new federal exemptions for consumers that may allow them to keep more property after bankruptcy than they could under state laws unless the states take contrary action; and (d) a new procedure that will allow small businesses to pay off their debts gradually under a proceeding similar to a reorganization. see *bankruptcy.*

Bankruptcy Tax Act of 1980: federal legislation that went into effect on January 1, 1981. In part, the law says that a company that buys back its own bonds at a discount price must pay income tax on the spread between the face value of the bonds, or the original sales price, and the discount repurchase price. see also *solvent debtor section.*

bank securities: a commercial bank offerings include convertible or nonconvertible capital debentures, convertible or nonconvertible preferred stock, and common stock.

Banks for Cooperatives: an organization that makes and services loans to eligible cooperative associations engaged in marketing agricultural products, purchasing farm supplies, or furnishing farm business services.

bank term loan: a loan terminating in a year or more. At times used instead of a long-term bond issue, especially during periods of high interest rates.

bank trust department: the unit of a bank involved in settling estates, administering trusts and guardianships, and performing agency services. Also acts as trustee for corporate bonds, administers pension and profit-sharing plans, and functions as a transfer agent.

banque d'arraires: a French bank involved in long-term financing and in the ownership of companies, usually industrial firms. see *merchant bank.*

Banque de France: the central bank of France, created by Napoleon Bonaparte in 1800.

BANs: see *bond anticipation notes.*

Ban Ser Corp: formed in 1974 to service insurance plans offered by savings banks to their employees, depositors, and/or mortgagors. Ban Ser does not handle general lines of insurance or service claims. Rather, it acts as liaison between savings banking and the insurance industry in developing new insurance plans to meet savings banks' changing needs and in monitoring existing plans for pricing, service, and standards of coverage. Ban Ser offers a complete insurance consulting service for thrift institutions.

bar chart: a chart showing the price action of a security; used to aid in shaping opinion about future movements.

bargain counter: describing stocks offered for sale at prices below their intrinsic value.

bargain hunter
(1) ***general:*** an individual who seeks out the store selling items at the lowest possible price.
(2) ***investments:*** a speculator or investor who waits until stocks are on the bargain counter.

bar graph: a graph having solid bars showing the comparisons of two or more amounts.

"barometers": business measurements used to determine the condition of a market or economy (e.g., Consumer Price Index, housing starts, gross national product, new plant expenditures).

barometer securities: stocks that move in the same direction as the market and are considered to be representative of the market.

barracudas: synonymous with *guerrillas.*

barren money: currency that does not earn interest or other forms of income.

Barron's: a weekly publication of financial and investment matters by Dow Jones & Company.

Barron's Confidence Index: the ratio of Barron's highest-grade corporate bond yield average to the Dow Jones composite bond yield average (including lower-grade bonds). This index changes with corresponding changes in these yields.

BAS: see *block automation system.*

base: a charted stock pattern showing a relatively narrow price range over an extended time frame which often follows a period of decline.

basebuilding: a period of sideways price trend over an extended time period. Following a long drop, a basebuilding period is required before an established price advance occurs.

base market value: the average market price of a group of securities at any given time; used in plotting dollar or percentage changes for purposes of market indexing.

base-year analysis: a method of analysis of financial statements, whereby the figures for each of a series of years are compared to those of a common base year.

BASIC: see *Banking and Securities Industry Committee.*

basic balance: the sum of the balance-of-payments current account plus long-term capital movements.

basic IS-LM Model: see *IS-LM model.*

basic yield: a concept similar to pure interest, that is, the annual rate of return in percent on a risk-free investment, such as a long-term U.S. government bond.

basis
(1) ***taxation:*** in calculating capital gains or losses, the value employed as the original property cost, which may or may not be the true cost.
(2) ***investments:*** the difference between the cash price of money market instrument that is hedged and a futures contract.

basis book: a book of mathematical tables used to convert bond yields-to-maturity to equivalent dollar prices at various rates of interest.

basis point: the smallest measure used for quoting yields on bonds and notes. A basis point is 0.01 percent of yield.

basis price
(1) ***investments:*** the price an investor uses to determine the long- or short-term capital gains when selling a bond or security.
(2) ***odd-lot trading:*** the price arbitrarily set by an exchange floor official at the end of a trading session for a buyer or seller of an odd lot when the market bid and asked prices are more than $2 apart, or if no round-lot transactions occurred that day. The investor receives the basis price plus or minus the odd-lot differential, if any.

basis quote: the sale or offer of a cash commodity measured as the difference less than or more than a futures price.

basis trading: synonymous with *relationship trading.*

basis value: the value of a security considered as an investment, and, with bonds, as bearing interest, if held to maturity.

basket purchase: the purchase of a group of assets for one price. So that the items can be recorded individually in the accounts, however, a cost is assigned to each asset.

batten: to grow wealthy at another's expense.

bay: space on a selling floor between four columns; a recess or opening in walls.

BB
(1) see *Big Board.*
(2) see *bond, baby.*
(3) see *bond, bearer.*
(4) see *buy back.*
(5) the quality rating for a municipal or corporate bond, lower than BBB and higher than B.

BBB: the quality rating for a municipal or corporate bond, lower than A and higher than BB.

BC: see *blue chip.*

BD
(1) see *bad delivery.*
(2) see *bill discounted.*

Bd.
(1) see *board.*
(2) see *bond.*

B/D: see *broker-dealer.*

BD form: a document filed by a brokerage house with the SEC describing the company's financial status and listing of its officers.

BDO: see *bottom dropped out.*

BDR: see *bearer depositary receipt.*

B/E: see *bill of exchange.*

bear: a person who thinks security prices will fall. A bear market is one that goes down over a period of time. see *bears.*

bear account: any short account.

bear campaign: the practice of selling securities short to lower prices, and then attempting to close out the short sales at a significant profit. synonymous with *bearing a market, bear raiding.*

bear clique: a group of people or organizations that attempt to depress the price of stocks and commodities by selling short. The formation of a bear clique for this manipulative objective is outlawed. see *bear raid, short sale.*

bear covering: the purchase by bears of the stock, commodity, or currency which they have sold.

bearer: any person holding a negotiable instrument.

bearer bond: see *bond, bearer.*

bearer certificate: a certificate that is not filled out in the name of a particular person. Since these certificates are negotiable without endorsement, they should always be kept in a safe place.

bearer check: a check payable to cash or the bearer rather than to a specific party.

bearer depositary receipt (BDR): a depositary receipt made out in bearer form; used to assist in the trading of foreign corporations.

bearer form: in a form payable to bearer, the security having no registered owner.

bearer instrument: a negotiable instrument payable on demand to the individual who holds the instrument. Title passes by delivery without endorsement.

bearer paper: in dealing with negotiable instruments, an instrument is called *bearer paper* when it is payable to bearer (i.e., the person having possession of it). Ownership of such a document is transferred by delivery, no indorsement being needed. If the person who originally issued the paper placed it in bearer form, it cannot thereafter receive a special indorsement.

bearer security: securities whose owners are not registered with the borrower; the securities are owned by those who possess them. The 1982 tax law requires the registration of all securities issued in the United States, with only a few exceptions.

bearer stock: capital stock evidenced by certificates that are not registered in any name. They are negotiable without endorsement and transferable by delivery. They carry numbered or dated dividend coupons.

bear hug: an unnegotiated corporate takeover proposal, made privately or publicly to directors. The major goal is to force a board into a decision.

bearing a market: synonymous with *bear campaign.*

bearish and bullish: when conditions suggest lower prices, a bearish situation is said to exist. If higher prices appear warranted, the situation is said to be bullish.

bear market: a declining stock market.

bear panic (squeeze): a condition resulting when securities advance in price, rather than declining, to the disappointment of the bears, thus forcing the bears to close out their positions at a loss.

bear pool: now prohibited, a type of manipulation consisting of a formally organized fund contributed by operators who desire prices to be forced downward.

bear position: a stance taken by a person who expects the market to fall. As a consequence, he or she sells securities short, hoping that the market will move downward.

bear raid: attempts to depress the price of a security or item by heavy selling.

bear raiding: synonymous with *bear campaign.*

bears: speculators who anticipate that prices are going to drop. see *bear, hammering the market.*

bear spread: an option technique where the investor purchases one type of option (either a put or a call), and sells the other on the same underlying security simultaneously. The option that is bought has a higher striking price than the one sold. The investor profits by a decrease in the market price of the underlying stock. cf. *bull spread.*

bear squeeze: a strategy by central banks which know that uncovered bears have sold their currency short. By temporarily bidding up the currency until the time comes for the bears to deliver the currency they had contracted to sell, the central bank forces the bears to take a loss.

bear straddle writing: an option writing technique involving an uncovered call and a covered put on the same underlying security, at the same striking price with the identical date of expiration. cf. *bull straddle writing.*

bear trap: when a stock declines, thereby attracting heavy selling, and then surges.

beat down: slang, to bargain to lower the cost of an item.

beating the gun: prohibited by the SEC, the practice of accepting customer orders for a new stock, and/or releasing significant data on a new offering. prior to the registration statement of the security's becoming effective.

bed and breakfast deals: short selling abuses. Arrangements whereby individuals or firms sell shares one day and buy them back the next morning in a previously agreed-upon transaction to establish a tax loss against future capital gains. Exists in Great Britain. In the United States, not allowed; a 30-day interval is required between a sale and repurchase to establish a tax loss.

bell: the signal opening and closing trading on major exchanges—sometimes the bell is replaced with a buzzer sound.

bellwether stock: any security used as a measure of the stock market's movement. In most cases, these are stocks that indicate the direction of the general market about two or three weeks before other securities follow a similar pattern.

below par: at a discount; less than face amount.

below the line: the classification applied to an out-of-the-ordinary revenue or expense, or an extraordinary and material nonrecurring item that requires a separate grouping in a company's balance sheet or income statement.

below the market: at a price lower than the prevailing level at which a security is currently quoted or traded.

Benef.: see *beneficiary.*

beneficial interest (owner): an individual, not the true owner of property, who enjoys all or part of the benefits to it, by reason of a trust or private arrangement.

beneficiary

(1) ***general:*** a person beneficially interested in a trust or estate.

(2) ***insurance:*** the person(s) to whom the proceeds of a life insurance contract are payable at the death of the insured.

(3) ***law:*** the person for whose benefit a trust, policy, will, or contract promise is made. synonymous with *cestui que trust.*

beneficiary, change of: process of altering the beneficiary endorsement to provide for payment to one other than originally named, or to provide for payment in a different manner.

beneficiary, contingent: a beneficiary who is entitled to benefits only after the death of a primary beneficiary.

beneficiary, endorsement: an endorsement placed on (or attached to in rider form) the policy setting forth the names of the beneficiaries, relationship to the insured, manner in which policy proceeds are to be paid, and conditions upon which each beneficiary's right to receive such payment is based.

beneficiary, irrevocable: a beneficiary for whom another may not be substituted by the insured.

benefit fund: the monies set aside by the plan sponsored with a trustee or insurance company for the payment of benefits.

bequeath: to offer personal property in a will.

bequest: a gift of personal property made by a testator.

Berne Union: established in 1934, with 26 member nations, works for "the international acceptance of sound principles of export credit and investment insurance."

best bid: the highest price a person is willing to pay for something offered for sale. This bid is the relevant one used in determining the market for a security.

best efforts offering: the public offering of a new stock where underwriters agree to use their best efforts to sell the entire issue by a given date. The underwriter does not buy and then resell the issue but rather leaves the risk with the issuer.

Best's rating: a rating by Best's Rating Service of the financial soundness of insurance firms. Useful to investors purchasing shares of insurance companies in addition to purchasers of insurance or annuities. The top rating is A+.

beta: a measure of a stock's sensitivity to the movement of the general market (S&P 500), in either direction over the last five years. A beta of 1.6 means that over the past five years, the stock has moved 60 percent greater than the S&P 500, both up and down. see also *alpha.*

BF: see *backdoor financing.*

Bfcy.: see *beneficiary.*

Bgt.: bought.

bicicleta: bicycle. A money manipulation system in which people invest money in short-term accounts at rates as high as 150 percent annually.

bicycle: see *bicicleta.*

bid: an offering of money in exchange for property (items, goods, etc.) put up for sale. Types of bids are: *best bid*—not necessarily the lowest or highest, but good for the organization seeking a bid; *competitive bid*—a bid secured from a public announcement of the competition; and *sealed bid*—a bid that is not disclosed until a specified time, when all other bids are revealed and compared. (This approach purports to guarantee the independence of bidders.)

bid ahead: used to explain to a prospective purchaser of securities that bids at the same price or at a higher price arrived on the trading floor before his or her's and therefore have priority for the same issue.

bid and asked: synonymous with *quotation.* c. *bids and offers.*

bid-ask spread: the difference between the buying (bid) and selling (ask) price.

bid bond: see *bond, bid.*

bidding

(1) ***general:*** the act of offering money as an exchange for an item or service.

(2) ***auction:*** an individual, or his or her representative, bids by raising a numbered paddle or by other signal arranged in advance with the auctioneer. Bids may also be submitted in written form before an auction. At major sales, arrangements are also made for bids to be submitted by telephone while the auction is in progress.

bidding up: the activity of raising the price bid for a security, for fear of failing to have an order executed before an upswing begins.

bid price: in the case of open-end shares, the price at which the holder may redeem their shares; in most cases, it is the current net asset value per share. In the case of closed-end shares, the highest price then offered for stock in the public market.

bids and offers: a "bid" is the quotation of a prospective buyer for the purchase; and an "offer" is the quotation of a seller for the sale of a trading unit or other specified amount of a security. Some of the established methods of trading in securities are: *for cash*—delivery and payment must be made on the same day; *regular way delivery*—securities must be delivered and paid for on the third full business day after sale; and *seller's option*—the seller has the right to deliver the securities within a period of not less than 4 nor more than 60 days.

bid wanted (BW): a request by the seller of a stock or commodity who wishes to locate a purchaser for it.

big bang: the peaking of deregulation in Great Britain in October 1986, when fixed charges on securities trading were abandoned in favor of negotiated commissions. In addition, barriers separating the activities of different kinds of financial institutions were reduced permitting big commercial and merchant banks positions in the brokerage business.

Big Board: the New York Stock Exchange, Inc. cf. *Little Board.*

big figure: used by foreign exchange dealers to denote the first three digits of an exchange rate.

bigger-fool theory: where investors know that they are not buying a quality issue, but believe they can foresee a desire by less informed investors, to take it off their hands at a later time.

big ticket: slang, the selling of an expensive item to a customer.

bilateral clearing: an international trade system to economize on the use of scarce foreign exchange by routing all payments through a central bank instead of with foreign trade banks or their equivalent demanding that the nations involved be required exactly to balance their mutual trade every year.

bilateral contract: an agreement containing promises, with each party serving as a promisor or promisee.

bill
(1) ***general:*** an invoice of charges for services or a product.
(2) ***general:*** paper currency.
(3) ***general:*** short for *bill of exchange*. see *bill of exchange.*
(4) ***government:*** short for *T-bill* or *Treasury bill*. see *Treasury bill.*

bill broker: any financial dealer in bills of exchange.

bill discounted: a promissory note or bill of exchange from which a bank deducts its interest in advance.

billed escrow: the amount of escrow payment that represents a total of the regular escrow payment plus arrears of minus prepaid escrow amounts.

billed principal: the amount of principal payment that represents a total of the normal principal amount plus any arrears.

bill for payment: an instrument given to a debtor or representative for the purpose of being paid, as differentiated from one that was presented for acceptance.

billing cycle: time interval, often a month, between regular periodic billing statement dates.

billing date: the month, day, and year when a periodic or monthly statement is generated, and when calculations for appropriate finance charges, minimum payment due, and new balance have been performed.

bill of exchange: instructions from one party to another party to pay a third party following completion of an assignment.

bills discounted overdue: bills, notes acceptances, and similar obligations that have passed their due date or matured and are as yet unpaid. Representing past due accounts of doubtful value, they are segregated from other assets.

bills payable: a comprehensive term that includes all notes and trade acceptances that are owed by a business to trade creditors and must be paid by the business at maturity.

bills receivable: a comprehensive term that includes the total of all notes and trade acceptances given by customers, usually in payment of merchandise, which the debtors must pay at maturity.

bimetallism: a double standard of metals used in coins. The ratio of content and weight must be specified in terms of, for example, gold and silver. cf. *real money.*

binding signature: a legally acceptable signature. One which when affixed to a legal document makes that document valid and enforceable.

bind the bargain: see *earnest money.*

BIR: Bureau of Internal Revenue. The division of the Treasury Department of the federal government which collects all internal taxes, including excise and income taxes.

bird-dog: to seek data to assist in studying a firm's position and potential earnings.

Bk.: see *bank.*

Bkg.: banking.

Bkr.: see *broker.*

Bks.: see *book(s).*

B&L ASSN: see *building and loan association.*

blackboard trading: the practice of selling commodities from a blackboard on a wall of a commodity exchange.

black box: a projected working model of a wholly electronic stock exchange that some predict will eventually replace the traditional stock exchanges.

Black Friday: September 24, 1869: the day of a business panic resulting from an attempt by financiers to corner the gold market. A depression followed. Coincidentally, the financial panics of 1873 and 1929 also first became serious on Fridays, hence the term, indicating a day of evil or calamity.

black market: buying or selling of products and commodities, or engaging in exchange of foreign currencies in violation of government restrictions. cf. *gray market.*

black market bond: see *bond, black market.*

Black-Scholes Option Pricing Model: a finance model using seven variables, such as strike price and stock volatility, to determine the value of an option.

Black Tuesday: Tuesday, October 29, 1929, the day the stock market crashed leading to the Great Depression of the 1930s.

blank bill: a bill of exchange with the payee's name not appearing.

blank-check tactic: where shareholders empower management to issue preferred stock with special voting rights to friendly parties, designed to discourage hostile bids. see also *staggered board amendment, Williams Act.*

blank endorsement: the signature or endorsement of a person or firm on an instrument such as a note or check making it payable to the bearer and therefore negotiable without restrictions.

blanket bond: see *bond, blanket.*

blanket certification form: see *NASD Form FR-1.*

blanket fidelity bond: see *bond, blanket.*

blanket mortgage: a mortgage covering all the property of a corporation and given to secure a single debt.

blanket recommendation: a notification from a brokerage house sent to all clients recommending that they purchase or sell a particular stock or stocks irregardless of individual investment goals or existing portfolio.

blank indorsement: the placing of one's name on a negotiable instrument without any qualification. synonymous with *general indorsement.*

blank stock: stock whose terms need not be set forth in the articles of incorporation but may be established by the board of directors at the time of issue.

blended credit: financial credit extended on the basis of more than one source of funding.

blind brokering: the practice of a business firm or individual, especially a dealer in government securities, trading indirectly through an intermediary person or firm instead of as the principal.

blind entry: a bookkeeping entry stating only the accounts and the amounts debited and credited, but not giving other data or accounting factors essential to an accurate record.

blind pool: a speculative device used in financial markets where a group of speculators allow one of their members to handle the operation of their obligated funds. The pool's composition, aside from the chosen member, is concealed from the public. see *bobtail pool.*

blind pool partnership: a limited real estate partnership investment where assets to be bought are unknown to investors at the time of investment.

blind trust: a trust established to protect a person from the claim of conflict in interest charge in which all financial affairs are handled by a fiduciary.

block

(1) ***general:*** a bundle of checks deposited for credit with a bank,

along with their relative deposit slips.
(2) ***investments:*** a large holding or transaction of stock popularly considered to be 10,000 shares or more.

block automation system (BAS): initiated in 1970 by the New York Stock Exchange, a computerized communications network to aid in large-block transactions by institutional investors. This approach enables such investors to identify buyers and sellers rapidly when they are considering a trade.

block house: a firm, sometimes not a member of a particular exchange, which specializes in block trades.

block positioner: a dealer, hoping to accommodate the seller of a block of stock, takes a position in the stocks, expecting to gain from a climb in the market price. Block positioners are required to register with the SEC.

block sale: the sale of a significant number of shares, with a buying price of usually more than $100,000.

block trade: the purchase and sale of blocks of stocks through brokers, who are sometimes not members of the particular exchange, working as negotiators between buyers and sellers. see also *block sale.*

block transaction: a transaction involving the trade of 10,000 shares or more of a specific security.

blood bath: slang, a tremendous loss suffered by investors when the stock market declines sharply.

blotter: a book of accounts or a journal used for entering the first or temporary list of transactions or occurrences.

blowing off: a temporary purchasing peak, often along with heavy trading volume and occurring after an extended advance.

blow it out: see *blowout.*

blowout: the rapid sale of all shares on a new stock offering. Firms desire to sell their securities in this fashion as they usually receive a high price for their stock, while investors have difficulty acquiring the quantity of shares they desire during a blowout. see *going away, hot issue.*

blue chip: a corporation maintaining a good dividend return and having sound management and good growth potential.

blue chip stock: synonymous with *quality stock.*

blue list: the trade offering sheets of bond dealers, listing dealers' offerings of municipal bonds for sale all over the country. A composite list published five days a week by The Blue List Publishing Company, New York City, showing current municipal bond offerings by banks and municipal bond houses all over the country.

blue room: the ancillary trading room that is part of the NYSE floor complex.

blue sky law: the name given to certain laws enacted by the various states to regulate the sale and issuance of securities, specifically, attempting to prevent fraud in their sale and disposition. cf. *SEC.*

Blumenthal bond: see *bond, Carter.*

BM
(1) see *bear market.*
(2) see *buyers' market.*

BN: see *bank note.*

BO
(1) see *buyer's option.*
(2) see *buy order.*

board: a standing comittee of high rank or importance (e.g., a board of directors).

board broker: an exchange member registered with an options exchange to serve as agent for other brokers and as a principal when trading for his or her own account. see also *order book official.*

board lot: synonymous with *round lot.*

board of arbitration: three to five persons chosen to adjudicate cases between securities houses. Approved by the National Association of Securities Dealers, all exchanges and other financial institutional associations, the board's rulings are final and binding.

board of directors: people chosen by stockholders of a corporation to manage the enterprise.

board of governors
(1) the governing body of the Federal Reserve System.
(2) the chief elective body of the National Association of Securities Dealers.

boardroom
(1) ***general:*** a room set aside for use by the board of directors of a business.
(2) ***investments:*** a room for registered representatives and customers in a broker's office, where opening, high, low, and last prices of leading stocks used to be posted on a board throughout the market day. Today such price displays are normally electronically controlled, although most board rooms have replaced the board with ticker and/or individual quotation machines.

bobtail pool: speculators acting independently of each other having a common goal and arrangement in mind. Commitments made by each member are his or her own responsibility. see *blind pool.*

bobtail statement: an abbreviated statement prepared for holders of demand deposit accounts.

BOC
(1) see *back office crunch.*
(2) see *breach of contract.*

BOD: see *board of directors.*

"body": see *corpus.*

Boerse: Dutch and German for stock exchange.

bogey: a threshold interest rate. As market rates drop, firms lower that threshold and put off financing.

boiler room tactic: selling of very speculative and often worthless securities through the use of high-pressured and misleading literature. see also *dynamiter.*

BOM
(1) beginning of the month.
(2) see *buying on margin.*

bona fide: "in good faith" (Latin); with honest intent. cf. *mala fides.*

bona fide arbitrage: any arbitrage in good faith, having offset buying and selling transactions that have a built-in profit.

bona fide purchaser: an individual who buys property in good faith, without notice of any defect in the title, and for a valuable consideration.

bonanza
(1) ***general:*** an enormously successful business venture.
(2) ***investments:*** a highly profitable investment resulting in sudden wealth for the owner.

bond
(1) an interest-bearing certificate of debt, usually issued in series, by which the issuer obligates itself to pay the principal amount at a specified time, usually five years or more after date of issue, and to pay interest periodically, usually semiannually. Bonds may be distinguished from promissory notes or other evidences of debt because of their formal execution under seal, and because a bank has certified that their issue has been authorized by the board of directors of a corporation or other governing body. Corporate bonds are usually secured by a lien against certain specified property.
(2) an instrument used as proof of a debt, usually secured by a mortgage. see other entries under *bond.*
(3) a promise, under seal (i.e., closed from view by the public) to pay money.
(4) the obligation to answer for the debt of another person.

bond, accumulation: a bond that is sold at a discount. If held to maturity, interest is realized up to the difference between the face value and the original purchase price. If sold before maturity, interest is the difference between the purchase and sale price.

bond, adjustment: see *bond, reorganization.*

bond, agency: a bond issued by U.S. agencies and corporations to cover their own debt. These agency securities rank just below Treasury paper.

bond, annuity: see *bond, perpetual.*

bond, approved: in the preparation for fiduciaries, *legal lists* are determined in some states. The bonds named in the *legal list* are approved bonds. see *legal list.*

bond, arbitrage: a bond issued by a municipality to gain an interest rate advantage by refunding a higher-rate bond in advance of its call date.

bond, assessment: a municipal bond created for improvements on property under municipal authority, including sidewalks or drainage, which is retired by property assessment taxes.

bond, assumed: a bond of one corporation whose liability is taken on by another corporation. see *bond, guaranteed.*

bond, authority: a bond issued by and payable from the revenue of a government agency or a corporation established to administer a revenue producing public enterprise.

bond, average: a bond given by an individual in receipt of freight, stating that the recipient will contribute to any standard claim.

bond, baby: a bond with a face value usually of $100 or less.

bond, banker's blanket: business insurance coverage guaranteeing banks against loss due to dishonest, fraudulent, or employee criminal activity. This bond insures against loss resulting from robbery, larceny, burglary, theft, holdup, misplacement, and other unexplained disappearances.

bond, bearer: a bond payable to the holder that does not have the owner's name registered on the books of the issuing company.

bond, bid: a guarantee that the contractor will enter into a contract, if it is awarded to him, and will furnish such contract bond (sometimes called performance bond) as is required by the terms of the bond.

bond, black market: a registered bond traded outside the offering syndicate between the effective date and the date pricing restrictions are removed from members of the account. Often harms the distribution efforts of the syndicate.

bond, blanket: a form of broad-coverage protection carried by financial institutions to cover losses from robbery, burglary. or employee dishonesty.

bond, bonus

(1) a security issued to war veterans, given in addition to their rated pay.

(2) a rare device in bond form given as with bonus stock. see *bonus stock.*

bond, borrowed: to meet specific requirements, banks and other financial institutions borrow bonds. Banks borrow bonds to comply with collateral requirements of governmental agencies, whereas brokers borrow bonds to make delivery on short sales.

bond, bridge: securities issued for bridge construction.

bond, callable: a bond issue, all of part of which may be redeemed by the issuing corporation under definite conditions, before the issue reaches maturity.

bond, called: a bond that the debtor has declared to be due and payable on a certain date, prior to maturity, in accordance with the provisions of an issue to be redeemed; the bonds to be retired are usually drawn by loss.

bond, Carter: a medium-term foreign currency obligation issued by the United States to government during President Carter's administration as a way of achieving foreign currency balances.

bond, cash flow: a hybrid security combining features of both traditional mortgage-backed bonds and conventional pass-through securities; a debt obligation of the issuer, with a fixed coupon and required payment schedule and is at the same time a fully amortizing instrument with an average life equal to (or less than) that of the mortgage collateral pool which secures it.

bond, circular: a complete description of a bond offering used to publicize the relevant facts about the issue. A circular is traditionally released by an underwriter and given to interested parties.

bond, citizen: a form of certificateless municipal; registered on stock exchanges, in which case its price is listed in daily newspapers, unlike other municipal bonds.

bond, city: see *bond, municipal.*

bond, civil: a bond circulated by any governmental agency.

bond, classified: a debt security that receives a designation such as "Series A" or "Series B" to differentiate it from another bond of the same debtor. The series differ as to maturity date and interest.

bond, clean: a bond of the coupon type that has not been changed by any endorsement or rephrasing of the original contract. see *stamped security.*

bond, collateral: further security for a loan.

bond, collateral trust: an issue of bonds for which collateral has been pledged to guarantee repayment of the principal. This type of bond usually arises out of intercompany transactions in which the parent company issues bonds with securities of a subsidiary as the underlying collateral.

bond, combination: a bond issued by a governmental unit which is payable from the revenues of a governmental enterprise but which is also backed by the full faith and credit of the governmental unit.

bond, commercial blanket: a bond issued for a stated amount on all regular workers of the covered firm, insuring against loss from an employee's dishonest acts. see also *bond, banker's blanket.*

bond, commodity-backed: a bond tied to the price of an underlying commodity; intended to be a hedge against inflation, which drives up the prices of most commodities.

bond, completion: a bond guaranteeing the construction for an improvement in connection with which, and prior to the completion of which, a mortgagee or other lender advances funds to an owner.

bond, consolidated: a debt instrument issued to replace two or more bonds issued earlier, often done to simplify a debt structure or to benefit from a lower prevailing rate of interest.

bond, consolidated mortgage: a bond issue covering several property units and can refinance separate mortgages on these properties.

bond, continued: a debt instrument that need not be redeemed at maturity but can continue to earn interest.

bond, convertible: a bond that gives to its owner the privilege of exchanging it for other securities of the issuing corporation on a preferred basis at some future date or under certain conditions.

bond, corporate: an obligation of a corporation. see *bond, long-term corporate.*

bond, coupon: a bond with interest coupons attached. The coupons are clipped as they come due and are presented by the holder for payment of interest. see *talon.*

bond, coupon-strip: a bond sold at a deep discount in a secondary market, separately from their interest-bearing coupons, that are treated like zero-coupon bonds.

bond, currency: in 1934 the U.S. Supreme Court decided that all bonds, even those with gold clauses, were henceforth to be paid in lawful currency.

bond, current coupon: a corporate, federal or municipal bond within half a percentage point of current market rates. Such a bond is less volatile than similarly rated bonds with lower coupons.

bond, cushion: a high-interest-rate bond of top quality that sells at a premium level above par and that usually results in a higher yield to maturity.

bond, debenture: a bond for which there is no specific security set aside or allocated for repayment of the principal.

bond, deep discount: a bond selling substantially below face value; a general measure is below $800 on a bond with a face value of $1000.

bond, deferred: see *bond, extended.*

bond, deferred interest: a bond paying interest at a later date.

bond, deferred serial: a serial bond in which the first installment does not fall due for two or more years from the date of issue.

bond, definitive: any bond issued in final form; used particularly with reference to permanent bonds for which temporary bonds or interim certificates were issued.

bond, discount: a bond which may be purchased below par (e.g., 1000), thereby producing a higher yield to maturity and, in most cases, reducing the risk of call. As a general rule, the greater the discount, the lesser the chances of call and the greater the bond's attraction. Interest is paid on presentation of coupon attached to the bond.

bond, dollar

(1) a bond denominated in U.S. dollars and issued outside the country.
(2) a municipal revenue bond quoted and traded on a dollar price basis rather than on yield to maturity.
(3) a bond denominated in U.S. dollars and issued outside the country by foreign firms.

bond, drawn: a bond that has been called for redemption by lot. see *bond, called.*

bond, endorsed: a bond that has been extraneously signed permitting it to be considered for normal delivery according to the regulations of the exchange and which therefore must be sold.

bond, equipment trust: a bond used to finance the purchase of equipment, such as railroad rolling stock.

bond, escrow: represents the safest and highest-quality bond in the tax-free market; created in conjunction with a process known as advance refunding, or prerefunding of an issuer's older bonds. Proceeds from the new bond sale go into an escrow account held by a trustee bank. The money is then used to buy U.S. Treasury securities tailored to meet the interest and principal payments on the old bonds. see also *advance refunding.*

bond, estate tax: a certain designated government bond redeemable at par less accrued interest for federal estate taxes to the extent that the entire proceeds are applied to such taxes due, providing the securities were owned by the decedent at the time of death.

bond, Eurodollar: a bond paying interest and principal in Eurodollars held in a bank outside of the United States, usually in Europe. Such bonds are not registered by the SEC and are sold at lower than U.S. interest rates.

bond, extended: a bond that has matured and on which the debtor has not yet paid the principal but has agreed to extend or continue to pay the principal at a later time. Upon the creditor's accepting the extension, the bonds are stamped to show such agreement. synonymous with *deferred bond.*

bond, external: a bond issued by a country or firm for purchase outside that nation, usually denominated in the currency of the purchaser.

bond, federal: the promissory note of a central government.

bond, first mortgage: a long-term debt instrument secured by a first mortgage on all or a portion of the property of the issuer.

bond, flat income: the price at which a bond is traded includes consideration for all unpaid accruals of interest. Bonds that are in default of interest or principal are traded flat. Income bonds, which pay interest only to the extent earned, are usually traded flat. All other bonds are usually dealt in *and interest,* which means that the buyer pays to the seller the market price plus interest accrued since the last payment date.

bond, floating-rate: a debt instrument issued by large corporations and financial organizations on which the interest rate is pegged to another rate, often the Treasury bill rate, and adjusted periodically at a specified amount over that rate. Some issues permit the holder the right to "put" or redeem the notes to the issuer at par value prior to the maturity date.

bond, flower: a U.S. government bond. Until the Tax Reform Act of 1976, flower bonds sold at a substantial premium in relation to other bonds issued at similarly low interest rates because the Treasury accepted them for estate tax payments at 100 cents on the dollar, whatever their cost at the time of purchase. Now this benefit is in part taxable as a capital gain.

bond, free: an unpledged bond; any bond disposable immediately.

bond, full coupon: a bond with a coupon rate near or above current market interest rates.

bond, full faith and credit: a financial obligation of a municipality not backed by any collateral other than its creditworthiness. Such a bond is the direct obligation of the municipality.

bond, funding: a bond issued to retire outstanding floating debt and to eliminate deficits.

bond, general mortgage: a bond secured by a blanket mortgage upon property already subject to prior mortgages.

bond, general obligation (GO): a bond secured by the pledge of the issuer's full faith and credit, usually including unlimited taxing power.

bond, gilt-edged: a high-grade bond issued by a company that has demonstrated its ability to earn a comfortable profit over a period of years and to pay its bondholders their interest without interruption. see also *blue chip.*

bond, GO: synonymous with *general obligation bond.*

bond, gold: a debt instrument giving the legal holder an option of being paid principal and/or interest in gold. Since 1935 these bonds are paid in legal currency instead of gold.

bond, government: an obligation of the U.S. government, regarded as the highest-grade issues in existence. see *Treasury bill, Treasury note.*

bond, guaranteed: a bond on which the principal or income or both are guaranteed by another corporation or parent company in case of default by the issuing corporation.

bond, high-grade: a bond rated triple-A or double-A by Standard & Poor's or Moody's rating services.

bond, high-yield: synonymous with *bond, junk.*

bond, honor: a consumer-size certificate of deposit with denominations as low as $5.00, many banks promoted these bonds and told purchasers that they were merely honor-bound to report the interest on their tax returns. The Internal Revenue Service moved swiftly to eliminate this irregularity.

bond, hospital revenue: a bond issued by a state or municipal agency to finance the building of a nursing home or hospital.

bond, housing: a short- or long-term bond issued by a local housing agency to finance short-term building of low-or middle-income housing or long-term commitments for housing, plants, pollution control units, or related efforts. Bonds are free from federal income taxes and based on rulings, also from state and local taxes.

bond, improvement: any bond issued by a municipality to finance a public improvement.

bond, improvement mortgage: a bond issued for financing improvements of the debtor business that are secured by a general mortgage.

bond, inactive: see *inactive stock (bond).*

bond, income: a type of bond on which interest is paid when and only when earned by the issuing corporation.

bond, indemnity: a bond that protects the obligee (the party for whom the applicant for bond, the *principal,* has undertaken to perform specified duties) against losses resulting from the principal's failure to fulfill his or her obligations. Examples of miscellaneous indemnity bonds are warehouse, lost instrument, and lien.

bond, indenture: a written agreement under which bonds are issued, setting forth maturity date, interest rate, and other terms.

bond, indexed: a bond where the values of the principal and the payout rise with inflation or the value of the underlying commodity. cf. *bond, nonindexed.*

bond, industrial: any long-term financial debt obligations issued by corporations other than utilities, banks, and railroads. Proceeds are used for expansion, working capital, and for retiring other debts.

bond, industrial development (IDB): a long-term, tax-exempt bond isued by a state or municipality for acquiring revenue-producing land, plant, and equipment, or to aid private firms for purposes of economic development in the area, the revenue and lease income is used to pay principal and interest. synonymous with *industrial revenue bond.*

bond, industrial revenue (IRB): see *bond, industrial development.*

bond, installment: synonymous with the *serial bond.* see *bond, serial.*

bond, insular: a bond issued by a unit of the United States (e.g., Alaska, New York). synonymous with *territoral bond.*

bond, insured municipal: a municipal bond issued with insurance covering both principal and interest. The insurance fee is paid by the issuer and the bond receives high ratings because of the protection against default.

bond, interchangeable: a bond in either a registered or coupon form that can be converted to the other form or its original form at the request of the holder. A service charge is often made for such a conversion.

bond, interim: sometimes used before the issuance of permanent bonds to raise funds needed only temporarily. synonymous with *temporary bond.* see *bond, temporary.*

bond, intermediate: a callable bond bearing no date of maturity. The call aspect usually is not effective until some stated time period has passed.

bond, interminate: a callable bond having no set maturity date. The call feature is usually not effective until some stated period has passed. see *bond, callable.*

bond, internal: a bond issued by a country payable in its own currency; to be distinguished from an external bond, which is a bond issued by one country and sold in another country and payable in the currency of that other country.

bond, internal revenue: a bond required by the U.S. government which guarantees payment of federal taxes and compliance with government regulations.

bond, irredeemable: a bond issued which contains no provisions for being "called" or redeemed prior to maturity date.

bond, jeopardy assessment: a bond remaining in jeopardy assessment pending appeal. This bond is required to guarantee payment of federal taxes due or claimed to be due.

bond, joint and several: any debt instrument where the holder seeks payment from more than one corporation up to the full face amount of the security.

bond, joint control: a bond needed prior to transfer of the assets of an estate to the custody of the principal.

bond, junior: those bonds that are not senior; they are subordinate or secondary to another issue which in the event of liquidation, would have prior claim to the junior bond.

bond, junk: a bond that typically offers interest rates three to four percentage points higher than Treasury issues. This is to compensate for the increased possibility of default. They are deemed less than "investment grade" by Standard & Poor's Corporation or Moody's Investors Service. That is, they are rated BB or lower according to S&P or Ba by Moody's. Fiduciaries generally must steer clear of them. synonymous with *high-yield bond.*

bond, legal: a bond that federal and state laws identify as an acceptable and legal investment for fiduciary institutions.

bond, letter: see *letter security.*

bond, limited tax: a bond that is secured by a tax that is limited as to amount and rate.

bond, long-term corporate: a debt of industrial corporations, finance companies, utilities, and telephone companies. Maturities range from 10 to 40 years, with intermediates running from 4 to 10 years. They are rated AAA and AA for high quality. A and BBB for medium quality. The face denomination for corporate bonds is $1000, but new issues are often marketed above or below par to adjust to current yields. Older bonds with lower interest coupons sell at discounts.

bond, lost-instrument: a bond that indemnifies the issuer of a document of consequences that may arise from possession of the document by others than the recognized owner.

bond, medium: a bond with a maturity of 2 to 10 years.

bond, moral obligation: a revenue-backed municipal bond issued by a state's agency. Although not a general obligation bond, it is assumed that, in the event of default, the state will offer funds for covering both interest and principal.

bond, mortgage: a bond that has as an underlying security a mortgage on all properties of the issuing corporation.

bond, municipal: a bond issued by a state or a political subdivision (county, city, town, village, etc.). Also, a bond issued by a state agency or authority. In general, interest paid on municipal bonds is exempt from federal income taxes and state and local taxes in the state of issue.

bond, municipal revenue: banks now may underwrite a few kinds of revenue bonds, which are obligations backed not by city or state tax revenues, but by revenue produced by the facilities that are financed—for example, a housing project. Banks want to be permitted to underwrite more kinds of revenue bonds. In addition, the Comptroller of the Currency is seeking to determine the legality of municipal revenue bonds underwriting, under which banks offer, in effect, to repurchase the bonds at par within five years. This recent activity in banking is testing the Glass-Steagall Act. see *Glass-Steagall Act.*

bond, new housing authority: a bond issued by a local public housing authority to finance public housing. It is backed by federal funds and the pledge of the U.S. government.

bond, noncallable: a bond that cannot, under the terms of the issue, be called by the obligor (the corporation) for redemption or conversion.

bond, nonindexed: a bond wherein inflation erodes the value of the principal because the investor will be paid back in dollars that are worth less. The value of the bond declines further as inflation also drives up interest rates, since bond prices move inversely with interest rates. cf. *bond, indexed.*

bond, noninterest bearing: a bond issued at a discount. Throughout the bond's life its interest is not earned, however the instrument is redeemed at maturity for full face value. U.S. Treasury bills are issued this way.

bond, obligation: a bond authorized by a mortgagor that is larger than the original mortgage amount. A personal obligation is created to safeguard the lender against any costs that may develop over the amount of the mortgage.

bond, open-end: a mortgage bond of an issue that has no limit on the number or quantity of bonds that can be issued under the mortgage. However, some relationship is often required of the number and quantity of bonds to the value of the property that has been mortgaged.

bond, optional: see *bond, callable.*

bond, optional payment: a bond that gives the holder the choice to receive payment of interest or principal or both in the currency of one or more foreign countries, as well as in domestic funds.

bond, original issue discount (OID): a bond offered below face value at time of the initial offering, the difference between redemption price and original issue price is treated as income, rather than capital gains, over the life of the bond.

bond, overlying: a junior bond, subject to the claim of a senior underlying bond having priority of claim.

bond, par: a bond selling at par, in line with prevailing new issues of estimated going yield rates.

bond, participating: a bond which, following the receipt of a fixed rate of periodic interest, also receives some of the profit held by the issuing business. A form of profit sharing, this bond is rarely used today.

bond, passive: a bond that does not carry any interest. Often these bonds are issued following a reorganization.

bond, pay-through: a mortgage-backed bond backed by pools of mortgages which are marketed through public offerings or private placements to major investors, such as pension funds.

bond, perpetual: any bond having no maturity date; rarely issued in the United States.

bond, petitioning on creditors': a bond providing that, if a petition in bankruptcy filed by creditors against a debtor is dismissed, the bonding company will pay to the debtor all expenses, costs, and damages.

bond, pickup: a bond having a relatively high coupon rate and is close to the date at which it can be paid off prior to maturity by the issuer. As interest rates fall, an investor can expect to pickup a redemption premium, since the bond will probably be called.

bond, plain: any debenture. see *certificates of debt.*

bond, preference: any income or adjustment bond.

bond, premium: in the United States, a bond that is selling above its face value. In Europe, a bond having a lottery feature. When called, as distinguished from regular maturity, a premium bond generally pays substantially more than the face amount. Also, the excess of the price at which a bond is acquired or sold, over its face value. The price does not include accrued interest at the date of acquisition or sale.

bond, prior-lien: a bond holding precedence over other bonds issued by the same corporation.

bond, privileged: a convertible bond that has attached warrants.

bond, profit-sharing: a bond that participates in the issuing company's profits as well as receiving a guaranteed interest rate.

bond, public: any bond issued by a governmental agency, domestic or foreign.

bond, Public Housing Authority (PHA): a longer-term debt security issued by municipalities to provide permanent financing for low and middle-income housing.

bond, public utility: a high-quality debt instrument issued by public utility firms. The bonds are traditionally backed by mortgages on buildings and equipment.

bond, purchase-money: a bond having as security a purchase-money mortgage. see *purchase-money mortgage.*

bond, purchasing-power: a bond in which the amount of annual interest and final repayment are not stated as a fixed sum but adjusted to an index.

bond, put: a bond where investors can sell back the securities at a specified date before the bond matures.

bond, real estate: a bond secured by a mortgage or trust conveyance of real estate.

bond, redeemable: any callable bond. see *bond, callable.*

bond, redemption: a *refunding bond.* see *redemption.*

bond, redemption value: guaranteed face amount of a bond payable at maturity.

bond, refunding: a bond issued to retire a bond already outstanding. Refunding bonds may be sold for cash and outstanding bonds redeemed in cash, or they may be exchanged with holders of outstanding bonds.

bond, registered: a bond in which the name of the owner is designated, and the proceeds are payable only to him or her. Bonds may be registered as to principal and interest, or principal only. Interest on a bond registered as to both principal and interest is paid to the owner by check as it becomes due. Bonds registered as to principal only have coupons attached which are detached and collected as the interest becomes due.

bond, registered coupon: a bond registered in the owner's name but for which the interest coupons are not registered and are negotiable merely by delivery. The coupons need to be presented to a disbursing agent for payment of interest.

bond, regular serial: a serial bond in which all periodic instalments of principal repayment are equal in amount.

bond, reorganization: a debt security issued in the recapitalization of a firm in financial difficulty: an *adjustment bond.*

bond, revenue: a bond whose principal and interest are to be paid solely from earnings; such bonds are usually issued by a municipally owned utility or other public service enterprise the revenues and possibly the properties of which are pledged for this purpose.

bond, Sarmurai: a corporate bond issued in Japan by a non-Japanese firm in the yen denomination and sold only on the Japanese domestic market.

Bond, Savings (U.S.): Series EE, introduced at the start of 1980, replaced the highly popular Series E bonds. These new bonds are available in face-value denominations of $50, $75, up to $10,000, and are sold at one-half their face value. EE bonds pay varying interest rates—as much as one percent at six-month intervals if market conditions warrant. Presently, the maturity on Series EE bonds is eight years, down from nine years, effectively boosting the rate on those bonds to 9 percent. The rate on HH bonds is 8.5 percent. HH bonds are bought at face value, pay interest semiannually, and mature in 10 years. In 1982 a variable-interest-rate U.S. Savings Bond was approved. The investment yield on these bonds was increased to a level equal to 85 percent of the yield on five-year Treasury securities when held five years.

bond, school: a municipal bond to help finance the building and equipment purchases for a school.

bond, second-mortgage: a bond issued on property that already has a first mortgage outstanding on it.

bond, secured: a bond secured by the pledge of assets (plant or equipment), the title to which is transferred to bondholders in case of foreclosure. synonym for *secured debt.*

bond, self-liquidating: a bond serviced from the earnings of a municipally owned enterprise, usually a utility. The earnings must be sufficient to cover the debt service with a reasonable margin of protection if the bonds are to be regarded as entirely self-liquidating.

bond, senior: those bonds having prior claim to the assets of the debtor upon liquidation.

bond, serial: an issue of bonds in which a certain proportion of the bonds is retired at regular intervals, issued when the security depreciates through use or obsolescence. These issues usually provide that the bonds outstanding shall not exceed the value of the security. synonymous with *installment bond.*

bond, serial annuity: a serial bond in which the annual installments of the bond principal are so arranged that the payments for principal and interest combined are approximately the same each year.

bond, series: a single bond issue offered on different dates to the public rather than on the issuance date. cf. *bond, serial.*

bond, short
(1) a bond with a short maturity, usually two years or less.
(2) a bond repayable in one year or less and thereby categorized as a current liability.
(3) a short coupon bond.

bond, sinking fund: a bond secured by the deposit of specified amounts. The issuing corporation makes these deposits to secure the principal of the bonds, and it is sometimes required that the funds be invested in other securities.

bond, special assessment: a bond payable from the proceeds of special assessments. The bond is payable only from the proceeds of special assessments levied against the properties presumed to be benefited by such improvements or services.

bond, special assistance: a bond payable from levies on the properties presumably benefited by the improvement being financed. The issuing government agrees to make the assessments and earmarks the proceeds for debt service on these bonds.

bond, special district: a bond issue of a local taxing district which has been organized for a special purpose, such as road, sewer, fire, drainage, irrigation, and levee districts.

bond, special lien: a special assessment bond that acts as a lien against a particular piece (or pieces) of property.

bond, special tax
(1) a municipal revenue bond to be repaid through excise taxes on purchases, such as gasoline, tobacco, and liquor. The bond is not backed by ordinary taxing power of the municipality issuing it. Interest from these bonds is tax free to resident bondholders.
(2) any special assessment bond.

bond, stamped: when a debtor fears default on a bond, should he or she receive approval from the holder, the maturity date and/or rate of interest can be altered and a stamp affixed to the bond to signify the holder's acceptance of the terms.

bond, state: a division of municipal bonds, or the promissory note of a state.

bond, sterling: a bond denominated in British pounds sterling as distinguished from a bond denominated in another currency unit (i.e., U.S. dollar).

bond, straight: a bond conforming to the standard description, that is, unquestioned right to repayment of principal at a specified future date; unquestioned right to fixed interest payments on stated dates; and no right to either additional interest, interest in assets or profits or voice in management.

bond, straight serial: a serial bond in which the annual installments of bond principal are approximately equal.

bond, strip: where traders clip the coupons off a fixed-interest bond or note and then sell the principal and interest parts separately to two groups of investors. Those seeking current income buy the strip of coupons and those wanting a lump sum at maturity, and, a capital gain, buy the principal or "corpus" portion. Because each portion is worth less than its whole before taxes, both are sold at a deep discount from their face values.

bond, super sinker: a bond with long-term coupons but with short maturity; for example, a housing bond.

bond, tax anticipation: any short-term, interest-bearing bond created to be bought by businesses with money assembled as a reserve in order to pay taxes.

bond, tax-exempt: any security of a state, city, or other public authority specified under federal law, the interest on which is either wholy or partly exempt from federal income taxes. see *bond, municipal.*

bond, temporary: similar to a definitive bond except that it has been printed rather than engraved. see *bond, definitive.*

bond, term: bonds of the same issue usually maturing all at one time and ordinarily to be retired from sinking funds. Sometimes a term bond has more than one maturity date—for example, a serial issue having postponed maturities in only a few late years of its term.

bond, terminable: any bond having a stated maturity.

bond, terminal: bonds secured by property in the form of railroad or grain terminals.

bond, territorial: see *bond, insular.*

bond, toll revenue: a municipal bond supported by revenues from tolls paid by users of the public project constructed with bond proceeds.

bond, Treasury: a U.S. government long-term security, sold to the public and having a maturity longer than five years.

bond, underlying: a bond that has a senior lien where subsequently claims exist.

bond, unified: see *bond, consolidated.*

bond, unlimited tax: a bond secured by pledge of taxes which may be levied by the issuer in unlimited rate or amount.

bond, unsecured: a bond backed up by the faith and credit of the issuer instead of the pledge of assets.

Bond, U.S. Savings: see *Bond, Savings (U.S.)*

bond, utility revenue: a municipal bond issued to finance the construction of electric generating plants, gas, water, and sewer systems, and other public utility services. They are repaid from revenues the project yields once put into operation.

bond, zero-coupon: a security sold at a deep discount from its face value and redeemed at the full amount at maturity. The difference between the cost of the bond and its value when redeemed is the investor's return. These notes provide no interest payments to holders.

bond amortization: indicating the premium over par that has been paid for a bond.

bond anticipation notes (BANs): short-term notes of a municipality sold in anticipation of bond issuance which are full faith and credit obligations of the governmental unit and are to be retired from the proceeds of the bonds to be issued. see *interim borrowing.*

bond averages: calculations of the mean price of selected bonds over a specific period of time. A series of such calculations reflects the general trend of the bond market.

bond broker: a broker who executes bond transactions on the floor of an exchange. The broker may also engage in trading corporate, U.S. government, and municipal debt issues over the counter, primarily for large institutional customers.

bond buy-backs: as prices for corporate bonds drop, often a result of soaring interest rates, the buying up of a firm's outstanding bonds at discounts creates yields of 15 to 20 percent, thus exceeding those on most other short-term investments. In addition, corporate buyers save interest while they get ahead of their required sinking fund payments and clean up their balance sheets. see *buy back, sinking fund.*

Bond Buyer, the: a daily publication identifying most of the leading indexes and statistics for the fixed-income markets.

Bond Buyer's Index: published daily by the Bond Buyer, an index of the municipal bond market.

bond circular: a full description of a bond offering used to communicate the major facts of the issue. The circular is prepared by the underwriters and distributed to interested persons and firms.

bond crowd: brokers working in the securities markets who specialize in the trading of bonds.

bond discount: the amount below the face or par amount of a bond at which the bond is purchased.

bond dividend: a rarely offered dividend paid in the form of a bond, not in cash or additional shares of stock.

bond equivalent yield: calculating the return on original-issue discount securities, such as U.S. Treasury bills, so that it can be compared to returns on long-term debt securities.

bond floor broker: a NYSE member that handles bond transactions in the NYSE bond room.

bond fund
(1) a fund established to receive and disburse the proceeds of a governmental bond issue.
(2) an investment company, the portfolio of which consists primarily of bonds.

bondholder: one who owns bonds and therefore is a creditor of the issuer.

bond house: a financial organization whose major activity is the selling of bonds.

bond immunization: approaches that attempt to match up investment income with future liabilities—the lack of certainty that they will always be able to reinvest a bond's coupon income at high enough rates.

bonding company: an organization whose business is the forming of contracts of surety and the providing of bonds.

bond interest: interest on bonds, often paid twice a year, as determined by the conditions of the bonds. Should the bond be registered, it might take the form of a check. If it is a bearer bond, the interest may be paid with a coupon.

bond interest coverage: the measure of bond safety as computed by the total income divided by annual interest on bonds (or earnings before interest and taxes divided by annual interest on bonds).

bond market
(1) the place where bonds are sold. Most are sold over the counter;

others, in large amounts, are sold on an exchange.
(2) financial institutions that buy bonds (e.g., trust funds, banks, insurance firms).

bond ordinance (or resolution): an ordinance or resolution authorizing a bond issue.

bond power: a form of assignment executed by the owner of registered bonds which contains an irrevocable appointment of an attorney-in-fact to make the actual transfer on the books of the corporation. see also *stock power.*

bond premium: the excess of the price at which a bond is acquired or sold over its face value.

bond puts: see *put bond option.*

bond quality ratings: symbolic ratings to various levels of investment qualities of bonds, measured according to their investment risk.

bond quotations: corporate bonds are usually issued with face values of $1000 and quoted in points based on face value. One point equals $10 with minimum variations of 1/8 of a point.

bond rating: appraising and rating, by a recognized financial organization (e.g., Moody's Investors Service) of the worth of a bond as a sound investment. Ratings are based on the reputation of the organization, its record of interest payments, its profitability, and the like. A triple A (AAA) bond is the most secure, followed by AA, A, B, and so on.

bond ratio: the total face value of bonds of a corporation divided by the total face value of bonds, preferred stock, common stock, reserve, and surplus.

bond register: a book of original entry, in bound or loose-leaf form, in which are recorded the details relative to the purchase and sale of bonds for the firm's own investment account.

bond resolution: a legal order or contract by the appropriate body of a governmental unit authorizing a bond issue. The rights of the bondholders and the obligations of the issuer are carefully detailed in this resolution.

bonds authorized and unissued: bonds that have been legally authorized but have not been issued and which can be issued and sold without further authorization.

bonds issued: bonds sold.

bonds payable, matured: bonds that have reached or passed their maturity date but remain unpaid.

bond swap: the simultaneous sale of one issue and the purchase of another. Ideally, a swap should consist of, in effect, trading a shorter maturity for a longer one because longer maturities tend to sell for less than shorter ones in today's market and have a greater potential for appreciation should interest rates drop.

bond value tables: tables of bond yields to bond values used to compute bond yields to maturity or to determine the price of a bond necessary to afford a given yield to a given maturity.

bond yield: the rate of return on bonds.

bond yield to maturity: the calculation of the precise return paid by a bond upon maturation, as a function of the purchase price.

bonus: an additional dividend paid to savers who have met all the requirements of a special savings account contract.

bonus account: a savings account that earns interest at a bonus rate if the customer makes regular deposits to the account, leaves a specified amount on deposit for a specified term, or fulfills other conditions of the account contract.

bonus bond: see *bond, bonus.*

bonus futures: a recently uncovered means for increasing executive bonuses. For example, an executive hedges his expectations of a substandard year-end bonus from the company by selling a future to a colleague. The purchaser agrees to guarantee the seller an amount equivalent to, say, 10 percent of the seller's annual salary. If the company at year-end grants a bonus of more than 10 percent, the futures buyer gets the excess and makes a nice profit. On the other hand, if the company gives out a disappointing bonus of 9 percent, the futures speculator suffers a loss.

bonus stock: securities given most often to top management and other employees as a bonus.

book: a notebook the specialist in a stock exchange uses to keep a record of the buy and sell orders at specified prices, in strict sequence of receipt, which are left with him or her by other brokers.

book, close: see books (close).

book, open: see *books (open).*

book credit: items shown on a ledger accounts representing commitments of firms and individuals which are not secured by notes or other security.

book crowd: synonymous with *cabinet crowd.*

book depreciation: the amount that can be deducted for depreciation purposes from the cost of an asset of the property owner.

book-entry security: an issued security, not in the form of a certificate, but merely as an entry in an account at a bank. Eighty percent of marketable Treasury securities are held in bookentry form.

bookkeeper: a person who makes entries on the general ledger of a business.

bookkeeping: the art, practice, or labor involved in the systematic recording of the transactions affecting a business.

bookkeeping cycle: the full bookkeeping process discharged in a fiscal period, including journalizing, posting, preparing a trial balance, and preparing financial statements.

bookkeeping equation: a one-line summary of a balance sheet. The basic equation is assets = liabilities + proprietorship.

book liability: the amount at which securities issued or assumed by the carrier and other liability items are recorded in the accounts of the carrier.

book of final entry: a book to which information is transferred from a book of original entry.

book of original entry: the record in which transactions are formally recorded for the first time, such as the cash journal, check register, or general journal. Where machine bookkeeping is used, it may happen that one transaction is recorded simultaneously in several records, one of which may be regarded as the book of original entry.

book of secondary entry: ledger; not books of original entry (i.e., journals).

book profit: the increase in the value of a stock that has not been sold. For example, a stock is bought at $50 and its prime climbs to $60, but it is not sold, leading to a book profit of $10. cf. *realized profit.*

books

(1) journals, ledgers, or other records containing a firm's accounts.
(2) the record kept by a specialist in a particular security of all orders that were not executed because they were limited to a price other than the one prevailing in the market.

books (close): the date the transfer agent closes the transfer books of a corporation and checks the stockholder list to determine eligibility to vote or receive dividends. see also *books (open).*

books (open): the date the transfer agent opens the transfer books of a corporation to commence transferring stocks after they had been closed to check the list of stockholders. see also *book (close).*

bookshares: a modern share-recording system which eliminates the need for mutual fund share certificates by gives the fund shareowner a record of his holdings. see also *uncertified shares.*

book value

(1) ***general:*** the amount of an asset found in the company's records, not necessarily that which it could bring in the open market. see *depreciated cost.*
(2) ***investments:*** determined from a company's records by adding all assets, then deducting all debts and other liabilities, plus the liquidation price of any preferred issues. The sum arrived at is divided by the number of common shares outstanding, and the result is "book value per common share."

boom

(1) ***general:*** a period of rapidly rising prices and an increased demand for goods and services, usually accompanied by full employment.
(2) ***investments:*** when business expands and the value of commodities and securities increases.

boot: payments by or to the U.S. Treasury that may be necessary in an advance refunding in order to align more closely the respective values of the eligible issues and the issues offered.

booth: the areas on the outside rim of an exchange trading floor occupied by a member firm; used to transmit orders from the firm's offices to the trading floor.

borrowed bond: see *bond, borrowed.*

borrowed funds: all direct or indirect nondeposit liabilities. Borrowings may be accomplished through the use of promissory notes, purchase of federal funds, bills payable, mortgages payable, due bills, securities borrowed, customer paper rediscounted, and assets sold with the bank's endorsement.

borrowed reserves: discounts and advances from Federal Reserve Banks; mainly advances secured by U.S. government securities or eligible paper.

borrowed stock: the security a broker borrows to complete the obligation of a short selling contract held by his or her client. see *loaned stock.*

borrowing power of stocks
(1) the amount of funds that clients can invest in stocks on margin, as listed each month on their brokerage account statements. Usually the margin limit equals 50 percent of the value of stocks, 30 percent of the value of bonds, and the full value of their cash equivalent assets, such as money market account funds.
(2) stocks pledged to a bank or another lender as loan collateral. The loan value fluctuates based on lender policy and type of stock.

Boston interest: ordinary interest computed by using a 30-day month rather than the exact number of days in a month. cf. *New York interest.*

Boston Stock Exchange: organized on October 13, 1834, this stock exchange has but once failed to perform its operations, when it closed from July 30, 1913 to December 10, 1914 during the frantic period at the beginning of World War I.

BOT: short for bought.

bottom: in a market decline, the point at which sufficient buyers absorb all selling, especially when it has been tested, and has held several times.

bottom dropped out: a situation of sharply falling prices occurring when the market is well liquidated, thus establishing a panic atmosphere.

bottom fisher: an investor searching for a stock or commodity that has dropped to a bottom level before turning around. In some situations, people who purchase stocks and bonds of bankrupt or near-bankrupt organizations.

bottom-fishing: buying stocks in countries whose currencies are lowest against the U.S. dollar.

bottom out: the point, following a period of declining prices, where demand for a stock begins to exceed supply and a rise in prices occurs. synonymous with *gravelled.*

bottom price: the lowest price for a stock or commodity in a given period of time, such as a day, week, year, or cyclical period.

bottom-up approach to investing: looking for quality performance of a stock prior to examining any impact of economic trends. This method presumes that individual firms can perform well even if the industry as a whole is not doing well. cf. *top-down approach to investing.*

bought deal: in securities underwriting, a firm commitment to buy the entire issue outright from an issuing company. Usually, to accomplish this, a syndicate puts up a portion of its own capital and borrows the remainder from commercial banks. Then the syndicate attempts to resell the issue to investors at a price higher than the purchase price.

bourse: French term for *stock exchange.*

boutique: slang, a specialized brokerage house that trades with a limited list of customers and offers a limited product line. cf. *financial supermarket.*

box: the physical location of stocks and other documents held in safekeeping.

box, short against the: selling short a stock which one already owned, especially, one held for over a year, as to protect a paper profit by postponing the effective tax year for taking that profit.

BP
(1) see *bills payable.*
(2) see *book profit.*

BR
(1) see *bills receivable.*
(2) see *bond rating.*
(3) depository institutions; borrowing from the Federal Reserve.

BRA: see *Bankruptcy Reform Act of 1978.*

bracket: groupings determined by underwriting amounts in a new issue or loan.

branch office manager: an individual responsible for activities of one or more of a member firm's branch offices, having satisfactorally completed a special exchange examination.

brassage: the charge made by a government for producing coins from bullion.

breach of contract: not fulfilling one's part in an agreement; breaking a promise to carry out one's contractual responsibility.

breach of trust: violation of a duty of a trustee to a beneficiary.

breach of warranty: when a warranty made by a seller is found to be false, the warranty is said to be breached.

breadth
(1) the strength and scope of a market direction; measured by several indicators including advance/decline and volume figures. Used to identify turning points in the market. When advances exceed declines the breadth is considered positive and vice-versa.
(2) for a single issue of stock, the extent to which a security is distributed—the number of shares outstanding and the number of stockholders.

break
(1) ***general:*** any discount.

(2) ***investments:*** an unexpected drop in the price of stocks and commodities.
(3) ***investments:*** any discrepancy in the accounts of brokerage houses.
(4) ***investments:*** slang, good fortune.

breakeven point
(1) ***general:*** a point of activity at which the company earns zero profit. It is reached when total revenue equals total expense.
(2) ***securities:*** the dollar price where a transaction yields neither a gain nor a loss.

breaking the syndicate: terminating the investment banking group established to underwrite a new issue. It leaves members of the syndicate free to sell remaining holdings without price restrictions.

break in the market: an unusually sharp drop in the price for a product.

breakout: when a specific security climbs above a level where strong selling resistance exists, or drops below a level of strong purchasing support.

break point: share increments permitting a reduction in commissions charged for purchasing certain mutual funds.

breakpoint sale: in mutual funds, the dollar investment needed to make the fundholder eligible for a lower sales charge.

breakup value: in an investment fund or an issue of a holding firm, the value of the assets available for the issue, taking all marketable securities at their market price.

bridge bond: see *bond, bridge.*

bridge financing: emergency financing whereby a short- or medium-term loan is secured to meet a debt obligation or to await favorable conditions for a longer-term loan.

bridge loan: a short-term loan made in expectation of intermediate- or long-term financing. synonymous with *swing loan.*

bring out: the offering to the public of a new security issue by one or more underwriters.

broad market: describing a time of considerable volume in the buying and selling of stocks and bonds.

broad tape: slang, the Dow Jones news ticker displayed in brokerage houses as a large rectangular screen on which lines of copy roll upward.

Brok.: see *broker, brokerage.*

broken lot: an odd lot, usually less than 100 shares of a stock.

broken period: a forward foreign exchange arrangement which is not for a standard maturity period.

broker
(1) ***general:*** a person who prepares contracts with third parties on behalf of the broker's principal.
(2) ***general:*** a specialist who represents buyers of property and liability insurance and deals with either agents or companies in arranging for the coverage required by the customer. The broker is licensed by the

state or states in which he or she conducts business.

(3) ***general:*** a state-licenses individual who acts as middleman in property transactions between a buyer and seller.

(4) ***investments:*** a member of a stock exchange firm or any exchange member who handles orders to buy and sell securities and commodities for a commission. cf. *street broker;* see also *floor broker.*

brokerage: the business of a broker.

brokerage account: a client's account managed by a broker subject to the client's order. The broker purchases and sells securities or commodities either on margin or for cash.

brokerage firm: synonymous with *brokerage house.*

brokerage house: any firm serving as a broker or dealer in stock transactions. synonymous with *brokerage firm.*

broker-dealer (B/D): a firm that retails mutual fund shares and other securities to the public.

broker loan rate: the interest rate that brokers borrow from banks to cover the securities positions of their customers. This rate is about one percentage point of the short-term interest rates as the Treasury bill rate.

broker's broker: a dealer, that is, one who buys or sells for his or her own account.

broker's free credit balance: the idle amount of funds in brokerage accounts reported by the New York Stock Exchange on a monthly basis.

broker's loan: a loan made to a stockbroker and secured by stock exchange collateral. synonymous with *general loan and collateral agreement.*

broker's market: exists when the investing public is generally inactive at the same time that brokers are trading quite heavily with their own accounts.

broker's ticket: a written statement of all buy and sell orders executed by a broker, giving the date, name, and amount of the security traded, the price, the customer's name, the broker's name, and so on.

BS

(1) see *back spread.*
(2) see *balance sheet.*
(3) see *bellwether stock.*
(4) see *block sale.*
(5) see *butterfly spread.*

Bt.: bought.

BTG: see *beating the gun.*

BTM: see *bulling the market.*

bubble: an unwise business venture in which the price of the item has little or no relationship to the value of the asset.

bubble company: a firm that never had any true business or did not intend to be honest, or a firm created to defraud the public.

bucketing: activity of a broker who executes a customer's order for his or her own account instead of on the market, with the expectation of profiting from a balancing transaction at a future time. This activity is forbidden by the SEC.

bucket shop
(1) ***general:*** slang, an institution engaged in securities dealings of doubtful legality.
(2) ***investments:*** an unlicensed, dishonest business; customers place bets on the increase or decrease of stock prices on the regular exchange. No orders are filled, but profits and losses are based on the actual price movement on the exchange, with a commission going to the broker. The SEC has declared the maintenance of a bucket shop illegal.

bucking the trend: going contrary to "the crowd," that is, buying long in a declining market or selling short in a rising market.

Buck Rogers: stocks that enjoy a sudden rise in a short period of time.

budget: an itemized listing, and frequently the allotment, of the amount of all estimated revenue a given business anticipates receiving; and the listing, and frequently the segregation, of the amount of all estimated costs and expenses that will be incurred in obtaining the revenue during a stated period of time. see also *cash.*

budget deficit: excess of expenditures over revenues.

budget document: the instrument used by the budget-making authority to present a comprehensive financial program to the appropriate body.

budget loan: a mortgage loan that requires a proportionate amount of tax, insurance, and assessment to be held in escrow, in addition to interest and principal payments.

budget plan: a system of buying or making expenditures in divided equal payments over a period of time.

budget surplus: excess of revenues over expenditures.

building and loan association: a cooperative or stock society for the saving, accumulation, and lending of money. Deposits in an institution of this kind may be represented by shares issued in the name of the depositor.

building loan: a mortgage loan made to finance the construction of a building. It is advanced in stages as the construction work progresses. see *construction loan.*

building societies: a British term for *public deposits* where a high interest rate is given to attract funds to finance home loans and property purchases. Similar to savings and loan associations in the United States.

bulge: a temporary, though sudden climb in the price of a stock or commodity.

bulk segregation: a client owned stock held in the street name but kept separate from firm-owned securities. Such securities are not individually registered in the name of a client or person.

bull: a person who believes security prices will rise.

bull account
(1) the total amount of securities held for anticipated appreciation.
(2) that portion of the market which believes that prices will rise.

bull campaign: an informal concentrated effort by financial interests or market operators to push security prices upward. see *bull clique.*

bull clique: an informal group of people or interests that carry out a bull campaign. see *bull campaign.*

"bullet": a borrowing that is not to be repaid gradually but in a lump sum at the end of its term.

bulletproof: slang, any document with no loopholes.

bulling the market: speculator trading purporting to force the level of prices upward. Techniques include spreading rumors and entering price orders at levels somewhat above the prevailing price.

bullion: usually gold or silver, formed in ingots or bars, for use as a coin.

bullion broker: a company or person dealing in precious metals.

bullionism
(1) the monetary policy of mercantilism that called for direct regulation of transactions in foreign exchange and in precious metals in order to maintain a favorable balance in the home country.
(2) followers of the monetary theories of the Bullion Report (England 1810).

bullish: see *bearish and bullish.*

bull market: an advancing stock market.

bull pool: now prohibited by law, a form of manipulation that consisted of a formally organized fund contributed by financial interest that sought to cause prices to rise. A pool manager was chosen and an agreement entered upon that stipulated the division of profits or losses and that none of the members should make individual transactions in the particular security being manipulated.

bull position: the existing position of market optimists or bulls.

bulls: speculators who anticipate that prices will rise.

bull spread: a spread option technique where an investor purchases one type of option, either a call or put, and sells the other on the same underlying stock simultaneously. The option sold has a higher striking price than the one purchased. The investor profits by an increase in the market price of the underlying stock. cf. *bear spread.*

bull straddle writing: an option writing technique involving an uncovered put option and a covered call option on the same underlying stock. cf. *bear straddle writing.*

bunching
(1) repeated sales of the same stock at similar or identical prices as shown repeatedly on the ticker tape of an exchange.
(2) combining many round-lot orders for execution at the same time on the floor of the exchange. It can

also be used with odd-lot orders when combining many small orders.

B-unit: a large trading unit whose value varies from day to day. It is composed of equal proportions of different currencies: American dollar, German mark, French franc, Swiss franc, and British pound.

buoyant: advancing stock; securities that continue to climb in value.

burnout: the exhaustion of a tax shelter's benefits, when an investor begins to receive income from an investment. Taxes are to be paid on this income and reported to the IRS.

business
(1) the buying and selling of goods and services.
(2) the activity of an individual, partnership, or organization involving production, commerce, and/or service.

Business Conduct Committee: established by NASD in each of 13 districts to serve as a court of first instance for a trade practice complaints, synonymous with *District Business Conduct Committee.*

business day: the day when exchanges and other financial marketplaces are open for trading.

business risk: that part of a firm's risk that is caused by the inherent risk of the firm's investment (asset) operations. It is not concerned with how the firm finances its assets.

business segment reporting: revealing any divisions, subsidiaries, or other aspects of a business separately enabling a comparison to income, sales, and assets.

business solvency: a situation where a company has more assets than liabilities.

business transaction: the act of business involving purchasing or selling or other exchanges in value.

busted convertible: a convertible whose convertibility is valueless because the underlying equity is low in price.

butterfly spread: the simultaneous purchase or sale of three futures contracts in the same or different markets. For example, buying 10 soybean futures contracts in January, and other 10 for an April delivery, and at the same moment selling (going short) 20 soybean contracts for May of the same year. Borrowing power and profits may result. In addition, any profits are held until after the tax year ends. see also *spread, straddle.*

buttonwood tree: on May 17, 1792, 24 men (the original founders of the New York Stock Exchange) declared themselves "brokers for the purchase and sale of public stocks." A buttonwood tree (sycamore) once stood at that location.

buy: slang, a security considered suitable for purchase as a good investment at a given time.

buy a call: where an investor pays a premium for a stock option contract giving him the right to buy 100 shares of a specific stock at a given price within a certain time frame.

buy and hold strategy: a technique for acquiring shares in a firm over a number of years, enabling the investor to pay favorable long-term capital gains tax profits and requires less involvement than a more active trading objective.

buy and put aside (away): see *buy and hold strategy.*

buy and write strategy: a conservative options technique involving purchasing securities and then writing covered call options on them. An investor receives both dividends from the stock and the premium income from the call options. A disadvantage is that the investor may be required to sell the security below the current market price if the call is exercised.

buy a put: where an investor pays a premium for a stock option contract giving him or her the right to sell 100 shares of a specific stock at a given price within a certain time frame.

buy back: buying an identical amount of the same stock that had been sold short in order to satisfy the agreement within the seller's contract and complete the sale. see *bond buy-backs, short covering, short sale.*

buyer: synonymous with *holder.*

buyer's market: a market characterized by low or falling prices, occurring when supply is greater than demand. The buyers tend to set the prices and terms of sale. synonymous with *soft market.*

buyer's monopoly: a characteristic of the market of many sellers and one purchaser.

buyer's option: a stock transaction where a buyer determines the delivery date for stock involved. If the seller delivers the stock prior to that date, the buyer has the option to reject them. cf. *seller's option.*

buyers over: a situation of more buyers than sellers. cf. *overbought.*

buyers' premium: see *fee.*

buy hedge: synonymous with *long hedge (2).*

buy-in: when a seller of securities fails to make delivery of them within the period stipulated. The purchaser can then buy them elsewhere if he or she had given prior written notice to the seller, and may charge the seller all costs and differences involved. cf. *sell-out.*

buying basis: the difference between the cost of a cash commodity and a future sold to hedge it.

buying climax: a sudden climb in a securities or commodities price setting the way for a rapid drop. This surge attracts most of the potential purchases of the stock or commodity, leaving them, with no one to sell to at higher prices, thus leading to a drop in prices.

buying hedge: a hedge that is initiated by taking a long position in the futures market equal to the amount of the cash commodity that is eventually needed. see also *hedge.*

buying in: when a seller does not hand over his securities at the expected time, the purchaser obtains shares wherever he or she can find them, and the seller becomes responsible for all added expenses.

buying long: buying stocks, bonds, or commodities outright with the expectation of holding them for a rise in price and then selling. cf. *selling short.*

buying on a shoestring: acquiring stocks or commodities with the minimum margin.

buying on balance: occurs when a stockbroker's orders to buy exceed his or her cumulative orders to sell.

buying on margin: purchasing securities without paying the full price immediately. Margin regulations are closely controlled by the SEC. see *margin, marginal trading, margin call.*

buying on scale: a procedure for purchasing securities where the broker is told to purchase a given number of shares at given intervals of a price decline. Since the buyer does not know how low the price can drop, by buying on scale as the price declines, their average cost per share also declines. synonymous with *scale buying.*

buying on the bad news: a technique based on the feeling that shortly following a firm's announcement of "bad news" the price of its stock will significantly fall. Investors who purchase at this time expect that the price is about as low as it will go, leaving room for a rise when the news becomes positive. cf. *bottom fisher, selling on the good news.*

buying order: instructions given to a broker or agent to purchase or sell securities or commodities.

buying outright: paying with cash only; buying an item with 100 percent cash. In securities, the opposite of margin.

buying power: money available for spending and consumption. A combination of liquid assets plus available credit.

buying range: a price range in a declining market determined by analysts to be a likely turnaround area and, therefore, a sound time to make an investment.

buying rate: the publicized quotation for buying such things as foreign exchange, commodities, and bills of exchange which a bank or other buyer employs to inform the trader of his desire to buy.

buying signals: a progression of prices on a stock chart that exceeds the normal range. It is used as an indication that self-stabilizing forces will soon respond to cause a reversal in trend.

buying the intermarket spread: an investment strategy involving taking a hedge position in two securities simultaneously. If the speculator believes that banks are going to come under increased pressure, buying a future contract for Treasury bills and, at the same time, selling short a futures contract for bank CDs. see *intermarket* *spread.* cf. *selling the intermarket spread.*

buy-in procedure: a purchaser's remedy should the selling broker-dealer fail to deliver a purchased security. Two business days following written notice of an intent to the delinquent seller, the buyer can purchase the promised amount of that stock in the market and hold the delinquent seller responsible for all incurred losses. synonymous with *close-out.*

buy-limit order: see *limited order.*

buy minus: an order to purchase a security at a price lower than the current market price. Investors attempt to execute a buy minus order on a temporary decline in the stock's price.

buy on bid: a strategy whereby an individual can purchase a listed stock from an odd-lot trader who is selling at the bid price instead of waiting to execute an odd-lot sale following the next round-lot sale, which may be an indefinite time.

buy on close (or opening): to buy at the end (or beginning) of the session at a price within the closing or (opening range).

buy on the offer: a strategy of purchasing an odd lot, thus avoiding the delay that might be involved with a market order. Instead of waiting for the next round-lot sale to establish the price of the odd-lot transaction, a buy on the offer order is executed at the lowest quoted asking price plus the odd-lot differential.

buy order: order to a broker, investment representative, bank, or manufacturer, to purchase a specified quantity of security or item.

buy out: to purchase all the assets, stock, and so on, of an ongoing organization; to purchase the interest in a firm that is owned by another.

buy signal: technical indicators showing that a security is in a pattern that will shortly lead to an up-reversal. cf. *sell signal.*

buy stop order: a buy order marked to be held until the market price climbs to the stop price. At that time it is to be entered as a market order to buy at the best available price. Buy stop orders are not permitted on the over-the-counter market. synonymous with *suspended market order.*

buy the book: instructions from a trader or institutional account to purchase all shares available from a specialist's book at the current offer price.

buy ticket: a form prepared in multiple copies, used by the investment department to instruct the order department to purchase a security.

buy-up: an act or an instance of buying up, as of business interest, such as stock.

BV: see *book value.*

BW: see *bid wanted.*

by-bidder: a person who makes fictitious bids at an auction, on behalf of the owner or seller of the items, to obtain a higher price or to encourage further bidding.

bypass trust: the agreement permitting parents to pass assets on to their heirs for purposes of reducing estate taxes. It is an irrevocable trust since the terms can never be altered. see also *irrevocable trust.*

C

C
(1) a liquidating dividend (in stock listings of newspapers).
(2) the lowest quality rating for a municipal or corporate bond.
(3) the current component of money.

C$: Canadian dollar.

CA
(1) see *capital account.*
(2) see *capital assets.*
(3) see *chartered accountant.*
(4) see *current account.*
(5) see *current assets.*
(6) in bond tables and offering sheets, meaning *callable.*

cabinet bid: an off-the-floor transaction closing an out-of-the money options contracts at $1.00 per contract.

cabinet crowd: the section of the bond trading unit of the New York Stock exchanges that handles trading in active bonds. synonymous with *book crowd, inactive crowd.*

cabinet security: a stock or bond listed on an exchange that is not actively traded. see also *cabinet crowd.*

cable: slang, the dollar/sterling spot exchange rate.

cage
(1) the location in a brokerage house's back office where funds are received and disbursed.
(2) an installation where a bank teller works.

calculated risk: a probability of succeeding; the unknowns pertaining to an investment or venture that is judged to be worth undertaking.

calendar: a list of stocks that are soon to be offered to the public for sale. Individual calendars are kept for corporate bonds, municipal bonds, government bonds, and new stock offerings.

calendar bear spread: synonymous with *horizontal bear spread.*

calendar bull spread: synonymous with *horizontal bull spread.*

calendar spread: synonymous with *horizontal spread.*

calendar spreading: the simultaneous purchase and sale of options within the same class having different expiration dates. see also *horizontal bear spread, horizontal bull spread.*

calendar year experience: experience developed on premium and loss transactions occurring during the 12 calendar months beginning January 1, irrespective of the effective dates of the policies on which these transactions took place.

call
(1) ***general:*** to demand payment of a loan secured by collateral because of failure by a borrower to comply with the terms of the loan.
(2) ***investments:*** to demand payment of an installment of the price of bonds or stocks that have been subscribed.
(3) ***bonds:*** the right to redeem outstanding bonds prior to their scheduled maturity. The first dates when an issuer may call bonds are given in the prospectus of all issues having a call provision in its indenture.
(4) ***options:*** the right to purchase a given number of shares at a state price by a fixed date.

callable [CA]
(1) that which must be paid on request, as a loan.
(2) a bond issue or preferred stock, all or part of which may be redeemed by the issuing corporation under definite conditions, before maturity.

callable bond: see *bond, callable.*

callable capital: that portion of a company's capital not paid up and on which the firm's directors can call for payments to be made.

callable preferred stock: a preferred stock which can be called in for payment at a price stated on the certificate by the corporation at its option.

call away: the right of a call option buyer to purchase, in 100-share lots, a specific stock at a particular price from a seller who has written an option contract on those shares.

call date: the date on which a bond may be redeemed before maturity at the option of the issuer.

called: see *redeem.*

called away
(1) a bond redeemed prior to maturity.
(2) a call or put option exercised against the shareholder.
(3) a delivery required on a short sale.

called bond: see *bond, called.*

called preferred stock: a preferred stock, containing call provisions, which is redeemed by a corporation.

call feature: a provision on a senior security (debt or preferred stock) that allows the firm to buy back the security at a prespecified price prior to maturity.

call loan rate: the interest rate charged by banks for call loans; often used as a base for the minimum margin interest charge. synonymous with *call money rate.*

call loans: loans from a broker, on deposit of proper collateral for financing margin activities of a client.

call money (CM): currency lent by banks, usually to stock exchange brokers, for which payment can be demanded at any time.

call money market: an activity of brokers and dealers having call funds secured by stock exchange collateral and government securities to meet their money needs to cover customers' margin accounts and their own securities inventory.

call money rate: synonymous with *call loan rate.*

call of more (CM): the right to call again for the same amount of goods previously bought. Used primarily in the purchase of options.

call option (CO): giving the option buyer the right to buy 100 shares of stock at a stated price at any time before a deadline, at which point the option expires.

call option buy/sell ratio: a call option buying divided by call option selling. The higher ratio during a decline often indicates a bearish reaction and a lower ratio during an upswing usually indicates a bullish reaction.

call premium

(1) the premium payable by the issuer if he or she redeems a callable bond before maturity. It will be fixed in the indenture and normally decreases as maturity approaches.

(2) the premium payable by an issuer when he or she redeems, if appropriate, preferred stock at an amount in excess of par or stated value.

call price: the price at which a callable bond is redeemable; used in connection with preferred stocks and debt securities having a fixed claim. It is the price that an issuer must pay to voluntarily retire such securities. Often the call price exceeds the par or liquidating price in order to compensate the holder of the called security for his or her loss of income and investment position resulting from the call.

call protection: convertibles issued in recent years offering protection of two to three years. After that, the company can force conversion of the bonds into stock. It usually does so when the convertible trades 25 to 30 percent above its call price. While the protection is in place, though, the convertible's price has unlimited potential and will continue to trade at a premium over the conversion value. If a bond is called, the investors runs the risk of losing some accrued interest.

call provision: the call provision describes the terms under which a bond may be redeemed by the issuer in whole or in part prior to maturity.

call purchase: the buying of commodities when the seller has some option of pricing at a later date within a given range of the existing price. cf. *call sale.*

calls: an option contract that entitles the holder to buy a number of shares of the underlying security at a stated price on or before a fixed expiration date. see *puts and calls*.

call sale: an agreement for the sale of a commodity where the price is set by the purchaser in the future. The setting of the price is at the "call" of the purchaser and is within a few points above or below the price of a stated future on the day of fixing the price of the contract. Opposite of *call purchase*.

call spread: an option spread position formed by buying a call on a specific stock and writing a call with a differing date of expiration, differing exercise price, or both on the same security.

cambism: engaging in the sale of foreign monies.

cambist

(1) ***general:*** an individual who buys and sells foreign currencies.

(2) ***international:*** a handbook in which foreign country funds are converted into currency tables of the country for which the handbook is issued.

cambistry: the study of exchange of foreign currencies, with emphasis on identifying the least expensive procedure for remitting to a foreign nation.

cancel (Cncld.) (Cnl.)

(1) ***general:*** to mark or perforate; make void.

(2) ***investments:*** to void a negotiable instrument by annulling or paying it.

(3) ***investments:*** terminating a bond or other contract prematurely.

(4) ***investments:*** voiding an order to buy or sell.

can crowd: bond brokers who trade cabinet securities.

capital

(1) the amount invested in a venture. see *equity, fixed capital*.

(2) describes a long-term debt plus owners' equity.

(3) the net assets of a firm, partnership, and so on, including the original investment, plus all gains and profits.

capital account (CA): an account maintained in the name of the owner or owners of a business and indicating his or their equity in that business—usually at the close of the last accounting period.

capital asset pricing model (CAPM): a model showing the relationship between expected risk and expected return. The model states that the return on an asset or a stock is equal to the risk-free return, such as the return on a short-term Treasury security, plus a risk premium.

capital assets (CA): a collective term that includes all fixed assets, consisting of furniture and fixtures, land, buildings, machinery, and so on: as differentiated from property consumed; that is, property that yields income or reduces expenses. cf. *capital expenditure, capital investment*.

capital budget: a budget that itemizes expenditures to be used for building and for purchasing capital goods, and which identifies the source of the funds required to meet the expenditures.

capital charges: sums required to satisfy interest upon, and amortization of, monies invested in an enterprise.

capital consumption: that portion of a firm's investment used in part or in its entirety in the process of production.

capital distribution: see *liquidating dividend.*

capital expenditure (CE): see *expenditure.*

capital gain (or loss)
(1) the gain or loss from the sale of a capital asset above or below the cost or appraised value.
(2) the difference (gain or loss) between the market or book value at purchase or other acquisition and that realized from the sale or disposition of a capital asset.

capital gains distribution: a distribution to investment company shareholders from net long-term capital gains realized by a *regulated investment company* on the sale of portfolio securities.

capital gains tax (CGT): a tax that is placed on the profit from selling a capital asset, often stock.

capital goods (CG): items ordinarily treated as long-term investment (capitalized) because of substantial value and life (e.g., industrial machinery).

capital growth: an increase in market value of securities; a long-term objective pursued by many investment companies.

capital investment: a collective term representing the amount invested in capital or fixed assets or in long-term securities, as contrasted with funds invested in current assets or short-term securities. Generally speaking, capital investments include all funds invested in assets that during the normal course of business are not expected to be returned during the coming fiscal period.

capital issues: stocks and bonds that are more or less permanent and fixed, as contrasted with short-term notes and accounts payable.

capitalization
(1) the sum of all monies invested in a firm by the owner or owners; total liabilities. see *undercapitalization.*
(2) the method of appraising property by deducting the estimated normal expenses from the amount of income the property is expected to yield. The resulting net profit does not necessarily represent the actual property value.
(3) the total value of all securities in a firm.

capitalization of income: estimating the existing investment value of property by lowering anticipated future income to its present worth.

capitalization rate
(1) the relationship of income to capital investment or value, expressed as a percentage.
(2) the (percentage) rate at which an anticipated future income stream is discounted to present worth (i.e., market value).

capitalization rate(s), basis for split: justification of the use of split rates is confined to two basic assumptions, as follows. (a) Investment in land and investment in building represent different degrees of risk and, therefore, require the application of a different rate in the capitalization of the income attributed to each: (i) land value is presumed to be stable and to earn a constant return to perpetuity; (ii) terminable lives of buildings require a higher rate to ensure return of capital investment within their estimated economic life, in addition to a return on the investment or capital value. (b) Income attributable to land and return to building are predictable, separable, and identifiable.

capitalization rate(s), methods of selection of: a band of investment, sometimes designated synthetic, in which the current mortgage rate and rate for equity capital are combined in the same proportion as each (mortgage and equity) bears to the total value estimate. The accuracy of this method depends upon the correctness of the appraiser's estimate of the availability of mortgage money at the rate and long-value ratio set forth, and the degree to which the rate of return on equity capital has been verified by reference to comparable sales.

capitalization rate(s), net
(1) the rate of interest expected to be earned on an investment.
(2) the rate of interest at which anticipated future net income is discounted, exclusive of provision for recapture of capital investment.

capitalization rate(s), over all: net (capitalization) rate plus provision for recapture of total investment (i.e., land and improvements). This is the rate used in the property residual technique and is applied to net income before depreciation.

capitalization rate(s), safe: the net rate of return on a virtually riskless and completely liquid investment, generally accepted as the savings bank interest rate or interest being paid on long-term government bonds, in a stable market; usually known as the *safe rate*.

capitalization rate(s), source of: the market is the only source of capitalization rates which provides provable support for those rates.

capitalization rate(s), split: in the capitalization process denoting an application of different rates to portions of total net income presumed to be earned by fractional parts of an improved property—for example, one rate applied to claimed earnings of land and another applied to net income said to be earned by the building.

capitalization ratios: the percent that each of the following or its components is of total capitalization: bonds, other long-term debt, preferred stock, common stock and retained income, capital surplus, and premium on capital stock.

capitalize
(1) to classify a cost as a long-term investment item instead of a charge to current operations.
(2) to divide income by an interest rate to obtain principal.
(3) to convert into cash that which can be used in production; to issue shares to represent an investment.

capitalized cost: the original cost of an asset plus the net charges incurred to prepare or complete it for its stated use.

capitalized surplus: the transfer of a corporation's paid in or earned surplus to capital stock by issuing a stock dividend; by increasing the par or stated value of the capital stock, or by simple resolution of the board of directors.

capitalized value: the asset value (principal) of a given number of income dollars determined on the basis of an assumed rate of return. For example, the capitalized value of a $500 perpetual income at a rate of 5 percent is $10,000 (obtained by dividing $500 by 0.05).

capital lease: the lease shown of a firm's balance sheet as an asset and corresponding liability. Traditionally, this applies to leases where the lessee acquires the economic benefits and risks of the leased property.

capital loss: a stock transaction where the proceeds of the sale is less than the adjusted cost of acquisition.

capital market line: the graphic indication of the average rate of return provided by the marketplace for various levels of risk.

capital net worth: the total assets of a business less the liabilities.

capital rating: a rating given by a mercantile organization when appraising the net worth of a firm.

capital requirement: the total monetary investment needed to create and operate any business.

capital risk: the risk that an investor may not recover all or a portion of their original capital at the time an investment has been liquidated.

capital stock (CS): the specified amount of stock a corporation may sell as authorized by the state granting the corporate charter. If the stock has a stated value per share, such value is known as *par value*. see *common stock*.

capital stock discount and expense: a balance sheet account. The excess of par value over the price paid in by the shareholder is capital stock discount. Expenses incurred in connection with the issuance and sale of capital stock which are not properly chargeable to "organization," and which have not been charged to "surplus" are included in capital stock discount and expense.

capital stock subscribed: the temporary capital account containing a record of capital stock subscribed for but as yet not issued because the subscriptions have not been fully paid.

capital stock tax: a tax on the stock of a corporation usually computed as a percentage of par value or assigned value. A special form of capital stock tax was the declared value capital stock tax, which was combined with an excess profits tax.

capital structure: the distribution of a corporation's capital among its several component parts, such as stock, bonds, and surplus.

capital sum: the original amount of an estate, fund, mortgage, bond, or other financial dealing, together with accrued sums not yet recognized as income.

capital surplus: synonymous with *paid-in capital.*

capital turnover: the rate at which an organization's assets are converted into cash. synonymous with *investment turnover.*

CAPM: see *capital asset pricing model.*

capping: a manipulative and/or illegal practice where individuals try to hold the market price of an underlying security from trading above a certain exercise price of a stock option contract.

captive: a mine or plant; the product of which is used entirely by a parent company instead of being sold to the public. A large user of coal, cement, paper, or oil which is not in the business of marketing these products but it is a large user of them, may own and operate captive mines, wells, or mills.

captive finance firm: an organization, usually a wholly owned subsidiary, that was formed primarily to finance consumer purchases from the parent firm. Organized in this manner, the parent company has higher leverage and assures their active participation in the commercial paper and bond markets.

capture: see *dividend capture.*

carat: the unit of weight for gems equal to approximately 3.2 grains; a twenty-fourth part of pure gold. cf. *karat.*

care of securities: the action of an investor following the purchase and payment for a security.

Carey Street: a British term for *bankruptcy.*

carry
(1) ***general:*** to enter or post.
(2) ***investments:*** the interest cost of financing the holding of securities.
(3) ***investments:*** the act of a broker in providing money to customers who trade by margin accounts; to hold stocks; to be *long* of stock.

carry income (loss): the difference between the interest yield of a dealer's portfolio and the cost of funds which support that portfolio.

carrying broker: any broker or commission house maintaining a client's account.

carrying charge
(1) ***general:*** the continuing cost of owning or holding any property or items.
(2) ***general:*** the amount of charges added to the price of a service to compensate for deferred payment.
(3) ***investments:*** a fee charged by investment brokers for handling margin accounts.
(4) ***real estate:*** the carrying cost, primarily interest and taxes, of owning land prior to its development and resale.
(5) ***commodities:*** a charge for carrying the actual commodity, including interest, storage, and the costs of insurance.

carrying market: a market in which more distant positions are quoted at a premium over the nearby positions, and where this premium is high enough to compensate for the carrying charges.

carrying-over day: any postponed day of delivery. Used on the London Stock Exchange. see *backwardation.*

carrying value: the value of a fixed asset remaining after its accumulated depreciation reserve has been deducted from its original depreciable cost.

carryover clause: a clause to protect a broker for a specified time, usually beyond the expiration date of the property listing.

cars: slang, used by commodity traders as a synonym for the term "contracts."

cartel: a group of separate business organizations that have agreed to institute approaches to alter competition by influencing prices, production, or marketing. Rarely as effective as a monopoly. cf. *consortium.*

Carter bonds: see *bond, Carter.*

cash: an all-embracing term associated with any business transaction involving the handling of currency and coins.

cash-and-carry: noting or involving a market that handles nonperishable commodities, such as cotton, copper, petroleum, and so forth. cf. *noncarry.*

cash basis

(1) ***general:*** a system of accounting under which revenues are accounted for only when received in cash, and expenditures are accounted for only when paid.

(2) ***bonds:*** paying the full tax on Series EE Savings Bonds on maturity. An alternative would be to prorate the tax each year until the bonds mature.

cash board: in a commodity exchange, the area of blackboard used for the recording of sales of cash commodity contracts.

cash buying: the purchase of securities or commodities outright for immediate delivery of the item.

cash commodity: a specific lot of a commodity bought through a cash transaction for immediate delivery, though delivery may be deferred.

cash cow: a business activity that yields a continuous flow of cash. Securities of cash cows usually generate dependable dividends.

cash delivery: the same-day delivery of traded securities.

cash dividend: declared dividends payable in cash, usually by check.

cash earnings (CE): the profits or net income of an organization. These earnings include all depreciation and amortization accruals.

cash equivalent

(1) the value of an asset if immediately exchanged for cash.

(2) an item readily converted to cash with little or no change in current market value (e.g., securities, notes).

cash flow
(1) ***general:*** the reported net income of a corporation, plus amounts charged off for depreciation, depletion, amortization, and extraordinary charges to reserves, which are bookkeeping deductions and not actually paid out in cash. Knowledge of these factors results in a better understanding of a firm's ability to pay dividends. cf. *net cash flow.*
(2) ***investments:*** the net income plus depreciation and other noncash charges. Investors study cash flow carefully because of the concern for the company's ability to pay dividends.

cash flow bond: see *bond, cash flow.*

cashiering department: see *cage.*

cash-ins: redemptions of investment company securities.

cash in the chips: slang, to conclude a business transaction; to sell one's share of a company.

cash items (CA): items listed in a firm's statement that are the equivalent of cash, such as bank deposits, government bonds, and marketable securities.

cash management account (CMA): a bank-type development of Merrill Lynch in partnership with Bank One of Ohio, based in Columbus, where affluent clients are offered a Visa credit card and checking to draw against their investment balances. The account was initially offered in 206 of Merrill Lynch's 382 offices in the United States. see also *central assets accounts.*

Cash Management Bill: U.S. Treasury bills introduced in 1975 to raise funds quickly for a short period; ranging from 9 to 20 days to maturity, with notice of their offering given up to 10 days ahead. All payment must be made in federal funds.

cash market: as contrasted with the *futures market;* synonymous with *spot market.*

cash on delivery (COD)
(1) ***general:*** any purchase made with the expectation that the item(s) will be paid for on delivery.
(2) ***investments:*** the requirement that delivery of stock to institutional investors be in exchange for assets of equal value, usually defined as cash. synonymous with *delivery against cost, delivery versus payment.*

cash position: the percentage of cash to the total net assets; the net amount after the deduction of current liabilities.

cash price: the current price of the cash commodity of a designated quality available for immediate delivery. synonymous with *spot price.*

cash ratio: the ratio of cash and marketable stocks to current liabilities. Describes the extent to which liabilities can be liquidated immediately.

cash sale
(1) ***general:*** the surrender of cash at the time of sale.
(2) ***investments:*** a transaction on the floor of an exchange that calls for delivery of the securities the same day. In "regular way" trades, the

seller is to deliver on the fifth business day.

cash trade (CT): any transaction in securities and commodities paid in full with cash for immediate delivery of goods. see *for cash.*

cash value: describes the amount available to the owner of a life insurance policy when the policy is surrendered to the insurer.

cash with fiscal agent: deposits with fiscal agents, such as commercial banks, for the payment of matured bonds and interest.

casino society: speculators or investors who gamble on the undervalued corporate asset, the out-of-sync security price, the volatile futures contract—anything, in fact, that can be leveraged and traded. People devoted to high-stakes financial maneuvering as a shortcut to wealth.

catcher: a clerk who records each transaction in the trading ring.

CATS: see *Certificate of Accrual on Treasury Securities.*

cats and dogs
(1) ***general:*** items that do not have satisfactory sales turnover and accumulate inventory.
(2) ***investments:*** highly speculative stocks.

CB
(1) see *bond, callable.*
(2) see *bond, coupon.*

CBOE: see *Chicago Board Options Exchange.*

CBT: see *Chicago Board of Trade.*

CC
(1) a quality rating for a municipal or corporate bond, lower than CCC and higher than C.
(2) see *chamber of commerce.*
(3) see *cold canvassing.*

CCC: a quality rating for a municipal or corporate bond, lower than B and higher than CC.

CCS: see *Central Certificate Service.*

CD
(1) see *certificate of deposit.*
(2) see *cum dividend.*

CE
(1) see *capital expenditure.*
(2) see *cash earnings.*

CEA: see *Commodity Exchange Authority.*

CEC: see *Commodities Exchange Center.*

CEDEL: Centrale de Livaison de Valeurs Mobilières; a computerized system for delivery and settlement for Eurobonds and related securities based in Luxembourg, with membership exceeding 850 institutions.

CEF: see *closed-end funds.*

CEFCO: Cooperative Export Financing Corporation. A plan for a co-op to borrow money cheaply, usually by using tax breaks or by obtaining funds in low-interest money markets abroad, and then relending it to foreign buyers of U.S. exports.

CEIC: see *closed-end investment company.*

Celler Antimerger Act: an extension of the Clayton Antitrust Act, this 1950 addition prohibits a corporation from acquiring the stock or assets of another corporation if the effect would be a substantial lessening of competition or a tendency to monopoly.

central assets accounts: an all-in-one account that combines banking and investment services. For example, see *cash management account.* see also *sweep.*

Central Certificate Service (CCS): a privately run depository through which members effect security deliveries between each other via computerized bookkeeping entries, thereby reducing the physical movement of stock certificates.

Centrale de Livraison de Valeurs Mobilières: see *CEDEL.*

central registration depository: a computerized record-keeping system for registrations of broker-dealer principals and agents under state securities regulations. Eliminates multiple filings.

CEO: see *chief executive officer.*

Cert.: see *certificate.*

certain: French term for *indirect quotation.*

certificate (Cert.) (Ctfs.)
(1) the piece of paper that is evidence of ownership of stock in a corporation. Watermarked paper is finely engraved with delicate etchings to discourage forgery.
(2) a form of paper money, issued against silver or gold deposited in the U.S. Treasury.
(3) any written or printed document of truth that can be used as proof of a fact.

certificate check: see *certified check.*

certificated securities: the quantity of a specific commodity held in warehouses that have been approved by a commodity exchange, and which is certified as deliverable on future contracts.

certificateless municipals: municipal bonds having no certificate of ownership for each bondholder. Instead one certificate is valid for an entire issue. Permits investors to trade their bonds without having to transfer certificates.

certificateless trading: a means for transacting the purchase and sale of stocks where no certificates of ownership are issued to the buyer of the stock. Evidence of ownership can be obtained by the buyer, usually in the form of a nonnegotiable certificate issued in the name of the broker who originally executed the transaction.

certificate of accounts: the statements released by a certified public accountant stating the accountant's evaluation of a company's books of account that have been audited and/or from which he or she has prepared statements.

Certificate of Accrual on Treasury Securities (CATS): U.S. Treasury issues sold at a deep discount from face value. However, as Treasury securities they cannot be called away. see *called away.* cf. *TIGER.*

certificate of beneficial interest: a statement of a share of a firm's business when such ownership has been deposited with a trustee. The certificate holder receives the income from and holds an interest in the firm's assets, but relinquishes management control. Used when a business is operated as a trust.

certificate of deposit (CD): a negotiable, nonnegotiable, or transferable receipt payable to the depositor for funds deposited with a bank, usually interest bearing. see also *certificate of deposit (demand), certificate of deposit (time), variable interest plus.*

certificate of deposit (demand): a negotiable or transferable receipt issued for funds deposited with a bank and payable on demand to the holder. These receipts do not bear interest and are used principally by contractors and others as a guarantee of performance of a contract or as evidence of good faith when submitting a bid. They may also be used as collateral.

certificate of deposit (time): a negotiable or transferable receipt for funds deposited with a bank, payable to the holder at some specified date (not less than 30 days after issuance) and bearing interest.

certificate of deposit rollover: an investment technique of deferring taxes from one year to the following year. An investor purchases a certificate of deposit on margin that will mature in the next year, then deducts the interest cost on the loan this year, and shifts the income from the certificate into the following year. The IRS allows the interest deduction be applied against $10,000 of earned income plus any net investment income, which included dividends, interest, royalties, and short-term capital gains.

certificate of incorporation (COI): the franchise or charter issued by a state to the original petitioners of an approved corporation. Such franchise or charter constitutes the authority granted by the state for the organization to transact business as a corporation.

certificate of indebtedness (COI):
(1) a short-term note issued by a governmental agency, describing the current debt.
(2) an unsecured promissory note, the holder having a general creditor's recourse against general assets.

certificate of participation: a certificate by an investment company issued in place of shares to show a proportionate interest. Also used to show interests in a loan or mortgage where there are many lenders.

certificate of stock: see *stock certificate.*

certificate of title: a title company certification that the seller possesses sound, marketable, and/or insurance title to the property. If a title company issues this certificate and a defect is identified at a later time, the title company will indemnify the holder. see *title insurance.*

certificates of debt: certificates indicating that a loan or some other form of debts remains to be paid.

certified check: the check of a depositor drawn on a bank; the face of the check bears the word "accepted" or "certified," with the date and signature of a bank official or authorized clerk. The check then becomes an obligation of the bank, the regulations require that the amount of the check be immediately charged against the depositor's account.

certified financial planner (CFP): an individual holding an official certificate issued by the College for Financial Planning in Denver, Colorado, having the required knowledge in personal finance to serve individual clients, as with regard to investments, insurance, estates, and so forth.

certified public accountant (CPA): an accountant who has been certified by the state as having met that state's requirements of age, education, experience, and technical qualifications. Not all who practice accounting are certified. see also *chartered accountant.*

cestui que trust: synonymous with *beneficiary.*

CF: certificates (in bond listings of newspapers).

CFA: see *chartered financial analyst.*

CFC: see *chartered financial consultant.*

CFO: chief financial officer.

CFP: see *certified financial planner.*

CFTC: see *Commodity Futures Trading Commission.*

CG
(1) see *capital gain (or loss).*
(2) see *capital goods.*

CGT: see *capital gains tax.*

chairperson of the board: the highest ranking executive of a corporation. In some cases the firm's president is also the chairperson of the board.

chamber of commerce (CC): an organization of business executives created to advance the interests of its members.

chancellor of the exchequer: the person in the United Kingdom in charge of the receipts and payments of the government. A function similar to the Secretary of the Treasury in the United States.

Chandler Act: passed by Congress in 1938, this Act revised the federal law on financial reorganization of corporations, including bankruptcy.

change column: see *plus.*

CHAPS: Clearing House Automated Payments Systems (London).

Chapter 11: see *Bankruptcy Reform Act of 1978.* see also *bankruptcy.*

Chapter 7: see *bankruptcy.*

charitable bequest: a gift of personal property to a legal charity by will.

charitable devise: a gift of real property to a legal charity by will.

charitable lead (or up-front) trust: a trust for a fixed term of year wherein a charity is the income beneficiary and the remainder goes to a noncharitable beneficiary.

charitable remainder: an arrangement wherein the remainder interest goes to a legal charity upon the termination or failure of a prior interest.

charitable remainder annuity trust: a trust that provides a certain sum, not less than 5 percent of initial fair market value of all property placed in trust, to be distributed at least annually to a noncharitable beneficiary, with remainder to a qualified charity.

charitable remainder trust: an arrangement wherein the remainder interest goes to a legal charity upon the termination or failure of a prior interest.

charitable remainder unitrust: a trust that provides a fixed percentage, not less than 5 percent of net fair market value of property, valued annually, to be distributed at least annually to a noncharitable beneficiary, with remainder to a qualified charity.

charitable trust: a trust created for the benefit of a community ordinarily without a definite beneficiary—for example, a trust for educational purposes. synonymous with *public trust.*

charter: the contract between a private corporation and the state, identifying the articles of association granted to the corporation by authority of the legislative act. Powers and privileges granted are included.

chartered accountant (CA): in the United Kingdom, Canada, and Australia, a certified accountant.

chartered financial analyst (CFA): an individual who has passed a series of examinations given by the Institute of Chartered Financial Analysts in Charlottesville, Virginia having the required knowledge and practices in accounting, evaluations of financial data and factors, management of portfolios, and so on, to work for institutions, banks' trust departments, pension funds, and so on.

chartered financial consultant (CFC) (ChFC): an individual who has passed a series of examinations after taking courses in investments, real estate and tax shelters given by the American College of Bryn Mawr, Pennsylvania.

chartered investment counsel (CIC): an individual who has passed a series of examinations after taking courses in accounting, economics, taxation, and portfolio management given by the Investment Counsel Association of America. Five years of experience is also required before certification.

Chartered Life Underwriter (CLU): the professional designation awarded by the American College of Life Underwriters to those who have completed the prescribed series of examinations and have satisfied the organization's experience requirement.

Chartered Property & Casualty Underwriter (CPCU): the professional designation awarded by the American Institute for Property and Liability Underwriters to those who have completed the prescribed series of examinations and have satisfied the organization's experience requirement.

charting: a graphic strategy of depicting stock prices and other relevant information that tends to influence prices. Chartists follow the belief that past and present patterns can be useful in predicting future price direction.

chartist: an individual who interprets stock market activity and predicts future movement, usually over a short period, from a graphic depiction of price and volume on charts. cf. *Dow theory.*

chartist's liability: an estimated risk involved in purchasing a security or selling it short following an analysis of a chart pattern.

chart of accounts: a list of account titles giving the order of arrangement and classification of accounts found in the general ledger.

charts: records of price changes in a security or market average placed on graph paper with the relevant volume of transactions.

chattel: derived from "cattle." All property that is not real property. A structure on real property is a chattel real; movable properties (e.g., automobiles) are chattels personal. see also *personal property.*

chattel, personal: any item of movable property besides real estate.

checking the market: see *check the market.*

check-kiting: overdrawing one's account.

check the market
(1) in over-the-counter markets, asking for price quotations from several firms to determine the best quotes and the depth of the market.
(2) determing if the market for an issue has changed since the last time it was quoted and/or sold.

ChFC: see *chartered financial consultant.*

Chicago Board of Trade (CBT): the world's largest grain exchange where spot or futures contracts are completed in a host of agricultural products.

Chicago Board Options Exchange (CBOE): an exchange set up by the Chicago Board of Trade and using the facilities provided by the Board for open-market trading of certain stock options. Prior to the 1973 opening of the CBOE, options had been handled on an individually negotiated basis.

Chicago Mercantile Exchange (CME): organized in 1919 as a national market place of trading in cash and futures contracts for commodity items, including butter, eggs, potatoes, pork bellies, hogs, cattle, sorghums, turkeys, and lumber. The CME is the leading currency futures and options exchange in the United States.

chief executive officer (CEO): the person accountable to the board of directors for the activities and profits of the firm.

chumming: artificially inflating the market's volume to attract other orders in some issues which stock exchanges compete in.

churning: the repetitive buying and selling of securities when such activity has a minimal effect on the market but generates additional commissions to a stockbroker.

CI
(1) see *cash items.*
(2) see *compounded interest.*

Cia: Compañía (Spanish company).

CIC: see *chartered investment counsel.*

Cie: Compagnie (French company).

CIF: see *Corporate Income Fund.*

Cincinnati Stock Exchange (CSE): created 1887; most of its traded stocks are *unlisted,* including securities listed and traded on other stock exchanges.

circle: an underwriter's technique for designating potential purchasers and amounts of a securities issue during the registration period, before selling is allowed.

circular: any prospectus; a publication providing information on a security and distributed widely.

circular bond: see *bond, circular.*

circumfiduciation: the shifting of certificates of deposit money to other investments.

citizen bond: see *bond, citizen.*

City: *The City* is London's financial center. synonymous with *The Square Mile.*

city bond: see *bond, municipal.*

civil bond: see *bond, civil.*

civil corporation: an artificial being, created by law for the purpose of engaging in the business purposes stated in its charter that has been granted by the state.

CL: see *current liabilities.*

class
(1) ***general:*** to place in ranks or divisions.
(2) ***investments:*** stocks having similar featues.
(3) ***investments:*** options having similar features.

Class A stock: as distinguished from Class B stock, common, a stock that usually has an advantage over other stock in terms of voting rights, dividend or asset preferences, or other special dividend provisions.

Class B stock: see *Class A stock.*

classical security analysis: a security analysis based on the valuation techniques developed by Benjamin Graham. Unfortunately this approach fails to quantify risk.

classified: see *classified stock.*

classified bond: see *bond, classified.*

classified stock: the separation of equity into more than one class of common stock, usually designated Class A and Class B. Usually the advantage is given to Class A shares related to voting power, although dividend and liquidation privileges can also be included. Rarely used today.

class life asset depreciation: see *asset depreciation range system.*

class of options: options contracts of the same type (call or put) covering the same underlying security.

class I railroads: railroad companies having gross annual operating revenues in excess of $1 million.

class price: the price established for a group of buyers of the same commodity, with other prices established for different groups of buyers of that commodity. In effect, price discrimination based on the ignorance of buyers.

class system: a term occasionally applied to the stagger system of electing directors. Only a portion of the board has to stand for election in any one year. Each director's term runs for more than one year, so only one class of directors, or one portion of the full board, must win stockholder support at any one annual meeting.

CLD: called (in stock listings of newspapers).

cld: of bond, called.

clean
(1) ***general:*** free of debt, as with a clean balance sheet.
(2) ***trade:*** without documents, as in clean versus documentary drafts.
(3) ***investments:*** a block trade that matches corresponding buy or sell orders, thereby minimizing the inventory risk to a block positioner.
(4) ***Great Britain:*** a price quoted excluding accrued interest. cf. *dirty.*

clean bond: see *bond, clean.*

clean float: see *floating currency.*

clean opinion: a choice made by an accounting firm when auditing financial reports of public companies. Consists of two paragraphs in which the auditor attests that the company's financial records have been examined and have been found to fairly present the firm's financial condition in accordance with generally accepted accounting principles. see also *except for opinion, statement disclaiming, subject to opinion.*

clear
(1) the comparison and verification of a stock trade as anticipation of final settlement.
(2) the performance of the clearing activity for another brokerage house.

clearance fees: the change incurred in a commodity exchange following the clearing of a trade.

cleared: the time when an individual who has contracted for a stock pays for it and receives delivery. Many brokerage firms make a specialty of clearing transactions, charging other firms for this service.

clearing
(1) ***general:*** freeing a machine or device from obstuction or other barriers that minimize efficiency; erasing unnecessary information or data.
(2) ***investments:*** the physical transfer of cash and securities between the purchasers and sellers.

clearing house funds: funds represented by a personal or business check that are processed by a bank clearing function prior to approval of credit. The majority of stock transactions are payable in *clearing house funds.*

clearing the market: in securities and commodities, the satisfying of all buyers or sellers by moving the price.

clear title: synonymous with *good title, just title,* and *marketable title.* see *just title.*

Clifford trust: a 10-year trust to reduce income taxes by diverting the income from property placed in trust from the grantor to a beneficiary, usually a member of the grantor's family in a lower income tax bracket. At the end of the trust period of 10 years or more, the trust property reverts to the grantor. synonymous with *10-year trust.*

climax: the termination of rather long-lasting rising or declining price movement, often accompanied by significant securities trading volume, see also *blowing off.* see *selling climax.*

clique: a gentleman's agreement by a number of persons to manipulate securities by matched orders and short or wash sales. An illegal practice based on the concerted action of individuals rather than any structured organization.

CLO: see *at the close.*

CLOB: see *composite limit order book.*

clone fund: synonymous with *clone money-market fund.*

clone money-market fund: a type of money-market fund that is readily created but is required under federal rulings to put up a certain percentage of its assets as a reserve. synonymous with *clone fund.*

close
(1) ***general:*** to transfer the balances of revenue and expense accounts at the end of an accounting period (e.g., close the books.) see *accounting cycle.*
(2) ***general:*** to sign legal paper indicating that the property has formally changed ownership.
(3) ***general:*** to conclude a sale or agreement.
(4) ***investments:*** the short period before the end of the trading session when all trades are officially declared to have been confirmed "at or on the close."

close a position: eliminating an investment from a person's portfolio, usually by selling a security and its delivery to the buyers in exchange for payment. Terminates any involvement with the investment. cf. *hedging.*

closed account: a brokerage account terminated by either the brokerage firm or client. By law all former records are retained on file, but stocks and money are forwarded to the client or their representative.

closed corporation: a corporation whose shares are held by only a few people, usually in positions of management. synonymous with *privately owned corporation.*

closed-end funds (CEF): investment companies with a fixed capitalization. Their shares, like those of public corporations are priced by the forces of supply and demand. These funds are traded on a securities exchange or over the counter, so buyers and sellers deal with one another (not with the fund itself), in acquiring or disposing of shares. These funds often trade at a discount below the net asset value, and at other times trade at a premium above the net asset value. synonymous with *closed-end investment trusts and publicly traded funds.*

closed-end investment company (CEIC): a management investment company that has raised its capital by means of a public offering, over a limited period of time, of a fixed amount of common stock (and which may also have raised capital by the issuance of senior securities). The stock of a closed-end investment company is bought and sold on securities exchanges or over-the-counter markets, as are the securities of business corporations.

closed-end investment trusts: synonymous with *closed-end funds.*

closed-end mortgage: a mortgage bond issue with an indenture that prohibits repayment prior to maturity and the repledging of the same collateral without the bondholders' permission. synonymous with *closed mortgage.* cf. *open-end mortgage.*

closed-end mutual fund: unlike ordinary mutual funds, which sell unlimited shares that can always be redeemed at their net asset value, closed-end funds have only a set number of shares outstanding. The shares are traded on the major exchanges and the price rises and falls with demand.

closed mortgage: synonymous with *closed-end mortgage.*

closed out: a situation where the margin purchaser or short seller is unable to "cover" or make up the new amount of margin resulting from the price fluctuation of his securities. He or she is now closed out or sold out by their broker.

closed trade: a transaction concluded by selling a security that has been paid for previously, or the converting of a short sale (e.g., purchasing a security that had earlier been sold short).

closely held: the ownership of a com- company's common stock by a single individual, family, or a few holders that is not placed on the market for significant trading.

close money: term applied when changes in prices between successive stock transactions are fractional, or when the last bid and asked quotations are hardly different.

close-out: synonymous with *buy-in procedure.*

close prices: a market condition whereby prices fluctuate only minor amounts and the spread between bid and asked prices is small. see *spread.*

close (closing) the books: the date set by a corporation's board of directors for the declaring of dividends resulting in the temporary closing of their stock transfer books.

close-to-the-money: an option contract, either put or call, for which the striking price is close to the current market value of the underlying stock.

closing of transfer book: in corporations, setting a date after which changes of stock ownership for purposes of dividends and notices of meetings will not be accepted for a period to avoid confusion at dividend and meeting times.

closing price (CP): the price of securities quoted at the end of the stock exchange day.

closing purchase (CP): a transaction in which a writer liquidates his or her position by purchasing an option previously written (sold).

closing quote: last bid and offer prices recorded by a market maker at the end of a trading day.

closing range: commodities, unlike securities, are frequently traded at differing prices at the opening or close of the market. Purchasing or selling transaction at the opening can be filled at any point in such a price range for a particular commodity.

closing sale (CS): a transaction in which an investor who had previously purchased an option demonstrates intent to liquidate his or her position as a holder by selling in a closing sale transaction an option having the same terms as the option previously purchased.

closing statement: an accounting of funds in a real estate sale.

closing the books

(1) the entries of a bookkeeper at the end of a period that permits balancing and preparation of financial statements.

(2) action by a transfer agent that records the stock transfer so that a list of stockholders eligible to receive a dividend is prepared. Stocks sell ex-dividend the day following the closing of the books. see *ex-dividend.*

closing (or passing) title: the formal exchange of money and documents when real estate is transferred from one owner to another. see *title defect.* synonymous with *passing title.*

closing transaction: the purchase or sale of an option contract terminating an open position ending all obligations and rights to purchase of sell shares on the underlying security. cf. *opening transaction.*

cloud on title: any claim or existing shortcoming that interferes with the title to real property. see *abeyance.* cf. *marketable title, perfect title.*

CLU: see *Chartered Life Underwriter.*

CM

(1) see *call money.*

(2) see *call of more.*

CMA: see *Cash Management Account.*

Cmdty.: see *commodity.*

CME: see *Chicago Mercantile Exchange.*

CMO: see *collaterized mortgage obligation.*

CMV: see *current market value.*

Cncld.: see *cancel.*

Cnl.: see *cancel.*

CNS: continuous net settlement. A means of securities clearing and settlement which eliminates multiple fails in the same stock. Accomplished by a clearing house which matches transactions to stocks available in a firm's position, resulting in one net receive or deliver position at the end of the day. By including the previous day's fail position in the following day's selling trades, a firm's position is always up to date and money settlement or withdrawals can be made at any time with the clearinghouse. cf. *window.*

CO
(1) see *call option.*
(2) see *covered option.*

COB: close of business (with date).

COD: see *cash on delivery.*

code of arbitration: see *board of arbitration.*

code of procedure: the National Association of Securities Dealers guide for its District Business Conduct Committees in handling and adjudicating complaints filed between or against NASD members under its Rules of Fair Practice.

COD transaction: a broker buying for a customer's account for delivery to the customer's agent. On delivery, the agent will pay for the cost of the purchase.

coefficient of determination (R^2): measures the percentage of total risk which is market-related, that is, systematic.

COI
(1) see *certificate of incorporation.*
(2) see *certificate of indebtedness.*

coincident indicator: an indicator that changes at the same time and same direction that the general economy shifts. Some of the indicators followed are employment, personal income, and gross national product. cf. *lagging indicator, leading indicators.*

Col.: column.

COLA: Cost-of-Living Adjustment.

cold call: contacting a potential investment customer without prior notice in order to make a sale or arrange for an appointment.

cold canvassing: (CC): determining potential investment customers without assistance from others or from references (e.g., selecting every tenth name in the telephone directory within a given location and having a salesman or other person, call on these persons).

cold in hand: slang, a person without funds.

collapse
(1) a sudden drop in business activity or business prices.
(2) failure or ruin of a specific firm.

collar: a maximum and minimum dividend rate, beyond which they will not fluctuate. see also *adjustable-rate preferred stocks.*

collar pricing (CP): rather than fix the exact stock price at the time of a merger agreement, companies agree on a range—the collar—within which the final price will fall. The actual price is based on an average of the buying company's stock price during the 10 to 20 days before the deal is actually closed. The purpose is to avoid the tendency of the buyer's stock to a dive on the merger news as traders and investors unload their shares through fears of dilution.

collateral: any asset pledged by a borrower to a lender.

collateral bond: see *bond, collateral.*

collateralize: placing an asset as a pledge that a loan will be repaid.

collateralized loan: a loan granted a customer upon the pledge of liquid assets or illiquid assets. Should the borrower be unable to repay, the lender sells the collateral.

collaterized mortgage obligation (CMO): permitting investors to choose whether they want a piece of the early, middle, or late maturities in a single pool of mortgages the uncertain lifespan and erratic mix of principal and interest payments each month are determined. The cash flow is managed so that investors get their share of interest payments, but principal payments initially go to investors having the shortest-maturity bonds. For convenience payments are made at six-month intervals. Introduced by Freddie Mac in 1983.

collateral mortgage: a document used in connection with a loan which effects a lien on real estate, where the purpose of the loan is not for the purchase of the property offered as security.

collateral mortgage bonds: collateral trust bonds that have been secured by a deposit of mortgage bonds.

collateral note: a promissory note secured by the pledge of specific property.

collateral surety: commercial paper, such as stocks or bonds, that has have been placed with a lender as security for the payment of a loan.

collateral trust bond: see *bond, collateral trust.*

collateral trust notes: bonds secured by the deposit of other stocks or bonds. These notes are usually issued by investment trusts, railroads, and holding companies.

collateral value: the estimate of value of the thing put up as security for a loan made by a lender. With securities and commodities, the lender is usually restricted in his or her valuation by rules of an appropriate agency, such as the exchange of Federal Reserve Board.

collectible: any rare object collected by an investor, such as stamps, books, coins, and antiques.

collection ratio: the ratio of a firm's accounts receivable to its average daily sales.

collective investment fund: a pooled investment trust under which the funds of pension and profit-sharing plans that are approved by the Internal Revenue Service are commingled for investment.

collective ownership: possession of an item in common, with no particular part or proportion assigned to anyone.

coll. tr.: see *bond, collateral trust.*

combination: a stock-option position similar to a straddle, involving a put and a call on the same underlying stock but having different striking prices.

combination bond: see *bond, combination.*

Comex: see *Commodity Exchange, Inc.*

comfort letter: a common condition of an underwriting agreement in connection with the offering for sale of securities registered with the SEC whereby an independent auditor issues a letter to the underwriter reporting on the limited procedures followed with respect to unaudited financial statements or other financial data.

comingled real estate funds: see *CREF.*

commercial bank: an organization chartered either by the Comptroller of the Currency and known as a national bank or chartered by the state in which it will conduct the business of banking. A commercial bank generally specializes in demand deposits and commercial loans. see also other entries under *bank.*

commercial bar: a brick, or bar of precious metal, usually gold or silver, used in the arts and industry area, as distinguished from one created for monetary use (e.g., a jeweler's bar which is usually smaller than the bar used for monetary purposes.

commercial blanket bond: see *bond, commercial blanket.*

commercial borrower: one who borrows for some purpose having to do with business or commerce.

Commercial Exchange of Philadelphia: first opened in 1854 as the Corn Exchange Association of Philadelphia, changing in 1868 to its present name. This exchange deals in grains, feeds, and flour commodities.

commercial hedgers: firms taking positions in commodities markets to lock in prices at which they purchase raw materials or sell their products. see also *hedging.*

commercial lending: loans to businesses to meet short- or long-term needs.

commercial letter of credit: an instrument by which a bank lends its credit to a customer to enable him or her to finance the purchase of goods. Addressed to the seller, it authorizes the individual to draw drafts on the bank under the terms stated in the letter.

commercial loan: loans made to businesses for the financing of inventory purchases and the movement of goods, as distinguished from personal loans or consumer credit loans. Commercial loans are short-term loans or acceptances (time drafts accepted). see also *loan.* cf. *borrowed funds.*

commercial mortgage: a loan secured by real estate, and for which the real estate is used or zoned for business purposes or multiunit dwellings, or is part of a real estate investment portfolio.

commercial paper (CP)
(1) ***general:*** any notes, drafts, checks, or deposit certificates used in a business.
(2) ***general:*** in 1978 the Bankers Trust Company sold several issues of clients' commercial paper—short-term IOU's issued by corporations. The securities industry has tried unsuccessfully to get the Federal Reserve Board to prohibit that sale on grounds that it violated the Glass-Steagall Act, which separates commercial from investment banking. see *Glass-Steagall Act of 1933.*
(3) ***investments:*** unsecured short-term (under 270 days) promissory notes issued by corporations of unquestioned credit standing and sold to corporate and individual investors.

commercial-paper house: principals and dealers who purchase commercial paper at one rate and attempt to sell it at another.

commercial paper names: established borrowers who are frequently in the commercial paper market.

commercial property: property to be used for business purposes, as contrasted with residential, agricultural, or industrial functions.

commercial stocks: U.S. Department of Agriculture stocks of grain at major grain centers.

commercial wells: oil and gas drilling locations that are productive enough to be commercially profitable.

commercial year: a business year; unlike the calendar year, it consists of 12 months of 30 days each, totaling 360 days.

commingled accounts: when several bank trust department accounts are managed as one account to take advantage of economies available to large investments, the accounts are referred to collectively as a commingled account. Banks may not sell shares to the public that would increase the size of these accounts and make them, in effect, open-ended investment companies or mutual funds. A recent Supreme Court decision, however, allows bank holding companies to advise, sponsor, and organize closed-end investment companies, which sell only a certain number of shares that are then traded in the open market like common stocks.

commingled fund: a common fund in which the funds of several accounts are mixed.

commingled investment fund: a bank-operated trust fund in which accounts of individual customers are commingled and lose their identity. Each customer, in effect, owns a share of the entire fund. Such a fund differs only in detail from a mutual fund.

commingling
(1) ***trusts:*** pooling the investment funds of individual accounts, with each bank customer owning a share of the total fund.
(2) ***investments:*** mixing customer-owned stocks with those

owned by a company in its proprietary accounts.

commission
(1) the amount paid to an agent, which may be an individual, a broker, or a financial institution, for consummating a transaction involving sale or purchase of assets or services.
(2) agents and brokers are usually compensated by being allowed to retain a certain percentage of the premiums they produce, known as a commission.

commission broker: an agent who executes the public's orders for the purchase or sale of securities or commodities. see *dealer.*

Commission des Opérations de Bourse: the French government agency responsible for supervising its stock exchange.

commissioners' values: the values of securities as determined by the National Association of Insurance Commissioners to be used by insurers for valuation purposes when preparing financial statements.

commission house: a broker who purchases and sells only for customers and does not trade his or her own account.

commission trade: securities or commodities transactions where the brokerage firm receives a commission, as contrasted with tradings, usually over-the-counter, in which it serves as a principal and buys and sells for its own account and does not charge any commission.

commitment: an advance agreement to perform in the future such as by an association to provide funds for a mortgage loan.

commitment fee: a lender's charge for contracting to hold credit available.

Committee on Uniform Securities Identification Procedures: see *CUSIP.*

committees: on stock exchanges, bodies that aid in the operation of the exchange performing responsibility for admissions, conduct, and so on.

commodities: a basic product, usually but not always agricultural or mineral, which is traded on a commodity exchange.

Commodities Exchange Center (CEC): a facility for the four major New York commodity exchanges, opened in July 1977. Each exchange retains its own autonomy, clears transactions through separate clearing units, and shares in a single computer quotation system. CEC combines the Commodity Exchange, the New York Coffee and Sugar Exchange, the New York Mercantile Exchange, and the New York Cotton Exchange. see also *New York Coffee and Sugar Exchange, New York Mercantile Exchange.*

commodities futures contract: a contract to purchase or sell a specific amount of a given commodity at a specified future date.

Commodities Futures Trading Commission: see *regulated commodities.*

commodity (Cmdty.): an item of commerce of trade. cf. *spot market.*

commodity-backed bond: see *bond, commodity-backed.*

commodity collateral loan: any loan made with a commodity, such as cotton, coffee, or sugar, as collateral.

commodity exchange (CE): an organization usually owned by the member-traders, which provides facilities for bringing together buyers and sellers of specified commodities, or their agents, for promoting trades, either spot or futures or both, in these commodities. see *Commodity Exchange, Inc.*

Commodity Exchange Act: federal legislation of 1936 establishing the Commodity Exchange Commission to regulate trading in the contract markets and other power to prevent fraud and manipulation in commodities and set limitations in trading for the purpose of preventing excessive speculation.

Commodity Exchange Authority (CEA): a unit of the U.S. Department of Agriculture, responsible for enforcing the Commodity Exchange Act of 1936.

Commodity Exchange Commission (CEC): the U.S. secretary of commerce, secretary of agriculture, and attorney general are designated by the Commodity Exchange Act of 1936 as the Commodity Exchange Commission.

Commodity Exchange, Inc. (Comex): formed in 1933 by the merger of the New York Hide Exchange, the National Metal Exchange, the National Raw Silk Exchange, and the New York Rubber Exchange. Presently, silver, copper, and mercury are the commodities futures traded. In 1980, Comex absorbed the Amex Commodities Exchange, an offshoot of the American Stock Exchange.

commodity futures: trading of futures in commodities, such as wheat, corn, sugar, cotton, lumber, and so on.

commodity-futures straddle: a two-part transaction that consists of buying a commodity contract for delivery in one month and selling a contract for the same commodity for delivery in another month, hoping to profit from a change in the difference between the two months' prices. see also *straddle.*

Commodity Futures Trading Commission (CFTC): a federal agency established in April 1975, responsible for coordinating the commodities industry in the United States, with primary concern for detecting and prosecuting violators of the Commodity Exchange Act. see also *Tax Reform Acts of 1976, 1984. see also National Futures Association.*

commodity income statement: an income statement prepared for each of the major traded commodities.

commodity market: the market or public demand for the purchase and sale of commodity futures.

commodity paper: notes, drafts, or other documents with warehouse receipts or bills of lading for commodities. Should default occur, the lender can sell the commodities up to the value of the loan and the expense of collection.

commodity price: a price for a commodity is quoted on a cash (spot) basis, or on a future basis, the difference to be accounted for by the charges involved in carrying the commodity for the period of the delivery of the future.

commodity rate: the rate of interest charged by banks on notes, drafts, bills of exchange, and other related documents issued on stable commodities.

commodity standard: a suggested monetary system that proposes to substitute a commodity or commodities for the precious metal or other base of a currency.

commodity surplus: the supply of a specific commodity that exceeds the market demands for a specific time period.

commodity tax straddle: a commodity investment in which a taxpayer has real capital gain that he or she wants to offset with a capital loss in order to defer his or her current-year tax liability. see also *straddle.*

commodity trading: the process of buying or selling contracts for future delivery of a commodity.

common: see *common stock.*

common-law voting: one vote for each stockholder in a corporation, regardless of number of shares held. cf. *cumulative voting, ordinary voting.*

common stock (CS): securities that represent an ownership interest in a corporation. If the company has also issued preferred stock, both common and preferred have ownership rights. The preferred normally is limited to a fixed dividend but has prior claim on dividends and in the event of liquidation, assets. Claims of both common and preferred stockholders are junior to claims of bondholders or other creditors of the company. Common stockholders assume the greater risk but generally exercise a greater degree of control and may gain the greater reward in the form of dividends and capital appreciation. Often used interchangeably with *capital stock.* see *leverage.* see also *voting right (stock).* synonymous with *equities.*

common stock dividends: dividends declared on common stock during the year whether or not they were paid during the year. Unless otherwise qualified, it is the amount of such dividends charged to retained income (earned surplus) and includes those payable in cash or stock.

common stock equivalent: a security which, because of its terms or the circumstances under which it was issued, is considered in computing earnings per share to be in substance equivalent to common stock (e.g., a convertible security).

common stock fund

(1) a mutual fund that invests exclusively in common stocks.

(2) an investment firm having a portfolio consisting primarily of com-

mon stocks. Such a company can reserve the right to take defensive positions in cash, bonds, and other senior securities whenever existing conditions appear to warrant such action.

common stock index: a compilation showing the average current market value of common stock compared with their average market value at an earlier, base period.

common stock ratio: the percentage of total capitalization represented by a common stock. For the investor a high ratio means a lack of leverage. When a firm's stock ratio is below 30 percent, analysts check on earnings stability and fixed charge coverage in bad times as well as good.

common trust fund: a fund maintained by a bank or a trust company exclusively for the collective investment and reinvestment of money contributed to the fund by the bank or trust company in its capacity as trustee, executor, administrator, or guardian and in conformity with the rules and regulations of the Board of Governors of the Federal Reserve System pertaining to the collective investment of trust funds by national banks, as well as with the statutes and regulations (if any) of the several states.

community income (or property): assets shared by both spouses, pursuant to the laws of nine states.

comparative balance sheet: a balance sheet showing information for more than one fiscal period.

comparative profit and loss statement: a profit and loss statement showing information for more than one fiscal period.

comparative reports: financial reports giving the figures for more than one fiscal period.

comparative statement: the income, expense, profit and loss, balance sheet, or other financial statement of the same concern for two or more consecutive years that are analyzed to determine the increase or decrease in their component items, frequently for credit purposes.

comparisons: the exchange of information between a broker and his bank or between two brokers to verify that each party's records of collateral held against loan are valid and in agreement. If there is disagreement, the parties can rapidly track down any difference.

compensated dollar: a monetary unit where the gold content is periodically changed to retain the purchasing power level with some commodity index.

competitive bid: the awarding of a new stock issue to the highest bidder. In most cases, this nonnegotiated bid is made by investment banking groups. cf. *negotiated bid.*

competitive bid underwriting: the bidding among various underwriters for the right to handle a portion of (or all of), a new issue. Offering price is set by the bidding process.

competitive price: a price determined in the market by the bargaining of a number of buyers and sellers, each acting separately and without sufficient power to manipulate the market.

competitive trader: synonymous with *floor trader.*

completed contract accounting: an accounting method that allows some companies with long-term contracts to deduct many expenses immediately but defer almost indefinitely reporting any revenue and profits to the Internal Revenue Service. The Treasury Department calls such deferrals an "interest-free loan" to the firms. This technique allows companys to report losses to the IRS while reporting profits to stockholders.

completed transaction: a sale property that has closed. In this transaction all legal and financial aspects are identified, and title to the property has transferred from seller to buyer.

completes: used in a floor report showing that an order to purchase or sell a block of stock has been carried out.

completion bond: see *bond, completion.*

completion program: an oil and gas limited partnership that takes over drilling when oil is found in commercial quantities.

compliance director: a member of a securities house who seeks to find fraud or unauthorized or unethical behavior, in the buying and selling of securities.

compliance registered options principal (CROP): an individual charged with the audit function for determining that a brokerage firm's option activities are handled in compliance with SEC regulations and current laws.

compliance unit: a department established in all stock exchanges to oversee market activity and to guarantee that trading complies with SEC and exchange regulations. Any firm not complying with these rules can be delisted, and a brokerage house or individual broker that violates these rules can be barred from trading.

component operating firms: corporations that function as a unit of a holding company system. They are operating units of one parent company, which may merely hold stock in, and control the movement of, the existing operation companies or may, itself be an operating corporation.

composite commodity standard: a monetary system concept where the value of the monetary unit is defined in terms of a selected number of commodities (composite commodity unit) instead of in terms of one or more precious metals.

composite limit order book (CLOB): a central electronic repository and display that automates all orders to buy and sell securities. It could eliminate the need for any exchanges by having buying and selling done directly by brokerage offices through a central computer system.

composite rate depreciation: a single depreciation rate to be applied against the total of depreciable assets or a group of such assets; based on an average of the rates applicable to individual items with some weighting of the relative importance of the several items.

composites: averages using information from various sources to measure results. For example, the Dow Jones Composite uses data from the industrial, transportation, and utility averages.

composite tape: a stock ticker printout that reports transactions occurring in national, regional, and over-the-counter exchange markets.

compound: to add interest to principal at time intervals for the purpose of establishing a new basis for subsequent interest computations.

compound arbitrage: arbitrage achieved by using four or more markets. cf. *arbitrage.* see *simple arbitrage.*

compounded: indicating the frequency with which interest is computed and added to the principal to arrive at a new actual balance.

compounded interest (CI): interest created by the periodic addition of simple interest to principal, the new base thus established being the principal for the computation of additional interest.

compound growth rate: the rate of growth of a number, compounded over several years. Analysts study a firm's compound growth rate of profits for five years to see the long-term trend in profitability.

compound-interest method of depreciation: taking the initial cost of a capital asset, deducting the expected salvage value at the time it is expected to be discarded and spreading the difference in equal installments per unit of time over the estimated life of the asset but then reducing the depreciation charge for each period by the amount of interest that such a charge would earn from the period of the charge to the time of discard.

computerized market timing system: a system of choosing buy and sell signals that puts together voluminous trading data to identify patterns and trends.

COMSAT: Communications Satellite Corporation.

concept fund: a mutual fund that invests in concept stocks or in some other unique equities, such as foreign securities. cf. *concept stock.*

concept stock: a stock, whether old or new, whose company offers a unique product or service with strong growth potential. cf. *concept fund.*

concession

(1) ***general:*** any deviation from regular terms or previous conditions.

(2) ***general:*** a reduction or rebate; an allowance from the initial price or rate.

(3) ***investments:*** the selling group's per-share or per-bond compensation in an underwriting.

concurrent authority: exists when two or more brokers are given an open listing for property.

concurrent insurance: two or more insurance policies that provide the same coverage for the same property and the same interests.

Cond.: see *condition.*

condensed balance sheet: a balance sheet where the details have been removed to give an easy, though accurate, reading of the assets, liabilities, and capital of the corporation. see *balance sheet.*

condensed statement: a financial statement grouping minor details together so that the statement can be more easily studied by the general public.

condition (Cond.): a contractual clause, implied or expressed, that has the effect of investing or divesting with rights and duties the members of the contract.

condominium: individual ownership of a portion of a building that has other units similarly owned. Owners hold a deed and title. Owners pay taxes independently of other owners and can sell, lease, or otherwise dispose of the portion that the individual owns. Common areas, including halls, elevators, and so on, are jointly owned by the other tenants. cf. *cooperative building.*

condominium conversion: changing rental units into condominiums, where the buyer gets title to a specified unit plus a proportionate interest in common areas. See *condominium.*

conduit concept: an IRS term for income received by qualified investment firms. Interest and dividends received, in addition to net capital gains, are passed along to investors for their personal tax liability without subjecting the investment firm to federal and state/local taxation.

confidence index: see *Barron's Confidence Index.*

confirmation

(1) ***investments:*** a written order or agreement to verify or confirm one previously given verbally, face to face, or by telephone. Executions of orders to buy or sell securities as substantiated in writing by brokers to their customers. see *dealer.*

(2) ***law:*** an assurance of title by the conveyance of an estate or right from one to another, by which a voidable estate is made sure or valid, or at times increased.

confirmation slip: an acknowledgment forwarded to a client by a brokerage house verifying the transaction made on the client's behalf. The slip includes the name of the stock, number of traded shares, whether bought or sold, price per share, commission and fees, and the net dollar amount of the transaction. synonymous with *transaction slip.*

conformed copy: a copy of an original document with the signature, seal, and other such features being typed or otherwise noted.

conforming mortgage loan: a mortgage loan that conforms to regularity limits such as loan-to-value ratio, term, and other characteristics.

conglomerate: the result of the merging of organizations producing differing items and services, to secure a large economic base, acquire sounder management, and gain greater potential profit. see *merger.* cf. *consortium.*

conglomerate merger: a merger between companies in unrelated business lines.

consent to service: a legal document authorizing a person to serve as attorney to accept orders of any lawful proceeding brought against the person who signed the document. The filing of a *consent to service* is required with all applications for registration as a broker-dealer or agent under the Uniform Security Agent regulations.

conservative portfolio: a portfolio of securities and bonds, created with safety as its primary objective.

conservator: a court-appointed official responsible for the protection of the interests on an estate.

consol(s):
(1) a bond that will never reach maturity; a bond in perpetuity.
(2) the name given to British government bonds.

consolidate: to bring together various financial obligations under one agreement, contract, or note.

consolidated: the results obtained when the accounts of a parent company and its subsidiary companies are combined to reflect the financial position and results of operations of the group as if operated as a single entity. Such a consolidation involves intercompany eliminations and minority interest adjustments.

consolidated accounting standards: the combined financial statements of a parent company and its subsidiaries. The consolidated accounting statements show assets, liabilities, and net worth for the total organization.

consolidated balance sheet: a balance sheet showing the financial condition of a corporation and its subsidiaries.

consolidated income statement: the combined statement of profit and loss for a group of firms controlled or owned by the same interests, thus eliminating duplications and intercompany profits and losses.

consolidated limit order book (CLOB): see *composite limit order book.*

consolidated mortgage: when two or more firms, each holding a mortgage on property, combine, and then the consolidated organization takes out a mortgage, the latter mortgage is referred to as a consolidated mortgage.

consolidated mortgage bond: see *bond, consolidated mortgage.*

consolidated sinking fund: one sinking fund that is established to serve two or more bond issues.

consolidated statement of financial position: a summary of a firm's financial position at a specific time.

consolidated statement of income: a financial summary of the activities of a firm at a specific time, noting the operations of all subsidiaries in which the company has a controlling interest.

consolidated tape: under the consolidated tape plan, the New York Stock Exchange and Amex ticket systems became the "consolidated tape" Network A and Network B, respectively, on June 16, 1975. Network A reports transactions in NYSE-listed securities that take place on the NYSE or any of the participating regional stock exchanges and other markets. Each transaction is identified according to its originating market. Similarly, transactions in Amex-listed securities, and certain other securities listed on regional stock exchanges, are reported and identified on Network B.

consolidated tax return: a return combining reports of firms in what tax laws call an *affiliated group*, if at least 80 percent is "owned" by a parent or other inclusive corporation. "Owned" refers to a nonvoting stock, excluding preferred stock.

consolidation: a combination of two or more organizations into one, to form a new entity.

consortium: a grouping of corporations to fulfill a combined objective or project that usually requires interbusiness cooperation and sharing of resources. cf. *cartel, conglomerate.*

constant dollar plan: the means of accumulating assets by investing a fixed amounts of dollars in stock at set intervals. An investor purchases more shares when the price is low and fewer shares when the price is high. The overall cost is lower than it would be if a constant number of shares were purchased at set intervals.

constant dollars: the actual prices of a previous year or the average of actual prices of a previous period of years. synonymous with *deflator.*

constant factor: the periodic amount of principal and interest that is required to retire a loan.

constant payment: a fixed or invariable payment, a continually recurring payment.

constant ratio: a method of comparing mortgage amortization (principal and interest) on an annual basis to the original amount of the mortgage. Expressed as a percentage. synonymous with *mortgage constant.*

constant yield rate: an installment finance method where a rate is computed on the total note as in the true discount rate for a contract of 12 monthly payments only.

construction loan: funds extended on the security of real property for the purpose of constructing or improving a building.

constructive receipt: the date, defined by the IRS, when a taxpayer received dividends or other income.

constructive side of the market: a long purchase of a stock with the anticipation that its market price will jump; a bullish position.

consumer debentures: investment notes sold directly to the public by a financial institution. These notes are much like the certificates of deposit sold by banks and savings and loans.

Unlike banks selling notes, these notes can be sold anywhere, at any interest rate determined to be found competitive by the institution.

Cont.: see *contract.*

contango

(1) ***general:*** the cost factors when calculating from one given period to a future point.

(2) ***investments:*** a basic pricing system in futures trading. A form of premium or carrying charge; for example, instead of paying for the cost of warehousing silver bullion, paying insurance finance charges and other expenses (silver users prefer to pay more for a futures contract covering later delivery).

contingent immunization: a technique in the pursuit of active bond management providing for a minimum compound annual return. Active management strategies are applied to the portfolio as long as the portfolio value exceeds an amount of money needed to achieve the minimum return.

contingent obligation: an obligation dependent upon other events; for example, in the case of income bonds, the payment of interest is contingent upon the earning by the corporation of an amount sufficient to pay the interest.

contingent order: a request to purchase or sell a security at a specific price which in contingent upon the earlier execution of another order; for example, "Purchase 50 *ABC* at _____, if you can sell 50 *XYZ* at _____."

contingent payment order: a payment order that is executed only upon the receipt of a stipulated covering payment.

contingent remainder: a future interest in property that is dependent upon the fulfillment of a stated condition before the termination of a prior estate; to be distinguished from vested remainder. see *remainder.*

contingent reserve: the setting aside of a certain amount of profits to meet unanticipated needs of the business or some unexpected loss, the amount of which cannot be definitely ascertained at the time of budgeting.

contingent trustee: a trustee whose appointment is dependent upon the failure to act of the original or a successor trustee.

continued bond: see *bond, continued.*

continuing agreement: that portion of the broker's loan arrangement with a bank purporting to simplify the borrowing since the broker need not seek a loan application and sign a note each time he or she borrows. Following the signing of this agreement, the broker can borrow within the terms of the agreement on a continuous basis.

continuous audit: an audit where the detailed work is carried out continuously or at short, regular periods throughout the fiscal year, usually at the shortest intervals (weekly, monthly) when subsidiary records are closed and made available for audit in controllable form.

continuous market: a securities or commodities market that is broad, enabling normal amounts to be sold with ease and little price variation.

continuous net settlement: see *CNS.*

contra: means that an account has an offsetting credit or debit entry.

contrabalance: a balance in an account which is the opposite of the normal balance of that account (e.g., an accounts receivable account with a credit balance; such a balance is correctly shown as a liability). Asset valuation accounts, such as bad debt reserve, are contrabalances to the asset.

contra broker: the broker on the opposite side—the buy side of a sell order or the sell side of a buy order.

contract (Cont.): an agreement between two or more persons, as established by law, and by which rights are acquired by one or more parties to specific acts or forbearance from acts on the part of others.

contract, breach of: see *breach of contract.*

contract broker: on the stock market, a member of the exchange trading for other members. Prior to 1919, the fee for this service was a flat $2 per 100 shares. Hence the contract broker is called a *two-dollar broker.* see *two-dollar brokers.*

contract for deed: a written agreement between the seller and buyer of a piece of property, whereby the buyer receives title to the property only after making a determined number of monthly payments.

contract grades: those grades or types of a commodity which may be delivered on the futures contract. Differentials based on federal standards have been established by the various commodity exchanges which provide premiums for superior grades or discounts for lower grades.

contract holder: the group, entity, or person to whom a group annuity on contract is issued, in jointly administered plans, by the trustee.

contract market: one of the 18 commodity exchanges, permitted under the Commodity Exchange Act to deal in futures contracts in the commodities.

contract month: the delivery month for a grain contract. Also, the month when grain is deliverable against future contracts.

contract sale: a sale of real estate in which the seller retains title to the property until the buyer has made the required number of monthly payments.

contract sheet: disseminated by the Securities Industry Automation Corporation of data received from brokers and contra brokers. Brokers compare their transaction records to prepare for settlement. Items not agreeing with these records are DKd (don't know), or market QT (questioned trade).

contracts in foreign currency: agreements to buy and sell an amount of one currency for another at an agreed rate of exchange.

contractual plan: by common usage, an accumulation plan with a stated paying-in period and provision for regular investments at monthly or quarterly dates. Substantially synonymous with *period charge plan.*

contrarian: popularized by David Dreman to describe the small investor who makes money in the stock market at a rate that exceeds the popular averages. By purchasing unpopular stocks, the buyer looks for investment-grade stocks that are out of favor in terms of their current price-earnings ratios. Obviously, the higher the price-earnings ratio on a stock—that is, the bigger the multiple of earnings that the market is paying for it—the less likely it is to outperform both the market itself and stocks currently less in favor.

contrary market: market movement in an unexpected direction.

contributed capital: the payments in cash or property made to a corporation by its stockholders, in exchange for capital stock, in response to an assessment on the capital stock, or as a gift; paid-in capital; often, though not necessarily, equal to capital stock and paid-in surplus.

contribution margin: the excess of total revenue over total variable cost.

contribution profit: sales revenue less the variable cost of producing the revenue.

control individual: a person able to influence a corporation' actions or policies, including directors, officers, and shareholders with 10 percent of or more of shares outstanding.

controlled account: where the principal authorizes the broker, with a power of attorney, to exercise his or her own discretion in the purchasing and selling of securities or commodities.

controlled commodities: commodities that are subject to the regulations of the Commodity Exchange Authority.

controlled company (corporation): a firm whose policies are controlled by another with ownership of 51 percent or more of its voting shares. see *Tax Reform Act of 1969.* cf. *working control.*

controlled wildcat drilling: drilling for oil and gas in any location adjacent to but outside the limits of a proven field. synonymous with *field extension.*

controller: the brokerage house officer responsible for preparing firm and client financial reports, complying with SEC net capital regulations, and issuing internal audits.

controlling account: an account, usually kept in the general ledger, which receives the aggregate of the debit and of the credit postings to a number of identical, similar, or related accounts called subsidiary accounts so that its balance equals the agggregate of the balance in these accounts.

controlling interest: any ownership of a business in excess of 50 percent. However, a small percentage of shareholders may control the firm if the remainder of the stock is distributed among many owners and is not active in voting. see *working control.* cf. *minority interest.*

control person: synonymous with *affiliated person.*

control stock: securities belonging to those who have controlling interest in a company.

Conv.: see *convertible.*

conventional fixed-rate mortgage: a mortgage with a fixed term, fixed rate, and fixed monthly payments which is fully paid off within 30 years or less. It is a mortgage without government insurance or guarantee. see also *conventional loan.*

conventional loan: a mortgage loan, usually granted by a bank or loan association. The loan is based on real estate as security rather than being guaranteed by an agency of the government. This loan has a fixed interest rate and fixed payments for the life of the loan. see also *conventional fixed-rate mortgage.*

conventional mortgage: see *conventional loan.*

conventional option: synonymous with *OTC option.*

convergence: the movement of the price of a futures contract toward the price of the underlying cash commodity. Initially the price is higher, but as the contract approaches expiration, the futures price and the cash price converge.

conversion
(1) ***general:*** a process of changing from one system or one type of equipment to another.
(2) ***insurance:*** the switching from short-term to permanent life insurance.
(3) ***investments:*** exchanging a convertible security, such as a bond, into a fixed number of shares of the issuing firm's common stock.
(4) ***investments:*** the transfer of mutual-fund shares without charge from one fund to another one in a single family. synonymous with *fund switching.*

conversion charge: the specified cost of converting from one class or series of an open-end fund to another issued by the same company or group of companies having the same sponsor. It is usually lower than the regular sales charge.

conversion parity: the common stock price where the conversion value of a bond is equal to the existing market price of the convertible bond. see *conversion price.*

conversion point: the price (adjusted for accrued dividends) at which stock into which a bond is convertible will just equal the current market price of the bond plus accrued interest on the bond.

conversion premium: the percentage that the price of the convertible trades above its conversion value. One of the axioms of convertible bond trading is that the lower the premium, the more closely it will trade in step with the common. The higher the premium, the more likely the issue will trade on its merits as a bond.

conversion price: the price for which a convertible bond, debenture, or perferred stock stock of a firm can be exchanged by an owner for common stock or another security of the same organization.

conversion ratio: the number of shares of common stock received when a convertible bond or convertible preferred stock is exchanged with the same firm. The price is frequently given at the issue date of the bond or preferred stock, and may not be the same as the market price when the conversion takes place.

conversion value
(1) ***general:*** a value created by changing from the state, character, form, or use to another.
(2) ***convertibles:*** the price at which the exchange is made for common stock.

convertibility: ease of exchanging one currency for that of another nation or for gold. see *soft currency.*

convertible (Conv. Cvt.): slang, any corporate stock that can be converted to a stock of another corporation.

convertible bond: see *bond, convertible.*

convertible debentures: like bonds, these carry a fixed interest rate and have a set maturity date. They may be traded in for a given amount of stock at any time at the option of the investor. The issuer, however, also has the investor. The issuer, however, also has the right to call them in, to be redeemed either in cash or for common stock.

convertible hedge: an investment strategy of selling common stock short at the same time a long position is created in convertible bonds of the same firm. This form of hedging occurs when a decline is anticipated.

convertible money: money that can be exchanged at par for the standard or legal money.

convertible mortgage: a mortgage where pension funds receive interest and appreciation, based on the increase in rent. The fund has the option (usually between the seventh and tenth year of the loan) to convert into equity ownership, ranging from 50–80 percentage. Primarily based on commercial properties.

convertible preferred stock (CPS): a security that can be exchanged at the owner's option for a fixed quantity of common shares of the same corporation.

convertibles: interest-paying debentures and dividend-paying preferred shares that can be exchanged for the common stock of the issuing company on a preset basis. The conversion privilege becomes valuable only if the market value of the debenture or preferred stock is below that of the total value of the common shares into which it can be converted. synonymous with *hybrid stock.*

convertible security: usually a bond or preferred stock that may be converted into common stock at the option or the owner.

convertible wraparound mortgage: see *CWM.*

conveyance: a written statement called a deed, whereby ownership of property is passed from one person or organization to another.

conveyancing: the act of transferring title to real property.

cooling-off period: the term for the period, usually 20 days, that must elapse before the filing of a registration for a new security and public sale, as declared by the SEC

cooperative: anything owned jointly to the same end.

cooperative apartment: dwelling units in a multidwelling complex in which each owner has an interest in the entire complex and a lease on his or her own apartment, although he or she does not own the apartment as in the case of a condominium.

cooperative building: tenants residing in the building are stockholders in a corporation that owns the real estate. All are part owners of the corporation. Stockholders sign a proprietary lease with an operating organization, and in place of rent pay a proportionate fixed rate to cover operating costs, maintenance, and so on. cf. *condominium.*

Cooperative Export Financing Corporation: see *CEFCO.*

cooriginator: in bonding, where the clients of more than one surety company join for a specific contract. Such surety is known as cooriginator for its client's share.

copartnership (partnership): a company of partners, as distinguished from a proprietorship or a corporation.

copper a tip: slang, a person who reacts negatively to a tipster's advice.

corner the market: to purchase a security on a scale large enough to give the purchaser control over the price.

Corp.: see *corporation.*

corporate agent: trust companies act as agents for corporations, governments, and municipalities for various transactions. In each case, a fee is charged for the particular service rendered.

corporate bond: see *bond, corporate.*

corporate bond equivalent: the semiannual equivalent rate of return for a security whose interest payments are not on a semiannual basis.

corporate-bond unit trusts: similar to GNMA trusts units, but without monthly return or principal. Yield is close to a point less. see *Government National Mortgage Association.*

corporate charter: a legal document, state-authorized certified articles of incorporation, giving the name of the corporation, its address, amount and form of capitalization, projected activities, types of securities to be issued, and the uses of funds accumulated.

corporate equivalent yield: the comparison made by dealers of government bonds used in their offering sheets to provided the after-tax yield or government bonds selling at a discount and corporate bonds selling at par.

Corporate Finance Committee: the standing committee of the National Association of Securities Dealers that reviews documentation from underwriters in compliance with SEC requirements to ensure that proposed markups are fair and in the public interest.

corporate funds: see *funds, corporate.*

Corporate Income Fund (CIF): a short-term series investment vehicle. It is a unit trust that is similar to a money market fund with a fixed portfolio of high-grade investment paper.

corporate indenture: an agreement made by a bank to act as an intermediary between a corporation making a public bond offering and the purchasers of the bonds. The bank agrees to act as a trustee by protecting the interest of the lenders (bondholders).

corporate profits after taxes: the earnings of U.S. corporations organized for profit after liability for federal and state taxes has been deducted.

corporate profits before taxes: the net earnings or corporations organized for profit measured before payment of federal and state profit taxes. They are, however, net of indirect business taxes. They are reported without deduction for depletion charges and exclusive of capital gains and losses and intercorporate dividends.

corporate profits tax liability: federal and state taxes levied on corporate earnings of a given year; a measurement of taxes for the year in which they are incurred, not necessarily for the year in which they are paid.

corporate reacquisition: a corporation's attempt to repurchase its own securities through a tender offer.

corporate records: the records of a corporation required by incorporation laws. A listing of all shareholders, their addresses, quantity of stock, date of purchase, and price paid for shares is obligatory.

corporate shell: a firm having no fixed assets except for it name, cash, and perhaps a stock exchange listing. Some shells are illegal or carry on illegal activities.

corporate stock
(1) equity shares of a corporation classified as common, preferred, or classified.
(2) sometimes, bonds of a municipality.

corporate surplus: as of the date of the balance sheet, the equity in the assets not offset by the capitalization, current or deferred liabilities, or unadjusted credits. It includes appropriations for additions to property, for retirement of funded debt, reserves for sinking and other funds, and other appropriations not specifically invested.

corporate tax equivalent: the rate of return needed on a par bond to produce the same after-tax yield to maturity as a given bond.

corporate trust: a trust created by a corporation, typical of which is a trust to secure a bond issue.

corporate trustee: a trust institution serving as a trustee.

corporate venturing: synonymous with *intrepreneurialism.*

corporation (Corp.)
(1) ***general:*** an organization having purposefulness, declared social benefit, derived powers, legal entity, permanence, and limited liability.
(2) ***law:*** individuals created by law as a legal entity, vested with powers and ability to contract, own, control, convey property, and discharge business within the boundaries of the powers granted. cf. *firm.*

corporation bond: see *bond, corporate.*

corporation de facto: despite a minor failure to comply with the regulations for incorporation, a legal entity that thereafter has exercised corporate powers.

corporation de jure: a corporation formed by fulfilling the requirements of the law permitting the formation of the corporation.

corporation finance: the function within a firm responsible for providing funds needed by the organization. This includes raising initial capital, working capital, emergency funds, expansion capital, and so on.

corporation securities: securities of a business corporation, as distinguished from municipal or government securities.

corporation sole: a one-man corporation, the authority, duties, and powers of which are attached to and go with the office and not the natural person who for the time being holds the office.

corporation tax: a federal or state tax levied on the profits of a corporation.

corpus: a term used in trust companies and trust accounting to describe all the property in a trust, also referred to as the "body" of the trust. A corpus may consist of real estate, stocks, bonds, and other personal property, cash in the form of bank accounts, and any items that the donor may wish to have included.

correct: changing the direction of movement in stock prices, especially following their sharp rise or decline in the previous trading sessions.

correction: any price reaction within the market leading to an adjustment by as much as one-third to two-thirds of the previous gain.

correspondency system: the origination and administration of mortgage loans for investors by independent loan correspondents.

correspondent: a securities firm, bank, or other financial organization that regularly performs services for another in a place or market to which the other does not have direct access. Securities firms may have correspondents in foreign countries or on exchanges of which they are not members. Correspondents are frequently linked by private wires. Member organizations of the New York Stock Exchange with offices in New York City may also act as correspondents for out-of-town member organizations that do not maintain New York City offices.

correspondent firm: see *correspondent.*

cost approach to value: a method of estimating the value of real porperty by deducting depreciation from the cost of replacement and adding the value of the land to the remainder. see *appraisal.*

cost basis: the original price or cost of an asset usually based on the purchase price or, in the case of assets received from an estate, on the appraised value of the assets at the death of the donor or some anniversary or other fixed date.

cost-benefit analysis (CBA): a branch of operations research that aids in evaluating the implications of alternative courses of action. This method is primarily concerned with the selection of equipment, products, and so on, before they become available.

cost effectiveness: see *cost-benefit analysis.*

cost factors: the various expenses that must be met by a supplier of consumer credit, and which therefore influence the charges he or she will make for credit services.

cost ledger: a subsidiary record wherein each project, job, production center, process, operation, product, or service is given a separate account where all items entering into its cost are posted in the required detail. Such accounts should be so arranged and kept that the results shown in them may be reconciled with and verified by a control account or in the general books.

cost of capital: the rate of return that a firm must pay to acquire investment funds.

cost of carry: out-of-pocket costs incurred while an investor maintains an investment position, among them interest on long positions in margin accounts, dividends lost on short margin positions, and incidental expenses.

cost of funds: interest (dividends) paid or accrued on savings, Federal Home Loan Bank advances, and other borrowed money during a period as a percent of average savings and borrowings.

cost records: all ledgers, supporting records, schedules, reports, invoices, vouchers, and other records and documents reflecting the cost of projects, jobs, production centers, processes, operations, products, or services, or the cost of any of the component parts thereof.

costs and expenses: costs of conducting business that are paid from revenues received by the firm.

costs theory of capitalization: where a firm's capitalization is determined by the out-of-pocket investments in fixed assets, the regular working capital needed to run the firm, advertising, and other related costs.

cosurety: one of a group of surety companies executing a bond. The obligation is joint and several, but common practice provides a stated limit of liability for each surety.

cotrustee: a person, trust organization, or bank permitted to provide trust functions, acting with another as a trustee.

Cotton Futures Act: the United States Cotton Futures Act was legislated in 1915 to standardize transactions in cotton futures. In 1936, the Commodity Exchange Act was amended to cover other commodities, including cotton.

counter: see *over the counter.*

counter-cyclical stocks: securities issued by corporations whose earnings fluctuate in the opposing direction of the general economic trend.

countermand: to cancel an order that has not yet been carried out.

counteroffer: if the one to whom an offer is extended proposes terms different from those set forth in the original offer and thus rejects the original offer, he or she is in effect making a counteroffer. An effort to accept an offer conditionally is a *counteroffer.*

countersignature
(1) the signature of a licensed agent or representative on a policy, which is necessary to validate the contract.
(2) a signature added to a document to authenticate it. cf. *attestation.*

counterspeculation: action by the government in a controlled economy designed to counteract the power of buyers or sellers to influence price (and thus speculate) by estimating the price that would prevail in the absence of restrictions by sellers or buyers and then guaranteeing that estimated price. The guaranteed price is achieved by government purchases of sales.

country risk: synonymous with *sovereign risk.*

coupon
(1) ***bonds:*** the portion of a bond that is redeemable at a given date for interest payments. cf. *talon.*
(2) ***securities:*** the interest rate on a debt security the issuer promises to pay to a holder until maturity, expressed as an annual percentage of face value.

coupon bond: see *bond, coupon.*

coupon collection: being negotiable, coupons are collectible like any other negotiable instrument. The owner of the bond from which the coupon was clipped signs a "certificate of ownership" and attaches the coupon to this certificate. It is then either cashed by the bank, or deposited by the depositor as a credit to his or her account. Coupons are collected by banks under special transit letters which require considerably more description than is required for check collections.

coupon collection teller: the person in a coupon collection department who processes coupons presented for payment.

coupon rate: synonymous with *nominal interest rate.*

coupon-strip bond: see *bond, coupon-strip.*

coupon yield: interest on a bond on an annual basis divided by its face value, stated in percentage. This is not usually equal to the current yield or yield to maturity.

courtage: a European term for brokerage fee.

courtier: French term for *broker.*

covariance: a measure of the degree to which two variables move together. A positive value means that on average, they move in the same direction.

covenant: a contract pertaining to an undertaking, a promise, or an agreement to do or forbear from doing that which has legal validity and is legally enforceable.

cover

(1) ***general:*** meeting fixed annual charges on bonds, leases, and other obligations, out of earnings.

(2) ***investments:*** purchasing back a contract sold earlier; said of an investor who has sold stock or commodities short.

(3) ***investments:*** the amount of net-asset value underlying a bond or equity stock. Considered an important criteria for a bond's safety rating.

coverage: in insurance, the ratio of assets to cover specific liabilities. see also *insurance, self-insurance.*

covered: a short position hedged by a long position in the same underlying stock or its equivalent.

covered arbitrage: arbitrage between financial instruments dominated in differing currencies, using forward cover to eliminate exchange risk.

covered call

(1) a call whose seller (writer) owns the underlying security (or a call thereon with an exercise price equal to or less than the exercise price of the call sold), or a security convertible into the underlying security.

(2) a call whose holder has sold the underlying security short.

covered call writer: a seller of a call stock option contract who holds a hedged position in the underlying stock. cf. *uncovered call writer.*

covered industries investing: investing monies in an investment vehicle that directly affects the employment environment of the industries in which the participants of the plan are employed. see *socially responsible investments.*

covered interest arbitrage: buying a country's currency spot, investing for a period, and selling the proceeds forward in order to make a net profit due to the higher interest rate in that country. This act involves "hedging" because it guarantees a covered return without risk. The opportunities to profit in this way seldom arise because covered interest differentials are normally close to zero.

covered interest parity: the gap between interest rates in foreign and domestic currencies will be matched by the forward exchange rate differential, such that the "covered" interest rate differential will be close to zero.

covered margin: the interest rate margin between two instruments denominated in differing currencies, after taking account of the cost of forward cover.

covered option (CO): an option in which the seller (or writer) owns the underlying security, as opposed to the uncovered (or naked) condition, under which the option is written against cash or other margin.

covered put

(1) a put whose seller (writer) owns a put on the same underlying security with an exercise price equal to or greater than the exercise price of the put written, or who has sold the underlying security short.

(2) a put whose holder owns the underlying security or a security convertible into the underlying security.

covered put writer: a seller of a put stock option contract holding a hedged position in the underlying stock.

covered writing: the most common, and perhaps easiest to understand, strategy is writing calls against a long position in the underlying stock. By receiving a premium, the writer intends to realize additional return on the underlying common stock in his or her portfolio or gain some element of protection (limited to the amount of the premium less transaction costs) from a decline in the value of that underlying stock. The covered writer is long the underlying stock or a convertible security such as warrants, convertible bonds, convertible preferreds, or a listed option of the same class. He or she is willing to forsake possible appreciation in his underlying issues in return for payment of the premium.

covering

(1) ***general:*** the act of meeting one's obligation.

(2) ***investments:*** buying a stock previously sold short.

(3) ***investments:*** where a firm can fix its own exchange rate at the time of the sale or purchase in the foreign exchange markets by selling or buying currencies for future delivery.

covering exchange risk: synonymous with *hedging*.

CP

(1) see *closing price*.

(2) see *closing purchase*.

(3) see *collar pricing*.

(4) see *commercial paper*.

CPA: see *certified public accountant*.

CPCU: see *Chartered Property & Casualty Underwriter*.

CPI-W futures contract: introduced in June 1985 by New York's Coffee, Sugar and Cocoa Exchange, a futures contract based on the U.S. government's monthly index of urban wages and salaries.

CPPC: cost plus a percentage of cost.

CPS

(1) see *convertible preferred stock*.

(2) see *cumulative preferred (stock)*.

crash: a sudden and disastrous drop in business activity, prices, security values, and so on, as occurred in October of 1929.

crawling peg: foreign exchange rates that permit the par value of a country's currency to change automatically by small increments, upward or downward, if in actual daily trading on the foreign exchange markets the price in terms of other monies persists on the floor or ceiling of the established range for a given period.

credit balance
(1) ***general:*** an account balance in a customer's favor. see *balance of account.*
(2) ***securities:*** money deposited and remaining in cash accounts with brokers after purchases have been paid for, plus all uninvested proceeds from stocks sold. In margin accounts, proceeds from short sales, held in escrow for the stocks borrowed for such sales and free credit balances or net balances, that can be withdrawn at will.

credit department: synonymous with *margin department.*

credit life insurance: synonymous with *mortgage life insurance.*

credit spread: the difference in value of two options, where the value of the one sold exceeds the value of the one purchased. cf. *debit spread.*

CREF: comingled real estate funds. A professionally managed, relatively liquid, diversified source of stable and profitable investment.

CROP: see *compliance registered options principal.*

crop share lease: a land rental arrangement whereby the farm operator pays to the landowner a rent in the form of a share of the crops. Usually the farm operator and the landowner share the cost of some of the production expenses.

crop year: a commodity term referring to the period from the harvest of a crop to the next year, varying with different crops.

cross: an arrangement for the sale and purchase of a listed security, usually in a large block, to be formally completed by a specialist on the exchange. see also *crossing.*

crossed market: see *crossed trades.*

crossed sales: synonymous with *crossed trades.*

crossed trades: forbidden by both the securities and commodities exchanges, a manipulative technique where a broker or several brokers offset an order to purchase with an offer to sell and fail to execute the orders on the exchange. The transaction, is therefore, not recorded and can suggest that one of the parties to the cross failed to obtain the price that would have been obtained on the exchange. synonymous with *crossed sales.*

cross hedge: hedging one instrument with a different one, such as commercial paper with Treasury bill futures or corporate bonds with Treasury bond futures.

crossing: a practice by a broker who performs the act of seller and purchaser of the same stock. When a broker has such an order, he or she is required by the exchange to put the stock up for sale at a price that is higher than his or her bid price to fulfill the minimum variation permitted in the security, prior to concluding the transaction. see also *cross.*

cross order: in the stock market, an order to a broker to buy and sell the same security. If the buy order and sell order are from two different persons, the broker must execute them through the exchange, and may not directly pair them. If the orders are from the same person or collusive where by two persons, it is a wash sale. see *wash sale*.

cross purchase: where a broker, without recourse to the market, fulfills an order to buy and an order to sell the same stock. The practice is forbidden by the New York Stock Exchange.

cross-shareholding: the practice where two or more firms hold shares of stock in the other, especially as a means of controlling a market or industry.

crowd

(1) ***general:*** the aggregate of key persons involved in any activity; those who control the day-to-day decisions of the firm.

(2) ***investments:*** brokers who transact business in securities on the trading floor of an exchange.

crown jewels: slang, preferred entities within a diversified corporation as determined by asset value, earning power, and projected business activity.

crown loan: a demand loan to a lender's parents or children.

Crude Oil Windfall Profit Tax Act of 1980: see *windfall profits tax*.

crunch: an economic squeeze; a crisis created by some financial pressure.

crush margin: the gross profit that a processor makes from selling oil and meal, minus the cost of buying the soybeans.

crush spread: a futures spreading position in which a trader attempts to profit from what he or she believes to be discrepancies in the price relationship between soybeans and its two derivative products.

CS

(1) see *capital stock*.
(2) see *closing sale*.
(3) see *common stock*.

CSE: see *Cincinnati Stock Exchange*.

CSVLI: the cash surrender value of life insurance.

CT: see *cash trade*.

CTA: commodities trading adviser.

CTB: see *bond, collateral trust*.

Ctfs.: see *certificate*.

Cum.: see *cumulative*.

cum coupon: an international bond market term for dealings in a bond where the purchaser acquires the right to receive the next due interest payment. cf. *cum-dividend, ex-coupon*.

cum dividend (CD): as distinguished from the *ex-dividend*, the dividend included. The purchaser of a stock cum dividend has the right to receive the declared dividend.

cum right: the stockholder's right to acquire shares of a new issue of stock in a company in direct proportion to existing holdings. see also *rights*.

cumulative (Cum.): an arrangement whereby a dividend or interest which, if not paid when due or received when due, is added to that which is to be paid in the future.

cumulative dividend: a dividend on cumulative preferred stock payable, under the terms of issue, at intervals and before any distribution is made to holders of common stock.

cumulative preferred (stock) (CPS): a stock whose holders are entitled, if one or more dividends are omitted, to be paid on the omitted dividends before dividends are paid on the company's common stock.

cumulative rate of return: a compounded rate of return covering more than one year.

cumulative voting: each share of stock may cast as many votes for one director of the firm as there are directors who seek elected office. cf. *statutory voting.*

CUNA: Credit Union National Association.

Curb broker: an old name for a member of the Curb Exchange. see *Curb Exchange.*

Curb Exchange: the name used before 1953 for the American Stock Exchange in New York City. See *American Stock Exchange.*

currency bond: see *bond, currency.*

currency devaluation: any action by a government or by the marketplace to reduce the value of a currency in relation to the currencies of other nations.

currency exchange (swap): a long-term exchange of currency between two firms in different nations.

currency futures: contracts in the futures markets set for delivery in a major currency. Firms selling products throughout the world can hedge their currency risk with these futures.

current: in budgeting and accounting, designates the operations of the present fiscal period as opposed to past or future periods.

current account (CA): a running account between two companies, reflecting the movement of cash, merchandise, and so on.

current and accrued assets: generally consists of items realizable or to be consumed within one year from the date of the balance sheet. Includes cash, working funds, and certain deposits, temporary cash investments, receivables, materials and supplies including fuel, and prepayments.

current and accrued liabilities: generally consists of obligations incurred, accrued, or declared, including short-term borrowing, all of which are either due and payable, payable on demand or, in any event, contemplated to be paid within one year.

current and collectable: money that flows or passes from hand to hand as a medium of exchange.

current (floating) assets (CA): the assets of a company that are reasonably expected to be realized in cash, or sold, or consumed during the normal operating cycle of the business.

current assets to current debt: obtained by dividing the total of current assets by total current debt. Current assets are the sum of cash, notes, and accounts receivable (less reserves for bad debts), advances on merchandise, merchandise inventories, and listed federal, state, and municipal securities not in excess of market value. Current debt is the total of all liabilities falling due within one year.

current budget
(1) the budget prepared for the succeeding fiscal year, or in the case of some state governments, the budget prepared for the succeeding biennium.
(2) the budget in force during the current fiscal year or biennium.

current capital: circulating capital or gross working capital.

current cost: what it would cost today to replace an asset or to require equivalent productive capacity.

current coupon bond: see *bond, current coupon.*

current debt: the sum of all liabilities due within the year from the statement date, including current payment on mortgages, funded debts, and serial notes. Liability reserves are included, but reserves for depreciation are excluded.

current debt to inventory: dividing the current debt by inventory; yields yet another indication of the extent to which a business relies on funds from the disposal of unsold inventories to meet its debts.

current debt to tangible net worth: obtained by dividing current debt by tangible net worth. Ordinarily, a business is in trouble when the relationship between current debt and tangible net worth exceeds 80 percent.

current delivery: delivery during the present period, such as this month for commodities.

current income: wages, salary, profit, or other income of the immediate period of time, this month, this year.

current liabilities (CL): money owed and payable by a company, usually within one year.

current market value (CMV): the value of stocks in an account determined by the closing price of the previous trading day.

current maturity: the interval between the present time and the maturity date of a bond issue.

current operation expenditures: expenditures for salaries and wages, supplies, material, and contractual services, other than capital outlays.

current prices: security prices prevailing in the market as a specified time period.

current production rate: the top interest rate permitted on current GNMA mortgage-backed securities, traditionally half a percentage point below the current mortgage rate to cover administrative expenses of the mortgage servicing organization.

current ratio: the relationship between total current assets and total current liabilities. It is calculated by dividing current assets by current liabilities.

current resources: resources to which recourse can be had to meet current obligations and expenditures. Examples are current assets, estimated revenues of a particular period not yet realized, transfers from other funds authorized but not received, and, in case of certain funds, bonds authorized and unissued.

current return: the present income from any investment.

current value accounting: an accounting approach that requires the measurement of individual assets (e.g., factories, machines, and supplies) in current prices rather than in terms of the actual dollar costs at which they were acquired in earlier years.

current yield (CY): an expression as a portion of the annual income to the investment; for example, if annual income is $10 and investment is $100, the current yield is 10 percent. see also *yield.*

cushion

(1) the interval between the time a bond is issued and the time it can be called. see also *call protection.*

(2) the margin of safety for a firm's financial ratios.

(3) see also *LIFO.*

cushion bond: see *bond, cushion.*

cushion theory: a concept that a stock's price must rise if many investors are taking short positions in it, because those positions need to be covered by purchases of the security. synonymous with *short interest concept.*

CUSIP: the American Bankers Association's Committee on Uniform Securities Identification Procedures that established alphabetical and numerical descriptions of securities traded on the exchanges and in over the counter markets. see also *CUSIP number.*

CUSIP number: a number assigned to every common stock, preferred stock, corporate and municipal bond for security identification needs. see *CUSIP.*

custodial arrangement: the simple warehousing of securities by a bank for purposes of safekeeping. The bank may collect income and do simple reporting on the value of the assets. The bank does not have fiduciary responsibility.

custodian: a person responsible for the activities in the brokerage account of another individual (e.g., a custodian of a minor's account).

custody: the banking service that provides safekeeping for a customer's property under written agreement, and additionally calls for the bank to collect and pay out income, and to buy, sell, receive, and deliver securities when ordered by the principal to do so.

customer agreement: see *margin agreement.*

customer ownership: the legal ownership of securities by customers of a corporation.

customer's agreement and consent: the form required by a member firm of the New York Stock Exchange of any client holding a margin account. The client's signature indicates agreement to follow the rules of the exchange, the SEC, and the Federal Reserve Board.

customer's broker(man): synonymous with *registered representative (trader).*

customer's free credit balance: the funds in a client's brokerage account, other than from a short sale, which is at the dispersal of the client.

customer's ledger: a ledger that shows accounts receivable of each customer.

customer's loan consent: an agreement signed by a margin customer authorizing a broker to borrow margined stocks to the limit of the customer's debit balance so as to cover the other customers' short positions and certain failures to complete delivery.

customers' man: synonymous with *registered representative (trader).*

customers' net debit balances: credit of New York Stock Exchange member firms made available to help finance customers' purchases of stocks, bonds, and commodities.

customer's representative: employees of security firms who are regularly employed in the solicitation of business or the handling of customers' accounts, or who advise customers about the purchase or sale of securities.

customer's room: the area within a broker's office available for customers. The space usually contains a quotation board, a ticker, and other information available from investment services.

cutoff point: in capital budgeting, the minimum rate of return acceptable on all investments.

cutting a loss
(1) ***general:*** ceasing development, production, or sales of a failing item.
(2) ***investments:*** terminating an unprofitable market position and accepting the loss involved before it grows larger.

cutting a melon: slang, making an extra distribution of money or stock to shareholders, usually when preceded by an unusually profitable transaction (e.g., the sale of a subsidiary).

Cv.: see *convertible.*

CVC: see *convertible security* (in bond and stock listing of newspapers).

Cvt.: see *convertible.*

CWM: convertible wraparound mortgage, a mortgage making it possible for builders to offer below-market, fixed-rate, fully amortized loans to home buyers during periods of high interest rates without requiring forfeiture of the builder's profit through interest rate buy-downs or subsidies.

CWO: cash with order.

CY: see *current yield.*

cycle
(1) one completed interval of up and down economic or market movements. Cycles tend to vary in both length and volatility.
(2) the months in which stock option contracts expire. see *expiration cycle.*

cyclical stocks: securities that go up and down in value with the trend of business, rising faster in periods of rapidly improving business conditions and sliding very noticeably when business conditions deteriorate.

cyclical theory: see *cyclical stocks.*

D

D
(1) see *delivery.*
(2) see *discount.*
(3) in stock tables, designates a price that is the low for the past year.

DA
(1) see *depletion allowance.*
(2) see *discretionary account.*
(3) see *dollar (cost) averaging.*

Daily Bond Buyer: see *official notice of sale.*

daily high: the highest price attained by a stock or market average during a particular trading day. This not not necessarily the opening or closing price.

daily interest account: a savings account that pays interest daily from the date of deposit to the date of withdrawal.

daily low: the lowest price attained by a stock or market average during a particular trading day. This is not necessarily the opening or closing price.

daily trading limit: the maximum that most commodities and options markets are permitted to rise or decline in one trading session.

daisy chain (DC): the practice or process of engaging in a series of manipulative dealings or transactions designed to create the appearance of an active trading, as with a particular security.

dancing, take to: to make abrupt, big swings in prices.

D&B: see *Dun & Bradstreet.*

Data Universal Numbering System: see *Dun's number.*

dated date: a date given by underwriters as the effective date of a new issue. Usually the dated date is the same as the issue date.

dated earned surplus: retained earnings of a corporation accumulated from the date of a reorganization. On a balance sheet the reorganization date is included when reporting retained earnings.

date of maturity: the date on which a debt must be paid. Usually applied to those debts evidenced by a written agreement, such as a note, bond, and so on.

date of payment of dividends: the date when declared dividends are to be paid.

date of the note: the date of issue.

date of trade: the day when an order to buy or sell is executed.

dawn raids: British, where a firm buys a large block of another firm's stock in a hurry, at a premium price. The name comes from the fact that the bids are usually made just as the stock exchange opens.

daylight trading: making a purchase followed by a sale of a security on the same day, to avoid a holding position in the shares traded overnight or longer.

day loan: a one-day loan, granted for the purchase of stock, for the broker's convenience. Upon delivery, securities are pledged as collateral to secure a regular call loan.

day order: an order to buy or sell that, if not executed, expires at the end of the trading day on which it was entered.

day trading: in anticipation of a rapid price change, the purchasing of a stock and selling it again, or selling it short, on the same day.

DC

(1) see *daisy chain.*

(2) deep discount issue (in bond listings of newspapers). see *bond, deep discount.*

DCF: see *discounted cash flow.*

DCFM: discounted cash flow method.

DD

(1) see *declaration date.*

(2) see *deferred delivery.*

(3) see *delayed delivery.*

(4) see *due date.*

DDB: double-declining-balance depreciation method. The IRS-approved means for determining accelerated depreciation, permitting twice the rate of annual depreciation as the straight-line method.

dead market

(1) ***general:*** a dull selling day, marked by low volume, lack of consumer interest, or other factors creating poor sales.

(2) ***investments:*** a market marked by minor price changes and low volume.

dealer: an individual or firm in the securities business acting as a principal rather than as an agent. Typically, a dealer buys for his or her own account and sells to a customer from the dealer's inventory. The dealer's profit or loss is the difference between the price he pays and the price he receives for the same security. The dealer's confirmation must disclose to the customer that he has acted as principal. The same individual or firm may function, at different times, as broker and dealer.

dealer activities: a bank operating as a securities dealer by underwriting, trading, or selling securities.

dealer bank
(1) a commercial bank that makes a market in government and agency securities.
(2) a department within the bank that is registered as a municipal securities dealer.

dealer market: a market for government securities trading, located primarily in New York City.

"death sentence": a clause in the Public Utility Holding Company Act of 1935 requiring that all such companies register with the Securities and Exchange Commission and that no more than three levels of corporations are permitted (a parent company, its subsidiary, and a subsubsidiary). All holding companies exceeding these three levels must be dissolved (the death sentence).

death stock: securities of corporations facing forced or voluntary liquidations.

debase: to reduce the quality, purity, or content, or otherwise alter the accepted intrinsic value of the coinage of a realm.

debenture
(1) used to describe indebtedness, usually in long-term obligations, which is unsecured.
(2) a corporate obligation that is sold as an investment.
(3) a voucher or certificate acknowledging that a debt is owed by the signor.

debenture bond: see *bond, debenture.*

debenture stock (DS): stock issued under a contract to pay a specified return at specified intervals. In this sense, it may be considered a special type of preferred stock. It is to be distinguished from a debenture, which represents a bond in form as compared with a share of stock.

debit
(1) ***general:*** any amount in dollars and cents that, when posted, will increase the balance of an asset or expense account and decrease the balance of a liability account. All asset and expense accounts normally have debit balances, and all liability, capital, and income accounts normally have credit balances.
(2) ***insurance:*** a weekly premium life insurance agent's list of all the premiums he or she is required to collect.
(3) ***investments:*** that portion of the purchase price of stock, bonds, or commodities covered by credit extended by a broker to margin customers.

debit balance: in a customer's margin account, that portion of purchase price of stock, bonds, or commodities covered by credit extended by the broker to the margin customer. see *balance of account.*

debit spread: a spread option position for which the long option price is greater than the short option price, thereby establishing a debit in the brokerage account. cf. *credit spread.*

debt discount: the difference between the proceeds of a loan and the face value of the note or bond, where the former is smaller.

debtee: a creditor.

debt/equity ratio: calculated by dividing long-term debt by shareholder's equity, this ratio is useful in measuring the risk associated with the capital structure of a corporation.

debt-equity swap: a transaction in which a company trades newly issued stock, or equity, for outstanding deep-discount bonds or debt.

debt financing: the long-term borrowing of money by a business, usually in exchange for debt securities or a note, for the purpose of obtaining working capital or other funds necessary to operational needs or for the purpose of retiring current or other indebtedness.

debt instrument: a written promise to repay a debt; includes bills, notes, and bonds.

debt limit: a maximum amount of money that a state or local government can borrow; usually set by legislation of the state involved.

debt monetizing: the procedure whereby the Federal Reserve issues new fiat money to pay for government debt obligations. This new money in effect replaces the debt.

debt ratio: total debt divided by total assets.

debt retirement: the slow reduction of a firm's debt through either a sinking fund or serial bonds. Debt reduction purports to improve the quality and the market price of a bond issue.

debt securities: fixed obligations that evidence a debt, usually repayable on a specified future date or dates and which carry a specific rate or rates of interest payable periodically. They may be non-interest bearing also.

debt service: interest payments and capital reduction on government, industrial, or other long-term bonds. see *debt service fund.*

debt service fund: a fund established to finance an account for the payment of interest and principal on all general obligation debt, serial and term, other than that payable exclusively from special assessments and revenue debt.

debt service requirement: the amount of money required to pay the interest on outstanding debt, serial maturities of principal for serial bonds, and required contributions to a debt service fund for term bonds.

debt to equity ratio

(1) total liabilities divided by total stockholder's equity; indicates to what extent owner's equity will cushion creditors' claims in the event of liquidation.

(2) the total long-term debt divided by stockholders' equity; a measure of leverage.

(3) the long-term debt and preferred stock divided by common stock equity; compares stocks with fixed charges to those without fixed charges.

decapitalize: withdrawing the financial capital from a firm.

declaration date (DD): the date on which payment of a dividend is authorized by a corporation's board of directors.

declaration of dividend: see *declare.*

declare: to authorize payment of a dividend on a given date, as declared by a firm's board of directors. Once declared, a dividend becomes an obligation of the issuing company.

decline: a downward slump, trend. A lowering of the price for a commodity or a security.

declining wedge: see *wedge.*

decreasing term insurance: often used to cover the outstanding balance of a home mortgage, has a fixed annual cost. Initially, it offers large coverage for a small premium, but since its benefits decline over time, it should not be used as a primary insurance policy.

dedicated bond portfolio: a portfolio designed to meet a specific set of future benefit payments with the most cash flow from the bonds held in a portfolio. The most common application of the dedicated portfolio concept is in funding benefits due to retired employees.

deep discount bond: see *bond, deep discount.*

deep in/out of the money: a call option where the exercise price is significantly lower than the market price of the underlying security or well above the market price. For a put option, the situation is opposite.

de facto corporation: following an effort, in good faith, to form a corporation under a value statute and there is a failure in some particular, the firm is said to be de facto (in fact) when there has been an exercise of corporate power. Only the state, not a third party, can challenge the firm's existence as a de facto corporation.

defaulted paper: any obligation whose principal or interest is in default. Such obligation, security, or investment should be distinguished on all financial statements where they normally appear by showing those in default separately from those not in default.

defeasance

(1) ***general:*** a clause that provides that performance of certain specified acts will render an instrument of contract void.

(2) ***investments:*** short for *in-substance defeasance*, a method whereby a firm discharges old, low-rate debt without repaying it prior to maturity. A firm uses newly bought securities with a lower face value by paying higher interest or having a higher market value.

defensive industry: an industry nót seriously affected by poor conditions within the economy as other industries. Stocks of such businesses often perform better than the market throughout economic declines because they are able to sustain relatively sound earnings (e.g., the utilities industry).

defensive investment: an investment policy that places its major effort on reducing both the risk of (eventual) loss and the need for special knowledge, skill, and continuous attention. cf. *speculation.*

defensive portfolio: the aggregate of investments unlikely to fluctuate greatly in value either up or down (i.e., preferred stocks, high-grade bonds).

defensive stocks: stocks that shift little in price movements and are rarely of interest to speculators. Held by long-term investors seeking stability, these stocks frequently withstand selling pressure in a falling market. synonymous with *protective stocks.*

defer: to delay payment to a future time.

deferral: a tax shelter device that accelerates deductions and postpones taxable income.

deferral of taxes: the postponement of tax payments from the present year to a future year.

deferred account: an account that postpones taxes until a later date.

deferred annuity: an annuity contract that provides for the postponement or start of an annuity until after a specified period or until the annuitant attains a specified age.

deferred asset: an asset that is not readily convertible into cash, subject to current settlement.

deferred bond: see *bond, extended.*

deferred charges: expenditures that are written off over a time period.

deferred compensation: the postponement of distribution of a portion of current earnings until a later date, usually at retirement. The object of deferred compensation is to reduce current income taxes by postponing receipt of taxable income until a time when the receiver will likely be in a lower income tax bracket.

deferred delivery (DD): the purchase of a cash commodity for delivery at some specified future date. synonymous with *forward delivery.*

deferred dividend: a stock dividend (preferred or common) that will not be paid until some action occurs.

deferred group annuity contract: an investment technique for insured pension plans where the funding of benefits is provided through the purchase of single premium deferred annuities for each plan participant in an amount equal to the benefit accrued for the participant each year.

deferred interest bond: see *bond, deferred interest.*

deferred payment annuity: see *deferred annuity.*

deferred serial bond: see *bond, deferred serial.*

deferred special assessments: special assessments that have been levied but are not yet due.

deferred stock: stocks whose dividends are not to be paid until the expiration of a stated date, or until a specified event has taken place.

deferred tax: a tax liability accrued on income that is reported but not subject to income tax until a later time period.

deficiency letter: an SEC written notice to a prospective issuer of stocks that the preliminary prospectus should be revised or expanded upon. Such letters require immediate action; otherwise the registration period can be prolonged.

deficit
(1) the excess of liabilities over assets; the excess of obligations and expenditures affecting a given budget period which is in excess of the budget established for the period.
(2) indicating obligations or expenditures for items that are in excess of the amount allotted for those items in a financial budget.

deficit financing: exists when government expenditures exceed revenues and the difference is made up by borrowing. The objective is to expand business activity and yield an improvement in general economic conditions. The deficit is covered by release of government bonds.

deficit net worth: the excess of liabilities over assets and capital stock, often resulting from an operating loss. synonymous with *negative net worth.*

defined benefit pension plan: an Internal Revenue Service ruling making possible tax-deductible pension plan contributions as high as 100% of salary for professionals and business managers.

defined contribution plan: a pension plan that provides for an individual account for each participant and for benefits based on the amount contributed to the participant's account, including any income, expenses, gains, or losses.

definitive: denoting a permanent stock certificate or bond issued to replace an existing document resulting from a change in the corporation involved, particularly a change impacting on the firm's financial structure.

definitive bond: see *bond, definitive.*

definitive certificate: see *definitive.*

deflator: synonymous with *constant dollars.*

deflection of tax liability: the legal shift of an individual's tax burden to another person, as with a Clifford Trust.

degree of combined leverage: a measure of the company's earnings-per-share variability created by the combined effects of operating leverage and financial leverage.

degree of financial leverage: a measure of the company's earnings-per-share variability created by fixed financing costs.

degree of operating leverage: a measure of the variability of the company's earnings before interest and taxes that is caused by fixed operating costs.

delayed delivery (DD): securities that were sold with the knowledge that delivery would not occur on the regular clearance date. see *clearing.*

delayed items: items representing transactions that occurred before the current accounting year.

delayed opening (Op. D.): the situation created when buy and sell orders accumulate prior to the opening of a stock exchange.

del credere agency: when an agency, factor, or broker attempts to guarantee to his or her principal the payment of a buyer's debt, the agent (etc.) is functioning under a *del credere agency.*

delist: activity resulting in the removal or cancellation of rights, by the SEC, previously given to a listed security. This situation occurs usually when a security fails to meet some of the requirements for the listing privilege.

delivery (D)

(1) ***general:*** the transfer of the possession of an item from one person to another.

(2) ***investments:*** the transmission of the certificate representing shares bought on a securities exchange; delivery is usually made to the purchaser's broker on the fourth business day after the transaction. see *good delivery, settlement day.* see also *seller's seven sale.*

delivery against cost: synonymous with *cash on delivery.*

delivery date

(1) formally, the first day of the month during which delivery is to be made under a futures contract. Since sales are made at the seller's option, however, the seller can make delivery on any day of the month, following proper notification to the buyer.

(2) the fifth business day following a regular way transaction on the NYSE. Seller's option delivery can be anywhere from 5 to 60 days, though there may be a purchase-price adjustment compensating for delayed delivery.

delivery month: a futures contract must stipulate one of the calendar months as the month of delivery.

delivery notice: the notification of delivery of the actual commodity on the contract, issued by the seller of the futures to the buyer. The rules of the various exchanges require that tender notices be issued on certain days, and in some cases, at certain hours.

delivery points: those locations designated by futures exchanges at which the commodity covered by a futures contract may be delivered in fulfillment of the contract.

delivery price: the price fixed by the clearinghouse at which deliveries on futures are invoiced and also the price at which the futures contract is settled when deliveries are made.

delivery versus payment: synonymous with *cash on delivery.*

delta: the measure of the relationship between an option price and the underlying futures contract or stock price.

demand-and-supply curves: the graphic representation of the maximum purchasing and minimum selling prices given and accepted to traders in a particular commodity at a specific time and place, and the resulting market price.

demand mortgage: a mortgage that may be called for payment on demand.

demand note: a note or mortgage that can be demanded at any time for payment by the holder. see also *scrip*.

demand price: the maximum price a purchaser is willing to pay for a stated quantity of a commodity or service.

demographic trends: a technique used for projecting population trends and their impact on particular industries and economic needs.

demonetarize: see *demonization*.

demonization (demonetization)
(1) the reduction in the number of government bonds and securities by a commercial bank, resulting in an increase in the value of deposit and paper currency, including federal reserve notes.
(2) the withdrawal of specified currency from circulation.

demonstration: the unexpected activity or sudden climb in value for any specific or group of stocks.

denomination value: the face value of all currencies, coins, and securities.

depleted: when all economically recoverable oil and gas have been recovered from a well or reservoir.

depletion
(1) an amount charged to current operating expenses over a period of time in order to write off the asset value of a wasting asset, such as a mine or an oil well. It is a noncash expense.
(2) the consumption or exhaustion of wasting property, such as royalties, patent rights, mines, oil and gas wells, quarries, timberlands, and other things that are consumed or worn out in the using.

depletion accounting: natural resources, such as metals, oils, and gas, which conceivably can be reduced to zero over the years, present a special problem in capital management. Depletion is an accounting practice consisting of charges against earnings based on the amount of the asset taken out of the total reserves in the period for which accounting is made. A bookkeeping entry, depletion does not represent any cash outlay, nor are any funds earmarked for the purpose.

depletion allowance (DA): as permitted by the Internal Revenue Code, a deduction from taxable income derived from a wasting asset. The basis of the allowance is either a percentage of the gross income from specified property or a per-unit-of-product condition.

deployment: the act of committing fund money among alternative asset categories.

deposit administration contract: a funding contract with an insurance company in which an unallocated account is kept for active participants. Annuities are purchased for employees when they retire.

depositary: an individual or institution identified as one to be entrusted with something of value for safekeeping (e.g., a bank or trust company).

depositary receipt: mechanism to allow for the trading of foreign stocks on U.S. stock exchanges when the overseas nation involved will not allow foreign ownership of the stock of domestic firms. The shares are therefore deposited with a bank in the country of corporation and an affiliated or correspondent bank in the United States issues depositary receipts for the securities. U.S. investors buy these receipts and can trade them on an appropriate American stock exchange in the same way as other stocks. The major purpose of the instrument is to officially identify ownership of the stock in the foreign country.

depositary trust company: a central securities certificate depositary in New York City through which clearing members of the Stock Clearing Corporation effect security deliveries between each other by computerized entries, thus minimizing the physical movement of certificates.

depository: a bank in which funds or securities are deposited by others, usually under the terms of a specific depository agreement. Also, a bank in which government funds are deposited or in which other banks are permitted by law to maintain required reserves.

depository agreement: see *mortgage certificate.*

Depository Trust Company (DTC): a central securities certificate depository through which members effect security deliveries between each other via computerized bookkeeping entries, thereby reducing the physical movement of stock certificates.

depreciate

(1) in accounting, the process of reducing the book value of a fixed asset at periodic intervals to charge a portion of the assets' cost as an expense of the period in which it provides a service.

(2) to decrease in service capacity or usefullness.

depreciated cost: cost less accumulated depreciation and less other valuation accounts, having the effect of reducing the original outlay to a recoverable cost; the book value of a fixed asset.

depreciated currency: resulting from the lowering in the exchange value of currency, funds not accepted at face or par value.

depreciation

(1) ***general:*** normally, charges against earnings to write off the cost, less salvage value, of an asset over its estimated useful life. It is a bookkeeping entry and does not represent any cash outlay, nor are any funds earmarked for the purpose. see also *book depreciation.*

(2) ***general:*** a decline in the value of property.

(3) ***foreign exchange:*** the decline in the price of one currency relative to another.

depreciation fund: funds or securities set aside for replacing depreciating fixed assets.

depreciation method: the arithmetic procedure followed for reducing the book value of an asset over the years of its useful life.

depressed price: the market price for a stock that is lower than justified considering the basic conditions of the firm.

depression: an economic condition: business activity is down over a long period, prices drop, purchasing power is greatly reduced, and unemployment is high.

Depression of the 1930s: the Great Depression, a severe economic crisis that afflicted the United States and also affected worldwide business, is thought to have begun with the collapse of the stock market in October 1929 and finally ended in the early 1940s, when defense spending for World War II strengthened the general economy.

depth
(1) the capability of the market to absorb either a large sell or buy order free of any significant price change in a security.
(2) the degree of general customer interest in the market.

derivate markets: synonymous with *shadow markets*.

derivative suit: in corporation law, a suit by a stockholder on behalf of the corporation, in which the stockholder alleges that the officers of the corporation have failed to act to protect the interests of the corporation and therefore the particular stockholder is suing on behalf of the corporation.

descending tops: a chart pattern wherein every new high price for a stock is lower than the preceding high; a bearish trend.

designated concession: an order given to a syndicate.

designated net: any order received by a municipal security syndicate from a nonmember of the Municipal Securities Rulemaking Board.

Designated Order Turnaround (DOT): the NYSE electronic system for handling orders, permitting member firms to place day market and limit orders. Using DOT, a specialist receives the order, presents it to the trading crowd for execution, and a confirmation of the execution is sent back to the firm placing the order. cf. *post-execution reporting*.

desk, the: the trading desk at the New York Federal Reserve Bank, through which open market purchases and sales of government securities are made. The desk maintains direct telephone communication with major government securities dealers. A "foreign desk" at the New York Reserve Bank conducts transactions in the foreign exchange market. see also *foreign exchange desk*.

destination clauses: marketing contracts to permit an oil monopoly to stipulate which countries should receive oil, preventing the oil from being diverted to the spot market. see *spot market*.

detailed audit: an audit in which an examination is made of the system of internal control and of the details of all transactions and books of account, including subsidiary records and supporting documents, as to legality, mathematical accuracy, complete accountability, and application of accepted accounting principles for governmental units.

determination date: the latest day of the month on which savings may be deposited and still earn interest from the first day of the month; set by an association's board of directors, but usually the tenth day.

detinue: a common law action to recover property.

Detroit Stock Exchange: established in Michigan in 1907, the majority of its transactions are in unlisted securities.

development drilling program: searching for oil and gas in an area with proven reserves to a depth known to have been productive in the past.

diagonal spread: an option technique requiring the simultaneous sale of options of the same class on the same underlying stock but with different striking prices and different expiration dates.

diamond investment trust: a unit trust that invests in high-quality diamonds.

diary: a record kept of maturity dates for notes, bonds, and other instruments. see *tickler.*

differential duty: a difference in the duty on the same commodity based on the origin of the commodity or some similar face. synonymous with *preferential duty.*

differentials: the premiums paid for the grades higher than the standard growth (basic grades) and the discounts allowed for the grades lower than the basic grades. These differentials are fixed by the contract terms.

digested securities: securities owned by investors who are not expected to sell them soon. cf. *stag.*

digits deleted: on a stock exchange tape, indicating that since the tape has been delayed, some of the digits have been dropped. For example, 35 . . . 36 becomes 5 . . . 6.

dilute: reducing the earnings per share of a security, as by the potential exchange of stock.

dilution: the effect of a drop in earnings per share or book value per share, caused by the potential conversion of securities or by the potential exercise of warrants or options.

dilutionary: causing stock dilution.

dilutive: reducing or conducive to a reduction of earnings per share of a security, as by the potential exchange of stock.

dip: referring to prices, a mild setback or reaction.

directed trust: a trust in which the trustee has less than full managerial authority. This will be the case whenever somebody else, who is not a trustee, has the power to control particular actions of the trustee.

direct financing: raising capital without resorting to underwriting (e.g., by selling capital stock.)

direct investment: an equity investment in real estate, service corporations, and securities.

direct obligation: a drawer's obligation as the instrument maker, as contrasted with the indirect obligation of an endorser of the instrument.

director: a person elected by shareholders to establish company policies. The directors appoint the president, vice-presidents, and all other operating officers. Directors decide, among many other matters, if and when dividends are to be paid.

directorate: a corporation's board of directors.

direct participation program: a program permitting investors to participate directly in the cash flow and tax benefits of the underlying investments.

direct placement: the negotiation by a borrower, such as an industrial or utility company, directly with the lender, such as a life insurance company or group of companies, for an entire issue of securities. No underwriter is involved and that transaction is exempt from SEC filing.

direct reduction mortgage (DRM): a direct reduction mortgage is liquidated over the life of the mortgage in equal monthly payments. Each monthly payment consists of an amount to cover interest, reduction in principal, taxes, and insurance. The interest is computed on an outstanding principal balance monthly. As the principal balance is reduced, the amount of interest becomes less, thereby providing a larger portion of the monthly payment to be applied to the reduction of principal. As taxes and insurance are paid by the mortgagee (lending association), these disbursements are added to the principal balance. This procedure follows throughout the life of the mortgage.

dirty: in Great Britain, a stock which is cum-divided and close to the date for payment of interest.

Dis.: see *discount.*

disbursing agent: an institution or individual that handles payment of dividends or interest to stockholders.

discharge of bankruptcy: an order that terminates bankruptcy proceedings, usually relieving the debtor of all legal responsibility for certain specified obligations.

disclosure: all publicly owned corporations are required by the SEC to immediately inform the public of all information, positive or negative, that may influence any investment decision. see *full disclosure, insider.*

discontinuous market: as differentiated from continuously listed securities, the unlisted stocks and bonds forming a separate market.

discount

(1) ***general:*** the amount of money deducted from the face value of a note.

(2) ***foreign exchange:*** the relationship of one currency to another. For example, Canadian currency may be at a discount to U.S. currency.

(3) ***investments:*** the amount by which a preferred stock or bond sells below its par value.

(4) ***investments:*** "to take into account," as "the price of the stock has discounted the expected dividend cut."

discount bond: see *bond, discount.*

discount broker: a broker who buys and sells stock. Since such brokers do not usually provide customers with other services, notably research, they tend to have lower fees than those of major brokerage firms.

discount brokerage house: a securities broker firm offering considerably lower commission rates on stock transactions than full-service brokerage houses. In 1975, the SEC ruled that fixed pricing for stock transactions would be eliminated, giving rise to the discount brokerage industry.

discount dividend reinvestment plan: see *dividend reinvestment plan.*

discounted cash flow (DCF): an investment technique that takes into account that a dollar of cash received today is worth more than a dollar received a year from now, because today's dollar can be invested to earn a return during the intervening time.

discounted value: the present value of future payments due to receivable, computed on the basis of a given rate of interest.

discount from asset value: the percentage expression of the price of a share divided by its asset value.

discount house: see *discount brokerage house.*

discounting: occurs when an institution lends money to a business with a customer's debt obligation to the firm as security on the loan.

discounting the news: when a stock's price or the level of a major market indicator climbs or falls in expectation of a good or bad occurrence, then barely moves when the actual development takes place and is announced, the stock is said to have "discounted the news."

discount on securities: the amount or percentage by which a security (a bond or a share of stock) is bought or sold for less than its face or par value; opposed to premium on securities. cf. *premium on securities.*

discount window: a loan facility provided by the Federal Reserve Bank where member banks borrow against the collateral value of eligible securities.

discount yield: the yield on a stock sold at a discount.

discretionary account (DA): an account in which the customer gives the broker or someone else the authority, which may be complete or within specific limits, as to the purchase and sales of securities or commodities, including selection, timing, amount, and price to be paid or received. see *discretionary order.*

discretionary order: the customer specifies the stock or the commodity to be bought or sold, and the amount. His or her agent is free to act as to time and price. see *discretionary account.*

discretionary pool: a group of people authorized by others to act on their behalf in buying or selling securities or commodities.

discretionary trust
(1) a trust that entitles the beneficiary to use only so much of the income or principal as the trustee in its uncontrolled discretion shall see fit to give him or her to apply for his or her use.
(2) an investment company that is not limited in its policy to any one class, or type, of stock or security but may invest in any or all of a broad range of securities.

dishonored: any negotiable instrument offered for acceptance of payment that is turned down or cannot be obtained. see *notice of dishonor.*

disintermediation: when an investor, who has left funds on deposit with a portfolio intermediary, removes these monies, and makes a direct investment in other securities. Occurs when rates on direct security investments are significantly higher than the rates paid by portfolio intermediaries.

disinvestment: the result of failure to invest funds into a community, leading to a decline of cities and the disappearance of industries.

dissolution (corporate): termination at the expiration of a corporation's charter, by order of the attorney general of the state, by consolidation, or by action of the stockholders.

dissolution (partnership): termination by the wishes of the partners at a specified time, or by operation of law because of incapacity, death, or bankruptcy of any partner.

Dist.
(1) see *discount.*
(2) see *exchange distribution.*

distant: the designating or specifying the month of delivery which is in some far-off future.

distress selling: selling because of necessity; what happens when securities owned on margin are sold because lowered prices have hurt equities.

distributing syndicate: synonymous with *underwriting group.*

distribution
(1) ***general:*** dividing up of something among several people or entities; the process of allocating income and expenses to the appropriate subsidiary accounts.
(2) ***general:*** a division of aggregate income of a community among its members.
(3) ***investments:*** selling, over a time period, of a large block of stock without unduly depressing the market price. cf. *secondary distribution.*
(4) ***mutual funds:*** the payout of realized capital gains on stocks in the portfolio of a fund.
(5) ***closed-end investment firm:*** the payout of realized capital gains on stock in the portfolio of a closed-end investment firm.

distribution area: the price range where a security trades for a long time.

distribution date: the date when a dividend or other payment or distribution is made to holders of an instrument. synonymous with *payment date.*

distribution of risk: the spreading of investments over a number of stocks.

distribution security: the security part of a block sold over a length of time to avoid upsetting a market price.

distributor: synonymous with *wholesaler.*

District Business Conduct Committee: synonymous with *Business Conduct Committee.*

Div.: see *dividend.*

Divd.: see *dividend.*

divergence
(1) a time when prevailing trends of a market average or a stock is not in line with technical indicators.
(2) in technical analysis, when two or more average or indexes fail to show confirming trends.

divergent investments: synonymous with *socially responsible investments.*

diversification
(1) spreading investments among different companies in different fields. Another type of diversification is offered by the securities of many individual companies whose activities cover a wide range.
(2) the purchase of varying assets in order to minimize the risk associated with a portfolio. see *diversified.*

diversified: when more than 75 percent of a management investment firm's assets are represented by cash, government securities, securities of other investment firms, and other securities.

diversified holding company: a corporation that controls several unrelated companies. Holding companies do not participate in management of operations of their subsidiaries.

diversified investment company: an investment company that practices diversification. The Investment Company Act of 1940 requires such a company to have at least 75 percent of its assets represented by cash, government securities, securities of other investment companies, and other securities limited in respect of any one issuer to an amount not greater than 5 percent of the value of the total assets of such investment company and not more than 10 percent of the outstanding voting securities of such an issuer.

divided account: synonymous with *Western account.*

dividend (Div.) (Divd.): a portion of the net profits that has been officially declared by the board of directors for distribution to stockholders. A dividend is paid at a fixed amount for each share of stock held by the stockholder. cf. *Irish dividend.*

dividend appropriations: an amount declared payable out of retained income (earned surplus) as dividends on actually outstanding preferred or common stock, or the amount credited to a reserve for such dividends.

dividend capture: when a corporation buys a stock just before the dividend is paid; holds it for a while, and then sells it without taking a loss. Since companies pay almost no tax on dividend income, the approach can yield two to three times the aftertax return on Treasury bills.

dividend claim: a request made by the purchaser of stock upon the registered holder for the amount of a dividend where the transaction took place prior to the ex-dividend rate, but the transfer could not be effected prior to the record date.

dividend exclusion: the subtraction from dividends qualifying as taxable income under IRS regulations—$100 for individuals and $200 for married couples filing jointly.

dividend on: the sale of a stock with an understanding that the purchaser will receive the next dividend.

dividend order: a form which, when properly filled out, instructs a corporation to forward dividend checks to a specified address.

dividend payer: a security or firm paying dividends, as contrasted with those firms and their securities which, because of poor performance or the process of plowing back their earnings, do not pay dividends.

dividend-paying agent: the agent of a corporation charged with the duty of paying dividends on the stock of the corporation out of funds supplied by the corporation.

dividend payout: the fraction of earnings paid out as common dividends.

dividend payout ratio: the ratio of dividends per share of common stock to earnings per share of common stock. cf. *retention rate.*

dividend-price ratio: the ratio of the current dividend rate to the market price of a stock.

dividend rate: the indicated annual rate of payment to a shareholder based on a company's latest quarterly dividend and recurring extra or special year-end dividends.

dividend-reinvestment plan (DRP): a service offered by a firm allowing its stockholders to buy stock at low or no commissions.

dividend requirements: the amount of annual earnings required to pay preferred dividends in full.

dividend rollover plan: a technique for purchasing and selling securities around their ex-dividend dates to collect the dividend and make a small profit on the trade. A short-term gain, taxed at regular rates.

dividends payable: the dollar amount of dividends expected to be paid, as given in financial statements. Such dividends are an obligation once declared by a firm's board and are listed as liabilities in annual and quarterly reports.

dividends per share (DPS): the dollar amount of dividends paid to stockholders for each share owned of a corporation's common stock.

dividend stripping: synonymous with *strip (3).*

dividend warrant: any order to release a corporation's dividend to its rightful shareholder.

dividend yield: a stock's dividend per share divided by its market price per share.

DJ: Dow Jones.

D&J: December and June (semiannual interest payments or dividends).

DJA: see *Dow Jones averages.*

DJI: see *Dow Jones Industrial Average.*

DJIA: see *Dow Jones Industrial Average.*

DJTA: Dow Jones Transportation Average.

DJUA: Dow Jones Utility Average.

DK
(1) see *don't know (the trade).*
(2) a stock transaction between a broker and another broker and which is under query because of some discrepancy in records.

DMJS: December, March, June, September (quarterly interest payments of dividends).

DNR: see *do-not-reduce order.*

DO: see *day order.*

dollar bond: see *bond, dollar.*

dollar control: guiding inventory by the amount of funds rather than by the number of physical items.

dollar (cost) averaging (DA): a system of buying securities at regular intervals with a fixed dollar amount. The investor buys by the dollars' worth rather than by the number of shares. If each investment is of the same number of dollars, payments buy more shares when the price is low and fewer when it rises.

dollar credit: a letter of credit permitting drafts to be drawn in dollars.

dollar premium: used in Great Britain for the added premium or cost that investors are required to pay to purchase dollars for investment outside the country.

dollar stabilization
(1) acts by monetary authorities (e.g., the Federal Reserve Board, International Monetary Fund) to reduce the fluctuation of the international exchange value of the dollar.
(2) an idea of economist Irving Fischer that would result in a compensated dollar tied to commodities rather than gold.

dollar stocks: an English term describing American stocks.

dollar-weighted rate of return: the dollar-weighted rate is affected by the amount and the timing of cash flows during a given time period. This rate is an effective measure of the fund's rate of growth, giving full weight to the impact of cash flows on fund assets. synonymous with *internal discount flow, real rate of return.*

domestic corporation: a corporation carrying out business in the same state where it was established or incorporated.

donated stock: to raise working capital, a corporation may receive back from a shareholder any or all of the paid issues. Often done when the stock is offered as a payment for services rendered. Donated stock is nonassessable.

donated surplus: surplus arising from contributions without consideration, by stockholders and others, of cash, property, or the company's own capital stock. Donated surplus is a form of paid-in surplus.

Donoghue's Money Fund Average: the average of all major money market fund yields, published weekly for 7 and 30 days yields.

do-not-reduce (DNR) order: trading instruction made by an investor preventing a sell-stop order, a sell-stop limit order, or a buy-limit order from being reduced by the amount of the ordinary cash dividend on ex-dividend date.

don't fight the tape: don't trade against a trend of the market, such as when stocks are falling; don't buy aggressively.

don't know (the trade) (DK): denotes a lack of knowledge by one party of a particular trade or transaction. Trades are also DKed due to conflicting instruction from one party or the other, such as money difference or payment instructions.

dormant partner: a partner not known to the public at large who is entitled to participate in the profits and subject to the losses.

DOT: see *Designated Order Turnaround.*

double: an option either to purchase or sell a security or commodity at a special price.

double auction market: on the stock market, the process of constant varying of prices by those bidding (buyers) and asking (sellers) in order to make a market. A sales occurs when the highest bidder meets the price of the lowest asker.

double auction system: see *auction market.*

double barreled: applied to tax-exempt bonds which are backed by a pledge of two or more sources of payment. For example, many special-assessment or special-tax bonds are additionally backed by the full faith, credit, and taxing power of the issuer.

double bottom (top): the price action of a security or market average where it has declined two times to the same approximate level, indicating the existence of a support level and a possibility that the downward trend has ended.

double-declining-balance method: see *DDB.*

double digit inflation: the rate of inflation annually amounting to 10 percent or greater.

double endorsement: a negotiable instrument or other document containing two endorsements, indicating that recourse can be made to the two companies or persons that endorsed the instrument.

double entry: the method of recording transactions that requires that any increase in one account reflect an increase or decrease in another account. The total debits of each entry must equal the total credits. cf. *single entry.*

double exemption: a municipal term applied to bonds that are exempt from both state and federal income taxation.

double liability: the liability of the stockholders of banks before banking legislation of the 1930s brought about the elimination of this feature for all national banks and most state banks. Under the double liability provision, the stockholders of a bank, in the event of its liquidation, were held legally responsible for an amount equal to the par value of their stock in addition to the amount of their original investment.

double option: synonymous with *spread and straddle.*

double top: see *double bottom (top).*

double witching hour: slang, the time between 3 and 4 P.M. when arbitragers and institutional traders have their final opportunity to close out both June stock-index options and futures positions. The third Friday of eight months of the year when just the corresponding stock and index options expire. cf. *triple witching hour.*

Dow: another name for Dow Jones Averages, or more specifically, the Dow Jones Industrial Average.

Dow Jones averages (DJA): the average of closing prices of 30 representative industrial stocks, 15 public utility stocks, 20 transportation stocks, and an average of the 65 computed at the end of a trading day on the New York Stock Exchange. cf. *NYSE Common Stock Index, Standard & Poor's 500 Composite-Stock Index.*

Dow Jones Bond Average: an index utilizing average prices from six different bond groups; used to measure bond market strength.

Dow Jones Commodity Futures Index: an index determined every hour during trading for 12 commodities taking into account their volume and production for each, unit trading prices and contract delivery dates.

Dow Jones Composite: composite of the Dow Jones Industrial, Transportation, and Utility averages. synonymous with *65 Stock Average.*

Dow Jones Industrial Average (DJIA): an average computed from 30 leading blue-chip industrial securities utilizing an unweighted arithmetic mean and quoted in terms of points rather than dollars. DJIA is used as a representative indicator of the movement of markets in general, but specifically on the NYSE.

Dow Jones Municipal Index: an average determined weekly using the market value of leading municipal bonds that sell at a discounted price.

Dow Jones Transportation Average (DJTA): an average computed from 20 firms in the transportation industry.

downdraft: a downward movement, as of the stock market.

down gap: an open space formed on a security chart when the lowest price of any market day is above the highest price of the next day.

down market: a time period when there is a declining trend in market prices.

down reversal: see *reversal.*

downside breakeven: the price to which a stock must drop before an investor incurs a loss. cf. *upside breakeven.*

downside risk: the probability that the price of an investment will fall.

downside trend: a time of extended declining prices which can last for several months where small reversals can occur.

downstairs merger: a merger of a parent corporation into a subsidiary.

downstream: describing movement of a business activity from a higher to a lower level (e.g., a loan from a parent company to one of its subsidiaries).

downstream borrowing: the borrowing of money by a corporation through the use of the credit standing of its subsidiaries.

down tick: a securities transaction at a price that is lower than the last different price. synonymous with *minus tick.* see *up tick.*

down trend: a stock's prevailing price direction is declining.

downturn: following a growth period, the downward movement of a business cycle or activity.

Dow theory (DT): a theory of market analysis based on the performance of the Dow Jones industrial and transportation stock price averages. The market is said to be in a basic upward trend if one of these averages advances above a previous important high, accompanied or followed by a similar advance in the other. When both averages dip below previous important lows, this is regarded as confirmation of a basic downward trend. The theory does not attempt to predict how long either trend will continue, although it is widely misinterpreted as a method of forecasting future action. see *Dow Jones averages.*

DPS: see *dividends per share.*

Dr.: a debt in a customer's account with a brokerage house.

draining reserve: the Federal Reserve System action to lower the money supply by curtailing the funds banks have available to lend.

drawn bond: see *bond, drawn.*

drawn securities: any securities called for redemption.

dried up: to come to a halt; the disappearance of either buying or selling order on the stock market.

drive

(1) a concerted upward or downward movement in the price of a security.

(2) the attempt to manipulate the price of securities or commodities by sellers to force prices downward. If proven, such action is illegal.

DRM: see *direct reduction mortgage.*

drop: slang, a decline in the price of a stock or commodity.

DRP: see *dividend-reinvestment plan.*

dry hole: a complete well not productive of oil or gas in paying quantities. synonymous with *dry well, duster.*

dry well: synonymous with *dry hole.*

D/S: days after sight; referring to the tenor of a bill of exchange.

DS: see *debenture stock.*

DT: see *Dow theory.*

DTC: see *Depository Trust Company.*

dual exchange market: exists when the authorities operate two exchange markets, prescribing the use of one market for exchange transactions relating to specified types of underlying transactions and the use of the other permitted dealing in foreign exchange.

dual listing: securities listed on more than one stock exchange.

dual mutual funds: funds that divide their portfolios between capital growth investments and income investments.

dual-purpose fund: synonymous with *split investment company.*

dual savings plan: a plan whereby two separate operations are required to post a savings deposit or a withdrawal to an account.

Du. Dat.: see *due date.*

due (annuity): annuity payments to commence immediately.

due bill: a document attached by the selling broker to delivered securities giving title to the buyer's broker for a stated number of shares or dollars. synonymous with *due bill check.*

due bill check: synonymous with *due bill.*

due date (DD) (Du. Dat.): the date on which an instrument of debt becomes payable; the maturity date.

due diligence session: bringing together a firm's officials whose securities are to be issued with an underwriting syndicate in compliance with the Securities Act, to be questioned pertaining to a prospectus, registration of the security, and other relevant financial matters.

due from: specifies an obligation owed to you.

due-on-sale: a clause in a conventional home mortgage stating that the balance of the existing mortgage must be paid to the lending bank when the home is sold by the owner.

due process of law: all actions of a court taken to ensure the rights of private individuals before the law; all legal steps to protect these rights. A court order to compel compliance with its wishes (e.g., a summons, issued to compel attendance in court).

due to: specifies an obligation owed by you.

dull: an inactive trading period; when prices of stocks move very little.

dummy: a person, such as a director elected to a board, who acts only for another person. The dummy has no material ownership in the firm and allows the individual who has sponsored his or her election to control their vote on the issues before the directors.

dummy incorporators: usually, a minimum of three people who, when creating a new corporation, act temporarily as the incorporators and directors, then resign and transfer their interest to the true owners. synonymous with *dummy directors.*

dummy stockholder: one who holds in his or her name stock that belongs to another party, whose identity is thus concealed.

dumping
(1) ***general:*** selling items to other countries below cost for purposes of eliminating surplus or to hurt foreign competition.
(2) ***general:*** in the United States, selling imported items at price less than the cost of manufacture.
(3) ***securities:*** offering large amount of securities with little or no concern for price or market impact.

Dun & Bradstreet (D&B): the oldest and largest mercantile agency in the United States, offering credit data and ratings on business concerns.

DUNS: Data Universal Numbering System (Dun's Number). see *Dun's number.*

Dun's Market Identifiers: a published system identifying firms with an absolute identification number and providing regular updated economic information on each company (e.g., address code, number of workers, and corporate affiliation).

Dun's number: short for Dun's (Data Universal Numbering System) Market Identifier. Published as part of a list of companies giving information, such as an identification number, address code, and so on.

duration: a measure of the price change of a bond to a change in its yield to maturity. It summarizes, in a single number, the characteristics which cause bond prices to change in response to a change in interest rates.

duster: synonymous with *dry hole.*

Dutch auction: an auction sale where the price on items is continuously lowered until a bidder responds favorably and buys.

DVP: delivery versus payment. synonymous with *cash on delivery.*

dynamiter: a securities broker who attempts to sell fraudulent or unregistered stocks and bonds over the telephone. cf. *boiler room tactic.*

E

E: declared or paid in the preceding 12 months (in stock listings of newspapers).

each way: trading on both the buying and selling sides of a transaction; the broker earns a commission of 3 percent each way (i.e., 3 percent for selling and another 3 percent for executing the purchase order).

E & OE: errors and omissions excepted.

early withdrawal penalty: a charge assessed against holders of fixed-term investments should they withdraw their funds prior to maturity.

earned growth rate: the compounded annual internal rate at which a corporation's equity per share grows following a reinvestment of earnings.

earned surplus (ES): a firm's net profits available after the payment of dividends to shareholders.

earnest money: money given by a contracting party to another at the time of the signing of a contract to "bind the bargain"; this sum is forfeited by the doner if he or she fails to carry out the contract.

earning assets: loans and investments that together are the assets responsible for most of the bank's earnings.

earnings before taxes: earnings of a firm following payment of bond interest but before the payment of federal and other taxes.

earnings multiple: see *price-earnings ratio*.

earnings per share (EPS): synonymous with *net income per share of common stock*.

earnings price (EP) ratio: earnings per share of common stock outstanding divided by the closing stock market price (or the midpoint between the closing bid and asked price if there are no sales) on a day as close as possible after the publication of the earnings.

earnings protection: see *times interest and preferred dividend earned, times interest earned, times preferred dividend earned.*

earnings report: a statement issued by a company showing its earnings or losses over a given period. The earnings report lists the income earned, the expenses, and the net result.

earnings statement: an analysis or presentation of the earnings of an enterprise in statement form. An income statement form is an earnings statement.

earnings yield: a ratio found by dividing the market price of a stock into its earnings.

earn-out: a strategy of acquisition allowing an individual to pay for about half the cost of acquisitions in stock now and the balance five years later, depending on the acquired company's earnings. The result is getting earnings growth with minimal stock dilution. Later, when further dilution results from full pay-out of shares, there should be continued acquisitions as an offset as well as internal growth.

Eastern account: synonymous with *undivided account.*

EBIT: earnings before interest and taxes.

EC: see *ex-coupon.*

Economic Recovery Tax Act of 1981 (ERTA): federal legislation, signed by President Reagan in August, 1981; includes the following provisions.

Tax rate cuts: (1981) credit of 1¼ percent against individual tax bills and 5 percent withholding rate reduction on October 1; (July 1982) tax rate reduction of 10 percent, followed by another in July 1983. By 1984, the top rate on $50,000 in earned income dropped from 49 percent to 38 percent; (1985) cost-of-living wage and salary increased offset by widening tax brackets, raising "zero bracket" at low end, boosting personal exemptions.

Unearned income and capital gains: (June 9, 1981) the maximum tax on capital gains realized a drop from 28 percent (gain after 60 percent exclusion taxed at 70 percent) to 20 percent (gain after 60 percent exclusion taxed at 50 percent). Minimum holding period for long-term capital gain remains 12 months. (1982) Top rate on dividends, interest, rents, and royalties dropped from 70 to 50 percent, equal to maximum tax on salary income.

Marriage tax offset: (1982) if both spouses work, a 5 percent deduction from the salary of the lower-paid partner, up to $1500; (1983) a 10 percent deduction, up to $3000.

Pension deductions: (1982) tax deductions for contributions to Individual Retirement Accounts raised to $2000 and the 15 percent limitation canceled. The IRA provision is extended to employees already covered by pensions. Voluntary thrift plans as well as separate IRA accounts qualify.

Interest deductions: (1981-1982) exempt interest income up to $1000 ($2000 joint return) on special "All-Savers" savings certificates was offered for one year only. A deduction of $750 ($1500 joint return) of public utility stock dividends was allowed if paid into a reinvestment plan; (1985) exclusion of 15 percent of savings interest, less interest paid on consumer (but not on mortgage) loans.

Estate and gift tax reductions: (1982-1986) progressive exclusion from taxation of the first $250,000 of estate up to the first $600,000 of estate; (1982) unlimited deduction for estate and gift transfers to a spouse; (1982) annual gifts excluded from taxation raised from $3000 to $10,000.

Stock option treatment: (1981) no tax at exercise on $100,000 per year in stock. Capital gains treatment on gain over option price at sale.

Depreciation and investment tax credits: (1981) accelerated depreciation rules and expanded tax credits for certain classes of real estate investment should shelter more income for investors. see also *All-Savers certificates, Individual Retirements Accounts, Keogh Plan, Tax Reform Act of 1984*.

ECT: estimated completion time.

ED: see *extra*.

EDD: estimated delivery date.

EDGAR: see *electronic data gathering and retrieval*.

EDR: see *European depository receipt*.

effective: a declaration by the SEC of final authorization to begin distribution of a new issue of stock or bonds.

effective annual yield: the return on an investment, expressed in terms of the equivalent simple interest rate.

effective date

(1) ***general:*** the date on which an agreement takes effect.

(2) ***insurance:*** the date on which an insurance binder goes into effect and from which time protection is provided.

(3) ***securities:*** the date when an offering registered with the SEC may commence; usually 20 days following the filing of a registration statement.

effective debt: the total debt of a firm, including the major value of annual leases or other payments that are equivalent to interest charges.

effective exchange rate: any spot exchange rate actually paid or received by the public, including any taxes or subsidies on the exchange transaction as well as any applicable banking commissions. The articles of agreement envisage that all effective exchange rates shall be situated within permitted margins around par value.

effective gross revenue: total income less allowance for vacancies, contingencies, and sometimes collection losses, but before deductions for operating expenses.

effective interest rate (or yield): the rate or earning on a bond investment based on the actual price paid for the bond, the coupon rate, the maturity date, and the length of time between interest dates; in contrast to *nominal interest rate*.

effective net worth: the net worth plus subordinated debt, as determined by senior creditors.

effective par: with preferred stocks, the par value that would ordinarily correspond to a given dividend rate.

effective sale: the price of a round lot that will determine the price at which the following odd lot will be sold.

effective yield: the rate of return realized by an investor who purchases a security and then sells it.

efficient market hypothesis: a stock market theory that says competition for stock market profits is so keen that observed stocks prices are good estimates of the "true" value of the stocks.

efficient portfolio: a fully diversified portfolio. For any given return no other portfolio has less risk, and for a given level of risk no other portfolio provides superior returns.

EI

(1) see *exact interest.*
(2) see *ex-interest.*

eighth stocks: stocks on which the odd-lot differential, when added to a purchase order or subtracted from a sell order, of one-eighth of a point is applied to the following round-lot sale. Eighth stocks sell below 60, while quarter stocks sell above 60.

either-or order: synonymous with *alternative order.*

EL: see *even lots.*

elect: making a conditional order into a market order.

electronic data gathering and retrieval (EDGAR): the SEC computerized system making it easier for firms to send in their financial data and making it possible for the public to gain instant access to this information via home or office computers.

electronic handshake: see *Intermarket Trading System.*

eligible commercial paper: a negotiable instrument, having met certain requirements, that is eligible for rediscounting at a special rate by member banks of the Federal Reserve System.

eligible investment: any income-producing investment that is considered to be a sound repository for the funds of savings banks and similar institutions.

eligible list: a list of stocks that financial firms can purchase as investments that are prepared by representatives of financial institutions. see also *approved list, legal list.*

eligible paper: instruments, securities, bills, and so on, accepted by a financial institution (e.g., a Federal Reserve Bank) for the purpose of rediscounting.

eligible stock: a stock in which banks, charitable organizations, trustees, and so on, may invest funds committed to their care.

elves: an index of technical market indicators that track 10 barometers of market momentum, investor psychology, and monetary conditions.

EMP: end-of-month payment.

Employee Retirement Income Security Act of 1974 (ERISA): on Labor Day, 1974, President Ford signed into law the Employee Retirement Income Security Act. The purpose of ERISA is to protect the interests of workers who participate in private pension and welfare plans and their beneficiaries. ERISA reaches 1.5 million plans and approximately 40 million workers and affects assets now held in private pension and welfare plans totaling more than $200 billion.

Title I, administered by the Department of Labor, deals with protection of employee benefit rights. Title II is composed of amendments to the Internal Revenue Code. Title III deals with the division of responsibilities among the Department of Labor, the Internal Revenue Service, and the Pension Benefit Guaranty Corporation. Title IV deals with plan termination insurance and establishes the Pension Benefit Guaranty Corporation.

ERISA is designed to guarantee that workers are not required to satisfy unreasonable age and service requirements before becoming eligible for pension plan participation, that persons who work for a specified minimum period under a pension plan are assured of at least some pension at retirement age; that the money will be there to pay pension benefits when they are due; that plans and plan funds are administered and managed prudently; that employees know their rights and their obligations under the plans; that spouses of pensioners are given adequate protection; that the benefits of workers in certain defined benefit pension plans are protected in the event of a plan termination; and that the federal taxing power is protected by ensuring the equitable operation and soundness of pension plans.

The law also allows an employee not covered by a pension plan other than Social Security to put aside, on a tax-defered basis, a certain amount of money for retirement. see *Individual Retirement Account.* see also *Keogh Plan.*

employee spending account (ESA): where employees allocate up to 50 percent of their profit-sharing revenues. Throughout a given year the worker has the option of using the ESA to reimburse himself or herself for certain benefit expenses—medical, dental, legal, or day-care—or buy medical insurance at group rates that often subsidized by the firm.

employee stock ownership plans (ESOPs): programs created to give the worker a feeling of participation in the management and direction of a company. Thus workers are encouraged to purchase stock of the company.

employee stock repurchase agreement: a plan under which stock in a corporation is sold to employees with an agreement providing for repurchase by the corporation.

End.: see *endorsement.*

endiguer: French term for to *hedge.*

endorse: the act of placing one's name on an instrument, usually on the back, either by signing or by rubber stamping, so as legally to pass title of the instrument to another party. May also refer to the endorsing of a note by a second party guaranteeing payment in the event of default by the maker. Also spelled "indorse."

endorsed bond: see *bond, endorsed.*

endorsee: the person to whom a negotiable item payable or endorsed to order is negotiated by endorsement and delivery. Also spelled "indorsee."

endorsement (END.)
(1) ***general:*** a show of support, a verification.
(2) ***general:*** a signature written on the back of an instrument constitutes an endorsement. An endorsement is required on a negotiable instrument in order to transfer and pass title to another party, who becomes a "holder in due course." The endorser, in signing the endorsement, guarantees that he or she is the lawful owner of the instrument, knows of no infirmity in the instrument, accepted it in good faith for the value received, and is a holder in due course and has the legal capacity to transfer title to another party in the normal course of business.
(3) ***insurance:*** when circumstances require that a policy be changed (e.g., change of name, addition of property, or change in coverage), such changes are made by attaching to the policy an endorsement—a form bearing the language necessary to record the change.
(4) also spelled *indorsement.*

endorsement date: the date appearing on the interchange advice and endorsed on paper by the clearing member first entering the paper into interchange. The date must be the same date as that on which the paper is mailed to the card issuer's clearing member.

endorser: one who endorses; the person who transfers his or her title to an instrument to another by endorsement. Also spelled *indorser.*

endorsing: signing a check, note, or other financial instrument purporting to transfer it to another person.

endosser: French term for *to endorse.*

endowment insurance: life insurance on which premiums are paid for at a given period, during which the insured is covered. If the person survives beyond the end of the premium period, he or she collects the face value.

endowment term: the period of time from date of issue to maturity of an endowment contract.

energy mutual fund: a mutual fund that invests only in energy securities, such as oil, oil service, gas, solar energy, and makers of energy-saving equipment.

enforced liquidation: the condition created by the failure of a security owner to maintain sufficient equity in a margin account.

engross: to purchase a sufficient quantity of a commodity to secure a monopoly for purposes of reselling at a higher price.

entrepreneur: one who assumes the financial risk of the initiation, operation, and management of a given business or undertaking. see *threshold companies.*

envelope: a sliding list of price extremes.

EDA: effective on or about.

EOD: every other day (advertising).

EOM: end of month.

EPR: see *earnings-price ratio.*

EPS
(1) electronic payment system.
(2) see *earnings per share.*

Epunts: a European financing technique whereby the unit of account is a payment guarantee, the value of which is expressed in terms of gold, as are free-world currencies. The unit is not a gold obligation itself but has a value based on gold. Each unit represents slightly less than nine-tenths of a gram of gold, the same as the basis of the value of the American dollar. The holder of a matured bond that is expressed in Epunts can request payment in any one of 17 currencies, irrespective of the kind of currency the holder used when he or she made the purchase. The name Epunts comes from the European Payments Union, formed in 1947 to facilitate currency exchange, to which 17 nations belonged. The union no longer exists.

Equ.: see *equity.*

equal coverage: a corporation indenture protective clause providing that in the case of an additional issue of bonds, the subject bonds shall be entitled to the same security as that of the earlier issue.

equalizing dividend: a dividend paid to correct irregularities caused by changes in established regular dividend dates.

equipment obligations: equipment bonds, equipment notes, or car-trust notes secured only by lien on specific equipment.

equipment trust bond: see *bond, equipment trust.*

equipment trust certificate: a type of security, generally issued by a railroad, to pay for new equipment (e.g., locomotives). Title to the equipment is held by a trustee until the notes are paid off. An equipment trust certificate is usually secured by a first claim on the equipment.

equities: synonymous with *common stock.*

equity
(1) ***general:*** the value placed on the distribution of income.
(2) ***general:*** the difference between liens against property and the current market value.
(3) ***investments:*** the ownership interest of common and preferred stockholders in a company.
(4) ***investments:*** the excess of value of securities over the debit balance in a margin account. see *margin call.* see also *common stock.*
(5) ***law:*** the law of trusts, divorce, injunctions, and other rules of performance are enforced in courts of equity to determine fairness, right, and justice.

equity capital: stockholders' or owners' investments made in an organization.

equity conversion: synonymous with *reverse-annuity mortgage.*

equity earnings: a portion of surplus earnings of a subsidiary company, over dividend payments, that are unreported by the parent company. synonymous with *indirect earnings, undisclosed earnings, unreported earnings.*

equity equivalent loans: loans secured by real property or interests therein, which carry the right to acquire a percentage of the ownership of such property through an associated option.

equity financing: the selling of capital stock by a corporation.

equity funding: any combination of mutual fund shares and insurance. In such a plan, the buyer purchases his or her mutual fund shares and then the shares are pledged as collateral for the loan that is used to defray the cost of the premium on an insurance policy. see *investment company.*

equity income: net operating income less loan interest.

equity income funds: funds holding both stocks and bonds that purport to achieve high dividend and interest income.

equity kicker: a participation in the equity position of a development by the lender as an inducement to lend funds. Used in periods of tight money or a lenders' market.

equity mortgage: a home-mortgage contract in which a lender reduces interest rates by a certain percentage in return for the same percentage of profit when a borrower sells his or her home.

equity net worth: expressing the interest of the shareholders of a company as measured by the amount of capital, surplus, and retained earnings.

equity REIT: a real estate investment trust that takes an ownership position in the invested real estate. Shareholders earn dividends on rental income from the buildings and earn appreciation if properties sell for a profit.

equity risk premium: the difference between the rate of return available from risk free assets, such as U.S. Treasury bills, and that available from assuming the risk inherent in common stocks.

equity securities: any stock issue, common or preferred. see *common stock.*

equity turnover: the ratio that measures the relationship between sales and the common stockholders' equity. It is used to compute the rate of return on common equity.

equivalent bond yield: a measurement of the rate of return on a security sold on a discount basis that assumes actual days to maturity and a 365-day year.

equivalent taxable yield: the yield comparison of tax-free interest income to after-tax income from another taxable investment.

ER

(1) see *earnings report.*
(2) see *ex-rights.*

(3) excess reserves of depository institutions.

ERISA: see *Employee Retirement Income Security Act of 1974.*

ERTA: see *Economic Recovery Tax Act of 1981.*

ES
(1) see *earned surplus.*
(2) see *exempt securities.*

ESA: see *employee spending account.*

escrow: a written agreement or instrument setting up for allocation funds or securities deposited by the giver or grantor to a third party (the escrow agent), for the eventual benefit of the second party (the grantee). The escrow agent holds the deposit until certain conditions have been met. The grantor can get the deposit back only if the grantee fails to comply with the terms of the contract, nor can the grantee receive the deposit until the conditions have been met. see also *billed escrow.*

escrow agent: see *mortgage department.*

escrow agreement: an arrangement whereby two parties agree to place a sum of money in the hands of a third party for conditional delivery under specified circumstances.

escrow analysis: the periodic examination of escrow accounts by the mortgagee to verify that current monthly deposits are sufficient to provide the necessary funds to pay taxes, insurance, and other bills when they are due.

escrow bond: see *bond, escrow.*

escrow officer: an officer of a financial institution designated as the escrow agent or the custodian of the funds, securities, deeds, and so on, deposited until their release by agreement upon the completion of the agreed-upon act.

escrow receipt: acknowledgment from an approved depository that guarantees funds or stocks are on deposit at that bank and will be delivered upon an option contract being exercised.

ESOPs: see *employee stock option plans.*

estate tax: a state or federal excise tax placed on an estate, to be paid before property is transferred to heirs. This is different from an inheritance tax, which is levied against the receivers of the estate. see *Tax Reform Act of 1976.*

estate tax bond: see *bond, estate tax.*

estimated balance sheet: the estimate of assets, liabilities, and proprietorship at the end of a future fiscal period.

ETA: estimated time of arrival.

ETD: estimated time of departure.

ETLT: equal to or less than.

EURCO: see *European Composite Unit.*

Eurobill of Exchange: a bill of exchange drawn and accepted in the usual fashion but expressed in foreign currency and accepted as being payable outside the country whose currency is being used.

Eurobond: a bond released by a U.S. or other non-European company for sale in Europe. In this market, corporations and governments issue medium-term securities, typically 10 to 15 years in length. see *Eurocredit sector.*

Euro-Canadian dollars: Canadian dollars dealt in the Euromarkets.

Eurocommercial paper: commercial paper issued in a Eurocurrency. see *Eurocurrency.*

Eurocredit: any lending made using Eurocurrency. see *Eurocurrency.*

Eurocredit sector: a sector of the Euromarket, where banks function as long-term lenders by constantly rolling over short- and medium-term loans at rates that fluctuate with the cost of funds. see *Eurobond.*

Eurocurrency: monies of various nations deposited in European banks that are used in the European financial market. synonymous with *Euromoney.*

Eurodollar: U.S. dollars retained on deposit and circulated among bank and financial firms around the world that are used for short-term trade financing.

Eurodollar bond: see *bond, Eurodollar.*

Eurodollar collaterized certificates of deposits (CDs): certificates of deposit of at least $100,000 to foreign investors issued by federally chartered and Federal Savings and Loan Insurance Corporation-insured institutions.

Eurofrancs: Swiss, Belgian, or French francs traded on the Eurocurrency markets.

Euroguilders: Dutch guilders traded in the Eurocurrency markets.

Euromarket (Euromart):
(1) see *Eurobond.*
(2) see *Eurocredit sector.*

Euromarks: Deutschmarks traded in the Eurocurrency market.

Euromoney: synonymous with *Eurocurrency.*

European Composite Unit (EURCO): a nonofficial, private unit of account based on member currencies of the European Community; includes a quantity of each of the European Communities' currencies, in a proportion that reflects the importance of the country.

European Currency Unit (ECU): money made up of nine European currencies: the Deutschemark, French franc, British pound, Italian lira, Belgian franc, Dutch guilder, Danish krone, Luxembourg franc, and Irish punt—plus 20 percent gold. synonymous with *European Monetary Unit.*

European Depository Receipt (EDR): patterned after the American depository receipt to facilitate investments by Americans in securities of foreign nations. The EDR was first issued in London in 1963, to facilitate international trading in Japanese securities. It is a negotiable receipt covering certain specified securities which have been deposited in a bank in the country of origin of the securities. Their use in trading eliminates the necessity of shipping the actual stock certificates, thus making transfer of ownership easier, faster, and less costly. cf. *American Depository Receipt*.

European Monetary Unit: synonymous with *European Currency Unit*.

European option: an option that can be exercised only on a specified date.

European terms: an exchange rate expressed as a number of dollars per currency unit.

Euroyen: Japanese yen traded in the Euromarkets.

evaluator: an independent expert who appraises the value of property for which there is limited trading, such as antiques in an estate.

evaluator's fee: a fee charged by an evaluator for portfolios examined periodically, either by law or for establishing redemption price. The evaluator is charged with setting an estimate of the resale value of bonds and charges a fee for rendering this service.

evening up: a profit to offset a loss.

even lots (EL): lots or number of stock shares sold in units of 100 or multiples thereof. see also *board lot*.

even-par swap: the sale of one block of bonds and the simultaneous purchase of the same nominal principal amount of another block of bonds, without concern for the net cash difference.

even spread: a spread position where the investor neither receives nor pays a premium. The premium received from the long position equals the premium owed on the short position.

even up: a securities term describing an evenly divided balance of security buyers and sellers. Prior to the opening of the exchange, it refers to the opening prices of the day which show minimal changes from the closing prices of the previous days trading.

evergreen loans: loans to countries to cover possible losses on sovereign lending because of continuous rollovers and government reluctance to take the bankruptcy option.

EW: see *ex-warrants*.

Ex.: see *exchange*.

exact interest: interest compounded on a 365-days-per-year basis. see *compounded interest, ordinary interest, simple interest*.

ex-all: indicates that the seller has sold a security but reserved for himself or herself the right to all pending advantages. These would include rights, warrants, and dividends in money or kind which may be granted to the security.

ex-ante saving: a form of planned saving which may be more or less than exante investment (planned investment).

except for opinion: a choice made by an accounting firm when auditing financial reports of public companies which indicates that the auditor was unable to audit a certain area of the firm. Federal regulations do not permit public companies to issue a financial report with *except for* qualifications and insist that the omitted data be obtained. see also *clean opinion, statement disclaiming, subject to opinion.*

excess equity: a situation where the cash value of an account is in excess of the amount required for margin in the buying of securities.

excess insurance: a policy or bond covering the insured against certain hazards, applying only to loss of damage in excess of a stated amount. The risk of initial loss or damage (excluded from the excess policy or bond) may be carried by the insured himself or herself or may be insured by another policy or bond, providing what is known as primary insurance.

excess(ive) interest: the difference between the minimum rate of interest contractually guaranteed on dividends, or proceeds left with a firm and the interest actually credited.

excess margin: an equity in a brokerage house's customer account, given in dollars, above the legal minimum for a margin account or the maintenance requirement.

excess profits: a firm's profits that are determined by the government to be excessive, based on a historical base period.

excess return: the return derived from a security (during a specified holding period) less the return from holding a riskless security (e.g., a short-term government obligation) during the same period.

Exch.: see *exchange.*

exchange (Ex.)
(1) ***general:*** an organization or place for carrying out business or settling accounts.
(2) ***general:*** the volume of monies available for use.
(3) ***investments:*** any exchange for trading in securities or commodities. see *stock exchanges.*

exchange acquisition: a method of filling an order to purchase a block of stock on the floor of an exchange. Under certain circumstances, a member broker can facilitate the purchase of a block by soliciting sell orders. All orders to sell the security are lumped together and crossed with the buy order in the regular auction market. The buyer's price may be on a net basis or on a commission basis.

exchange against actuals: synonymous with *exchange of spot.*

exchange distribution: a method of selling large blocks of stock on the floor of an exchange. Under certain circumstances a member-broker can facilitate the sale of a block of stock by soliciting and inducing other member-brokers to solicit orders to buy. Individual buy orders are lumped together with the sell order in the regular auction market. A special commission is usually paid by the seller; ordinarily the buyer pays no commission.

exchange floor: the area of a stock exchange where stock trading between dealers and brokers occurs.

exchange for futures: transferring to a seller the cash commodity of a long futures position by the purchaser of a cash commodity. Any difference between the spot and futures contract is settled with cash.

exchange for physical: synonymous with *exchange of spot.*

exchange of securities: resulting from a merger or consolidation, a technique where the securities of one corporation are exchanged for those of a second firm on a mutually agreeable basis.

exchange of spot (or cash commodity) for futures: the simultaneous exchange of a specified quantity of a cash commodity for the equivalent quantity of futures, usually due to both parties' carrying opposite hedges in the same delivery month. In grain the exchange is made outside the "pit." synonomous with *exchange for physical,* or *exchange against actuals.*

exchange option contract: see *listed option.*

exchange privilege: enables a mutual fund shareholder to transfer his or her investment from one fund to another within the same fund group if the shareholders needs or objectives change, generally with a small transaction charge.

exchange rate: the price of one currency in relation to that of another.

exchanges: all checks, drafts, notes and other instruments that are presented to a clearinghouse for collection. synonymous with *clearing house exchanges.*

exchange seat: the membership on a stock exchange; required for transacting business on any exchange. Seats are limited in number and sold on the open market when a member leaves a specified exchange.

exchange-traded option: synonymous with *listed option.*

ex-clearing house: see *XCH.*

exclusive listing: an arrangement whereby a broker becomes the sole agent of the owner of a property, assuming the sole right to sell or rent the property within a specified time period.

ex-coupon (ec): without the coupon. A stock is sold ex-coupon when the coupon for the existing interest payment has been removed.

Ex. D.: see *ex-dividend.*

Ex. Div.: see *ex-dividend.*

ex-dividend (ex div; XD): identifying the period during which the quoted price of a security excludes the payment of any declared dividend to the buyer, and the dividend reverts to the seller.

ex-dividend date: the day on and after which the right to receive a current dividend is not transferred automatically from seller to buyer.

execute an order: to fulfill an order to buy or sell. When an execution is referred to as "good," it generally means that both the broker and the customer are satisfied that the price obtained is fair.

execution

(1) ***general:*** the actual filing of a customer's order.

(2) ***securities:*** carrying out a trade, usually by a broker.

exemption

(1) ***income taxes:*** a token deduction from gross income allowed for the taxpayer and others in his or her family where at least half of their support can be shown. Additional deductions are given for people over 65 years of age and for blindness. see *Tax Reform Act of 1976.*

(2) ***law:*** a person free from a duty required by some law (e.g., one relieved from jury duty because of prejudice of the subject).

exempt securities (ES): stocks that do not require the regular margin when bought on credit.

exercise

(1) to exchange a right or warrant for its equivalent in stock.

(2) the procedure when a holder of an option contract informs the writer of the contract that they want to purchase or sell shares of the underlying security. This is accomplished through the brokerage firm which must tender an exercise notice to the Options Clearing Corporation.

exercise assignment: a notification to a stock option contract writer that the option has been exercised against him or her.

exercise cut-off time: the time, determined by exchanges, by which option holders are required to inform their brokerage houses that they desire to exercise their options. Usually the cut-off time if is 5:30 P.M. Eastern time on the business day preceding the expiration date.

exercise limit: a rule of the option exchanges requiring that no investor or group of investors cooperating with each other can exercise more than 2000 options for each class, within five consecutive days.

exercise notice: a notice issued by a clearinghouse that was formed to ensure stock deliveries, obligating a customer to send the securities covered by an option against payment of the exercise price. see *exercise price.*

exercise price: the fixed price for which a stock can be purchased in a call contract or sold in a put contract. see *puts and calls.* synonymous with *striking price.*

exercise ratio: number of shares of common stock that may be exchanged for each warrant owned.

ex gratia payment: a payment made by an insurance company, but one for which it is not liable under the terms of the insurance policy.

exhaust price: the price at which a broker is forced to sell a security that was margined and subsequently dropped in price.

Ex. Int.: see *ex-interest.*

ex-interest: synonymous with *flat (1).*

exit: a time when holdings can be converted to cash or stocks which can be liquidated over a period of time.

exit fee: a charge by a financial institution to discourage transfers to another trustee.

ex-legal: a municipal bond not having the legal opinion of a bond law firm printed on it, as do most municipal bonds. When traded, purchasers must be warned that legal opinion is absent.

expansion: synonymous with *recovery (2)*.

expected rate of return: on an asset or portfolio, the weighted arithmetic average of all possible outcomes, where the weights are the probabilities that each outcome will occur; the expected value or mean of a probability duration.

expected yield: the ratio of expected return over the investment total, usually expressed as a percentage of an annual basis.

expendable fund: a fund whose assets may be applied by administrative action for general or specific purposes.

expenditure: an actual payment, or the creation of an obligation to make a future payment, for some benefit, item, or service received. If the expenditure is for the purpose of acquiring or improving a relatively permanent asset, it is termed a *capital expenditure*. If the amount involved is charged to some operating account, it is a *revenue expenditure*.

expense: the cost of resources used to create revenue. Expense is the amount shown on the income statement as a deduction from revenue. Expense should not be confused with cost. All expenses are costs, but not all costs are expenses.

expense ratio: a ratio, expressed in cents per $100 of investment, that compares mutual fund expenses for a management fee and other overhead costs to average the net asset value of outstanding securities. Usually this ratio is reported in a corporation's annual report.

expiration
(1) ***general:*** termination, cessation.
(2) ***general:*** the date on which a policy will cease to be in effect, unless previously canceled.
(3) ***investments:*** the last day on which the option may be exercised.

expiration cycle: the set of months when listed options can trade. Three expiration cycles exist. Options contracts on the same underlying stock can trade in only one of three cycles. First cycle: January, April, July, October. Second cycle: February, May, August, November. Third cycle: March, June, September, December.

expiration date
(1) the date when stocks of value, such as rights or warrants, expire and are no longer of value.
(2) the latest date a listed stock option contract can be exercised prior to expiration, which is presently the Saturday following the third Friday of the expiration month.

expiration month: the month in which a stock option contract expires.

expiration time: the latest time a listed stock option contract can be exercised prior to expiration, which is presently 11:59 A.M. Eastern time on the expiration date.

expire: to lapse. A right, warrant, or stock option contract that becomes worthless because it was not exercised within the specific time period permitted.

ex-pit transaction: the buying of cash commodities at a specified basis outside the authorized exchange.

exploratory drilling program: any very risk search for an undiscovered reservoir of gas or oil. Such programs are often syndicated, and units are sold to limited partners.

ex post: used to distinguish backward-looking, or historical, variables.

exposure: a prominent, often overextended position or commitment, as in investment, that is considered precarious and risky.

Ex. R.: see *ex-rights.*

ex-rights: without the rights. Corporations raising additional money may do so by offering their stockholders the right to subscribe to new or additional stock, usually at a discount from the prevailing market price. The buyer of a stock selling ex-rights is not entitled to the rights. see *ex-dividend, rights.*

ex-rights date: the date when a buyer of common stock is not entitled to the rights that had been declared for the security.

ex-stock dividend: without any stock dividend; for example, when the stock dividend is held as the property of the seller. cf. *ex-dividend.*

extendable notes: debt securities whose maturities can be stretched out at the option of the issuer. With extendables, investors have the right to get their cash back at an early maturity date or to accept an offer by the issuer to extend the maturities once, twice, three times, or more.

extended: an advance or decline in the price of a stock that extends the earlier established trend and suggests a high probability that a subsequent consolidation will take place.

extended bond: see *bond, extended.*

external bond: see *bond, external.*

external funds: funds brought in from outside the company, such as a bank loan, proceeds from a bond offering, or funds from venture capitalists.

externalization: the practice or process of purchasing and selling securities for customers by brokers by sending, as normal, orders to the floor of an exchange for execution.

extra (ED): short form of "extra dividend." A dividend in the form of stock or cash in addition to a company's regular or usual dividend. Not to be confused with *ex-dividend.*

extra dividend: synonymous with *special dividend.*

extra-market covariance: the tendency for prices of related securities to move together in such a way that is independent of the market as a whole.

extraordinary: any one-time income or charges on corporation income statements, that is, the write-off of a significant loss, the sale of a subsidiary firm.

ex-warrants: without warrants. When a security is sold ex-warrants, the warrants are retained (exercised) by the seller. see *ex-rights*.

F

F

(1) dealt in *flat* (in bond listings in newspapers).
(2) used on a ticker tape after a foreign stock symbol to show that the stock has been sold by a foreign owner.

FA

(1) see *face amount.*
(2) see *facilitating agency.*
(3) see *fixed assets.*

FAC: see *face-amount certificate company.*

face amount: the principal sum involved in a contract. The actual amount payable by the company may be decreased by loans or increased by additional benefits payable under specified conditions or stated in a rider.

face-amount certificate company (FAC): an investment firm that issues only debt securities that pay a fixed guaranteed rate of return.

face of a note: synonymous with *principal.*

face value: the principal value of an instrument. It is on the face value that interest is computed on interest-bearing obligations such as notes and bonds. The legal entity issuing a note, bond, or other obligation contracts to repay the face value of the obligation at maturity. synonymous with *par value.*

facilitating agency: any organization aiding an individual or firm in taking tile to goods (e.g., a stock exchange).

facsimile signature: a mechanically imprinted signature placed on an instrument, check, bond, security, and the like.

FACT: factor analysis chart technique.

fail(s)

(1) ***general:*** a business venture that does not prove financially viable.
(2) ***investments:*** a broker's inability to deliver stocks he or she owes another broker within the required

five business days. One broker's failure to deliver results in another broker's failure to receive.

fail float: the cash balance remaining when security transactions are not consummated on contractual settlement date by delivery of the securities.

fail position: see *fail(s).*

fail to deliver: a situation where a broker-dealer on the sell side of a contract fails to deliver securities to the broker-dealer on the buy side. Under these conditions, the seller will not receive payment for the stocks. cf. *fail to receive.*

fail to receive: a situation where a broker-dealer on the buy side of a contract does not receive delivery of securities from the broker-dealer on the sell side. Under these conditions, the buyer does not make payment for the stocks. cf. *fail to deliver.*

failure: the inability to fulfill normal business obligations; becoming insolvent or bankrupt.

FAIR Certificate: *f*ree from tax *a*fforda-ble, *i*nsured *r*ewarding; the 1981 Savings and Loan Association strategy with Congress to allow a savings certificate that would be free from federal income tax, offered in affordable denominations, insured by a federal agency, and pay a significant net turn. see *All-Savers certificates.*

fair market value
(1) the price at which a buyer and a seller are willing to exchange any asset.
(2) swaps against syndicate offerings—the price that a dealer usually pays for a security in the ordinary course of business if there was no swap involved.

fair-price: a rule to ensure that a bidder makes the same offer for all shares. Encourages an acquirer to seek out management first instead of making an unfriendly bid.

fair return
(1) the income or profit a person expects to receive on an investment, taking into account the amount invested and the involved risk.
(2) the approved profit of regulated industries, such as gas, electric, and telephone.

fair value: under the Investment Company Act, value determined in good faith by the board of directors for those securities and assets for which there is no market quotation readily available.

fairy godfather: slang, a potential business supporter.

fall: the failure of a seller to deliver securities to the purchaser or to a specific place of delivery as contracted.

fallen angel: a high-priced security of a large, widely known corporation whose price has abruptly fallen owing to some setback or adverse news.

fall out of bed: a crash in stock prices; a sharp drop in the market.

false pretense: any untrue statements or representations made with the intention of obtaining property or money.

family income rider: a special policy provision added to a basic term life insurance policy, stating that a specified monthly income is to be paid to the beneficiary for the remainder of the income period if the insured dies before the expiration of the term.

family of funds: a group of mutual funds that are managed by the same investment management firm, where each fund has a different objective.

F&A: February and August (semiannual interest payments or dividends).

Fannie Mae: see *Federal National Mortgage Association.*

far option: that side of a stock spread option position that will expire after the other side. see *spread.* cf. *near option.*

farther in: see *farther out.*

farther out: farther in; the relative length of option-contract maturities with reference to the present.

FASB8: Statement of Financial Accounting Standards No. 8; governs corporations' financial accounting and reporting for foreign currency transactions, and sets standards for foreign currency financial statements incorporated in the financial statements of a firm by consolidation, combination, or the equity method of accounting.

fast market: see *options in a fast market.*

FAT: fixed asset transfer.

fate (inquiry): an inquiry on the position of a bill of exchange to determine if it has been accepted, paid, and so on. short for *please advise fate.*

FC
(1) see *fixed capital.*
(2) see *floating capital.*
(3) see *futures contract.*

FCA: Fellow of the Institute of Chartered Accountants.

FCU: see *Federal Credit Union.*

Fd.
(1) see *fund.*
(2) see *funding.*

FDIC: see *Federal Deposit Insurance Corporation.*

FE
(1) see *foreign exchange.*
(2) see *futures exchange.*

feature
(1) ***general:*** the components of an item or service that yield a benefit.
(2) ***investments:*** the more active stocks in the general list.

Fed, the: see *Federal Reserve System.*

Federal agency security: a debt instrument issued by an agency of the federal government. Though not a general obligation, these stocks are sponsored by the government and consequently have the highest safety ratings.

federal bonds: see *bond, federal.*

Federal Credit Union (FCU): a cooperative association organized under the Federal Credit Union Act for the purpose of accepting savings from people, making loans to them at low interest rates, and rendering other financial services to members.

federal debt limit: a limit imposed by law on the aggregate face amount of outstanding obligations issued, or guaranteed as to principal and interest, by the United States; guaranteed obligations held by the secretary of the Treasury are exempted.

federal deficit: a public or federal debt; the difference that exists between revenue and government expenditures.

Federal Deposit Insurance Corporation (FDIC): a government corporation that insures the deposits of all banks that are entitled to the benefits of insurance under the Federal Reserve Act. The FDIC was created through the Banking Act of 1933 and was affected by amendments of 1935. All national banks and all state banks that are members of the Federal Reserve System are required by law to be members of the FDIC. Mutual savings bank are also encouraged to join.

federal discount rate: the interest rate charged on federal funds. The interest is charged on a discount basis and is a key factor in determining the prime rate charged for commercial loans.

Federal Financing Bank (FFB): established by the Federal Financing Bank Act of 1973 to consolidate and reduce the cost of financing a variety of federal agencies and other borrowers whose obligations are guaranteed by the federal government. The FFB is authorized to purchase any obligation that is issued, sold, or guaranteed by a federal agency.

federal government securities: all obligations of the U.S. government. see *Treasury bill, Treasury note.*

Federal Home Bank: one of 11 regional banks established in 1932 to encourage local thrift and home financing during the Depression. The banks are owned jointly by various savings and loan associations. The Federal Home Loan Bank Board serves as a management body.

Federal Home Loan Bank Consolidated Discount Notes: a new (first issue short-term investment which is sold in minimum denominations of $100,000 with 30–270-day maturities to be fixed at buyer's discretion. Have no regular offering schedule. Like commercial paper, the difference between discounted purchasing price and 100 at maturity reflects the interest received. They are not guaranteed by the U.S. government.

Federal Home Loan Mortgage Corporation (FHLMC) (Freddie Mac): established in 1970, responsible for aiding the secondary residential mortgages sponsored by the Veterans Administration and Federal Housing Administration in addition to nongovernment protected residential mortgages.

Federal Housing Administration (FHA): the government agency that carries out the provisions of the National Housing Act, approved in June 1934. The FHA promotes the ownership of homes and also the renovation and remodeling of residences through government guaranteed loans to home owners.

Federal Housing Administration mortgage: a mortgage made in conformity with requirements of the National Housing Act and insured by the Federal Housing Administration.

Federal Housing FHA Insured Loans: insured mortgages from private lending institutions to stimulate homeownership and rental opportunities to American families. Applicants who wish to participate in a single-family mortgage insurance program must apply to a HUD-approved mortgage lender, who then applies to HUD. Interest rates are set by the FHA on these loans.

Federal Loan Bank: one of 12 district banks, originally established in 1916, to make available long-term mortgage loans, at equitable terms, to farmers to enable them to own their own farms. The Federal Loan Bank System is the largest holder of farm mortgages in the world.

Federal National Mortgage Association (FNMA): an independent agency, originally chartered in 1938 and reconstituted in 1954. Its major function is to purchase mortgages from banks, trust companies, mortgage companies, savings and loan associations, and insurance companies to help these institutions with their distribution of funds for home mortgages. Nicknamed *Fannie Mae.*

Federal Open Market Committee (FOMC): the Federal Reserve System's most important policy-making group, with responsibility for creating policy for the system's purchase and sale of government and other securities in the open market.

Federal Reserve Act: legislation signed by President Wilson on December 23, 1913, establishing the Federal Reserve System to manage the nation's money supply.

Federal Reserve agent: chairman of the board of a Federal Reserve District Bank (a Class "C" director) who is responsible for maintaining the collateral for all Federal Reserve notes held within his bank.

Federal Reserve Bank: one of 12 banks created by and operating under the Federal Reserve System. Each Federal Reserve Bank has nine directors.

Federal Reserve Bank account: as mandated by Federal Reserve regulations, the account kept by all member banks and clearing member banks with a Federal Reserve Bank in its district. It shows the cash balance due from a Reserve Bank to guarantee that the member bank has sufficient legal reserves on hand.

Federal Reserve Bank collections account: shows the sum of monies for out-of-town checks distributed for collection by a Federal Reserve check collection system that are not presently available in reserve but being collected.

Federal Reserve bank float: Federal Reserve Bank credit on uncollected deposits.

Federal Reserve bank note: U.S. paper money released prior to 1935 by

Federal Reserve Banks and secured by U.S. bonds and Treasury notes authorized to be used for that purpose. These notes have been retired from circulation.

Federal Reserve Board: the seven-member governing body of the Federal Reserve System; the governors are appointed by the President, subject to Senate confirmation, for 14-year terms. Created in 1913 to regulate all national banks and state-chartered banks that are members of the Federal Reserve System, the board possesses jurisdiction over bank holding companies and also sets national money and credit policy.

Federal Reserve Bulletin: a monthly journal issued by the Board of Governors of the Federal Reserve System dealing with issues in banking and finance.

Federal Reserve Chart Book: a monthly and semiannual publication of the Board of Governors of the Federal Reserve System, presenting charts of interest to the financial community.

Federal Reserve check collection system: the system, established in 1916, by which the Fed accepts out-of-town checks from the banks at which they were deposited or cashed, routes the checks to drawees, and credits the sending bank. It handles over 60 million checks each business day.

Federal Reserve credit: the sum of the Federal Reserve credit as measured by the supply that its banks have given to member bank reserves. It is composed primarily of earning assets of the Federal Reserve Banks.

Federal Reserve currency: paper money issued by the Federal Reserve Banks that circulates as a legal medium of exchange and is legal tender.

Federal Reserve discount rate: the interest rate charged on funds that member banks borrow directly from any Federal Reserve District Bank. The rate, set by the Federal Reserve Board, changes based on their desirability to affect the expansion of credit and money.

Federal Reserve notes: when certain areas require large volumes of currency, or in seasons of the year when the public demand for currency is very heavy, Federal Reserve Banks have the power under the Federal Reserve Act to issue notes. When the need for currency relaxes, Federal Reserve Banks retire these notes. Federal Reserve notes are issued to member banks through their respective Federal Reserve Banks in denominations of $1, $5, $10, $20, $50, $100, $500, $1000, $5000, and $10,000. Federal Reserve notes answer the need for an elastic currency with full legal tender status.

Federal Reserve notes of other banks: the total amount of Federal Reserve notes held by Reserve Banks other than the Reserve Bank that issued them.

Federal Reserve Open Market Committee: a committee of the Federal Reserve System that has complete charge of open market operations, through which the Fed influences the growth of the nation's money supply. It includes the members of the Board of Governors of the Federal Reserve System and five representatives of the 12 Federal Reserve Banks.

Federal Reserve requirements: the amount of money that member banks of the Federal Reserve system must hold in cash or on deposit with a Federal Reserve Bank, in order to back up their outstanding loans. The requirement is expressed as a percentage of outstanding loan volume.

Federal Reserve System: the title given to the central banking system of the United States as established by the Federal Reserve Act of 1913. The system regulates money supply, determines the legal reserve of member banks; oversees the mint, effects transfers of funds, promotes and facilitates the clearance and collection of checks, examines member banks, and discharges other functions. The Federal Reserve System consists of 12 Federal Reserve Banks, their 24 branches, and the national and state banks that are members of the system. All national banks are stockholding members of the Federal Reserve Bank of their district. Membership for state banks or trust companies is optional. see *Federal Reserve Board.* slang, *The Fed.*

Federation International. des Bourses de Valeurs (FIBV): headquartered in Paris, the International Federation of Stock Exchanges. The organization develops policies that allow international financial investing. Worldwide stock exchanges belong to the *FIBV.*

Fed Funds Bill: see *Cash Management Bill.*

fed funds rate: the rate of interest payable on federal funds; considered the key short-term interest rate because it indicates the intentions of the government.

Fed intervention hour: the period when the Fed typically enters the market to conduct its various open market operations, usually shortly before noon Eastern time.

Fed open-market operations: the Fed increases the supply of bank reserves by buying U.S. government securities, and reduces reserves by selling them. Temporary reserve injections are made through repurchase agreements (RPs), while temporary draining is accomplished through matched sale-purchase agreements (reverse RPs). Traders and analysts analyze these operations to determine whether the Fed is making reserves more or less plentiful, resulting in lower or higher interest rates.

fee

(1) an inheritable estate in land.

(2) a remuneration for services.

(3) in an auction, a buyers' premium; the fee added to the winning bid price of an item, usually 10 percent at leading auction houses. The sellers' commission consists of a standard fee at auction houses of 10 percent of the final bid for amounts more than $3000, 15 percent for items sold for $3000 or less. The fee

is negotiable on important consignments.

feeding the ducks: selling off positions as stocks climb.

fee ownership: all of the mineral ownership, both the mineral (royalty) and working interest, are owned by the same party.

fees and royalties from direct investments: reported by companies with direct investments abroad. They represent income received by U.S. parent companies from their foreign affiliates for patent royalties, licensing fees, rentals, management services, other home office charges, and research and development.

feverish market: a condition of a stock or commodity market where prices change rapidly and no direction is easily identified.

FF&C: see *full faith and credit.*

FFB: see *Federal Financing Bank.*

FHA: see *Federal Housing Administration.*

FHB: see *Federal Home Bank.*

FHLMC: see *Federal Home Loan Mortgage Corporation.*

FIBV: see *Federation International des Bourses de Valeurs.*

fictitious credit: a credit balance in a securities margin account representing the proceeds from a short sale and the margin requirement under Regulation T of the Federal Reserve Board.

fiduciary: an individual, corporation, or association, such as a bank, to whom certain property is given to hold in trust, according to an applicable trust agreement. The property is to be utilized or invested for the benefit of the property owner to the best ability of the fiduciary. Administrators and executors of estates, and trustees of organizations, are common examples of fiduciaries. Investments of trust funds, are usually restricted by law.

fiduciary loan: an unsecured loan.

field extension: synonymous with *controlled wildcat drilling.*

FIFO (first in, first out): a method of computing dividends or interest and the effect withdrawals have on the earnings for the period. The FIFO method is considered to be using the oldest money on deposit for withdrawals during the interest period. It was originally designed to discourage withdrawals by exacting the maximum penalty.

fill

(1) ***general:*** to complete an order for goods or services.

(2) ***investments:*** to satisfy the demand for a security at a specific time by selling an amount equivalent to the quantity of shares bid for at the highest quoted price. see *hit the bid.*

fill order: an order that must be filled immediately (or cancelled).

finance

(1) ***general:*** to raise money by sale of stock, bonds, or notes.

(2) ***general:*** describes the theory and practice of monetary credit, banking, and comprehensive promotion methods. This theory covers in-

vestment, speculation, credits, and securities.
(3) ***government:*** to raise money by taxation or bond issue, and to administer revenue and expenditures in a governmental organization. More recently, this activity has become known as *public finance.*

finance and control: planning, directing, and measuring the result of a firm's monetary activities.

finance bill: any draft drawn by one bank on a foreign bank against securities retained by the overseas institution.

finance company: any institution other than a bank that makes loans to businesses or individuals.

Financial Accounting Standards Board (FASB): an independent accounting organization formed in 1973, responsible for creating "generally accepted accounting principles." FASB is a self-regulatory organization whose impact is on accounting firms and practitioners.

Financial Accounting Standards No. 8: see *FASB8.*

Financial and Operational Combined Uniform Single report (FOCUS report): a report filed by broker-dealers each month and each quarter with self-regulatory organizations, such as exchanges, securities associations, clearinghouses.

financial expense: the interest expense on long-term debts.

financial flexibility: the ability of an enterprise to take effective actions to alter the amount and timing of future cash flows so that it can respond to unexpected needs and opportunities.

financial futures: contracts traded on financial instruments that will be delivered in the future. These contracts state the price, interest rate, terms, and date of delivery.

financial guaranty: a bond the insurer guarantees that it will pay a fixed or determinable sum of money.

financial insolvency: a situation created when a company is unable to pay its debts as they mature even though its assets may exceed the liabilities.

financial institution: an institution that uses its funds chiefly to purchase financial assets (deposits, loans, bonds) as opposed to tangible property. Financial institutions can be classified according to the nature of the principal claims they issue: nondeposit intermediaries include, among others, life and property/casualty insurance companies and pension funds, whose claims are the policies they sell, or the promise to provide income after retirement; depositary intermediaries obtain funds mainly by accepting deposits from the public.

Financial Institutions Regulatory and Interest Rate Control Act: federal legislation of 1978; modified authority to invest in state housing corporation obligations; increased Federal Savings and Loan Insurance Corporation insurance limits for IRA and Keogh accounts from $40,000 to $100,000; permitted FSLIC to issue cease-and-desist orders against associations, directors, officers, employees, and agents; authorized cease-and-desist orders against associations, holding companies, their subsidiaries, and service corporations; expanded criteria for removal of a director interlocks among depository institutions; created interagency Federal Bank Examination Council to encourage uniformity in financial institutions supervision; authorized Federal Home Loan Mortgage Corporation purchase of secured home improvement loan packages; amended Consumer Credit Protection Act establishing rights and responsibilities for electronic funds transfer; established procedural safeguards for dissemination of financial institution records to federal agencies; extended Regulation Q authority for rate control and rate differential until December 15, 1980.

financial instrument: any written instrument having monetary value or evidencing a monetary transaction.

financial intermediaries: organizations operating in money markets that permit buyers and sellers, borrowers, and lenders, to meet easily.

financial investment: purchasing sound stocks or bonds as contrasted to real investment in a capital asset such as real estate or plant equipment.

financial lease: a long-term, noncancelable lease.

financial leverage: the ability of fixed-charge financing to magnify the effects of profits (losses) on earnings per share.

financial markets: the money and capital markets of the economy. The money markets buy and sell short-term credit instruments. The capital markets buy and sell long-term credit and equity instruments.

financial paper: accommodation paper, that is, a short-term loan not supported by a specific commercial transaction or transfer of goods. cf. *commercial paper, commodity paper.*

financial plan: the pattern of stocks and bonds issued at the time the corporation is organized, or after failure when it is reorganized.

financial planning: determining a person's financial needs and goals to identify short- and long-term financial requirements, investment strategy, insurance needs, and estate planning.

financial principal: a NASD's examination for an individual qualified to prepare and approve a member firm's financial statements and compute net capital requirements.

financial pyramid

(1) the risk structure investors seek in spreading their investments over differing risk vehicles. The largest section of the pyramid contains securities with liquidity and safety, while the tip of the pyramid contains the highest risk securities.

(2) the acquisition of holding company assets through financial leverage.

financial ratios: the relationship that exist between various items appearing in balance sheets and income accounts and occasionally other items. These ratios are used to measure and evaluate the economic condition and operating effectiveness of a firm.

financial risk: in investments, used in contradistinction to interest rate risk and purchasing power risk to refer to the risk of default in performing the obligations of a security.

financial statement: any statement made by an individual, a proprietorship, a partnership, a corporation, an organization, or an association, regarding the financial status of the "legal entity."

financial structure: mix of the firm's total financing sources, both long and short term.

financial supermarkets: a firm offering a wide variety of financial services.

Financial Times (of London): considered by professionals as one of the best English-language newspapers for business and financial news.

financial uncertainty: the probability of financial changes occurring in the company issuing a specific security.

financing statement: the statement, filed by a creditor, giving a record of a security interest or lien on the debtor's assets.

fine metal: the degree of purity of precious metals.

fineness: the degree of purity when speaking of gold or silver coin. United States coin was formerly nine-tenths fine or pure and one-tenth alloy.

finite-life real-estate investment trusts (FREITs): equity-oriented investments that are self-liquidating after 4 to 15 years. The termination date is specified in the documents provided to shareowners when the trust is formed. Share-price fluctuations are less than they are for standard REITs. cf. *Real Estate Investment Trust.*

fireworks: slang, the rapid climb in price for a security or group of securities.

firm

(1) ***general:*** the acceptance of an obligation to perform, deliver, or accept, as "a firm bid," "a firm offer."
(2) ***general:*** any business, corporation, proprietorship, or partnership.
(3) ***law:*** an unincorporated business or a partnership. Unlike a corporation, a firm is not recognized as a separate person apart from those managing it (i.e., it is not an entity).

firm bid (or offer): in over-the-counter markets a number of bids are nominal or informational and can vary with the order size. To guarantee that the bid or offer quoted is for a given size transaction, the inquirer requests a firm quotation that is binding upon acceptance, as distinguished from the informational quotation.

firm commitment

(1) ***underwriting:*** an arrangement where investment bankers make outright purchases from an issuer of stocks to be offered to the public.

(2) ***lending:*** an agreement to make a loan to a borrower within a given time period and, if applicable, on a stated property.

firming of the market: a period when security prices tend to stabilize around a certain level after a downward movement.

firm maintenance excess: an on-going minimum equity requirement of the long market value of margined stocks. Most brokerage houses use a maintenance requirement of 30 percent.

firm market: the price that is either not negotiable or minimally negotiable. see *firm price*.

firm order
(1) ***general:*** a definite order that cannot be canceled. It may be written or verbal.
(2) ***securities:*** an order to purchase or sell for the proprietary account of the broker-dealer firm.
(3) ***securities:*** a buy or sell order not conditional on the client's confirmation.

firm price: the price quoted by a securities dealer that is not negotiable or only slightly negotiable and is quoted for that specific time only. The price may change depending on market conditions.

firm quote: any round-lot bid or offer price of a stock stated by a market maker and not identified as a nominal or subject quote.

first board: the delivery dates for futures as determined by the administration of an exchange.

first call date: the first date stated in the indenture of a corporate or municipal bond contract on which part or all of the bond can be redeemed at a set price.

first in, first out: see *FIFO*.

first lien: a first mortgage.

first mortgage: the mortgage on property that takes precedence over all other mortgages. A first lien. see also *prior lien, underlying mortgage*.

first mortgage bond: see *bond, first mortgage*.

first notice day: the first day on which transferable notices can be issued for delivery in a specified delivery month.

first preferred stock: dividend stocks that are preferred over common stock of the corporation. It ranks ahead of the second preferred issue.

firsts: the top grade of any item.

fiscal agency services: services performed by the Federal Reserve Banks for the U.S. government. These include maintaining accounts for the Treasury Department, paying checks drawn on the Treasury, and selling and redeeming Savings Bonds and other government securities.

fiscal agent: a bank or trust company acting under a corporate trust agreement with a corporation. The bank or trust company may be appointed in the capacity of general treasurer of the corporation, or may be appointed to perform special functions as fiscal agent. The principal duties of a fiscal agent include the disbursement of funds for payment of dividends, redemption of bonds and coupons at maturity, and the payment of rents.

fiscal period: A 12-month accounting period for which business activities are reported.

fiscal policy: a planned course of action on budgetary issues.

fiscal year (FY)
(1) ***general:*** a corporation's accounting year. It can be any 12 consecutive months (e.g., February 1 of one year through January 31 of the next). Most companies operate on a calendar year basis.
(2) ***government:*** the fiscal year of the U.S. government begins October 1.

FIT: federal income tax.

fit: slang, a situation where the features of a specific investment perfectly match the portfolio needs of an investor.

fitch sheets: published by Fitch Investor's Service, sheets showing the successive trade prices of stocks listed on the exchanges.

FITW: federal income tax withholding.

five hundred dollar rule: the Regulation T provision of the Federal Reserve exempting deficiencies in margin requirements amounting to $500 or less from mandatory remedial action. Brokers in this situation are not required to resort to the liquidation of an account to correct a trivial deficiency when, for example, a client is out of town for a few days and cannot be contacted.

five percent rule: the Rule of Fair Practice of the National Association of Securities Dealers proposing an ethical guideline for spreads in dealer transactions and commission in brokerage transactions.

fixation: the setting of a price in the future, as used in commodity call purchase and call sale trades.

fixed annuity: an annuity contract providing payments that remain constant throughout the annuity period. These payments do not vary with investment experience.

fixed assets: permanent assets required for the normal conduct of a business, which normally are not converted into cash during the period after they were declared fixed (e.g., furniture, land, buildings). see *illiquid*.

fixed-balance bonus account: a savings account that pays earnings above the passbook rate if the balance in the account exceeds a specified minimum for a specified term.

fixed capital: capital invested, usually by stock-and bondholders; as distinguished from current assets, which are partly supplied by banks.

fixed-charge coverage: the ratio of profits before payment of interest and income taxes to interest on bonds and other contractual long-term debt, showing how many times interest charges have been earned by the firm on a pretax basis. synonymous with *times fixed charges*.

fixed cost (or expense): a cost or expense, for a fixed period and a range of activity, that does not change in total but becomes progressively smaller per unit as the volume increases. synonymous with *period cost*.

fixed debt: the permanent debt extending over a length of time, such as that represented by bonds.

fixed exchange rate: a concept within the European Monetary System, where all members except Britain maintain fixed exchange rates between their currencies, promoting monetary stability in Europe and throughout the world.

fixed-income market: any debt-bearing instrument, among them U.S. government bonds, tax-exempt bonds, corporate bonds, financial futures, and money market funds.

fixed income security: a preferred stock or debt security with a given percentage or dollar income return.

fixed investment trust: synonymous with *unit trust*.

fixed liabilities: all liabilities that will not mature within the ensuing fiscal period (e.g. mortgages due 20 years hence, bonds outstanding).

fixed obligation: an obligation that is fixed at the time the agreement is made and continues to run during the life of the agreement (e.g., interest on bonds except income or adjustment bonds).

fixed price (FP)
(1) ***securities:*** the lowest sale price of a new issue, below which a purchase cannot be made. This price is usually set by the underwriter of the security.
(2) ***contracts:*** a type of contract where the price is preset and invariable, regardless of the actual production costs.

fixed rate: see *fixed exchange rate*.

fixed-rate mortgage: a home mortgage with a fixed interest rate, usually long term; there are equal monthly payments of principal and interest until the debt is paid in full.

fixed return dividend: a dividend that neither increases nor decreases over time (i.e., preferred stocks).

fixed trust: synonymous with *unit trust*.

fixing the price
(1) ***general:*** establishing a price on something arbitrarily rather than through the free enterprise system.
(2) ***investments:*** computing the price at which a commodity will be billed for rapid delivery. see *spot market*.

flag: a charted stock trend that represents a plateau in prices. cf. *pennant*.

flash: a tape display designation when volume on an exchange is so heavy that the tape runs more than five minutes late. see *flash prices*.

flash prices: a technique used whenever an exchange ticker tape runs late. The latest prices of two groups of 50 stocks are printed at five-minute intervals.

flash reporting
(1) a technique for exchanges when transaction reporting falls six

minutes behind the market activity. In lieu of normal procedures, every five minutes prices of 15 securities are presented. The word *flash* precedes the reports.
(2) a news or financial release giving highlights of a story which will then be followed by a more thorough report.

flat
(1) ***general:*** with no interest.
(2) ***investments:*** a price at which a bond is traded including consideration for all unpaid accruals of interest. Bonds that are in default of interest or principal are traded flat. Income bonds, which pay interest only to the extent earned, are usually traded flat. cf. *loaned flat*.
(3) ***investments:*** the inventory of a market maker with a net zero position, such as neither long, nor short.
(4) ***investments:*** the position of an underwriter whose account is fully sold.

flat bond: see *bond, flat income*.

flat income bond: see *bond, flat income*.

flat market: a market characterized by horizontal price movements, often resulting from limited trading.

flat scale: in municipal bonds, a condition where shorter- and longer-term yields show little difference over the maturity range of a new serial bond issue.

FLB: see *Federal Loan Bank*.

fleece: slang, to take money or property from an unknowing person (the "sheep") by unfair activity. synonymous with *swindle*.

flexible exchange rates: where exchange rates of varying world currencies freely change in reaction to supply and demand conditions, free from governmental maneuvers to hold a fixed rate where one currency is exchanged for another.

flexible loan insurance plan (flip): a new type of mortgage, this device calls for using a portion of the borrower's down payment to set up a savings account. The account is then pledged over to the lender and gradually drawn upon to supplement the low monthly payments made by the borrower during the initial years of the loan. Popularly referred to as *flip*. An example of a *pledged-account mortgage*.

flexible manager: an investment manager who will change the securities in the portfolio, rotating from sectors to sectors, industries to industries, companies to companies, including varying amounts of cash equivalents.

flexible mortgage: see *renegotiable-rate mortgage, rollover mortgage, variable-rate mortgage*.

flexible-payment mortgage: an interest-only type of loan for the first five years. Two major restrictions apply: each monthly payment must cover at least the interest due, and after five years, payments must be fully amortizing. A rarely used mortgage because it offers the home buyer only a slight reduction in monthly payments during the early years. see also *graduated-payment mortgage, pledged-*

account mortgage, reverse-annuity mortgage, rollover mortgage, variable-rate mortgage.

flexible prices: see *sticky prices.*

flier: a speculative purchase of investment, usually made by an individual who does not usually speculate or actively trade in the market.

flight of capital: the movement of capital, which has usually been converted into a liquid asset, from one place to another to avoid loss or to increase gain. see also *flight of the dollar.*

flight of the dollar: purchasing foreign securities with dollar exchange, to escape the adverse impact of inflation, deflation, or other economic condition.

flight to quality: shifting capital to the safest possible investment to protect oneself from loss during an unsettling period in the market.

flip: acronym for *flexible loan insurance plan.*

flip mortgage: a graduate-payment scheme offered in some states.

flip-over provision: a provision to force management to issue new common shares if it proceeds with a takeover. As a strategy to thwart a takeover bid, it purports to dilute control of a corporation by any individual or family.

flipper: an investor who is by turns in and out of a stock for taking a fast profit, usually in a matter of days.

flipping: when professional money managers buy stock in a new issue in the morning and sell it after its first rise, generating considerable amounts of commission dollars. Unsophisticated investors may get caught up in the initial excitement, often of an initial public offering, but wind up holding a position that others are selling off. see also *initial public offering.*

float: the portion of a new security that has not yet been bought by the public. cf. *undigested securities.*

floatation (flotation)
(1) ***general:*** the process of financing a business activity.
(2) ***investments:*** launching an issue of securities. see *float.*

floater: see *floating-rate CD, floating-rate note.* see also *floaters.*

floaters: high-yielding, liquid securities sold mostly by banks and pegged to the going rate on six-month bank deposits (the London Interbank Offered Rate).

floating capital: synonymous with *working capital.*

floating charge: a business loan that is secured on assets rather than on a particular item. The lender has priority of repayment from the fund of assets that exist when a receiving order is made against the firm.

floating currency: one whose value in terms of foreign currency is not kept stable (on the basis of the par value or a fixed relationship to some other currency) but instead is allowed, without a multiplicity of exchange rates, to be determined (entirely or to some degree) by market forces. Even where a currency is floating, the authorities may influence its movements by official intervention; if such intervention is absent or minor, the expression *clean float* is sometimes used.

floating debt: any short-term obligation; usually, the portion of the public debt held in Treasury bills or other short-term obligations.

floating exchange rates: see *floating rates*.

floating-rate bond: see *bond, floating-rate*.

floating-rate CD (FRCD): a certificate of deposit whose coupon is variable and normally linked to the interbank money market rate.

floating-rate note (FRN): used by banks to raise dollars for their Euromarket operations, a mixture of the rollover credit market with the Eurosecurities market.

floating rate preferred security: a preferred stock which has a dividend rate pegged to the Treasury bill rate or another rate and periodically adjusted at some set amount over that rate.

floating rates: the automatic determination of appropriate exchange rates by market forces, not a nation's reserve holdings. Nations that do not follow these rates are pressured into line; otherwise, they would see the value of their currency driven to unacceptably low levels or driven up to the point where no other nation would be able to purchase their goods.

floating securities

(1) securities purchased for speculation and resale, retained in the name of a broker.

(2) stock of a corporation ready for sale on the open market.

(3) new issues of securities that have not been completely purchased.

floating supply

(1) ***securities:*** the number of shares of a stock available for purchase.

(2) ***municipal bonds:*** the overall amount of securities believed to be available for immediate purchase, in the hands of dealers and speculators who wish to sell as distinct from investors who may be willing to sell only for a special reason.

floor

(1) ***government:*** the minimum level determined by regulation, law or contract for wages, prices, and so on.

(2) ***investments:*** the huge trading area where stocks and bonds are bought and sold on an exchange. see also *pit*.

floor broker: a member of a stock exchange who executes orders on the floor of the exchange to buy or sell listed securities.

floor official: a securities exchange employee who settles disputes in the auction procedure on the floor of an exchange. This person makes decisions on the spot and his or her judgment is rarely questioned.

floor partner: a member of a stock exchange and a brokerage firm partner who transacts his or her firm's business on the floor of that exchange.

floor report: confirmation of an executed order on an exchange trading floor, such as price, number of shares, and the name of the security.

floor ticket: a summary of the information entered on the order ticket by a registered representative on receipt of a buy or sell order from a customer. The floor broker is provided with information required to execute a stock transaction.

floor trader: any member of the stock exchange who trades on the floor for his or her own account. An exchange member who executes his or her own trades by being personally present in the pit or place provided for futures trading.

flotation: see *floatation.* synonymous with *competitive trader, registered competitive trader.*

flower bond: see *bond, flower.*

flow of funds: a statement in the bond resolutions of municipal revenue issues listing the priorities by which municipal revenues will be applied.

fluctuation: the ups and downs of prices. see *hedging, yo-yo stocks.*

fluctuation harnessing: applied to the investment formula known as dollar cost averaging because a constant dollar amount is invested at regular intervals, regardless of price.

fluctuation limit: limits on the daily ups and downs of futures prices by the commodity exchanges. Should a commodity reach its limit, it cannot trade any more that day.

fluid savings: savings that have neither been spent nor invested.

flurries: unexpected, short-lived price fluctuations in the trading of securities, usually brought on by news.

FMAN: February, May, August, November (quarterly interest payments or dividends).

FNMA: see *Federal National Mortgage Association.*

FOCUS report: see *Financial and Operational Combined Uniform Single report.*

FOMC: see *Federal Open Market Committee.*

for a turn: a commitment in a stock made with the expectation of gaining a quick, though small profit.

Forbes 500: an annual listing by *Forbes* magazine of the largest U.S. publicly owned corporations ranked by sales, assets, profits, and market value. cf. *Fortune 500.*

for cash

(1) ***general:*** items or services sold for 100 percent of funds.

(2) ***investments:*** a transaction demanding that sold stocks be delivered to the purchaser on the same day.

forced conversion: when a convertible security is called in by its issuer.

forecast

(1) predicting market prices and/or volume patterns utilizing varying analytical data.

(2) estimating future sales, costs, and earnings of a company.

foreclose (foreclosure): a legal process whereby a mortgagor of a property is deprived of his or her interest therein, usually by means of a court-administered sale of the property.

foreign exchange desk: the foreign exchange trading desk at the New York Federal Reserve Bank. The desk undertakes operations in the exchange markets for the account of the Federal Open Market Committee, as agent for the U.S. Treasury and as agent for foreign central banks. see also *desk, the.*

foreign exchange markets: those in which the monies of different countries are exchanged. Foreign exchange holdings—sometimes referred to as foreign exchange—are holdings of current or liquid claims denominatea in the currency of another country.

foreign exchange rate: the price of one currency in terms of another.

foreign exchange risk: the risk of suffering losses because of adverse movement in exchange rates.

foreign exchange speculation: the act of taking a net position in a foreign currency with the intention of making a profit from exchange rate changes.

foreign exchange trading: the buying and selling of foreign currencies in relation to either U.S. dollars or other foreign currencies.

foreign exchange transactions: the purchase or sale of one currency with another. Foreign exchanges rates refer to the number of units of one currency needed to purchase one unit of another, or the value of one currency in terms of another.

Foreign Investors Tax Act: federal legislation of 1966 establishing a tax ceiling (30 percent) for overseas investors in U.S. securities, the purpose of which is to stimulate foreign investment in the United States and aid in lowering the deficit in the U.S. international account.

foreign securities

(1) the investment in the securities issued by a company incorporated outside of the United States and which generates a major portion of its business outside the United States.

(2) securities issued by governments other than the U.S. government.

forex: short, for foreign exchange.

form 8-K: the SEC form that a publicly held corporation is required to file, indicating any significant happening that might alter its financial situation or the value of its shares.

form 4: the SEC form used for reporting changes in the holdings of those who own at least 10 percent of a firm's outstanding stock and directors and officers, even those not owning stock in the company.

form S-16: see *registered secondary offering.*

form 10-K: an annual report that all corporations having securities registered with the SEC are required to release and provide to the public.

form 10-Q: the SEC requirement for filing of a quarterly report for all firms with listed stocks.

form 3: the SEC form required from all holders of 10 percent or more of a firm's stock registered with the commission, providing information on number of shares owned, rights, and so on.

formula investing: an investment technique. One formula calls for the shifting of funds from common shares to preferred shares or bonds as the market, on average, rises above a certain predetermined point—and the return of funds to common share investments as the market average declines. see *dollar (cost) averaging.*

Fortune 500: *Fortune* magazine's annual listing of the 500 largest U.S. industrial corporations, ranked by sales. see also *Forbes 500.*

forward: a financial instrument, such as a mortgage-backed security (i.e., a Ginnie Mae), sold for future delivery in violation of securities laws.

forward buying: the buying of an actual or spot commodity where delivery is for the future rather than as a current delivery.

forward commitment: an investor's agreement to make or purchase a mortgage loan on a specified future date.

forward contract: a cash market transaction in which two parties agree to the purchase and sale of a commodity at some future time under such conditions as the two agree. The terms of forward contracts are not standardized, is not transferable, and usually can be canceled only with the consent of the other party, which often must be obtained for consideration and under penalty. Forward contracts are not traded in federally designated contract markets.

forward cover: an arrangement of a forward foreign exchange contract to protect a foreign currency buyer or seller from unexpected exchange rate fluctuations.

forward deal: an operation consisting of purchasing or selling foreign currencies with settlement to be made at a future date.

forward delivery: synonymous with *deferred delivery.*

forward exchange: a foreign bill of exchange purchased or sold at a stated price that is payable at a given date.

forward exchange rate: the price of foreign currency for delivery at a future date agreed to by a contract today.

forward exchange transaction: a purchase or sale of foreign currency for future delivery. Standard periods for forward contracts are one, three, and six months.

forward-forward: a deal for a future date in an instrument maturing on a further forward date; the instrument is usually a certificate of deposit and the object may be to extend the term of the deal.

forward interest rate: the prevailing interest rate for a contract in a specific future, "forward," time period.

forward margin: the margin between today's price of a currency and the price at a future date.

forward market: the claim to sell or purchase securities, foreign currencies, and so on, at a fixed price at a given future date. This market is one that deals in futures.

forward movement: the rising tendency in the price of a security or commodity or an average.

forward pricing: a requirement that open-end investment firms, whose share price is always set by the net asset value of the outstanding shares, base all incoming buy and sell orders on the next net asset valuation of fund shares.

forward rate: see *forward exchange rate.*

forward selling: indicates when commodity trading investors sell at present market prices for delivery in the future while anticipating lower price movements.

foundation: any non-profit private organization with a tax-free status from the IRS that receives and distributes funds for charitable and other approved causes.

founders' shares: see *founder's stock.*

founder's stock: stock given to the developers of founders of a new corporation for services rendered by them.

fourth market: the buying and selling of unlisted securities directly between investors.

401 (K) plan: synonymous with *salary reduction plan.*

FP: see *fixed price.*

FPS: see *first preferred stock.*

FRA: see *Federal Reserve Act.*

fraction: generally applied to holdings of less than one share, resulting from rights and stock dividends. Because they are not entitled to dividends, they are usually disposed of by sale or rounded out, by the purchase of additional fractions, to full shares.

fractional discretion order: a buy or sell order for securities permitting the broker discretion within a stated fraction of a point.

fractional lot: less than a round lot. see *fraction.*

fractional share: a unit of stock less than one full share.

FRB: see *Federal Reserve Bank.*

FRCD: see *floating-rate CD.*

Freddie Mac: see *Federal Home Loan Mortgage Corporation.*

free and clear: any ownership of property that is free of all indebtedness. Property that never had a mortgage encumbering it, or in which the mortgage has been paid in full.

free bond: see *bond, free.*

free box: slang, a secure storage plan for fully paid stocks of a client, such as a bank vault.

free credit balance: cash retained by a broker in a client's account that can be withdrawn by the client at any time.

free crowd: see *active bond crowd.*

freed up: slang, for members of an underwriting syndicate no longer bound by the price agreed upon and fixed in the agreement among underwriters.

free riding
(1) prohibited by law, the buying and rapid sale of securities, where no personal funds are given for the original purchase.
(2) the withholdings by brokerage firms of new stocks that are expected to climb higher than the initial public offering. Prohibited by the SEC.

free right of exchange: an ability for transferring stocks from one name to another without paying a charge associated with a sales transaction.

free supply: in the commodities industry where total stocks are less than what is owned or controlled by the government.

free surplus: that portion of retained earnings available for common stock dividends, that is, after deducting any amounts appropriated or legally restricted by reason of such items as preferred stock dividends in arrears, the repurchase of treasury stock, or loan agreements calling for a minimum cash balance or a minimum liability ratio. Dividends payable in common stock are a general exception to most restrictions on dividends arising from loan agreements.

free wheeling: when a stock makes new highs after having successfully penetrated a resistance area.

FREITs: see *finite-life real-estate investment trusts.*

FRN: see *floating-rate note.*

front-end commission: see *front-end load.*

front-ending an order: block orders where the broker-dealer agrees to purchase a portion of a block with the provision that he or she will execute the remainder of the order as the agent.

front-end load: a sales charge on some mutual funds at the start of the contract to buy shares, usually from 6 to 8 percent.

front running: the illegal practice where an option client acts on information not yet transmitted on the exchange tape where the underlying security is traded.

frozen account
(1) ***general:*** an account on which payments have been suspended until a court order or legal process again makes the account available for withdrawal. The account of a deceased person is frozen pending the distribution by a court order grant to the new lawful owners of the account.
(2) ***general:*** where a dispute has arisen regarding the true ownership of an account, it is frozen to preserve the existing assets until legal action can determine the lawful owners of the asset.
(3) ***investments:*** a brokerage account under disciplinary action by

the Federal Reserve Board for violation of Regulation T. During this period an account is frozen for 90 days and the customer cannot sell stocks until their purchase price has been completely paid and certificates have been delivered.

FRS: see *Federal Reserve System.*

FS
(1) see *financial statement.*
(2) see *futures spread.*

full: when a bond trades with accrued interest. A seller receives and the purchaser pays all accrued interest from last payment date up to but not including settlement date. cf. *flat.*

full-bodied money: gold; currency that is worth its face value as a commodity.

full coupon bond: see *bond, full coupon.*

full disclosure: as described by the Securities Exchange Act of 1934; every company that has securities listed on an exchange must register with the SEC and file annual and other reports disclosing financial and other data for the information of the investing public. Management must also disclose basic financial information used in stockholder's meetings.

full faith and credit: a pledge of the general taxing power for the payment of obligations.

full faith and credit bond: see *bond, full faith and credit.*

full lot: synonymous with *round lot.* cf. *odd-lot orders.*

full-paid stock: see *capital stock.*

full-service broker: a broker able to provide a wide variety of services to customers.

full service fund: a mutual fund that permits stockholders to have their capital gains and dividends automatically reinvested in more shares of that fund.

full stock: an equity stock with a par value of $100. see also *capital stock.*

full trading authorization: an approval for a person other than the brokerage client to have trading authority in the client's account.

fully diluted earnings per (common) share: indicating earnings per common share after assuming the exercise of warrants and stock options, and conversion of convertible bonds and preferred stocks.

fully distributed: any new securities issue having been completely resold to the investing public.

fully invested: when an investor, either institutional or individual, has all or nearly all available cash invested and thereby cannot make further investments unless some present investment is liquidated.

fully managed funds: mutual funds and/or other investment firms permitted by their charter to invest in more than one specific type of investments. synonymous with *general management investment company.*

fully modified pass-through: see *participation certificate.*

fully paid stocks: legal issues where the corporation has received at least the equivalent of its par value in goods, services, or currency.

fully registered: generally applied to bonds that are registered as to principal and income. In this form, a bond is not negotiable and interest is remitted by the disbursing agent to the registered owners.

fully valued: a stock having attained a price at which analysts believe the underlying firm's fundamental earnings power has been seen by the market. Should the price of the stock rise, it is referred to as being *overvalued;* stock declines, it is termed *undervalued.*

fund

(1) an asset of any organization set aside for a particular purpose. Not to be confused with general fund. see *sinking fund.*

(2) cash, securities, or other assets placed in the hands of a trustee or administrator to be expanded as defined by a formal agreement.

(3) any investment company.

(4) see also *mutual fund.*

fundamental analysis: an analysis based on factors, such as sales, earnings, and assets that are "fundamental" to the enterprise. The usefulness of fundamental analysis is challenged by the semi-strong form of the efficient market hypothesis which holds that the analysis of publicly available fundamental information cannot improve an investor's rate of return. cf. *efficient market hypothesis, technical analysis.*

fundamentalist: an individual who believes that the best investment results are obtained by studying the record of a firm and its industry, and the economy in general, as distinct from examining investment cycles.

fundamental product: offering to the market that is immediately recognized as what is being sold, such as a savings account.

fundamentals: a Wall Street school of thought that purports to predict stock market behavior by examining the vital statistics of a stock, the firm's management, earnings, and so on.

fund balance: the excess of the assets of a fund over its liabilities and reserves except in the case of funds subject to budgetary accounting where, prior to the end of a fiscal period, it represents the excess of the fund's assets and estimated revenues for the period over its liabilities, reserves, and appropriations for the period.

funded debt

(1) ***general:*** exists when the method of paying off the debt and its interest is determined for specific periods.

(2) ***investments:*** usually, interest-bearing bonds of debentures of a company; may include long-term bank loans but does not include short loans or preferred or common stock.

funded debts to net working capital: funded debts are all long-term obligations, as represented by mortgages, bonds, debentures, term loans, serial notes, and other types of liabilities maturing more than one year from the statement date. This ratio is obtained by dividing funded debt by net working capital. Analysts tend to compare funded debts with net working capital in determining whether or not long-term debts are in proper proportion. Ordinarily, this relationship should not exceed 100 percent.

funded debt unmatured: unmatured debt (other than equipment obligations), maturing more than one year from date of issue.

funded deficit: a deficit eliminated through the sale of bonds issued for that purpose. see also *bond fund.*

funded reserve: a reserve invested in earmarked interest-bearing securities.

fund group: a group of funds which are similar in purpose and character. For example, several special revenue funds constitute a fund group.

funding: the gathering together of outstanding debts of a business, leading to a reissuing of new bonds or obligations for the purpose of paying off debts.

funding bond: see *bond, funding.*

funds: a sum of money or stock convertible to money, assets.

funds, corporate: a general funds mix of industrial and utility issues of varying maturities. Typically, about half the securities mature in more than 20 years. High-yield funds have less than 20 years maturity periods.

funds, government: the U.S. government has a large selection of load and no-load funds of high quality.

funds, municipal: most big fund sponsors have muncipal bond funds, some general funds with securities of good grade, and some "high-yield" filled with speculative issues.

funds management: the continual arrangement and rearrangement of a bank's balance sheet in an attempt to maximize profits, subject to having sufficient liquidity and making safe investments.

funds to acquire under-performing properties: synonymous with *vulture funds.*

fund surplus: see *fund balance.*

fund switching: synonymous with *conversion (4).*

fungibles: bearer instruments, stocks, or goods that are equivalent, substitutable, and interchangeable, such as soybeans, wheat, common shares of the same firm, and dollar bills.

funny money: convertible preferred stocks, convertible bonds, options, and warrants that appear to have characteristics of common stock equity but which did not reduce reported earnings per share before 1969.

furthest month: in commodities or option trading, the month that is furthest away from settlement of the contract.

future exchange contract: a contract for the purchase or sale of foreign exchange to be delivered at a future date and at a rate determined in the present.

futures

(1) ***general:*** foreign currencies bought or sold based on a rate that is quoted as of some future date.

(2) ***investments:*** contracts for the sale and delivery of commodities at some future time, made with the expectation that no commodity will be received immediately. see *gray market, hedging, Tax Reform Act of 1976.*

futures call: the sale of commodities where delivery is made upon the request of the seller on any trading date for a specified month.

futures commission broker: a firm or party engaged in soliciting or accepting and handling orders for the purchase or sale of any commodity for future delivery on or subject to the rules of any contract market and who, in or in connection with such solicitations or acceptance of orders, accepts any money, securities, or property (or extends credit in lieu thereof) to margin any trades or contracts that result therefrom. They must be licensed under the Commodity Exchange Act when handling business in commodities covered thereby.

futures commission merchant: see *futures commission broker.*

futures contract: the right to buy or sell a commodity at a specified price on a specified future date. The price is established when the contract is made in open auction on a futures exchange.

futures exchange: an organization created for the trading of commodity futures.

futures market: any commodity exchange trading in futures.

futures spread: the simultaneous purchase and sale of contracts in either the same or different commodities. In the case where one commodity is involved, the contracts must be in different delivery months. The aim of a futures spread is to take advantage of the difference, or spread, in the prices of two future contracts that have some direct economic relation to each other. A trader buys one contract, and sells the other short—sells it without owning it—in the hope that one part will move more than the other. see *spread, straddle.*

future value of the dollar: the amount by which $1 grows at a given rate of interest if compounded for a specified number of periods.

future worth: the equivalent value at a future date on time value of money.

FV: see *face value.*

F/X: foreign exchange.

FY: see *fiscal year.*

G

G
(1) gold
(2) dividends and earnings in Canadian Dollars (in stock listings of newspapers).

GA: see *general account.*

GAAP: generally accepted accounting principles. see *Financial Accounting Standards Board.*

GAAS: generally accepted auditing standards.

GAI: guaranteed annual income.

gain: any benefit, profit, or advantage, as opposed to a loss.

gain on disposal: the sale of a noncurrent asset for more than book value.

gambling: in securities, the random buying and selling of these items without intelligently investigating prospects.

gap
(1) ***general:*** the amount of financing need for which a provision has to be made. Financing is usually made available from state and local governments interested in promoting economic development.
(2) ***securities:*** the price movement of a security or commodity when one day's trading range for a stock or commodity fails to overlap the following day's, creating a range, or gap in which no trade has taken place.

garage, the: slang, the annex to the New York Stock Exchange trading floor where Post 30, for inactive stocks, and six of the other 18 trading posts are lodged.

Garnet St Germain Depository Institutions Act of 1982: instructs the Depository Institutions Deregulation Committee to authorize money market deposit accounts (MMDAs), requiring that the account be "directly equivalent to and competitive with money market mutual funds." In addition, it specified that the account have no minimum maturity and that it allowed up to three preauthorized or automatic transfers and three transfers to third parties (checks) per month.

gather in the stops: synonymous with *uncover the stops*. see *snowballing*.

GB: see *bond, guaranteed*.

GD
(1) see *good delivery*.
(2) see *gross debt*.

gearing: in Great Britain, the relationship between equity capital and fixed interest capital. synonymous with *leverage* in United States.

general account (GA)
(1) ***general:*** an account appearing in a bank's general ledger; all accounts other than those of depositors and depositories.
(2) ***investments:*** a Federal Reserve Board term for brokerage customer margin accounts that are subject to Regulation T, covering extension of credit by brokers for the purchase and short sale of stocks. All transactions in which a broker advances credit to a client must be made in this account.

general bonded debt: the outstanding bonded indebtedness of a governmental unit with the exception of utility and special assessment bonds.

general indorsement: synonymous with *blank indorsement*.

generalists: stocks trading at more than $100 a share. The name is derived from the General Electric Company. Its stock used to trade above the century mark.

general ledger
(1) the most important bank record. Every transaction that takes place in the bank during the business day is reflected through various departmental subsidiary records to the general ledger.
(2) the formal ledger showing all the financial statement accounts of a business venture.

general loan and collateral agreement: synonymous with *broker's loan*.

general long-term debt: a long-term debt legally payable from general revenues and backed by the full faith and credit of a governmental unit. see *long-term debt*.

generally accepted accounting principles: see *Financial Accounting Standards Board*.

general management investment company: synonymous with *fully managed fund*.

general management trust: a trust that is not limited to any particular stock in which to invest.

general mortgage: a mortgage covering all properties of a debtor and not restricted to one parcel.

general mortgage bond: see *bond, general mortgage*.

general obligation bond: see *bond, general obligation*.

general obligations (GO): long-term borrowings that are backed by the full faith, credit, and taxing powers of the issuing locality rather than income generated by a specific project.

general partner: a partner who, along with others, is liable for the partnership debts.

general partnership: an unincorporated business firm formed by at least two people where each partner shares in the profits and has unlimited liability.

gen-saki: a Japanese short-term money market; a market for conditional bond sales. A market where securities firms sell or buy bonds, usually for two or three months, while simultaneously including an agreement to repurchase them.

GICs
(1) see *guaranteed income contracts.*
(2) see *guaranteed investment contracts.*

Gifts to Minors Act: state regulations which permit an adult to serve as custodian of an investment account for a minor without a court appointment. Monies and purchases of securities are considered gifts and cannot be rescinded. All purchases, sales, dividends, and interest are made in the name of the minor.

gilt-edged: high grade stocks issued by corporations having a known record for profit and payment of dividends and interest over the years.

gilt-edged bond: see *bond, gilt-edged.*

Ginnie Mae: see *Government National Mortgage Association (GNMA).*

Ginnie Mae pass-through securities: under this program, principal and interest payments collected on mortgages in specified pools are "passed through" to holders of GNMA-guaranteed certificates after deduction of servicing and guaranty fees. Actual maturity of these certificates is 40 years, but the average life is approximately 12 years because of prepayments. The minimum denomination of certificates is $25,000 and issuance is in registered form only.

Ginnie Mae trusts: closed-end unit investment trusts made up of Ginnie Mae certificates. The cost is $1000 per unit with a sales charge of around 4 percent. The monthly payments cover earned interest and amortization—the same as having direct participation in Ginnie Mae certificates, which are available only in the larger denominations. see *Government National Mortgage Association.*

Ginnie Mae II: started in July 1983, similar to the original Ginnie Mae with other advantages. Lets originators join together to issue jumbo pools, which combine mortgages from different issuers into a single package, as well as continue to be sole issuers. There is only one central paying agent, the Chemical Bank, leading to greater efficiency in payments and transfers. Holders of Ginnie Mae II are paid on the twenty-fifth day of the month, in contrast to the fifteenth day of the month for the original Ginnie Mae; thereby the 10-day delay lowers the yield on the securities by about five points. see also *Ginnie Mae trusts.*

Giscards: French government-backed bonds formerly known as Pinay bonds. Backed by the gold Napoleon, which trades at a premium to its gold content, and for the French people, the proposed capital gains tax would not apply to bonds.

give an indication: expressing an interest in a new security issue by entering a firm buy order for a stated amount.

give an order: directing a broker to purchase or sell a security in a certain amount which may include specifications of a price or time limit.

give-out order: in securities and commodities, an order to a broker given out by him or her to a specialist for execution.

give-up: occurs when a member of a stock exchange on the floor acts for a second member by executing an order for him or her with a third member. see *two-dollar brokers.*

give-up order: securities not accepted for direct sale by a participating underwriter.

GL: see *go long.*

glamour stock
(1) ***general:*** any popular security.
(2) ***investments:*** a successful security that attracts a substantial following and whose price rises on a continuous basis.

Glass-Steagall Act of 1933: a legislative safeguard designed to prevent commercial banks from engaging in investment banking activities; also authorized deposit insurance. In recent years, attempts have been made to change this act. After a long period of contentment with the restrictions, the banking industry, especially the American Bankers Association, has begun to test the limitations on several fronts, including commercial paper, commingled accounts, money market funds, municipal revenue bonds. see *bond, municipal revenue, commercial paper, commingled accounts, money market fund.*

glut: to oversupply (e.g., a glut of oil on the market).

GmbH: Gesellschaft mit beschränkter Haftung (West German limited liability company).

GNMA: see *Government National Mortgage Association.*

GNMA certificate unit trusts: backed by government-guaranteed mortgages. Maturities of 12 years or less. Big brokerage houses sweep monthly checks for interest and returned principal from mortgage amortization into a market-rate money fund. Requires periodic reinvestment decision.

GNMA mortgage-backed securities: securities guaranteed by GNMA and issued primarily by mortgage bankers (but also by others approved by GNMA). The GNMA security is pass-through in nature, and the holder is protected by the "full faith and credit of the U.S. government." It is collateralized by FHA or VA mortgages.

gnomes: financial and banking people involved in foreign exchange speculation. The term was coined by Great Britain's Labour ministers during the 1964 sterling crisis.

GO
(1) see *general obligations.*

(2) see *government obligations.*

go around: a means whereby the trading desk at the New York Federal Reserve Bank, acting on behalf of the Federal Open Market Committee, contacts primary dealers for bid and offer prices.

go-go fund: an investment purporting to acquire sizable earnings in a short time period, resulting in risky, speculative market activity.

going ahead: when a broker decides to make a trade for his or her own account, fair practice requires that he or she fill all his or her customer's orders first. A dishonest broker will "go ahead" (i.e., transact his or her own business first).

going away
(1) ***bonds:*** bonds bought for dealers for immediate resale to investors.
(2) ***bonds:*** for new offerings of serial bonds, large purchases, usually by institutional investors, of the bonds in a particular maturity grouping.

going business: any business that over a period of years has been profitable, properly managed, and financially responsible, and holds prospects for continued prosperity.

going-concern value: the value of a firm as an operating business to another firm or individual.

going long: buying a security, bond, or commodity for investment or speculation.

going private: the shift from public ownership to private ownership of a firm's shares either by the firm's repurchase of shares or through purchases by outside private investors.

going public: describes a situation when a firm's shares become available on a major exchange, as distinguished from being held by a few shareholders.

going short: selling a stock or commodity short.

gold bas: see *bullion.*

gold bond: see *bond, gold.*

gold brick: slang, worthless, and often fraudulent, securities that initially appear sound and worthy.

goldbug: an analyst fascinated by gold as an investment.

gold bullion standard: a monetary standard according to which (a) the national unit of currency is defined in terms of a stated gold weight, (b) gold is retained by the government in bars rather than coin, (c) there is no circulation of gold within the economy, and (d) gold is made available for purposes of industry and for international transactions of banks and treasuries.

gold certificate: any legal tender backed by gold and readily converted into gold on demand. Most world currencies today are backed by the full faith and credit of the issuing nation rather than by gold.

gold certificate account: gold certificates on hand and due from the Treasury. The certificates, on hand and due from the Treasury, are backed 100 percent by gold owned by the U.S. government. They count as legal reserve, the minimum the Reserve Banks are required to maintain being 25 percent of their combined Federal Reserve note and deposit liabilities.

golden handcuffs: a contract tying a broker to a brokerage house; a response by the brokerage industry to the frequent change from one firm to another. Usually includes an agreement to return to the original firm much of the compensation received while employed there.

golden parachute: a lucrative contract given to a senior executive of a firm; provides significant benefits should the firm be taken over by another, which may result in job loss.

golden passbook: see *time deposit (open account).*

gold exchange standard: an international monetary agreement according to which money consists of fiat national currencies that can be converted into gold at established price ratios.

gold fixing: in London, Paris, and Zurich, at 10:30 A.M. and again at 3:30 P.M., gold specialists or bank officials specializing in gold bullion activity determine the price for the metal.

gold hoarding: with the hope of guaranteeing the value of their money, people who convert their funds into gold bullion and hold on to it over an extended time period.

gold market: a foreign exchange market dealing in gold.

goldminers: synonymous with *golds.*

gold mutual funds: a mutual fund that invests in shares of gold mining companies.

gold points: the range within which the foreign exchange rates of gold standard countries will differ. Gold points are equal to the par rate of exchange plus and minus the cost of transporting gold. The cost of insurance is included.

Gold Pool: seven representatives of central banks of the United States, the United Kingdom, Belgium, Italy, Switzerland, the Netherlands, and the Federal Republic of Germany, who, operating through the Bank for International Settlements of Basle, seek to maintain equilibrium in the price of gold by purchasing and selling on the markets within certain minimum and maximum levels.

golds: stocks of gold-producing firms. synonymous with *goldminers.*

gold shares: issues of firms engaged primarily in gold-mining operations.

go long: purchasing stock for investment or as speculation. see *short sale.*

good buying: said when a stock is accumulated by strong, informed buyers.

good delivery: certain basic qualifications must be met before a security sold on an exchange may be delivered; the security must be in proper form to comply with the contract of sale and to transfer title to the purchaser.

good faith: trust.

good-faith check: the bid that must be included with a bid on a bond sale. The bidding notice ordinarily provides that if the bonds are awarded to a syndicate that does not pick them up as agreed, the good-faith check will be held as liquidated damages. The good-faith checks of unsuccessful bidders are returned.

good faith deposit
(1) ***general:*** a token amount of money advanced to show intent to pursue a contract to completion.
(2) ***securities:*** a deposit, traditionally 25 percent of a transaction, required by securities firms of individuals who are not known to them but desire to enter orders with them.
(3) ***bonds:*** a deposit left with a municipal bond issuer by a firm competing for the underwriting business.
(4) ***commodities:*** the initial margin deposit required when purchasing or selling a futures contract.

good quality: corporate stocks with sound financial status, paying satisfactory dividends and interest over an extended time period.

good-this-month order (GTM): a customer's request to a broker for the purchase or sale of stocks or commodities, the order being good this month only. see *day order, open order.*

good-this-week order (GTW): a customer's request to a broker for the purchase or sale of stocks or commodities, the order being good this week only. see *day order, open order.*

good through: a request to purchase or sell stock at a stated price limit for a stated time period, unless it is executed, canceled, or altered as to price. May appear as GTW (good through week), GTM (good through month), and so on.

good ticket: slang, financially successful.

good-'til-canceled order (GTC): an order to buy or sell that remains in effect until it is either executed or cancelled. synonymous with *open order.* cf. *orders good until a specified time, resting order.*

good title: synonymous with *clear title, just title, marketable title.* see *just title.*

good to the last drop: an exchange system whereby all clearinghouse members are required to make good in the event that one of their number does not or cannot comply with transferring the debits and credits that have resulted from the day's trading. see also *mark to the market.*

go private: changing a public corporation to one that is held privately. This involves purchasing back the outstanding shares of securities in conformance with SEC regulations. synonymous with *private.*

go public: to raise money for a corporation by offering stock for public sale. see *new issue, registration.*

go (going) short: selling a security short, that is, selling a security not owned, or owned but not delivered, cf. *go long.*

governing committee: a governing body of a recognized stock exchange.

government agency stock: a debt security issued by agencies of the federal government (i.e., Government National Mortgage Association). Agency securities, unlike treasury issues, are not guaranteed by the federal government.

government bills: debt securities issued by the U.S. government maturing in one year or less.

government bond: see *bond, government.*

government funds: see *funds, government.*

Government National Mortgage Association (GNMA): an agency of the Department of Housing and Urban Development. Its primary function is in the area of government-approved special housing programs, by offering permanent financing for low-rent housing. Nickname, Ginnie Mae. see *Ginnie Mae trusts.*

Government National Mortgage Association Participation Certificates: infrequently issued bonds which are fully guaranteed as to principal and interest by the U.S. government. Maturities range from 3 to 14 years presently, and there is a fairly active secondary market providing moderate liquidity. Interest is paid semiannually and the minimum unit of purchase if $5000.

government notes: debt securities issued by the U.S. government or one of its agencies. Such notes usually mature in 2 to 10 years and are readily traded. They are extremely safe investments.

government obligations (GO): instruments of the U.S. government public debt that are fully backed by the government, as contrasted with U.S. government securities—that is, Treasury bills, notes, bonds, and savings bonds.

"governments": as used in the United States, all types of securities issued by the federal government (U.S. Treasury obligations), including, in its broad concept, securities issued by agencies of the federal government.

government securities: securities issued by U.S. government agencies; for example, Federal Land Bank bonds and Federal Home Loan Bank notes. These securities are not guaranteed by the federal government.

government securities dealers: firms, including a few large banks with their own dealer units as well as nonbank dealers, that finance significant inventories of U.S. government stocks via borrowing from banks and corporations.

GP
(1) see *going public.*
(2) see *gold points.*
(3) see *grace period.*
(4) see *gross profit.*

GPAM: see *graduated-payment adjustable mortgage.*

GPMs: see *graduated-payment mortgage.*

grace period
(1) most contracts provide that the policy will remain in force if premiums are paid at any time within a period

(the "grace period") varying from 28 to 31 days following the premium-due date.
(2) the period when a mortgage payment becomes past due, before it goes into default.

grades (grading): the classification into well-defined grades of major commodities. The standardization in quality difference of staple commodities for purposes of identification during trading periods.

graduated-payment adjustable mortgage (GPAM): a GPM with an adjustable rate; the borrower and lender share interest rate risk. see *graduated-payment mortgage, price-level-adjusted mortgage.*

graduated payment adjustable mortgage loan: a mortgage instrument that combines features of the graduated payment mortgage and the adjustable mortgage loan was authorized by the Federal Home Loan Bank Board in July 1981. Lenders are now able to offer mortgage loans where the interest rate may change to reflect changes in the market place and where the monthly payments for the first 10 years may be set at a lower amount than required to fully amortize the loan.

graduated-payment mortgage (GPM): first insured by the Federal Housing Administration in 1977, where payments are much lower at first than for traditional level-payment mortgages. Prices then rise gradually and level off after a few years. The idea is to put homeownership within reach of young people who might otherwise be forced by spiraling housing prices and high interest rates to remain renters. see also *flexible-payment mortgage, pledged-account mortgage, price-level-adjusted mortgage, reverse-annuity mortgage, rollover mortgage, variable-rate mortgage.*

graduated securities: stocks that have moved from one exchange to another (e.g., from the American Stock Exchange to the New York Stock Exchange).

Graham method: a method developed by Columbia University finance professor Benjamin Graham in 1934. He believed that the only sound investment strategy was to buy a portfolio of stocks priced by the market below their intrinsic value, which eventually would be recognized by other investors. Often called the *value-oriented investing philosophy.*

grain bill: a bill of exchange drawn against grain shipments.

grain exchanges: commodity exchanges that trade in spot and futures of grain.

grain pit: that part of a trading area of a commodity or grain exchange where pit traders or commodity brokers transact business. The pit is really a series of concentric rings, with each ring indicating a different contract period.

Gramm-Rudman Act: 1985 federal legislation which requires that the federal deficit be eliminated by fiscal 1991.

grantor
(1) ***general:*** an individual who makes a grant; a person who exe-

cutes a deed giving up title to property.
(2) ***investments:*** an options trader who sells a call option or a put option and receives premium income for this act. The grantor sells the right to purchase a stock at a given price in the case of a call, and the right to sell at a given price in the case of a put.

gratuity fund: a special fund providing death benefits to the next of kin of deceased members of an exchange derived from contributions made by exchange members.

gravelled: a London Stock Exchange term, synonymous with *bottom out.*

graveyard market: a securities market where those who are in cannot get out and those who are out cannot get in.

gray chips: as distinguished from blue chips which represent the larger corporations in the United States, the smaller and mid-size companies that are considered the backbone of the nation.

gray knight: an opportunistic second bidder in a company takeover, not sought out by the target, who attempts to take advantage of the problems between the target and the initial bidder. cf. *white knight.*

gray market: sources of supply from which scarce items are bought for quick delivery at a premium well above the usual market price. Individuals engaged in this legal activity speculate on future demands. cf. *black market.*

Great Crash: the crash of the New York stock market on October 29, 1929. see *Depression of the 1930s.*

greemail: which occurs when a hostile investor buys a sizable portion of a company's stock. Desperate to rid itself of the raider, the company buys back the investor's shares for more than the going rate.

green shoe: an underwriting agreement clause stating that in the event of exceptional public demand, the issuer will authorize further shares for distribution by the syndicate.

gross bonded debt: the total amount of direct debt of a governmental unit represented by outstanding bonds before deduction of sinking fund assets.

gross book value: the dollar amount at which an asset is carried on a firm's books, without making a deduction for accumulated depreciation or any other contra accounts.

gross charge: the ratio between the interest charge on a discount interest loan and the discounted amount disbursed to the borrower.

gross debt: all long-term credit obligations incurred and outstanding, whether backed by a government's full faith and credit or nonguaranteed, and all interest-bearing short-term credit obligations.

gross deposits: all deposits, without any exclusions or deductions. This would include all forms of demand and time deposits (i.e., those due banks and government deposits).

grossed-up net redemption yield: British term for net redemption yield on a security, divided by the proportion of marginal income retained by the investor following tax.

gross profit: operating revenue less the cost of goods sold.

gross profit ratio: the ratio to sales of the difference between sales and the cost of merchandise sold.

gross sales: total sales, over a specified period, before customer returns and allowances have been deducted.

gross savings: the sum of capital consumption (depreciation), and personal and corporate savings.

gross spread: the dollar difference between the public offering price of a new issue and the proceeds to an issuer. It is also subdivided into a manager's fee, the dealer's or underwriter's discount, and the selling concession.

gross yield: the return obtained from an investment before the deduction of costs and losses involved in procuring and managing the investment. see *net yield*.

gross yield to redemption: British term for interest yield on a security plus the annual capital gain should the security be held to redemption.

ground floor: slang, a low price security with expectations of considerable increase in value.

group annuity contract: a contract issued by a life insurance company that may be used as the funding instrument for benefits to be made in accordance with a pension plan. A single master contract provides that a group of persons participating in the plan will receive annuities during retirement. Individual certificates stating coverage may be issued to members of the group. Forms of group annuity contracts include: deposit administration, immediate participation guarantee, pension investment, deferred annuity, and group permanent.

group average: the average of market prices, price/earnings ratios, earnings per share, and so on, for a group of firms within a specified industry.

group net: a purchase order given to a manager of a municipal securities syndicate.

Group of Ten: composed of the prosperous countries of the world who fix and regulate their policies in international monetary activities. Members today are Belgium, Canada, France, Great Britain, Italy, Japan, the Netherlands, Portugal, Spain, Sweden, the United States, and West Germany. Switzerland is an unofficial member. see also *Paris Club*.

group sale: a sale of securities shared pro rata by each of the selling syndicate members, as contrasted to a designated sale, where only certain members participate.

growth fund: a mutual fund whose holdings are made up primarily of growth stocks. The more speculative of these are often referred to as go-go stocks.

growth industry: a business or industry having increases in both sales and earnings, with projected improvement.

growth in earnings per share: annual percentage growth in primary earnings per share for the restated five-year period ending December 31, based on the least-squares method.

growth portfolio: a portfolio of common stocks that are expected to return rapid appreciation rather than current income.

growth stock: stock of a corporation whose existing and projected earnings are sufficiently positive to indicate an appreciable and constant increase in the stock's market value over an extended time period, the rate of increase being larger than those of most corporate stocks. synonymous with *performance stock.*

GS
(1) see *glamour stock.*
(2) see *government securities.*
(3) see *gross sales.*
(4) see *growth stock.*

GSA: see *Glass-Steagal Act of 1933.*

GTC: see *good-'til-canceled order.*

Gtd.: guaranteed.

GTM: see *good-this-month order.*

GTW: see *good-this-week order.*

Guar.: see *guarantee.*

guarantee (Guar.)
(1) at an auction, a promise to the seller that the sale will fetch a certain minimum. Top auction houses deny giving them. But dealers maintain that a global reserve amounts to a guarantee.
(2) at an auction, a warranty of the accuracy of the statements made in the catalogue about items to be sold. Excluded from the guarantees are paintings, drawings and sculptures done before 1870. Other exclusions are contained in the fine print of catalogues.

guaranteed bond: see *bond, guaranteed.*

guaranteed certificate of deposit: certificates of deposit issued by banks having flexible terms, guaranteed principal, and reinvestment rates similar to the guaranteed investment contracts issued by insurance companies.

guaranteed debt: obligations of certain semipublic and public corporations that are guaranteed by the federal government as contingent liabilities.

guaranteed deposits: see *Federal Deposit Insurance Corporation.*

guaranteed division: a dividend on the capital stock of a firm, which has been guaranteed to be paid at specific intervals.

guaranteed income contracts (GICs): agreements that promise a rate of return no matter how well or poorly an insurance company's investment portfolio performs.

guaranteed insurability: an option that permits the policyholder to buy additional amounts of life insurance at stated times with evidence of insurability.

guaranteed interest
(1) the rate of interest return specified in the policy as the rate at which reserves will be accumulated.
(2) the rate of interest paid on funds deposited with the company, either for advance premium deposits or in accordance with the settlements options.

guaranteed investment contracts (GICs): public bonds which typically promise a fixed rate of return for relatively short periods—3 to 10 years.

guaranteed stock: usually, preferred stock on which dividends are guaranteed by another company; under much the same circumstances as a bond is guaranteed.

guarantee mortgage certificate: a pass-through security representing an undivided interest in a package of conventional mortgages purchased by the Federal Home Loan Mortgage Corporation. see *Federal Home Loan Mortgage Corporation.*

guarantee of signature: a certificate affixed to the assignment of a stock certificate or registered bond or to other documents by a bank or stock exchange house, vouching for the genuineness of the signature of the registered holder.

guaranty: a contract, agreement, or undertaking involving three parties. The first party (the guarantor) agrees to see that the performance of a second party (the guarantee) is fulfilled according to the terms of the contract, agreement, or undertaking. The third party is the creditor, or the party, to benefit by the performance.

guaranty fund: a fund which a mutual savings bank in certain states must create through subscriptions or out of earnings to meet possible losses resulting from decline in value of investments or from other unforeseen contingencies. In other states, such a fund is known as the *surplus fund.*

guaranty savings bank: a savings bank with features of both a mutual savings bank and a stock savings bank.

guaranty stock: basic stock that is not withdrawable and which protects the interest of all other investors against losses.

GUC: see *good-'til-canceled order.*

guerrillas: municipal bond syndicates that attempt to outbid independent bidders on new bond issues. synonymous with *barracudas.*

gun jumping
(1) trading stocks on information prior to the information becoming publicly disclosed.
(2) illegally soliciting buy orders in an underwriting, before a SEC registration is terminated.

gunslinger: Wall Street slang for *speculator.*

gutter market: the outdoor securities market that existed in 1914 during World War I when the exchange was closed. Trading was conducted on New Street near the New York Stock Exchange building.

guy to the head: a disguise to divert attention away from an intended takeover; often used during a proposed friendly takeover.

gyp 'ems: slang, for graduated-payment mortgages. see *graduated-payment mortgage.*

H

H: declared or paid after stock dividend or split-up (in stock listings of newspapers).

HA: see *house account*.

hacking the pie: slang, what occurs at the end-of-the-year meeting of partners when they divide up a firm's profits.

haircut finance: a borrowing made against securities as collateral.

half-hedged option: a stock-option writing technique where the option writer sells two option contracts for every 100 shares of an underlying stock that are owned.

half-life: the time when half the principal has been repaid in a mortgage-backed security issued by the Government National Mortgage Association, the Federal National Mortgage Association, or the Federal Home Loan Mortgage Corporation. Usually it is assumed that such a security has a half-life of 10 years, but some mortgage pools can have longer or shorter half-lives, depending on interest rate trends.

half-stock: common or preferred stock having a par value of $50.

hallmark: an impression made on gold and silverware introduced in the beginning of the fourteenth century in England to identify the quality of the metal used.

hammering the market: the persistent selling of securities by speculators operating on the short side who believe that prices are inflated and that liquidation is imminent. When the market is primarily affected by the bears, these individuals are said to be *hammering the market*.

handling charge: a charge for handling small transaction orders made by a brokerage house.

hand signals: a system used by brokers during the early days of the American Stock Exchange to communicate executions and quotations to their clerks.

hard dollar: payments made by a client for services, including research, rendered by a brokerage house. cf. *soft dollars.*

harden: following a drop in the price for securities, a surge in buying leading to a price increase.

hard spot: a security or group of securities holding strong in a generally weak market.

Hart-Scott-Rodino Act: federal legislation of 1976, requiring companies to notify the Federal Trade Commission and the Justice Department of their plans to buy more than $15 million or 15 percent of a company. see also *Herfindahl index.*

HC: see *holding company.*

head and shoulders: a charter price trend. A series of peaks with the central peak higher than the earlier or following peaks. Can be used for interpreting when to sell reflecting the end of an upward pattern.

heart attack market: the market's reaction following President Eisenhower's heart attack in 1955 when the Dow Jones Industrial Average dropped 31.89 points, 6.5 percent.

heavy industry: traditional basic industries, such as steel and mining.

heavy market: a declining securities and commodities market created when the supply of bids for buying shares exceeds the demand for them, resulting in a price drop.

hedge: to offset. Also, a security that has offsetting qualities. Thus one attempts to "hedge" against inflation by the purchase of securities whose values should respond to inflationary developments. Securities having these qualities are "inflation hedges." see *arbitrage, puts and calls, short sale.* see also *inflation hedge.*

hedge clause: a disclaimer found in market letters, stock research documents and other printed materials having to do with evaluating investments, which attempts to absolve the writer from responsibility for the accuracy of information obtained from usually sound sources. Although liability may not exist, writers can be charged with negligence in their use of information.

hedged tender: when a seller anticipates that less than the full amount of stock tendered will be accepted by a buyer. The tenderer sells short a portion of the amount tendered to be protected if the total amount of tender is not accepted.

hedge fund

(1) a mutual fund that uses hedging practices by purchasing stocks on margin, selling short, or trading in options in an effort to maximize its profits at risk.

(2) any limited partnership of investors that invests in speculative stocks.

hedger: an individual who is unwilling to risk a serious loss in his or her cash position and takes a counterbalancing position in order to avoid or lessen loss.

hedging: when foreign currency is sold forward into local currency, so that its value is not affected by subsequent exchange rate changes. synonymous with *covering exchange risk*.

hedging clause: a protective statement of warning for securities customers that customarily reads: "The information furnished herein has been obtained from sources believed to be reliable, but its accuracy is not guaranteed."

held to maturity: see *Moody's Bond Yield*.

hemline concept: an amusing theory that security prices move in the same direction as the hemlines of a women's dress.

Herfindahl index: a mathematical standard for determining when an industry is so concentrated that mergers will be anticompetitive. see also *Hart-Scott-Rodino Act*.

H/F: held for.

HFR: hold for release.

HI: see *hot issue*.

hiccup: slang, a short-lived drop in the stock market.

Hicksian IS-LM framework: see *IS-LM model*.

hidden assets: assets of a firm that are not easily identifiable by examining the balance sheet.

hidden clause: in a contract, any obscure provision that stipulates requirements that may be against the buyer's interests.

high: see *highs*.

highballing: a fraudulent swap method, where a customer's holdings are purchased by a dealer above the current market value so the dealer does not have a loss. The customer swaps for a new holding above its market value and the dealer accepts the loss on the purchase so as to build in a present gain on the sale.

high flyers: high-priced speculative securities that move up or down several points in a trading day.

high grade: describes an item of superior quality (e.g., high-grade stock).

high-grade bond: see *bond, high-grade*.

high/low index: an index indicating yearly highs and lows on a moving average basis; used to predict major pattern changes.

high-premium convertible debenture: a bond with a long-term equity kicker packaged to offer some protection against inflation. Designed primarily for the bond buyer, it carries a higher return than conventional convertible debentures.

high quality stock: an investment attraction where a corporation shows strong financial standing and management, displays a sound interest and dividend record over an extended time period, and possesses high standing in the industry.

high-ratio loan: mortgage loans in excess of 80 percent of the sales price or value, whichever is less.

high-risk stock: an investment situation with significant price volatility.

Price earnings ratios are usually high and the firm's capital structure is often small.

highs: securities that have attained new high prices in daily trading for a current 52-week period. Used by analysts in predicting stock market trends.

high-speculative security: a security that carries a relatively high price-earnings ratio, which is generally considered of speculative or risky nature.

high tech: a high technology firm dealing with technological goods or services.

high-tech stock: securities of firms engaged in high-technology fields, such as computers, biotechnology, robotics, and so forth.

high-yield bond: see *bond, junk.*

high-yield financing: synonymous with *junk financing.*

hi-lo index: the moving average of individual stocks that attain new highs and new lows each day, indicating a weakening or improving market in general. At the same time, an established indicator (e.g., Dow Jones Industrials) might show no action or even opposite movement in blue-chip issues.

H. in D.C.: see *holder in due course.*

historical cost: the principle requiring that all information on financial statements be presented in terms of the item's original cost to the entity. The dollar is assumed to be stable from one time period to another.

historical-cost profits: the net aftertax income from continuing operations before extraordinary items are reported.

historical trading range: the price range within which a security, bond, or commodity has traded after going public.

historical yield: the yield provided by a mutual fund, usually a money market fund, over a stated time period.

hit the bid: selling at the highest bid price quoted for a stock.

HOI: see *house of issue.*

hokeys: see *Home Owners' Loan Corporation Bonds.*

hold: a stock which has been purchased and currently considered suitable for keeping, as for long-term growth or pending further market conditions.

holder

(1) owning a stock or bond or other instrument of value.

(2) intending to own something of value for an extended time period.

(3) an option client having bought a contract giving him or her the right either to purchase the underlying stock in the case of a call or sell it in the case of a put, at a predetermined price, and within a given time period. synonymous with *buyer.*

holder in due course: a person who has taken an instrument under the following conditions; (a) that it is complete and regular upon its face; (b) that he or she become a holder of it before it was overdue, and without notice that it had been previously dishonored, if such was the fact; (c) that the holder took it in good faith and for value; and (d) that at the time it was negotiated to him or her, the holder had no notice of any infirmity in the instrument or defect in the title of the person negotiating it. see *endorsement.*

holder of record: dividends are declared payable to stockholders owning shares on a specific date. Such stockholders are said to be "holders of record."

holding company: a corporation that owns the securities of another, in most cases with voting control. synonymous with *parent company, proprietary company.* see *holding company (multiple-bank), holding company (one-bank).*

holding company (multiple-bank): a bank holding company, however defined, that owns or controls two or more banks.

holding company (one-bank): at present, there is no legal definition of a one-bank holding company. A very broad definition would be any company that owns or controls a single bank.

holding company affiliate: a legal term fully defined in the Banking Act of 1933. Generally, it pertains to any organization that owns or controls any one bank either through stock ownership or through any means that allows it to elect a majority of the bank's directors.

holding page: a client account record held by the brokerage house showing all transactions and current holdings.

holding period: the time when an investment or other asset is owned. Used to determine whether a profit or loss is long or short-term and whether sales of stocks are wash sale transactions.

holding the market: to minimize the decline in the price of a security, a sufficient quantity of the stock is purchased to support the interest in a particular share.

Home Loan Bank Board: an agency that roughly parallels for the Federal Loan Bank System the duties of the Board of Governors of the Federal Reserve Bank.

Home Mortgage Disclosure Act: a federal law requiring certain financial institutions to disclose information about their home mortgage activities to the public and to government officials.

homeowner's equity account: the credit line offered by banks and brokerage houses permitting a homeowner to tap the built-up equity in his or her home.

Home Owners' Loan Act of 1933: federal legislation establishing the Home Owners' Loan Corporation with $200 million from the Reconstruction Finance Corporation; the Corporation was authorized to release up to $2 billion in bonds to exchange for mortgages.

Home Owners' Loan Corporation Bonds: authorized by the Home Owners Loan Act of 1934, $2 billion of bonds could be sold or exchanged for mortgages by the Home Owners Loan Corporation. Nicknamed "hokeys." The Corporation is now defunct and all bonds have been recalled.

home run: any significant gain by an investor in a short time period; a risky form of investing.

honeycombed with stops: a securities market containing entries of many stop orders.

honor bond: see *bond, honor.*

horizon analysis: a means of measuring the discounted cash flow from an investment, utilizing time periods or series that differ from the investment's contractual maturity; allows comparison with alternative investments that is more realistic in terms of individual portfolio needs than traditional yield-to-maturity calculations.

horizontal audit: a method of testing the practical operation of internal controls by observing the accounting procedures. This is done by a public accountant.

horizontal bear spread: a spread option position involving the purchase and sale of options within the same class whereby the option purchased has a closer expiration date than the option sold. synonymous with *calendar bear spread.* cf. *horizontal bull spread.*

horizontal bull spread: a spread option position involving the purchase and sale of options within the same class, whereby the option sold has a closer expiration date than the option bought. synonymous with *calendar bull spread.* cf. *horizontal bear spread.*

horizontal merger: a combination formed when two or more businesses producing the same goods or service merge.

horizontal price movement: synonymous with *sideways price movement.* cf. *flat market.*

horizontal spread: a spread option technique involving the purchase and sale of option contracts within the same class and on the same underlying stock, and having the same striking price, but different expiration dates. synonymous with *calendar spread, time spread.* cf. *vertical spread.*

hours of trading: see *trading hours.*

hot issue
(1) a security that has been stolen.
(2) a stock in great demand, often when sold for the first time. A typical symptom is a rapid price increase with the original purchaser making a quick profit.

"hots": in Great Britain, Treasury bills on the day they are issued, with their full term to run.

hot stuff: an indication for good selling propaganda within literature pertaining to a stock issue, whether truthful or not.

house
(1) an individual or organization engaged in business as a broker-dealer in stocks and/or investment banking and related services.

(2) the London Stock Exchange (nickname).

house account
(1) ***general:*** any account belonging to a client that has not been nor ever may be assigned to a firm's representative.
(2) ***investments:*** an account created by a brokerage company for its own use.
(3) ***house bill:*** any bill of exchange drawn by a central office against a branch or affiliate.

house call: a brokerage firm notification that the client's equity in a margin account is below the maintenance level. Should the equity drop below that point, a broker is required to call the customer, asking for more cash or securities. Should the client fail to deliver the required margin, the client's position will be liquidated. see also *house maintenance call.*

house maintenance call: a brokerage house's request for its client to put up more funds or securities when the equity in the margin account drops below the firm's minimum maintenance requirement. see also *house call.*

house maintenance requirement: internally determined and enforced regulations of individual broker-dealer in stocks with respect to a client's margin account; determines levels of equity that should be maintained to avoid putting up further equity or having collateral sold out.

house of issue: an investment banking firm engaged in underwriting and distribution of security issues.

housepaper: a commercial bill of exchange drawn and accepted by firms in the same group, as a subsidiary, and accepted by its parent firm.

house rules: internal regulations and policies of broker-dealer houses concerning the opening and handling of customer's accounts and the activities of the clients in such accounts; assures that firms are in compliance with outside regulatory agencies.

HQ: headquarters.

HR 10: see *Keogh Plan (HR 10).*

Hulbert rating: a rating by *Hulbert Financial Digest* of how well the recommendations of various investment advisory newsletters perform over a number of years by ranking several dozen newsletters and calculating the profits and losses of their readers who followed their recommendations.

Humpty-Dumpty fund: a unit investment trust comprising shares of AT&T and the regional operating companies lumped together as though AT&T were united again.

hung up: a situation of an investor whose money is tied up in securities that have dropped in value below the original purchase price, the selling of which will lead to a major loss.

hurdle rate: required rate of return, or minimum acceptable rate of return imposed on a proposed investment.

hybrid annuity: a contract from an insurance firm permitting an investor to mix the benefits of both fixed and variable annuities.

hybrid stock: synonymous with *convertibles.*

hypothecated asset: things pledged without transferring possession or title.

hypothecated stock
(1) stock pledged as collateral for a loan.
(2) a pawned stock.

hypothecation
(1) ***general:*** an agreement or contract that permits a bank or a creditor to utilize the collateral pledge to secure a loan, in case the loan is unpaid at maturity.
(2) ***investments:*** the pledging of securities as collateral; for example, to secure the debit balance in a margin account.

hypothecation agreement: synonymous with *margin agreement.*

I

I

(1) see *interest.*
(2) the nominal market interest rate.
(3) paid this year, dividend omitted, deferred, or no action taken at last dividend meeting (in stock listings of newspapers).
(4) see *interlocking directorate.*
(5) the discount rate.

IA: see *intangible asset.*

IAA: see *Investment Advisers Act.*

IBA: see *Investment Bankers Association.*

IBES: Institutional Broker's Estimate System. A service providing analysts' estimates fo future earnings for thousands of publicly traded firms.

ICA: see *Investment Company Act of 1940.*

ICE: see *International Commercial Exchange.*

ICS: see *issued capital stock.*

ID

(1) see *immediate delivery.*
(2) see *income debenture.*
(3) see *interim dividend.*

IDB: see *bond, industrial development.*

idea: an insight, or apparent insight, concerning the effect on a company or an industry of some perceived economic or social trend.

identified shares: shares from a multiple holding of the same stock bought at different prices that the owner states as being the shares to be sold. The result is to show a short-term capital loss or long-term capital gain on the sale of securities for tax purposes.

IET: see *interest equalization tax.*

if issued: see *when issued.*

II: see *institutional investor.*

IID: see *investment in default.*

illegal: describes behavior contrary to the basic principles of law. An illegal act is forbidden by law, whereas an unlawful act, though not forbidden by law, is not given the protection of the law.

illegal dividend: a dividend declared by a corporation's board of directors in direct violation of state regulations or its charter. Shareholders who receive such dividends may be required to return them so as to fulfill the claims of creditors.

illiquid
(1) possessing inadequate liquid assets to meet short-term obligations.
(2) any investment that is not readily converted into cash.

imbalance of orders: too many buy or sell orders of one kind without matching orders of the opposite kind. Should it occur prior to the opening of an exchange, trading in the security may be delayed. Taking place during the trading day, a suspension in trading may occur until sufficient matching orders are found to make an orderly market.

IMM: see *International Money Market.*

immediate delivery: an arrangement whereby an investor selects mortgages, generally from a mortgage banker's off-the-shelf inventory, for delivery, acceptance, and payment within a limited period, usually 30 days.

immediate family: as stipulated by NASD regulations on freeriding and withholding, certain sales are prohibited to brokerage employees and their immediate family, such as parents, in-laws, siblings, children, and other relatives to whose support the prohibited employee contributes.

immediate or cancel order: an order to buy or sell with trading instructions that the order should be executed immediately in part or in its entirety as quickly as it is presented to the trading floor. Any portion not immediately filled is canceled. cf. *fill order.*

immediate participation guarantee contract: a group insurance contract under which the employer's unallocated account is credited with its share of actual investment income for the year. There is generally no guarantee of principal or a minimum rate of interest. Annuity payments are charged directly against the account as they are paid.

immediate payment annuity: an annuity contract purchased with one payment and with a stated payout plan.

immunization: a technical method of protecting bond-investment income against a loss resulting from lower bond prices at the time of high interest rates. synonymous with *bond immunization.*

immunized: undergoing bond immunization. see *immunization.*

impaired capital: when the capital of a firm is indeed less than the capital stated.

impaired risk: a risk that is substandard or under average.

impair investment: a money or near-money expenditure which does not result in capital formation, being either for consumption or a transfer and acquisition of existing capital.

impairment
(1) the total, where liabilities exceed assets by reason of losses.
(2) the amount by which stated capital is reduced by dividends and other distributions, and by losses.

implicit interest: synonymous with *imputed interest.*

improvement mortgage bond: see *bond, improvement mortgage.*

imputed: describes a value estimated when no cash payment is made, in order to establish that value.

imputed cost: a cost that is not specified but instead is implied to exist by the policies of the organization (e.g., interest that would have been earned on cash spent to purchase inventories).

imputed income: income received in some form other than money, usually stated in terms of goods or services. Imputed income includes wages paid in kind, rental value of owner-occupied homes, food and fuel produced and consumed on farms, and interest payments by financial intermediaries, which do not explicitly enter the national accounts.

imputed interest: an estimate of value, charge, or interest due for using capital even though a cash payment has not been made. synonymous with *implicit interest.*

In.: see *income.*

inactive asset: that part of total assets that are not in continuous productive use in any business. An emergency generator not in use for an extended time period would be an inactive asset.

inactive bond crowd: see *cabinet crowd.*

inactive corporation: one which neither operates property nor administers its financial affairs. If it maintains an organization, it does so only for the purpose of complying with legal requirements and maintaining title to property or franchises.

inactive crowd: synonymous with *cabinet crowd.*

inactive market: a market condition characterized by a lower volume of activity than its usual.

inactive post: synonymous with *Post 30.*

inactive stock (bond): an issue traded on an exchange or in the over-the-counter market in which there is a relatively low volume of transactions. Volume may be a few hundred shares a week or even less. see *cabinet crowd.*

inalienable: not able to be sold or transferred. synonymous with *non assignable.*

in-and-out: the purchase and sale of the same security within a short period—day, a week, even a month. An in-and-out trader is generally more interested in day-to-day price fluctuations than dividends or long-term growth.

Inc.
(1) see *income.*
(2) see *incorporate.*

incentive fee: synonymous with *performance fee.*

incentive stock options (ISO): a form of stock option provided under the Economic Recovery Tax Act and subject to tax preference over unqualified stock options.

incestuous share dealing: the buying and selling of one another's company securities for purposes of creating a tax or other financial advantage.

inchoate: newly begun or incomplete.

inchoate interest: a future interest in real estate.

income (In.) (Inc.)
(1) personal or business revenues received for a stated period.
(2) funds received from an investment as either interest or dividends.

income and expense statement: synonymous with *profit and loss statement.*

income and profit: income and profit involve net or partially net concepts and refer to amounts resulting from the deduction from revenues, or from operating revenues, of cost of goods sold, other expenses, and losses, or some of them. The terms are often used interchangeably and are generally preceded by an appropriate qualifying adjective or term such as "gross," "operating," "net . . . before income taxes," and "net."

income approach to value: a procedure for property appraisal in which the value on the net amount of income produced by the property is used. This value is determined by subtracting the total income of the property from expenses to determine net profit.

income available for fixed charges: total income less miscellaneous deductions, which consist of expenses of miscellaneous operations, taxes on miscellaneous operating property, miscellaneous rents and tax accruals, loss on separately operated properties, maintenance of investment organizations, income transferred to other companies, and miscellaneous income charges.

income averaging: see *averaging.*

income basis: the ratio of the dollars of interest or dividend to the price paid for the security rather than to the face or par value.

income beneficiary: a person who, by the terms of a will or a trust instrument, is entitled to receive income from property for a specified number of years or for life.

income bond: see *bond, income.*

income coverage
(1) ***direct:*** the extent to which net income from portfolio investments (after deduction of any prior interest or preferred dividend requirements) covers the requirements of a specific senior obligation, whether bank loans, debentures or preferred stock; in computing the coverage for bank loans or debentures, interest actually paid is added back to net income. The coverage figure may be expressed in dollars, as a percentage, or as a ratio.
(2) ***overall:*** the amount by which net income from portfolio invest-

ments plus interest actually paid covers total interest charges, if any, senior preferred dividends, if any, and the dividend requirement of the subject issues.

income debenture: a corporate bond paying interest only when earned. By means of a subordinate venture, the interest it bears is senior to stock dividends.

income deductions: includes interest on long-term debt, amortization of debt discount, expanse and premium-net, taxes assumed on interest, interest on debt to associated companies, other interest charges, interest charged to construction (credit), miscellaneous amortization and income deductions (any nonrecurring income deductions of a material amount should be noted).

income dividends: payments to mutual fund shareholders of dividends, interest, and short-term capital gains earned on the fund's portfolio securities after deduction of operating expenses.

income fund: an investment company whose primary objective is generous current income. May be a balanced fund, common stock fund, bond fund, or a preferred stock fund.

income investment firm: a management company operating an income-oriented mutual fund for investors who value income over growth.

income limited partnership: a real estate, oil and gas, or equipment leasing limited partnership seeking high income, much of which is taxable. Used often for tax sheltered accounts, such as Keogh Plan accounts and pension plans.

income portfolio: stock holdings of individual or institutional investors purporting to give high current income rather than growth of capital.

income property: property, usually commercial, industrial, or residential, owned or purchased for a financial return expected.

income return: monies earned from an investment over the period of one year. see *yield.*

income shares: one of two kinds or classes of capital stock issued by a dual-purpose fund or split investment company. Dividends to such shareholders receive both classes of shares which usually have a minimum income guarantee, which is cumulative.

income stock: a stock, the earnings on which are mainly in the form of dividend income, as opposed to capital gains. It is considered a conservative, dependable investment, suitable to supplement other income. Well-established corporations with a consistent record of paying dividends are usually considered income stock.

income tax: a tax on annual earnings and profits of a person, corporation, or other organization. Traditionally, there are federal, state, and city taxes, although not all states and not all cities tax income.

income yield: in Great Britian, the return during the next 12 months in interest payments on a security.

incorporate (Inc.): to form into a corporation; become a corporation.

incorporated trustee: any trust company or bank under its charter and by law that can serve as a fiduciary.

incorporation: the procedure in obtaining a state charter to form a corporation.

incremental: describes the additional investment required for a project or additional cash flows resulting from a project.

incremental cash flow: the net of cash outflows and inflows attributable to a corporate investment activity.

incubate: an SEC statement that mutual funds cannot operate internally until they demonstrate a sound track record.

incurred losses: loss transactions occurring within a fixed period, usually a year. For example, calendar-year incurred losses are customarily computed in accordance with the following formula: losses paid during the period, plus outstanding losses at the end of the period, less outstanding losses at the beginning of the period.

indebtedness: a debt is owed; any form of liability.

indefeasible: incapable of being annulled or rendered void; as, an indefeasible title to property.

indemnify: to compensate for actual loss sustained. Many insurance policies and all bonds promise to "indemnify" the insureds. Under such a contract, there can be no recovery until the insured has actually suffered a loss, at which time he or she is entitled to be compensated for the damage that has occurred (i.e., to be restored to the same financial position enjoyed before the loss).

indemnity

(1) ***general:*** payment for damage; a guarantee against losses.

(2) ***general:*** a bond protecting the insured against losses from others failing to fulfill their obligations. see *bond, indemnity.*

(3) ***investments:*** an option to buy or sell a specific quantity of a stock at a state price within a given time period.

(4) ***law:*** an act of legislation, granting exemption from prosecution to certain people.

indemnity bond: see *bond, indemnity.*

indenture

(1) a written agreement under which debentures are issued, setting forth maturity date, interest rate, and other terms. see *Trust Indenture Act.*

(2) a formal agreement between an issuer of bonds and the bondholder covering such concerns as form of the bond, amount of the issue, property pledged, protective covenants, working capital, current ratio, and redemption rights or call privileges. Provides for appointment of a trustee to act on behalf of the bondholders.

indenture bond: see *bond, indenture.*

independent audit: an audit performed by an independent auditor. see also *audit report, independent auditor.*

independent auditor: an auditor who is independent of the governmental unit or agency whose accounts are being audited.

independent broker: members on the floor of the New York Stock Exchange who execute orders for other brokers having more business at that time than they can handle themselves, or for firms who do not have their exchange member on the floor. Formerly known as the two-dollar brokers—from the time when these independent brokers received $2 per 100 shares for executing such orders. Their fees are paid by the commission brokers. see *commission broker.*

index
(1) ***general:*** an ordered reference list of the contents of a file or document, together with keys or reference notations for identification of location of those contents.
(2) ***government:*** a statistical yardstick expressed in terms of percentages of a base year or years. For example, the Federal Reserve Board's index of industrial production is based on 1967 as 100. In April 1973 the index stood at 121.7 which meant that industrial production during that month was about 22 percent higher than in the base period.

index bond: see *bond, indexed.*

indexed bond: see *bond, indexed.*

index fund: a mutual fund whose investment objective is to match the composite investment performance of a large group of publicly traded common stocks, generally those represented by the Standard & Poor's 500-Composite-Stock Index.

index futures: where contracts are promises to buy or sell a standardized amount of a stock index by a specified date. Futures are regulated by the Commodity Futures Trading Commission, and the contracts are available only from brokers licensed by the CFTC. cf. *index options.*

indexing: an increasingly popular form of investing: investments are weighted in line with one of the major stock indices (e.g., Standard & Poor's 500-Composite-Stock Index.).

Index of Industrial Production: a government index for measuring and comparing changes in the actual output of the nation's industries, mining activities, and utility production. It is a coincident indicator used to verify market moves and the health of the economy.

index options: option contracts issued by the Options Clearing Corporation, based on a stock index instead of an underlying security. When exercised, settlement is made by a cash payment, not delivery of shares. cf. *index futures.*

indicated interest: synonymous with *open interest.*

indicated market: synonymous with *indication.*

indicated yield: used to describe the current return or yield to maturity of stocks and bonds.

indication: the approximation of what a stock's trading range may be when trading continues following a delayed opening or after being stopped because of an imbalance of orders or another justifiable reason. synonymous with *indicated market.*

indication of interest (IOI): orders for purchasing shares of a new offering that are not firm commitments to purchase. These orders are taken during the period before final registration and must be either canceled or confirmed once the final prospectus is completed.

indicators: any quantity (average, composite, or index) that is correlated to the performance of the stock market or to general economic conditions. Indicators are observed in an attempt to predict market conditions.

indirect control: control of an individual, a corporation, or other legal person, as exercised through an intermediary.

indirect costs: costs not usually identifiable with or incurred as the result of the manufacture of goods or services, but applicable to a productive activity generally. Included are costs from manufacturing operations (wages, maintenance, overhead, etc.).

indirect earnings: synonymous with *equity earnings.*

indirect exchange: a strategy employed in arbitrage of foreign exchange in purchasing foreign exchange in one market and quickly selling it in another market at a rate that produces a profit over the purchase price plus the expenses of the transaction.

indirect expense: expenses such as rent, taxes, and insurance which cannot be specifically charged to the department or cost center that benefit from them. They are generally accumulated for a period and the total then distributed on some equitable basis.

indirect quotation: a quotation of fixed units of domestic currency in variable units of foreign currency.

indirect standard: the monetary system that does not directly convert its currency into a standard metal such as gold or silver but allows, as a right of ownership, the exchange of the domestic currency into the currency of a nation that is on a metal standard. The ratio of exchange is credited and held with only occasional changes.

individual account: an account in the name of one individual, as contrasted with an account or a corporation, a partnership, or an account in two or more names.

individual proprietorship: synonymous with *proprietorship.*

Individual Retirement Account Rollover (IRA Rollover): a provision of the IRA law permitting individuals receiving lump-sum payments form the firm's pension or profit-sharing plan because of retirement or termination of employment to roll over the amount into an IRA investment plan within 60 days. With an IRA rollover, the capital continues to accumulate tax-deferred until the time of its withdrawal.

Individual Retirement Accounts (IRA): originally, individual pension accounts available to anyone not covered at work by a qualified pension plan. Effective January 1, 1982, all wage earners, including those already in company pension plans are able to make tax-deductible contributions to IRAs. An individual can now put away an extra $2000 a year, or a total of $2250 if there is a nonworking spouse, and let the earnings accumulate tax-free until age 59½. see also *Economic Recovery Tax Act of 1981, Keogh Plan.*

individual segregation: a technique employed by a broker to identify fully paid customer securities left with the broker. The segregation can be effected by the security in the customer's name, or by attaching an identification with the customer's name to certificates registered in the name of the broker.

Indm.: see *indemnity.*

indorse: see *endorse.*

indorsee: see *endorsee.*

indorsement: see *endorsement.*

indorser: see *endorser.*

industrial average: see *Dow Jones Industrial Average.*

industrial bond: see *bond, industrial.*

industrial collateral: a category of stock exchange collateral where brokers who borrow in the call money market present to the lending institution either industrial or regular collateral. This collateral is represented by the firm's traded stocks.

industrial development bond: see *bond, industrial development.*

industrial revenue bond: see *bond, industrial development.*

industrials: corporate securities of firms involved in the production and/or sale of services or commodities.

industrial stock: see *industrials.*

industry funds: mutual funds whose investment is restricted to high-yield, senior securities. The goal of an industry fund is to obtain high levels of income and preserve capital.

inflation: an increase in the price level creating a decrease in the purchasing power of the monetary unit.

inflation accounting: the bookkeeping practice that shows the impact of inflation on corporate assets and profits.

inflationary gap: the amount by which government and private spending exceeds the amount needed to maintain a stable price level and full employment.

inflationary risk: the risk that an investment has less purchasing power when it is liquidated than when it was originally invested.

inflation hedge: an investment projected to increase in value at a rate to offset the decline in purchasing power of the dollar during inflationary periods. Some investments increase in value as inflation grows, while others will decline. see also *hedge.*

inflation proofing: protecting savings and other fixed income investments from inflation by linking them to an objective standard reflecting changes in purchasing power, such as the Consumer Price Index.

inflation rate: the rate of change in prices, determined on an annual, monthly, or other basis.

in gear: the parallel rise of two or more indicators of an economic condition or activity; for example, when the Dow Jones Industrial Average and the Transportation Averages both rise, they are *in gear.*

ingot: a bar of metal. Investors can take delivery of an ingot of a precious metal, such as gold or silver, or can purchase a certificate entitling them to a share in an ingot.

initial equity: money or stocks needed to open a margin account. see *initial margin.*

initial margin: the amount a buyer is requested to deposit with a broker before commencing trading. cf. *maintenance margin.* see also *margin, margin call.*

initial public offering (IPO): a firm's first offering of stock to the public. see also *flipping.*

initiation fee: in the securities business, the initial membership levy for a newly elected member to an exchange. Thereafter, most exchanges have annual dues.

in play: a situation where attention is called to a potential target enabling sharks to prepare for a takeover. see *shark.*

Ins.: see *insurance.*

inscribed: government bonds such as savings bonds whose records are held by the Federal Reserve Banks rather than the U.S. Treasury.

in shape for sale: describing the condition in which a security will make a good delivery.

inside buying: buying of stock by officers and other key members of a corporation in their publicly traded corporation.

inside director: a director of a corporation who maintains a significant stock interest and may be employed by the corporation.

inside information: facts pertaining to the condition and plans of a firm that have not been revealed to the public and employees. see also *tips.*

inside market: bid or asked quotes between dealers trading for their own inventories. synonymous with *interdealer market, wholesale market.*

insider: an individual who, because of his or her employment position, has special information dealing with the financial status of a firm before that information is released to the public or to stockholders. see *smart money.*

insider reports: monthly reports required by the SEC that must be filed by officers, directors, and stockholders owning more than 10 percent of a corporation whose securities are listed on any national securities exchange.

insider selling: selling securities by officials and other key members of a corporation in their publicly traded corporation.

Insider Trading Sanctions Act of 1984: federal legislation allowing the Securities and Exchange Commission to seek civil penalities of up to three times the profit gained, or loss avoided, by persons who illegally buy or sell securities.

insider transaction: purchasing or selling securities by officers, large shareholders, or other key members in a corporation. The SEC rules that such transactions must be reported to them within 10 days after the close of the month in which the transactions are made.

in sight: a commodities term describing the quantity of goods that are to be delivered to a particular location.

insolvency: the inability to pay one's debts as they mature. Even though the total assets of a business might exceed its total liabilities by a wide margin, the business is said to be insolvent if the assets are such that they cannot be readily converted into cash to meet the current obligations of the business as they mature.

insolvent: an individual who has ceased to pay his or her debts or is unable to pay such debts as demanded by creditors. see *bankrupt, bankruptcy.*

Inst.
(1) see *installment (instalment).*
(2) see *instrument.*

installment (instalment): a partial payment on the purchase price for any item, sold with the agreement that the remaining monies will be paid on a specified due date.

installment bond: see *bond, serial.*

installment refund annuity: see *annuity, installment refund.*

installment sale
(1) ***general:*** a sale made with an agreement that the bought items or services will be paid for in fractional amounts over a stated period of time.
(2) ***securities:*** a transaction with a set contract price, paid in installments over a period of time.

installment sales contract: a contract for the sale of property in which the buyer receives possession of the property, but not title to it, upon signing the contract. The buyer makes regular installment payments until the contract is fulfilled and then receives the deed and title.

INSTINET: Institutional Networks Corporation; a computerized service enabling subscribers to complete transactions in the fourth market bypassing brokerage or dealer involvement.

institution: an organization (e.g., bank, insurance company, investment company pension fund) holding substantial investment assets, often for others.

institutional broker: a broker who services institutions.

institutional brokerage firm: firms specializing in servicing the requirements of the institutional investor.

Institutional Broker's Estimate System: see *IBES.*

institutional buy/sell ratio: institutional buying divided by institutional selling, measuring the degree of optimism or pessimism among institutional investors.

institutional house: a brokerage firm that serves financial institutions and profit-sharing plans rather than individual investors.

institutional investors: a company having substantial funds invested in securities (e.g., a bank, labor union, college).

institutional lender: a financial institution that invests in mortgages either directly or through the purchase of mortgages or mortgage-backed securities in the secondary mortgage market.

institutional market: the market for short terms and commercial paper. This market is used by corporations and financial institutions needing cash or having cash to invest in large quantities for short periods of time.

Institutional Networks Corporation: see *INSTINET.*

institutional pot: the percentage, usually 20 percent, of an offering of a security that has been set aside by managers for large institutional orders.

Instl.: see *installment (instalment).*

instrument: any written document that gives formal expression to a legal agreement or act.

instrumentalities: agencies of the federal government whose obligations are not the direct obligation of the federal government.

instrumentality: a subordinate agency.

in-substance defeasance: see *defeasance.*

insular bond: see *bond, insular.*

insurable interest (life version): the monetary interest of the beneficiary of a life insurance contract in the continued life of the person insured. Insurable interest exists only to the extent that the beneficiary will suffer financial loss as the result of the death of an insured.

insurance (Ins.)

(1) ***general:*** a method whereby those concerned about some form of hazard contribute to a common fund, usually an insurance company, out of which losses sustained by the contributors are paid. see also *self-insurance.*

(2) ***law:*** a contractual relationship that exists when one party (the insurer), for a consideration (the premium), agrees to reimburse another party (the insured) for loss to a specified subject (the risk) caused by designated contingencies (hazards or perils), or to pay on behalf of the insured all reasonable sums for which he or she may be liable to a third party (the claimant).

insurance binder: a written evidence of temporary hazard or title coverage that runs for a limited time and must be replaced by a permanent policy.

insurance company: an organization chartered under state or provincial laws to act as an insurer. In the United States, insurance companies are usually classified as fire and marine, life, casualty, and surety companies and may write only the kinds of insurance for which they are specifically authorized by their charters.

insurance coverage: the total amount of insurance that is carried.

insurance policy: broadly, the entire written contract of insurance. More specifically, it is the basic written or printed document, as well as the coverage forms and endorsement added to it.

insurance premium: see *premium.*

insurance trust: an instrument composed wholly or partially of life insurance policy contracts.

insurance trust expenditures: cash payments to beneficiaries of contributory social insurance programs (employee retirement funds, unemployment compensation, sickness insurance, etc.). Excludes cost of administration, intergovernmental expenditures for social insurance, and noncontributory payments to former employees.

insured, the: synonymous with *policyholder.*

insured account: an account at a bank, savings and loan association, credit union, or brokerage firm that is associated with a federal or private insurance organization. Brokerage accounts are insured by the Securities Investor Protection Corporation.

insured deposit: a deposit that is guaranteed against loss if failure of the financial organization occurs.

insured loan: a loan in which the lender is assured partial or full payment in the event of a default by the borrower.

insured municipal bond: see *bond, insured municipal.*

insurer: the party to the insurance contract who promises to indemnify losses or provide service.

intangible asset: an asset that has no substance or physical body; it is incorporeal. The most widely known types of intangible asset are goodwill and patented rights. These assets are purchased, sometimes for very substantial outlays of capital. Their value to the purchaser lies in the use he or she can make of them, although they cannot be seen.

intangible (personal) property: rights to personal property as distinguished from the property itself (e.g., stocks, bonds, notes, and contracts).

intangible tax: a state tax levied on all deposits in a bank (stocks, bonds, notes, etc.), excluding certain exempted items. The tax is against the individual accounts.

intangible value: the value of a company's intangible assets.

intensity: the degree to which the market is overbought or oversold in a particular session or day of trading.

interbank bid rate: the rate at which the clearing member purchased or made a bona fide offer to purchase

U.S. dollars for immediate delivery from another financial institution in exchange for transaction currency.

interbank rate: see *London Interbank Offered Rate (LIBOR).*

interchangeable bond: see *bond, interchangeable.*

interchange authorization: an amount at or below which an authorizing member may authorize transactions on behalf of an issuer and over which authorization must be obtained from such issuer.

intercommodity spread: a position between two related commodities; for example, a long wheat and a short corn position is an intercommodity spread. see *interdelivery spread, intermarket spread.*

intercorporate stockholding: an unlawful condition where a corporation holds stock in other corporations and this interferes with competition (e.g., restraint of trade).

interdealer market: synonymous with *inside market.*

interdelivery (or intramarket) spread: the most common type of spread consisting of buying one month and selling another month in the same commodity. An example of such a spread would be long December corn/short September corn. see also *intercommodity spread, intermarket spread.*

interest: the price paid for the borrowed use of a commodity, usually money. see *money rates.*

interest accrued: interest earned but not yet due or payable.

interest assumption: the expected rate of investment return (for actuarial purposes) on a plan's assets. In calling the return interest, it is recognized that in addition to interest on debt securities, the earnings of a pension fund may include dividends on equity securities, rentals on real estate, and gains or (as offsets) losses on fund investments.

interest bearing: a debt instrument (e.g., note bond or mortgage) upon which interest is computed. This is distinguished from equities, upon which dividends are declared.

interest bearing note: a note in which the maker agrees to pay the face of the note with interest.

interest charges: the carrying charges on a client's margin account that compensates a broker for his or her responsibility and the cost of finding funds needed to maintain it. This rate is usually somewhat higher than a broker's rate at the bank.

interest equalization tax (IET): a form of foreign-exchange control established by the U.S. government in the early 1960s whereby any U.S. resident has to pay a special tax on any purchase of overseas securities.

interest expense: the expense incurred for interest on a debt.

interest on long-term debt: interest on outstanding bonds (mortgage and debenture), receivers' certificates and miscellaneous long-term debt, notes, and so on, issued or assumed by the utility and which are due one year or more from date of issuance.

interest only account: an account which in the last two calendar months has made one or more payments of which nothing was applied to the principal (ledger card balance). Loans made during the last two calendar months are excluded.

interest rate: a percentage expressing the relationship between the interest for one year and the principal.

interest rate arbitrage: the movement of funds from one money market center to another through the foreign exchange market in order to obtain higher rates of interest.

interest rate futures: a transferable agreement to make or take delivery of a fixed income security at a specific time, under terms and conditions established by the federally designated market upon which futures trading is conducted.

interest rate option: an option contract to purchase or sell a specified quantity of a specific underlying financial instrument at a specific future date at a predetermined price. cf. *stock index options.*

interest rate peg: monetary policy followed from 1942 to 1951 where the Federal Reserve System adjusted the amount of money in order to maintain a constant interest rate on Treasury securities.

interest rate risk
(1) the risk that interest rates will change above current levels on a locked-in or fixed rate instrument.
(2) the risk that longer-term fixed income stocks will drop in market value if general interest rates climb. If a stock of this type is liquidated before maturity, the investor can also face capital risk.

interest-rate spread: the difference between the price a bank pays its depositors and the price it charges its borrowers.

interest rate swap: the exchange of two financial assets (liabilities) which have the same present value but which generate different streams of receipts (payments). see also *swap.*

interest rate uncertainty: the market price of the security may change as interest rate levels change.

interest receivable on investments: the amount of interest receivable on investments, exclusive of interest purchased. Interest purchased should be shown in a separate account.

interest table: a broad term given to any mechanical indexing device, or chart, permitting independent calculation of simple or compound interest, the discount or present value, and the like, on varied amounts for certain or varied times.

interest warrant: a firm's request for payment of interest due on its notes, debts, and so on. see *warrant.*

interest yield: the uniform rate of interest on investments computed on the basis of the price at which the investment was purchased, giving effect to the periodic amortization of any premiums paid or to the periodic accrual of discounts received.

interest yield equivalent: the measurement of the rate of return on a security sold on a discount basis, which assumes actual days to maturity and a 360-day year.

interim bond: see *bond, interim.*

interim borrowing: the sale of short-term paper in anticipation of bond issuance. see also *bond anticipation notes.*

interim closing: any closing of the books of account that occurs at some time other than at the end of a fiscal year and which does not involve the summarizing of the income and expense accounts.

interim dividend: any dividend given to shareholders ahead of the full (regular) dividend.

interim financing: short-term, temporary financing, that is, generally in effect during a building's construction or until a permanent, long-term loan can be obtained.

interim report: a report, made monthly, quarterly, or semiannually, to stockholders informing them of current developments and results. The interim report serves as a supplement to an annual report.

interim statement: a financial statement prepared before the end of the current fiscal year and covering only financial transactions during the current year to date. see *statement.*

interim warrants: see *interim borrowing.*

interlocking directorate: the condition in which one or more members of the board of directors of one business also are members of the board of directors of other corporations.

intermarket spread: involves purchasing a commodity deliverable on one exchange and selling the same commodity deliverable on another exchange (e.g., long Chicago December wheat/short Kansas City December wheat). see *intercommodity spread, interdelivery spread.*

Intermarket Trading System (ITS): a computerized system connecting the six exchanges in the nation (American Stock Exchange, Boston Stock Exchange, Midwest Stock Exchange, New York Stock Exchange, Philadelphia Stock Exchange, and Pacific Stock Exchange) which transmits commitments to buy or sell to each simultaneously. Price information is displayed on a video screen at each exchange where traders then accept or reject the prospective transaction on the basis of the price. sometimes referred to as *electronic handshake.*

intermediaries: financial organizations (e.g., commercial banks, savings and loan associations), that accept deposits on which they pay interest and then reinvest those funds in securities with a higher yield.

intermediate bond: see *bond, intermediate.*

intermediate credit bank: one of the 12 Federal Intermediate Banks established in 1923 to provide banks and other financial institutions with a rediscounting facility for agricultural paper of an intermediate term.

intermediate term: several weeks to several months; used by technical analysts when making recommendations.

intermediate-term credit: credit that is generally extended over a period of 3 to 10 years.

intermediate trend: movements within the framework of the primary or major trend. The price of a security can move in one direction 10 to 30 points and then back the opposite way. It is composed of many smaller movements in price.

intermediation: the investment process in which savers and investors place funds in financial institutions in the form of savings accounts and the financial institutions in turn use the funds to make loans and other investments.

interminate bond: see *bond, interminate.*

internal audit: a business audit carried out by the firm itself on a continuous basis. cf. *look back.*

internal bond: see *bond, internal.*

internal discount flow: synonymous with *dollar-weighted rate of return.*

internal expansion: the asset growth financed out of internally generated cash or through accretion or appreciation.

internal financing: covering the cost of expansion through use of retained earnings avoiding the need to issue stocks or bonds.

internal rate of return: see *IRR.*

internal revenue: in the United States, federal income from all taxation other than customs duties.

internal revenue bond: see *bond, internal revenue.*

Internal Revenue Code (IRC) of 1954: federal legislation; provided for a complete revision of the Internal Revenue Code of 1939. Includes provisions for dividend credit and exclusion, retirement income credit, and accelerated depreciation. Changes in tax laws since 1954 have been enacted as amendments to this code.

Internal Revenue Service (IRS): the federal agency empowered by Congress to administer the rules and regulations of the Department of the Treasury, which includes the collection of federal income and other taxes. It is divided into nine regions with 64 districts and is also responsible for the investigation and prevention of tax frauds.

international banking: bank operations dealing with foreign exchange, making of foreign loans or serving as investment bankers for foreign nations, provinces, municipalities, and companies.

International Commercial Exchange: established in 1970, following the passage of the Commodity Exchange Act, to create a currency futures trading market. An international commercial exchange clearing association was also formed. This institution replaced the New York Produce Exchange.

international corporation: a corporation participating in commerce in several countries.

international funds: funds that buy securities traded on stock exchanges outside the United States.

internationalization: purchasing or selling securities for customers by stockbrokers entirely within the brokerage house instead of sending, as traditional, orders to the floor of an exchange for execution. cf. *externalization.*

International Monetary Fund (IMF): to restore orderly exchange practices following World War II, the IMF was formed and became operational on March 1, 1947. Member nations can borrow foreign currencies from the fund under specified conditions. Membership in the fund is a prerequisite to membership in the International Bank for Reconstruction and Development.

international money management: strategies used by firms with multinational cash flows to maximize earnings from interest and exchange rate movements while reducing exposure to risk.

International Money Market (IMM): a unit of the Chicago Mercantile Exchange providing a marketplace for futures contracts in foreign countries, silver, and U.S. Treasury bills and notes.

International Mutual Fund: a mutual fund that invests in stocks from around the world so that should one market be in a slump, money can still be made in others.

international securities: securities traded in major securities markets of the world, with trading on a listed or unlisted basis.

interpolation: a statistical method for approximating either the price of yield when the actual bond's maturity falls between listed maturity dates.

interpositioning: when brokerage houses create an arrangement to create business when acting in behalf of two principal companies in a stock transaction. Abuses of interpositioning are illegal under SEC regulations.

interproduct competition (direct): firms offering products from different product classes to the same market, such as a brokerage firm's securities competing with high-interest CDs for corporate dollars.

intersympathy between stocks: the tendency for price action of securities within the same group to be similar.

intervals: an established schedule of exercise prices for a new series of options. These standard intervals are:

Price of Underlying Stock	Interval
$50 or less	5 points
$50 to $200	10 points
Over $200	20 points

intervention: a monetary agency's transaction to maneuver the exchange rate for its currency or the level of its foreign exchange reserves.

intervention currency: the foreign currency a country uses to ensure by means of official exchange transactions that the permitted exchange rate margins are observed. Intervention usually takes the form of purchases and sales of foreign currency by the central bank or exchange equalization fund in domestic dealings with commercial banks.

in the black: slang, describing a business that is functioning with a profit.

in the money: a situation in which the striking price is below the market price of the underlying stock for a call, or the striking price is above the market price of the underlying stock for a put.

in the red: slang, describes a business that is functioning at a loss.

in the tank: slang, when market prices decline quickly.

intracommodity spread: a position in the same commodity but different months on the same exchange.

intraday high and low: the highest and lowest price obtained by a security during a specific market session which defines the trading range for a day.

intragovernmental service fund: a fund established to finance and account for services and commodities furnished by a designated department or agency to other departments and agencies within a single governmental unit. Amounts expended by the fund are restored thereto either from operating earnings or by transfers from other funds, so that the original fund capital is kept intact. Formally called a *working capital fund.*

intramarket spread: see *interdelivery spread.*

intrastate securities: over-the-counter shares issued and distributed within only one state.

intrepreneurialism: where large corporations play venture capitalist by investing in fledgling companies to get a toehold on new technologies. synonymous with *corporate venturing.*

intrinsic value

(1) ***general:*** the market value of the material in a thing (e.g., the value of the metal in a gold tooth filling).

(2) ***investments:*** the excess of the market value of the underlying stock over the striking price of the option for a call, or the excess of the striking price of the option over the market value of the underlying stock for a put.

(3) ***options:*** the difference between the exercise price or strike price of an option and the market value of the underlying security.

inventory

(1) ***general:*** the name given to an asset of a business. Inventories are of two general types: direct and indirect. (a) Direct inventory in an industrial concern consists of raw materials, work-in-process, and finished goods. Direct inventories represent various steges of fabrication; in commercial and retail businesses, they are inventories purchased for resale. (b) Indirect inventories, in

general, are all supplies used to carry on the business and not purchased for resale. Indirect inventories are usually considered as deferred assets.
(2) ***general:*** a list of all assets owned by a person and the value of each, based on cost, market value or both.
(3) ***securities:*** the net long or short position of a dealer or specialist.
(4) ***securities:*** stocks bought and held by a dealer for later resale.

inventory turnover: the measure of a firm's efficient use of assets based on turnover of salable items.

inverse demand pattern: exists when price and volume vary at the same time and more is sold at a high price than at a lower one.

inverse saucer: see *saucer.*

inverted market: a commodity futures market where distant-month contracts are selling lower than near-month contracts.

inverted scale: a serial bond offering where earlier maturities have higher yields than later ones.

inverted yield curve: a condition where short-term interest rates are higher than long-term rates, resulting in lenders receiving a higher yield when committing their money for a longer period of time. synonymous with *negative yield curve.*

investable: synonymous with *investible.*

invested capital: the amount of capital contributed to a company by its owners.

investible: an object suitable for investment, such as a rare coin, stamps, and so on. synonymous with *investable.*

investment: the use of money for the purpose of making more money, to gain income or increase capital, or both.

investment adviser: an organization or person engaged in offering investment guidance or supervision of investment portfolios for a charge. These advisors must comply with SEC rules and state registration requirements.

Investment Advisers Act: federal legislation of 1940 to regulate investment advisers, in order to protect the public from misrepresentation and dishonest investment tactics, by identifying specific unlawful activities. All investment advisers are required to register with the SEC, the administrator of the Investment Advisers Act.

investment advisory service: a service providing investment advice for a fee. Such organizations are required to register with the SEC. see also *Hulbert rating.*

investment analysis: the examination and evaluation of information available on differing investment alternatives to determine risk, price movements, and so on, and to recommend courses of action.

investment analysts: individuals whose profession is the study and comparison of securities. Investment analysts usually serve brokerage houses or investment institutions.

investment banker: the middleman between the corporation issuing new securities and the public. The usual practice is for one or more investment bankers to buy outright from a corporation a new issue of stock or bonds. The group forms a syndicate to sell the securities to individuals and institutions. The investment banker is the underwriter of the issue.

Investment Bankers Association: a national fraternity of investment bankers engaged in investment banking activities. The IBA was founded in 1912.

investment banking: the financing of the capital requirements of an enterprise rather than the current "working capital" requirements of a business.

investment banking group: synonymous with *underwriting group.*

investment banking house: one that engages in the merchandising of corporate and government securities by purchasing them in large blocks and selling them to investors. It helps to finance the capital, or long-term, credit requirements of business organizations, whereas the commercial bank finances their short-term credit requirements.

investment bill: a bill of exchange purchased at a discount with the intention of holding to maturity as an investment.

investment broker: one who negotiates only cash transactions and not those on margin.

investment certificate: a certificate issued by an association which shows the amount of money an individual has invested with it. Such certificates do not carry any stockholders' liability and have no voting rights.

investment club: a voluntary grouping of people who pool their monies to build up an investment portfolio, which it is hoped, will give members a better return per individual than each would have expected separately.

investment company: a company or trust that uses its capital to invest in other companies. There are two principal types: the closed-end type and the open-end, or mutual fund. (a) Shares in closed-end investment companies are readily transferable in the open market and are bought and sold like other shares. Capitalization of these companies remains the same unless action is taken to change, which is seldom. (b) Open-end funds sell their own new shares to investors, stand ready to buy back their old shares, and are not listed. Open-end funds are so called because their capitalization is not fixed; more shares are issued as people want them. see *reinvestment privilege.* synonymous with *investment fund, securities company.* cf. *hedge fund, monthly investment plan, no-load funds, regulated investment companies, split investment company.*

Investment Company Act of 1940: federal legislation requiring the registration and regulation of investment companies with the SEC. see also *unit investment trust.*

investment cost theory of rate making: in utility and railroad rate making, investment cost is the cost of acquisition by the present owner of property devoted to public use. On this base the rate of return is computed.

investment counsel: one whose principal business consists of acting as investment adviser; a substantial part of the person's business consists of rendering investment services. see also *investment advisor.*

investment credit: a direct credit of up to 10 percent of the cost of tangible personal property used in one's business. The amount of the credit reduces the tax liability in the year of purchase. Any excess credit may be carried backward or forward, subject to limitations.

investment dollars: dollars in London that are available for the purchase of dollar securities. In times of great demand these dollars are quoted at a premium, and the amount of the premium changes daily. As there are only so many dollars available in the investment pool, the rate changed to secure them changes rapidly throughout the business day, whenever there is an unusual demand for American securities. synonymous with *security dollars.*

investment feature: characteristics of a specific investment. The five basic features are: income potential, growth potential, safety of principal, tax advantages, and a balance of features.

investment fund: synonymous with *investment company.*

investment grade
(1) an investment situation where the firm shows a very strong balance sheet, is well capitalized, has a record of continuous dividends, and is recognized as a leader in the industry.
(2) a bond rating of Baa/BBB or higher. Bonds recognized as investment grade quality are suitable for purchases by fiduciaries.

investment income: any income resulting from monies invested in securities or other property.

investment in default: investment in which there exists a default in the payment of principal or interest.

investment letter: a letter of intent between the issuer of stocks and the purchaser establishing that the stocks are being bought as an investment and are not for resale; used in private placement of new securities.

investment manager: those individuals or companies that perform the service of managing the investments of institutions or individuals. Investment managers charge a fee for performing this service.

investment market
(1) a place where securities and other investments are sold.
(2) the state of trade in investments.

investment media: any area in which capital is invested (e.g., securities, certificates, insurance, commodities, and business ownership).

investment multiplier: the reciprocal of the marginal propensity to save. The ratio of the change in national income consequent upon a change in investment to that change in investment. When there is an increment of aggregate investment, other things unchanged, national income will change by an amount that is *X* times the investment. *X* is the investment multiplier. Hence, the greater the marginal propensity to consume, the greater the investment multiplier.

investment objective: the goal (e.g., long-term capital growth, liberal current income, etc.) which an investor (whether an individual, and investment company, or other institution) pursues.

investment policy statement: the communication of a risk policy to the fund's investment manager(s), stating unambiguously the degree of investment risk which fiduciaries are willing to undertake with pension trust assets. An investment policy prescribes acceptable courses of action; a policy can be acted upon, implemented. An investment objective (such as a performance standard) is a desired result. A manager cannot implement an objective; he or she can only pursue a course of action, consistent with investment policy, which he or she believes offers a reasonable likelihood of realizing the objectives.

investment portfolio: the list of securities owned by a bank, an individual, or a business enterprise.

investment powers: the power of a fiduciary regarding the investments in the account.

investment program: the course of action (stated policy) followed by an individual or an institution in investment matters.

investment property: real estate acquired for profit.

investment savings account: a savings account, usually represented by a certificate for each unit of savings placed in the account, on which earnings ordinarily are mailed to the account holder when payable rather than credited to the account.

investment securities: investments purchased for a portfolio, as opposed to those purchased for resale to customers. Those eligible for investments by banks include U.S. Treasury and government agency bonds, notes, and bills, state and municipal bonds, and corporate bonds.

investment strategy: a quest of active management to achieve additional return that more than compensates for the additional risk assumed. Generally relates to the intent of permissible portfolio changes within a broader policy context.

investment strategy committee: the unit in a brokerage house's research department responsible for setting the overall investment strategy the house recommends to customers.

investment tax credit: an incentive for making long-term investments that reduces a firm's federal tax obligation by a specified percentage of the new investment costs.

investment trust: any firm, company or trust that takes its capital and invests it in other companies. see *closed-end investment company, mutual fund.*

investment turnover: synonymous with *capital turnover.*

investment underwriting: see *underwriting.*

investment value (convertible securities): the price at which a bond or preferred stock would theoretically sell if it had no convertibility feature; determined by estimating the price at which the convertible would sell to provide a yield comparable to that of a nonconvertible security having similar investment characteristics (i.e., current yield, investment quality, etc.).

investment year method: synonymous with *new money approach to investment income.*

investor: an individual whose principal concerns in the purchase of a security are regular dividend income, safety of the original investment, and if possible, capital appreciation. see *long position.* cf. *speculator.*

investors funds: synonymous with *money funds.*

Investors Service Bureau: a facility of the New York Stock Exchange which answers written inquiries from individual investors on all aspects of securities investing. Major areas of inquiries involve finding local brokerage firms that take small orders or accounts, explaining investing methods and listed securities, clarifying exchange operations, and providing instructions for tracing dubious securities.

invoice: an instrument prepared by a seller of goods or services and rendered to the buyer. The instrument usually lists all items making up the bill for the convenience of the buyer, and to prevent disagreements, the amount is stated on the instrument.

involuntary alienation: the forced sale of real estate.

involuntary bankruptcy: see *bankruptcy.*

involuntary investor: an investor who has purchased securities at a high price and therefore cannot sell his or her shares without a substantial loss; he or she becomes an investor. see *locked in, trader.*

involuntary lien: a lien on property demanded without the consent of the owner. Construction of sewers and sidewalks near an owner's property and property tax increases are examples. synonymous with *lien in invitum.*

IOC: see *immediate-or-cancel order.*

IOI: see *indication of interest.*

IOU: an informal written agreement acknowledging a cash debt (i.e., I owe you).

IP: see *issue price.*

IPO: see *initial public offering.*

IR: investor relations.

IRA: see *individual retirement accounts.*

IRA Rollover: see *Individual Retirement Account Rollover.*

IRB: industrial revenue bond. see *bond, industrial development.*

IRC: see *Internal Revenue Code.*

Irish dividend: a trade term for an assessment imposed on a security instead of a dividend.

IRR: internal rate of return. A discount rate where the present value of the future cash flows of an investment equals the cost of the investment. When the IRR exceeds the required return, the investment is acceptable.

irredeemable bonds: see *bond, irredeemable.*

irregular: a commodity or security market condition where some prices or averages advance while others decline, with no recognized movement of the overall market in any particular direction.

irregular savings account: a savings account containing a contractual variation as to time, notice, systematic buildup, additional earnings, earnings penalty, or similar provision.

irrevocable letter of credit: a contract by an issuer to accept drafts as conditioned by the contract and to charge them against his or her account. The letter is good for a given period of time.

irrevocable trust: a trust that cannot be set aside by its originator.

IRS: see *Internal Revenue Service.*

ISB: see *Investors Service Bureau.*

ISBN: International Standard Book Number.

IS-LM model: explains the notion of policy mix, where the *IS* curve (depicts equilibrium in goods and services market) is the locus of combinations of interest rate and real economic activity consistent with equilibrium in the goods and services market. The curve is downward sloping because lower interest rates induce higher levels of investment, which increase real income through the multiplier. The *LM* curve (depicts equilibrium in money market) is the locus of combinations of interest rate and real economic activity consistent with the equilibrium in the money market.

ISO: see *incentive stock options.*

ISSN: International Standard Serial Number.

issue

(1) any of the company's securities, or the act of distributing such securities.

(2) stocks or bonds sold by a corporation or a government entity at a particular time.

(3) selling new securities, either by private placement or through an underwriter.

(4) descendants, such as children and grandchildren.

issued and outstanding: shares of a firm, authorized in the charter of the corporation, which have been issued and are outstanding.

issued capital stock: a portion of a firm's stock retained by stockholders or repurchased by the firm to be held as treasury stock. Such stock represents the difference between authorized and unissued capital stock.

issue price: the price for a new security sold to the public, determined by an underwriter or syndicate. see *syndicate, underwriter.*

issuer
(1) a corporation offering or already offered bonds, notes, or securities for public sale or private placement.
(2) for listed option contract, the Options Clearing Corporation.

issue value: the value of a share of stock at which it is issued by a corporation.

IT: see *income tax.*

ITC: see *investment tax credit.*

itemized deductions: a listing of allowed expenses which are subtracted in arriving at taxable income. see *Tax Reform Act of 1976, Tax Reform Act of 1984.*

ITS: see *Intermarket Trading System.*

J

JA: see *joint account.*

JAJO: January, April, July, October (quarterly interest payments or dividends).

J&D: June and December (semiannual interest payments or dividends).

jeeps: 9.5 percent GPMs. see *graduated-payment mortgage.*

jeopardy clause: a Eurocurrency agreement clause stating that should certain events curtail a lender's activity or the operation of the Euromarkets, other designated actions (i.e., the substitution of another agreed rate of interest) will come into effect.

Jnt. Stk.: see *joint stock company.*

job: in foreign exchange, a bank dealing on its own behalf with other banks.

jobber: in Great Britain, an individual or firm dealing in stock as a principal rather than as a broker. Stockjobbers are not permitted to deal with the public since this function is reserved to stockbrokers.

job lot: a form of contract having a smaller unit of trading than is featured in the regular contract.

John Doe: a name given in legal proceedings to a party whose true name is unknown.

joint account: an account owned by two or more people, subject to deposit or withdrawal by all signatures of all joint owners. In banks, any account owned by two or more parties is referred to as a joint account regardless of whether all parties or any one of the parties may sign checks.

joint account agreement: the form used for opening a joint account at a bank or brokerage house.

joint and survivor annuity: see *annuity, joint and survivor.*

joint and survivorship: a phrase usually applied to annuities under which during the lifetime of both husband and wife, they are joint beneficiaries of the annuity and, after the death of either, the survivor becomes the sole beneficiary.

joint bond: see *bond, joint and several.*

joint contract: two or more people who make a promise to another are joint obligors to the contract and to the other party identified.

joint control bond: see *bond, joint control.*

joint demand: demand created when two or more commodities are used together, if at all, and are therefore wanted at the same time.

joint deposit: see *joint account.*

joint liability: a liability shared by two or more people. In the event of legal proceedings, persons jointly liable must be acted against as a group.

joint life insurance: insurance on two or more persons, the benefits of which are payable on the first death to occur.

jointly and severally

(1) ***general:*** in loan transactions when several persons sign a note for a loan, where each person is legally obligated to become liable for the payment of the note; the group involved must also become liable.

(2) ***securities:*** a municipal bond underwriting where the account is undivided and syndicate members are fully responsible for unsold bonds in proportion to their participation.

joint mortgage: any mortgage that has been signed by two or more mortgagors, being the joint obligation of all signers.

joint note: a note with more than one maker. Should there be a default, the holder sues all the makers on a joint basis as distinguished from a "joint and several" action that is against one or all the makers.

joint operating agreement: an agreement between two or more lease owners providing for the operation of a lease in which one operates the lease with all owners sharing in the cost.

joint-stock banks: in England, the name for all commercial banks. This term does not apply to the Bank of England, private banks, and so on.

joint stock company: an association that is neither a partnership nor a corporation but has some of the characteristics of each.

joint tenancy: two or more people holding equal ownership of property. Upon the death of one of the parties, the decedent's interest automatically passes on to the surviving owner(s). see *undivided right.*

joint tenants account: an account where cash and/or stocks are owned jointly by two or more parties. Each party shares equally in liabilities and profits of the account. Upon the death of either tenant, their interest passes to the surviving tenants without becoming part of the deceased's estate.

joint tenants by the entireties: an account held in two or more names from which either owner may withdraw funds but for which each owner is considered to own all the funds.

joint tenants with right of survivorship: property (bank account, safe deposit box) held in two or more names, to which any single owner has access without notifying the others. Right of survivorship indicates that in the event of the death of one owner, the remaining tenant(s) immediately becomes owners of the property.

joint venture: a commercial undertaking by two or more people, differing from a partnership by relating to the disposition of a single lot of goods or the termination of a specific project. cf. *partnership.*

joint will: a single will of two or more individuals.

JOJA: July, October, January, April (quarterly interest payments or dividends).

Jr.: see *junior.*

JSC: see *joint stock company.*

JSDM: June, September, December, March (quarterly interest payments or dividends).

judgment: a debt or other obligation, as determined by the decision or decree of a court.

judgment currency clause: a clause found in a Eurocurrency credit agreement protecting lenders against any loss arising from the fact that the loan is made in one currency and judgment given by the courts in still another.

judgment rates: rates established by the judgment of the underwriter utilizing his or her professional skills and experience, without the application of a formal set of rules or schedule.

jumbo certificate of deposit: a certificate with a minimum denomination of $100,000. Jumbo CDs are traditionally purchased and sold by large institutions, such as banks, pension funds, money market funds, and insurance firms. see also *certificate of deposit.*

junior: an exchange by holders of securities maturing within one to five years for issues with original maturities of five or more years.

junior advance refunding: an operation where the securities eligible for exchange mature in from one to five years.

junior bond: see *bond, junior.*

junior equity: common stock. The junior position refers to the fact that the claims of holders of common stock are subordinate to holders of preferred stock, in the event of the liquidation of a corporation.

junior interest
(1) a legal right that is subordinate to another interest.
(2) a mortgage participation junior to another participation.

junior issue: an issue whose claim for dividends or interest, or for principal value, comes following that of another issue, called a senior issue.

junior lien: a lien against a property that has a senior lien made and recorded. The rights are enforceable only after previous liens have been satisfied.

junior mortgage: a second or third mortgage that is subordinated to a prior mortgage.

junior refunding: an exchange by holders of securities maturing within one to five years for issues with original maturities of five or more years.

junior securities: common stocks and other issues whose claims to assets and earnings are contingent upon the satisfaction of the claims of prior obligations. see also *senior securities*.

junior stock plan: in executive compensation, where executives swap specially issued shares for common stock after a term of years.

junk bond: see *bond, junk*.

junk financing: involves the use of unsecured, high-interest securities with low ratings from credit-rating agencies. synonymous with *high-yield financing*.

junk securities: see *junk financing*.

jurisdiction

(1) ***general:*** the authority given by the Constitution to the courts to try cases and determine causes. Different courts get differing cases, based on the nature of the offense, the amount of the claim involved, and other factors.

(2) ***general:*** the legal right to hear and determine a cause of various regulatory authorities, including the Federal Reserve Board.

(3) ***investments:*** the authority to resolve disputes with respect to Eurocurrency loan agreements, where it is possible for a loan to be funded in one country but made in another by a group of international banks each from different nations, to a borrower in still another country.

justified price: a fair market price that a buyer will give for property.

just title: a title that will be supported against all claims. Considered to be a proper title. synonymous with *clear title, good title, marketable title*.

K

K
(1) declared or paid this year on a cumulative issue with dividends in arrears (in stock listings of newspapers).
(2) Kilo—(prefix meaning multiplied by one thousand).

Kaffirs: used by European investors when describing mining shares from South Africa.

Kansas City Board of Trade (KCBT): a futures exchange where contracts for wheat and the Value Line Stock Index are traded.

karat: the unit for measuring the content of gold. One karat equals $^1/_{24}$ proportion of pure gold. cf. *carat.*

Karat count: used in the profession and measured as follows:

24	100 percent gold purity
22	91 percent gold purity
18	75 percent gold purity
14	58 percent gold purity
10	41 percent gold purity

KCBT: see *Kansas City Board of Trade.*

KD: see *knocked-down* (disassembled).

keep-well agreements: lending institution agreements which morally bind partners to come up with additional money, if needed, to keep the project solvent, synonymous with *letter-of-comfort agreements.*

Keogh Plan (HR 10): a form of tax-qualified retirement plan established by a nonincorporated business or self-employed individual. Investment contributions and appreciation are generally tax deferred until actually received in the form of benefits. Formerly defined under the Self-Employment Individuals Tax Retirement Act of 1962. Until January 1, 1982, in each taxable year, the contributed amount could not exceed $7500 or 15 percent of annual earned income, whichever was less. Under the Tax Reform Act of 1976, for individuals with less than $15,000 of adjusted gross income, the minimum contribution would remain at the lesser of $750 or 100 percent of self-employed income. Effective January 1, 1982, a self-employed person or an individual who has outside self-employment income can put as much as $15,000 every year in a Keogh plan, double the old limit. But the 15 percent of earnings restrictions stays in effect for Keoghs. see *Economic Recovery Tax Act of 1981, Individual Retirement Accounts.*

kerb dealing: dealing in commodity markets which occur once the official market has closed.

kickback
(1) ***general:*** an illegal rebate given secretly by a seller for granting an order or contract, as with a payoff.
(2) ***investments:*** a practice where sales finance firms reward dealers for discounting installment purchase paper through them with cash payments.

killer bees: slang, those who assist a firm in fending off a takeover bid; usually investment bankers who implement procedures purporting to make the target less attractive or more difficult to acquire.

killing: slang, describes an unusually profitable trade.

kill order: see *immediate or cancel order.*

kin: persons of the same blood or members of the same family.

kinked demand: a firm's demand curve which becomes continuous at the market price. This is associated with the phenomenon of an industry in which there are few firms but no price leader.

kite (kiting)
(1) ***general:*** writing a check in an amount sufficient to overdraw the account, but making up this deficiency by depositing another check, likewise in excess of deposits, and issued on some other bank. This unorthodox procedure is considered to be evidence of fraudulent intent.
(2) ***securities:*** driving securities prices to high levels through manipulative trading procedures, such as creating an artificial trading activity by the buyer and seller working together and utilizing the same funds.

KK: Kabushiki-Kaisha (Japanese stock company).

knocked-down: a lowered or reduced price; a seller's asking price that has been lowered for purposes of making the sale.

know your customer rule: the New York Stock Exchange regulation demanding that the broker learn essential facts relative to clients and the nature of the accounts prior to approving the opening of an account with the brokerage house.

KP: see *Keogh Plan.*

Krugerrand: the gold bullion coin minted by the Republic of South Africa having one troy ounce of gold. Kruggerrands traditionally sell for 4 to 5 percent more than the current value of their gold content.

KS: kiting stocks. see *kite.*

KYC: see *know your customer rule.*

L

L

(1) listed (securities).

(2) a new definition of money supply of the Federal Reserve Board: a broad measure of liquid assets, equaling M3 plus other liquid assets not included elsewhere, such as term Eurodollars held by U.S. residents other than banks; bankers' acceptances; commercial paper; Treasury bills and other liquid Treasury securities; and U.S. Savings Bonds. see also *M3.*

LA

(1) see *legal assets.*

(2) see *liquid assets.*

lag: see *leads and lags.*

laggard: stock that is not performing as well as the average of the stock market or of its group.

lagging indicator: a numerical index which exhibits trends similar to those of the stock market, after the fluctuations have taken place in the stock market. Lagging indicators are followed by those seeking to verify specific trends.

lamb: an inexperienced speculator.

lame duck

(1) ***general:*** an individual going out of office shortly; thus thought to be ineffectual or helpless.

(2) ***investments:*** a speculator whose venture has failed.

(3) ***investments:*** a member of a stock exchange who is unable to meet his or her debts.

land certificate: a legal document indicating proof of ownership of land or property. Contains a description of property and the owner's name and address.

land contract: an installment contract drawn between buyer and seller for the sale of property. Occasionally used as a substitute for a mortgage, except that ownership of the property does not pass until payment of the last installment.

land development loan: an advance of funds, secured by a mortgage, for the purpose of making, installing, or constructing those improvements necessary to produce construction-ready building sites from raw land.

land sale leaseback mortgage: buying the underlying land of a building and leasing it back on a long-term lease (sometimes as long as 90 years) to the seller of the land (often a developer). The leasehold interests are the improvements (structures) on the land that do not carry with them ownership interests in the ground. At the end of the ground lease, the owner of the land (the fund) owns whatever improvements were made on the land.

land tax: a tax levied on the ownership of real property. An assessed valuation determines the rate of the tax. see also *cadastre.* synonymous with *ad valorem taxes, property tax.*

land trust: title to land held by a trustee in the interest of the beneficiaries of a trust.

land trust certificate: an instrument granting participation in benefits of the ownership of real estate, while the title remains in a trustee.

land value tax: a governmental levy on the value of land only (i.e., not including structures or agricultural produce on it).

land warrant: a government document given as proof of ownership to anyone buying public land.

lapse

(1) the failure of the insured to pay the cost of the premium when due, or within the days of grace allowed.

(2) the discontinuance of a right of the passage of time, as when the grace period of a mortgage ends of the date of a lease has passed.

(3) the termination of a right through disuse or failure to meet standard obligations over a fixed time period.

lapsed option: an option that reached its expiration date without being exercised, thereby being without value.

larceny: the unlawful taking of the personal property of another without the individual's consent and with intent to deprive him or her of the ownership and use of it. This offense is defined by statute in nearly all states and provinces, but there are some differences in the definitions.

La Salle Street: the financial center of Chicago.

last in, first out: see *LIFO.*

last sale: the final price in the transacting of a security during the trading day or at the end of the day.

last trading day: the last day during which trading in a futures contract is permitted during the delivery month. All contracts which have not been offset by the end of trading on that day must therefore be settled by delivery or agreement.

late tape: any delay in displaying price changes because trading on an exchange is excessively heavy. Should the tape be more than five minutes late, the first digit of a price is deleted; for example, a trade at $52^1/_2$ is shown as $2^1/_2$.

laying off: synonymous with *lay off.*

lay off: in investment banking, a means of reducing the risk in a standby commitment, under which bankers agree to buy and resell to the public any portion of a security issue not subscribed to by stockholders who hold rights. The risk is that the market value will fall during the two to four weeks when stockholders are deciding whether to exercise or sell their rights. synonymous with *laying off.*

LB: see *bond, legal.*

LBO: see *leveraged buyout.*

LC
(1) see *leverage contract.*
(2) see *loan capital.*
(3) see *loan crowd.*

LCM: least common multiple (mathematics).

lead: see *leads and lags.*

leaders
(1) ***general:*** any item that shows strong selling power in a market situation.
(2) ***investments:*** individual securities or groups of shares that set the pace of a climbing or declining market.

leading: the quick conversion of all soft foreign currencies into the stronger dollar to be sent home.

leading indicators: 12 indicators, issued by the Bureau of Economic Analysis, chosen for their record in predicting turns in the business cycle, released late in the month for the previous month.

lead-manage: to handle or arrange a loan, bond issue, and so on as the initial broker, underwriter, and so on.

lead manager: see *lead-manage.*

leads and lags: changes in the pattern of international payments terms. Should a devaluation of a nation's currency be feared, its importers with overseas currency obligations will rush to pay to avoid their debts becoming greater following devaluation; they *lead* payments. Conversely, exporters will benefit by not rushing to convert export receipts in foreign currency; they *lag* payments.

lead underwriter: an insurance underwriter who is the first of a number of underwriters to accept a line on a risk.

lease: a form of contract transferring the use or occupancy of land, space, structures, or equipment, in consideration of a payment, usually in the form of rent. Leases can be for a short period or as long as life. In a lease, the lessor gives the use of the property to a lessee.

lease (regular or commercial): agreement to occupy and use space for a definite term at a fixed monthly rental.

lease acquisition cost: the price paid by a real estate limited partnership, when securing a lease, including legal fees and other expenses. Such charges are prorated to the limited partners.

lease broker: an individual in the business of securing leases for speculation and resale in areas where land plays or exploration work is being carried out.

leased fee interest: an interest of the owner in a leased property.

leasehold: an estate or interest a tenant holds for a number of years in the property he or she is leasing.

leasehold improvement: the sums expended to improve or upgrade the property over a period of years. Because such improvements normally accrue to the landlord, or owner at the expiration of the lease, their costs must be amortized over the life of the lease.

leasehold obligation: an obligation in a leasehold, to pay a specified rental for a specified number of years.

leasehold value: the market value of a lease may increase or decrease over what was originally paid.

Led.: see *ledger.*

ledger: a record of final entry in bookkeeping. An account is established for every type of transaction, and a ledger account is posted with every transaction affecting this particular account.

ledger debit balance: money that a client owes a brokerage house for transactions, commisssions, interest, and other fees.

left-hand financing: a practice whereby issuers sell investors a stake in a particular asset, such as a plant or piece of property, instead of selling shares in a whole company.

leg

(1) a sustained pattern in stock market prices. For example, a prolonged bull or bear market can have first, second, and third legs.

(2) one side of a spread transaction. Utilizing two options is called *legs of the spread.* Selling one of the options is called *lifting a leg.*

LEGAL: the computerized data base of the NYSE for tracking enforcement actions against member firms, audits of member firms, and customer complaints.

legal asset: any property, including securities, that can be used for payment of a debt.

legal bond: see *bond, legal.*

legal capital

(1) that portion of the paid-in capital of a corporation that comprises the par or stated value of the stock.

(2) that portion of a corporation's net under corporate law.

legal common trust fund: a common trust fund invested wholly in property that is legal for the investment of trust funds in the state in which the common trust is being administered. The term is employed most often in or with respect to common trust funds in states that have a statutory or court-approved list of authorized investment for trustees where the terms of the trust do not provide otherwise.

legal entity: any individual, proprietorship, partnership, corporation, association, or other organization that has, in the eyes of the law, the capacity to make a contract or an agreement and the abilities to assume an obligation and to discharge an indebtedness. A legal entity is a responsible being in the eyes of the law and can be sued for damages if the performance of a contract or agreement is not met.

legal investments
(1) investments that savings banks, insurance companies, trustees, and other fiduciaries (individual or corporate) are permitted to make by the laws of the state in which they are domiciled, or under the jurisdiction of which they operate or serve. Those investments which meet the conditions imposed by law constitute the legal investment list.
(2) investments that governmental units are permitted to make by law. see *legal list.*

legal list: a list of investments selected by various states in which certain institutions and fiduciaries, such as insurance companies and banks, may invest. Legal lists are often restricted to high-quality securities meeting certain specifications. see *prudent man rule.*

legal monopoly: a privately owned organization that is granted an exclusive right by the government to function in a specified market under strict control and pricing by the government (e.g., public utilities).

legal name: an individual's personal first and last name, used as identification when entering into certain transactions. The name must be currently in use for financial purposes and must be used without fraudulent intent.

legal opinion: a counsel's statement offered to an issuer of municipal securities stating that interest income is exempt from federal taxation, that enabling legislation permits the issue, and that no restrictive covenant or prior issues is violated by such an issue.

legal ownership: an estate of interest in property which is enforceable in a court of law.

legal partnership: an estate or interest in property that is enforceable in a court of law.

legal person: often applied to a corporation that is allowed to own property, to sue, to be sued, and to exercise many of the rights accorded to natural persons.

legal rate of interest: the maximum rate of interest that is permitted by the laws of the state having jurisdiction over the legality of a transaction. Interest in excess of this legal rate is termed usury.

lending at a premium: when a broker lends stocks to another to cover customer's short position and imposes a charge for making the loan.

lending at a rate: paying interest to a client on the credit balance created from the proceeds of a short sale; held in escrow to secure the loan of securities, often made by another broker, to cover the client's short position. Lending at a rate is the exception rather than the rule.

lending flat: when a security sold short is borrowed for purposes of delivery and the borrower does not have to pay a charge for the privilege of borrowing it. When a security is lent flat, no fee is charged the borrower.

lending securities: securities that can be borrowed by a broker representing a short seller.

lessee member: an individual who has leased the use of the membership on any exchange from another member for a fixed time period for a stated fee.

letter bond: see *letter security.*

letter-of-comfort agreements: synonymous with *keep-well agreements.*

letter of dispute: a letter with a customer's signature explaining the nature of his or her dispute.

letter of hypothecation: an instrument executed by the pledgor of items or the documents of title.

letter of intent (L/I)
(1) a pledge to purchase a sufficient amount of open-end investment company shares within a limited time (usually 12 to 13 months) to qualify for the reduced selling charge that would apply to a comparable lump-sum purchase.
(2) a letter expressing the intention to take, or not take, an action that may be subject to other action being taken.
(3) an agreement between two firms that intend to merge.
(4) a promise by a mutual fund stockholder to invest a specific sum of money monthly for about one year. In return, the stockholder is entiled to lower sales charges.
(5) an investment letter for a letter security. see *letter security.*

letter security: a stock or bond not registered with the SEC and, therefore, which cannot be sold in the public market. If an issue is sold directly by the issuer to the investor, registration with the SEC can be avoided if a letter of intent is signed by the purchaser establishing that the securities are being bought for investment and not for resale.

letters patent: a government-issued instrument granting a right or conveying title to a private person or organization.

letter stock: see *letter security.*

level accrual: an accrual method of recognizing earned income by dividing interest balance by the number of months to maturity.

level charge plans: mutual fund plans for adding shares over a period of time. A sales charge occurs each time more shares are purchased and is based on the dollar amount of the investment.

level debt service: the provision in a municipal charter stipulating that payments on a municipal debt be approximately equal each year.

level I service of NASDAQ: a subscription service providing, on an electronic screen, the highest bid and lowest offer of all NASDAQ-traded securities. cf. *level II service of NASDAQ, level III service of NASDAQ.*

level II service of NASDAQ: a subscription providing, on an electronic screen, the market makers and their bids and offers for all NASDAQ-traded securities. cf. *level I service of NASDAQ, level III service of NASDAQ.*

level III service of NASDAQ: a subscription service providing, on an electronic screen, the market makers and their bids and offers for NASDAQ-traded securities, permitting subscribers to compete by entering their own bids and offers for securities in which they are registered. cf. *level I service of NASDAQ, level II service of NASDAQ.*

level-premium life insurance: life insurance for which the premium remains the same from year to year. The premium is more than the actual cost of protection during the earlier years of the policy and less than the actual cost in the later years. The building of a reserve is a natural result of level premiums. The overpayments in the early years, together with the interest that is to be earned, serve to balance out the underpayments of the later years.

leverage

(1) the effect on the per share earnings of the common stock of a company when large sums must be paid for bond interest or preferred stock dividends, or both, before the common stock is entitled to share in earnings. Leverage may be advantageous for the common stock when earnings are good but may work against the common stock when earnings decline.

(2) a means of enhancing return or value without increasing investment. Purchasing stocks on margin is an example of leverage with borrowed money. Extra leverage is possible if the leveraged stock is convertible into common stock.

(3) see also *gearing.*

leverage contract: the right to buy or sell a commodity at a specified price on a specified future date without rigid variation margin requirements of recognized commodity exchanges. The customer puts up 25 percent of the value of the contract and pays a premium of 2 percent over the prevailing market price, commissions, and interest on the unpaid balance of the contract.

leveraged buyout: where loans are used to finance most of the purchase price. A company is considered highly leveraged when debt far outweighs equity as a percentage of its total capitalization, and most of its cash flow is used to cover debt service. synonymous with *leveraged takeover.*

leveraged company: a firm with debt in addition to equity in its capital structure. see also *leverage investment company.*

leveraged ESOP: a strategy to avoid unwanted takeover. The company makes an annual payment to Employee Stock Option Plan (ESOP) from revenues and deducts the full amount from taxable income. Stock is allocated to each employee's ESOP account as the loan is paid off. When employees retire or quit, they withdraw their stock or sell it, often back to ESOP. see also *employee stock option plans.*

leveraged investment company
(1) an open-end investment company, or mutual fund, permitted by its charter to borrow capital from a bank or another lender.
(2) a dual-purpose investment company, which issues both income and capital shares, where in effect, each class of stockholder leverages the other.

leveraged lease: a lease involving a lender, usually a bank or insurance firm, in addition to the lessor and lessee.

leveraged takeover: synonymous with *leveraged buyout.*

leverage factor: the ratio of working assets to price of the leverage security.

leverage funds: shares in closed-end investment companies, which function along the lines of mutual funds except that once the original underwriting is completed, no additional shares are issued.

leverage stock: a junior security of a multiple-capital-structure company, generally a common stock, but the term may also be applied to a warrant, or to a preferred stock if the latter is preceded by funded debt of bank loans.

L/I: see *letter of intent.*

liabilities: see *liability.*

liability
(1) ***general:*** all the claims against a corporation.
(2) ***investments:*** a claim on the assets of a firm or person, excluding ownership equity. It represents a transfer of assets or services at a determinable date; the firm or person has little or no discretion to avoid the transfer; and the event causing the obligation has already taken place.

liability hedge: a strategy for a bank to make its liabilities less sensitive to rate changes. When a bank takes in interest-sensitive deposits (e.g., six-month money market certificates, it can fix, or very nearly fix, the cost of reissuing or rolling over the certificates simply by short-selling securities for future delivery.

LIBOR: see *London Inter-Bank Offered Rate.*

license: a right to engage in certain activities for which permission is needed.

liée: French for *swap.*

lien: a claim on property to secure payment of a debt or the fulfillment of a contractual obligation. The law may allow the holder of the lien to enforce it by taking possession of the property.

lien affidavit: an affidavit either stating that there are no liens against a particular property or documenting and describing any existing liens. see *recordation.* cf. *no lien affidavit.*

lienee: a person possessing a right of lien on the property of another person.

lien in invitum: synonymous with *involuntary lien.*

lienor: the holder of a lien. see *voluntary conveyance or deed.*

lien placement fee: the cost of recording with the secretary of state the security interest of a bank on the title of any new or used car.

lien theory: a theory of real estate law which holds that a mortgage conveys to the mortgagee a claim to, or lien on, the mortgaged property.

"life": synonymous with *LIFFE* (London International Financial Futures Exchange).

life annuity: see *annuity, life.*

life beneficiary: a person who receives benefits from an estate, generally in the form of income, during his or her lifetime; sometimes called a life tenant if the estate consists of real property.

life expectancy: the age to which an average person can be expected to live, as determined by an actuary.

life insurance: insurance providing for payment of a stipulated sum to a designated beneficiary upon the death of the insured. Various plans of life insurance are available to fit the differing needs of many classes of insureds—for example, endowment plans, which pay back the face amount of the policy to the insured if he or she survives the specified period of the policy, of annuity contracts, under which savings are accumulated and paid back in periodic payments of guaranteed lifetime income to the annuitant if he or she survives the specified period.

life insurance in force: the sum of the face amounts, plus dividend additions, of life insurance policies outstanding at a given time. Additional amounts payable under accidental death or other special provisions are not included.

life insurance trust: a trust created by an individual for the benefit of his or her heirs, the major portion of which is in the form of life insurance.

life interest: the estate or interest that a person has in property for his or her own life or for another person's life, or for an indefinite period limited by a lifetime.

life of delivery: the time period from the beginning of commodity trading in the delivery to the date of the last transaction.

LIFFE: London International Financial Futures Exchange. synonymous with *"life."*

LIFO (last in, first out)
(1) dealing with the valuation of inventories: the price shown on the last incoming shipment of a particular item is the one that will be used for current valuations and cost.
(2) a method of determining the effect of withdrawals on savings account dividends or interest computations. With LIFO, withdrawals are made from money that was deposited last. The withdrawal penalty under this plan is loss of interest on the last money deposited. cf. *FIFO.*

lift: the climb in securities prices as measured by the Dow Jones Industrial Averages or other averages.

lifting a leg: see *leg.*

limit

(1) in commodities, the maximum allowed price fluctuation in any day before trading is suspended.

(2) the restriction on the number of futures contracts any one individual or firm may hold.

limited (Ltd.): see *limited company.*

limited audit: an audit in which the effectiveness of the system of internal control and the mathematical accuracy, legality, propriety, and completeness of all transactions are determined by examining only selected items. The assumption is that the transactions selected for examination are representative of the entire group from which selected, and, therefore, if no errors are found in them, the unchecked items in the group are also correct.

limited company: a British business corporation; "Ltd."; indicates registration under the Companies Act and formally establishes the limited liability of stockholders.

limited discretion: an agreement between client and broker permitting the broker to make specific trades without the need to consult the client.

limited-dividend corporation: a corporation upon which a limitation is placed regarding the maximum amount of dividends on its capital stock. Following creation of the needed and desirable surplus and reserves, such a corporation's prices can be reduced to the point where earnings were sufficient to meet the maximum dividend requirements and to maintain reserves.

limited liability: the legal exemption of stockholders from financial liability for the debts of the firm beyond the amount they have individually invested. see *partnership.* cf. *nonassessable stock.*

limited life: a characteristic of a single proprietorship or partnership in both cases the business ceases to exist on the death of either of the owners.

limited open-end mortgage: an indenture under which additional bonds may be issued, but which establishes certain limits, or measures, of maximum amounts that may be issued.

limited order: an order in which the customer has set restrictions with respect to price. see *composite limit order book, no-limit order, percentage order, stop limit order.*

limited partner: a member of a partnership who is not personally liable for incurred debts of the partnership. By law, at least one partner must be fully liable.

limited partnership: see *limited partner.*

limited price order: an order to buy or sell a stated amount of a security at a specified price, or at a better price according to the directions within the order. cf. *limited order.*

limited risk

(1) the risk in buying an options contract.

(2) a stock that has recently fallen in price, and is unlikely to drop much further.

limited tax bond: see *bond, limited tax.*

limited trading authorization: the approval for an individual other than the brokerage client to have trading rights in the account of the client. Such authorization is limited to purchases and sales.

limit move: the greatest change in the price of a futures contract allowed during any trading period, as determined by the contract market's regulations.

limit order: see *limited order.*

limit-or-market-on-close: an order to purchase or sell a given number of shares of a particular stock at a limit price. Should the order not be executed as a limit order, it is then to be executed as a market order at, or as near to the close of trading as possible. see also *limit price.*

limit player: a broker selling short any margined stock held for customers and investing the proceeds to earn interest. At the same time, broker purchases calls and sell puts on the stock.

limit price: the price set in a limit order. A broker executes an order at the limit price or higher.

limit (limitation) system: an electronic system informing subscribers about stocks traded on all participating exchanges, showing the specialist, exchange, order volume, and the bid and offer prices.

limit up, limit down: commodity exchange restrictions on the maximum upward or downward movement permitted in the price for a commodity during any trading session day.

line

(1) in Great Britain, a large quantity of stock or shares.

(2) in Great Britain, an acceptance of a risk by an insurance underwriter and, should there be more than one underwriter, each underwriter's proportion of the sum assured.

line chart: a chart constructed on graph paper showing the price range of a security on a particular day, week, or month. The closing price is noted and a separate chart of volume is usually recorded, helping chartists so predict future price movements.

Lipper Mutual Fund Industry Average: a publication of Lipper Analytical Services of New York, giving the average performance level of all mutual funds, ranked quarterly and annually, by type of fund.

liquid: capable of being readily converted to cash. Usually the assets of an entity are considered to be most liquid when they are in cash or marketable securities. see also *collectible.*

liquid.: see *liquidation.*

liquid asset fund: see *money market fund.*

liquid assets: those assets that are easily converted into cash (e.g., government bonds). see also *flight of capital.*

liquidate
(1) to convert (assets) into cash.
(2) to discharge or pay off an indebtedness.
(3) to settle the accounts of, by apportioning assets and debts.

liquidating dividend: the declared dividend in the closing of a firm, to distribute the assets of the organization to qualified stockholders.

liquidating market: a securities market where aggressive selling occurs at relatively low prices.

liquidating value: the anticipated value of a particular asset that will be realized in case of liquidation of a business.

liquidation
(1) dissolving a business by selling all assets, paying outstanding obligations, and distributing the remaining to stockholders.
(2) in an account, closing out positions an investor is holding for cash.

liquid cushion: the protection provided by holdings of cash or of securities (such as short-term marketable government bonds) that are readily convertible into cash.

liquidity
(1) the investor's ability to convert stocks into cash on short notice with minimal or no loss in current market value.
(2) the ability of the market to absorb major increases in the trading volume of a stock with only minor price adjustments.
(3) a firm's ability to meet obligations out of liquid assets.

liquidity diversification: the purchase of bonds whose maturities range from short- to medium- to long-term, thereby helping to prevent dramatic fluctuations in interest rates.

Liquidity Fund: a California firm that will purchase a limited partner's interest in a real estate limited partnership for cash at 25 percent to 30 percent below the appraised value.

liquidity ratio: a measure of corporate liability, the ratio comparing cash and marketable securities owned by a firm to its present liabilities.

liquid market: a market where selling and buying can be accomplished with ease, due to the presence of a large number of interested buyers and sellers willing and able to trade substantial quantities at small price differences.

liquid ratio: see *liquidity ratio.*

liquid saving: an individuals' saving consisting of, or easily and quickly convertible into, cash. These consist of currency, bank deposits, shares in savings and loan associations, and securities. Included are holdings of persons, unincorporated businesses, trusts, and not-for-profit institutions.

liquid securities: stocks, bonds, and so on, easily marketable and converted to cash.

liquid yield option notes (LYONs): combines zero-coupon bonds and convertibles. Corporations do not pay interest to holders until the bonds mature, while interest accumulates on top of the purchase price. For tax purposes, the corporation can deduct interest as it accrues. With the added feature of convertibility into the common stock, the corporation can pay less than the going interest rate for long-term funds. cf. *CATs, TIGER*.

listed option: a put or call option authorized by an exchange for trading. synonymous with *exchange-traded option*.

listed option contracts: stock option contracts, issued by the OCC, that trade in an organized auction market on the floor of a member exchange. Striking prices and expiration dates are determined earlier, and adjustments are made should the stock split or provide dividends. Listed options trade in a liquid market, allowing buyers and sellers to close out their positions at any time or to exercise their contracts at will. cf. *unlisted option*.

listed securities (stocks): any bonds or stocks that have been admitted for trading on a stock exchange and whose issues have complied in every way with the listing requirements of the exchange.

lister: a broker who sells property from a listing.

listing: a stock or bond's admission to trading rights on a stock exchange, based on its size, profitability, shareholders, and so on.

listing agreement: a mutual agreement between a firm seeking to have its securities identified on that exchange. see *listed securities (stocks), listing requirements*.

listing requirements: securities listed on the New York Stock Exchange require that (a) the corporation have net tangible assets of $16 million; (b) the corporation issue a minimum of 1,000,000 publicly held shares, including at least 2000 round-lot shareholders; (c) the publicly held shares have a market value of at least $16 million; (d) the corporation have had $25 million of net income or more prior to federal taxes in the latest year and $2 million or more in each of the preceding two years; and (e) the corporation fulfill certain other requirements as to debt, capital, national interest, and so on.

litigant: a person engaged in a law suit.

litigation: the act of carrying on a lawsuit.

Little Board: the American Stock Exchange. cf. *Big Board*.

little man: see *small investor*.

LL: see *limited liability*.

Lloyd's: an association of English insurance underwriters, the oldest of its kind in the world. The Corporation of Lloyd's also provides a daily newspaper *(Lloyd's List and Shipping Gazette)*, a classification of ships *(Lloyd's Register of Shipping)*, and other publications.

L.M.E.: see *London Metal Exchange*.

LMV: see *long market value*.

LO

(1) see *limited order*.
(2) see *lowest offer*.

load: the portion of the offering price of shares of open-end investment companies that cover sales commissions and all other costs of distribution. The load is usually incurred only on purchase; there is seldom any charge when the shares are sold. cf. *no-load funds*.

load charge: the commission charged to a mutual fund shares purchaser covering sales, promotion, and distribution costs.

load funds: mutual funds sold by sales representatives. For the shares they sell, there is a sales charge or load. cf. *no-load funds*.

loading
(1) ***general:*** the amount added to net premiums to cover a company's operating expenses and contingencies; includes the cost of securing new business, collection expenses, and general management expenses. Precisely: the excess of the gross premiums over net premiums.
(2) ***general:*** money added to an installment agreement to cover selling and administrative overhead, interest, risk, and so on.
(3) ***investments:*** monies added to the prorated market price of underlying securities, representing fees and overhead.

loading charge: a premium, usually from 6 to 8 percent, charged by open-end investment funds on selling new securities, to cover selling costs.

load-loading charge: the premium of a net asset value, generally 6–8½ percent, charged by open and investment companies to cover sales commissions and all other distribution costs on the sale of new shares. Normally incurred only on purchase.

load spread option: a means of payment funds issued on a contractual plan basis.

load up: to buy a security or commodity to one's financial limit, for purposes of speculation.

loan: a business transaction between two legal entities whereby one party (the lender) agrees to "rent" funds to the second party (the borrower). The funds may be "rented" with or without a fee. This fee is called interest or discount. Loans may be demand or time loans, depending on the agreement as to maturity. Loans may also be short term or long term.

loan capital: a part of a corporation's capital formed by long- and short-term creditors (i.e., banks, noteholders).

loan-closing payments: expenses incurred when a mortgage loan is set (mortgage costs, legal fees for preparing the papers, appraisal and recording fees, etc.).

loan consent agreement: the agreement that a securities broker must receive authorizing him or her to lend securities carried for a customer's account. A loan consent agreement is required by the SEC.

loan crowd: stock exchange members who will borrow or lend securities to investors who have sold short. These individuals usually meet at a designated place of the exchange. see *short sale*.

loaned flat: sometimes securities are sold short, requiring the seller to borrow them if this becomes necessary to make delivery. When he or she is able to borrow without making an interest payment for the shares, the seller is dealing in a stock that is *loaned flat.* see also *loaned stock.*

loaned stock: stock loaned to a short seller of his or her broker to fulfill the terms of a short selling contract by delivering shares. The borrower pays the lender of the security the market value of the stock in money and the lender either pays interest on the money or receives a premium for lending it.

loans and investments adjusted: the total of loans adjusted, U.S. government securities, and other bank eligible securities.

loan stock: see *loaned stock.*

loan value

(1) ***general:*** the amount a lender is willing to loan against collateral.

(2) ***investments:*** the maximum percentage of the current market value of eligible securities that a broker can lend a margin account customer. Set by Regulation T of the Federal Reserve Board, it applies only to securities formally registered or having an unlisted trading privilege on a national exchange.

(3) ***insurance:*** the amount of money that can be borrowed on a life insurance policy.

(4) ***mortgages:*** the amount a lending organization will lend on property.

loan-value ratio: the ratio of a property's appraised value in proportion to the amount of the mortgage loan.

local: the trader in a pit of a commodity exchange who buys and sells for his or her account.

local bill: printed confirmations of trades prepared and mailed to investors for the transactions and open orders.

lock-away: a British term for a long-term security.

locked in

(1) when an investor does not sell a security because its profit would immediately become subject to the capital gains tax. see *Tax Reform Act of 1976.*

(2) a commodities position in which the market has an up or down limit day, and investors cannot get in or out of the market.

(3) the rate of return that has been assured for a period of time through an investment, such as a CD or a fixed rate bond.

(4) profits or yields on stocks or commodities that have been protected through hedging techniques.

locked market: a highly competitive market environment with identical bids and ask prices for a security. The appearance of more buyers and sellers unlocks the market.

lockup

(1) ***general:*** a note or obligation that has been renewed, the time of repayment having been extended beyond the original due date.

(2) ***investments:*** securities that have been withdrawn from circula-

tion and placed in a safe deposit box as a long-term investment.

loco: in the commodities market, meaning "at" (i.e., silver may be traded "loco London").

Lombard loan: a central bank loan supported by collateral such as stock and bonds. Term used primarily in England and parts of Europe.

Lombard Street: the financial area in London.

London Interbank Offered Rate (LIBOR): a measure of what major international banks charge each other for large-volume loans of Eurodollars, or dollars on deposit outside the United States.

London Metal Exchange: members, approximately 110, deal in copper, lead, zinc, and tin.

London options: contracts on commodities, such as cocoa and gold, traded in London.

London Stock Exchange: a major European stock exchange, formed in 1773.

long: signifies ownership of stocks. "I am long 100 U.S. Steel" means that the speaker owns 100 shares. Specifically, holding a sizable amount of a security or commodity in anticipation of a scarcity and price rise. see *carry*.

long account: synonymous with *long interest*.

long call: a call option contract purchased on an opening purchase transaction. cf. *short call*.

long coupon

(1) a bond issue's first interest payment covering a longer period than remaining payments, or the bond issue itself. Occurs when a bond is issued more than six months prior to the date of the first scheduled payment.

(2) an interest-bearing bond maturing later than 10 years.

long hedge

(1) buying of futures made as a hedge against the sale of a cash commodity.

(2) a futures contract bought to protect against a rise in the cost of honoring a future commitment. synonymous with *buy hedge*.

(3) a futures contract or call option purchased with the expectation of a fall in interest rates, so as to lock in the present yield on a fixed-income stock.

long interest: the collective retention of a particular stock, or group of stock. synonymous with *long account*.

long leg: the part of an option spread indicating a commitment to purchase the underlying security.

long market: an overbought market.

long market value (LMV): the current market value calculated on a daily basis of long stocks held in a brokerage account. cf. *short market value*.

long of exchange: when a trader in foreign bills in an amount exceeding the bills of his or her own that have been sold and remain outstanding, the trader is long of exchange.

long on the basis: one who has bought cash or spot goods and has hedged them with the sale of futures. He or she has therefore bought at a certain basis on or off futures and expects to sell at a better basis with the future for a profit.

long option position: a stock option contract bought on an opening purchase transaction.

long position: describes a holder of securities who expects an increase in the price of his or her shares or holds these securities for income.

long pull: the buying of a security with the expectation of a holding position over a period of time hoping for a rise in the value of the stock.

long put: a put option contract bought on an opening purchase transaction. cf. *short put*.

long sale: in the commodities market, hedging sales or sales created due to spot commitments. see *short sale*.

long side: a long interest.

long squeeze: a market situation in which longs are forced to liquidate their positions because of falling prices.

long stock: securities that have been bought in anticipation of increasing prices.

long term

(1) the holding period of six months and a day, or longer, defined by the Tax Reform Act of 1984. Investors under this condition pay the lower long-term capital gains tax rate on profits.

(2) an investment approach to the market where the investor seeks appreciation by retaining a stock for a year or longer.

(3) a bond with a maturity of 10 years or longer.

long-term corporate bond: see *bond, long-term corporate*.

long-term debt: liabilities that become due more than one year after the signing of the agreement. Usually, these are formal legal agreements demanding periodic payments of interest until the maturity date, at which time the principal amount is repaid.

long-term financing: the issuance and sale of debt securities with a maturity of more than one year and preferred and common stock for the purpose of raising new capital refunding outstanding securities, or for the divestment of investments in securities not permitted to be held under the Public Utility Holding Company Act of 1935.

long-term gain: the profit on a securities or capital transaction when the interval between purchase and sale is longer than six months. cf. *long-term loss*.

long-term institutional equity: financing with more preferred stock and convertible debt to give institutions a longer-term stake. Seen as an alternative to the way most corporations are presently financed.

long-term investment

(1) a security or other asset purchased for its income flows rather than for rapid capital gains.

(2) investment held for more than six months.

long-term liability: a debt obligation coming due in more than one year; usually 10 or more years.

long-term loss: the loss incurred as a result of selling an asset held for six months or longer. A long-term loss can be offset by a long-term gain. cf. *long-term gain.*

long-term mortgage: a home mortgage running 40 or more years.

long-term receivables and investments: a group of assets, including money owed to the firm on a long-term installment basis, plus the firm's investments in affiliated and other firms.

long-term trend: the direction in which market prices appear likely to move over a future time period.

look back: the auditing of past records to locate errors that have come to the attention of a bank's auditing department. cf. *internal audit.*

lookback option: a call option or put option whose striking price is determined when the option is exercised instead of when it was purchased, giving the holder a chance to purchase at the lowest price or sell at the highest price prior to its expiration date.

loophole: an ability to circumvent a law's intent without violating its letter.

loophole certificate (CD): under present regulations, federally insured banks are permitted to pay the market interest rate—that pegged to the weekly auction of Treasury bills—only on deposits of $10,000 or more. With the loophole certificate of deposit, the saver is loaned, generally at an annual rate of 1 percent, the difference between his or her deposit sum and the $10,000. For example, if the depositor has only $5000, the bank issues a passbook loan for the other $5000. The loan is automatic and requires no collateral. It is only a paper transaction and the consumer never touches the money. It is credited to their account at the beginning and extracted six months later.

Los Angeles Stock Exchange: see *Pacific Stock Exchange.*

loss

(1) any item that can be listed as an expense.

(2) the excess of the cost or depreciated cost of an asset over its price of sale.

losses

(1) the difference between the amount invested and the amount recovered when the amount invested exceeds what is realized on liquidation.

(2) the difference between all income and expense when income is less than expense.

lost opportunity: a professional money managers description for investments that are not earning the current available rate of interest.

lot

(1) ***general:*** any group of goods or services making up a single transaction.

(2) ***general:*** a parcel of land having measurable boundaries.
(3) ***investments:*** a quantity of shares, usually 100. cf. *block, odd-lot orders*.

low: the lowest price paid for a purchase of securities at a specific time period.

lowest offer: the lowest price that a person will accept in the sale of a stock at a specific time.

low grade: in rating stocks, the uncertainty of the issuer's ability to fulfill financial obligations, management strength, and its position in its industry.

low interest: an account on which the rate has been reduced to 12 percent per annum simple interest or less.

LP
(1) see *limited partner*.
(2) see *long position*.

LR: see *listing requirements*.

LS
(1) see *letter security*.
(2) see *listed securities (stocks)*.

LSE: see *London Stock Exchange*.

Lshld.: see *leasehold*.

LT
(1) see *legal tender*.
(2) see *legal title*.

LTD: limited to any security or purpose.

Ltd.: see *limited company*.

lucrative title: a title that is obtained by a person who pays less than the true market value of the property; title to property obtained as a gift.

lump sum: full payment made in one sum, and at one time.

lump-sum distribution: the one time payment to a beneficiary covering the entire amount of an agreement. Used extensively with IRAs, pension plans, and executive stock option plans when taxes are not too burdensome when they become eligible.

LYONs: see *liquid yield option notes*.

M

M

(1) matured bonds (in bond listings in newspapers).

(2) mega- (prefix meaning multiplied by one million).

(3) mill- (prefix meaning divided by one thousand).

(4) one thousand (Roman Numeral).

(5) the equilibrium nominal money stock.

m: see *matured.*

M1: see *M-1A.*

M-1A: a money supply definition of the Federal Reserve Board (1980), replacing the old M1 definition; currency plus demand deposits at commercial banks. This is essentially the same as the old M1 with one exception: it excludes demand deposits held by foreign banks and official institutions. see also *L, M-1B, M2, M3, M4, M5.*

M-1B: a money supply definition of the Federal Reserve Board (1980); equals M-1A plus other checkable deposits at all depositary institutions, including NOW accounts, automatic transfer service, credit union share drafts, and demand deposits at mutual savings banks. see also *L, M-1A, M2, M3, M4, M5.*

M2: a money supply definition of the Federal Reserve Board (1980); equals M-1B plus savings and small-denomination time deposits at all depositary institutions, overnight repurchase agreements (RPs) at commercial banks, overnight Eurodollars held by U.S. residents other than banks at Caribbean branches of member banks, and money-market mutual fund shares. see also *L, M-1A, M-1B, M3, M4, M5.*

M3: a money supply definition of the Federal Reserve Board (1980); equals M2 plus large-denomination time deposits at all depositary institutions and term repurchase agreements at commercial banks and savings and loan associations. see also *L, M-1A, M-1B, M2, M4, M5.*

M4: (defunct) includes M2 plus large negotiable CDs at banks.

M5: (defunct) includes M3 plus large negotiable CDs at banks, savings banks, credit unions, and savings and loans.

MA
(1) see *margin account.*
(2) see *market averages.*

MAC: Municipal Assistance Corporation; created in 1975 to save New York City from bankruptcy by issuing MAC bonds.

macro-hedge: a hedge designed to reduce the net portfolio risk of an organization. cf. *micro-hedge.*

"made to the order of": see *order.*

magic mortgage: a lending method enabling buyer to purchase a house with a very low down payment but requiring a yearly interest fee to the insurer of the loan. The term derives from MGIC, Mortgage Guarantee Insurance Corporation, which promoted the idea.

magic sixes: a group of stocks, often considered undervalued, that meet certain requirements, all of them having to do with the number 6. A magic six stock must trade at less than 60 percent of book value. It must also have a maximum price-earnings ratio of six. Finally, the annual dividend, or yield, is equal to more than 6 percent.

maintenance
(1) ***general:*** the upkeep of any form of property (land, machinery, tools, etc.).
(2) ***general:*** all expenditures made to preserve an asset's value.
(3) ***investments:*** the sum of cash or securities deposited in a brokerage account to fulfill the broker's margin requirements.
(4) ***law:*** support or sustenance that a person is legally bound to give to another.
(5) ***law:*** interfering unlawfully in a suit between others by assisting either party (e.g., giving one party money).

maintenance call: the demand on a brokerage client to deposit money in his or her margin account to bring it up to the minimum maintenance margin requirement.

maintenance excess: the dollar amount of a client's equity that exceeds the minimum maintenance requirements in a margin account.

maintenance fee
(1) a fee charged by a mutual fund that is deducted quarterly for paying the reinvestment of dividends and capital gains.
(2) an annual charge to maintain some brokerage accounts.

maintenance margin: the amount of money required by a clearinghouse to retain a futures position. It is less than the initial margin and allows the flexibility needed to permit minor price fluctuations.

maintenance of investment organization: the charges to income for the directly assignable organization and administration expenses that are incident to the carrier's investments in leased or nonoperating physical property, and in stocks, bonds, or other securities.

maintenance requirement: see *minimum maintenance.*

major bottom: an expected situation when market prices reach their lowest values.

majority-owned subsidiary: a subsidiary for which more than 50 percent of the outstanding voting capital stock is owned by the parent company or by another of the parent's majority-owned subsidiaries.

majority stockholders: those who own more than 50 percent of the voting stock corporation, thus having controlling interest. see *working control.*

major trend: the direction stock prices move over a period of time regardless of temporary shifts contrary to trend. synonymous with *primary movement.*

make (making) a line: a stock's price pattern which fluctuates within a relatively narrow range for some time, indicating either accumulation or distribution of the security. Chartists follow these formations for clues on price direction.

make a market: when a broker or dealer is prepared to purchase and sell stocks in creating, regulating, and maintaining a market.

make a price: the price a seller gives indicating a willingness to accept at the request of the purchaser, or vice versa.

maker: an individual, firm, or other legal entity who signs a note, check, or other negotiable form as a responsible party.

making a market: see *make a market.*

making a price: see *make a price.*

making-up price: the price of a delivered security.

mala fides: see *bad faith.*

malfeasance: a wrong doing; a criminal act (e.g., a public official taking graft).

malicious: describes an improper act done purposefully without excuse.

Maloney Act: see *National Association of Securities Dealers and Investment Managers.*

managed account: an investment account comprised of money that one or more customers entrust to a manager, who determines when and where to invest it.

management audit: a system for examining, analyzing, and appraising a management's overall performance. Ten categories of the audit are economic function, corporate structure, health of earnings, service to stockholders, research and development, directorate analysis, fiscal policies, production efficiency, sales vigor, and evaluation of executive performance.

management company: a firm that manages and sells the shares of open-end investment companies and claims a fee or commission.

management enrichment stock ownership plans: see *MESOPs.*

management fee: the charge made to an investment company for supervision of its portfolio. Frequently includes various other services and is usually a fixed percentage of average assets at market.

management stock
(1) stock owned by the management of a corporation.
(2) stock having extra voting privileges, thus gaining control over a corporation.

manager: a bank involved in managing a Eurocredit or an issue of a security.

manager's fee: see *management fee.*

managing underwriter: the syndicate organizer, also referred to as the syndicate manager or the principal underwriter. synonymous with *principal underwriter.*

M & L: see *matched and lost.*

M & N: May and November (semiannual interest payments or dividends).

M & S: March and September (semiannual interest payments or dividends).

MANF: May, August, November, February (quarterly interest payments or dividends).

manipulation
(1) ***general:*** an artful approach, often in an unfair or fraudulent fashion.
(2) ***investments:*** an illegal operation. Buying or selling a security for the purpose of creating a false or misleading appearance of active trading or for the purpose of raising or depressing the price to induce purchase or sale by others. see *rigged market, stock jobbing.* see also *SEC.*

Marg.: see *margin.*

marge à terme: French for *forward margin.*

margin
(1) ***general:*** the difference between the cost of sold items and the total net sales income.
(2) ***general:*** the difference between the market value of collateral pledged to secure a loan and the face value of the loan itself.
(3) ***investments:*** the amount paid by the customer when he or she used a broker's credit to buy a security. Under Federal Reserve regulations, the initial margin required in past decades has ranged from 50 to 100 percent of the purchase price. see *Regulation T.*
(4) ***futures trading:*** the good-faith deposit an investor is required to put up when purchasing or selling a contract. Should the futures price move adversely, the investor is required to put up more money to meet margin requirements.

marginable stocks: stocks approved for purchase on a margin basis.

margin account: any brokerage account where listed stocks can be bought with the aid of credit given by the buyer's broker.

margin agreement: a document signed by a client before opening a margin account where the client agrees to abide by regulations and allow the brokerage house to have a lien on the account. synonymous with *hypothecation agreement.*

marginal activity: a commercial venture barely able to meet its expenses from its revenues.

marginal analysis: the analysis of economic information by examining the results of the value added when one variable is increased by a single unit of another variable.

marginal borrower: a borrower who will reject an opportunity to borrow if the interest charge is increased.

marginal buyer: a buyer who will refuse to buy at any given price if the price is increased.

marginal efficiency of capital: the annual percentage yield earned by the last additional unit of capital. synonymous with *marginal productivity of capital, matural interest rate, net capital productivity, rate of return over cost.*

marginal lender: a lender or investor who will refuse to lend or invest if the rate of interest is lowered.

marginal pair: the marginal seller and marginal buyers plus the first seller whose price is above the market price and the first buyer whose price is just below the market price.

marginal productivity of capital: synonymous with *marginal efficiency of capital.*

marginal seller: a seller who refuses to sell if the price is lowered.

marginal tax rate: a tax rate paid on any additional dollars of income.

marginal trading: the purchase of a security or commodity by one who borrows funds for part of the purchase price rather than paying for the entire transaction with his or her own money.

margin buying: using credit given by a broker to purchase securities.

margin call (MC)

(1) if a borrower has securities pledged as collateral for a loan, and a declining market for the securities forces the value of the securities downward, the bank is responsible for seeing that the margin requirements are maintained. The bank will request more margin from the borrower, who will either have to pledge more collateral or partially pay the loan, to meet the established margin requirements. synonymous with *margin notice.*

(2) a demand upon a customer to put up money or securities with a broker. The call is made when a purchase is made or when a customer's equity in a margin account declines below a minimum standard set by the exchange or firm.

margin department: a unit within a brokerage house that monitors client compliance with margin regulations, maintaining records of debits and credits, short sales, and purchases of stock on margin, and other extensions of credit by the broker. synonymous with *credit department.*

margined securities: stocks purchased on credit or held as collateral in a margin account. The securities cannot be withdrawn until the debit balance owing in the account has been fully paid.

margin minimum requirement: the minimum dollar amount of cash or value of marginable stocks an inevstor is required to place on deposit so as to purchase more stocks on margin. The Federal Reserve Board determines margin requirements.

margin notice: synonymous with *margin call.*

margin of profit: operating income divided by sales. Income taxes are usually excluded, and depreciation is usually included in the operating expenses.

margin of safety (MOS) (MS)
(1) ***general:*** the balance of income left after payment of fixed charges.
(2) ***investments:*** the difference between the total price of a bond issue and the true value of the property for which it is issued.

margin requirement: the portion of a total purchase price of securities that must be put up in cash.

margins: the limits around the par value within which a spot exchange rate of a member nation's currency is allowed to move in actual exchange market dealings and public transactions.

margin security: a security that can be bought or sold in a margin account with a broker. Regulation T controls margin buying and divides securities into categories. see also *taxable estate.*

marital deduction: a provision of the Economic Recovery Tax Act of 1981 permitting all the assets of a marriage partner to pass to the surviving spouse free of estate taxes.

Mark: see *market.*

markdown
(1) any reduction of an originally established selling price.
(2) the revaluation of stocks based on a decline in their market quotations.
(3) the amount subtracted from the selling price when a client sells stocks to a dealer in the over-the-counter market.
(4) any reduction in the price that underwriters offer municipal bonds after the market has indicated a lack of interest at the original price.
(5) a downward adjustment of the value of stocks by banks and investment houses.

marked to the market: see *mark to the market.*

market (Mkt.)
(1) the place where purchasers and sellers gather to publicly trade, usually the stock exchanges.
(2) when buyers and sellers gather for trading purposes.
(3) the highest bid and lowest offer at a given time for a stock.
(4) the supply and demand for a particular stock or item.
(5) the availability of shares of any stock.
(6) promoting a product or stock.

marketability: the speed and ease with which a specific stock can be bought and sold.

marketable securities: securities for which there is always a ready market available, such as active, listed securities.

marketable title: synonymous with *clear title, good title, just title.* see *just title.*

market analysis: an aspect of market research involving the measurement of the extent of a market and the determination of its characteristics. see *chartist, Dow theory.*

market area: that territory within which the purchase of sale of a commodity affects the price generally prevailing for that commodity.

market averages: a major securities barometer showing the trend and conditions of the market; that is, the American Stock Exchange Index, the Dow Jones averages, the New York Stock Exchange Index, and Standard & Poor's 500-Composite-Stock Index.

market bottom: the lowest point that a market indicator reaches for a stated time frame. A bottom must, therefore, be followed by some form of recovery.

market breadth

(1) the number of shares of a stated stock publicly traded.

(2) the scope and strength of the market's direction. Breadth is usually measured by several indicators including advance/decline figures and volume momentum.

market capitalization: the value of a firm as determined by the market price of its issued and outstanding common stock.

market cycle: in securities, a period of rising prices followed by a period of lower prices. These cycles roughly correspond to a business cycle of recovery, prosperity, recession, and depression.

market equilibrium: the balance that occurs when buyers and sellers decide to stop trading at the prevailing prices.

market excess return: a forecast of annual expected return (percentage) in excess of risk free rate of return derived from predicted market return.

market-if-touched order (MIT): an order to buy or sell at the market immediately if an execution takes place at a certain price stated in the oder.

market index: data expressed as a percentage of a base in which a part of the market is stated as a percentage of the entire market.

market instinct: the ability to interpret accurately the significance of the price and volume shifts in securities.

market is off: the analysis of the state of the market which shows that prices have dropped from an earlier closing.

market leaders: securities of major corporation (e.g., Standard Oil of New Jersey, International Business Machines), because of their importance in their own industry, are considered primary indicators of the economic health of the economy in general and the security market in particular.

market letter: printed sheets mailed by brokerage houses and investment advisory services which attempt to interpret conditions in the market and make recommendations for investment opportunities.

market liquidity: the condition of a securities market reflecting the supply and demand forces, assisting an investor to purchase or sell stocks at prices relatively close to the previous sale.

market maker: a broker or bank that is prepared to make a two-way price to purchase or sell, for a security or a currency on a continuous basis.

market off: an expression indicating that prices on the various stock exchanges were down for the day.

market-on-the-close order: a market order for purchasing or selling stocks requiring execution at the close of that day's trading, or as close to it as possible.

market-on-the-opening order: a market order for purchasing or selling stocks requiring execution at the opening of that day's trading.

market opening: the initial opening transaction on an exchange, usually 10 A.M. for trading. At that time, most listed stocks become open and commence trading.

market order: synonymous with *at the market.*

market out clause: found in underwriting statements of securities; the underwriter reserves the privilege of terminating an agreement to sell securities at a stated price if unfavorable market conditions occur, rendering sale at this price unprofitable.

market oversight surveillance system: see *MOSS.*

marketplace: a general term identifying business and trade activities.

market portfolio: includes all risky assets in proportion to their market value. In the capital asset pricing model, it is the optimum portfolio of risky assets for all investors. Graphically, it is located at the point of tangency of a line drawn from the risk free rate of return to the efficient frontier of risky assets.

market potential: the expected sales of a commodity, a group of commodities, or a service for an entire industry in a market during a stated period.

market price

(1) the price established in the market where buyers and sellers meet to buy and sell similar products; a price determined by factors of supply and demand rather than by decisions made by management.

(2) the last reported price at which the stock or bond sold.

market ratio: the power of one good to command another in exchange for itself in a free market. Often used with reference to the relative value of gold and silver.

market report

(1) any news about or condition of the securities market.

(2) a report from the trading floor of an exchange that a particular transaction has been executed at the stated price found in the report. The report can be either written or verbal.

market risk: the possibility of a decline in the price of a specific security; the loss that the holder of an investment may have to assume at the time of sale. synonymous with *systematic risk.*

market securities

(1) as a verb, to offer securities for sale on a market.

(2) as an adjective, those securities traded in a public market as distinguished from those with a limited market.

market sentiment: the public or mass psychology that affects the buying or selling trend of securities. They may be positive, negative, or mixed.

market share: the percentage of industry sales of a specific corporation or product.

market stabilization: attempts to stop the working of the full and free forces in a market by some agency, such as the underwriter of an issue or a sponsoring investment banker; usually prohibited by the SEC. One exception is made when an initial offering is registered with the SEC receiving authorization to "peg" or stabilize prices of an issue. Sometimes a secondary offering receives such permission.

market swing: movements of the average prices of a security or commodity market which are of a cyclical or secondary trend.

market timing: based on economic factors, including interest rates, decisions on when to buy or sell securities.

market tone: the general health and vitality of the stock market.

market top: the highest point that a market indicator reaches for a stated time period. A top is, therefore, followed by some degree of decline.

market trend: the prevailing direction, either up or down, of markets as a whole.

market uncertainty: the probability that investor's attitudes may shift, thus causing the market price of the investment to change.

market value (MV)

(1) the price that property will command on the open market. The price for which an owner is prepared to sell property and the amount a purchaser is willing to pay. see *reasonable value.*

(2) the price of a security or commodity on the daily quotation, indicating the amount required for buying or selling.

market value-weighted index: an index having components weighted according to the total market value of their outstanding shares. The index changes with the price moves of the securities.

market volume

(1) the number of shares traded on a particular exchange in one day.

(2) the number of shares traded for a specific stock in one day.

market vs. quote: the market price of a security is the price at which the last order was executed; a quote designates the current bid and ask.

marking: a manipulative strategy of an investor or trader involving the execution of an option contract at the close that fails to represent the fair value of the contract resulting in a net improved equity position in the customer's account.

mark (marking) time: the condition of a commodity or security market where no trend or direction appears to be indicated by the prices of various transactions.

mark to the market
(1) ***investments:*** checking the last sale prevailing for stocks retained in a margin account to determine if the account fulfills minimum margin requirements of the Federal Reserve Board, the Stock Exchange, and/or the brokerage house involved. see also *good to the last drop.*
(2) ***mutual funds:*** the daily net asset value reported to stockholders resulting from the marking the fund's current portfolio to current market prices.

married put: the stock put option and shares of the underlying stock bought on the same day and identified as such.

Massachusetts rule: a term frequently applied to a rule for the investment of trust funds enunciated by the Supreme Judicial Court of Massachusetts in 1830; now commonly referred to as the prudent man rule. see *prudent man rule.*

master limited partnership (MLP): an investment vehicle that combines the tax-shelter attractions of conventional limited partnerships with the marketability of publicly traded issues like stocks. There are two types of MLPs: (1) the *roll out,* in which a company spins off assets to stockholders and (2) the *roll up,* in which dozens of private partnerships are combined and exchanged for publicly traded units.

master notes: paper issued by big credit-worthy companies. Unlike commercial paper, which may be sold to another company, these notes are issued only to banks. cf. *commercial paper.*

master trust
(1) a pooling of directed and/or discretionary trusts.
(2) the pooling of one sponsor's assets, which includes multiple managers and multiple plans under one trust agreement.

Mat.
(1) see *matured.*
(2) see *maturity*

matched and lost (M&L): when two bids of the same stock are made on the trading floors simultaneously, and each bid is equal to or larger than the amount of stock offered, both bids are considered to be of an equal basis. The two bidders then flip a coin to decide who buys the stock.

matched book: accounts of dealers when their borrowing costs equal the interest earned on loans to clients and other brokers.

matched maturities: the coordination of the maturities of a financial institution's loans made to borrowers and certificates of deposit issued to depositors.

matched orders
(1) manipulation by a person entering an order to purchase a specific security with one broker and simultaneously, an order to sell the identical security with a second broker. This practice is prohibited as a means of trying to either increase or decrease security prices.
(2) a specialist in a particular stock who buys and sells a security purporting to arrange an opening price that is reasonably close to the previous day's close.

matched sale-purchase agreements: when the Federal Reserve makes a matched sale-purchase agreement, it sells a security outright for immediate delivery to a dealer or foreign central bank, with an agreement to buy the security back on a specific date (usually within seven days) at the same price. The reverse of repurchase agreements, matched sale-purchase agreements allow the Federal Reserve to absorb reserves on a temporary basis. see also *repurchase agreement.*

matched sales: see *repurchase agreement.*

matching: equating assets and liabilities denominated in each currency so that losses due to foreign exchange rate changes are minimized.

matrix trading: bond swapping where traders try to take advantage of temporary aberrations in yield spread differentials between bonds of the same class but with different ratings or between bonds of different classes.

matural interest rate: synonymous with *marginal efficiency of capital.*

matured (M) (Mat.): fully paid up, fully carried out as to terms, completed as to time or as to contract.

matured bonds payable: see *bonds payable, matured.*

maturity (Mat.)
(1) ***investments:*** the date on which a note, time draft, bill of exchange, bond, or other negotiable instrument becomes due and payable. A note, time draft, or bill of exchange drawn for a future date has a maturity date that is set starting with the date of the loan or acceptance and runs the specified number of days from date of loan or acceptance of maturity. Presentation and request for payment of the instrument are made on the maturity date.
(2) ***law:*** the completion of a contract, as with an insurance policy.

maturity basis: the ratio of the dollars of interest payable on a bond to the maturity value, ignoring any premium or discount at the time of acquisition. cf. *yield to maturity.*

maturity date
(1) ***general:*** the date on which a financial obligation becomes due for payment and/or an obligation or contract expires.
(3) ***factoring:*** the average due date of factored receivables, when the factor remits to the seller for receivables sold each month.

maturity distribution of loans and securities: shows the amounts of loans, holdings of acceptances, and government securities that mature or are payable within the various period specified.

Max: maximum.

maximum capital gains mutual fund: a fund whose goal is to produce significant capital gains for its stockholders.

May Day: May 1, 1975; the date when fixed minimum brokerage commissions were terminated in the United States. Now brokers are allowed to charge whatever they wish. Ushered in the concept of the discount brokerage house that executes buy and sell orders for low commissions, but renders no investment advice. Also, May Day encouraged the diversification of the brokerage industry into a wider range of financial activities.

MB: see *bond, municipal.*

MBA: see *Mortgage Bankers Association of America*

MBIA: see *Municipal Bond Insurance Association.*

MC: see *margin call.*

MCC: mutual capital certificate.

MCIC Indemnity Corporation: a subsidiary of MGIC Investment Corporation that offers insurance on specific municipal bonds.

MD: see *maturity date.*

Md: the demand for nominal money.

mean return: the expected value in security analysis, of all the likely returns of investments comprising a portfolio.

measuring gap: a price gap duplicating the most recent move. see *gap.*

medium bond: see *bond, medium.*

medium of exchange: any commodity (commonly money) which is widely accepted in payment for goods and services and in settlement of debts, and is accepted without reference to the standing of the person who offers it in payment.

medium other than cash: checks, notes, credit.

medium term: see *intermediate term.*

medium-term notes (MTNs): unsecured promissory notes that have maturities ranging from 9 months to 15 years—most of them are between 1 and 7 years.

meeting bond interest and principal: an expression indicating that payments are being made when due.

megagoths: firms with at least $25 billion in capital and offering more services than anything today.

member corporation: a securities brokerage firm, organized as a corporation, having at least one person who is a member of a stock exchange as a director and a holder of voting stock in the corporation.

member firm: a securities brokerage firm organized as a partnership and having at least one general partner who is a member of a stock exchange.

membership corporation: a corporation that does not issue stock but which members join by paying a membership fee.

membership dues: an annual fee paid to an exchange by members, as distinguished from an initiation fee.

member's rate: the amount of commission charged a member of an exchange who is not a member of the clearing association. This amount is less than the regular charge paid by the average customer.

members' short sale ratio: determined by dividing all shares sold short by members for their personal accounts by total short sales for the identical period. It shows a negative feeling when member short selling is 85 percent or more and positive feeling when the ratio is 68 percent or lower.

member-takedown: when a syndicate member buys bonds from an account at the takedown or member's discount price and sells them to a client at the public offering price.

Memo: memorandum.

merchant bank: used in Great Britain for an organization that underwrites securities for corporations, advises such clients on mergers, and is involved in the ownership of commercial ventures (e.g., Rothschild's, Hambro's).

merger: the combining of two or more entities through the direct acquisition by one of the net assets of the other. A merger differs from a consolidation in that no new entity is created by a merger, whereas in consolidation a new organization comes into being and acquires the new assets of all the combining units. see *conglomerate.* cf. *takeover.*

merger conversion: where mutual institution's depositors can vote on a merger but are not given any cash or stock by the acquirer. They do stand first to buy the acquirer's stock, in an offering equal to the mutual's market value, as appraised by, for example, an investment banker.

MESOPs: management enrichment stock ownership plans. A form of ESOPs; often violates the law. see *ESOPs.*

mezzanine bracket: members of a stock underwriting group whose participations are of such a size as to place them in the tier second to the largest participations. In a newspaper advertisement announcing a new security offering, the underwriters are listed in alphabetical groups, first the lead underwriters, then the mezzanine bracket, then the remaining participants. see also *mezzanine level.*

mezzanine financing: a preferred stock with a sinking fund that retires the issue within eight years.

mezzanine level: in venture capital, the stage of a firm's development immediately before going public.

MF: see *mutual fund.*

MGIC Investment Corporation: a holding company that, via its subsidiaries, offers insurance for commercial and residential mortgages, commercial leases, and some municipal bonds.

micro-hedge: a hedge designed to reduce the risk of holding a particular asset or liability. cf. *macro-hedge.*

middle-of-the-road stand: to be noncommittal about the future movement of security prices, that is, neither optimistic nor pessimistic.

Midwest Stock Exchange (MSE): formed in 1949 with the merger of the Cleveland, Minneapolis-St. Paul, and St. Louis Stock Exchanges with the Chicago Stock Exchange (1882). In trading volume, this exchange is the second largest among the "regional" securities exchanges.

MIG-1: see *Moody's Investment Grade.*

mill: equals one percent or .001; used in establishing rates for property taxes.

Min: minimum

mini-manipulation: trading in a stock underlying an option contract in order to manipulate the stock's price, so as to encourage an increase in the value of the options. In this way, the manipulator's profit is multiplied several times.

minimum maintenance: the equity level maintained in brokerage customers' margin accounts as required by the NYSE, the National Association of Securities Dealers, and separate brokerage houses. Under Regulation T, $2,000 in cash or securities must be deposited with a broker before any credit can be extended. An initial margin requirement needs to be met, presently 50 percent of the market value of eligible stocks long or short in a client's account.

minimum variation:
(1) 1/8th of a point differences found in the trading of securities.
(2) 1/32nd of a point differences found in the trading of government notes and bonds.

minimum yield: the lesser of yield to call and yield to maturity.

minipriced security: see *penny stocks.*

mini-warehouse limited partnership: a partnership that invests in small warehouses where people rent space to store personal effects and other belongings.

minority interest: the part of the net worth of a subsidiary relating to shares not owned by the controlling company or other members of the combined group.

minority investment: retaining less than 50 percent of a corporation's voting stock.

minority stockholder: a shareholder with less that 50 percent of a coproration's stock, individually or collectively.

minor trend: day-to-day shifts in security prices as contrasted to the longer intermediate and primary trends.

mint par of exchange: the figure derived by dividing the pure gold or silver weight of the monetary unit of one country by the pure similar metal weight of the monetary unit of another country.

mint price of gold: the price for gold which the government will pay upon delivery to the mint.

mint ratio: the ratio of the weight of one metal to another, and their equivalent in terms of the national unit of currency, such as the dollar (e.g., × grains of silver = × grains of gold = $1).

minus: the symbol (−) preceding a fraction or number in the change column at the far right of a newspaper stock tables designating a closing sale lower than that of the preceding day.

minus tick: synonymous with *down tick.*

minus yield: a situation where a convertible bond sells at a premium greater than the interest yield on the bond.

minute book: an official record of a corporation's scheduled meetings (e.g., stockholders' gathering, board of director's meeting, etc.).

miscellaneous stock: a security that does not properly belong to any particular industrial grouping.

missing the market: failing to execute a transaction on terms favorable to a client and thereby being a negligent broker. Should the order be executed later at a price shown to be less favorable, the broker, as the client's agent, may be required to make good on the amount lost.

MIT
(1) see *market-if-touched order.*
(2) modern investment theory. see *modern portfolio theory.*
(3) see *Municipal Investment Trust.*

mixed: a stock or commodity market characterized by generally uneven or trendless price shifts, with some prices advancing and others declining.

mixed account: a brokerage account where some securities are owned and some are borrowed.

mixed collateral: different forms of securities that are pledged against the payment of borrowed funds.

mixed currency: a currency consisting of (a) precious metals and notes, or (b) various kinds of precious metals.

mixing rates: used in the foreign exchange rate system, the use of varying rates of exchange for specific categories of overseas traded goods.

MJSD: March, June, September, December (quarterly interest payments or dividends).

Mkr.: see *maker.*

Mkt.: see *market.*

MLP: see *master limited partnership.*

MM: see entries under *money market.*

MMC: see *money market certificate.*

MMDA: see *money market deposit account.* see *Garnet St Germain Depository Institutions Act of 1982.*

MMF: see *money market fund.*

MO: in newspaper listings, stock traded on the Montreal Stock Exchange.

Mobile Home Certificates: lesser known variations of the Ginnie Mae. They are fully guaranteed pass-through securities consisting of mobile home mortgages carrying shorter maturities.

modern investment theory: synonymous with *modern portfolio theory.*

modern portfolio theory (MPT): the theoretical constructs that enable investment managers to classify, estimate and control the sources of risk and return; encompasses all notions of modern investment, as well as portfolio, theory. synonymous with *modern investment theory (MIT), new investment technology (NIT), portfolio theory.*

modified legal list: in some states, investment guidelines permitting fiduciaries to invest the majority of funds in legal list stocks and a portion in other stocks not found on that list.

momentum: the rate of acceleration in price or volume expansion, best noted by developing gaps in velocity figures, or gaps in an on-balance volume series. Upside momentum is greatest just short of price maturity, and downside momentum tends to reach a peak at or near an important bottom.

momentum indicator: a market indicator utilizing price and volume statistics for predicting the strength or weakness of a current market and any overbought or oversold conditions, and to note turning points within the market.

monetary indicator: an indicator showing the actions and policies of the Federal Reserve and Treasury Department that impact on equity and bond markets. Measures the liquidity presently available in the economy that can be added to the markets, and measures yield relations between alternative investments.

money: any denomination of coin or paper currency of legal tender that passes freely as a medium of exchange; anything that is accepted in exchange for other things (e.g., precious metals). Major characteristics of money include easy recognition, uniformity in quality, easy divisibility, and a relatively high value within a small area.

money broker: a person or institution serving as a go-between for borrowers and lenders of money.

money center bank: a bank in one of the primary financial centers of the world that, because they are significant lenders, affect a role in the movement of the markets.

money funds: a type of mutual fund. Though they have been marketed practically as bank accounts, the individual owns shares in a fund. The value is usually $1 per share, to make the accounting simple. The purchaser doesn't actually have a cash balance. The shares owned purchased prior to March 14, 1980 were free from new Federal Restrictions. synonymous with *investor funds.*

money manager: see *portfolio manager.*

money market: an international dealer market of trading short-term financial instruments released by governments, firms, and financial organizations. The major money market securities are Treasury bills, commercial paper, banker's acceptance, and negotiable certificates of deposit.

money market (brokers): all financial organizations that handle the purchase, sale, and transfer of short-term credit instruments and notes.

money market certificate (MMC): a six-month Federal Home Loan Bank Board certificate at federally insured savings and loan associations.

money market deposit account (MMDA): a market-sensitive bank account available since December 1982. Such accounts are required to have a minimum of $1000 (until Jan. 1, 1986) and only three checks can be drawn per month. Interest rates are comparable to rates on money market funds, though any particular bank's rate can be higher or lower.

money market fund (MMF)
(1) many investment banking firms sponsor money-market mutual funds, which invest in such short-term credit instruments as Treasury bills. Customers earn high interest rates on the accounts and can write checks against their investment. Commercial banks contend that these accounts are offering traditional commercial banking services without the restrictions that apply to commercial banks, such as reserve requirements on deposits. see *Glass-Steagall Act of 1933.*
(2) an investment vehicle whose primary objective is to make higher-interest securities available to the average investor who wants immediate income and high investment safety. This is accomplished through the purchase of high-yield money market instruments, such as U.S. government securities, bank certificates of deposit, and commercial paper.

money market instruments: private and government obligations with a maturity of one year or less. These include U.S. Treasury bills, bankers acceptances, commercial paper, finance paper, and short-term tax-exempts.

money market preferred stock: an adjustable-rate preferred stock, with an interest rate set by investor bidding for the stock, rather than by a formula.

money market rates: current interest rates on various money market instruments. The rates reflect the relative liquidity, security of investment, size of investment, term of investment, and general economic factors.

money markets: markets where short-term debt instruments are traded.

money market securities: high-quality and generally accepted senior securities whose market prices expressed on a yield basis relate more closely to the prevailing interest rate for money than to the risks in a company's operations or in general business conditions.

money multiplier: see *M-1A.*

money pinch: see *pinch.*

money price: the number of money units that must be sacrificed to purchase a particular commodity.

money rates: interest rates that lenders charge their borrowers.

money spread: see *calendar spreading, vertical spread.*

money stock: see *M-1A, M2, M3.*

money supply: the total sum of currency circulating in a country. see *price.* see also *money supply (Federal Reserve).*

money supply (Federal Reserve): measures several variants in the amount of money in the economy, issued each Thursday for the week that ended eight days earlier. It has been criticized as very erratic, subject to frequent revision.

monthly investment plan (MP): a pay-as-you-go method of buying odd lots of exchange listed shares on a regular payment plan for as little as $40 a month or every three months, and up to $1000 per payment. Under MIP the investor buys a stock designated by a securities broker by the dollar's worth. If the price advances, he or she gets fewer shares; if it declines, more shares. The investor may discontinue purchases at any time without penalty. cf. *investment company.*

monthly statement: in securities, an account issued by a brokerage house to its clients, stating the date, amount, prices, and so on, of any transaction for the month; plus a listing of dividends, interest, securities received or delivered, and the existing debit or credit balance.

mooch: slang, a person lured into purchasing securities with hopes of significant profits, without first making a careful investigation.

Moody's Bond Ratings and Stock Quality Groups

(a) bonds

Aaa: best quality, generally referred to as "gilt edge."

Aa: high quality by all standards; generally known as high-grade bonds.

A: possessing many favorable investment attributes and considered as high-medium-grade obligations.

Baa: considered as lower-medium-grade obligations—that is, neither highly protected nor poorly secured. Such bonds lack outstanding investment characteristics as well.

(b) preferred and common stocks

high quality: high quality by all standards.

good quality: possesses many favorable high-grade investment attributes.

medium quality: medium-grade equity securities.

Moody's Bond Yield (Annual Averages of Monthly Yield): represents the average yield on 40 operating utility companies' bonds (10 each of Class Aaa, Aa, A, and Baa) as determined and rated by Moody's Investors Service. This "yield" is the arithmetical average of 12 months and is calculated on the basis of market price, coupon rate, and on being "held to maturity."

Moody's Investment Grade: the rating by Moody's Investors Service, to some municipal short-term debt securities, classified as MIG-1, 2, 3, and 4 to indicate best, high, favorable, and adequate quality, respectively.

All four are investment grade or bank quality.

Moody's Investors Service: an independent service that examines, compares, and offers ratings for stocks, at the same time providing other financial data for investors.

MOP: see *margin of profit.*

moral obligation: a debt or responsibility whose payment or fulfillment is not based on legal rights or action.

moral obligation bond: see *bond, moral obligation.*

morning loan: bank loans to stockbrokers on an unsecured basis enabling the broker to handle stock deliveries until reimbursed by the customer.

mortgage

(1) a written conveyance of title to property, but not possession, to obtain the payment of a debt or the performance of some obligation, under the condition that the conveyance is to be void upon final payment.

(2) property pledged as security for payment of a debt. see *chattel.* cf. *conventional loan.*

mortgage-backed certificates: several banks, notably the Bank of America, have issued certificates covering pools of conventional mortgages insured by private mortgage insurance companies. These certificates are issued in big denominations, so the market is limited mainly to institutions.

mortgage-backed securities: bond-type investment securities representing an interest in a pool of mortgages or trust deeds. Income from the underlying mortgages is used to make investor payments.

mortgage banker: a banker who specializes in mortgage financing; an operator of a mortgage financing company. Mortgage financing companies are mortgagees themselves, as well as being mortgage agents for other large mortgages.

Mortgage Bankers Association of America (MBA): the professional and business organization of persons operating under the correspondency system whose major purpose is continuing improvement in the quality of service to investors.

mortgage banking: the packaging of mortgage loans secured by real property to be sold to a permanent investor with servicing retained by the seller for the life of the loan in exchange for a fee. The origination, sale, and servicing of mortgage loans by a firm or individual.

mortgage banking company: a specialist in purchase and sale of government-backed mortgages.

mortgage bond: see *bond, mortgage.*

mortgage broker: a firm or individual that brings the borrower and lender together, receiving a commission. A mortgage broker does not retain servicing.

mortgage certificate: an interest in a mortgage evidenced by the instrument, generally a fractional portion of the mortgage, which certifies as to the agreement between the mortgagees who hold the certificates and the mortgagor as to such terms as principal, amount, date of payment, and place of payment. Such certificates are not obligations to pay money, as in a bond or note, but are merely a certification by the holder of the mortgage, generally a corporate depository, that he or she holds such mortgage for the beneficial and undivided interest of all the certificate holders. The certificate itself generally sets forth a full agreement between the holder and the depository, although in some cases a more lengthy document, known as a *depository agreement*, is executed.

mortgage chattel: a mortgage on personal property.

mortgage clause: see *mortgagee clause.*

mortgage company: mortgage financing companies are mortgages themselves, as well as being mortgage agents for other large mortgagees. Serving as mortgage agents, these mortgage bankers collect payments, maintain complete mortgage records, and make remittances to the mortgagees for a set fee or service charge.

mortgage constant: synonymous with *constant ratio.*

mortgage correspondent: an agent of a lending institution authorized to handle and process loans.

mortgage credit certificates: devices that the 1984 Congress created to boost homeownership among less affluent families. The certificates give first-time home buyers as well as low- and middle-income families a tax credit for a portion of their mortgage interest. These credit certificates were designed as substitutes for the mortgage revenue bonds issued by states and cities to create low-interest mortgages.

mortgage debenture: a mortgage bond. see *bond, mortgage.*

mortgage debt: an indebtedness created by a mortgage and secured by the property mortgaged. A mortgage debt is made evident by a note or bond.

mortgage department: a department in banks, building and loan, savings and loan associations, and trust companies, where mortgage counselors, mortgage loan officers, and mortgage recording personnel handle all phases of mortgage work for mortgagors. This department may also act as "escrow agents" for mortgagors, in that they collect in the monthly payment from the mortgagor a portion of the real estate taxes, assessments on real estate, and hazard insurance. They hold these in escrow funds until payable, and then disburse the funds for the benefit of the mortgagor, and also the mortgagee, to prevent the development of liens against the property. In some states, they administer escrow funds in connection with closing mortgages, whereas in other states mortgage closings are required to be handled by attorneys-at-law.

mortgagee: the creditor or lender, to whom a mortgage is made. The mortgagor retains possession and use of the property during the term of the mortgage (e.g., the bank holds the mortgage on your house).

mortgagee clause: a clause in an insurance contract making the proceeds payable to a named mortgagee, as his or her interest may appear, and stating the terms of the contract between the insurer and the mortgagee. This is preferable usage but the same as *mortgage clause.*

Mortgage Guarantee Insurance Corporation: see *magic mortgage.*

mortgage guarantee policy: a policy issued on a guaranteed mortgage.

mortgage in possession: a mortgagee creditor who takes over the income from the mortgaged property upon default of the mortgage by the debtor.

mortgage insurance policy: issued by a title insurance firm to a mortgage holder, resulting in a title policy.

mortgage insurance premium (MIP): the consideration paid by a mortgagor for mortgage insurance—either to FHA or to a private mortgage insurer (MIC).

mortgage investment trust: a specialized form of real estate investment trust that invests in long-term mortgages, usually Federal Housing Administration-insured or Veterans Administration-guaranteed, and makes short-term construction and development loans.

mortgage lien: in a mortgage given as security for a debt, serving as a lien on the property after the mortgage is recorded.

mortgage life insurance: insurance on the life of the borrower that pays off a specified debt if he dies. synonymous with *credit life insurance.*

mortgage loan: a loan made by a lender, called the mortgagee, to a borrower, called the mortgagor, for the financing of a parcel of real estate. The loan is evidenced by a mortgage. The mortgage sets forth the conditions of the loan, the manner of repayment or liquidation of the loan, and reserves the right of foreclosure or repossession to the mortgagee. In case the mortgagor defaults in the payment of interest and principal, or if he or she permits a lien to be placed against the real estate mortgaged due to failure to pay the taxes and assessments levied against the property, the right of foreclosure can be exercised.

mortgage loan commitment: a written statement by a lender to grant a specific loan amount, at a given rate, for a certain term, secured by a specific property, if the real property transaction is closed before the expiration date.

mortgage loan ledger record: a document that contains a complete record of all transactions—payments of principal and interest, special disbursements, fees, charges, and the like—on a particular mortgage loan.

mortgage loan report: an updated report that requires the same kind of information as the full report plus a statement certifying that all Federal Housing Administration or Veterans Administration specifications, including public record items have been met.

mortgage note: a note that offers a mortgage as proof of an indebtedness and describes the manner in which the mortgage is to be paid. This note is the actual amount of debt that the mortgage obtains, and it renders the mortgagor personally responsible for repayment.

mortgage origination: the part of a mortgage banker's service involving performance of all details concerned with the making of a real estate loan.

mortgage-participation certificate: a pass-through security representing an undivided interest in a pool of mortgages purchased by the Federal Home Loan Mortgage Corporation. These mortgages are packaged and resold through these certificates. see *Federal Home Loan Mortgage Corporation.*

mortgage pass-through securities: a security consisting of a pool of residential mortgage loans with monthly distribution of 100 percent of the interest and principal to the investor. There are nongovernment-sponsored issues of these securities, as well as the government versions, Freddie Macs and Ginnie Maes.

mortgage pattern: the arrangement or design of payments and other terms established by a mortgage contract.

mortgage pool: a group of mortgages sharing similar characteristics, such as class of property, interest rate, and maturity. Investors purchase participations and receive income derived from payments on the underlying mortgages, providing liquidity, diversification, and a significantly attractive yield.

mortgage portfolio: the aggregate of mortgage loans or obligations held by a bank as assets.

mortgage premium: an additional bank fee charged for the giving of a mortgage when the legal interest rate is less than the prevailing mortgage market rate and there is a shortage of mortgage money.

mortgager(or): a debtor or borrower who gives or makes a mortgage to a lender, on property owned by the mortgagor.

mortgage REIT: the real estate investment trust that lends stockholder capital to real estate builders and buyers; also borrows from banks and relends that money at higher interest rates.

mortgage risk: the hazard of loss of principal or of anticipated interest inherent in an advance of funds on the security of a mortgage.

mortgage securities: see *Freddie Mac, Government National Mortgage Association, mortgage-backed certificates.*

mortgage servicing: the administration of a mortgage loan, including collecting monthly premiums and penalties on late payments, maintaining records of the amount of principal and interest already paid at a given time, serving as escrow agent for funds to cover taxes and insurance, and when needed, curing defaults and foreclosing when a homeowner is unnecessarily delinquent.

mortgagor: an owner who conveys his or her property as security for a loan (the debtor).

Mos.: months

MOS: see *margin of safety.*

MOSS: market oversight surveillance system; proposed by the Securities and Exchange Commission, a $12 million computerized surveillance network capable of monitoring every facet of securities trading in the country.

most active list: securities having the largest number of shares traded on a given day.

Mother Goose: a brief, nontechnical summary of what the full prospectus means; usually found at the very beginning of the prospectus.

movable exchange: instruments quoted in the currency of the nation in which payment is to be made rather than that in which the instrument is drawn.

movement: an increase or decrease in the price of a specific stock.

moving average: a technique for correcting small fluctuations of the stock market indicator to yield a general market trend.

moving bogeys: see *bogey.*

MP: see *market price.*

MPT: see *modern portfolio theory.*

MS

(1) see *majority stockholders.*
(2) March, September (semiannual interest payments or dividends).
(3) see *margin of safety.*
(4) see *minority stockholder.*
(5) see *money supply.*

M^s: the supply of nominal money, composed of checkable deposits and currency.

MSB: see *mutual savings bank.*

MSE: see *Midwest Stock Exchange.*

MSRB: see *Municipal Securities Rulemaking Board.*

Mtg.: see *mortgage.*

Mthly.: monthly.

MTNs: see *medium-term notes.*

multimanagement system: the use of more than one investment manager by the plan sponsor in order to provide diversification of management as well as diversification of styles and classes of investments.

multiple: see *price-earnings ratio.*

multiple capital structure company: a company having more than one class of outstanding securities.

multiple-commodity reserve dollar: a scheme to maintain a constant value ratio between gold and other commodities in terms of dollars, purporting to set a reserve of selected items. Money is redeemed in either gold or in these reserve goods, and gold and the reserve goods can always be exchanged for dollars. A constant ratio should be maintained between the value of the commodities, the gold, and the dollar.

multiple currency practice: arises when two or more effective exchange rates exist simultaneously, at least one of which, as the result of official action, is more than 1 percent higher or lower than the par value. Such practices are usually to be found where a dual exchange market exists or where the monetary authorities set different exchange rates for imports, exports, current invisibles, and capital. They often result from taxes or subsidies on specified exchange transactions.

multiple currency securities: securities, mostly bonds, payable in more than one currency at the election of the holder. In the event of devaluation of a currency, the holder can elect to be paid in the currency of a nation that has not devalued its currency.

multiple currency system: a means of controlling foreign exchange where domestic currency can be exchanged for foreign currency only through a government unit or controlled bank.

multiple exchange: three or more principals involved with various pieces of property.

muni: a *municipal bond.*

Munic.: municipal.

Municipal Assistance Corporation: see *MAC.*

municipal bond: see *bond, municipal.*

municipal bond fund: a mutual fund that invests in tax-exempt municipal bonds.

municipal bond insurance: policies underwritten by private insurers guaranteeing municipal bonds in the event of default.

Municipal Bond Insurance Association (MBIA): a pool of insurance firms that insure payment of both principal and interest on specific municipal bonds at maturity. All municipal bonds with MBIA insurance are rated AAA.

municipal funds: see *funds, municipal.*

municipal improvement certificates: certificates issued in lieu of bonds for the financing of special improvements.

municipal investment trust (MIT): a unit investment trust that purchases municipal bonds and passes the tax-free income on to stockholders. Sold through brokers, usually for a sales charge of about 3 percent of the principal paid, many MITs invest in the securities of just one state.

municipal notes: short-term securities of several months up to several years issued by a municipal authority.

municipal revenue bond: see *bond, municipal revenue.*

municipals: a popular word for the securities of a governmental unit.

Municipal Securities Rulemaking Board (MSRB): the self-regulation board that determines the regulations and registration requirements for the municipal securities industry.

Munifacts: a subscription service providing data about new municipal bond offerings.

munifund: synonymous with *mutual fund.* see *investment company.*

munis: Wall Street slang for municipal bonds. see *bond, municipal.*

mutilated security: a certificate that cannot be read for the name of an issue or issuer, or for the detail needed for identification and transfer, or for the exercise of the holder's rights. The seller has the obligation to take proper action, which frequently means having the transfer agent guarantee the rights of ownership to the purchaser.

mutual association: a savings association that issues no capital stock, but is owned and controlled solely by its savers and borrowers, who are called members. Members do not share in profits, because a mutual institution operates in such a way that it makes no "profit," but they exercise other ownership rights.

mutual company: a corporation without capital stock (e.g., mutual savings bank); the profits, after deductions, are distributed among the owner-customers in proportion to the business activity carried with the corporation.

mutual fund: an investment company which ordinarily stands ready to buy back (redeem) its shares at their current net asset value; the value of the shares depends on the market value of the fund's portfolio securities at the time. Also, mutual funds generally continuously offer new shares to investors. see also *investment company, money funds.* synonymous with *munifund, mutual investment fund.*

mutual fund cash ratio: the percentage of mutual funds' cash in relation to their total assets. More than ten percent is considered positive and 6 percent or less is considered unfavorable. A high ratio of cash to total assets is considered bullish since funds are available for investment. However, an increasing cash percentage is bearish because it indicates that mutual funds are withdrawing from the market.

mutual fund corporation: a trust company or commercial bank that provides safekeeping of securities owned by a mutual fund; may serve as a transfer agent, making payments to and collecting investments from stockholders.

mutual fund custodian: a trust company or commercial bank holding for safekeeping securities owned by a mutual fund.

mutual improvement certificate: a certificate issued by a local government in place of bonds to finance improvements or services, such as installing a sewer line, repaving a street, etc. The obligation is payable from a special tax assessment against those who benefit from the improvement, and the payments can be collected by the contractor doing the work.

mutual investment fund: synonymous with *mutual fund.*

mutual savings bank (MSB): a banking organization without capital stock, operating under law for the mutual benefit of the depositors. The depositor is encouraged to practice thrift, and the savings of these small depositors are invested in very high grade securities and some first-class mortgages. Dividends from these investments are mutually distributed after deduction of expenses of the association and reserves for a guaranty fund for depositors. The principal idea of a mutual savings bank is to perform a social service for small depositors who cannot invest their savings at high yield. see also *mutual company*.

mutual wills: a common arrangement executed pursuant to an agreement in which the husband and wife leave everything to each other.

MV: see *market value*.

N

N
(1) new issue (in stock listings of newspapers.)
(2) see *note.*

NA
(1) see *net assets.*
(2) no approval required (full discretion.)

NAIC: see *National Association of Investment Clubs.*

naked: synonymous with *uncovered.*

naked calls: the selling of options on stock that is not owned by a customer.

naked option: see *naked calls.*

naked option writer: synonymous with *uncovered writer.*

naked position: a stock position that is not hedged from market risks.

name
(1) as in a street name, used for easing security transfers.
(2) shorthand in foreign exchange markets referring to other participants (e.g., "I can't do the name," meaning "I am not allowed to trade with that institution").
(3) in Great Britain, a marking name. synonymous with *street name.*

name day: see *settlement day.*

N & M: November and May (semiannual interest payments or dividends).

narrowing the spread: closing the spread between a bid and asked price of a stock, resulting from bidding and offering by market makers and specialists in a stock.

narrow market: a condition that exists when the demand for a security is so limited that small alterations in supply or demand will create major fluctuations in the market price.

NASD: see *National Association of Security Dealers and Investment Managers.*

NASDAQ: see *National Association of Securities Dealers Automated Quotations.*

NASDAQ indexes: includes trading price averages computed by utilizing more than 3000 domestic over-the-counter firms. The seven NASDAQ indexes are the industrials, banks, insurance firms, other financial institutions, utilities, transportations, and the composite.

NASD 5 percent policy: a flexible rule for NASD members suggesting that commissions and markups and markdowns be about 5 percent on a traditional trade, but in all cases be fair. Exceptions to this rule include mutual fund sales, small transactions, exempt securities, and transactions that are difficult to complete.

NASD Form FR-1: the statement required of foreign dealers in stocks subscribing to new securities issues about to be distributed, where they agree to abide by the National Association of Securities Dealers regulations covering a hot issue. synonymous with *blanket certification form.*

NASDIM: see *National Association of Security Dealers and Investment Managers.*

NASD Rules of Fair Practice: the NASD rules dealing with ethics within the securities industry ensuring fair and just dealings between clients and members.

National Association of Investment Clubs (NAIC): a nation wide association that assists investment clubs in getting started.

National Association of Securities Dealers (NASD): see *National Association of Security Dealers and Investment Managers.*

National Association of Securities Dealers Automated Quotations (NASDAQ): an automated information network that provides brokers and dealers with price quotations on securities traded over the counter.

National Association of Security Dealers and Investment Managers (NASDIM): the Maloney Act, passed in 1938, which amended the Securities Exchange Act of 1934, provides for self-regulation of the over-the-counter securities market by associations registered with the SEC. The NASD (National Association of Security Dealers) became the only association so registered, and most companies offering variable annuities became NASD members. On January 1, 1984, the National Association of Security Dealers and Investment Managers was awarded official government recognitition as a self-regulatory body. NASDIM represents the efforts of a number of licensed securities dealers and its members no longer are required to apply for an annual license to deal in securities.

National Daily Quotation Service: the quotation service of the National Quotation Bureau. see *National Quotation Bureau.*

National Exchange Market System (NEMS): see *National Market Advisory Board.*

National Exchange Market System Act: synonymous with *Securities Act Amendments of 1975.*

National Farm Loan Association: an agricultural cooperative of local operation created as a result of the Federal Farm Loan Act. Upon subscription to shares of the Federal Land Bank in its area, the association can secure financing for farm mortgages.

National Futures Association (NAF): founded in 1982, a private-sector regulatory body in the futures markets. see also *Commodity Futures Trading Commission.*

National Housing Act of 1934: created the Federal Housing Administration to insure home mortgage, low-income housing project, and home inprovement loans made by private lenders; established the Federal Savings and Loan Insurance Corporation to insure savings accounts at member savings associations up to $5000.

National Market Advisory Board (NMAB): an SEC appointed board under provisions of the 1975 Securities Act to study and advise the commission on a National Exchange Market System (NEMS), a projected highly automated national exchange. cf. *National Market System.*

National Market System (NMS)
(1) the system of trading over the counter securities under the sponsorship of the National Association of Securities Dealers and NASDAQ. Trading in this system must fulfill specific criteria for size, profitability, and trading activity. National Market System stocks provide the stock name, dividend, high and low price for the past 52 weeks, trading volume, high and low price during the trading day, closing price on that day, and price change for that session.
(2) the national system of trading where the prices for stocks and bonds are listed simultaneously on the NYSE and on all regional exchanges. see also *National Market Advisory Board.*

National Mortgage Association: see *Federal National Mortgage Association.*

National Quotation Bureau (NQB): an organization that releases quotations on over-the-counter securities. see *pink sheets, white sheets, yellow sheets.*

National Securites Clearing Corporation (NSCC): the securities clearing organization established in 1977 by merging subsidiaries of the New York and American Stock Exchanges with the National Clearing Corporation; functions as a vehicle for brokerage houses, exchanges, and other clearing corporations to reconcile accounts with one another.

National Securities Trade Association (NSTA): the organization of brokerage houses and dealers involved in over-the-counter markets.

National Security Exchange: not to be confused with the National Stock Exchange; any exchange labeled by the SEC. Included are most of the larger exchanges. Only a few smaller exchanges are not designated as National Security Exchanges.

National Stock Exchange (NSE): the third stock exchange of New York City, established in 1960.

natural financing
(1) a real estate transaction requiring no outside financing, as is demanded in cash sales.
(2) the selling of properties that do not call for a third party.

natural interest rate: the interest rate at which the demand for loanable funds just equals the supply of savings. The interest rate that keeps the flow of money incomes constant rather than the interest rate, which keeps the price level constant.

natural monopoly
(1) a monopoly due to natural conditions (e.g., a crop that demands special climate is subject to monopolization by a grower in the area having that climate).
(2) among industries that experience economies of scale, the cost per unit is lowest when there is only one company in the industry.

NAV: see *net asset value.*

NC
(1) see *net capital.*
(2) see *net cost.*
(3) no charge.
(4) on bond offering sheets designating bond, the abbreviation for noncallable. see *bond, noncallable.*

NCB: see *bond, noncallable.*

NCS: see *noncallable securities.*

NCV: no commercial value.

ND: next day delivery (in stock listings of newspapers). see *next day.*

NE: see *net earnings.*

nearby delivery: the closest active month of delivery, as stated in a commodity futures agreement.

nearest month: in option trading or commodity futures, the date of expiration given in months, closest to the present. Nearest month contracts are always more heavily traded than furthest month contracts.

near money: highly liquid assets (e.g., government securities) other than official currency.

near option: that side of a stock spread option position expiring before the other side does. see *spread* cf. *far option.*

near term: research analysis of market performance over a one-to-five-week time frame.

negative amortizer: when a home buyer gets a bank mortgage below the going rate and the difference is added to the principal. Payments are low to start but much higher later.

negative carry: a condition when the cost of funds borrowed to finance stocks is higher than the yield on the stocks. cf. *positive carry.*

negative cash flow: the condition of a firm spending more cash than it receives through earnings or other transations in an accounting period.

negative coverage: a property financed by a mortgage with a debt service that tops its earnings.

negative float: see *float.*

negative income tax: proposed by some to provide financial aid to individuals with incomes below a certain minimum. Rulings of the Internal Revenue Service would be followed, but the procedure would be to distribute rather than collect revenue.

negative interest: money deducted from or paid on interest.

negative investment: see *disinvestment.*

negatively sloping yield curve: a yield curve where interest rates in the shorter dates are above those in the longer dates.

negative net worth: synonymous with *deficit net worth.*

negative working capital: the condition where current liabilities of a company exceeds its current assets. Unless corrected, the company will be unable to pay debts when due. Bankruptcy may then follow.

negative yield: when the return from savings is less than the rate of inflation and taxes, the result is loss of capital.

negative yield curve: the condition where yields on short-term stocks are higher than those on long-term stocks of the same quality. synonymous with *inverted yield curve.*

Negb.: see *negotiable.*

Neg. Inst.: see *negotiable instrument.*

negotiable
(1) ***general:*** anything that can be sold or transferred to another for money or as payment of a debt.
(2) ***investments:*** a security, title to which is transferable by delivery.

negotiable certificate of deposit: a time deposit at a fixed rate of coupon interest. An issuer must redeem at maturity at the face value ($100,000 minimum) plus the stated interest rate. Holders may resell the instrument in the secondary market at prevailing rates.

negotiable instrument: the Uniform Negotiable Instruments Act states: "An instrument, to be negotiable, must conform to the following requirements: (a) it must be in writing and signed by the maker or drawer; (b) it must contain an unconditional promise or order to pay a certain sum in money; (c) it must be payable on demand, or at a fixed or determinable future time; (d) it must be payable to order or to bearer; and (e) where the instrument is addressed to a drawee, he or she must be named or otherwise indicated therein with reasonable certainty."

negotiable order of withdrawal: see *NOW account.*

negotiable paper: negotiable instruments that are used in the borrowing of money on a short-term period for business objectives.

negotiable securities: bearer instruments that result in the transfer of title by assignment or delivery. Bearer bonds, bearer notes, bearer warrants, stock certificates, and coupons can be negotiated, as distinguished from registered securities.

negotiate: in finance, to transfer a written obligation such as a note or bond. To handle successfully.

negotiated bid: in underwriting, when the issuer and a single underwriting syndicate agree on the price through mutual understanding. Most common stock underwritings are negotiated. cf. *competitive bid.*

negotiated purchase: the process of preparation of a security issue by the issuing company by negotiation with the underwriting investment banking firms. cf. *competitive bid.*

negotiated sale: a private arrangement between two or more parties to finance the sale of securities by an issuer, without competitive public bidding.

negotiated underwriting: the underwriting of new issues where the spread between the purchase price paid to an issuer and the public offering price is set through negotiations rather than multiple competitive bidding. Most corporate stock and bond issues and municipal revenue bond issues are priced through negotiation, while municipal general obligation bonds and new issues of public utilities are usually priced through competitive bidding.

NEMS: National Exchange Market System. see *National Market Advisory Board.*

net

(1) ***general:*** that which remains after certain designated deductions have been made from the gross amount.

(2) ***investments:*** the dollar different between proceeds from the sale of a stock and the seller's adjusted cost of acquisition, either the gain or loss.

net assets: the property of a business, corporation, organization or estate, remaining after all obligations have been met.

net asset value (NAV): it is common practice for investment companies to compute assets daily, or even twice daily, by totaling the market value of all securities owned. All liabilities are deducted; the balance is divided by the number of shares outstanding. The resulting figure is the net asset value per share.

net avails: the funds given to a borrower in the discounting of a note. It is equal to the face value of the note minus the discount.

net balance: the amount due at a particular time, after all refunds have been calculated. Often called *net payoff.*

net bonded debt: gross bonded debt less applicable cash or other assets.

net borrowed reserves: borrowings less excess reserves.

net capital: a firm's net worth (assets minus liabilities) minus certain deductions, for assets that may not be easily converted into cash at their full value. In the securities industry, net capital is used to determine whether a brokerage house can be considered solvent and capable of operating.

net capital productivity: synonymous with *marginal efficiency of capital.*

net capital ratio: synonymous with *net captial requirement.*

net capital requirement: the SEC requirement that member firms as well as nonmember broker-dealers in stocks maintain a maximum ratio or indebtedness to liquid capital of 15 to 1. synonymous with *net capital ratio, net capital rule.*

net capital rule: synonymous with *net capital requirement.*

net change: the change in the price of a security between the closing price on one day and the closing price on the following day on which the stock is traded. The net change is ordinarily the last figure on the stock price list. The mark is +1¼ means "up $1.250 a share from the last sale on the previous day the stock had been traded."

net charge-offs as percent of average net loans: loan charge-offs less recoveries as percent of net average loans outstanding. Net loans are gross loans outstanding minus unearned income and the valuation portion of loan loss reserves on an average daily basis for the year. A minus sign indicates that recoveries exceeded share-offs.

net cost

(1) ***general:*** the true cost of an item. The net cost is determined by subtracting all income or financial gain from the gross cost.

(2) ***insurance:*** the total premiums paid on a policy less any dividends, and the surrender value as of the time the net cost is determined.

net current assets: the dollar difference, if a positive number, between the current assets of a firm and its current liabilities. synonymous with *net working capital.*

net debt: the sum of fixed and existing liabilities less the sinking fund and other assets that are earmarked for payment of the liabilities.

net earnings (NE): the excess of gross operating income over gross operating expenses is referred to as "operating earnings before taxes." Income taxes applicable to operating earnings are deducted, to arrive at "net earnings" or "net operating earnings."

net estate: the part of an estate remaining after all expenses to manage it have been taken out.

net federal funds borrowed as percent of average net loans outstanding: net federal funds borrowed are the bank-calculated average federal funds purchased and securities sold under agreements to repurchase, less the bank-calculated average federal funds sold and securities purchased under agreements to resell. A minus sign indicates that the bank was a net seller of federal funds. see *net charge-offs as percent of average net loans.*

net for common stock: net income less dividends on preferred stock applicable to the period on an accrual basis.

net foreign investment: the net change in the nation's foreign assets and liablilites, including the monetary gold stocks, arising out of current trade, income on foreign investment, and cash gifts and contributions. It measures the excess of (a) exports over imports, (b) income on U.S. public and private investment abroad over payments on foreign investment abroad over payments on foreign investment in the U.S., and (c) cash gifts and contributions of U.S. (public and private) to foreigners over cash gifts and contributions received from abroad.

net income: the remains from earnings and profits after all costs, expenses, and allowances for depreciation and probable loss have been deducted.

net income after dividends: net income less dividends on preferred stock applicable to the period and dividends declared on common stock during the period.

net income multiplier: a figure which, times the net income of a property, produces an estimate of value of that property. It is obtained by dividing the selling price by the monthly net rent (net income).

net income per share of common stock: the amount of profit or earnings allocated to a share of common stock after all costs, taxes, allowances for depreciation, and potential losses have been deducted; given in dollars and cents. synonymous with *earnings per share (EPS).*

net income to net worth ratio: see *return on equity.*

net interest cost: the average rate of interest over the life of a bond which an issuer must pay to borrow funds.

net investment income per share: the income received by an investment firm from dividends and interest on stock investments during a given accounting period, less management fees and administrative expenses and divided by the number of outstanding shares.

net liquid assets: the dollar difference between a firm's cash and readily marketable securities and its current liabilities.

net listing: the broker receives as commission all monies received above minimum sales price agreed to by owners and broker.

net long-term debt: total long-term debt, less cash and investment assets of sinking funds and other reserve funds specially held for redemption of long-term debt.

net loss: the excess of expenses and losses during a specified period over revenues and gains in the same time frame.

net operating earnings: see *net earnings.*

net operating income: net current operating income after minority interest and taxes but before securities gains and losses and preferred dividends for the year ending on December 31.

net option: a written instrument granting the right to buy a property at a specified price to the owner.

net out: determining a customer's position by calculating how much margin must be posted at the exchange.

net payoff: see *net balance.*

net position: the difference between the open contracts long and the open contracts short held in any one commodity by an individual or group.

net present value (NPV): a technique for evaluating investments where all cash outflows and cash inflow are determined by utilizing a discount rate, usually a required rate of return. An investment is acceptable when the NPV is positive.

net proceeds: an amount, traditionally cash, received from a sale or disposition of property, from a loan, or from the sale or issuance of stocks following deduction of all costs incurred in the transaction.

net profit: the excess of all revenues over all costs and expenses incurred to obtain the income in a given enterprise during a given period of time. If the total expenses exceed the income, such amount is known as the net loss. synonymous with *net revenue.*

net profit on net sales: obtained by dividing the net earnings of the business, after taxes, by net sales (the dollar volume less returns, allowances, and cash discounts). This is an important yardstick in measuring profitability.

net profits on net working capital: net working capital represents the equity of the owners in the current assets, as obtained by subtracting total current debt from total current assest, as obtained by subtracting total current debt from total current assets. This equity, or margin, represents the cushion available to the business for carrying inventories and receivables, and for financing day-to-day operations. To illustrate how net working capital is computed: if a concern has current assets of $1 million and current debt of $400,000, its net working capital is $600,000.

net profits on tangible net worth: tangible net worth is the equity of stock holders in the business, as obtained by subtracting total liabilities from total assets, and then deducting intangibles. The ratio is obtained by dividing net profits after taxes by tangible net worth. The tendency is to look increasingly to this ratio as a final criterion of profitability. Generally, a relationship of at least 10 percent is regarded as a desirable objective for providing dividends plus funds for future growth.

net quick assets: cash, marketable securities, and accounts receivable, minus current liabilities. Inventory is not included.

net realized capital gain per share: the amount of net capital gains realized on the sale of portfolio securities during an accounting period after deducting losses realized, divided by the number of shares outstanding.

net revenue: synonymous with *net profit.*

net revenue available for debt service: gross operating revenues of an enterprise less operating and maintenance expenses but exclusive of depreciation and bond interest. "Net revenue" as thus defined is used to compute "coverage" on revenue bond issues.

net sales: gross sales, minus returns and allowances, over a stated period.

net sales to inventory: obtained by dividing annual net sales by merchandise inventory as carried on the balance sheet. This quotient does not yield an actual physical turnover. It provides a yardstick for comparing stock-to-sales ratios of one concern with another or with those for the industry.

net sales to net working capital: net sales are divided by net working capital. This provides a guide as to the extent the company is turning its working capital and the margin of operating funds.

net sales to tangible net worth: obtained by dividing net sales by tangible net worth. The result gives a measure of the relative turnover of capital. If capital is turned over too rapidly, liabilities build up excessively, as amounts owed to creditors become a substitute for permanent capital. And if capital is turned too slowly, funds become stagnant, and profitability suffers.

net surplus: the earnings or profits remaining to a corporation after all operating expenses, taxes, interests insurance, and dividends have been paid out. The surplus is determined before deducting dividends while the net surplus is determined following the deduction of dividends.

net tangible assets per share: the total assets of a firm, less all intangible assets, such as goodwill, patents, and trademarks, minus all liabilities and the par value of preferred stock, divided by the number of common shares outstanding.

net transaction: in securities trading, where no further fee is levied on either a buyer or a seller.

net unrealized appreciation: the appreciation between investment cost and current market value of a person's holdings.

net unrealized depreciation: the decline between investment cost and current market value of a person's holdings.

net volume: the difference between uptick and downtick volume.

Network A: a subscription service from the Consolidated Tape Association providing successive round-lot transaction statements received for NYSE-listed securities regardless of the marketplace on which the transaction occurred. cf. *Network B.*

Network B: a subscription service from the Consolidated Tape Association providing successive round-lot transaction statements received for ASE-listed securities regardless of the marketplace on which the transaction occurred. cf. *Network A.*

net working capital: synonymous with *net current assets.*

new worth

(1) ***general:*** the owner's equity in a given business, represented by the excess of the total assets over the total amounts owing to outside creditors at a given moment of time.

(2) ***investments:*** the sum of preferred stock, common stock, capital surplus, and retained earnings.

net yield: the return from an investment following subtractions for costs and losses incurred in operating the investment.

net yield to redemption: the gross yield to redemption on a security, adjusted to take account of taxation.

neutral money: a system under which the dollar would be convertible into commodities at a fixed price with the object of stabilizing the price level.

neutral spread: an investment strategy, since on the downside it is impossible to lose more than commission costs. It involves buying a call option on a stock for a specific time period and selling two call option on the same stock for the same period, but at a higher exercise price. The idea is to pick a stock whose options at the high exercise price are trading at about half the price, or premium, of the option bought. The out-of-pocket costs are just the commissions on doing the deal. synonymous with *ratio bull spread, twofer.*

neutral trend: the sideways price direction of a stock.

new account report: a statement completed by a broker detailing vital information about a new customer's financial conditions and investment goals.

New England NOW Accounts: a 1979 federal law that expanded NOW account authority to federally chartered associations in Connecticut, Maine, Rhode Island, and Vermont. see also *NOW account.*

new high: usually, the highest price that a security has attained since its exchange listing.

new housing authority bond: see *bond, new housing authority.*

new investment technology: synonymous with *modern portfolio theory.*

new issue: a stock or bond sold by a corporation for the first time. Proceeds may be issued to retire outstanding securities of the company to finance new plant or equipment, or to secure additional working capital.

new issue market: the market for new issues of securities (as opposed to the secondary market on securities already issued.)

new low: the lowest price a stock or market index has ever attained.

new money: the amount of further long-term financing provided by a new issue(s) in excess of the amount of a maturing issue or by being refunded.

new money approach to investment income: an investment income allocation technique used by insurance companies whereby an attempt is made to allocate investment income under a group annuity contract on the basis of the rate of return earned on new investments made in the year in which each block of contributions was received. synonymous with *investment year method.*

new money preferred: a preferred stock issued after October 1, 1942 when the tax exclusion for corporate investors receiving preferred stock dividends was increased from 60 percent to 85 percent, to equal the exclusion on common stock dividends. cf. *old money preferred.*

news ticker: a machine, often located in brokerage houses, providing up-to-the-minute news stories on world affairs, business conditions, market information, corporation actions and so on. synonymous with *news wire.*

news wire: synonymous with *news ticker.*

New York call money: funds borrowed by brokerage houses to meet short-term financial requirements for clients who maintain margin accounts.

New York Coffee and Sugar Exchange (NYCSCE): founded in 1982, when it was originally known as the New York Coffee Exchange, it is the principal U.S. exchange for the trading of coffee and sugar futures contracts. see *Commodities Exchange Center.*

New York Cotton Exchange: see *securities and commodities exchanges.*

New York Curb Exchange (NYCE): the former name for the American Stock Exchange.

New York Futures Exchange (NYFE): created in 1980, resulting from the absorption of the Amex Commodities Exchange (ACE). The new exchange began with trading futures in Treasury bonds, and contracts in five foreign currencies: British pounds, Canadian dollars, Japanese yen, Swiss francs and West German marks.

New York Insurance Exchange: opened in March 1980, allows insurance brokers to place large business orders with a variety of underwriters on one exchange floor.

New York Interest: interest computed by the exact days in a month rather than by use of a 30-day month or other. cf. *Boston interest.*

New York Mercantile Exchange (NYME): founded in 1872 as a market for cheese, butter, and eggs, its principal commodities include potatoes, silver coins, and platinum. see *Commodities Exchange Center.*

New York NOW accounts: legislation passed in 1978 permitting FSLIC-insured institutions in New York State to offer NOW accounts. see *NOW account.*

New York plan: the technique for transferring ownership of equipment bought through the use of equipment trust certificates, where title to the equipment passes to the purchaser as the debit is retired. see *equipment trust certificate.* cf. *Philadelphia plan.*

New York Stock Exchange (NYSE): the largest, most prestigious security exchange in the world, reorganized under its existing name in 1863. In 1817, the New York Stock and Exchange Board moved indoors to a second-floor room at 40 Wall Street in New York City. On January 2, 1863, the title was changed to the New York Stock Exchange, and on the next day, the first subsidiary, the New York Stock Exchange Building Company, was created. see also *NYSE Common Stock Index.*

New York Stock Exchange Averages: a general market indicator comprised of the prices of 25 industrial and railroads stocks.

New York Stock Exchange Composite Index: the average calculated using all of the common shares of NYSE list companies. This composite index uses a base-weighted aggregate method for calculating its average. The four subgroup indexes are: NYSE Industrials, NYSE Transportations, NYSE Utilitles, and NYSE Financials.

New York Stock Exchange volume: the total shares traded on any given day on the New York Stock Exchange.

next-day (ND): commitments to provide usable, or same-day funds on day two.

NFA: see *National Futures Association.*

NH
(1) see *new high.*
(2) see *not held.*

NI
(1) see *negotiable instrument.*
(2) see *net income.*

niche: a particular specialty where a company has garnered a significant share of the market.

NICs: newly industrializing countries (e.g., Mexico, South Korea, Brazil, and Taiwan).

NIFs: see *note issuance facilities.*

NIL: negotiable instruments law. see *negotiable instrument.*

nine-bond rule: the NYSE regulation requiring any order received by a member firm for nine or less bonds that are listed on the NYSE to first be sent to the floor of the exchange, then should the order not be filled in one hour, it can be filled in the over-the-counter market.

ninety-day savings account: an account paying interest usually equivalent to that paid on 90-day deposits in savings certificates. The account is a passbook account and is subject to substantial interest penalties if funds are withdrawn prior to the end of the 90-day period. If funds are left on deposit after 90 days, the pledge is automatically renewed for an additional period.

NINOW's: noninterest-bearing NOW accounts.

NIP: see *normal investment practice.*

NIT
(1) see *negative income tax.*
(2) see *new investment technology.*

NL
(1) see *net loss.*
(2) see *no-load funds.*

NLF: see *no-load funds.*

NLO: see *no-limit order.*

NM: see *narrow market.*

NMAB: see *National Market Advisory Board.*

NMF: see *nonmember firm.*

NMS: see *National Market System.*

N/O: registered in name of.

no-action letter: an SEC letter in response to a request for clarification of whether federal regulation may prohibit a proposed action. In such a communication, the SEC agrees to take neither civil nor criminal action.

no-brainer: the direction of a market that is obvious, thereby requiring little or no analysis, suggesting that most of the stock will climb in a strong bull market and fall in a bear market.

no lien affidavit: a written document by a property owner that the work has been finished on an identified property and that no liens or mortgages encumber it. cf. *lien affidavit.*

no-limit order: a request to buy or sell a security without any stipulation about price. cf. *limited order.*

no-litigation certificate: a statement issued by the bond attorney that there are no legal suits pending (and that as far as he or she knows none is being planned) that might result in an impairment of the validity of the bonds.

no load: without any sales charge. With mutual funds, shares sold at net asset value.

no-load funds: mutual funds that are not sold by a salesperson. They do not involve extensive marketing schemes and contain no sales charge or load.

nominal

(1) the face value of a bond.

(2) the probable level of a market, but that level is not based on actual transactions.

nominal account: an account established to analyze the changes in the surplus account. These include expense and income accounts which are closed into surplus at the end of each fiscal period. cf. *real accounts.*

nominal asset: an asset whose value is inconsiderable, to be questioned, or difficult to evaluate such as claims or judgments in reorganization. Accounting tradition suggests that nominal assets be written down and carried as some token value, usually one dollar. Copyrights, goodwill, and other such assets can be considered nominal assets.

nominal capital: the par value of issued shares of a corporation, as differentiated from the book or market value.

nominal cost: cost measured in monetary units at the time it was incurred, that is, ignoring changes in the purchasing power of money. cf. *real costs.*

nominal exercise price: the exercise price of a Government National Mortgage Association option contract.

nominal interest rate: the contractual interest rate shown on the face and in the body of a bond and representing the amount of interest to be paid, in contrast with the effective interest rate. synonymous with *coupon rate.*

nominally issued: capital stock, funded debt, and other securities when they are signed and sealed or certified and placed with the proper officer for sale and delivery, or pledged or placed in some special fund of the issuing corporation.

nominally outstanding: securities reacquired by or for the issuing corporation under each circumstance as requires them to be considered as held alive, and not canceled or retired. see *actually outstanding.*

nominal partner: an individual who lends his or her name to a business organization but is not a true partner because he or she may not have given sufficient financial backing or he or she does not take a full share of the profit.

nominal price
(1) ***general:*** an amount of money so small in relation to the item purchased that it hardly justifies the use of the word "price."
(2) ***investments:*** an estimated price for a security or commodity that is not traded often enough to warrant the setting of a definite market price.

nominal quotation: bid and offer prices given by a market maker for the purpose of valuation, not as a suggestion to trade. Regulations require that nominal quotations be identified as such. synonymous with *numbers only.*

nominal rate of exchange: the post rate of exchange, allowing a person to have a sound idea of what the foreign exchange rate is and which is used for small foreign exchange transactions.

nominal return on an asset: the rate of return in monetary terms (i.e., unadjusted for any change in the price level).

nominal value: used in the United Kingdom for face value, or par value. In the United States, this term is equivalent to *par value.* see *face value.*

nominal yield: the rate of return stated on a security calculated on its par or face value.

nominee name: the registered name issued by the controller of the currency into which a bank or a trust company registers the securities it holds as custodian and/or investment agent for its trust department portfolios thereby facilitating the making of "good" delivery to brokers at time of sale or exchange.

nonassented securities: securities whose holders have not agreed to some change in the terms or status of a defaulted security. cf. *assented securities.*

nonassessable stock: most securities; stock whose owners cannot be assessed in the event of failure or insolvency. cf. *limited liability.*

nonassignable: synonymous with *inalienable.*

noncallable bond: see *bond, noncallable.*

noncallable securities (NCS): stocks that cannot be redeemed prior to maturity, even if the issuing company can afford to do so. They are not subject to call.

noncarry: involving a market that handles perishable commodities, such as cattle, sugar, coffee, and so on.

noncash: constituting financial sources other than cash.

nonclearinghouse stock: securities that do not clear through the New

York Stock Exchange Clearing Corporation, including stocks traded on other exchanges or over the counter.

nonclearing member: an exchanges' member firm without adequate operational equipment for clearing transactions and turns to another member firm to provide these services. A fee is involved.

noncompetitive bid: the means of purchasing Treasury bills without having to meet the high minimum purchase requirements of the regular dutch auction. Treasury bills are bid either as competitive or noncompetitive bids. synonymous with *noncompetitive tender.*

noncompetitive tender: synonymous with *noncompetitive bid.*

noncontingent preference stock: cumulative preferred stock.

noncontributory: describing a group insurance plan under which the policyholder (employee) pays the entire cost.

Non. Cum.: see *noncumulative.*

noncumulative: a preferred stock on which unpaid dividends do not accrue. Omitted dividends are, as a rule, gone forever.

noncumulative dividends: dividends not distributed by a corporation at its usual payment date, they do not accrue for the benefit of the stockholders and, therefore, are lost forever.

noncumulative preferred stock: a preferred stock issued with the agreement that should a dividend not be paid out by the corporation it will not accrue for the benefit of the preferred stockholders.

noncumulative voting: see *statutory voting.*

noncurrent asset: an asset not expected to be converted into cash, to be sold, or exchanged within the normal operating cycle of the firm, usually one year.

noncurrent liabilities: claims against the assets of an entity that will become due a year or more later.

no near bid-offer: where the highest bid or lowest offer is relatively far below or above the price of the previous sale.

nonexempt: a bond exempt from redemption for stated period of time.

nonforfeiture options: privileges allowed under terms of a life insurance contract after cash values have been created. Four privileges exist: (a) surrender for full cash value; (b) loans up to the full amount of the cash value; (c) paid-up policy for the amount of insurance that cash value, as a single premium, will buy at net rates; and (d) term insurance for full face amount of the original policy for as long as the cash value will last to pay necessary premiums.

nonindexed bond: see *bond, nonindexed.*

noninsured fund: a pension or other fund invested through channels other than deposit with an insurance company.

non-interest-bearing bond: see *bond, noninterest bearing.*

non-interest-bearing note: a note whose maker does not have to pay any interest.

noninvestment property: property that will not yield income.

nonledger asset: assets not carried in the general ledger, such as accrued dividends, uncollected and deferred premiums, and excess of market value of securities over book value.

nonlegal investment: an investment that is outside the classes designated by statute or by some governmental agency as proper for the investment of trust funds. cf. *unauthorized investment.*

nonlegals: securities that do not conform to the requirements of the statutes, in certain states, concerning investments for savings banks and for trust funds; opposed to legals. see *legal list.*

nonmarketable liabilities of U.S. government (including medium-term securities): other medium-term securities include foreign holdings of nonmarketable, medium-term U.S. government securities, payable before maturity only under special conditions. Examples of these are nonconvertible "Roosa Bonds" issued by the Treasury, and Certificates of Participation representing Export-Import Bank loans sold mainly to foreign governments and central banks.

nonmarket risk: the volatility of returns of securities in a portfolio not related to the movement of the market in general.

nonmember firm: any brokerage firm that is not a member of the New York Stock Exchange. Usually such houses sell securities in the third market, often at lower fees than those charged by New York Stock Exchange members. see *member firm.*

nonmortgage loan: an advance of funds not secured by a real estate mortgage.

nonnegotiable: wanting in one of the requirements of a negotiable instrument, and as a consequence not entitled to the benefits of negotiability, such as freedom from many defenses that could otherwise be raised by the maker (e.g., fraudulent inducement). A nonnegotiable document is transferable by assignment. To prevent transfer, the label "nontransferable" should be used.

nonnegotiable certificate of deposit: a nonnegotiable instrument issued by banks and other financial organizations to the public, offering considerable safety, and sound return. They are not negotiable and carry high penalties for early withdrawal.

nonnegotiable instrument: a legal instrument of value that cannot be freely or readily sold or transferred to another party.

nonnegotiable title: a title that cannot be transferred by delivery or by endorsement.

nonparticipating group annuity contract: a contract with an insurance company providing income to participants (usually 10 or more) for which the insurance company alone assumes the mortality and investment risk.

nonparticipating preferred stock: see *participating preferred.*

nonpublic information: data about a firm that will significantly alter the price of its stock when it is released to the public. Insiders are prohibited from using this information before it has reached the public.

nonpurpose loan: a loan for which stocks are pledged as collateral but are not used to purchase or carry securities.

nonqualified: the failure to meet the requirements in the pertinent provisions of the applicable regulations for tax preference (e.g., a nonqualified stock-option plan).

nonqualifying annuity: an annuity purchased outside of an IRS-approved pension plan. The earnings from this annuity can accumulate tax deferred until withdrawn. cf. *qualifying annuity.*

nonqualifying stock option: an employee stock option not fulfilling the IRS regulations for favorable long-term capital gains treatment. Gains from the exercise of nonqualifying options are treated as ordinary income in the tax year in which the options are exercised.

nonrecourse loan: where a limited partner borrows funds to partially fund his or her participation in the partnership and pledges as collateral his or her ownership in the venture. Allows the lender to attach the ownership but not other assets of the partnership.

nonrecurring charge: any one-time income or expense entered on the income statement of the firm.

nonrefundable: a bond indenture provision that either prohibits or sets limits on the issuer's retiring the bonds with the proceeds of a subsequent issue. shortened to *not rated.*

nonresident-owned (NRO) funds: open-end investment companies, notably in Canada, the shares of which are sold to U.S. investors.

nonrevenue receipts: collections, other than revenue, such as receipts from loans where the liability is recorded in the fund in which the proceeds are placed and receipts on account of recoverable expenditures.

nonstock corporation: the type of nonprofit corporation in which the members hold no stock. Among these are religious, charitable, mutual insurance, and municipal corporations.

nonstock money corporation: any corporation operating either under the banking law or the insurance law which does not issue stock (e.g., mutual savings banks, credit unions, mutual insurance companies).

nontaxable dividend: funds paid to stockholders that are specified as return of capital. Though nontaxable at distribution, the cost basis of the stock must be reduced by the amount received.

nontaxable securities: securities having some tax-exempt features, the most common being the exemption for holders of municipal securities when filing their income taxes.

nonvoting stock: securities of any class within a firm other than voting stock. They cannot be listed by the New York Stock Exchange. see *listing requirements.*

non-par value: having no face value.

non-par-value stock: stock of a corporation without designated par value.

no-passbook savings: the same as a regular passbook savings account, except that no passbook is used. Deposits and withdrawal slips are receipted by the teller, with a copy returned to the depositor for personal records. A periodic statement is rendered in place of a passbook. Withdrawals must be made by the depositor personally.

normal beta: sponsors desired portfolio beta (exposure to systematic risk).

normal investment practice (NIP): the history of investment in a client account with a member of the National Association of Securities Dealers as defined in their fair practice's rules; used for testing the bona fide public offerings requirement that applies to the allocation of a hot issue. A record of purchasing only hot issues is not considered acceptable as a normal investment practice. see also *NASD Form FR-1.*

normal lending territory: synonymous with *regular lending area.*

normal price: the price to which the market price tends to return following fluctuations up or down.

normal profit: the lowest price that an entrepreneur will accept as compensation for his or her activity. It is part of an organization's total economic costs, since it is a payment that must be received by the owner to keep him from withdrawing capital and effort that might have to be used in another way.

normal return: the income on a specific investment, computed at a standard interest rate.

normal sale: a transaction that pleases both the seller and buyer of property and in which no unforeseen or abnormal situations surface.

normal trading unit (NTU): synonymous with *round lot.*

not a delivery: when an instrument or document does not meet the requirements of an exchange and contains a fault.

notarial acknowledgment: the acknowledgment of the due execution of a legal instrument before a notary public. The statement of the notary public as to the face and date of the acknowledgment, with the notary public's signature and seal of office and date of expiration of commission to serve as notary public.

notarial certificate: the certificate of the notary public as to the due acknowledgment of the instrument.

notarial protest certificate: see *notice of dishonor (protest jacket).*

notarized draft: a withdrawal order signed and acknowledged before a notary public, who affirms that the person who signed the draft personally appeared before him or her, was known to be the person indicated, and executed the draft for the purpose indicated.

notary public: a person commissioned by a state for a stipulated period (with the privilege of renewal) to administer certain oaths and to attest and certify documents, thus authorizing him or her to take affidavits and depositions. A notary is also authorized to "protest" negotiable instruments for nonpayment or nonacceptance. see *notice of dishonor (protest jacket).*

note (N): an instrument, such as a promissory note, which is the recognized legal evidence of a debt. A note is signed by the maker, called the borrower, promising to pay a certain sum of money on a specified date at a certain place of business, to a certain business, individual, or bank, called the lender.

note broker: see *bill broker.*

note issuance facilities (NIFs): spawned issues similar to Euro-commercial paper.

not-for-profit: describes an activity of an organization established with the sole goal of providing service for society rather than for the purpose of making a profit.

not held: a customer's instructions accompanying a market order to a broker, giving the broker some discretion over the execution and relieving him or her of any responsibility if he or she temporarily misses the market.

notice account: a passbook savings account on which the customer agrees to give the association specified notice before making a withdrawal. As long as the customer gives the agreed notice, his or her funds earn at a higher interest rate than that paid on passbook accounts; insufficient notice from a withdrawal may incur a penalty.

notice day: the day on which notices of intention to deliver may be issued.

notice of dishonor (protest jacket): when a "holder in due course" presents an instrument for payment or acceptance by a drawee, and the maker or drawee fails to honor the instrument, the holder in due course gives it to a notary public. The notary public also presents the instrument to the maker or drawee as a legal formality. If the maker or drawee again dishonors the instrument by refusing to pay for or to accept it, the notary public prepares a "notice of dishonor," or in the terminology of some states, a "mandate of protest" or a "notarial protest certificate."

notice of intention to deliver: a certificate supplied by a short seller indicating his or her intention to fulfill his or her contract obligation by delivering the actual commodity.

notice of protest: a declaration made and witnessed by a notary public, stating that a check, bill of exchange, or note has been presented and payment has been refused.

notice price: the fixed price at which futures deliveries are invoiced.

noting a bill: the notation on a bill of exchange by a notary public after presentation of the bill protesting its nonpayment. The notation consists of the date, notary's initials, reason for nonpayment, and the notary's charges.

not rated

(1) short for *nonrefundable.*

(2) in bonds and preferred stocks, securities not rated by a national service. No credit risk judgments are offered.

(3) in tombstones of debt issues, especially municipals, the designation that a serial maturity is not reoffered for sale.

(4) showing that a stock has not been rated by a recognized rating agency. The NR does not imply any indication of quality or lack of quality.

not subject to call: those bonds or notes that cannot be paid off and retired prior to their maturity date. cf. *callable.*

novation

(1) the replacement of a new debt or obligation for an older one. see *open-end mortgage.*

(2) the replacement of a new creditor or debtor for a former creditor (or debtor).

NOW (negotiable order of withdrawal) account: a savings account from which the account holder can withdraw funds by writing a negotiable order of withdrawal (NOW) payable to a third party. Until January 1, 1980 NOW accounts were available only in New England, New York, and New Jersey. Effective with new federal regulations, all savings and loans as well as banks, for the first time nationally, are allowed to offer interest-bearing checking accounts (NOW accounts). see also *super-NOW account.*

NP

(1) see *net position.*

(2) see *net profit.*

(3) see *notary public.*

NPV

(1) net present value.

(2) no par value.

NPVS: see *no-par-value stock.*

NQB

(1) see *National Quotation Bureau.*

(2) no qualified bidders.

NR: see *not rated.*

NRO: see *nonresident-owned funds.*

NSCC: see *National Securities Clearing Corporation.*

NSE: see *National Stock Exchange.*

NSTA: see *National Securities Trade Association.*

NSTS: National Securities Trading System.

NTU: see *normal trading unit.*

numbers only: synonymous with *nominal quotation.*

numeraire: French, a standard by which values are measured, such as exchange rates in the international monetary system.

numismatic: pertaining to coins and the collection of coins and medals.

NV: Naamloze Vennootschap (Dutch corporation).

NVS: see *nonvoting stock.*

NW: see *net worth.*

NWC: see *net working capital.*

NY: see *net yield.*

NYCE: see *New York Curb Exchange.*

NYCSCE: see *New York Coffee, Sugar and Cocoa Exchange.*

NYCTN: New York Cotton Exchange.

NYCTN, CA: New York Cotton Exchange, Citrus Associates.

NYFE: see *New York Futures Exchange.*

NYM: see *New York Mercantile Exchange.*

Nymex: see *New York Mercantile Exchange.*

NYSE: see *New York Stock Exchange.*

NYSE Common Stock Index: a composite index covering price movements of all common stocks listed on the "Big Board." It is based on the close of the market December 31, 1965, as 50.00 and is weighted according to the number of shares listed for each issue. The index is computed continuously and printed on the ticker tape each half-hour. Point changes in the index are converted to dollars and cents, to provide a meaningful measure of changes in the average price of listed stocks. The composite index is supplemented by separate indices for four industry groups: industrials, transportation, utilities, and finances. cf. *Dow Jones averages.*

O

O

(1) old (in options listing of newspapers).

(2) in newspaper reports of corporate earnings, designating the principal market for their securities is over-the-counter.

O&A: October and April (semiannual interest payments or dividends).

OAPEC: see *Organization of Arab Petroleum Exporting Countries.*

OARS: see *Opening Automated Report Service.*

OB

(1) see *bond, obligation.*

(2) see *operating budget.*

(3) see *or better.*

objectives

(1) investment goals for a person or institutional investors anticipated by stated investment plans.

(2) the price an investor expects a specific stock will attain during a stated time period.

obligation bond: see *bond, obligation.*

obligator: synonymous with *obligor.*

obligatory maturity: the compulsory maturity of any bond or note, as distinguished from optional maturity dates or early redemption dates.

obligee: a creditor or promisee.

obligor: a debtor or promisor; principal. synonymous with *obligator.*

OBO: see *order book official.*

obsolete securities: abandoned or defunct corporation securities. Any bond that has matured or been withdrawn.

OBV: see *on-balance volume.*

OC: see *operating company.*

OCC: see *Options Clearing Corporation.*

OCC prospectus: the formal disclosure statement required by the SEC that is to be sent to all options customers prior to their approval for trading stock option contracts.

OCO: see *one-cancels-the-other order.*

odd lot: an amount of stock less than the established 100-share unit or 10-share unit of trading: from 1 to 99 shares for the greatest majority of issues, 1 to 9 for so-called inactive stocks. see *inactive stock (bond), round lot.* synonymous with *uneven lot.*

odd-lot buy/sell ratio: an indicator of feeling toward the market by odd-lot investors. A ratio of odd-lot purchasing divided by odd-lot selling.

odd-lot dealer: a member firm of an exchange that buys and sells odd lots of stock—1 to 9 shares in the case of stocks traded in 10-share units and 1 to 99 shares for 100-share units. The odd-lot dealer's customers are commission brokers acting on behalf of their customers.

odd-lot differential: the added cost charged to a customer for executing an odd-lot transaction. The differential charge is usually one eighth of a point ($12^1/_2$ cents).

odd-lot house: a brokerage company specializing as a dealer in handling orders from investors for amounts less than 100 shares (round lots). The broker takes positions in the market and draws on his or her own inventory to satisfy demand for stocks.

odd-lot index: a measurement determined by dividing total odd-lot sales by off-lot purchases on a 10-day moving average. When sales outnumber purchases, this is judged as unfavorable because the public is hesitant to buy. When purchases outnumber sales, the reverse is true.

odd-lot orders: any purchase or sale of stock not in 100-share units. cf. *round lot.*

odd-lot short sales ratio: odd-lot shares shorted divided by all other odd-lot sales. When the ratio exceeds or reaches 3 percent the indicator is considered positive and when the ratio drops to 0.7 percent or less it is considered negative.

odd-lot theory: a concept stating that investors who buy odd-lot quantities of stocks are usually late in the timing of their investments.

odd-lot trader: a person who purchases and sells securities in less than 100-share lots, as contrasted by professional investors and others of considerable means who deal in larger, more economical amounts.

odd-lot trend: an indicator for comparing odd-lot buying volume to odd-lot selling volume.

OEF: see *open-end funds.*

OEIC: see *open-end investment company.*

OEIT: see *open-end investment trust.*

OF: see *offshore funds.*

Ofd.: see *offer(ed).*

off: describes a given day on which the prices of stocks and commodities drop. see also *on.*

off-balance sheet financing: financing that is not clearly displayed on the balance sheet (i.e., some leasing).

off-board: synonymous with *off the board.*

offer(ed)
(1) ***general:*** to present for acceptance or refusal.
(2) ***investments:*** the price at which a person is ready to sell. Opposed to bid, the price at which one is ready to buy.

offered ahead: a situation created when an individual who has placed an order to sell at a given price finds that other or lower offers have been given earlier on the same security; these obviously take precedence over his offer.

offered down: securities that are offered for sale at levels lower than the last sale or quoted price of the same stock.

offered firm: a firm offer to sell a stated amount of something at a stated price for a stated time period.

offeree: one to whom an offer has been made.

offering: used to indicate an issue of securities or bonds offered for sale to the public. see *secondary distribution, special offering.*

offering book: see *offering list.*

offering circular: the required prospectus made available to any potential investor during an initial stock offering. Includes information on the corporation, its officers, financial status, and planned use of funds to be received from the offering. see also *prospectus.*

offering date: the date when a distribution of stocks or bonds is to be made available for sale to the public for the first time.

offering list: a document showing the price, amount, and description of the item printed by a seller or dealer.

offering price: synonymous with *asked (asking) price.*

offering sale: prices when different maturities of a serial bond issue are offered to the public by an underwriter. The offering sale can also be expressed as yields to maturity. see *yield to maturity.*

offering sheet: see *offering list.*

offeror: one who makes an offer.

offers to sell: see *matched and lost.*

offer wanted (OW): a notice by a possible purchaser of a stock that he or she is seeking an offer by a possible seller of the stock. Abbreviation OW is found on pink sheets (stock listings) and on yellow sheets (corporate bond listings) released by the National Quotation Bureau for securities traded by over-the-counter dealers. see also *pink sheets, yellow sheets.*

off-exchange: commodity firms registered with the Commodity Futures Trading Commission that are not members of any of the 10 regulated futures exchanges that keep an eye on the daily operations of their members. In fact, these "off-exchange" houses, in practice, are barely regulated.

off-floor order: an order to buy or sell a stock originating away from the floor of an exchange. These are client orders originating with brokers. Exchange regulations require that such orders be executed before orders initiated on the floor.

Office of Supervisory Jurisdiction: an office supervised by a parent office of a member of the NASD. Each member of NASD is required to have at least one office of supervisory jurisdiction.

official exchange rate: the ratio that is applied by the monetary authority of one nation in exchanging its money for that of another nation.

official notice of sale: the notice released by a municipality inviting investment bankers to present competitive bids for an upcoming bond issue. The *Daily Bond Buyer* carries these notices.

official statement: a statement giving the details of a new municipal bond offering. Modeled after the *offering circular.* see *offering circular.*

offset

(1) ***general:*** either of two equivalent entries on both sides of an account.

(2) ***options:*** a closing transaction involving the purchase or sale of an option having the same features as one already held.

(3) ***options:*** hedge, such as a short sale of a security to protect a capital gain or the purchase of a future to protect a commodity price, or a straddle representing the purchase of offsetting put and call options on a stock.

offsets to long-term debt: cash and investment assets of sinking funds, bond reserve, and other reserve funds held specifically for the redemption of long-term debt, and assets of credit funds that are pledged to redeem debt incurred to finance loan activities of such funds.

offshore funds: as they affect U.S. citizens, mutual funds that have their headquarters outside this country or off its shores. Usually, such funds are not available to Americans but are sold to investors in other parts of the world.

offshore trusts: a personal trust that is foreign, not domestic. Its situs is usually in a country that does not have significant taxes on these trusts.

off the board: a transaction made over the counter or involving a block of listed securities that were not executed on an organized exchange. synonymous with *off-board.* see *secondary distribution, third market.*

of record: as shown by the record; usually employed in such entries as "attorney of record," showing that the one named is the recognized representative of the party at interest.

OI

(1) see *operating income.*

(2) see *ordinary interest.*

OID: see *bond, original issue discount.*

oil and gas limited partnership: a partnership of one or more limited partners and one or more general parties that is organized to seek, extract, and market commercial quantities of natural gas or oil.

oil and gas lottery: the Bureau of Land Management program that allows anyone filing an application to be chosen for the right to drill for gas and oil or selected parcels of federal land. A winner can sublet the property to an oil firm, which will pay royalties if the land produces commercial quantities of gas and/or oil.

OJAJ: October, January, April, July (quarterly interest payments or dividends).

OL
(1) see *odd lot.*
(2) see *operating losses.*

old money: synonymous with *old money preferred.*

old money preferred: preferred securities of U.S. firms held before October 1, 1942 are eligible for a 60 percent exclusion of dividends from taxable income. synonymous with *old money.* cf. *new money preferred.*

OM
(1) see *on margin.*
(2) see *open market.*

omitted dividend: synonymous with *passed dividend.*

Omnibus Reconciliation Act of 1980: federal legislation; imposed restrictions on use of mortgage subsidy bonds plus other miscellaneous tax changes.

on: the number of points that a cash commodity is higher than a specified futures month. see also *off.*

on account
(1) describes a payment made toward the settlement of an account.
(2) a purchase or sale made on open account.

on a scale: in buying or selling securities, the customer purchases or sells equal amounts of a stock at prices that are spaced by a constant interval, as the market price rises or drops.

on balance
(1) ***general:*** the net effect or result.
(2) ***investments:*** the difference between offsetting sales and purchases; for example, if an investor sells 1000 shares of securities, then purchases 2200 shares of the same security, he has purchased 1200 shares on balance.

on-balance volume: an indicator that attempts to pinpoint where futures contracts are being accumulated or bought, and when they are being distributed or sold by controlling market forces, the hedgers, and large traders.

on bid (or offer): a method that an odd-lot trader transacts in a listed stock without waiting for an actual round-lot trade in the security to occur. A transaction is made by selling at the bid price or purchasing at the offering price.

one-cancels-the-other order (OCO): synonymous with *alternative order.*

on-floor order: an order originating on the floor of an exchange. Assures that people who are members cannot utilize inside data or floor situations to take advantage of buyers or sellers not privy to this information.

ongoing buyer (ongoing seller): a buyer (or seller) wishing to accumulate if a buyer, or distribute, if a seller, by making numerous purchases or sales of a security. If done with limit or scale orders will usually result in a better average price than a one-time order to buy or sell in a preferred average price than a one-time order to buy or sell a large quantity of a security.

onlend: British term, to lend (borrowed funds) to others.

on margin: describes securities purchased when the buyer has borrowed part of the purchase price from the broker.

on opening: used to specify execution of an order during the opening call.

OO: see *open order.*

OP
(1) see *offering price.*
(2) see *opening price.*
(3) see *opening purchase.*
(4) see *operating profit.*

Op.D.: see *delayed opening.*

OPEC: see *Organization of Petroleum Exporting Countries.*

open
(1) ***general:*** an unpaid balance.
(2) ***general:*** to form an account or letter of credit.
(3) ***investments:*** establishing an account with a broker.
(4) ***securities:*** the status of an order to purchase or sell stocks that has not yet been executed.

open contracts: contracts that have been bought or sold without the transaction having been completed by subsequent sale or repurchase or actual delivery or receipt of the commodity.

open credit: credit that is allowed without immediate proof of a customer's credit worthiness.

open-end bond: see *bond, open-end.*

open-end clause: an optional mortgage clause, used in states that recognize its validity, which provides that the pledge of real estate will cover additional advances of funds that the borrower may request and the lender agrees to grant at unknown times in the future. Under the terms of this clause, all subsequent advances represent a claim on the property dating from the time of recording of the original mortgage.

open-end funds: mutual funds where new shares of the fund are sold whenever there is a request, with the expectation that the seller will eventually request to buy back the shares, at no additional charge. see *investment company.*

open-end investment company: an investment firm that sells and reclaims its capital stock continuously, selling it at book value, adding a sales charge, and redeeming it at a slight discount or at book value.

open-end investment trust: an investment trust in which the trustee, by the terms of the trust, is authorized to invest in shares of stock other than those in the trust at the time of the inception of the trust or of the participation in the trust.

open-end lease: a lease that may involve an additional payment based on the value of property when returned.

open-end management firm: the investment company that sells mutual funds to the public, and continuously creates new shares upon demand. see also *open-end investment company.*

open-end mortgage: a mortgage that permits the borrower to reborrow money paid on the principal up to the original amount.

open-end mutual fund: see *open-end funds.*

open fund: an open-end investment firm of mutual funds, so identified because it does not have fixed capitalization. Money is raised by selling its own stock to the public and investing the proceeds in other securities.

opening
(1) ***general:*** the first price given in an auction or sales marketplace.
(2) ***investments:*** the initial price at which a transaction in a security takes place on every day; the first quoted price of a new stock issue.
(3) ***investments:*** the short time frame of a market opportunity.

Opening Automated Report Service (OARS): a computerized service available to specialists with the NYSE and AME to facilitate opening and reopening of the market for individual securities.

opening block: the first transaction of a trading session for a particular stock. It can be as a single block transaction, but is usually an accumulation of a number of individual orders.

opening price
(1) ***general:*** the first price given in an auction or sales marketplace.
(2) ***investments:*** the initial price at which a transaction in a security takes place on every day; the first quoted price of a new stock issue.

opening purchase: a transaction in which an investor becomes the holder of a security or an option.

opening range: commodities, unlike securities, are often traded at several prices at the opening or close of the market. Buying or selling orders at the opening might be filled at any point in such a price range for the commodity.

opening rotation: a trading rotation to set an initial price level where buy and sell orders will be in balance with regard to both price and volume.

opening sale: a transaction in which an investor becomes the writer of an option.

opening transaction: the purchase or sale of an option contract that establishes an open position and gives the right or obligation to purchase or sell shares on the underlying security.

open interest: the number of outstanding contracts in the exchange market, or in a particular class or series. synonymous with *indicated interest.*

open market: a general term describing a condition of trading that is not limited to any area or persons.

open-market credit: short-term financing enabling commercial paper houses to purchase notes and resell them in the open market.

open-market paper: bills of exchange or notes drawn by one with high credit standing, made payable to himself or herself and indorsed in blank. These are sold to financial institutions other than banks.

open mortgage: a mortgage that can be paid off, without penalty, at any period prior to its maturity.

open on the print: a block trade that has been completed with an institutional client and "printed" on the consolidated tape, but leaves a block positioner open, that is, with a risk position to be covered.

open option: see *outstanding option.*

open order: synonymous with *good-'til-canceled order.*

open outcry: see *outcry market.*

open prospectus: a brochure that aims to obtain financial backing and does not clearly identify the use to be made of the investment.

open REPO: a repurchase agreement where the repurchase date is not stated and the agreement can be terminated by either party at any time. see also *repurchase agreement.*

open trade: any transaction that has not yet been closed.

operating assets: those assets that contribute to the regular income from the operations of a business. Thus stocks and bonds owned, unused real estate, loans to officers, and so on, are excluded from operating assets.

operating budget: a budget that applies to all outlays other than capital outlays. see *budget.*

operating capital: funds available for use in financing the day-to-day activities of a business.

operating company: a company whose officers direct the business of transportation and whose books contain operating as well as financial accounts.

operating costs: costs of maintenance, utilities, office equipment, salaries, and such required to keep a business operational.

operating earnings before taxes: see *net earnings.*

operating expense
(1) the actual expense incurred in the maintenance of property (e.g., management, repairs, taxes, insurance); not included as operating expenses are mortgage payments, depreciation, and interest paid out.
(2) any expense incurred in the normal operation of a business. This is to be distinguished from expenditures, which are disbursements that are

capitalized and depreciate over a period of years. see *margin of profit.*

operating income
(1) income to a business produced by its earning assets and by fees for services rendered.
(2) rental monies obtained from the operation of a business or from property.

operating income as percent of net interest income: net operating income before securities gains and losses, divided by total interest income, minus total interest expense, minus provision for loan losses.

operating interest: the mineral interest minus the royalty interest. This interest in burdened with the cost of development and operation of the property.

operating lease: an equipment lease, where the contract is written for considerably less than the life of the equipment and the lessor handles all maintenance and servicing. synonymous with *service lease.*

operating leverage: see *leverage.*

operating losses: losses incurred in the normal (i.e., nonnegligent) operation of a business.

operating profit: profit arising from the regular operation of an enterprise engaged in performing physical services (e.g., public utilities), excluding income from other sources and excluding expenses other than those of direct operation.

operating profit (for purposes of marketing): gross margin (gross profit), less operating expenses (including salaries of managers, whether proprietors or employees), fixed plant and equipment cost, and sometimes interest on invested capital.

operating profit ratio: the ratio of a firm's operating profit to its net sales. see *turnover ratio.*

operating ratio: the total of expenses of operation divided by total of operating revenues. Usually, this includes only the ratio of (a) cost of goods sold plus selling, administrative, and general expenses to (b) net sales.

operating reserves: a group of balance sheet accounts reflecting the net accumulated balances provided for property insurance, injuries and damages, pensions and benefits, and amortization.

operating statement: a statement providing net sales, costs, expenses, and the net operating profit or loss for a fixed period.

operating surplus: the remaining profit after deducting all operating costs of the business over a given time period. Items such as interest on capital and indebtedness are not deducted prior to determining the operating surplus.

operations unit: a brokerage house's back office where clerical functions deal with clearance, settlement, and execution of trades are to be handled.

operator: slang, any person who makes a career in speculation on the prices of securities or commodities.

OPG: the security trading designation, derived from the word "opening" requiring that a buy or sell order be executed at the market price at the opening of trading. Any portion not executed is automatically canceled.

opinion of title: a legal opinion stating that title to property is clear and marketable; serves the same purpose as a certificate of title.

opinion shopping: when a company seeks an auditor who is willing to support a favorable accounting treatment that isn't consistent with generally accepted accounting principles.

OPM
(1) options pricing model. see *Back-Scholes Option Pricing Model.*
(2) other people's money. Slang, borrowed money for increasing the return on invested capital.

opportunity cost
(1) ***general:*** the maximum alternative profit that could have been obtained if the productive good, service, or capacity had been applied to some other use.
(2) ***investments:*** the cost of forgoing a safe return on an investment with the expectation of making a larger profit.

OPRA: see *Options Price Reporting Authority.*

Opt.: see *option.*

optics: a form of debt instrument proposed to increase the offering price of a corporation during an attempted takeover.

option (Opt.)
(1) the privilege to buy or sell, receive, or deliver property, given in accordance with the terms stated, with a consideration for price. This privilege may or may not be exercised at the option holder's discretion. Failure to execise the option leads to forfeiture.
(2) an agreement, often for a consideration, to buy or sell a security or commodity within a stipulated time in accordance with the agreement. see *puts and calls.* cf. *covered option, straddle.*
(3) see also *call option* and *put option.*

option account: a charge account in which the consumer may choose either to pay at the end of 30 days or to spread payments over a longer period of time. If he or she chooses to spread payments beyond 30 days, he or she pays a service charge.

option account agreement form: a special brokerage account form completed and signed by all option customers, disclosing their financial status and previous investment experience. They also agree to comply with the Options Clearing Corporation and exchange regulations.

option agreement: a form completed by a brokerage house's client when opening an option account, where the customer agrees to abide by the regulations of options trading. synonymous with *option information form.*

optional bond: see *bond, callable.*

optional date: the date at which a municipality or corporation has the right to redeem its obligations under certain condtions.

optional dividend: the stockholder has the choice of receiving either a stock dividend or a cash dividend.

optional payment bond: see *bond, optional payment.*

option contract
(1) a contract in foreign exchange to deal in foreign exchange, wherein the date of completion of the deal, but not its existence, is at the customer's choice with a specified period.
(2) in the securities market, buying an option that gives the choice of dealing in the securities at a certain price prior to a certain date. This differs from the foreign exchange option in that the deal itself, rather than its date, is optional.

option day: the specified date when an option expires unless exercised.

optionee: the holder of an option; a prospective buyer.

optioner: any property owner.

option holder: an individual who has purchased a call or put option but has not yet exercised or sold it.

option income fund: the investment objective of these funds is to seek a high current return by investing primarily in dividend-paying common stocks on which call options are traded on national securities exchanges. Current return generally consists of dividends, premiums from expired call options, net short-term gains from sales of portfolio securities on exercises of options or otherwise, and any profits from closing purchase transactions.

option information form: synonymous with *option agreement.*

option mutual fund: a mutual fund that either buys or sells options so as to increase the value of fund shares; may be either aggressive or conservative.

option premiums: the dollar amounts paid to the writer for the option. This amount is generally determined by supply and demand, duration of the contract difference between the fluctuations, among other considerations.

Options Clearing Corporation (OCC): the issuer of all options contracts on the American Stock Exchange.

option series: options of the same class that also have the same exercise price and month of maturity.

options in a fast market: a situation occuring when trading volume on an options exchange is heavy or when volume is considerable for a specific option. Traditional reporting is impossible and the options are declared by an official of the exchange to be in a "fast market". Quotes are behind trading and the specialist is no longer held responsible for reporting.

options market: a market in which contracts are traded that gives a purchaser the right but no obligation to buy (call) or to sell (put) a currency in the future at a given price.

option spreading: the simultaneous purchase and sale of options within the same class. The options may be either at the same striking prices with different expiration months, or at different striking prices with the same or different expiration months. The spread is the dollar difference between the buy and sell premiums.

Options Price Reporting Authority (OPRA): a subscription service that announces option transactions and quotations on a ticker tape or CRT.

options principal member: a person who has bought from an exchange or from another member the right to buy and sell listed options on the floor of that exchange.

option writer: synonymous with *writer.*

or better (OB): shown on an order ticket of a limit order to buy or sell stocks. States that the broker should transact the order at a price higher than the specified limit price should a better price be obtainable.

order: legally enforceable instructions, stated or written, from a customer to the broker to purchase or sell a given quantity of a particular stock at market price or at a specific price. Special trading instructions may also be added.

order book official (OBO): in the Pacific or Philadelphia stock exchanges, employees who accept orders for options not readily executed. When and if such orders can be transacted, the OBO makes the trade on an agency basis, and informs the member firm that they have entered the orders. On the Chicago Board Options Exchange, such employees are called *board brokers.*

order department: synonymous with *wire room.*

order party: a party instructing the sender to execute the transaction.

order room: synonymous with *wire room.*

orders

(1) ***general:*** requests made for the delivery of goods or services.

(2) ***investments:*** instructions to a broker to buy or sell shares.

orders good until a specified time: a market or limited price order that is to be represented in the "trading crowd" until a specified time, after which such order or the portion not executed is treated as canceled. cf. *good-'til-canceled order.*

order support system (OSS): implemented in 1979 by the Chicago Board Options Exchange to speed public order information in and out of the exchange. cf. *trade support system.*

order ticket: a form completed by a registered representative of a brokerage house, upon receiving order instructions from a client. Regulations require that the house retain these forms for a certain period of time.

ordinary asset: an asset that is bought and sold as a regular component of a continuing business activity. What may be an ordinary asset to one firm may be a capital asset to another. A real estate broker selling property would be selling an ordinary asset, whereas a retailer would be selling a capital asset if he sold land.

ordinary discount: the difference between the value at maturity and the present value which at an assumed rate of interest will accumulate to the value of maturity.

ordinary gain (or loss): the gain or loss realized from the sale or exchange of property that is not a capital asset, such as inventory.

ordinary income: in income tax filing, reportable income that does not qualify as capital gains.

ordinary interest: interest that is calculated based on 360 days to the year.

ordinary life: a type of insurance policy continuing in force throughout the policyholder's lifetime and payable on his or her death or when he or she attains a specified age. synonymous with *straight life, whole life insurance.*

ordinary shares: British term for the junior stock issue of a corporation, similar to common stock in the United States.

ordinary stock: common or equity stock.

ordinary voting: the stockholder under this principle is entitled to one vote for each voting share and directors are elected one at a time. cf. *cumulative voting.*

Organization of Arab Petroleum Exporting Countries (OAPEC): includes members of OPEC less Ecuador, Gabon, Indonesia, Iran, Nigeria, and Venezuela, plus Bahrain, Egypt, and Syria; aids in setting international oil prices and acts as liaison between the Arab oil states and other Arab nations, see also *Organization of Petroleum Exporting Countries.*

Organization of Petroleum Exporting Countries (OPEC): the group's 13 members are concentrated in the Middle East but also include countries in Africa, South America, and the Far East. By virtue of their large exports, Saudi Arabia and Iran have been the most powerful influences. see also *petrodollars.*

organized exchange: the place where goods or property rights are bought and sold according to recognized rules. Examples are stock and bond exchange, grain, butter, sugar, and other exchanges.

organized market: a group of traders, operating under recognized rules, for the purpose of buying and selling a single commodity or a small number of related commodities—for example, the Chicago Board of Trade.

original asset: stocks, bonds, or other property received in a trust at the time of its creation, or an estate at the time of appointment of the executor or administrator.

original investment: an investment received by the trustee as part of the decedent's estate or from the settlor of a living trust.

original issue discount: the discount from par value at the time a bond is issued.

original issue discount bond (OID): see *bond, original issue discount.*

original (originally) issue (issued) stock: securities initially issued at the time the corporation was established and which are part of the starting capitalization.

original margin: margin required at the onset of a transaction.

original maturity: the time interval between the issue date and the maturity date of a bond. cf. *current maturity.*

originator
(1) a banking house or individual investment banker who is the first to promote a proposed new issue for a corporation.
(2) an investment banking firm that worked with an issuer of a new stock and whom is frequently appointed manager of the underwriting syndicate.

OS: see *option spreading.*

OSS: see *order support system.*

O/T: overtime.

OTB: see *off the board.*

OTC: see *over the counter.*

OTC margin stock: shares of come large companies traded over-the-counter that qualify as margin securities under Regulation T of the Federal Reserve Board.

OTC option: a call or put whose strike price, expiration and premium are negotiated. synonymous with *conventional option.*

OTC stock-index futures: over-the-counter contracts to make or take delivery at a set time in the future, based on the quoted value of an index of stock prices. see also *stock index future.*

other loans for purchasing or carrying securities: loans to other than brokers and dealers for the purpose of purchasing or carrying securities.

other long-term debt: long-term debt other than mortgage bonds and debentures. This includes serial notes and notes payable to banks with original maturity of more than one year.

other people's money: see *OPM.*

other securities: all securities other than U.S. government obligations—that is, state, municipal, and corporate bonds. (Member banks are generally not permitted to invest in stocks other than Federal Reserve bank stock.)

outbid: to offer a higher price for an item than that offered by other bidders.

outcry market: commodity tradings by private contract that must be shouted out, as on the floor of an exchange, in order that the agreement be recorded. synonymous with *open outcry.*

out for a bid: a dealer lets municipal bonds to an agent in order to solicit their sale. The broker receives a fee should the bonds be sold and is in a position to offer the bonds to prospective customers.

out-of-favor industry (or stock): an industry (or stock) that is presently unpopular with most investors. Such stocks tend to have a low price/earnings ratio.

out of line: a stock whose price is determined to be either too low or too high. This is often determined by noting the corporation's price-earnings ratio.

out of the money: a situation in which the striking price is above the market price of the underlying stock for a call, or the striking price is below the market price of the underlying stock for a call, or the striking price is below the market price of the underlying stock for a put.

outright purchases (or sales): net purchases (or sales) by the Federal Open Market Committee. Excludes buys or sells that are partially offset by repurchase or reverse repurchase agreements.

outright transaction: a purchase sale or forward exchange without a corresponding transaction spot.

outside broker: not a member of a regular stock exchange; a dealer in unlisted stocks.

outside director: the member of a firm's board of directors who is not employed by the company.

outside financing: the process of raising funds for a business expansion through the sale of securities, as opposed to the use of retained earnings.

outside market: an over-the-counter market, or a market where unlisted securities are handled.

outsiders: the general investing public.

outside security: any security not listed or quoted on a major local exchange. For example, a security for the City of Los Angeles not traded on the Pacific Stock Exchange.

outstanding

(1) ***general:*** any unpaid or uncollected debt.

(2) ***investments:*** stock in the hands of stockholders, as distinguished from stock that has not yet been issued or, if issued, has not been released by the corporation. cf. *absorbed.*

outstanding option: an option contract issued by the OCC that has not expired, been closed, or exercised.

out the window: a new issue of securities or bonds that moves out rapidly or is sold quickly to investors.

overall market price coverage: the ratio of net assets to the sum of all prior obligations at liquidating value plus the issue in question taken at market price.

overallotting: when more shares in a public offering are confirmed than are available in anticipation that some orders may not be confirmed by the investors.

overbanked: underwritings whose initial allotment to syndicate members exceeds the number of securities to be offered. To achieve 100 percent, some members drop out while others decrease their allotment, or should too many members drop out, others will increase their allotments.

overbooked: see *oversubscribed.*

overbought: reflecting an opinion about price levels. May refer to a security that has had a sharp rise, or to the market as a whole after a period of vigorous buying, which some are arguing, has left prices "too high."

overbought market: see *oversold market.*

overcapitalized: a situation where the capital stock of a firm is valued at a dollar amount greater than the value of the assets of the corporation.

overcommitment: synonymous with *overextension.*

overextension

(1) ***general:*** the expansion by a business concern of buildings, equipment, and so on, in excess of the company's present or prospective future needs. synonymous with *overcommitment.*

(2) ***general:*** credit received or extended beyond the debtor's ability to pay.

(3) ***investments:*** the condition of a dealer in securities who becomes obligated for an amount beyond his or her borrowing power or ability to pay.

overflow account: synonymous with *sweep account.*

overinvestment theory: a business cycle concept which holds that economic variations are a function of too much investment in the economy as business managers try to measure increasing demands during an upswing, and of major cutbacks in investment during a downswing when they realize that they expanded too much in the previous prosperity. synonymous with *oversaving theory.*

overissue: the release of stock in excess of the authorized or ordered amount. see *registrar, undigested securities.*

overlapping debt: in municipal securities if there are co-issuers of a stock, or if a higher-ranking municipality and a lower-ranking one share responsibility for an issue.

overlying bond: see *bond, overlying.*

overlying mortgage: a junior mortgage subject to the claim of a senior mortgage, which has a claim prior to the junior mortgage.

overnight position: a broker-dealer's long position or short position in a stock at the trading day's end.

overnight REPO: an overnight repurchase agreement where dealers and banks finance their inventories of Treasury bills, notes and bonds.

oversaving theory: synonymous with *overinvestment theory.*

oversold

(1) ***general:*** the situation of a manufacturer who has become obligated to deliver more than he or she is able to supply within the stated period.

(2) ***investments:*** an opinion—the reverse of overbought. A single security or a market that is believed to have declined to an unreasonable level.

oversold market: when the speculative long interest has been drastically reduced and the speculative short interest increases, actually or relatively, a market is said to be oversold. At such times, sharp rallies often materialize. On the other hand, when the speculative short interest decreases sharply, a market is said to be overbought. At such times, the market is often in a position to decline sharply.

overspeculation: a market situation wherein activity is abnormally high, caused not by the normal needs of legitimate buyers and sellers, but by speculators.

overstay the market: holding a position in stocks for too long a period of time; for example, a sustained advance when the market appears overbought and about to have a price correction.

oversubscribed: a situation in which, for a given issue of shares, more orders have been received than can be filled. cf. *undigested securities.*

over the counter (OTC): securities not listed or traded on any of the regular exchanges. Such securities are traded through dealers in unlisted stocks. Sales or purchases are arranged by these dealers or through a chain of them until the desired securities and prices are obtained. However, members of regular stock exchanges also handle trades in unlisted securities, but not through the exchange. see *National Association of Securities Dealers Automated Quotations.* cf. *offboard.* synonymous with *unlisted.*

over-the-counter index option: first traded on the Philadelphia Stock Exchange in 1985, made up of the 100 most highly capitalized stocks in the unlisted market. It provides investors with a vehicle for guessing short-term price movements in the vast over-the-counter arena. It is designed to provide investors with a tool for limiting risks by hedging against their portfolios of over-the-counter securities.

over-the-counter option: see *unlisted option.*

overtrading

(1) ***general:*** the activity of a firm that even with high profitability cannot pay its own way for lack of working capital and finds itself in a liquidity crisis.

(2) ***underwriting:*** a procedure whereby a member of an underwriting group convinces a brokerage client to purchase a portion of a new issue by buying other securities from the client at a premium.

(3) ***securities:*** excessive buying and selling by a broker in a discretionary account. see also *churning.*

overturn: synonymous with *turnover.*

overvalued: a security whose current price is not justified by the earnings outlook or the price/earnings ratio. cf. *undervalued.* see also *fully valued.*

overwriting: a speculative practice by an option writer who expects a security to be overpriced or underpriced and sells call options or put options on the stock in quantity, hoping that they will not be exercised.

OW: see *offer wanted.*

OWC: see *owner will carry.*

owner financing: a creative home-financing approach where the potential buyer bypasses the bank and borrows money directly from the person selling the house. Owners often find that this type of financing is the only way they can sell their houses because so many potential buyers cannot qualify for bank loans. The buyer; for example, might borrow half the needed money from the owner at 8 percent interest and the rest from a bank at 14 percent.

owner of record: a person or organization whose name appears on a corporation's transfer agent's book as the proper owner of securities in that firm as of a specified date. This name is identified to be entitled to receive any benefits or dividends declared.

owner's equity: see *net worth.*

ownership certificate: a form required by the government and furnished by the Collector of Internal Revenue which discloses the real owner of stocks registered in the name of a nominee. Such a form must also accompany coupons presented for collection on bonds belonging to nonresident aliens, or partially tax-free corporate bonds issued prior to January 1, 1934.

owner will carry (OWC): mortgages carried at below-market rates permitting an investor to knock costs down farther.

P

P

(1) paid this year (in stock listings of newspapers).

(2) see *partnership.*

(3) see *private trusts.*

(4) put (in options listings of newspapers). see *put option.*

PA

(1) see *paying agent.*

(2) see *per annum.*

Pa: in newspaper reports, designating that the principal marketplace for securities is the Pacific Stock Exchange.

PAC: put and call (options market).

Pacific Stock Exchange: formed in January 1957, by a consolidation of the San Francisco Stock Exchange (1882) and the Los Angeles Stock Exchange (1899), it is the most active U.S. securities exchange outside New York City.

packet: a London Stock Exchange term for *block,* as in a block purchase of securities.

paid-in capital: indicated on a corporation's balance sheet, the dollar difference between the aggregate par value of issued common shares and the price at which they were sold. synonymous with *capital surplus.*

paid-in surplus: a balance sheet entry in the shareholder's equity portion showing the difference between dollar value received on the actual issuance of shares and the part or stated value of those particular shares.

paid-up capital: the total of par value stock and the given value of no-par securities for which full consideration is received by a corporation.

paid-up insurance: a policy on which no further premium payments need to be made; the company will be held liable for any benefits claimed under terms of the contract.

paid-up shares: see *paid-up stock.*

paid-up stock: a capital stock on which the initial buyer has paid in services, goods, or funds an amount at least equal to the par value.

painting the tape
(1) creating an interest in a particular stock by trading constantly in it, thus causing it to appear on the ticker tape at frequent intervals.
(2) an unusual public interest in a specific security.

paired shares: common stocks of two firms under the same administration, sold as a unit; usually appearing as one certificate printed front and back. synonymous with *Siamese shares, stapled stock.*

P & L statement: a profit and loss accounting statement released by a corporation, providing sources of income and expense and net profit or loss.

panic: a sudden, spreading fear of the collapse of business or the nation's economy, resulting in widespread withdrawal of bank deposits, stock sales, and similar transactions. A depression may but does not always follow a panic.

paper: synonymous with *stock option contract.*

paper capital: long-term, low interest notes issued by the FSLIC.

paper gain or loss: an expression for unrealized capital gains or losses on securities in a portfolio, based on comparison of current market quotations and the original costs.

paperless: evidence of ownership of a security or bond recorded electronically without the physical issuance of a certificate.

paper loss: a decrease in the market value of a stock below the price at which it was bought. It is an unrealized loss until the stock has been liquidated.

paper money: currency on which a value is printed, although unlike coins, the bills have no value in themselves; usually represents bullion held in government vaults.

paper profit: an unrealized profit on a security still held. Paper profits become realized profits only when the security is sold. see *short sale.*

paper title: a written document that appears to convey proof of ownership but may not in fact show proper title. cf. *cloud on title.*

Papilsky regulations: NASD rules regarding securities taken in trade by an underwriter, selling concessions made in an exchange for bona fide research services, and the allocation of new issues to related individuals.

PAR: a price-adjusted rate preferred (security).

par: when the exchangeable value of an instrument is equal to that expressed on its face without consideration of any premium or discount. see also *face value.*

parachutes: see *golden parachute.*

paramount title: the foremost title, a title that is superior to all others. Often the original title used to prepare later ones.

par bond: see *bond, par.*

par cap: in GNMA forward delivery contracts under yield maintenance procedures, when a seller is precluded from delivering substitute GNMA securities with an interest coupon rate requiring adjusting the contract's dollar price above the issue's par value.

parent company: synonymous with *holding company.*

par exchange rate: the free market price of one country's money in terms of the currency of another.

Paris Bourse (PB): the national stock exchange of France, established in 1724.

Paris Club: synonymous with *Group of Ten.*

par item: any item that can be collected at its par or face value upon presentation.

parity
(1) ***general:*** the equivalence established between the wage schedules of some categories of employees.
(2) ***government:*** a farm policy established to keep the purchasing power of a unit of farm output equal to the purchasing power of the units of production bought by a farmer in the same ratio that existed during a chosen period.
(3) ***investments:*** the state or quality of being equal or equivalent; equivalence of a commodity price expressed in one currency to its price expressed in another.
(4) ***investments:*** equality of purchase power established by law between different kinds of money at a given ratio.

parity clause: a mortgage clause by virtue of which all notes obtained by the mortgage have "equal dignity"; that is, none has priority.

parity price: the price for a service or commodity that is pegged to another price or to a composite average of prices based on a given prior period.

parking: putting assets in a safe investment while other investment alternatives are being considered. For example, parking the proceeds of a stock or bond sale in an interest-bearing money market fund while evaluating what other stocks or bonds to buy.

par of exchange: the market price of money in one national currency that is exchanged at the official rate for a specific amount in another national currency, or another commodity of value (gold, silver, etc).

partial covered writing: an option posture of a combination of covered and uncovered calls written against the same underlying stock.

partial delivery: when a broker fails to deliver the total amount of a stock or commodity called for by a contract.

partially amortized mortgage: a mortgage partly repaid by amortization during the life of the mortgage and partly repaid at the end of the term.

partial write: a strategy for investors with a large position in stock. The investor writes calls against a portion of his or her owned stock. If the stock's price stays low, the investor keeps the premium and thus increases their cash flow. If the stock's price rises, the investor can buy back the calls to prevent the stock from being called away. The premium is lost, but the stock is worth more. The investor then writes more options, this time on double the amount of stock.

participant: a bank, brokerage house, or investment firm that has agreed to sell a stock issue to the public as part of a syndicate.

participate but do not initiate: trading instructions when a significant order is involved, asking that the order should not initiate market activity but that it be filled out of the normal market trading. Used to minimize any adverse price effect on the market price of the stock.

participating bond: see *bond, participating.*

participating brokers/dealers: brokers and dealers not associated with an underwriting syndicate but who participate in the selling of the new offering. synonymous with *selling concession, selling group.*

participating certificate
(1) an instrument that specifies a partial owner interest in a stock.
(2) a federal security sold in multiples of $5000 and guaranteed by the Federal National Mortgage Association.
(3) see also *participation certificate.*

participating exchange: a national securities exchange approved by the SEC to trade listed options issued by the Options Clearing Corporation.

participating group annuity contract: a contract with an insurance company providing income to participants (usually 10 or more) in which both the mortality risk and the investment experience are shared in varying degrees between the policyholder and the insurance company.

participating investment trust: synonymous with *unit trust.*

participating life insurance: insurance on which the policyholder is entitled to receive policy dividends reflecting the difference between the premium charged and actual experience. The premium is calculated to provide some margin over the anticipated cost of the insurance protection.

participating mortgage: a mortgage with a basic interest rate, plus a participation such as additional interest in the future or present income of the property. The investor can benefit from other aspects, such as participation in the sale of the property.

participating preferred: describing a preferred stock that is entitled to its stated dividend and, also, to additional dividends on a specified basis (i.e., with respect to the plan participated in) on payment of dividends on the common stock.

participating trust: synonymous with *unit trust.*

participation: an ownership interest in a mortgage.

participation agreement: an understanding, the terms of which are usually specified in writing between institutional investors, to buy or sell partial ownership interest in mortgages.

participation certificate (PC): a mortgage pass-through certificate, which represents an interest in a group of mortgages purchased by the Mortgage Corporation. The PC was designed to shift capital from mortgage deficit areas to mortgage surplus areas. Certificate rates are chosen by the corporation for each issue. Secondary market conditions are similar to GNMAs, but the scale or the market is smaller. Timely payment of interest and full payment of principal are guaranteed by the Mortgage Corporation. synonymous with *pass-through security.*

participation dividends: earnings of a cooperative that are distributed to every member in direct proportion to the amount of business that he or she has done with the cooperative during the fiscal period.

participation loan
(1) ***general:*** a loan having two or more banks as creditiors. Laws prohibit banks from lending more than a fixed percentage of their capital and surplus to any one borrower. Thus, banks invite other banks to participate in making large loans.
(2) ***mortgages:*** a mortgage loan, made by a lead lender, in which other lenders own an interest.

partly paid: in securities, those stocks held in a margin account (i.e., a ballance is owned by an investor to his or her broker on the full amount of the stock bought).

partner: a person who is a member of a partnership; usually for the purpose of operating a business.

partnership: a contractual relationship between two or more people in a joint enterprise, who agree to share, not necessarily equally, in the profits and losses of the organization. cf. *joint venture.*

partnership certificate: a certificate filed with a bank showing the interest of each partner in a business enterprise operating as a partnership. This certificate also shows the limited partners (partners who specify a maximum amount for which they may be held responsible in settlement of obligations incurred by the partnership), and also "silent partners" (partners who have invested funds in the partnership, but who, for certain reasons, do not wish to be publicly known as partners).

party at interest: individual or group of individuals having a vested interest in a commercial enterprise.

par value: synonymous with *face value.*

par value (of currency): the value of a currency in terms of gold as formally proposed to the International Monetary Fund, normally subject to fund concurrence. The fund's Articles of Agreement envisage that each member country shall have an effective par value (i.e., a unitary, fixed exchange rate for spot transactions that is established and maintained in accordance with the provisions of the Articles).

P & S: the purchase and sales (of securities).

passbook savings: customer accounts deposited with commercial banks and savings institutions, permitting easy withdrawal of funds. Effective April 1, 1986, all of these federally insured institutions were free to pay whatever interest rate they wished.

passed dividend
(1) a regular or scheduled dividend that has been omitted.
(2) a dividend anticipated on common shares that the board of directors fails to declare. synonymous with *omitted dividend.*
(3) an omitted dividend on cumulative preferred shares. A passed dividend on such shares accrues until paid and all such dividends in arrears are to be paid before common stock dividends.

passing title: synonymous with *closing title.* see *closing (or passing) title.*

passive bond: see *bond, passive.*

passive management: a style of investment management that seeks to attain average risk-adjusted performance.

pass-through security: synonymous with *participation certificate.* see also *Ginnie Mae pass-through securities.*

pawned stock: see *hypothecated stock.*

pay
(1) to pay a check in cash, as when a check is paid by the paying teller.
(2) to charge a check against a customer's account, as in the case of a check coming through the clearings.
(3) slang, currency of denomination of a bond.

payable in exchange: the requirement that a negotiable instrument be paid in the funds of the place from which it was originally issued.

payables: a bookkeeping term for any and all accounts or notes payable total. cf. *receivables.*

pay-by-phone: a service enabling customers to instruct their financial institution via telephone to initiate one or more payments from their accounts.

paydown
(1) ***lending:*** the repayment of principal short of full payment.
(2) ***bonds:*** refunding by a firm of an outstanding bond issue through a smaller new bond issue, frequently to reduce interest costs. The amount of the net deduction is the *paydown.*

PAYE: pay as you earn.

payer: the party primarily responsible for the payment of the amount owed as evidence by a given negotiable instrument.

pay-in: a monetary contribution or deposit in a fund or account, usually on a periodic basis.

paying agent: an agent to receive funds from an obligor to pay maturing bonds and coupons, or from a corporation for the payment of dividends.

payment: the total sum of money borrowed, plus all finance charges, divided by the number of months in the terms of the loan.

payment bill: a bill of exchange presented for payment instead of acceptance.

payment date: synonymous with *distribution date.*

payout: the annual proportionate amount of corporate earnings to be disbursed to stockholders as dividends.

payout ratio: the amount of dividends per share given as a percentage of annual earnings per share.

Payroll-based Stock Ownership Plan: see *PAYSOP.*

payroll deduction plan (mutual fund): an arrangement whereby an employee may accumulate shares in a mutual fund by authorizing shares in a mutual fund by authorizing his or her employer to deduct and transfer to a fund a specified amount from their salary at stated times.

PAYSOP: Payroll-based Stock Ownership Plan. Created by the Economic Recovery Tax Act of 1981 permitting a tax credit of one-half percent of payroll if the employer contributed that much to ESOP.

pay-through bond: see *bond, pay-through.*

pay to bearer: see *bearer instrument.*

pay to order: a negotiable instrument having such words is negotiable by endorsement of the within named payee and his or her delivery to another.

pay up
(1) a condition when an investor who wishes to purchase a stock at a specific price hesitates and the stock begins to climb in price. Instead of letting the stock rise, the investor "pays up" to purchase the shares at the higher prevailing price.
(2) when an investor purchases shares in a high quality company at which is determined to be a high price.

PB: see *Paris Bourse.*

PBGC: see *Pension Benefit Guaranty Corporation.*

PBWSE: see *Philadelphia-Baltimore-Washington Stock Exchange.*

PC
(1) see *participation certificate.*
(2) see *professional corporation.*

PCS: see *preferred capital stock.*

Pd.: paid.

PE: see *price earnings ratio* (in stock listings of newspapers).

peak: synonymous with *top.*

peg (pegging): to fix or stabilize the price of something (e.g., stock, currency, commodity) by manipulating or regulating the market. For example, the government may peg the price of gold by purchasing all that is available at a stated price. see also *crawling peg.*

pegged price
(1) the agreed, customary, or legal price at which any commodity has been fixed.
(2) the price level for a specific stock at which buying support nearly always evolves and prevents a decline—thus "pegging" the price. see also *peg (pegging).*

penalty syndicate bid: a stabilizing bid made by a manager of a syndicate providing that selling concessions will be withheld, and often a dollar penalty issued, against members of an account whose clients reoffer to the account manager securities just sold them by members of the account.

penetration pricing: strategy of using a low initial price means to capture a large share of the market as early as possible.

pennant: a technical chart trend appearing as a pointed flag, with the point facing to the right. Formed as the rallies and peaks that give it its form become less pronounced. A *pennant* is characterized by declining trade volume. cf. *flag.*

Pennsylvania Rule: a rule that requires credit of extraordinary dividends received in trust on the basis of the source of such dividends; to income if declared from earnings of the corporation during the life of the trust, and to principal if from earnings accumulated before commencement of the trust.

penny ante: slang, involving an insignificant amount of cash.

penny stocks: low-priced issues, often highly speculative, selling at less than $1 a share. Frequently a term of disparagement, although a few penny stocks have developed into investment-caliber issues.

pension: French for a money market borrowing against securities held in pension by the lender until repayment.

Pension Benefit Guaranty Corporation (PBGC): a federal corporation created under the Employee Retirement Income Security Act of 1974 to guarantee basic pension benefits in covered plans by administering terminated plans and placing liens on corporate assets for some pension liabilities that were not funded.

pension fund: a fund out of which pensions are to be paid either to those entitled thereto under specific agreement or to those who may be selected by persons in control of the fund.

pension plan: a method used by a firm or union to pay annuities or pensions to retired and/or disabled employees. Sections 401 and 404 of the Internal Revenue Code identify conditions enabling an organization to establish a pension plan. see *Employee Retirement Income Security Act of 1974.*

pension reserve: an actuarial computation of the financial obligation for future payments to be made on account of a pension or retirement allowance or benefit.

pension trust: a trust established by an employer (commonly a corporation) to provide benefits for incapacitated, retired, or superannuated employees, with or without any contributions made by the employees.

PER
(1) see *par exchange rate.*
(2) see *post-execution reporting.*
(3) see *price-earnings ratio.*

per annum: by the year.

Per. Cap.: per capita.

per capita: by the individual.

per capita debt: the total bonded debt of a municipality, divided by its population.

per capita tax: by the individual; a tax based on the result of dividing stated sums of money by a specified group of people to show the amount to be paid by each person.

percentage lease: a lease providing for payment of rent based on a percentage of the gross sales or the sales over a fixed amount.

percentage order: either a market or a limited price order to buy (or sell) a stated amount of a specified stock after a fixed number of shares of such stock have traded.

percent return on investment: profit received from the firm as compared to the money and property invested in the firm.

per centum: by the hundred.

perfected lien: a security interest in an asset that is properly documented and has been filed with the appropriate legal authority. Thus the claim of the creditor has been protected.

perfect title
(1) property displaying total right of ownership.
(2) a title that is not open to dispute or challenge because it is complete in every detail, and has no legal defects. see also *quiet title suit.* cf. *cloud on title.*

performance fee: fees charged by some mutual fund managers when their purchasing and selling for the fund portfolio helps it to outperform certain market averages over a stated time period. synonymous with *incentive fee.*

performance fund: a mutual fund that places more of its monies into speculative risky investments, such as some common stocks, rather than more conservative investments, such as bonds.

performance index: a "total return" index of investment performance. A performance index differs from the popular market indexes (or so-called averages) in that the popular measures do not include the return derived from dividends and other distributions to shareholders. see also *total return.*

performance securities: issues expected to demonstrate strong short-term growth in market price.

performance stock: synonymous with *growth stock.*

performance unit plans (PUPs): a form of incentive compensation that provides executives with cash or stock awards for attaining corporate profit goals.

period cost: synonymous with *fixed cost.*

periodicity: a condition of a market as affected by cyclical shifts.

periodic payment plan: a contractual mutual fund where an investor agrees to make regular payments to the plan company. In return the investor receives benefits from the plan firm, traditionally plan completion insurance and asset withdrawal privileges, and other benefits from the underlying fund including sharing in a diversified portfolio of common stocks and reinvestment privileges.

periodic purchase deferred contract: an annuity contract for which fixed-amount payments (premiums) are paid either quarterly or monthly and that does not commence paying out until a time chosen by the holder.

period of digestion: a time immediately following the release of a new or large security offering, during which sales are made primarily to regular investment customers.

period of redemption: the length of time during which a mortgagor may reclaim the title and possession of his or her property by paying the debt it secured.

permanent accounts: see *real accounts.*

permanent asset: any fixed or capital asset.

permanent capital: common and preferred stock as well as retained earnings that do not have to be paid back.

permanent financing: a long-term mortgage, amortized over 15, 20, or more years at a fixed rate of interest.

permanent income: the average income anticipated to be received over a number of years.

permanent life insurance: a phrase used to cover any form of life insurance except term; generally insurance that accrues cash value, such as whole life or endowment.

permanent stock association: see *stock association.*

perpendicular spread: see *vertical spread.*

perpetual bond: see *bond, perpetual.*

perpetual warrant: an investment certificate giving a holder the right to purchase a given number of common shares of stock at a stated price with no expiration date.

perpetuity

(1) endless; the quality of going on forever (e.g., an estate willed in perpetuity).

(2) anything that is removed from the ordinary channel of commerce by limiting its capacity to be sold for a period longer than that of a life or lives in being and 21 years thereafter, plus the period of development, is said to be *removed in perpetuity.*

per share net: after tax earnings of a firm divided by the total number of common shares outstanding.

personal estate: synonymous with *personal property.*

personal finance company: a business that lends small sums of money to people, usually for personal needs, at relatively high interest rates. Most states require these organizations to be licensed.

personal financial statement: an account of an individual's personal resources and obligations. A personal financial statement is comparable to a balance sheet for a business.

personal holding company: a holding company which under income tax law derives at least 80 percent of its gross income from royalties, dividends, interest, annuities, and sale of securities, and in which over 50 percent of the outstanding stock is owned by not more than five persons.

personal property: the rights, powers, and privileges an individual has in movable things such as chattels, and choses in action. synonymous with *personal estate.*

personal saving: the difference between disposable personal income and personal consumption expenditures; includes the changes in cash and deposits, security holdings, indebtedness, reserves of life insurance companies and mutual savings institutions, the net investment of unincorporated enterprises, and the acquisition of real property net of depreciation.

personal security: an unsecured accommodation in which the net worth and the stature of the business borrower are relied on rather than some collateral which is pledged.

personal surety: surety provided by an individual as contrasted with surety provided by an insurance company.

personalty: personal property.

petition in bankruptcy: the form used for declaring voluntary bankruptcy. see *bankruptcy.*

petitioning on creditors' bond: see *bond, petitioning on creditors'.*

petrobonds: instruments that are backed by a specific number of barrels of oil. Since 1977, the Mexican government has been raising money by selling these bonds that trade in direct relations to the rapidly rising official price of Mexico's crude oil.

petrodollars: huge sums of money from oil-producing nations other than the United States or Great Britain. These funds are initially converted into Eurocurrency and deposited with international banks to be used for future investment and for paying debts. These banks traditionally set limits on the sum they will accept from any one country. see *Organization of Petroleum Exporting Countries.*

PFD: see *preferred stock.*

PHA: see *bond, Public Housing Authority.*

phantom stock: used in executive compensation programs, the executive is granted a number of shares of the company; each share entitles the executive to the amount, if any, by which the market price of the stock at some future time exceeds the current market price.

Philadelphia exchange: an affiliate of the Philadelphia Stock Exchange having a futures contract on its own OTC index.

Philadelphia plan: a technique for transferring ownership of equipment purchased with equipment trust certificates where the title to the equipment is retained by the trustee until the debt has been retired in full. see *equipment trust certificate.* cf. *New York plan.*

Philadelphia Stock Exchange: in 1919, the Philadelphia Stock Exchange became the Philadelphia-Baltimore Stock Exchange. In July 1953, the Washington Stock Exchange merged with the PBSE and in 1969, the Pittsburgh Stock Exchange consolidated with the Philadelphia-Baltimore-Washington Stock Exchange.

phony dividends: rather than paying dividends from stock earnings, dividends that are paid immediately from a portion of the money that comes in from the public's purchasing of that stock. This is an illegal activity.

physical commodity: the actual commodity that is delivered to the contract purchase at the completion of a commodity contract in either the spot or the futures market.

physical market: synonymous with *spot market.*

physical(s): actual commodities rather than futures contracts.

physical verification: when an auditor reviews the assets of a company, especially inventory, to confirm their existence and value, instead of depending on written records.

pickup: the gain in yield resulting from the sale of one block of bonds and the purchase of another block with a higher yield.

pickup bond: see *bond, pickup.*

picture: slang, the requesting bid and asked prices and quantity information from a specialist or from a dealer related to a specific stock.

piece-of-the-action financing: a lending arrangement in which the mortgagee receives, besides regular loan interest, a negotiated percentage of the gross income of an income property, of increases in rentals over a stated period of the life of an income property, or the gross or net profit of a commercial or industrial enterprise.

piggyback registration: the condition when a securities underwriter permits existing holdings of shares in a firm to be sold in combination with an offering of new public shares.

Pinay bonds: see *Giscards.*

pinch

(1) a bind or tight situation.

(2) a sudden, unanticipated rise in prices; when money rates go up suddenly, it is called a *money pinch.*

pink sheets: price quotations of many over-the-counter stocks that are published on pink sheets. synonymous with *"sheets," the.* cf. *white sheets.*

pip: foreign exchange dealers' term for 0.00001 of a unit.

pipeline, in the: an underwriting procedure involving securities being proposed for public sale. In the municipal bond market, the pipeline is called the *Thirty Day Visible Supply* in the *Daily Bond Buyer newspaper.* see also *official notice of sale.*

pit: a circular area in the middle of the floor of a stock exchange; steps lead down into the pit, giving greater visibility to the trading action occurring there. synonymous with *ring.* see *floor, outcry market.*

PITI: common abbreviation for principal, interest, taxes, and insurance, used when describing the monthly carrying charges on a mortgage.

pivotal stock: a stock that is accepted as the leader of its group and often influences the activity of other stocks.

PL: price list.

place: to locate a market for a security; to sell it to an investor.

placement: negotiating for the sale of a new securities issue, or the arranging of a long-term loan.

placement memorandum: a document prepared by the lead manager of a syndicate in the Eurocredit market; seeks to provide information to other potential leaders to assist them in deciding whether to participate in the credit.

placement ratio: the ratio determined at the end of business each Thursday, showing the percentage of the past week's new municipal bond offerings that have been purchased from the underwriters. Published by the *Daily Bond Buyer* newspaper.

placing power: the ability of a bank or broker to sell securities to investors (i.e., to place the securities).

plain bond: see *bond, plain.*

plaintiff: a complaining party or the person who begins a legal action against another person or organization, seeking a court remedy.

PLAM: see *price-level-adjusted mortgage.*

plan company: a sales firm registered with the SEC as a participating unit investment trust selling contractual-type funds on behalf of the fund's underwriter. A purchaser receives two propectuses—one for the plan company and one for the mutual fund.

plan completion insurance: decreasing term life insurance sold to subscribers to a mutual fund contractual plan at group rates. Should the planholder die prior to the completion of the plan contract, the difference between the planholder's contribution and the plan amount is paid to the custodian bank.

planholder: a pension plan shareholder.

plateau: a sideways price-movement period following a time of increasing prices. A plateau indicates a period of uncertainty or confusion, but is usually followed by a drop in security prices.

play

(1) any speculation in the stock market.

(2) any speculative security.

(3) a business whose success largely depends on a speculative stake or stakes.

PLC: (British) Public Limited Company.

please advise fate: see *fate (inquiry).*

pledged-account mortgage: a variation on graduated-payment mortgages, where a portion of the borrower's down payment is used to fund a pledged savings account, which is drawn on to supplement the monthly payment during the first years of the loan. The net effect to the borrower is lower payments at first. Payments gradually rise to slightly above those on conventional mortgages. see also *flexible-payment mortgage, graduated-payment mortgage, reverse-annuity mortgage, rollover mortgage, variable-rate mortgage.*

pledged assets: securities owned by a bank, generally U.S. government bonds and obligations, specified by law, which must be pledged as collateral security for funds deposited by the U.S. government, or state or municipal governments.

pledged loan: a mortgage loan that has been pledged as security for a borrowing; particularly, one that has been pledged as security for a Federal Home Loan Bank advance.

pledged securities: securities issued or assumed by the accounting company that have been pledged as collateral security for any of its long-term debt or short-term loans.

pledgee: the person or firm to whom the security for a loan is pledged.

pledgor: the person or firm that makes a pledge of real or personal property as the collateral for a loan.

plum: slang, extra profits or additional stock dividends.

plunge
(1) a sudden decline in the price of a stock within a day or two, indicating an immediate purchase signal if other technical factors are favorable.
(2) a reckless speculation.

plunger: an individual speculator who takes great risks, resulting in substantial profits or losses.

plunk down: slang, to make a payment in cash.

plus
(1) the sign (+) following a price quotation on a Treasury note or bond, showing that the price is refined to 64ths.
(2) the sign following a transaction price in a listed stock showing that the trade was at a higher price than the previous regular way transaction.
(3) the sign before the figure in the column labeled "change" in the newspaper stock tables, indicating that the closing price of the stock was higher than the previous day's close by the amount stated in the "change" column.

plus tick: synonymous with *up tick.*

plus tick rule: synonymous with *short-sale rule.*

PM: see *primary market.*

PMM: see *purchase-money mortgage.*

PN: see *project notes.*

PNI: see *participate but do not initiate.*

PO
(1) see *public offering.*
(2) see *purchase order.*

POB: point of business.

POD: pay on delivery.

point: a unit of measure in revealing stock prices. Usually one point equals one percent. In bond quotes, one point is one percent of the bond's face value, usually $10. In mortgages one point equals one percent. In securities one point equals $1, and in releasing market indicator figures one point merely equals a one-point move from the base level.

point and figure chart: a means of showing market price changes and the direction of such shifts. Volume is not included and time is not precisely measured.

poison pen: special corporate warrants that deny shareholders the right to consider tender offers for their shares and that transfer that right to the board.

poison pill: a stock issue of warrants or preferred stock authorized by a corporation, usually in its shareholders' meeting, purporting to prevent any unfriendly takeover by making it excessively expensive.

policy dividend: a refund of part of the premium on a participating life insurance policy reflecting the difference between the premium charged and actual experience.

policyholder: a person or company protected by an insurance contract. synonymous with "the insured."

policy loan: funds borrowed from a life insurance organization, usually at low interest rates, using as security the cash value of the holders' policy.

policy value: the amount of money available to the insured upon the maturity of the policy.

political investments: synonymous with *socially responsible investments.*

political risk: synonymous with *sovereign risk.*

polyopsony: the market situation in which the number of buyers is so few that their actions materially affect the market price, yet large enough that each buyer cannot with confidence judge the effect of his or her actions on the conduct of other buyers in the market.

polypoly: the market situation in which the number of sellers is so few that their actions materially affect the market price, yet large enough that each seller cannot with confidence judge the effect of his or her actions on the conduct of the other sellers in the market.

Ponzi Scheme: a fraud where investors are promised enormous returns. Initially these investors are impressed as they are paid by utilizing later subscribers' investments. Eventually the entire system collapses. synonymous with *Pyramid Club.*

pool
(1) ***general:*** any combination of resources of funds, and so on, for some common purpose or benefit.
(2) ***general:*** an agreement between two or more companies to curtail output, divide sales areas, or in any other way avoid competition.
(3) ***general:*** firms joined to share business over a fixed time.
(4) ***investments:*** a combination of persons (brokers, traders) organized for the purpose of exploiting stocks. The SEC prohibits pool operations. see *SEC.*

pooled income fund: a fund to which several donors transfer property, retaining an income interest, and giving the remainder to a single charity.

pool financing: in municipal financing, when a sponsor floats an issue whose proceeds are used by a number of cities allowing municipalities to share underwriting expenses and get the lower interest rates available to large borrowers.

pooling of interests: a method of accounting for business combinations under which the net assets are accounted for in the combined corporation's financial statements at their book value as recorded in the combining corporations, and comparative figures are restated on a combined basis.

pooling operation: a business similar to an investment trust or syndicate, which solicits, accepts, or receives from others funds for the purpose of trading in any commodity for futures delivery. see *pool.*

POR: pay on return.

pork belly (bellies): the class of hog commodity in frozen form; one of the major speculative items in the commodity exchange.

portfolio: holdings of securities by an individual or institution. A portfolio may contain bonds, preferred stocks, and common stocks of enterprises of various types.

portfolio beta score: the volatility of a person's stock portfolio, taken as a whole, as measured by the Beta coefficients of the securities making it up. see also *Beta.*

portfolio management theory: synonymous with *portfolio theory.*

portfolio manager: the person from an investment advisory firm who supervises an investor's portfolio, as contrasted with a broker, who sells particular securities.

portfolio optimization: starting with a universe of securities that has been valued in terms of (a) expected return, (b) variances of expected return, and (c) covariance of return with every other security under consideration, the process involves selecting the portfolio that minimizes risk for a given level of risk.

position
(1) ***general:*** a job; an employment situation.
(2) ***general:*** a bank's net balance in a foreign currency.
(3) ***general:*** a company's financial situation.

(4) ***investments:*** an investor's stake in the market, in general, or a particular security.
(5) ***investments:*** (as a verb) to take on a long or a short position in a stock.

position building: purchasing shares to accumulate a long position or of selling shares to accumulate a short position.

position limit
(1) ***commodities:*** the number of contracts acquired in a given commodity before a speculator is identified as a large trader. A position limit will vary with the kind of commodity.
(2) ***options:*** the maximum number of exchange-listed option contracts that can be owned or controlled by an individual holder, or by a group of holders acting jointly, in the same underlying stock. The present limit is 2000 contracts on the same side of the market with the limit applying to all expiration dates.

position traders: traders who take the long-term approach to the commodity markets, meaning anywhere from six months to a year or more.

positive carry: a condition where the cost of money borrowed to finance stocks is lower than the yield on the stocks. cf. *negative carry.*

positive yield curve: a condition where interest rates are higher on long-term debt securities than on short-term debt securities of the same quality. cf. *negative yield curve.*

post
(1) ***general:*** to record onto detailed subsidiary records (ledgers) amounts that were recorded in chronological records of original entry. see also *suspense account.*
(2) ***investments:*** the horseshoe-shaped fixture on the New York Stock Exchange trading floor where 100-share unit stocks and active 10-share unit stocks are bought and sold.

postdate: dating an instrument a time after that on which it is made.

post-execution reporting (PER): on the AME, a computerized order routing system for member-firm market, limit, and odd-lot orders that transmits these orders and returns the particulars of executed orders. cf. *designated order turnaround.*

Post 30: the trading post at the New York Stock Exchange where usually inactive issues are traded in 10-share units rather than the normal round lots of 100 shares. No odd-lot differential is involved on sales or purchases. Post 30 is located in the Exchange's annex, popularly referred to as the garage. see *garage*; synonymous with *inactive post.*

pot: that part of a security issue set aside by a syndicate manager for distribution to dealers or institutions. see *pot protection.*

potential stock: the difference between the total authorized capital stock and the actually issued one.

pot is clean: slang, an announcement made by a syndicate manager to members of the account that all stocks set aside for institutional sales have been bought.

pot protection: an arrangement guaranteeing that an institution receives a specified amount of stocks or bonds from a *pot.*

pp
(1) see *paper profit.*
(2) see *purchase price.*

PPS: see *preferred stock, prior.*

Pr.
(1) preferred.
(2) see *principal.*

PR: see *pro rata.*

praecipium: in the Euromarket, the manager of a credit or bond who negotiates a fee payable by the borrower. From this the manager deducts a specified amount for itself—the praecipium before dividing the balance of the fee between the rest of the management group.

precautionary liquidity balance: cash and securities held for use in emergencies.

precedence of order: the priority that one security has over another for buying or selling. When bids arrive, a priority exists to determine whose buy or sell order is accepted first.

preemptive right: synonymous with *subscription privilege.*

preference as to assets: in the event of dissolution of a firm, before disbursement of a declared dividend, stockholders holding preferred shares are entitled to claim payments before payments are made to common stockholders.

preference bond: see *bond, preference.*

preference shares (preferred stock): shares that receive a dividend at a stated rate prior to the paying out of any dividend on the firm's common shares.

preferential duty: synonymous with *differential duty.*

preferred capital stock: capital stock to which preferences or special rights are attached (i.e., preferred as to dividends and/or proceeds in liquidation) as compared to another class of stock issued by the same company.

preferred dividend coverage: a ratio of corporate after-tax income to annual dividends payable to preferred stockholders.

preferred dividends payable: an account containing a record of the amount owed to the preferred stockholders for dividends.

preferred stock: corporate stock whose owners have some preference as to assets, earnings, and so on, not granted to the owners of common stock of the same corporation. see also *adjustment preferred securities, Class A stock, cumulative preferred (stock), effective par, guaranteed stock, privilege issue, voting right (stock).*

preferred stock, cumulative: see *cumulative preferred (stock).*

preferred stock, noncumulative: see *noncumulative.*

preferred stock, participating: see *participating preferred.*

preferred stock, prior: ranks ahead of any other preferred and common in claim on dividends and assets.

preferred stock funds: mutual funds emphasizing investments in preferred securities with a primary goal of higher current income and capital preservation.

preferred stock ratio: a preferred stock at par value divided by total capitalization. The result is the percentage of capitalization shown by preferred stock.

pregnancy notes: notes that postpone payment for 10 months.

preliminary official statement: the preliminary statement issued for municipal securities offering that gives details about the upcoming offering. Modeled after a preliminary prospectus.

preliminary prospectus: an advance report giving the details of a planned offering of corporate stock. The issue is still in the process of being registered by the SEC and cannot be sold until clearance is received. synonymous with *red herring*. see also *open prospectus*.

preliminary title report: the results of a title search by a title company prior to issuing a title binder of commitment to insure.

Prem.: see *premium*.

premium

(1) ***general:*** the sum paid for a policy, not to be confused with premiums. An earned premium is the portion of the written premium covering the part of the policy term that is included in the time period. The pure premium is found by dividing losses by a hazard or contingency, and to which no operating expenses of the firm has been added (e.g., commissions, taxes).

(2) ***general:*** the amount by which one form of funds exceeds another in buying power.

(3) ***investments:*** the amount by which a preferred stock or bond may sell above its par value. In the case of a new issue of bonds or stocks, a premium is the amount the market price rises over the original selling price.

(4) ***investments:*** a charge sometimes made when a stock is borrowed to make delivery on a short sale.

(5) ***investments:*** the redemption price of a bond or preferred stock, if this price is higher than face value.

(6) ***investments:*** the price of a put or call determined through the auction process.

premium bond: see *bond, premium*.

premium for risk: the actual yield on an investment minus the basic yield prevailing at the time.

premium income: the investor's income from selling a put option or a call option. The investor receives premium income by writing a covered option, if the investor owns the underlying stock, or a naked option, if the investor does not own the underlying stock. The investor who sells options to collect premium income expects that the underlying security will not increase much in the case of a call, or drop much in the case of a put.

premium on bonds: the amount or percentage by which bonds are purchased, sold, or redeemed for more than their face value.

premium on capital stock: the excess of the cash or cash value of the consideration received from the sale of capital stock (excluding accrued dividends) over the par or stated value of such stock.

premium on funded debt: the excess of the actual cash value of the consideration received for funded debt securities (of whatever kind) issued or assumed over the par value of such securities and the accrued interest thereon.

premium on securities: the amount by which a security (a bond or a share of stock) is bought or sold for more than its face or par value. opposed to *discount on securities.*

premium over bond value: the upward difference between the market value of a convertible bond and the price at which a straight bond of the same firm would sell in the same open market.

premium over conversion value: the amount that the market price of a convertible preferred stock or convertible bond exceeds the price at which it is convertible.

premium raids: the unannounced lightning-quick buying sprees that several companies have mounted to build up large stakes in other companies by offering a bonus over the prevailing stock market share price.

premium recapture: the time it takes for the convertible's yield advantage (the difference between what the bond pays in interest yearly and what the underlying common would pay in dividends) to recoup the premium paid over the conversion value. The shorter, the better. Anything less than two years is considered good.

premiums on bonds: the amount or percentage by which bonds are bought, sold, or redeemed for more than their face value.

premium stock

(1) a stock that lends at a premium (i.e., an amount charged for loaning it to a person who borrowed it to make delivery on a short sale).

(2) an average, superior stock; any confirmed leader.

prepaid charge plan: see *contractual plan.*

prepaid expense: the pro rata portion of a fully paid charge for a service should a portion of the service overlap the end of a firm's fiscal year.

prepayment

(1) ***general:*** the payment of a debt before it actually becomes due.

(2) ***general:*** paying a loan prior to maturity.

(3) ***credit:*** making payments prior to maturity.

(4) ***securities:*** paying a seller for a stock before its settlement date.

prepayment penalty: a penalty placed on a mortgagor for paying the mortgage before its due date. This applies when there is no prepayment clause to offset the penalty.

prepayment privilege: an optional clause in a mortgage which gives the mortgagor the right to pay all or part of a debt prior to its maturity.

prerefunding: an exchange by holders of securities maturing in less than one year for securities maturing in less than one year for securities of longer original maturity, usually due within 10 years.

prerogatives: the rights, powers, privileges (e.g., diplomatic immunity) of an individual that others do not possess.

presale estimates: in an auction, a range of prices stated in the catalogue within which the auction house believes an item will sell. The reserve is usually set below the low estimate.

presale order: an order to buy part of a new municipal bond issue that is accepted by an underwriting syndicate manager prior to the announcement of the price or coupon rate and before any public offering.

present value: the discounted value of a certain sum due and payable at a certain specified future date.

present value of expected cash flow: the net cash that a company expects to realize or pay out from holding an asset or liability, discounted by an appropriate rate of interest.

preservation of capital: a form of investment, with the objective of preserving capital by way of avoiding high-risk situations. cf. *go-go fund.*

presidential election cycle concept: the belief by some investors that major stock market shifts are predictible based on the four-year presidential election cycle where stocks decline shortly after the election, midway stocks will begin to rise in value.

presold issue: an issue of government or municipal bonds that is completely sold out prior to a public announcement of its price or yield. Corporate bond issues under SEC regulation cannot be presold.

price alert: a price breakout occurring when a security exceeds its highest or lowest price during a stated time period. The total number of stocks that have upside or downside breakouts are used to measure the strength or weakness of the market.

price averaging: buying equal share amounts of a stock at varying price levels.

price change: the net rise or fall of the price of a stock at the end of a trading day, compared to the previous session's closing price.

price/dividend ratio (P/D): showing the relationship between the current market price of a security and its annual dividend. It is determined by dividing current market value per share by the annual dividend per share.

priced out of the market: a market situation wherein the asked-for price of an item eliminates possible buyers, leading to a decline in sales volume.

Price-earnings multiple: see *price-earnings ratio.*

price-earnings (P/E) ratio: the price of a share of stock divided by earnings per share for a 12-month period.

For example, a stock selling for $50 a share and earning $5 a share is said to be selling at a price-earnings ratio of 10:1.

price gap: when a stock's price either leaps up or down from its last trading range without overlapping the trading range; considered by some analysts as indications of an overbought or oversold position.

price-level-adjusted adjusting mortgage (PLAM): a unique mortgage plan in which the outstanding loan balance is indexed. The interest rate is a rate net of any inflation premium. The payments on a PLAM are based on this real rate, and at the end of each year, the then outstanding balance is adjusted by an inflation factor. The principal benefit of a PLAM is the much lower initial payment than either a GPM, GPAM, or a shared appreciation mortgage. see *graduated-payment mortgage, shared-appreciation mortgage.*

price limit: the price that is entered on the trading floor of an exchange for placing an order to buy or sell. see *limited order.*

price loco: the price at the place where a purchase occurs.

price potential: an estimate employing anlysis of a securities future market value, either near-, intermediate-, or long-term price appraisal.

price range: high and low limits within which a stock has traded over a stated time frame, quoted for a day or a year of the past 52 weeks.

price spread: synonymous with *vertical spread.*

price taker: a relatively small purchaser or seller who has no impact on the market price.

price talk: the early discussions among underwriters concerning the range within which they will offer a negotiated issue or within which they will bid on a competitive issue.

price/volume alert: a price breakout where a security exceeds its highest or lowest price during a given time period that is also accompanied by a volume breakout, indicating extremely dynamic stock movement.

price-weighted index: an index where component stocks are weighted by their price.

pricey: slang, an unrealistically low bid price or high offer price.

primary dealer: a select group of banks and investment dealers authorized to purchase and sell government securities in direct dealings with the Federal Reserve Bank of New York in its execution of Fed Open Market Operations.

primary distribution: the original sale of a company's securities. synonymous with *primary offering.*

primary earnings per (common) share: earnings available to common stock divided by the number of common shares outstandings.

primary market
(1) ***general:*** the initial market for any item or service.

(2) ***investments:*** the initial market for a new stock issue.
(3) ***investments:*** a firm, trading market held in a security by a trader who performs the activities of a specialist by being ready to execute orders in that stock.

primary movement: synonymous with *major trend, underlying movement.*

primary offering: synonymous with *primary distribution.*

primary points: primary trading centers for agricultural commodities (e.g., Chicago, Kansas City).

primary trend: the direction in stock values that last for many months and usually for years.

PRIME: Prescribed Right to Income and Maximum Equity.

prime: a very high grade or quality.

prime investment
(1) ***general:*** a quality, first-class investment.
(2) ***investments:*** a high-grade investment, considered so safe and sound that dividends or interest payments are assumed.

prime paper: the highest quality commercial paper, as rated by several rating services; considered investment grade. Moody's prime paper ratings are: P-1, highest quality; P-2, higher quality; P-3, high quality. Below P-3, commercial paper is not considered prime paper.

principal
(1) ***general:*** one of the major parties to a transaction; either the seller or purchaser.
(2) ***general:*** the original amount of a deposit, loan, or other amount of money on which interest is earned or paid.
(3) ***investments:*** the face value of an instrument, which becomes the obligation of the maker or drawee to pay to a holder in due course. Interest is charged on the principal amount. synonymous with *face of a note.*
(4) ***investments:*** exclusive of earnings, the basic amount invested.
(5) ***investments:*** a person for whom a broker executes an order, or a dealer buying or selling for his or her own account.

principal amount: the face value of an obligation to be repaid at maturity, as separate from the interest.

principal balance: the outstanding total of a mortgage or other debt, excluding interest or premium.

principal beneficiary: synonymous with *ultimate beneficiary.*

principal shareholder: a shareholder owning a significant number of shares in a corporation, usually 10 percent or more of the voting stock of a registered firm.

principal sum: the amount specified under a life insurance policy, such as the death benefit.

principal underwriter: synonymous with *managing underwriter.*

print: see *block trade.*

prior deductions method: an improper method of determining bond interest or preferred dividend coverage: the requirements of senior obligations are first deducted from earnings and the balance is applied to the requirements of the junior issue.

priority: in the auction market, an approach where the first bid or offer price is executed before other bid and offer prices even when subsequent orders are greater. Orders originating off the floor of an exchange also have priority over on-floor orders.

prior lien: a mortgage that ranks ahead of another.

prior-lien bond: see *bond, prior-lien.*

prior preferred (stock): see *preferred stock, prior.*

prior redemption: an obligation that a debtor has paid prior to stand maturity.

prior redemption privilege: a privilege frequently extended by a debtor to the holders of called bonds permitting them to redeem their holdings prior to the call date or maturity. There are chiefly three types of offers prior redemption: (1) with interest in full to the call date; (2) with interest in full to the call date less a bank discount (usually 1/4 percent per annum) based on the period from the date of collection to the date of call; and (3) with interest to the date of collection only.

prior sale: when the supply of an item or commodity is limited, the owner or his or her broker can offer it, at a price subject to the fact that more than one buyer may wish the item. Thus the first bid for the item will purchase it. The public is told that bids after the first may not be effective because of some prior sale.

prior stock: any preferred stock.

private distribution: the distribution of a corporation's stock to a limited number of investors.

private financing: synonymous with *private placement.*

private limited partnership: a partnership not registered with the SEC having a maximum of 35 accredited limited partners. Private partnerships are sold by financial planners, brokerage houses, and other SEC-registered investment advisors.

privately owned corporation: synonymous with *closed corporation.*

private offering: an offering for sale of a new issue of stock to a small number of investors; usually limited to $300,000 or less and cannot be offered to more than 25 people.

private placement: usually associated with debt instruments where marketability is not required, but not always the case, the private placement of a loan with an institutional investor such as a pension fund or insurance company precludes the borrower from any SEC registration requirements, eliminates problems connected with changing market interest rates and provides the investor with a higher interest rate and often a tailor-made maturity that might be difficult for him to obtain in a public offering. synonymous with *private financing.*

private sector pass-through: nongovernmental mortgage-backed securities issued by some financial institutions. Some of these are privately guaranteed.

private trust
(1) a trust created for the benefit of a designated beneficiary or designated beneficiaries; as, a trust for the benefit of the settlor's or the testator's wife and children; opposed to a charitable (or public) trust.
(2) a trust created under a declaration of trust or under a trust agreement; as, a living trust or an insurance trust; opposed to a trust coming under the immediate supervision of a court.

private trust fund: a trust fund that will ordinarily revert to private individuals or will be used for private purposes. For example, a fund that consists of guarantee deposits.

private wire firm: brokerage companies that are sufficiently large to allow them to rent telegraph wires for their own branch office communications.

privilege: see *spread, straddle.* see also *privilege dealer.*

privilege broker: see *privilege dealer.*

privileged bond: see *bond, privileged.*

privilege dealer: a broker or dealer in the business of selling puts and calls and variations of such options, which are also referred to as *privileges.*

privilege issue: a preferred stock or bond having a conversion or participating right, or having a stock purchase warrant on it.

privileges: see *privilege dealer.*

proceeds
(1) the actual amount of funds given to a borrower, following deductions for interest charges, fees, and so on.
(2) the monies remaining after a business has paid all its bills. see also *contribution profit.*
(3) the reward to the entrepreneur for the risks assumed by him or her in the establishment, operation, and management of a given enterprise or undertaking.

proceeds sale: an over-the-counter securities sale where the proceeds are used to buy another security.

process effects: the increase in consumer spending and private investment created by the spending on a public-works project.

processing: the preparation of a mortgage loan application and supporting documents for consideration by a lender or insurer.

produce exchange
(1) a spot market for perishable agricultural products.
(2) a contract market where futures contracts are transacted for agricultural products.

producer: a stockbroker in the employ of a brokerage firm who regularly generates or earns a lot of commissions for it, resulting from high-volume sales of stocks he or she derives from big or wealthy customers.

production rate: the current coupon rate for issuance of pass-through securities of GNMA. It is the interest rate set 50 basis points (.5 percent) below the prevailing FHA mortgage rate.

professional: in the securities business, a student of the market or a person who makes a living buying and selling securities. A professional may direct the investments of a pension fund or other institution, or be a member of a brokerage firm who advises or acts for his firm's clients.

professional corporation (pc): a corporation created to practice a professional trade, such as law or medicine.

profit
(1) ***general:*** the excess of the selling price over all costs and expenses incurred in making a sale.
(2) ***general:*** monies remaining after a business has paid all its bills.
(3) ***general:*** a reward to the entrepreneur for the risks assumed by him or her in the establishment, operation, and management of a given enterprise or undertaking.
(4) ***investments:*** the difference between the selling price and the purchase price of commodities or securities when the selling price is higher.

profitability: a firm's ability to earn a profit and the potential for future earnings.

profitability index: the present value of future cash flow benefits divided by the initial investment.

profitability ratios: ratios indicating how efficiently a firm is being managed.

profit and loss account: an account transferred from accounts receivable to a separate ledger. An amount deducted from the accounts receivable balance. An account deemed to be uncollectable, or a certain number of months past due, becomes eligible for transfer to the "profit and loss account" ledger.

profit and loss reserve: an amount set aside by a firm to provide for anticipated "P & L accounts" during the fiscal period. Usually calculated as given percentage of the total "accounts receivable."

profit and loss statement (operating statement; P & L): the summary listing of a firm's total revenues and expenses within a specified time period. synonymous with *income and expense statement.*

profit and loss summary account: an account to which balances of all the income and all the expense accounts are transferred at the conclusion of the fiscal period.

profit center: a segment of a business that is responsible for both revenues and expenses.

profit margin: the ratio of sales less all operating expenses divided by the number of sales.

profit on fixed assets: the profit resulting when the book value of a fixed asset is less than the actual value at the time the asset is sold.

profit on net worth ratio: a profitability ratio (net profit after taxes divided by net worth) indicating how well invested funds are used.

profit-sharing bond: see *bond, profit-sharing.*

profit-sharing securities: participating bonds or participating preferred stock.

profit taking: the sale of stock that has appreciated in value since purchase, in order to realize the profit that has been made possible. This activity is often cited to explain a downturn in the market following a period of rising prices. cf. *unloading.*

program buying: the initial purchase of stock dictated by a big premium between the price of stock and the price of futures. cf. *program selling.*

program selling: occurs when the premium disappears. cf. *program buying.*

progressive tax: an income tax that rises as income increases. The rate of increase varies. see *ability to pay.* cf. *regressive taxes.*

projection: forecasting future prices or conditions utilizing past and projected data.

project notes (PN): short-term debt obligations issued by the government to provide funds for public housing construction. Upon completion of the construction, permanent bonds are issued to retire and replace the project notes.

promoter: one who acts as a middleman in business in order to bring together those with money to risk and those who have a business proposition. His or her duties may include securing new funds for old or new business ventures, discovering new ventures, or merging established businesses.

prompt date: on the London Metal Exchange, the date on which a metal has to be delivered to fulfill the terms of the purchase contract.

property

(1) ***general:*** the exclusive right or interest of a person in his or her belongings.

(2) ***law:*** that which is legally owned by a person or persons and may be used and disposed of as the owner(s) see fit.

property assessment: the valuation of real property for tax purposes.

property capital: stocks, bonds, mortgages, and notes are examples, but currency and bank deposits are not.

property dividends: dividends paid by one corporation in the form of stocks of another corporation, which the former may have acquired by purchase or received from the sale of property.

property tax: synonymous with *land tax.*

proportional representation: a strategy of shareholder voting, providing stockholders increased power over the election of directors than they have under statutory voting, which, by permitting one vote per share per director, makes it possible for a majority stockholder to elect all the directors.

proportional tax: a tax whose percentage rate stays constant as the tax base increases, resulting in the amount of paid tax being proportional to the tax base (e.g., property tax).

proprietary accounts: those accounts which show actual financial condition and operations such as actual assets, liabilities, reserves, surplus, revenues, and expenditures.

proprietary company: synonymous with *holding company.*

proprietor: a person who has an exclusive right or interest in property or in a business.

proprietorship: a business owned by one person. The individual owner has all the rights to profits from the business as well as all the liabilities and losses. synonymous with *individual proprietorship.*

pro rata: "according to the rate" (Latin); in proportion to a total amount. For example, if a contract is terminated prior to the end of the period for which payment has been given, a pro rata return of the payment is made, in proportion to the unused period of time remaining.

pro rate cancellation: the termination of an insurance contract or bond, with the premium charge being adjusted in proportion to the exact time the protection has been in force. cf. *short-rate cancellation.*

prospect: a potential customer.

prospectus: a formal statement legislated by the Securities Act of 1933 describing all facts and figures related to a stock issue being sold to the public. The document must be issued to each prospective purchaser of a public offering. Its purpose is to ensure thorough disclosure of material pertaining to the firm, its financial status, products and services, officers, litigations, cost of the offering, and the projected use of the funds received from the offering. The prospectus must be filed with the SEC and is called an *offering circular.* see also *offering circular.*

protective committee: a committee formed to represent security holders in negotiations on defaulted securities.

protective covenant: see *covenant.*

protective stocks: synonymous with *defensive stocks.*

proximo: in the following month.

proxy: a power of attorney given by a stockholder to an individual or individuals to exercise the stockholder's rights to vote at corporate meetings.

proxy battle: synonymous with *proxy fight.*

proxy fight: the contest between or among two or more factions of shareholders in a corporation, in which each group tries to control the firm, as in the election of its directors, by soliciting signed proxy statements for sufficient votes. synonymous with *proxy battle.*

proxy statement: printed information required by the SEC to be given to potential holders of securities traded on a national exchange, supplying minimum descriptions of the stock, timing of the proposed sale, and so on.

prudent investment-cost standard: a means of defining the value of an organization by subtracting the costs of unwise, inappropriate, or wasteful investments from the original costs of the assets.

prudent man rule: an investment standard. In some states, the law requires that a fiduciary, such as a trustee, may invest the fund's money only in a list of securities designated by the state—the so-called legal list. In other states, the trustee may invest in a security if it is one that would be bought by a prudent person of discretion and intelligence, who is seeking a reasonable income and preservation of capital.

PS
(1) see *penny stocks.*
(2) see *pink sheets.*
(3) see *preferred stock.*
(4) see *price spreading.*

PSA: Public Securities Association.

PSE: see *Pacific Stock Exchange.*

PT
(1) see *paper title.*
(2) see *passing title.*
(3) see *perfect title.*
(4) see *profit taking.*

public bond: see *bond, public.*

public corporation: any corporation that has issued securities through a public offering and whose shares are traded on the open market. Under some conditions, two stockholders or more can constitute a public corporation. In other regulations, 25 or fewer shareholders constitute a private corporation. synonymous with *publicly owned corporation.*

public credit: the capacity of political units to acquire funds in return for their promise to pay. Represented by government, municipal, and other public agencies' bonds and notes.

public debt financing: synonymous with *backdoor financing.*

public finance: see *finance(3).*

public housing authority bond: see *bond, Public Housing Authority.*

public limited partnership: a partnership registered with the SEC and offered to the public through registered broker/dealers. Such partnerships are found in real estate, oil and gas, equipment leasing, etc. cf. *private limited partnership.* see also *limited partner.*

publicly held: a corporation having shares available to the public are large. These corporations are regulated by the SEC.

publicly owned corporation: synonymous with *public corporation.*

publicly traded funds: synonymous with *closed-end funds.*

public offering: new or subsequent issues of stocks sold to the general public. cf. *private financing (private placement).*

public offering price: the price at which a new issue of stocks is offered to the public by underwriters.

public ownership: ownership by the public of the common or other equity stock of a New York Stock Exchange firm.

Public Securities Association: a trade association representing banks, dealers, and brokers who underwrite and trade municipals, governments, and federal agency securities.

public trust: synonymous with *charitable trust.*

public utility: an economic unit that supplies a basic service to the public, such as natural gas, water, electricity. Such organizations tend to function as a monopoly and are highly regulated by the government.

public utility bond: see *bond, public utility.*

Public Utility Holding Company Act of 1935: federal legislation to regulate the securities industry which reorganized the financial structures of holding companies in the gas and electric utility industries and regulated their debt and dividend policies.

public utility securities: equity shares issued by public utilities paying a high yield; considered stable and safe due to their regulated position.

PUDs: abbreviation for the bonds of a public utility district.

PUHCA: Public Utility Holding Company Act. Passed by Congress in 1935 to regulate public utility holding companies. For the principal provisions, see *"death sentence."*

pull: raising the offering price, or lowering the bid price of a stock, or if neither, then to cancel completely.

pull the plug on the market: removing or canceling supporting bids which had earlier been entered just below the market prices prevailing for certain leading stocks.

punt: slang, shares that will rarely turn out to be profitable.

pup: slang, a low-priced, inactive security.

PUPs: see *performance unit plans.*

purchase acquisition: an accounting technique applied in a merger where the purchasing firm treats the acquired company as an investment and adds the acquired firm's assets to its own at their fair market value.

purchase agreement: synonymous with *underwriting agreement.*

purchase contract: synonymous with *underwriting agreement.*

purchase group: synonymous with *underwriting group.*

purchase-money bond: see *bond, purchase-money.*

purchase-money mortgage: for those who put their homes on the market and find that, to sell their property, they must act as the lender themselves. The mortgage is actually a short-term instrument, that runs no more than five years and often only a year or two. In most cases, a purchase-money mortgage is a second mortgage, supplementing the buyer's partial bank financing.

purchase option: fair market; an option given to a lessee to buy equipment at the end of a lease.

purchase order: a document that authorizes the delivery of specified merchandise or the rendering of certain services and the making of a charge for them.

purchase outright: to pay the full amount in cash for purchased stocks.

purchase price
(1) the amount for which any item is bought.
(2) the combination of monies and mortgages given to obtain a property.

purchaser: a buyer; a person who obtains title to or an interest in property by the act of purchase.

purchasing power
(1) ***general:*** the value of money measured by the items it can buy.
(2) ***investments:*** the amount of credit available to a customer in a brokerage account for buying further stocks.

purchasing-power bond: see *bond, purchasing-power.*

purchasing power risk: in investments, used in contradistinction to financial risk and interest rate risk to refer to the risk the price level may move, thus affecting the market value of bonds, for example, relative to common stocks. synonymous with *purchasing power uncertainties.*

purchasing power uncertainties: synonymous with *purchasing power risk.*

pure play: slang, a firm that is virtually dedicated to one line of business. An investor wishing to invest in that line of business looks for such a pure play. cf. *conglomerate.*

pure premium: a premium arrived at by dividing losses by exposure, and to which no loading has been added for commission, taxes, and expenses.

purpose loan: a loan backed by securities and utilized in purchasing other securities under Federal Reserve Board margin and credit rules.

purpose statement: a form filed by a borrower detailing the objective of a loan backed by securities. The borrower agrees not to use the loan proceeds to purchase securities in violation of Federal Reserve Board regulations.

put: see *put option.*

put and call broker: a broker who deals in options or privileges, which are contracts to exercise some right or privilege during a specified time period. Put and call brokers are not allowed on a stock exchange floor.

put bond: see *bond, put.*

put bond option: see *put option.*

put option
(1) ***bond:*** a bondholder's right to redeem a bond prior to its maturity.
(2) ***options:*** a contract granting the right to sell at a specified price a given number of shares by a stated date. A put option purchaser gains this right in return for payment of an option premium. The put option seller gains this right in return for receiving this premium.

put option contract: a contractual agreement giving the holder the right to sell, and the writer the obligation to purchase, 100 shares of the underlying stock per contract at a stated strike price within a stated time period.

put out a line: the selling short of a considerable amount of the stock of one or more firms over a period of time with the hope of falling prices. cf. *take on a line.* see *short sale.*

puts and calls: options that give the right to buy or sell a fixed amount of certain stock at a specified price within a specified time. A put gives the holder the right to sell the stock; a call conveys the right to buy the stock. Puts are purchased by those who think a stock may go down. A put obligates the seller of the contract, commonly known as the option writer, to take delivery of the stock and to pay the specified price to the owner of the option within the time limits of the contract. The price specified in a put or call is usually close to the market price of the stock at the time the contract is made. Calls are purchased by those who think a stock may rise. A call gives the holder the right to buy the stock from the writer at the specified price within a fixed period of time. Put and call contracts are written for 30, 60, or 90 days, or longer. Six months and 10 days is the most common term. If the purchaser of a put or call does not wish to exercise the option, the price paid for the option becomes a loss. see *spread.*

put spread: an option spread position formed by writing a put contract and buying a put contract on the same underlying security with varying expiration dates, different exercise prices, or both.

put to: the right of a put option purchaser to sell, in 100 share lots, a specific security at a stated price to the writer who has sold an option contract on that security. see *exercise.*

put to seller: when a put option is exercised.

PV
(1) see *par value.*
(2) see *present value.*

PVR: profit/volume ratio.

PX: an abbreviation for the price on an offering sheet or on other releases dealing with securities.

Pyramid Club: synonymous with *Ponzi Scheme.*

pyramiding
(1) employing profits of open or unliquidated positions to add to the holder's original position; buying additional stocks or commodities by offering unrealized paper profits as additional margin. Used with commodities; rarely with stocks.
(2) using unrealized profits from one stocks or commodities position as collateral to purchase additional positions with funds borrowed from a broker. This use of leverage creates increased profits in a bull market, and causes margin calls and significant losses in a bear market.

Q

Q
(1) in receivership or bankruptcy proceedings.
(2) quarterly.

QA: see *quick assets.*

QB: qualified buyers.

QI: quarterly index.

QP: see *quoted price.*

QPC: see *quasi-public company.*

Q-ratio: developed in the early 1960s by Yale University economist James Tobin, a way of explaining how the level of stock market prices affects capital spending—and thus the overall economy—even though the vast majority of firms never consider raising fresh equity capital. The *Q*-ratio relates the market value of a company's physical assets to the cost of replacing those assets. A ratio greater than one means that the stock market values a dollar of a company's assets at more than a dollar. Conversely, if *Q* is less than one, the assets, are being valued at less than dollar for dollar.

QS: see *quality stock.*

QT
(1) questioned trade.
(2) see *quotation ticker.*

Q-tip trust: qualified terminable interest property trust. Permits assets to be transferred between spouses. A Q-tip trust grantor directs income from the assets to his or her spouse for life having the power of distribute the assets upon the spouse's death. Qualifies the grantor for the unlimited marital deduction should the spouse die first.

Qtr.: quarter

qualification: a statement in an auditor's report directing attention to any limitation to the examination, or any doubt concerning a reported item in a company's financial statements.

qualified: meeting the requirements in the pertinent provisions of the applicable regulations for tax preference, as with a qualified stock option.

qualified acceptance: any counteroffer.

qualified employee stock options: a corporate program permitting workers to purchase shares in their corporation at a fixed price within a specified time period. Should the purchase not be made within that time frame, the option expires.

qualified endorsement: an endorsement by which the endorser seeks to avoid the usual liabilities inherent in his or her act. "Without recourse" is the most common example. If the instrument is not honored, the endorser does not want to become responsible for it. cf. *recourse.*

qualified plan (or trust): an employer's trust or plan that qualifies under the Internal Revenue Code of 1954 for the exclusive benefit of his or her employees or their beneficiaries in such manner and form as to entitle the employer who makes the payments to the plan or trust to the deductions and income tax benefits as set forth in that Code.

qualified retirement plan: a private retirement plan that meets the rules and regulations of the Internal Revenue Service. Contributions to a qualified retirement plan are in almost all cases tax deductible, and earnings on such contributions are always tax sheltered until retirement.

qualified stock option: synonymous with *restricted option.*

qualified terminable interest property trust: see *Q-tip trust.*

qualifying annuity: an annuity approved by the IRS for inclusion as an investment in IRAs, Keogh Plans, and other approved pension and profit-sharing plans. cf. *nonqualifying annuity.*

qualifying coupon rate: with GNMA contracts, whether options, cash, or forwards, when GNMAs with coupon rates below the current production rate are deliverable against the contract. An adjustment is made in the aggregate exercise price taking into account the lowered coupon rate on the certificates delivered.

qualifying dividends: dividends from taxable U.S. corporations, $100 of which can be excluded from an individual's income, $200 for married taxpayers filing a joint return.

qualifying period: see *waiting period.*

qualifying share: a share of common stock owned so as to qualify as a director of the issuing company.

qualifying stock option: the right given to an employee of a corporation permitting the purchase, for a special price, of a limited number of shares of its capital stock under conditions sustained in the IRS Code. All funds received from the exercise of employee stock options are treated as paid-in capital.

qualifying utility: a utility where stockholders can defer taxes by reinvesting up to $750 in dividends in the firm's stock. When the stocks is sold the taxes are due. The program, created by the Economic Recovery Tax Act of 1981 was phased out at the end of 1985.

qualitative analysis: value judgments pertaining to a stock based on nonfinancial data. cf. *quantitative analysis.*

quality rating: the rating of a stock based on the financial structure and viability of the firm, its history of dividend payments, executive competence, etc.

quality stock: a stock of high grade of superior merit. synonymous with *blue chip stock.*

quantitative analysis: value judgments pertaining to a stock based on financial data, found in a balance sheet, income statement of a firm, or other source. cf. *qualitative analysis.*

quarterly (Q)

(1) ***general:*** every three months; a quarter of a year.

(2) ***securities:*** the basis on which earnings reports to stockholders are made.

(3) ***securities:*** the traditional time period for payment of dividends.

quarter stock: stock with a par value of $25 for each share.

quartile: the grouping of statistics in four equal sections. Performance measurement results are commonly grouped into "quartiles" (i.e., first quartile would include those funds ranking from one to 25 in a sample of 100 funds).

quasi-arbitrage: see *arbitrage.*

quasi-corporation: any political subdivision of an organization or group (e.g., an unincorporated town).

quasi-money: assets that have properties similar to those of money in the strict sense, namely notes and icon plus bank deposits payable at sight.

quasi-public company: a corporation operated privately in which the public has a special interest (e.g., eleemosynary institutions).

quasi-rent: the yield on an investment in capital goods (sunk cost). If there is no alternative use, the total yield, and if there is an alternative use, the yield over the alternative. The capital good is not a determinant of the product since it will continue to be used as long as the price is greater than the average variable cost. Thus any return on such goods is similar to a rent.

quasi-reorganization: a restructuring that does not lead to the formation of a new company, undertaken for purposes of absorbing a deficit, avoiding bankruptcy, and affording an opportunity to begin again. see also *reorganization.*

quick asset ratio: synonymous with *quick ratio.*

quick assets

(1) assets that in the ordinary course of business, will be converted into cash within a reasonably short time.

(2) assets that can be readily converted into cash without appreciable loss. see *liquidity.*

quick (quickie) buck: slang, money made rapidly; a windfall.

quick ratio
(1) a ratio between existing liabilities and quick assets; shows a firm's ability to pay off its liabilities rapidly with available funds.
(2) cash, marketable securities, and accounts receivable divided by current liabilities. synonymous with *quick asset ratio.* see also *acid test ratio.*

quick turn: any quick buy and sale transaction over a brief time period, often within hours. see *day trading.*

quid pro quo
(1) ***general:*** "Something for something" (Latin). A mutual consideration; securing an advantage or receiving a concession in return for a similar favor.
(2) ***securities:*** an arrangement by a company utilizing institutional research that it will execute all trades based on that research with the firm providing it, instead of directly paying for the research.

quiet title suit: a legal action to remove a defect or any questionable claim against the title to property. cf. *cloud on title.*

quotation: the highest bid to buy and the lowest offer to sell a security in a given market at a given time. For example, if you ask a broker for a "quote" on a stock, the reply may be something like "$45\frac{1}{4}$ to $45\frac{1}{2}$." This means that $45.25 is the highest price any buyer wanted to pay at the time the quote was given on the floor of a stock exchange, and $45.50 was the lowest price any seller would take at the same time. The word is often shortened to *quote.* synonymous with *bid and asked.*

quotation board: a display board where current daily market prices are posted either by clip-on numbers or more popularly today, by electronic circuitry. Shows the ticker symbol, shares traded, latest traded price. May also include high, low, and open prices, and the previous trading day's closing price.

quotation ticker: the ticker of an exchange carrying prices of actual transactions.

quote: see *quotation.*

quoted price: the stated price of a security or commodity.

quote machine: any of various types of electronically operated stock-quotation devices, frequently found in a brokerage firm.

quote wire: the direct wire from a brokerage house to the quotation department of the New York Stock Exchange by which a firm can learn the highest bid and lowest offer for a listed security. A quotation can be obtained during regular business hours by dialing the number assigned to the stock.

Quotron: the trademark for a type of quote machine.

quo warranto: Latin for "by what authority." A suit to test the authority of a person in office or of a corporation to its franchise or charter.

R

R

(1) declared or paid in the preceding 12 months plus stock dividend (in stock listings of newspapers).

(2) option not traded (in option listings in newspapers).

(3) see *range.*

(4) see *register.*

(5) see *right.*

RA

(1) see *restricted account.*

(2) see *Revenue Act of 1962, Revenue Act of 1964, Revenue Act of 1971, Revenue Act of 1976, Revenue Act of 1978.*

radar alert: the careful monitoring of trading trends in a firm's stock by senior executives to uncover unusual purchasing activity that might signal a takeover attempt. see also *shark watcher.*

rag stock: slang, low-priced securities.

raid: a deliberate attempt by professionals, traders, and others to depress the market price of a stock.

raider: a person or corporate investor who wishes to gain control of a firm by purchasing a controlling interest in its stock and installing new management. Raiders who accumulate 5 percent or more of the outstanding shares in the target firm must report their purchases to the SEC, the exchange of listing, and the target itself. see also *bear raid, Williams Act.*

raise

(1) ***general:*** any increase in value or amount (e.g., wages or prices).

(2) ***investments:*** a fraudulent increase in the face value of a negotiable instrument.

raise (raising) funds: acquiring money, financing, or credit from surplus earnings of the firm, to stockholders, the public, creditors, customers, or employees.

rally: a brisk rise following a decline in the general price level of the market, or in an individual stock.

RAM: see *reverse annuity mortgage.*

RAN: see *revenue anticipation notes.*

R & D: see *research and development.*

random walk: see *efficient market hypothesis.*

range
(1) the difference between the high and low price of the future during a given period.
(2) the high and low end of a security, commodity future, or market's price fluctuations in a given time period.

ranking: the evaluation of a stock's price performance throughout a time period relative to all other stocks being ranked.

rapid amortization: a program that permits owners of facilities to write off all or a part of their cost for income tax purposes in a short space of time, usually five years. see also *amortization.*

ratable distribution: the proportionate distribution of an estate according to a percentage. For example, if all the legacies cannot be paid in full and each of them is reduced by the same percentage, there is ratable distribution.

rate
(1) to categorize and rank in terms of special qualities or properties.
(2) the cost of a unit of insurance. cf. *premium.*
(3) a charge, fee, or price.

rate covenant: a provision in municipal revenue bond agreements or resolutions covering the rates, or means of setting rates, to be charged users of a facility being financed. The covenant promises that rates will be adjusted when needed covering the cost of repairs and maintenance while continuing to provide for payment of bond interest and principal.

rated: see *rating.*

rate-making: synonymous with *rating (3).*

rate of return (ROR)
(1) the yield obtainable on a security based on its purchase price or its current market price. This may be the amortized yield to maturity on a bond or the current income return.
(2) the income earned by a public utility company on its property or capital investment, expressed as a percentage.

(rate of) return on investment (capital): see *return on invested capital.*

rate of return over cost: synonymous with *marginal efficiency of capital.*

rating
(1) ***bonds:*** a system of rating that provides the investor with a simple system of gradation by which the relative investment quality of bonds are indicated.
(2) ***credit:*** an evaluation of securities investment and credit risk by ratings services.
(3) ***insurance:*** applying statistics, mortality tables, probability theory, experience, judgment, and mathematical analysis to set the rates on which insurance premiums are based. synonymous with *rate-making.*

ratio
(1) a number relationship between two things (e.g., ratio of births to deaths).
(2) any relationship that can be used in measuring the rating or financial position of a firm (e.g., the relationship of a company's earnings to the firm's market price for its stock).
(3) one of the various analyses made by a money-lending or credit agency, of the financial statements of a given individual, company, or other business enterprise seeking credit, to determine the desirability of granting the requested credit.
(4) the relative values of silver and gold in a monetary system based on both. see *bimetallism*.

ratio analysis: the analysis of the relationships of items in financial statements. see listings under *ratio*.

ratio bull spread: synonymous with *neutral spread*.

ratio of accounts payable to purchases: this ratio, determined for the present period and compared with a similar ratio for previous periods, indicates the trend toward or from prompt payment of current obligations.

ratio of capital to fixed assets: this ratio is usually determined for a number of years to ascertain whether there is a trend toward converting the investment of the owners into fixed assets, thereby indicating a possible reliance on creditors for furnishing the required working capital.

ratio of collateral to debt: a measure for determining how effectively stock margin is achieved. It is shown as a fraction with full collateral value as the numerator and the total securities margin as the denominator.

ratio of finished goods inventory to the cost of goods sold: this ratio is determined by dividing the cost of goods sold by the average finished goods inventory. The resulting figure is the number of times the investment in the finished goods inventory has turned over during the period under consideration. The present ratio is compared with a similar ratio for several previous periods, since it tends to portray the stability and trend of sales, or the possible overstated or expanded inventory.

ratio of fixed assets to fixed liabilities: this ratio tends to indicate the margin of safety to the present mortgage and bond holders, if any. Failure of the ratio to meet the minimum requirement frequently suggests that additional funds should be raised from the owners rather than by mortgaging fixed assets.

ratio of notes payable to accounts payable: three quantitative factors are frequently considered when determining whether the resulting ratio (notes payable/accounts payable) is desirable: (a) notes issued in payment of merchandise, (b) notes issued to banks and brokers, and (c) notes issued to others. If a relatively large amount of the outstanding notes was issued to merchandise creditors, this might indicate that the firm is unable to take advantage of the cash discounts offered in the trade, and, also, that other lending agencies might consider the firm's credit unfavorably.

ratio of notes receivable to accounts receivable: if a financial statement discloses a large ratio of notes receivable to accounts receivable, as compared with other firms in a similar line of business, the firm with the high ratio may have a lax credit policy, or it may be extending credit to customers whose ability to pay promptly is dubious.

ratio of owned capital to borrowed capital: this ratio is considered to be important in determining the advisability of extending additional long-term credit to an applicant. If this ratio is not considered favorable, it frequently suggests that the funds desired should be raised from the owners of the business (i.e., the applicants themselves) rather than through the additional pledging of any assets.

ratio of raw materials inventory to cost of manufacture: this ratio is determined by dividing the cost of goods manufactured by the average raw materials inventory. The resulting figure is the number of times the investment in the raw materials inventory has turned over during the period under consideration. When the present ratio is compared with a similar ratio for previous periods, it tends to portray the trend and steadiness of production, or to indicate an overstated or overexpanded inventory.

ratio spreading: a spread option strategy involving the simultaneous buying and sale of option contracts on the same underlying stock where the number of contracts sold changes from the number of contracts bought. see also *variable spread.*

ratio write: an option writing strategy where a holder of an underlying stock writes more calls than he or she has round lots to cover the short options. synonymous with *variable ratio writing.*

ratio writer: an options writer who sells more call contracts than he or she has underlying shares.

RB

(1) see *bond, redeemable.*
(2) see *bond, revenue.*

RC

(1) see *recurring charges.*
(2) see *risk capital.*

Rcd.: received.

RCMM: see *Registered Competitive Market Maker.*

Rcpt.: see *receipt.*

Rct.: see *receipt.*

RE: see *real estate.*

reachback: the ability of a limited partnership or other tax shelter to offer deductions at the close of the year that reach back for the entire year. Reachback on tax shelters was considered to be abusive by the Internal Revenue Service, and consequently was substantially eliminated in 1983.

reacquired securities: securities, once outstanding, that have been acquired by the issuing corporation and are legally available for reissue or resale (in some states these securities cannot be reissued without approval of regulatory authorities).

reaction: a drop in securities prices following a sustained period of increasing prices.

read(ing) the tape: a technique for judging the performance of various stocks by following their price changes as given on the ticker tape.

Reaganics (Reaganomics): describes a set of economic policies introduced by President Reagan in 1981 designed to reduce inflation, increase investment and economic growth and shift emphasis from short-term demand management policies to a long-term orientation.

real accounts: those accounts—asset, liability, reserve and capital—whose balances are not canceled out at the end of an accounting period but are carried over to the next period. These accounts appear on the post-closing trial balance and the statement of condition. sometimes called *permanent accounts.*

real costs

(1) costs measured in dollars of constant purchasing power or adjusted by some index serving the same purpose. cf. *nominal cost.*

(2) costs that involve effort or sacrifice.

real earnings: earnings adjusted to exclude the effects of price change.

real estate: tangible land and all physical property. Includes all physical substances below, upon, or attached to land; thus houses, trees, an fences are classified as real estate. All else is personal property.

real estate bond: see *bond, real estate.*

Real Estate Investment Trust (REIT): an organization, usually corporate, established for the accumulation of funds for investing in real estate holdings, or the extension of credit to others engaged in construction. These funds are usually accumulated by the sale of share of ownership in the trust. cf. *FREITS.*

real-estate limited partnerships: a public investment program requiring $5,000 or $10,000 that are SEC registered. Designed chiefly to yield annual cash returns.

real estate loans: loans secured by real estate, regardless of the purpose. see *mortgage.*

real estate owned: all real estate directly owned by a bank, usually not including real estate taken to satisfy a debt.

Real Estate Settlement Procedures Act: federal legislation of 1974, this act provided comprehensive guidelines for loan closing costs and settlement practices; effective in June 1975. see *Real Estate Settlement Procedures Act amendments.*

Real Estate Settlement Procedures Act amendments: federal legislation of 1976 which eased the requirement of the Real Estate Settlement Procedures Act by permitting lenders to disclose good faith estimates of closing costs instead of actual charges, and by tying disclosure timing to receipt of the application instead of the date of closing; also eliminated disclosure of the property's previous selling price. see *Real Estate Settlement Procedures Act.*

real estate sold on contract: real estate that has been sold for which the buyer does not have sufficient down payment to warrant the seller giving title; the contract generally provides that when the contract balance is reduced to a certain amount, the buyer may refinance the contract to get title to the property.

real estate tax: a pecuniary charge laid upon real property for public purposes.

real income: the sum total of the purchasing power of a nation or individual.

real interest rate: the rate at which a person earns future purchasing power on monetary assets. It equals the money rate minus the rate of inflation.

real investment: an expenditure that establishes a new capital asset, thus creating a new capital formation.

realization (realize)
(1) ***general:*** the act or process of converting into cash an asset, or the total assets, of an individual or business.
(2) ***investments:*** receiving a profit from selling a security following an increase in its price.

realization account: an account established to summarize and adjust the accounts of a business being liquidated. The account reflects the item-by-item realization of the assets through reduction to cash or application to the reduction of liabilities.

realized profit (or loss): a profit or loss resulting from the sale or other disposal of a security, as distinguished from a paper profit or loss.

realized yield: the return a bond earns over a stated time period, based on the purchase price and on the assumption that the incoming cash is reinvested at a stated rate.

realizing: when a profit is realized either by a liquidating sale or the repurchase of a short sale.

realizing sale: a sale to convert a paper profit into an actual profit.

reallowance: the maximum part of the selling concession that an underwriter gives up or "reallow" to another NASD member, who need not be a syndicate member. Reallowance is specified at the time of pricing.

real money: money containing one or more metals having intrinsic value, as distinguished from representative money such as currency issued by a realm, and checks, drafts, and so on, issued by legal entities. see *bimetalism.*

real-money balances: the amount of goods and services that can be bought from a given stock of money retained by individuals. Shifts in real-money balances are computed by adjusting changes in the level of prices.

real property: the property that is devised by will to a party known as the devisee; or all fixed, permanent, immovable property, such as land and tenements.

real property transaction: an extension of credit in connection with which a security interest is or will be retained or acquired in real property, as defined by the law of the state in which it is located.

real rate of return: synonymous with *dollar-weighted rate of return.*

real return: an inflation-adjusted return. see *nominal return on an asset.*

real stock: as contrasted with stock that is sold short, any long stock.

real terms: how purchasing power is affected by inflation.

realtor: a real estate broker or an associate holding active membership in a local real estate board affiliated with the National Association of Realtors.

realty: synonym for *real estate.*

reappraisal: the term applied when property is appraised a second time.

reasonable value: a value placed on property that parallels the existing market value. cf. *market value.*

reassessment: the result of a change in the assessed value of property or reappraisal of property.

recapitalization: altering the capital structure of a firm by increasing or decreasing its capital stock.

recapitalization surplus: the surplus resulting upon a recapitalization, which usually arises from reduction in the par value of stocks and the exchange of bonds for securities of lesser value.

recapture: the amount of a gain on the sale of depreciable property that represents depreciation charges previously taken for tax purposes. Recapture taxes must be paid on investment tax credits taken at the time of purchase if the assets are sold before a sufficient holding period has elapsed.

recasting a mortgage: reconstructing an existing mortgage by increasing its amount, interest rate, or time period.

Recd.: received.

recede: any drop in prices.

receipt: any written acknowledgment of value received.

receipts outstanding for installments paid: receipts for payments on account of subscriptions to capital stock.

receivables: accounts receivable owned by a business. These may be pledged as collateral for a loan secured from a bank or other financial institution. cf. *payables.*

receivables turnover: a computation done to evaluate the quality of a company's accounts receivable. Receivables turnover is calculated as the ratio of net sales to current value of receivables. The resulting figure gives an indication of the average length of time for which the firm's receivables remain outstanding.

receive (advice to): an advance notice to an account-maintaining bank that it will receive funds to be credited to the sender of the message.

receive against payment: synonymous with *receive versus payment.*

receiver: a court-appointed, neutral party named to handle property under litigation or the affairs of a bankrupt person. The receiver is required to maintain the property and its assets for the benefit of those having equity in it until a court decision as to its disposition is made. see also *remaindermen.*

receivers' and trustees' securities: evidences of indebtedness (other than equipment securities or obligations) issued by a receiver or trustee acting under orders of a court.

receiver's certificates: certificates representing the debt and equity stocks of a corporation in receivership. These certificates are usually traded on the open market.

receivership: a form of bankruptcy permitting reorganization. The courts appoint a trustee to oversee the reorganization and try to ameliorate the financial difficulties of the firm.

receive versus payment: an instruction accompanying sell orders by institutions that only cash will be accepted in exchange for delivery of the stocks at the time of settlement. synonymous with *receive against payment.*

reciprocal business: a business favor where a request to purchase or sell stocks by one person is expected from another in return for a similar order.

reclaim: recovering money or a certificate following discovery of an irregularity in the settlement of a security contract.

reclamation
(1) ***general:*** a business term to describe the act of obtaining useful materials from waste products.
(2) ***general:*** a sum of money due or owing by a bank resulting from an error in the listing of the amount of a check on a clearinghouse balance.
(3) ***securities:*** the right of either party to a securities transaction to recover losses resulting from bad delivery or other irregularities in the settlement process.

reclassification of stock: a change or modification of the capital structure of an organization.

recognizance: the acknowledgment of a former debt upon the record.

recognized quotations: statements regarding the highest bid and lowest offer prevailing for a specific stock listed on an exchange.

reconditioning property: improving a property's value by repairing it or making changes to enhance it.

reconveyance: the transfer of title of property back to a former owner.

recordation: the public acknowledgment in written form that a lien exists against a specific property that is identified in a mortgage. see *lien affidavit.*

record date: the date on which a person must be registered as a shareholder on the stock book of a company in order to receive a declared dividend, or among other things, to vote on company affairs. cf. *ex-dividend.* synonymous with *date of record.*

recording fee: cost of recording necessary documents with the appropriate state or county administrative office.

records of original entry: the general journal, the cash receipts record, and the cash disbursement record. All transactions must first be analyzed and recorded in one of these records before posting to the general ledger accounts.

recourse: the rights of a holder in due course of a negotiable instrument to force prior endorsers on the instrument to meet their legal obligations by making good the payment of the instrument if dishonored by the maker or acceptor. The holder in due course must have met the legal requirements of presentation and delivery of the instrument to the maker of a note or acceptor of a draft, and must have found that this legal entity has refused to pay for, or defaulted in payment of the instrument. see also *notice of dishonor (protest jacket).*

recourse loan

(1) a loan for which a guarantor or endorser is liable for payment in the event a borrower defaults.

(2) a loan made to a direct participation program or limited partnership whereby the lender, in addition to being secured by particular assets, has recourse against the general assets of the partnership.

recovery

(1) ***general:*** the period of the business cycle that follows a depression.

(2) ***investments:*** following a period of declining prices, the rise in stock prices. synonymous with *expansion.*

Recover Act: see *Economic Recovery Tax Act of 1981.*

Rect.: see *receipt.*

recurring charges: those financial obligations of a recurring nature that a potential borrower must pay or has obligated himself to pay, including taxes, debt repayments, legal obligations such as alimony, and other items.

redeem

(1) a process where note or bondholders are paid the face value of their instruments at the time of maturity. The issuing corporation purchases back the bond/note releasing them of any continuing obligation.

(2) a repurchase of mutual fund shares from investors by the issuing fund.

redeemable bond: *bond, redeemable.*

redeemable preferred stock: see *redeemable stock.*

redeemable stock: a preferred stock that can be called in, at the option of the issuing company. see *redemption price.*

redemption

(1) the liquidation of an indebtedness, on or before maturity, such as

the retirement of a bond issue prior to its maturity date.
(2) purchasing back; a debtor redeems his mortgaged property when he has paid his debt in full.

redemption bond: see *bond, redemption.*

redemption fund: a fund created for the purpose of retiring an obligation.

redemption notice: information mailed to concerned stockholders whose securities are being redeemed or which is printed in financial periodicals according to requirements of the indenture of the issue. The notice provides the time and terms of the redemption.

redemption period: the time in which a mortgagor may buy back property by paying the amount owed (with principal and interest) on a foreclosed mortgage. The specific time is subject to state law.

redemption price
(1) the price (usually at its par value) at which a bond may be redeemed before maturity, when retired at the option of the issuing company.
(2) the amount a company must pay to call in certain types of preferred stock.

redemption right: a defaulted mortgagor's right to redeem his property after default and court judgment, both before and after its sale.

redemptions: cash-ins made of investment company shares.

redemption value
(1) the price at which bonds can be redeemed; old bond issues were often redeemable at par value.
(2) the cash-in value of investment company shares.

redemption value bond: see *bond, redemption value.*

red herring: synonymous with *preliminary prospectus.* see open *prospectus.*

redlining: the alleged practice of certain lending institutions of making it almost impossible to obtain mortgages, improvement loans, and insurance by homeowners, apartment house landlords, and business in neighborhoods outlined in red on a map, usually areas that are deteriorating or considered by the lending institution as poor investments.

reference currency: a currency used in making payments to a bondholder.

refinance
(1) to extend existing financing or to acquire new monies. Usually done when a mortgage is withdrawn so that a larger one can be placed on the property. see *refunding mortgage.*
(2) to revise a payment timeable and, frequently, to modify interest charges on the obligation.

reflect reaction: the downward shift in direction of a price trend that does not reverse that established trend, but will correct an overbought condition. cf. *reflex rally.*

reflex rally: an upward shift in the direction of a price trend that does not reverse the established trend but will correct an oversold situation. cf. *reflex reaction.*

refund
(1) an amount paid back of credit allowed because of an overcollection or on account of the return of an object sold.
(2) to pay back or allow credit for an amount because of the return of an object sold.
(3) to provide for the payment of a loan through cash or credit secured by a new loan.
(4) to replace one bond issue with another, usually in order to extend the maturity, to reduce the interest rate, or to consolidate several issues.

refunding
(1) replacing an old bond issue with a new issue, either before or at maturity of the older one. It is often done to change the interest rate on the debt.
(2) the act of returning a portion of money to the giver from an amount already paid out.

refunding bond: see *bond, refunding.*

refunding mortgage: refinancing a mortgage with monies derived from a new loan.

regional exchange: a small-scale stock exchange located outside of New York City, designed for trading in securities of firms in their own geographical regions, but on which some of the major stocks are also traded.

regional fund: a mutual fund that specializes in investments in stock of firms geographically close by.

register
(1) formally submitting data to and receiving approval from the SEC and/or state agencies as legislated regarding the release of new stocks and a subsequent public sale.
(2) formally recording the names of stockholders on the books of a corporation.

registered as to principal: a term applied to a coupon bond, the name of the owner of which is registered on the bond and on the books of the company. Such bonds are not negotiable and cannot be sold without an assignment.

registered bond: see *bond, registered.*

registered competitive market maker (RCMM)
(1) a securities dealer registered with the National Association of Securities Dealers as a market maker in a specific over-the-counter issue—that is, an individual who maintains firm bid and offer prices in the stock by standing prepared to buy or sell round lots.
(2) a registered competitive trader on the NYSE. see also *registered competitive trader:*

registered competitive trader: synonymous with *floor trader.*

registered coupon bond: see *bond, registered coupon.*

registered equity market maker: an ASE member firm registered as a trader for its own account. These firms are expected to make stabilizing purchases and sales when needed to adjust for imbalances in specific stocks. see also *registered competitive market maker.*

registered exchange: a registered security exchange that subscribes to the regulation of the SEC or a commodity exchange which has registered and subscribed to the regulation of the Commodity Exchange Commission.

registered form: an instrument that is issued in the name of the owner and payable only to the owner.

registered investment company: an investment company which has filed a registration statement with the SEC, fulfilling the requirements of the Investment Company Act of 1940.

registered options principal (ROP): a member firm employee responsible for option transactions placed by customers of that particular firm.

registered option trader: a specialist working on the ASE floor who is responsible for maintaining a fair and orderly market in an assigned group of options.

registered over-the-counter securities: an unlisted, over-the-counter stock that has been authorized for trading in a margin account.

registered representative (trader): present name for "customer's man," a full-time employee of a stock exchange member organization who has met the requirements of the exchange with respect to background and knowledge of the securities business. Also known as an *account executive* or *customer's broker.*

registered secondary offering: an investment banker's offering of a significant block of stocks that were previously issued to the public, utilizing the abbreviated Form S-16 of the SEC which relies heavily on previously filed documents such as the S-1, the 10-K, and quarterly filings.

registered securities

(1) securities officially filed with the SEC and/or state agency for sale to the public.

(2) shares registered on the books of the firm as to holder of record.

registered traders: exchange members who utilized their floor trading privileges primarily to purchase and sell for their own account and others that they have an interest. Their transactions must fulfill exchange requirements. see also *floor trader.*

registrar: an agency, usually a trust company or a bank, charged with the responsibility of preventing the issuance of more stock that has been authorized by a company. The registrar's primary function is to authenticate the issuing of securities. see *overissue.* see also *Torrens certificate.*

registration: before a public offering may be made of new securities by a company, or of outstanding securities by controlling stockholders, the securities must be registered under the Securities Act of 1933. A registration statement is filed with the SEC by the issuer, disclosing pertinent information relating to company's operations, securities, management, and purpose of the public offering. On security offerings involving less than

$300,000, the information required is less detailed.

registration fee: a charge made by the SEC and paid by the issuer of a stock when a public offering is recorded with the SEC.

registration statement: a statement filed with the SEC showing all pertinent information pertaining to a corporation's sale of stocks to the public.

regression analysis: a technique for estimating future conditions of behaviors, as in business, based on known or observable values of some variables.

regressive taxes: rates in a tax system that decrease as the base amount taxed increases (a rate of 5 percent applied to a base of $2000, etc.). A sales tax is a regressive tax. cf. *progressive tax.*

regular delivery: in government securities market, delivery of a security made on the business day following purchase or sale. cf. *cash delivery.*

regular dividend: the established rate of dividend set by a firm on its stock which is usually paid every three or six months.

regularity of dividends: the pattern of constant payment of dividends by a corporation. Confidence by the public is often related to a firm's regularity of dividends.

regular lending area: the geographical boundaries within a security property must be located in order for a savings association to invest in a mortgage loan secured by the property, without the loan and the association being subject to special limitations set by regulatory and supervisory agencies. synonymous with *normal lending territory.*

regular lot: the unit of trading on a specific stock or commodity exchange; the full or board lot.

regular mortgage: the legal document used in most states to pledge real estate as security for the repayment of a debt.

regular serial bond: see *bond, regular serial.*

regular-way delivery: unless otherwise specified, securities (other than government) sold on the New York Stock Exchange are to be delivered to the buying broker by the selling broker and payment made to the selling broker by the buying broker on the fourth business day after the transaction. Regular-way delivery for government bonds is the following business day. see *delivery, transfer.*

regular-way sale: any securities transaction that is not a short sale.

regular-way settlement: the normal settlement of a stock transaction, including, certificate delivery, payment of fund due no later than the fifth business day following that transaction date. Other securities have a next business day settlement, such as option transactions.

regulated commodities: those commodities over which the Commodity Exchange Authority has supervision are known as "regulated." This does not mean that the prices are controlled. The CEA simply concerns itself with the orderly operation of the futures market and, at times, investigates abnormal price movements. Under the Commodity Exchange Act, approved June 15, 1936, definite regulations are established providing for the safeguarding of customers' money deposited as margin. Commodities currently supervised by the CEA are wheat, cotton, corn, rice, oats, barley, rye, flaxseed, grain sorghums, bran, shorts, middlings, butter, eggs, potatoes, onions, wool tops, wool futures, lard, tallow, soybean oil, cottonseed meal, cottonseed, peanuts, soybeans, and soybean meal.

regulated investment companies: investment companies that can avoid income tax on its ordinary income and capital gains by distributing profits as dividends and by conforming to other statutory rules.

regulated T-Call: see *margin call.*

Regulation A: the regulation governing registration of a stock offering of more than $50,000 but less than $300,000. This Regulation requires using a prospectus, but a less complicated one than for offering in excess of $300,000.

Regulation G: the regulation governing credit size that can be advanced for purchasing stocks in circumstances that are otherwise unregulated.

Regulation Q: a ruling of the Federal Reserve Board governing the rate of interest imposed on banks. Deposits in excess of $100,000 extended beyond 30 days are exempt from Regulation Q.

Regulation T: the Federal Reserve Board criterion governing the amount of credit that may be advanced by brokers and dealers to customers for the purchase of securities. see *margin.*

Regulation U: the Federal Reserve Board criterion governing the amount of credit that may be advanced by a bank to its customers for the purchase of listed stocks when the requested loan is to be secured by listed stocks.

Regulation W: a ruling of the Federal Reserve Board governing down payments of commercial credit and loan maturities for consumer items, such as cars, revolving charge accounts, and so on.

rehypothecation: pledging by brokers of stocks in clients' margin accounts to banks as collateral for broker loans under a general loan and collateral agreement. Broker loans cover the positions of brokers who have made margin loans to clients for margin purchases and selling short. Margin loans are collateralized by the hypothecation of clients' securities to the broker. Their *rehypothecation* is authorized when the client originally signs a general account agreement.

reinvestment: using proceeds of dividends, interest, or sale of stocks to buy other securities. One popular feature of some securities of investment companies is that the proceeds can be reinvested at favorable terms.

reinvestment privilege: the automatic investment of dividends from holdings in a mutual fund in additional shares of the fund, at times without a sales charge.

reinvestment rate: the rate of return resulting from reinvestment of the interest from a fixed-income security or a bond. Other than zero-copuon bonds, the reinvestment rate on coupon bonds has little predictability because it rises and falls with market interest rates.

REIT: see *Real Estate Investment Trust.*

rejection

(1) ***general:*** the refusal to grant credit to an applicant because of inadequate financial strength, or another reason.

(2) ***insurance:*** the refusal to underwrite a risk, that is, to release a policy.

(3) ***securities:*** the refusal of a broker or client to accept the stock presented to complete a trade; usually occurs because the stock lacks the needed endorsements, or because of other exceptions to the rules for good delivery.

relationship trading: applying hedging techniques to pounce on pricing quirks which occur in the markets and then disappear. Investors buy or sell stocks, and at the same time hedge by taking the opposite position with futures or option contracts. synonymous with *basis trading.*

relative priority: a principle of reorganization under which each group of creditors and stockholders, based on seniority, survives the reorganization, but the losses of each group are inversely proportional to its seniority.

relative strength: a measure of the market performance of a stock in comparison to its own industry and/or a market index for a stated time period.

relative value: the comparative attractiveness of an investment over another investment.

release clause: a clause in a mortgage permitting payment of a part of the debt in order that a proportionate part of the property can be freed.

release date and time: the date and time the sender authorizes the service to forward the instructions to the receiver.

release letter: a letter sent by a manager to others in a syndicate showing final details of an offering, whether the offering will or will not be advertised, the handling of the good faith deposit, the participation, and how the delivery of the certificates are to be handled at distribution time. synonymous with *release-terms letter, syndicate account letter.*

release of liability: an agreement in which a lender terminates the personal obligation of a mortgagor for the payment of a debt.

release of lien: an instrument discharging secured property from a lien.

release of mortgage: dropping a claim against property established by a mortgage.

release of premiums on funded debt: a credit to income each fiscal period of a proportion of the premium realized at the sale of funded securities, based on the ratio of such fiscal period to the remaining life of the securities.

release-term letter: synonymous with *release letter.*

reloader: slang, an individual who is clever in selling further securities to a person who has just purchased a small amount of the same stock.

remainder: upon completion of a life estate, the property reverts to the owner or goes to an heir. If the owner does not take the property back, a remainder estate is created by the same instrument. This estate begins upon the termination of the temporary estate (i.e., the life estate) that preceded it.

remainder beneficiary: the beneficiary of a trust who is entitled to the principal outright after the prior life beneficiary or his or her interest has been terminated.

remainder estate: an estate in property created simultaneously with other estates by a single grant and consisting of the rights and interest contingent upon and remaining after the termination of the other estates.

remainder interest: a future interest which will become an interest in possession after the termination of a prior interest created at the same time and by the same instrument as the future interest. For example, H leaves his estate in trust with income to be paid to W, and on her death the trust is to terminate and the property is to be delivered to C. C has a remainder interest.

remaindermen: those persons who receive the proceeds from the final distribution of a trust or estate.

remargining: placing added margin against a loan. Remargining is one option when brokers require additional cash or collateral when their securities have lost some of their value.

remit: to pay for bought goods or services by cash, check, or electronic payment.

removed in perpetuity: see *perpetuity.*

renegotiable-rate mortgage (RRM): authorized by the Federal Home Loan Bank Board, requires home buyers to renegotiate the terms of the loan every three to five years—a distinct advantage if interest rates drop but a poor hedge against inflation if they go up. cf. *variable-rate mortgage.* sometimes called the *rollover mortgage.*

renewable term insurance: insurance that offers a guaranteed option to renew without a health examination up to retirement age and sometimes beyond.

renewal certificate: an insurance policy is sometimes renewed by issuing a certificate rather than writing out a new policy. The certificate refers to the policy but does not enumerate all its items.

renounce
(1) an act by which an individual or trust institution named under a will as executor or trustee declines to accept such appointment.
(2) the act of a surviving husband or wife under the decedent's state law declining to take the provision made for him or her under share of the estate had the other died without a will.
(3) any action by which the beneficiary of any interest in real or personal property therewith refuses to accept such interest.

rent: income received from leasing real estate.

rentes: the annual interest payable on the bonded debt of France, Austria, Italy, and a few other countries. The term is also applied to the bonds themselves.

rentier: a person living on income received from fixed investments.

REO: see *real estate owned.*

REOP: the reopening after a halt in trading.

reopen an issue: when the Treasury sells more of an issue that is already outstanding. Contains the same terms and conditions, at prevailing price levels.

reorganization: the altering of a firm's capital structure, often resulting from a merger, that affects the rights and responsibilities of the owners. The objectives of a reorganization are to eliminate the cause of failure, settle with creditors, and allow the firm to remain in business. see also *bankruptcy.* cf. *quasi-reorganization.*

reorganization bond: see *bond, reorganization.*

reorganization department: that portion of a cashiering function handling the exchange of one security for another.

repatriation: the liquidation of overseas investments and the return of the proceeds to the country of the investor.

repeat prices omitted: a designation of the consolidated tapes, that the tape is late, and in order to save time, only the first transaction in a series of trades for the same security will be printed.

replacement cost accounting: balance sheets tend to value assets at cost plus installation. To overcome this problem, assets can be valued at replacement cost. For fiscal years ending on or after December 25, 1979 the Financial Accounting Standards Board requires approximately 1350 of the largest U.S. corporations to report supplementary information based on constant (inflation-adjusted) dollars and current (replacement) costs.

REPO: see *repurchase agreement.*

report (or certificate): the report (or certificate) of an independent accountant (or auditor) is a document in which he or she indicates the nature and scope of the examination (or audit) that he or she has made and expresses the opinion that was formed in respect to the financial statements.

reportable position: synonymous with *reporting limit.*

reporting limit: the number of futures contracts, as determined by the exchange and/or the Commodity Futures Trading Commission, above which one must report daily to the exchange and/or the CFTC with regard to size of one's position by commodity, by delivery month and by purpose of the trading (i.e., bona fide hedging or speculating). synonymous with *reportable position.*

representative money
(1) ***general:*** paper money secured by monetary metal (i.e., gold or silver certificates) deposited in the treasury of a country.
(2) ***investments:*** funds that are backed in full by a commodity.

repurchase agreement (REPO): an arrangement allowing the owner of debt securities (usually Treasury bills) to borrow money by selling the securities to a buyer while promising to repurchase them at a fixed price on a specified date. see also *open REPO, overnight REPO,* retail *REPO.*

repurchases: in closed-end companies, voluntary open market purchases by investment companies of their own securities, usually for retirement. In open-end funds, the term represents stock taken back at approximate liquidating value.

request for a report: a request on the status of a security order made through the order room of a brokerage house to the broker concerned on the stock exchange floor.

request for proposal: see *RFQ.*

required rate of return: the rate of return to be achieved in order to avoid a drop in the value of an investment or portfolio as a result of systematic risk.

required return: the lowest return of profit needed to justify an investment.

Res.: see *reserve.*

res: in the phrase trust res, the same as trust property. The corpus of the trust.

research and development (R&D)
(1) ***general:*** applying the findings of science and technology to create a firm's products or services.
(2) ***investments:*** the dollar amount spent on company-sponsored research and development for the year as reported to the SEC. The total excludes any expenditures for research and development performed under contract for others, such as U.S. government agencies.

research and development limited partnership: a concept where investors place money for financing new product research and development. In return the investors receive a percentage of the product's profits, if any, along with investment credits and depreciation of equipment.

research unit: a department within a brokerage house, investment firm, bank trust unit, insurance company, or other institutional investing organization that analyzes markets and securities.

reserve: in an auction, a minimum price, agreed upon in confidence between the seller and the auctioneer, below which the item will not be sold. The auction firm buys in, or bids, through a representative on behalf of the seller, for items that fall to meet the minimum price.

reserve for bad debts: synonymous with *allowance for bad debts.*

reserve for retirement of sinking fund bonds: a reserve that indicates the amount of cash and other resources that should have been accumulated at a certain date in order eventually to redeem bonds outstanding.

reserve for revenue bond contingency: a reserve in an enterprise fund which represents the segregation of a portion of retained earnings equal to current assets that are restricted for meeting various contingencies as may be specified and defined in the revenue bond indenture.

reserve for revenue-bond-debt-service: a reserve in an enterprise fund which represents the segregation of a portion of retained earnings equal to current assets that are restricted to current servicing of revenue bonds in accordance with the terms of a bond indenture.

reserve fund: any asset such as cash or highly liquid securities created to meet some expense.

reserve split: reduction in the number of shares of a class of capital stock, with no reduction in the total dollar amount of the class, but with an increase in the par or stated value of the shares. This is achieved by substituting one new share for so many outstanding shares. see also *split.*

residential mortgage: a loan extended for which real estate is usually a single owner-occupied home or a small number of dwelling units.

residential real property: improved real property used or intended to be used for residential purposes, including single-family homes, dwellings for from two to four families, and individual units of condominiums and cooperatives.

residual cost (or value): the difference between the cost of a particular asset and any amortized or expensed account. see also *book value.*

residual securities: stocks that derive most of their value from conversion rights. see *conversion price, conversion ratio.*

residual value

(1) the realizable value of a fixed asset following costs associated with a sale.

(2) the amount remaining following all allowable depreciation charges that were subtracted from the original cost of a depreciable asset.

residuary clause: the provision in the will or trust agreement that disposes of all of the decedent's property remaining after the payment of all taxes, debts, expenses, and charges and the satisfaction of all other gifts in the will or trust agreement.

residuary devise: a gift by will of the real property remaining after all specific devices have been made.

residuary devisee: a recipient by will of any real property after all other claimants to the estate have received payment.

residuary estate: what remains in an estate after all claims to the estate have been properly disposed of.

residuary legatee: a person to whom is given the remainder of a testator's personal property after all other legacies have been satisfied.

residuary trust: a trust composed of the property of the testator that remains in the state after the payment of all taxes, debts, expenses, charges, and the satisfaction of all other gifts under the will.

residue: (rest, residue, and remainder); that portion of a decedent estate remaining after the payment of all debts, expenses, and charges and the satisfaction of all legacies and devises.

resistance area: synonymous with *resistance level.*

resistance level: the point where the rise in the price of a particular security seems to be repeatedly arrested due to more substantial selling than buying. synonymous with *resistance area, resistance zone.* cf. *support level.*

resistance points: points or areas of price fluctuation at which a security or security average comes to a resistance or stop before moving in a direction.

resistance zone: synonymous with *resistance level.*

resting order: an order that can remain open or good until canceled when (a) an order to purchase securities is limited to a price lower than the market, or (b) an order to sell is limited to a price above the market.

restoration premium: the premium charged to restore a policy or bond to its original value after payment of a loss.

restricted account: any margin account where the debit balance exceeds the maximum loan value of stocks retained in that account.

restricted assets: money or other resources, the use of which is restricted by legal or contractual requirements. The most common examples of restricted assets in governmental accounting are those arising out of revenue bond indentures in enterprise funds.

restricted funds: see *restricted assets.*

restricted list: a periodically updated list received by sales-personnel from broker-dealers providing the names of issuers and specific security issues that cannot be traded or may be sold by customers only should the order to sell be unsolicited.

restricted retained earnings: synonymous with *restricted surplus.*

restricted securities: see *restricted shares.*

restricted shares: common stock shares released under an agreement whereby they do not rank for dividends until some event has taken place—usually the attainment of certain levels of earnings. Any unregistered stock acquired in private transactions as employment bonuses and the like.

restricted stock option: a privilege granted to an employee of a corporation to purchase during a specified period, at the market price at the date of the option, a specified number of shares of its capital stock. synonymous with *qualified stock option.*

restricted surplus: that portion of retained earnings which is not regarded as available for dividends. This may be because of legal requirements or loan agreements. synonymous with *restricted retained earnings.*

resyndication limited partnership: a partnership where present properties are sold to new limited partners who can gain tax advantages that have already been exhausted by the old partnership.

retail broker: see *registered representative.*

retail firm: a brokerage house that services retail investors instead of institutions. see also *boutique, wire house.*

retail investor

(1) an investor who purchases stocks and commodities futures on his or her own behalf, not for an organization. retention.

(2) in securties underwriting, the number of units earmarked to a participating investment banker minus the units retained by the syndicate manager for easing institutional sales and for allocation to firms in the selling group that are not also members of the syndicate.

retail repo: arrangements in which a lender lends the bank cash for a flexible period—usually a week to 89 days, and the bank promises to return the principal to the lender, plus interest. They are more liquid than bank savings certificates because there are usually no penalties for early withdrawal. The interest rate is competitive with money market mutual funds and much higher than the rate on passbook savings. The minimum denomination is typically $1000. However, a retail repo is an investment, not a deposit, and the money is not insured. see also *repurchase agreement.*

retained earnings: the net income key by firm's management and reinvested on common stockholders' behalf rather than paid as dividends.

retained earnings, appropriated: the net accumulated balance reflecting reservations of retained earnings bring held for a special purpose, and not available for dividends.

retained earnings, restricted: see *restricted surplus.*

retained earnings, unappropriated: formerly earned surplus; accumulated net income less distribution to stock holders and transfers to other capital accounts. It is the connecting link between the income account and the balance sheet and represents the excess of the book value of the depreciated assets (and other debits) over the sum of long-term debt, current and accured liabilities, deferred credits, operating reserves, contributions in aid of construction, accumulated in aid of construction, accumulated deferred income taxes (when used by the company), and proprietary capital other than retained earnings.

retention: the percentage of a syndicate member's underwriting participation retained for his or her own retail sales.

retention rate: a percentage of aftertax profits credited to retained earnings. cf. *dividend payout ratio.*

retention requirement: see *restricted account.*

retire
(1) redeeming a debt stock at maturity or prior to maturity.
(2) where an issuer withdraws a stock from the market, cancels it, and will not permit it to be resold or distributed.

retired securities: Treasury shares or outstanding shares that are called-in and canceled. Such shares are removed from a list of authorized shares and may no longer be sold or distributed.

retirement accounts: see *Individual Retirement Accounts, Keogh Plan.*

retirement annuity: see *annuity, retirement.*

retreat: any drop in the price level of securities or commodities.

retroactive restoration: a provision in a policy or bond whereby, after payment of a loss, the original amount of coverage is automatically restored to take care of prior undiscovered losses as well as future losses.

return: synonymous with *yield (2).*

return of capital: cash payments to stockholders considered a return of invested capital instead of distribution of dividends. A nontaxable event but the investor is required to reduce the original cost of investment by the amount returned.

return on assets (ROA): a profitability ratio defined as net income divided by total assets.

return on equity (ROE): a profitability ratio defined as net income divided by equity.

return on invested capital: the amount, expressed as a percentage, earned on a firm's total capital—its common and preferred stock equity plus its long-term funded debt. synonymous with *return on investment.*

return on investment (ROI): synonymous with *return on invested capital.*

return on investment ratio: a profitability ratio (net profit divided by total assets) representing the total investment in a firm.

return on net worth: the ratio of an organization's net profit following taxes to its net worth, providing a measure of the rate of return on a shareholder's investment.

return on total assets: the ratio of an organization's net profit following taxes to its total assets, providing a measure of the rate of return on, or productivity of, total assets.

return premium: the amount due the insured if a policy is reduced in amount, canceled, or—if subject to audit—the audit yields a finding of less exposure(s) than the original estimate(s).

Revenue Act of 1962: federal legislation; provided investment tax credit of 7 percent on new and used property other than buildings. see also *Revenue Act of 1964, Revenue Act of 1971, Revenue Act of 1978, Revenue Adjustment Act of 1975.*

Revenue Act of 1964: federal legislation; provided for two-stage cut in personal income tax liabilities and corporate-profits tax liabilities in 1964 and 1965. see also *Revenue Act of 1962, Revenue Act of 1971, Revenue Act of 1978, Revenue Adjustment Act of 1975.*

Revenue Act of 1971: federal legislation; accelerated by one year scheduled increases in personal exemptions and standard deduction. Repealed automobile excise tax retroactive to August 15, 1971; on trucks and buses to September 22, 1971. Reinstated 7 percent investment tax credit and incorporated depreciation range guidelines.

Revenue Act of 1976: much of this act was revised by the Revenue Act of 1978. see *Revenue Act of 1978.*

Revenue Act of 1978: federal legislation affecting the following areas.

(a) *Individual and corporate tax cuts:* lowers tax rates and widens brackets so that raises will not bring people so quickly into higher tax levels; the personal exemption deduction goes to $1000 beginning with 1979; the top corporate rate will be 46 percent in 1979 and after, with new graduated rates for lower income corporations.

(b) *Capital gains:* sellers of capital assets held more than a year can exclude 60 percent of the gain for sales on or after November 1, 1978. Capital gains have no adverse impact on the maximum tax on earned income on or after that date; nor are they subject to the add-on 15 percent preference tax in 1979 and later.

(c) *New alternative tax on capital gains:* the excluded portion of capital gains and adjusted itemized deductions are no longer subject to the regular add-on preference tax to be replaced by a new alternative minimum tax. If a person has heavy capital gains or itemized deductions, he or she must now figure two taxes—regular taxes and an alternative tax, which is at graduated rates (25 percent maximum) above an exclusion base of $20,000; the individual pays whichever is higher.

(d) *Homeowners:* personal residence sales will no longer produce gains subject to the old add-on minimum tax or to the new alternative minimum tax described above. There is also the right to exclude all gain up to $100,000 if the individual is 55 years of age or over. Both changes apply to home sales after July 26, 1978.

(e) *Tax shelter rules:* these are broader, causing more entities to be subject to the "at risk" rules that keep people from deducting more than their equity investment. Entertainment facilities such as hunting lodges and yachts are no longer to be accepted as business deductions. Partnerships face more stringent reporting requirements, with stiff new penalties if partnership returns are not sent in on time.

(f) *Carryover basis rules postponed:* a stepped-up basis for inherited property is back. The carryover basis rules enacted in 1976 did not apply until 1980. Refund possibilities abound for those who have reported gains using carryover basis for assets inherited from someone who died in 1977 or 1978.

(g) *Other provisions:* there are changes on deductions and credits—for example, there is a new targeted jobs credit, and the investment credit is set permanently at 10 percent. The new law also contains important changes for employee benefits. See *Tax Reform Act of 1976.* see also *Energy Tax Act of 1978.*

Revenue Adjustment Act of 1975: federal legislation; provided extensive redrafting of tax laws. Restricted use of tax shelter investments and made changes in taxing of gifts and estates. Increased taxes on very wealthy. Continued tax cuts passed in 1975.

Revenue and Expenditure Control Act of 1968: federal legislation; levied 10 percent surtax on personal income corporate taxes effective April 1, 1968, and on corporate taxes effective January 1, 1968. Postponed reduction in excise tax rates on automobiles and telephone service.

revenue-anticipation notes (RANs): short-term municipal borrowings that fund current operations and are to be funded by revenues other than taxes, especially federal aid.

revenue application notes: short-term notes sold in anticipation of receipt of revenues and payable from the proceeds of those revenues.

revenue bond: see *bond; revenue.*

revenue bonds payable: a liability account which represent the face value of revenue bonds issued and outstanding.

revenue expenditure: see *expenditure.*

reversal

(1) a shift in direction in the stock or commodities futures markets, as charted by analysts. For example, when the Dow Jones Industrial Average has been rising from 1000 to 1100, chartists talk of a *reversal* if the average begins a sustained drop back toward 1000.

(2) a shift in the near-term trend of market price that continues for a number of days. If the change is from advancing to declining it is called a *down-reversal;* from declining to advancing it is called an *up-reversal.*

reversal pattern: any shift in the direction of a stock's market price.

reverse-annuity mortgage: designed for retirees and other fixed-income homeowners who owe little or nothing on their houses. Typically, it permits them to use some or all of the equity already in the home as supplemental income, while retaining ownership. In effect, they are borrowing against the value of the house on a monthly basis. The longer they borrow, of course, the less equity they retain in the house. The loan becomes due either on a specific date or when a specified event occurs such as the sale of the property or death of the borrower. see also *graduated-payment mortgage, pledge-account mortgage, rollover mortgage, variable-rate mortgage.* synonymous with *equity conversion.*

reverse a swap: restoring a bond portfolio to its earlier position following a swap of one bond for another to gain the advantage of a yield spread or a tax loss.

reverse conversion: a method allowing brokerage houses to earn interest on their clients' stock holdings. For example, a brokerage house sells short the stocks it holds in its clients' margin accounts, then invests this money in short-term money market instruments. To guard against a sudden climb in the markets, the house hedges its short position by purchasing call options and selling put options. To unwind the reverse conversion, the house purchases back the stocks, sells the call, and buys the put.

reverse hedge: when a client, owning a common stock, sells short a convertible stock that can be converted into common stock. The client speculates that the premium over the conversion parity will decline and the total position can be closed out with a profit.

reverse repos: see *repurchase agreement.*

reverse repurchase agreement: see *repurchase agreement.*

reverse repurchases: where a lender purchases securities with a commitment to resell them at the same price plus a specified interest charge.

reverse split: a technique where a firm reduces the number of shares outstanding. The total number of shares will retain the same market value immediately following the reverse split as before it, but each share will now be worth more. Such splits are started by firms wishing to raise the price of their outstanding shares because they believe the price is too low to attract investors. synonymous with *split down.* see *split.*

reverse stock split: synonymous with *stock split-down.*

reverse yield gap: a situation where fixed-interest securities yield more than industrial shares.

reversible term insurance: insurance that is generally the cheapest policy for healthy people who gamble on continuing to stay healthy. However, it is not automatically renewable. In later years a person who becomes sick would not be able to renew at the cheap rate and might have to pay a higher rate, sometimes much higher.

RFC: Reconstruction Finance Corporation (defunct).

Rfg.: see *refunding.*

RFQ: request for quotation. synonymous with *request for proposal.*

RH: see *red herring.*

rialto: slang, a stock exchange or other financial center.

rich: an expression applied to security prices when the current market quotation appears to be high (or the income return low) in comparison with either the past price record of the individual security or the current prices of comparable securities.

rigged market: the situation that exists when purchases and sales are manipulated to distort a normal supply and demand price.

right
(1) the privilege attaching to a share of stock to subscribe to other securities in a fixed ratio.
(2) that which is reserved by a settlor, as the right of amendment or revocation; opposed to the power granted to the trustee.

right of accumulation: a privilege offered by open-end investment companies to current fundholders. The right becomes active should the value of current holdings in any, or all, of the funds managed by the fund manager exceed set breakpoints for fund purchases. The *rights of accumulation* for a particular fund is described in the prospectus of that fund.

right of rescission: a contract cancellation privilege because the purchase was carried out in contravention of existing laws.

rights: when a company wants to raise more funds by issuing additional securities, it may give its stockholders the opportunity, ahead of others, to buy the new securities in proportion to the number of shares each owns. The piece of paper evidencing this privilege is called a right. Because the additional stock is usually offered to stockholders below the current market price, rights ordinarily have a market value of their own and are actively traded. In most cases they must be exercised within a relatively short period. Failure to exercise or sell rights may result in actual loss to the holder. see also *cum right.*

rights offering: see *rights.*

rights on: when a security is selling at a price and on a basis including the privilege to purchase a pro rata amount of additional securities offered.

ring: synonymous with *pit.*

ringing out (or up): a practice of commodity brokers and commission merchants of settling existing futures contracts among themselves before the instruments mature and become deliverable. For example, A has agreed to purchase in the future from C and at the same time to sell the same item to C. In the meantime, B has agreed to sell the item to C. The ring is complete and the transaction can be approved. The ringing-out process permits incomplete ring participants to clear up their responsibilities and commitments.

rising bottoms: a bullish formation that reveals the ability of a futures contract to turn up above each preceding important low point. To be complete, however, there should also be an accompanying series of rising tops. Rising bottoms precede rising tops and are thus the first technical requirement that must be met if a situation is to be termed bullish.

rising wedge: see *wedge.*

risk: the possibility of loss; specifically chance of nonpayment of a debt.

risk-adjusted discount rate: in capital budget analysis and portfolio theory, the rate needed to identify the present value of an uncertain or risky stream of income. It is the risk-free rate, usually the return on short-term U.S. Treasury securities, plus a risk premium that is based on an analysis of the risk characteristics of the specific investment.

risk arbitrage: the risky practice of purchasing long stock of a corporation to be acquired and selling that of an acquiring firm in the expectation of a concluded merger, in which event the shares of the former will climb and those of the latter will decline.

risk aversion: the attitude of an investor who is not willing to accept increasing amounts of uncertainty about future investment returns without commensurate increases in the level of return anticipated. Another manifestation of this attitude is the investor who prefers less risk for the same rate of return expectation.

risk capital

(1) ***general:*** capitalization not secured by a lien or mortgage.

(2) ***general:*** long-term loans or capital invested in high-risk business activities.

(3) ***investments:*** common stock from a new enterprise.

risk free asset: a noncallable, default free bond such as a short-term government security. While such an asset is not risk free in an inflation sense, it is (under the rationale that the government can always print money) risk free in a dollar sense.

risk free return: a theoretical return that is earned with perfect certainty; it is without risk. We approximate the risk free return with 91-day Treasury bill yields.

riskless transaction

(1) a trade guaranteeing a profit to the trader that initates it.

(2) an approach in assessing whether dealer markups and markdowns in over-the-counter transactions with clients are reasonable or excessive. In order to avoid NASD inquiry, broker-dealers usually disclose the markups and markdowns to clients in transactions where they serve as dealers.

risk of capital: a risk that all or a part of one's original investment may be lost.

risk of inflation: a risk that the return of principal on an investment has lower purchasing power than when the investment was first made or that the yield on an investment will not keep pace with inflation.

risk of selection: the risk that the investor, given an equal choice of investment alternatives, will not choose wisely.

risk of timing: the risk that the investor will seek investments at the wrong time based on market conditions.

risk premium: the additional required rate of return due to extra risk incurred.

risk rating: a systematic process of analyzing mortgage risk that results in estimation, in precise relative terms, of the soundness of individual transactions.

risk-reward spectrum: a construct used to illustrate that (in a rational marketplace) higher and higher anticipated rewards are always accompanied by incremental increases in risk (measured as the deviations between expected and actual results). The left end of the spectrum represents the lowest risk investment-typically short-term government obligations. Moving to the right on the spectrum—through a continuum of common stock investments—each incremental increase in expected return in accompanied by an incremental increase in risk.

RL: see *round lot.*

ROA: see *return on assets.*

Robinson-Patman Act of 1936: federal legislation amending the Clayton Antitrust Act of 1914. Price discrimination practices are more clearly identified. Quantity discounts in excess of the cost savings realized by selling in such quantities are declared illegal, as are false brokerage deals. Promotional allowances must be made to all buyers on a proportionately equal basis, and price discrimination is acceptable if made to meet a proper low price of a competitor so long as the price does not restrict competition.

ROC: return on capital.

ROE: see *return on equity.*

ROI: see *return on invested capital, return on investment.*

roll down: a shift from one option position to another one having a lower exercise price and assumes that the position with the higher exercise price is closed out.

roll forward: synonymous with *rolling over.*

rolling over: a substitution of a far option for a near option on the same underlying stock at the same striking price. synonymous with *roll forward.*

rolling stock: with transportation firms, designating movable equipment.

rollover
(1) applying proceeds from a maturing bond into a new bond issue of identical or near identical type.
(2) refunding of a debt obligation by issuing a new bond of identical or near identical type. see also *tax-free rollover.*

rollover CD: a certificate of deposit package with a maturity of three years, divided into 12 six-month periods for which CDs are issued. synonymous with *roly-poly* CD.

rollover mortgage: a short-term mortgage where the unpaid balance is refinanced, or "rolled over," every few years; at that time, the interest rate is adjusted up or down, depending on prevailing market conditions. Before the Depression of 1929, such loans were common, but since then the fixed-rate mortgage has generally been standard. During the early 1980s, the rollover mortgage again became popular. see also *flexible-payment mortgage, graduated-payment mortgage, pledged-account mortgage, reverse-annuity mortgage, variable-rate mortgage.* see *renegotiable-rate mortgage.*

roll up: see *master limited partnership.*

roll-up fund: an investment fund outside of Great Britain, investing in world currencies on which no dividend is paid and the return is taxed as a capital gain instead of income.

roly-poly CD: synonymous with *roll over CD.*

rook: slang, to misrepresent, overcharge, or cheat another.

Roosa Bonds: see *nonmarketable liabilities of U.S. government.*

ROP: see *registered options principal.*

ROR: see *rate of return.*

ROS: return on sales.

round down: leaving a credit in a client's account by purchasing the closest share number under his or her deposit. IRAs and Keoghs are rounded down since the IRS does not allow debits in such accounts. cf. *round up (2).*

round lot: this is a unit of trading. On the New York Stock Exchange, the unit is generally 100 shares. In some inactive stocks, the trading unit could be 10 shares. An amount of stock less than the established unit of trading is called an add lot. synonymous with *board lot, full lot, normal trading unit.*

round lot cash buy/sell ratio: the cash account purchasing of round lots divided by cash account selling of round lots.

round lot margin buy/sell ratio: a margin account purchasing divided by margin account selling.

round lot short/cover ratio: the total round lot shares shorted divided by total shares covered.

round-lotter: an individual who purchases or sells a security in any quantity of 100 shares that are active or 10 shares that are inactive.

round trip trade: any complete transaction, made up of a buy followed by a sale of the same stock, or vice versa. synonymous with *round turn.*

round turn: synonymous with *round trip trade.*

round up
(1) a practice to achieve a normally used price variation (i.e., a stock goes exdividend).
(2) a client's instruction if a fixed dollar amount is invested such as "buying a number of shares that leaves a debit in the account." The client pays the added amount. cf. *round down.*

royalty: compensation for the use of a person's property based on an agreed percentage of the income arising from its use (e.g., to an author on sales of his book, to a manufacturer for use of his machinery in the factory of another person, to a composer or performer, etc.) It is a payment reserved by the grantor of a patent, lease, or similar right, while a residual payment is often made on properties that have not been patented or are not patentable. see also *syndicate.*

royalty trust: the oil or gas firm spin-off of an oil-producing property to stockholders. The corporation is not taxed if most of its income is distributed to shareholders, and shareholders receive a tax benefit from depletion allowance.

RP: see *repurchase agreement.*

RPQ: request for price quotation.

RR: see *registered representative (trader).*

RRM: see *renegotiable-rate mortgage.*

RRP: reverse repurchase agreement. see *repurchase agreement.*

RS: see *redeemable stock.*

R-squared: the percentage of the portfolio's total return explained by the market risk level (i.e., the portfolio's beta).

RT: see *royalty trust.*

Rule 405: the NYSE codification of an ethical principle. see *know your customer, rule.*

Rule of '78: the technique for calculating interest refunds in the event of early payoff of a debt.

Rule of 72: a means for determining how long it will take for money to double at various interest rates. By dividing the rate of return into 72, the result is the number of years required to double money at that rate of interest, assuming annual compounding.

Rule 144: the SEC rule covering the sale of control stocks and restricted stocks.

rules of fair practice: a National Association of Securities Dealers' rule designed to foster just and equitable principles of trade and business; highest standards of commercial honor and integrity among members; the prevention of fraud and manipulation practices; safeguards against unreasonable profits, commissions, and other charges; and interaction with governmental agencies, to protect investors and the public interest in accordance with the Maloney Act.

rules of the class: the terms and conditions, established by the association's board of directors and included in the savings account contract, applicable to each savings account classification, such as time and amount of deposit, rate of interest, penalty provisions, and the account designation.

rumor: in securities, hearsay of unfounded gossip intended to create a rise or drop in security prices. Stock Exchange members are restricted from circulating any information detrimental to the well-being of the exchange.

run

(1) ***general:*** an action of a large number of people (e.g., a run on a bank occurs when a great many customers make massive withdrawals of funds).

(2) ***securities:*** a list of available securities, along with current bid and asked prices, which a market maker is presently trading. For bonds the run may include the par value as well as current quotes.
(3) ***securities:*** when a stock's price rises rapidly, analysts state that it had a quick run up.

rundown
(1) ***general:*** a status report or summary.
(2) ***bonds:*** a summary of the amounts available and the prices on units in a serial bond that has not been fully sold to the public.

running ahead: the illegal practice of purchasing or selling a stock for a broker's personal account before houses prohibit their brokers from making such trades for a stated period of time, such as two full days from the time of the recommendation.

running book: one function of the individual who specializes in certain stocks on the trading floor of a stock exchange. A list of orders that are limited to a price other than that currently prevailing is kept in the book.

running in the shorts: purchasing different securities where there is a substantial short position for the purpose of advancing the price so that those short will purchase their securities back, or cover their short selling contracts, and hence lead to an additional climb in price. see *short covering, short sale.*

running through the pot: when a manager of a syndicate recalls a portion of the stocks or bonds taken down by the syndicate and selling group members for retail sales and then includes them in the pot set aside for institutional sales.

running yield: see *current yield.*

runoff: the closing prices printed by the stock exchange ticker following the closing of the daily market. During a heavy trading session, the runoff may be hours late.

S

S

(1) no option offered (in option listings of newspapers).

(2) signed (before signature on typed copy of a document, original of which was signed). see *signed instrument.*

(3) split or stock dividend (in stock listings of newspapers).

SA

(1) Sociedad Anónima (Spanish corporation).

(2) Société Anonyme (French corporation).

SAA: see *special arbitrage account.*

SAB: special assessment bond. see *bond, special assessment.*

saddled: a situation describing an individual holding an undesirable security purchased at a price above the prevailing market price.

safe harbor

(1) ***general:*** an accounting step for avoiding legal or tax consequences. Used in particular with safe harbor leasing, as allowed by the Economic Recovery Tax Act of 1981.

(2) ***general:*** a legal provision that excuses liability if the attempt to comply in good faith is demonstrated.

(3) ***investments:*** a defense against a hostile takeover whereby a target firm acquiring a heavily regulated business must clear all the paperwork dealing with regulation, clearance, and licensing, thereby making the target less attractive.

safekeeping: protective measures that a broker-dealer uses for protecting clients' fully paid securities, including adequate segregation, identification, and so on.

safe rate: see *capitalization rate(s), safe.*

safety of income: the assumption that a firm will sustain its interest and dividend payments on time.

safety of principal: the major characteristic of a sound investment.

safety stock: inventory maintained to avoid stockouts.

sag: a minimal drop or price weakness of shares, usually resulting from a weak demand for the securities.

salary reduction plan: a program permitting employees to place a percentage, usually no more than 10 percent, of their gross salary withheld and invested in the worker's choice of a stock, bond, or money-market fund. synonymous with *401 (K) plan.*

sale
(1) ***general:*** the transfer of title for a sum of money and conditions, for the change of ownership of property.
(2) ***general:*** the transfer of title to an item or items or the agreement to perform a service in return for cash or the expectation of cash payment.
(3) ***securities:*** in trading, when a buyer and a seller have agreed on a price for the stock.

sale and leaseback (S&L): a transaction in which the seller remains in occupancy by simultaneously signing a lease (usually of long duration) with the purchaser at the time of the sale. By so doing, the seller receives cash for the transaction, while the buyer is assured a tenant and thus a fixed return on his or her investment.

sale and servicing agreement: in secondary-market transactions, a contract under which the seller-servicer agrees to supply, and the buyer to purchase, loans from time to time; the contract sets forth the conditions for the transactions, and the rights and responsibilities of both parties.

sale on approval: a contract under which title does not pass to the buyer until he or she indicates an approval (or fails to disapprove within a stated time). Unless otherwise specified, risk of loss stays with the seller until approval is indicated.

sale or return: a contract under which there is a sale and title immediately passes to the buyer, who has the right to revest title in the seller by returning the goods. The buyer takes risk of loss, however, while the goods are in his or her hands.

sales
(1) the sum of the income received when goods and services are sold.
(2) revenue received from the sale of goods.

sales agreement: a written document by which a seller agrees to convey property to a buyer for a stipulated price under specified conditions.

sales charge: the amount charged in connection with the issuance of shares of a mutual fund and their distribution to the public. It is added to the net asset value per share in determining of the offering price.

sales literature: literature used by an issuer, underwriter, or dealer to inform prospective purchasers concerning an investment company the shares of which are offered for sale. Such literature is governed by the SEC's Statement of Policy and various regulations issued by the state.

sales load: see *sales charge.*

sales tax: a tax placed by a state or municipality on items at the time of their purchase. It may be a tax on the sale of an item every time it changes hands, or only upon its transfer of ownership at one specific time. The sales of manufacturers are taxed when the items are considered to be completed goods; the sales of wholesalers are taxed when their goods are sold to retailers; and retail sales are taxed when the goods are purchased by consumers. see *tax.*

Sallie Mae: see *Student Loan Marketing Association.*

salt-down stock: buying securities and keeping them over a long time period, disregarding paper profits that evolve.

salvage value: see *residual value.*

SAM: see *shared-appreciation mortgage.*

same-day substitution: offsetting changes in a margin account in the course of one day, leading to neither a margin call nor a credit to the special miscellaneous account.

Samurai: in Japan, the public debt market.

Samurai bond: see *bond, Samurai.*

S&L
(1) see *sale and leaseback.*
(2) see *savings and loan association.*

S&P: see *Standard and Poor's Corporation.*

S&P index: see *Standard & Poor's 500-Composite-Stock Index.*

sandwich spread: see *butterfly spread.*

San Francisco Stock Exchange: see *Pacific Stock Exchange.*

SARs: see *stock-appreciation rights.*

satisfaction of mortgage: a document issued by mortgagee when a mortgage is paid off.

satisfaction piece: an instrument acknowledging payment of an indebtedness due under a mortgage.

saturation: a market condition where the supply of a commodity or stock is so large that price reductions are needed to absorb any additional offerings. see also *saturation point.*

saturation point: the time when the supply of stocks for purchase starts to exceed the public demand. see *distribution, undigested securities.*

Saturday night special: a direct tender offer, made without any forewarning, that expires in one week. Such offerings were made possible by the Williams Act of 1968, which permits tender offers to run as short as seven days and does not require the bidder to tip his hand in advance with any notification.

saucer: a pattern developed by a chartist, indicating that the price of a stock or a commodity has formed a long-term bottom and is shifting upward. An *inverse saucer* shows a long-term top in the stock's price and signals a downturn.

Sav.: see *saving.*

saver's surplus: the differences between the amount of interest that savers actually get and the amount of interest for which they would have been willing to lend it the demand for loans (quantity demanded) had been less.

saving: the amount of existing income that is not spent on consumption.

savings account: money that is deposited in a bank, usually in small amounts periodically over a long period, and not subject to withdrawal by check. Savings accounts usually bear interest and some banks levy a service charge for excess withdrawal activity on an account. synonymous with special *interest account, thrift account.*

savings and investment theory: developed by John Maynard Keynes and D. H. Robertson: business cycles occur because people save either more or less than the amounts invested in new capital.

savings and loan association: a mutual, cooperative quasi-public financial institution, owned by its members (depositors), and chartered by a state or by the federal government. The association receives the savings of its members and uses these funds to finance long-term amortized mortgage loans to its members and to the general public. Such an association may also be organized as a corporation owned by stockholders.

savings bank: a banking association whose purpose is to promote thrift and savings habits in a community. It may be either a stock organization (a bank with a capital stock structure) or a "mutual savings bank." Until passage of the Cincotta-Conklin Bill in New York State or other similar bills, a savings bank had no power to perform commercial functions, but specialized in interest-bearing savings accounts, investing these savings in long-term bonds, mortgage loans, and other investment opportunities for the benefit of all depositors. see *NOW account.*

Savings Bank Life Insurance (SBLI): insurance written in several states through savings banks. Characterized by having no agents selling the insurance. It is bought over the counter and is available in statutory limited amounts in the form of whole life, limited-payment life, endowment, term, and annuities on a participating basis.

Savings Bond: see *Bond, Savings (U.S.)*

SB

(1) savings bond.
(2) short bill.

SBI: see *share of beneficial interest.*

SBIC: see *Small Business Investment Company.*

SBLI: see *Savings Bank Life Insurance.*

SC: see *stock certificate.*

scale: in serial bonds, critical information for each of the scheduled maturities in a new issue, including the number of bonds, the date they will mature, the coupon rate, and the offering price.

scale buying: synonymous with *buying on scale.* see *scaling.*

scale order: an order to buy (or sell) a security specifying the total amount to be bought (or sold) and the amount to be bought (or sold) at specified price variations.

scaling: trading in securities by placing orders for purchase or sale at intervals of price instead of giving the order in full at the market or at a stated price.

scalper
(1) a speculator who constantly sells his or her shares at fractional profit or at one or two points profit per share.
(2) an investment advisor who takes a position in a stock prior to recommending it, then sells out after the price has climbed as a result of the recommendation.
(3) a market maker who, in violation of the rules of fair practice of the National Association of Securities Dealers, adds an excessive markup or takes an excessive markdown on a transaction. see also *scalping.*

scalping: a speculative attempt to derive a quick profit by the purchase of a security at an initial offering price with the hope that the issue being oversubscribed will then advance in price at this time the security can then be sold. Scalping is also found on commodity exchanges where a scalper pruchases and sells during the trading day in equal amounts so that at the end of the trading time he or she has no position either long or short. see also *scalper.*

SCC: see *Stock Clearing Corporation.*

schedule: a systematic plan for future operations over a given period.

Schedule C: a bylaw of NASD stating the criteria which some individuals associated with a member must fulfill to be registered as a principal, financial principal, or representative.

schedule of charges: a schedule showing the rate charged by an international department for handling various transactions.

schedule of distribution: a form of accounting which sets forth in detail the estate property contained in each share to be distributed.

schedule supply: see *supply.*

Schedule 13D: the form required under section 13D of the Securities Act of 1934 within 10 business days of acquiring direct or beneficial ownership of 5 percent or more of any class of equity securities in a publicly held firm. In addition to SEC filing, the buyer of such stock must also file the 13D with the exchange on which the shares are listed, if any, and with the firm itself.

Schedule 13G: a short form of Schedule 13D filed by an individual who, at the end of a calendar year, owns 5 percent or more of an equity security of a corporation registered under Section 12 of the Securities Exchange Act of 1934.

school bond: see *bond, school.*

scorched-earth policy: a strategy used by a firm that has become a takeover target to make itself less attractive to the potential acquirer. For example, the firm will announce that its entire debt will become due immediately following a merger.

SCORE: see *special claim on residual equity.*

screen: to search, usually with the aid of computers, for securities that fulfill specific predetermined investment and financial criteria.

scrip: any temporary document that entitles the holder or bearer to receive stock or a fractional share of stock in a corporation, cash, or some other article of value upon demand, or at some specified future date. Some industries issue scrip to their employees as a supplement to salary for use in company-owned stores.

scrip certificate: a certificate showing ownership of a fractional share of stock that can be converted into a full share when presented in amounts equal to a full share.

scrip dividend: a type of dividend issued by a corporation to its stockholders, entitling the holder or bearer to receive cash, stock, or a fractional share of stock, or one or more units of the product manufactured, upon presentation or at a specified future date.

scripophile: an individual who practices scripophily.

scripophily: a hobby of collecting or trading in old financial documents, such as now-defunct bonds and security certificates.

SD
(1) see *secondary distribution.*
(2) see *stock dividend.*

SDB: special district bond. see *bond, special district.*

SDBL: sight draft, bill of lading attached.

SDMJ: September, December, March, June (quarterly interest payments or dividends).

SE
(1) see *shareholder's equity.*
(2) see *stock exchanges.*

sealing: concealed bids that are simultaneously revealed; the most attractive one is accepted on the spot, without further bidding.

seasonal trend: advances and declines in the market for a short time period that have appeared consistently, such as a year-end rally.

seasoned: a new issue widely distributed to a large number of buyers that trades often and with good liquidity in the secondary market.

seat: membership on a national securities exchange.

SEC: the Securities and Exchange Commission, established by Congress to protect investors. The SEC administers the Securities Act of 1933, the Securities Exchange Act of 1934, the Trust Indenture Act, the Investment Company Act, and the Public Utility Holding Company Act. The principal provisions of these acts are: (a) the Securities and Exchange Commission, created in 1934, administers the federal laws applying to securities; (b) corporations issuing securities and investment bankers selling them must make "full disclosure" of the character of the securities (i.e., they must state all relevant facts in registration statements to the

SEC and in prospectuses submitted to the public). see also *waiting period;* (c) any omission of fact or insertion of false information makes all persons (bankers, lawyers, accountants, etc.) whose names appear on the prospectus and the registration statement liable to the purchasers of the securities for any losses suffered; (d) the organization of people (brokers, traders, etc.) to manipulate the price of securities is forbidden. see *pool;* (e) dealings by corporation officers in securities of their own corporations are restricted; (f) the Board of Governors of the Federal Reserve System is given power to fix margin requirements on loans secured by bonds and stocks. see also *National Association of Securities Dealers and Investment Managers, unlisted trading privileges.*

SEC fee: a statutory fee of one cent per $300, or fraction, levied on the sale of equity securities registered on an exchange, irregardless of where the transaction took place. Usually this fee is paid by the seller.

SECO: see *Securities and Exchange Commission Organization.*

secondaries: slang, for smaller companies to which investors are attracted. They usually involve considerable risk but offer the opportunity for possible large gains.

secondary bank reserve: high-grade securities that are readily convertible into money.

secondary distribution: the redistribution of a block of stock sometime after it has been sold by the issuing company. The sale is handled off the exchange by a securities firm or group of firms, and the shares are usually offered at a fixed price that is related to the current market price. synonymous with *secondary offering.*

secondary financing: see *junior mortgage.*

secondary market: the market, referred to as the aftermarket, that exists for a new stock issue following distribution to the public. see *primary market.*

secondary mortgage market: an informally constituted market that includes all activity in buying, selling and trading mortgages among originators and purchasers of whole loans and interests in blocks of loans.

secondary movement: security price movements consisting of sharp rallies in a bear market and sharp reaction in a primary bull market; part of Dow theory.

secondary offering: synonymous with *secondary distribution.*

secondary reaction: a movement against the main trend of the market.

second market: the over-the-counter market.

second mortgage: a mortgage on real property that already possesses a first mortgage.

second-mortgage bond: see *bond, second-mortgage.*

second mortgage lending: advancing funds to a borrower that are secured by real estate previously pledged in a first mortgage loan. Should default occur, the first mortgage has priority of claim over the second.

second partner: an active partner in an organization whose capacity as a partner is not known to the public. cf. *silent partner.*

second preferred stocks: a series of preferred security issues that rank behind first preferred stock but in front of any third preferred issue or common stock in dividends or assets.

second round: the intermediate stage of venture capital financing, coming after the early start-up or seed money stage and prior to the mezzanine level, when the firm has matured to the point where it can consider a leveraged buyout by management or an initial public offering.

secret partner: a firm's member not known to the public, who may play a significant role in the firm's operations.

Section 403(b) plan: Section 403(b) of the Internal Revenue Code permits employees of certain charitable organizations and public school systems to establish tax-sheltered retirement programs which may be funded with annuities and mutual fund shares.

sector: a specific group of securities, often found in one industry, such as automobile or steel stocks.

sector funds: funds dedicated to gold, precious metals, and technology issues, that concentrate on trading a range of securities within a broad industry group, such as technology, energy, or financial services.

secular trend: a long-term trend either up or down in the price or level of a commodity, price structure, inflation rate, etc., that is not influenced by seasonal variations or distortions. The maxim is that a trend in force tends to perpetuate itself.

secured: guaranteed as to payment by the pledge of something valuable.

secured account: an account against which collateral or other security is held.

secured bond: see *bond, secured.*

secured debt: synonym for *secured bond.*

securities: pledges of corporations used to gain funds to meet financial obligations and needs.

Securities Act of 1934: federal legislation regulating activities dealing with trading of outstanding shares. The Act regulates securities exchanges and the over-the-counter market and those individuals and organizations involved in selling stocks. The Act is enforced by the SEC. see also *Securities Acts Amendments of 1975.*

Securities Acts Amendments of 1975: federal legislation of June 4, 1975 amending the Securities Exchange Act of 1934. These amendments directed the SEC to work with the industry toward creating a National Market System along with a nationwide clearance and settlement of securities transaction system. Additionally, amendments dealt with the handling and processing of securities; required transfer agents to register with the SEC; a Board was established for regulating brokers and dealers who handle municipal securities; and the prohibition of fixed commission rates. synonymous with *National Exchange Market System Act.* see also *National Market Advisory Board.*

securities analyst: see *analyst.*

securities and commodities exchanges: national exchanges where securities, options, and futures contracts are traded by members for their client's and personal accounts. The exchanges are registered with and regulated by the SEC; the commodity exchanges are registered and regulated by the Commodity Futures Trading Commission; and options which are traded on an exchange, their activity is also regulated by the SEC.

Securities and Exchange Commission Organization (SECO): an identification of nonmembers of NASD that are broker-dealers registered with the SEC. The SEC has jurisdiction over their trades and activities.

securities company: synonymous with *investment company.* see *holding company.*

securities depository: a physical location or organization where securities certificates are deposited and transferred by bookkeeping entry.

Securities Exchange Act: see *SEC.*

Securities Industry Association (SIA): a trade association representing brokers-dealers. A primary responsibility of SIA is to lobby for legislation affecting its members. The SIA also has a large education program to inform the public about the industry.

Securities Industry Automation Corporation (SIAC): established in 1972 to provide communications and computerized networks for the NYSE and the AMEX. It is two-thirds owned by the NYSE and one-third owned by the AMEX.

Securities Investor Protection Corporation: see *SIPC.*

securities loan: the lending of a stock or bond certificate to another broker-dealer for use in the completion of short sales. The borrowing broker-dealer must fully collateralize the loan of the certificates with cash equal to the full market value of the certificates to protect the lending broker, or the broker's client if the certificates were borrowed from a client. synonymous with *stock loan.*

securities trading: anyone who sells or buys securities through recognized channels is said to engage in securities trading; also applies to the operations of brokers in the various exchanges.

securitization: in Great Britain, the packaging of mortgage and other loans into exchange-traded shares and other securities.

security

(1) ***general:*** property pledged as collateral.

(2) ***investments:*** stocks and bonds placed by a debtor with a creditor, with authority to sell for the creditor's account if the debt is not paid.

(3) ***law:*** any evidence of debt or right to a property.

(4) ***law:*** an individual who agrees to make good the failure of another to pay.

security agreement: an agreement between the seller and the buyer stating that the seller will have a security interest in the goods.

security analysis: the application of comprehensive examination of the factors concerning a security, including variables of growth of sales and earnings, ratio analysis of financial statements, and evaluation of trends that affect a security.

security dollars: synonymous with *investment dollars.*

security element: the property that will secure a loan.

security exchange: see *stock exchanges.*

security instrument: the mortgage or trust deed evidencing the pledge of real estate as security for the repayment of the mortgage note.

security loan: any loan secured by the pledge of securities collateral.

security market: the places for sale and purchase of stocks and bonds; on the organized exchange and in the unorganized market.

security price level: the existing price level for a specified stock, any group of stocks, or the general securities market at a given period.

security ratings: ratings placed on securities according to the degree of investment risk incurred by the purchaser.

security valuation models: typically based on the precept that the value of a share of common stock is the sum of the discounted present value of the estimated future stream of dividends.

seed company: see *seed money.*

seed money: a venture capitalist's first contribution towards the financing or capital needs of a start-up firm. It usually takes the form of a loan, or an investment in convertible bonds or preferred stock.

seek a market: seeking a buyer (if a seller) or a seller (if a buyer) of stocks.

segregation of securities: SEC regulations (8c and 15c2-1) purporting to protect customers' securities used by broker-dealers to secure broker loans. Broker-dealers are refrained from commingling the securities of different clients without written approval from each client; refrained from commingling a client's securities with those of any individual other than a bona-fide client; or borrowing more against clients' securities than the clients, in the aggregate, owe the broker-dealer against the same securities.

selected dealer agreement: an agreement governing the selling group in a stock underwriting and distribution.

self-dealing: a financial transaction conducted on a personal, nonbusinesslike basis, such as lending or borrowing of money among corporate directors or their associates, often without concern for interest payment or principal repayment.

self-directed IRA: an Individual Retirement Account that is actively managed by an account holder who identifies a custodian to carry out investment instructions. Most corporate and U.S. government securities, and limited partnerships are eligible to be held by a self-directed IRA.

Self-Employed Retirement Plan: see *Keogh Plan.*

self-insurance: a system whereby a firm or individual, by setting aside an amount of monies, provides for the occurrence of any losses that could ordinarily be covered under an insurance program. The monies that would normally be used for premium payments are added to this special fund for payment of losses incurred.

self-liquidating: describing an asset that can be converted into cash or subject to the total recovery of invested money, over a period of time.

self-liquidating bond: see *bond, self-liquidating.*

self-regulatory organization: see *SRO.*

self-supporting: in the analysis of municipal securities, when the revenues generated by a project are adequate to pay the debt service without further revenues from another source.

sell: a stock considered suitable for sale in order to either take a profit or cut a loss.

sell at best: in over-the-counter transactions, when traders use other broker-dealers to aid them in selling portions of a market order, usually at the best available bid price.

sell (or buy) at the close: an order to be executed at the market (best price obtainable) at the close of the market on the day the order is entered.

sell (or buy) at the opening: an order to be executed at the market (best price obtainable) immediately after a stock exchange opens for business.

sell-down: where a security or syndicated borrowing is offered to other possible participants outside the syndicate that is underwriting the deal, the proportion which these outsiders take.

seller financing: to aid buyers who cannot come up with enough cash upon assuming a loan, sellers will sometimes provide a secondary trust by which the buyer pays back part of the money owed in monthly installments over a period of years, often at a rate two or three percentage points below the current mortgage rate. In some cases, sellers who do not immediately need cash from the sale of a home may hold onto the entire mortgage and allow the buyer to make monthly payments until mortgage rates drop and more attractive financing can be arranged.

seller's call: the buying of a commodity of a given quality identified in a contract that freezes the future price.

sellers' commission: see *fee.*

seller's market: a descriptive term: demand is greater than supply in this type of market, resulting in seller's setting the prices and terms of sale. It is a market characterized by rising or high prices.

seller's option: a special transaction on an exchange: the seller holding the option can deliver the stocks or bonds at any time within a specified period, ranging from not less than six business days to not more than 60 days.

seller's put: see *put option, puts and calls.*

seller's seven sale: an agreed-upon delay of several or more days for the delivery of a security. see *settlement day.*

seller's surplus: the difference between the price a seller actually receives and the lowest price that he or she would accept.

seller's 30: a security contract giving the seller an option of delivering a security which has been sold at any time within 30 days of the date of sale.

selling against the box: see *short sale.*

selling below the market: an expression indicating that a security is currently quoted for less than similar securities of comparable quality and acceptance.

selling charge: see *load.*

selling climax: the unsystematic dumping of stocks; a burst of panic selling indicating the termination of a declining period, as in a bear market. The rebounding rally after this climax is often short-lived, but strong. see *blowing off.*

selling concession: synonymous with *participating brokers/dealers.*

selling dividends: questionable methods of sales personnel dealing in mutual funds whereby a client is induced to purchase shares in a fund in order to receive the benefit of a dividend scheduled in the near future. However the client derives no real benefit since the dividend is already part of the net asset value of the fund and, therefore, part of the share price.

selling flat: when a purchaser of securities is not required to pay an additional sum beyond the purchase price of the principal of a bond. This added sum is the payment for accrued interest that the issuer pays the holder. The bonds that typically sell flat are bonds in default or income bonds.

selling, general, and administrative expenses (SG & A): the grouping of expenses reported on a firm's profit and loss statement between cost of goods sold and income deductions, including salespersons salaries and commissions, advertising expenses, travel and entertainment, office expenses, etc.

selling group: synonymous with *participating brokers/dealers.*

selling group pot: a percentage of an offering set aside for a selling group.

selling hedges: synonymous with *short hedges.*

selling-off: synonymous with *sell-off.*

selling on balance: selling-off stocks on declining market prices that is accompanied by high volume. Supply is greater than demand and surplus shares can be bought by the specialists and dealers.

selling on the good news: a method of selling a security shortly after a positive news development has been announced. The majority of investors, impressed with such information, purchase a stock assuming it will then climb in price. It usually does push up the price. A person selling on this good news expects that the security will have reached its top price once all those encouraged by the development have bought the security. Consequently, it is preferable to sell at this point than to wait for more good news or to be left holding the security if the next announcement is not positive. cf. *buying on the bad news.*

selling short: a technique employed with the expectation of a drop in the market with the expectation of a drop in the market price of the security. A temporarily borrowed stock is sold to effect delivery. If the price drops, the trader can purchase the security for less than he or she sold it, pay the borrowing cost, and clear a profit. see *bear position, loaned flat.*

selling the intermarket spread: buying a futures contract in bank CDs and selling Treasury bill futures short. see *intermarket spread.* cf. *buying the intermarket spread.*

sell-off: a sudden and marked drop in stock or bond prices resulting from widespread demand to sell. synonymous with *selling-off.*

sell order: a verbal or written request made by a stockholder to a broker to liquidate an identified number of shares of a specific stock at a specified price or at market with or without any other trading instructions.

sell out: to close out a customer's account by selling held securities or commodities.

sell-out notice (notification): an urgent notice sometimes sent by a brokerage house to a client stating that an amount due must be immediately paid or the house will be obliged to sell enough of the client's stocks to satisfy the liability. This final warning is usually made when a client fails to pay for stocks bought, or needs to deposit cash or securities to maintain sufficient margin in his or her account.

sell plus: a sell order with instructions to execute only if the trading price in a stock is higher than the last different preceding price.

sell signal: indicators showing that a security is in a pattern that could shortly lead to a down-reversal. cf. *buy signal.*

sell-stop order: see *stop order.*

sell the book: a client's instructions to a broker by the holder of a significant quantity of shares of a stock to sell all that can be absorbed at the current bid price.

SEM: see *shared equity mortgages.*

senior bond: see *bond, senior.*

senior debt: loans or debt securities having claim prior to junior obligations and equity on a firm's assets in the event of liquidation.

senior equity: a preferred stock that ranks before junior equity (common stock) in the event of the liquidation and distribution of assets of the issuing company.

senior interest: a participation senior or ahead of another participation.

senior issue: see *senior securities.*

senior obligations: synonymous with *senior securities.*

senior refunding: an exchange by holders of securities maturing within 5 to 12 years for issues with original maturities of 15 years or longer.

senior registered option principal: a general partner or office responsible for the overall authority and responsibility for client options transactions and accounts.

senior securities: preferred securities and bonds that receive consideration before common stock when a firm is at the point of being dissolved or actually fails, synonymous with *senior obligations.* see also *junior securities.*

sensitive market: characterized by fluctuations determined by the announcement of favorable or unfavorable news.

sentiment indicator: a measure of the bullish or bearish attitude of investors. For example, analysts believe that when investors are bullish, the market is soon to fall, and vice versa.

SEP: see *Simplified Employee Pension.*

separate account: an account established by an insurance company under which income, gains and losses, whether or not realized from assets allocated to the account, are credited to or charged against the account without regard to other income, gains or losses of the insurance company.

separate customer: a concept of the Securities Investor Protection Corporation in allocating insurance coverage. Should there be a difference in the way investment accounts are owned, each account is viewed as a separate client entitled to the maximum protection. see also *SIPC.*

separate property: property that is owned individually and is not jointly held.

serial annuity bond: see *bond, serial annuity.*

serial bond: see *bond, serial.*

serial bond issue: bonds of a single issue which mature on staggered dates rather than all at one time. The purpose of a serial bond issue is to enable the issuer to retire the bonds in small quantities over a long period.

serial bonds payable: a liability account that records the face value of general obligation serial bonds issued and outstanding.

serial issue: see *serial bond issue.*

series: options of the same class having the same exercise price and expiration time.

series bond: see *bond, series.*

Series EE Bond: see *Bond, Savings (U.S.).*

Series HH Bond: see *Bond, Savings (U.S.).*

series of options: all option contracts of the same class on the same underlying security having the same striking price and the same date of expiration.

service: meeting periodic payments on interest and a sinking fund for a long-term obligation.

service charge: a payment by a financial institution against an individual or organization for services rendered or are about to be rendered.

service corporation: a corporation, owned by one or more savings associations, that performs services and engages in certain activities for its owners, such as originating, holding, selling, and servicing mortgages; performing appraisal, brokerage, clerical, escrow, research, and other services; and acquiring, developing, or renovating, and holding real estate for investment purpose.

service lease: synonymous with *operating lease.*

servicing: in mortgage financing, the performance by the mortgagee or his or her agent of the many services which must be taken care of while the mortgage is held by the institution, such as title search, billing, collection of interest and principal payments, reinspections and reappraisals of the real property readjustment of the terms of the mortgage contract when necessary, and tax follow-up work.

servicing contract: in secondary-market transactions, a document that details servicing requirements and legally binds the servicing institution to perform them. Such a contract refers to the seller of mortgage participations, binding it to continue accepting loan payments.

session: in securities, the period of trading activity which usually coincides with a stock exchange's hours of business (e.g., volume was 100 million shares in today's session).

settle: completing a securities trade between brokers serving as agents or between a broker and his or her client. The trade is settled when the client has paid the broker for stocks purchased or when the client delivers stocks that have been sold and the customer receives the proceeds from the sale.

settlement

(1) closing out a brokerage account.

(2) completing a stock transaction by delivering the required stock certificates and/or funds.

settlement day: the deadline by which a purchaser of stock must pay for what has been bought and the seller must deliver the certificates for the securities that have been sold. The settlement day is usually the fifth business day following the execution of an order. cf. *shave.*

settlement options: provisions in a life policy or annuity contract for alternative methods of settlement in place of lump-sum payments.

settlor: synonymous with *trustor.*

severally and jointly: in underwritings, where syndicate members agree to purchase an issue and are both individually (severally) and as an account (jointly) responsible for the purchase price of the securities. cf. *severally but not jointly.*

severally but not jointly: an agreement used for establishing responsibility for selling a part of the securities in an underwriting. Underwriting group members agree to purchase a given number of shares of an issue (severally) but do not agree to joint liability for shares not sold by other members of the syndicate. cf. *severally and jointly.*

SF: see *sinking fund.*

SG&A expenses: see *selling, general, and administrative expenses.*

SH.: see *stockholder.*

shade: a small reduction in price or terms.

shading: giving a small reduction in a price or terms of a sale.

shadow calendar: a backlog of securities issues in registration with the SEC that have no offering date set pending clearance.

shadow markets: the manipulation of options and futures stemming partly from the huge leverage they afford. synonymous with *derivative markets.*

shadow price: considering the market price as a "real" price, the "equilibrium" price is a "shadow" price—the price that would prevail under equilibrium conditions.

shadow security: shares that don't actually exist but on which key executives receive dividends or deferred compensation.

shadow warrants: tying additional interest payments over the life of a loan to the market performance of a common stock.

shake out

(1) ***general:*** a trend or shift in a industry that forces weaker members toward bankruptcy.

(2) ***investments:*** any shift in activity that forces speculators to sell their shares.

share

(1) a unit of equity ownership in a corporation.

(2) a unit of stock naming the holder and indicating ownership in a corporation.

(3) a unit of ownership in a mutual fund.

(4) interest, often represented by a certificate, in a general or limited partnership.

share broker: a discount broker whose charges are determined by the number of traded shares. The greater the shares in a trade (usually, at least 500 shares), the lower the pershare cost will be.

Sharebuilder Investment Plan (SIP): developed by Merrill Lynch and Chase Manhattan Bank, a plan whereby a depositor's account is debited automatically on a prescribed date and the money transferred to a special sharebuilder account at Chase. The broker buys stock for the depositor the next morning. Chase and Merrill Lynch split the commissions on sales of the plan. There is a three-way split if a correspondent institution makes the sale. Customers benefit from rates discounted from the standard Merrill Lynch schedule, and they can buy stock with weekly or monthly installments too small to cover investments made through normal channels.

share capital: the total direct ownership in a corporation. When all stock to be issued by a firm is ordered and paid for, the funds collected constitute the share capital of the corporation.

shared-appreciation mortgage (SAM): a home-financing technique whereby the borrower receives a mortgage rate that is one-third lower than the prevailing level. But the borrower must agree to give the lender one-third of the profits from the eventual sale of the house. A shared-appreciation mortgage has payments that are based on a long amortization schedule, but the loan becomes due and payable no later than at the end of 10 years. It has an interest rate below that on a conventional mortgage. It has a contingent interest feature, whereby at either the sale or transfer of the property or the refinancing or maturity of the loan, the borrower must pay the lender a share of the appreciation of the property securing the loan.

shared equity mortgages (SEM): when an investor makes the down payment for the buyer and sometimes part of the monthly mortgage payment in return for a percentage of the home's future appreciation.

shareholder: synonymous with *stockholder.*

shareholder's equity: the total assets minus total liabilities of a corporation. see also *equity, net worth.* synonymous with *stockholder's equity.*

share of beneficial interest (SBI): an equity security representing the undivided interest in a pool of debt securities.

share of stocks: units of ownership in a firm.

shareowner: synonymous with *stockholder.*

share register: the records of a corporation indicating ownership of shares of that firm by the public. A share register is required by law for every corporation.

share repurchase plan: a plan where a corporation purchases back its own shares in the open market; often done when shares are considered to be undervalued. The result will be to increase the market value of the remaining shares held by stockholders since it reduces the number of shares outstanding and thereby increases earnings per share.

shares: equal interests into which the capital stock of a corporation is divided, the ownership being evidenced by certificates called stock certificates. see also *capital stock.*

shares authorized: the number of shares of securities provided for in the articles of incorporation of a firm.

shares outstanding: the shares issued by a corporation, excluding treasury stock.

share turnover: see *volume.*

sharing the market: any scheme by which sellers limit their individual efforts to given parts of the total market for a product or service (e.g., the "sharing" may be on a geographical basis).

shark: a takeover strategy that moves in when the potential target appears "wounded" and therefore vulnerable for takeover. see also *in play.*

shark repellent: a state statute that demands strict notification and disclosure of tender offers for companies incorporated or transacting business within its boundaries.

shark watcher: an organization specializing in the spotting of takeover activity. The firm's primary effort is to solicit proxies for a client corporation, monitor trading trends in a customer's stock and determine the identity of parties accumulating shares. see *radar alert.*

shave
(1) a charge that is higher than the accepted rate, made for the handling of a note or other instrument of low quality or when the seller will take a smaller amount for any other reason.
(2) the additional charge (premium) made for the right to extend the delivery time on a security.

sheared: an unsuccessful trader of securities or commodities.

"sheep": see *fleece.*

"sheets;" the: synonymous with *pink sheets.*

shelf distribution: a method of selling securities. Stocks, owned by stockholders, are placed on the shelf for sale at a later time. To be contrasted with the usual public offering of stocks to when all are sold at one time at a fixed price through underwriters.

shelf registration: a Securities and Exchange Commission ruling effective March 1983 permitting an issuer to register one big issue of bonds with the SEC. Instead of selling the bonds all at once, issuers will put at least some of them aside—on the shelf—to be sold piecemeal whenever they see a need for funds, find favorable market conditions, or receive a call from a trader or institution offering attractive terms. see also *shelf distribution.*

shell firm: an organization that is incorporated but does not function or produce any goods or services.

Shibosai: in Japan, the private placement market.

shoestring trading: existing on minimal, barely adequate margin.

shop
(1) the office of a broker-dealer in securities and commodities.
(2) the act of surveying dealers for the most favorable price, as in shopping securities dealers for the best bid or offer.

short: an individual who sells a futures contract in anticipation of purchasing it back at a lower cost. see *short hedges, short interest, short sale.* see also *shorts.*

short account: the account of a company or person who is short.

short against the box: see *short sale.*

short bond: see *bond, short.*

short call: a call option contract sold on an opening sale transaction.

short coupon
(1) a bond with a relatively short maturity, traditionally two years or less.
(2) a bond interest payment covering less than the conventional six-month period. This payment occurs when the original issue date is less than a half year from the first scheduled interest payment date.

short covering: buying a stock to return stock previously borrowed to make delivery on a short sale.

shortcut foreclosure: a method of foreclosure in which a power of sale clause in the mortgage allows the lender to sell a property if it goes into default. The borrower must be informed, but the issuing of a public statement need not be carried out. Upon property foreclosure, the junior mortgage holders' positions are wiped out, unless the sale yields more than the outstanding first mortgage.

short dates: usually periods up to one week, but sometimes periods up to a month.

short exempt
(1) the indication marked on specific short-sale orders sent to an exchange for execution.
(2) member firm orders made to correct a floor error.
(3) specialist orders for completing specific odd-lot buy transactions.

short-form mortgage clause: a mortgage clause permitting the buyer to take over the mortgage, subject to and not assuming liability for its payment.

short-fund(ed): buying short-term money at high rates of interest, in the expectation that rates would soon fall and lendable funds could then be more cheaply obtained.

short hedges: sales of futures created as hedges against holdings of the spot commodity or product. see *hedge.* synonymous with *selling hedges.*

short interest: measures the practice of selling borrowed shares in a bearish bet that a stock's price will fall; the number of shares that haven't yet been purchased for return to lenders.

short interest concept: synonymous with *cushion theory.*

short interest ratio: a ratio determined by dividing the reported short interest by the average NYSE volume for a 30-day period. A ratio above 1.60 is considered bullish and a ratio below 1.00 is considered bearish.

short leg: a short option forming a part of a spread.

short market value (SMV): the current market value of stocks sold short in a margin account.

short of the market: holding a short position in stock with the expectation that lower prices will occur. see *short sale.*

short position
(1) stocks sold short and not covered as of a particular date. On an exchange, a tabulation is usually issued once a month listing all issues on the exchange in which there was a short position of 5000 or more shares and issues in which the short position had changed by 2000 or more shares in the preceding month.
(2) the total amount of stock an individual has sold short and has covered, as of a particular date.
(3) a contract in which a trader agrees to sell a commodity at a future date for a stated price.

short purchase: buying a stock to cover an earlier short sale of the same stock.

short put: a put option contract sold on an opening sale transaction. cf. *long put.*

short-rate cancellation: describes the charge required for insurance or bonds taken for less than one year. Also in some cases, it denotes the earned premium for insurance or bonds canceled by the insured before the end of the policy period or term of bond. cf. *pro rate cancellation.*

shorts
(1) bear traders on the short side. see *short sale.* see also *short.*
(2) in Great Britain, gilt-edged securities with less than five years to maturity.

short sale: a transaction made by a person who believes a stock will decline and places a sell order, though he or she does not own any of these shares. Stock exchange and federal regulations govern and limit the conditions under which a short sale may be made. Sometimes a person will sell short a stock already owned to protect a paper profit. This is known as *selling against the box.*

short-sale rule: an SEC regulation requiring that short sales can only be made in a climbing market. The rule was created to minimize abuses perpetuated by pool operators, who attempt to drive down the price of a security by heavy short selling, then pick up the shares for a large profit. synonymous with *plus tick rule.*

short seller: a securities pessimist, that is, bearish on the trend of securities prices and substantiates this feeling by selling short.

short selling: selling a stock and purchasing it at a lower price to receive a profit.

short side: pessimists who sell short as contrasted with being on the long side. see *short sale.*

short squeeze: a sharp runup of prices that forces shorts to make offsetting purchases in order to avoid larger losses. A short squeeze occurs when people who have sold borrowed shares, in anticipation of replacing them at lower prices, are forced to cover those borrowed shares by buying shares, even at higher price. When a confluence of short covering occurs, price tend to jump because of the increased demand.

short stock: securities that have been sold short and not yet covered. see *short covering, short sale.*

short tender: using borrowed stock to respond to a tender offer. Prohibited by the SEC.

short term
(1) ***investments:*** an investment with a maturity of one year or less.
(2) ***taxes:*** stock, bonds, or other property held six months or less, the capital gains on which are taxed as ordinary income.

short-term capital gain: a profit received on an investment held for one year or less. The gain is treated as an addition to ordinary income.

short-term capital loss: a loss incurred on an investment held for one year or less. The loss is treated as a deduction against ordinary income.

short-term debt: an obligation that is usually due within the year.

short-term funds: money borrowed from 30 days up to one year.

short-term gain or less: in tax accounting, the profit or loss realized from the sale of securities or other capital assets held six months or less.

short-term savings account: ordinarily, an account that is to be withdrawn within less than 24 months from the date the account is opened.

short-term securities: securities payable on demand or which mature not more than one year from date of issue.

short-term trading: purchasing stocks and retaining them only long enough to take advantage of short-term price fluctuations.

short-term trading index (TRIN): the advance/decline ratio divided by advancing/decline volume ratio. TRIN is calculated every minute and used for identifying intraday movements. An index of 1.00 or less is considered bullish and an index of 1.00 or more is considered bearish. see also *trading index.*

Shr.: see *share.*

shrinking stocks: stocks of corporations that are bought by the firms of their own shares, thus drastically reducing the number of shares outstanding. These corporations feel that they can earn a higher return on the money spent for their stock than on investing in new business schemes.

shrinks: slang, open-market purchases of common stock.

shut-off rates: high mortgage rates that are designed to turn away prospective buyers.

SI: see *simple interest.*

SIA: see *Securities Industry Association.*

SIAC: see *Securities Industry Automation Corporation.*

Siamese shares: synonymous with *paired shares.*

SIBOR: Singapore Interbank Offered Rate.

SIC: see *split investment company.*

sick market: in securities, a weak, tremulous market, giving an appearance of being sick.

side collateral: security for a loan that is less than the required margin, less than the principal amount of the loan or not to be held for the full term of the loan. A loan secured only by side collateral is classified as unsecured.

sideliner: any person who withdraws temporarily from an active role in the market after closing out their long and/or short position.

sideways: the movement of a stock when its price changes minimally each day.

sideways price movement: the period where prices trade within a narrow range, showing only small shifts up or down. synonymous with *horizontal price movement.*

sign: see *technical sign.*

signal: an indicator showing a security is in a pattern that would soon lead to an important shift in its trend. Such patterns indicate either a buy signal or sell signal.

signed instrument: any legal agreement, or note which is written and signed.

silent partner: an individual who gives funds for a business partnership but takes no part in the management of the firm.

Silver Thursday: March 27, 1980, when the commodity industry and the entire financial community was imperiled after a major brokerage house, Bache Halsey Stuart Shields, was momentarily unable to get a commodity customer, the billionaire Hunt brothers, to cover a margin call for $100 million.

simple arbitrage: arbitrage achieved by using only three markets. cf. *compound arbitrage.*

simple interest: interest calculated on a principal sum and not on any interest that has been earned by that sum. cf. *compounded interest.*

Simplified Employee Pension (SEP): made possible by the Revenue Act of 1978; a retirement plan that increases the limit on yearly contributions to $7500 an employee. This plan combined element of both Keogh plans and Individual Retirement Accounts. The SEP option permits an employee to establish an IRA whether or not the worker is covered by a company pension plan. An SEP also increases the amount that can be contributed annually to an IRA from the usual $1500 to $7500. Earnings from investments are tax-free until after age 59½. Upon the death of the person, any undistributed funds can escape the estate tax by going to the heirs in installments over at least 36 months.

single capital structure company: a company having only one class of security outstanding.

single debit reporting: the normal method used by mortgage bankers for reporting the current status of its mortgages when making a regular remittance to an investor.

single debt: a system of mortgage accounting by which a servicer reports current installments as a lump sum. A detailed payment analysis is given only on uncollected and unscheduled payments.

single entry: a bookkeeping approach in which each transaction is entered only once on the account books. The single-entry system is primarily used by small businesses. cf. *double entry.*

single liability: the situation in which the stockholder is liable for the corporation's losses only to the extent of his or her investment.

single option: as contrasted from a spread or straddle, any put or call. see *option.*

single-premium deferred annuity: see *SPDA.*

single purchase annuity contracts: group single premium annuity contracts designed to provide annuities for participants in an uninsured pension or profit-sharing plan that has terminated. Under a single purchase contract, immediate annuities are provided for present pensioners and deferred annuities for those who are below retirement age.

single-state municipal bond fund: a mutual fund that invests entirely in tax-exempt obligations of governments and government agencies within one state. Dividends paid on fund shares are not taxable to residents of that particular state when filing state tax returns, although capital gains, if any, are taxable.

singular property title: property title granted to only one person.

sinkers: synonymous with *sinking fund bonds.* see *bond, sinking fund.*

sinking fund: a fund used to accumulate the cash needed to pay off a bond or other security. By accumulating cash in a sinking fund, the firm is in a better position to pay its securities when due, and the risk is therefore reduced to the security holder.

sinking fund bond: see *bond, sinking fund.*

sinking fund depreciation: a system for calculating depreciation: the yearly amount is presumed to be deposited in a sinking fund that will also increase as a result of earnings from the fund investment.

sinking fund requirements: the amount by which a sinking fund must be increased periodically through contributions and earnings so that the accumulation thereof will be sufficient to redeem sinking fund bonds as they mature.

sinking fund reserve: see *reserve for retirement of sinking fund bonds.*

SIP: see *Sharebuilder Investment Plan.*

SIPC: Securities Investor Protection Corporation; provides funds for use, if necessary, to protect customers' cash and securities which may be on deposit with an SIPC member firm in the event the firm fails and is liquidated under the provision of the SIPC

Act. SIPC is not a government agency. It is, however, a nonprofit membership corporation created by an act of Congress. see also *separate customer.*

sites: on the London exchange, sales made in sealed parcels, where the purchaser does not even see what he or she is getting until after purchase is completed.

65 Stock Average: synonymous with *Dow Jones Composite.*

size
(1) the number of shares or bonds available for sale.
(2) used when a large number of shares are for sale. For example, a trader will say that "shares are available in size."

size of the market: the number of round lots bid for at the highest price showing on the specialist's book and the total number being offered for sale simultaneously at the lowest price quoted, at any specified time.

skimming prices: a high introductory price followed by a series of price reductions, designed to get all the trade the market will bear at one price level before lowering the price, as well as to appeal to the more price-conscious consumer.

skip-day settlement: a negotiated settlement calling for delivery and payment on the second business day following the trade date.

skip-payment privilege: a privilege provided in certain mortgage contracts that allows the borrower to skip monthly payments at any time the loan is paid ahead of schedule as long as the loan is prepaid.

skyrocketing: slang, a sharp rise in stock prices within a relatively short time period.

SL: sold.

slaughter: slang, the indiscriminate selling of securities at very low levels, often unnecessarily low.

Sld.: sold.

SLD last sale: sold last sale. Appears on the consolidated tape when a greater than normal change occurs between transactions in a stock. The designation is used when the change is a point or more on lower-priced issues or two points or higher on higher-priced issues.

sleeper: a slow-moving security that has a sound potential for growth.

sleeping beauty: a possible takeover target that has not yet been approached by an acquirer. Such a firm usually has attractive features such as a significant amount of cash, or undervalued real estate.

slice: slang, having a portion or interest in a business venture or activity.

slide: a posting error by which an amount is wrongly recorded by a bookkeeper who unintentionally places the decimal one or more digits to the right or left of the true decimal position.

sliding parity: see *crawling peg.*

slid off: a drop in the price of stocks.

slipping: slang, a downward movement in the prices of securities or commodities which is not severe.

SLMA: see *Student Loan Marketing Association.*

SLO
(1) see *stop-limit order.*
(2) see *stop loss order.*

sluggish market: a slow-moving, inactive securities trading where volume is unusually low. Few stocks are traded with only minimal price fluctuations.

slugs: slang, Treasury securities. see *treasury securities.*

S&M: September and March (semiannual interest payments or dividends).

SM
(1) see *secondary market.*
(2) see *second mortgage.*

SMA
(1) Society of Management Accountants.
(2) see *special miscellaneous account.*

small-caps: firms with small capitalizations.

Small Business Investment Company (SBIC): a federal agency that provides capital to small businesses, licensed and regulated by the Small Business Administration as authorized by Congress in 1958. The SBICs may make long-term loans or buy convertible debentures or stock in small enterprises, as defined as having less than $5 million in assets, net worth less than $2½ million, and average net income following taxes the previous two years not exceeding $250,000.

small investor: an investor who purchases small amounts of stock or bonds, frequently in odd lot quantities.

small-saver certificates: certificates issued in denominations of less than $100,000 with maturities of 2.5 years or more.

smart money: experienced and professional security traders who exploit inside information to make profits at the expense of other investors.

smash: a severe drop in the market, approaching a panic.

smokey process: determining a pricing structure by reviewing prevailing rates across the nation and estimating the future cost of funds.

SMV: see *short market value.*

SN: stock number.

Snafu: situation normal, all fouled up.

sniping: unloading securities for four and five point losses in a single day.

snowballing: a resulting transaction following stop orders that become market orders, during periods of either advance or decline. see *touch off the stops.*

SO
(1) see *seller's opinion.*
(2) see *stock option.*

social consciousness mutual fund: a mutual fund that is administered for capital appreciation and at the same time investing in corporations that do not conflict with social priorities.

socially responsible investments: generally concluded to include those investments which: (a) carry a lesser rate of return and/or (b) have a lower credit rating and quality and/or (c) have less liquidity or marketability than other forms of investment or specific investments readily available in the marketplace, but which will: (i) create employment opportunities for plan participants and/or (ii) have a greater social or moral quality. Includes "socially sensitive" investments which otherwise are equal when compared to other investments by traditional financial analysis, but have favorable non-economic characteristics. Socially responsible investments are known as "divergent," "political," and "target" investments.

Society for Worldwide Interbank Financial Telecommunications (SWIFT): an automated communication network facilitating transfer of currencies and financial data.

soft: a security or general market that moves toward a lower price level.

soft arbitrage: arbitrage between public-sector and private paper.

soft dollars: brokerage house payments for their services through commission revenue instead of direct payments. cf. *hard-dollars.*

soft market: synonymous with *buyer's market.*

soft spot: while the general securities market is holding or even moving ahead, the sudden decline in specific stocks or groupings of securities.

sold last sale: see *SLD last sale.*

sold-out market: a market in which liquidations of weakly held contracts has largely been completed and offerings have become scarce.

sold to you: in over-the-counter trading, when traders reconfirm that their offer has been accepted by the contratrader.

sole owner: the only person holding the title to a specific property or business.

sole proprietorship: a proprietorship in which all equity lies with one individual.

solvent debtor section: a part of the Bankruptcy Tax Act of 1980 whereby a company that buys back its own bonds at a discount price must pay income tax on the spread between the face value of the bonds, or the original sales price, and the discount repurchase price.

Sonnie Mae: New York State Mortgage Authority.

SOP: see *statement of policy.*

sophisticated investor: an affluent investor with considerable market knowledge and experience and time for studying the market opportunities. He or she invests considerable funds.

SOR: see *stockholder of record.*

source and applications of funds statement: the analysis of shifts in the financial position of a company from one accounting period to another. synonymous with *sources and uses of funds statement.*

sources and uses of funds statement: synonymous with *source and applications of funds statement.*

sovereign risk: a risk that a foreign government will default on its loan or fail to honor business obligations because of a shift in national policy. synonymous with *country risk, political risk.*

SOYD: sum of the years' digits method.

SP
(1) see *short position.*
(2) see *spot price.*

SpA: Società per Azioni (Italian corporation).

SPDA: single-premium deferred annuity. A tax-deferred investment similar to an Individual Retirement Account, but free of the IRA restrictions. An investor makes a lump-sum payment to an insurance firm or mutual fund selling the annuity. The value of the annuity depreciates over the years according to fixed or variable terms established on the issue date. Proceeds are only taxed when distributions are taken, often later in life when the investor expects to be in a lower tax bracket. Unlike the IRAs, there is no maximum to the amount that can be invested in an SPDA, nor must the holder wait until age 59½ to draw the benefits.

special arbitrage account (SAA): a special margin account with a broker reserved for transactions where the client's risk is hedged by an offsetting security transaction or position. The margin requirement is considerably lower than in the case of stocks bought on credit and subject to price declines.

special assessment bond: see *bond, special assessment.*

special assistance bond: see *bond, special assistance.*

special bid: a method of filling an order to buy a large block of stock on the exchange floor. The bidder for the block of stock pays a special commission to the broker who represents him or her in making the purchase. The seller does not pay a commission. The special bid is made on the floor of the exchange at a fixed price, which may not be below the last sale of the security or the current bid in the regular market, whichever is higher. Member firms may sell this stock for customers directly to the buyer's broker during trading hours.

special bond account: a separate account created by brokerage houses for bookkeeping purposes identifying the amount of buying power available on bonds bought on margin.

special claim on residential equity (SCORE): a certificate issued by the Americus Shareowner Service Corporation; giving its holder the right to all the appreciation on an underlying security above a specified price, but none of the dividend income from the stock.

special convertible debt security account: a margin account where a client finances the purchase of short sale of debt securities that are convertible into a margin stock, or carry a warrant or right to subscribe to a margin stock.

special deal: prohibited by the rules of fair practice of the NASD, where an underwriter of an investment company pays or gives away anything of material value (worth more than $25 in one year) other than selling concessions granted in the prospectus to an employee of another dealer in concurrence with the sale of the fund's shares.

special depository: any bank authorized by the U.S. Treasury to receive as deposits the proceeds of sales of government bonds.

special devise: a gift, by will, of a specific parcel of real property.

special district bond: see *bond, special district.*

special dividend: synonymous with *extra dividend.* see *extra.*

special interest account: synonymous with *savings account.*

special issues: securities issued by the U.S. Treasury for investment of reserves of government trust funds and for certain payments to veterans.

specialist: a member of an exchange who has two functions: to maintain an orderly market, insofar as is reasonably practicable, in the stocks in which he or she is registered by an exchange as a specialist; and to act as a broker's broker.

specialist block purchase: a purchase by the specialist for his or her own account of a large block of stock outside the regular market on the exchange. Such purchases may be made only when the sale of the block could not be made in the regular market within a reasonable time and at reasonable prices, and when the purchase by the specialist would aid him or her in maintaining a fair and orderly market. cf. *specialist block sale.*

specialist block sale: opposite of *specialist block purchase.* Under exceptional circumstances, the specialist may sell a block of stock outside the regular market on the exchange for his or her own account at a price above the prevailing market. The price is negotiated between the specialist and the broker for the buyer.

specialist manager: an investment manager who confines research activity to either a single class of investments or otherwise implements a more narrowly defined strategy than a balanced manager.

specialist's book: a book where the specialist enters all limit and stop orders for each stock that have been left with him or her. The book also indicates market orders to sell short. Orders are entered according to price in the order they are received.

specialist's short-sale ratio: the ratio of the amount of stock sold short by specialists on the floor of the NYSE to total short sales; indicates whether specialists are more or less bearish on the outlook for stock prices than other NYSE members and the public in general.

specialist unit: a stock exchange specialist authorized by an exchange to deal as principal and agent for other brokers in maintaining a stable market in one or more specific stocks. A specialist unit on the NYSE must have sufficient capital to purchase at least 5000 shares of the common stock of a firm it handles and 1000 shares of the firm's convertible preferred stock.

specialized management trust: an investment firm whose investment policy is limited to securities of businesses found in one industry, such as oils, chemicals, or electronics.

specialized mutual fund: a fund limiting its investments to a specific sector of the marketplace.

special lien bond: see *bond, special lien.*

special loan: a loan involving unusual collateral; consequently, a higher rate of interest is often required. Over-the-counter securities are usually classified in this category.

special miscellaneous account (SMA): a memorandum account of the funds in excess of the margin requirement. This account exists enabling the broker to determine how far the client might be from a margin call. All withdrawals require the broker's authorization.

special offering: occasionally a large block of stock that becomes available for sale requires special handling because of its size and the market in that particular issue. A notice is printed on the ticker tape announcing that the stock will be offered for sale on the exchange floor at a fixed price. Member firms may buy this stock for customers directly from the seller's broker during trading hours. The price is usually based on the last transaction in the regular auction market. Only the seller pays a commission on a special offering. Special offerings must be approved by the SEC.

special omnibus account: the title of an account with one broker-dealer opened by another broker-dealer registered with the SEC. In such an account, the second broker-dealer is able to transact for its clients without disclosing the names of the clients.

special partner: a partner in a financial organization whose liability is limited to the interest he or she has in the company and is not active in the management. see *general partner, limited partner, silent partner.*

special-purpose funds: mutual funds that invest exclusively in securities from one industry. see *investment company.*

special security: effective September 1981, banks and savings and loan associations are able to take the deposits resulting from their new tax-exempt savings certificates and reinvest the money in securities offered by the Federal National Mortgage Association. see *All-Saver certificates.*

special situation: usually describes a venture capital type of investment, but may also refer to a conservative but relatively unknown investment or to heavy commitments in investments which, in the opinion of the management, are temporarily undervalued by the market.

special subscription account: a margin account where a client obtains advantageous credit to acquire a margin security through the exercise of a right or a warrant.

special tax bond: see *bond, special tax.*

specialty (specialized) fund: an investment company concentrating its holdings in specific industry groups (insurance, oil, aviation stocks, etc.).

specialty stock: a security from a particular industry or grouping.

specific issue market: a subsector of the repurchase agreement market. A reverse repurchase agreement is made in respect of a specific security issue whose price is expected by the dealer to drop.

specific risk: uncertainty in the return of an asset that arises from events that are specific to that firm. It is unrelated or, at most, distantly related, to events that impact other firms.

spectail: a broker-dealer who is part retail broker but primarily dealer-speculator.

speculate: investing in securities with the expectation of making a profit over a relatively short period.

speculation: the employment of funds by a speculator. Safety of principal is a factor secondary to increasing capital. see *letter security.* cf. *defensive investment, digested securities.*

speculation indicator: an indicator that purports to measure the amount of risk that investors are willing to take.

speculative market: an organized exchange where speculative buying and selling regularly occurs.

speculative position: an open position held by a trader that is unhedged.

speculative purchasing: buying items when prices appear lowest, with the expectation that there will be a future price increase, making possible a profit.

speculative stocks: securities issued by relatively new firms of unproven financial status, etc., and by firms with less than average financial strength.

speculator: one who is willing to assume a relatively large risk in the hope of gain. His or her principal concern is to increase capital rather than dividend income. Speculators may buy and sell the same day, or may invest in enterprises they do not expect to be profitable for years.

spike: a sharp rise in price in a single day or two. May be as great as 15 to 30 percent indicating the time for an immediate sell signal.

spilling stock: disposing of securities out of necessity, throwing the stocks on the market for sale.

spinoff: with respect to federal income taxes, a transfer by a firm of a portion of its assets to a newly formed organization in exchange for the latter's capital stock, which is thereupon distributed as a property dividend to the stockholders of the initial corporation.

split: the division of the outstanding shares of a corporation into a larger number of shares. A 3-for-1 split by a company with 1 million shares outstanding would result in 3 million shares outstanding. Each holder of 100 shares before the 3-for-1 split would have 300 shares. Of course his or her proportionate equity in the company would remain the same, since 100 parts of 1 million is the equivalent of 300 parts of 3 million. Ordinarily, a split must be voted by directors and approved by shareholders. Such action by a corporation does not alter the total contributed capital but merely increases the number of shares issued and outstanding and the par value per share. cf. *stock split-down.*

split close: variations in price; for example, the Dow Jones shows a higher closing price for the industrial averages, but a lower closing price for the utility average.

split commission: sharing a comission with someone else who has assisted in procuring the business for the broker, agent, or counselor. see *giveup.*

split down: synonymous with *reverse split.*

split funding: a program which combines the purchase of mutual fund shares with the purchase of life insurance contracts or other products.

split funds: originated in Great Britain, mutual funds with two classes of stock, income shares and capital shares. All income of both classes is assigned to the income shares, and all the capital gains are assigned to the capital shares.

split investment company: a closed-end investment firm issuing two types of capital stock. The first (income shares) receives dividends from investments; the second (capital shares) receives dividends from the appreciation of investments. synonymous with *dual-purpose fund.*

split-off: the exchange of stock by the shareholders of a parent (controlling) corporation in return for stock in a subsidiary corporation. cf. *spinoff.*

split offering: a new municipal bond issue, a portion of which is represented by serial bonds and part by term maturity bonds.

split opening: a situation where a security or commodity has simultaneous opening prices which are spread or different. This occurs when a number of traders at a trading post break up into groups and the sales occur in two groups at the same time but at differing prices.

split order: a large order that is separated into smaller units that are sold over a period of time. When purchasing or selling a security or commodity, a very large transaction could cause substantial price fluctuation which splitting may prevent.

split quotation: a quotation expressed in a different unit than the adopted standard quotation (e.g., a quote at $1/16$ of a point).

split rating: a condition where two major rating agencies give a different rating to the same stock.

split-schedule loan: a mortgage that establishes interest for only a few years and then a complete amortization schedule. The loan is usually accomplished through split amortization schedules on the loan.

split stock: new outstanding securities of a corporation resulting from a stock split.

split-up: the issuance of two or more stock shares replacing each outstanding share, used for financial and tax purposes. This increase, although lowering the value per share, does not alter the total liability of the issuing firm for the outstanding capital stock. see *split.*

Sp. Off.: see *special offering.*

sponsor

(1) ***securities:*** an important investor; usually an institution, mutual fund, or larger trader, whose positive attitude toward a specific security influences other investors and generates further demand for the stock.

(2) ***mutual fund:*** an investment company that offers shares in its funds. cf. *underwriter.*

(3) ***limited partnership:*** a general partner that organizes and sells a limited partnership.

sponsorship: the banking institution holding an interest in the selling price of a specific securities issue.

spot: a characteristic of being available for immediate (or nearly immediate) delivery. Refers to a cash market price for stocks of the physical commodity that are available for immediate delivery, or conversely and depending upon the noun it modifies, the stock themselves that are available for delivery if transactions are usually grouped into two kinds—spot and forward contracts. Sometimes used in reference to the futures contract of the current month, in which case trading is still "futures" trading but delivery is possible at any time.

spot delivery: see *immediate delivery.*

spot delivery month: the nearest delivery month among all those traded at any point in time. The actual contract month represented by the spot delivery month is constantly changing throughout the calendar year as each contract month reaches its last trading day.

spot exchange rate: the price of one country's currency in terms of another country's currency that is effective for immediate (today) delivery.

spot/fortnight: see *spot/next.*

spot market: a market where commodities are sold for cash and quickly delivered. see *fixing the price.* synonymous with *actual market, cash market, physical market.*

spot month: see *spot delivery month.*

spot news: any type of sudden news or condition that can temporarily impact on the general market action.

spot/next: a purchase of currency on Monday for settlement on Thursday is transacted at the exchange rate for spot delivery plus an adustment for the extra day. The adjustment is referred to as the *spot/next. Spot/week* refers to delivery a week after spot; *spot/fortnight* refers to delivery a fortnight after spot.

spot price: synonymous with *cash price.*

spot sale: the sale of a product for cash and current delivery rather than for at a future date.

spot secondary: a secondary offering of a bond or security that is being sold without an effective registration statement.

spotted market: a market condition characterized by small price movement either upward or downward and no general price trend or movement is observable.

spot trading: cash sales for immediate delivery.

spot/week: see *spot/next.*

spousal IRA: an IRA designed for the nonworking spouse of a couple with one wage earner. The maximum amount the family can save annually rises to $2250. Rules also permit a nonworking divorced wife to contribute to a spousal IRA after divorce.

spousal remainder trust: a method for shifting income-earning assets to an individual who is taxed at a lower rate.

SPP: see *stock purchase plan.*

SPQR: small profits, quick returns.

spread

(1) ***general:*** two prices given instead of one.

(2) ***general:*** the difference between two prices.

(3) ***investments:*** two different options, a put (price below the prevailing market), and a call (price above the prevailing market), with both options pertaining to the same stock and expiring on the same day. Thus the trader is guaranteed a sale not lower than the put price if the market drops and a buy at a price not higher than the call price if the market increases. see also *butterfly spread, straddle.*

(4) ***securities:*** the differences between the bid and asked prices of securities. synonymous with *double option.*

(5) ***commodities:*** in futures trading, the difference between delivery months in the same or different markets.

(6) ***fixed-income securities:*** the difference between yields on securities of the same quality but different maturities, or the difference between yields on securities of the same maturity but different quality.

(7) ***arbitrage:*** a larger-than-normal difference in currency exchange rates between two markets.

(8) ***underwriting:*** the difference between the proceeds an issuer of a new stock receives and the price paid by the public for the issue. The spread is taken by the underwriting syndicate as payment for its services.

spreading: purchasing and selling option contracts of the same class on the same underlying stock so as to profit from shifts in the price of that security.

spread loan: in contractual-type mutual funds where the principal part of the sales charge is paid over the first four years of the contract, with the remainder of the sales charge paid in equal installments over the remainder of the contract.

spread option: a spread position of the purchase of an option at one exercise price and the simultaneous sale of another option on the same underlying stock at a different exercise price and/or expiration date.

spread order: an option order indicating the series of listed options the client wants to buy and sell, along with the desired spread, or difference in option premiums, shown as a net debit or net credit. The transaction is completed should the floor broker execute the order at the requested spread.

spread position: the status of an account in which a spread has been executed.

SPRL: Société de Personnes à Responsabilité Limitée (Belgian corporation).

SPS: see *second preferred stocks.*

spurt: any short, but considerable climb in prices.

square: a position in a currency, security, or commodity which is balanced (i.e., neither long nor short).

Square Mile, the: see *City.*

squeeze

(1) ***general:*** when interest rates are high and money is difficult to borrow.

(2) ***investments:*** results when people who have sold stocks short in a climbing market are obligated to buy back their securities at a loss in order to fulfill their short-selling contract obligations. see *short covering, short sale.*

Sr.: senior.

SRO: self-regulatory organization. The primary method anticipated by the SEC for the enforcement of fair, ethical, and efficient practices in the securities and commodities futures industries. SROs include all national securities and commodities exchanges, the National Association of Securities Dealers, and the Municipal Securities Rulemaking Board. Rules made by MSRB are subject to approval by the SEC and are enforced by the National Association of Securities Dealers and bank regulatory agencies.

SRP: see *salary reduction plan.*

SRT: see *spousal remainder trust.*

SS

(1) see *selling short.*
(2) see *senior securities.*
(3) see *short sale.*
(4) see *shrinking stocks.*

SSD: see *stock split-down.*

ST

(1) see *sales tax.*
(2) see *stamped security.*
(3) see *stock transfer.*
(4) stopped. On the consolidated tape, showing that an execution on the floor was at a guaranteed price, it was "stopped" by the specialist or by another member.

stabilization

(1) ***securities:*** action by registered competitive traders on the NYSE complying with exchange requirements that 75 percent of their trades are stabilizing, that their sell orders follow a plus tick and their buy

orders a minus tick. see *down tick, up tick.*

(2) ***currency:*** purchasing and selling of a nation's own currency to protect its exchange value.

(3) ***underwriting:*** intervention by a managing underwriter so as to prevent the market price from dropping below the public offering price during the offering period. The underwriter places orders to purchase at a given price, that in any other situation would be a violation of the law suggestive of manipulation by the SEC.

stabilizing bid: a bid price offered by underwriters of a new stock offering to sustain the market price of a stock immediately after a public offering.

stag: an individual speculator who rapidly buys and then sells shares for profit, having had no intention of retaining the securities for any length of time. cf. *digested securities.*

staggered board amendment: a firm's ruling adopting two, three, and four-year terms for its directors to prolong any change in control. see also *blank-check tactic.*

staggered board of director: the board of directors of a firm where a percentage of the directors are elected each year. This process of staggering is intended to minimize attempts of an unfriendly takeover attempt.

staggering maturities: a method used to lower risk by a bond investor. Investors hedge against interest rate movements by purchasing short-, medium- and long-term bonds. Should interest rates drop, the long-term bonds will climb faster in value than the shorter-term bonds. Should rates climb however, the shorter-term bonds will hold their value better than the long-term debt obligations, which could fall precipitously.

stagnation

(1) ***general:*** a condition of minimal growth rate, or growth increasing at a rate lower than expected.

(2) ***securities:*** a period of low volume and inactive trading.

stamped bond: see *bond, stamped.*

stamped security: a stock that has been stamped to show any alteration made on it since it was first released—for example, a change in the date of maturity.

stamp tax: a government tax collected through the sale of stamps that are affixed to certain products (e.g., liquor, tobacco, stock certificates, or title deeds). see *transfer tax.*

Standard & Poor's Corporation (S&P): a subsidiary of McGraw-Hill, Inc. that provides numerous investor services, including rating bonds, common stocks, preferred stocks, and commercial paper. see also *Standard & Poor's 500-Composite-Stock Index.*

Standard & Poor's Corporation Records: see *tear sheet.*

Standard & Poor's 500-Composite-Stock Index: an index of stock prices composed of 400 industrials, 40 utilities, 40 financial firms, and 25 transportations. cf. *Dow Jones averages.*

Standard & Poor's rating: the classification of stocks and bonds according to risk. S&P's top four investment grades are: AAA, AA, A, and BBB indicating minimal risk that a bond issue will default. Stocks or bonds rated BB or lower are rated by S&P as speculative. Fiduciaries are not permitted to invest in them.

standardized expiration dates: options issued by the OCC have fixed expiration dates that run in three month cycles. Three expiration cycles exist. See *expiration cycle.*

standard stocks: securities of established and well-known firms.

standard underwriting: the purchase pursuant to agreement by investment banking firms of the unsold portion of an issue offered by the issuing company directly to its own security holders or some other restricted group.

standby offering: an offering of rights by a firm where an underwriter offers to stand-by to purchase any of the rights the firm is unable to sell.

standby underwriter: an investment banker who agrees to buy, at a price below the subscription price, any shares remaining unsubscribed after they have been offered to current shareholders through a rights offering.

STANY: Security Traders' Association of New York.

stapled stock: synonymous with *paired shares.*

start-up: any new business venture. The earliest stage at which a venture capital investor or investment pool will provide funds to an enterprise, often on the basis of a business plan containing the background of management and market and financial projections.

state bond: see *bond, state.*

stated capital: the sum of capital amounts contributed by stockholders.

stated value: the given value of a firm's stock for accounting purposes in lieu of par value. This value of stock has no relation to its market price. It is the amount per share that is credited to the capital stock account for each share outstanding and is thereby the legal capital of the corporation.

statement

(1) a summary of transactions between a creditor and his or her debts or a presentation of names and amounts of accounts to show a financial condition (e.g., an IRS statement).

(2) a summary for clients of the transaction that occurred over the preceding month; gives all stock, bond, commodity futures, or options trades, interest and dividends received, margin debt outstanding, and other transactions, in addition to a summary of the worth of the accounts for the month.

(3) a statement showing the status of a business' assets and liabilities and the results of their activities as of a given date.

statement analysis: applying such ratios as a current ratio, turnover ratio, and other accounting and credit measuring the devices for the purpose of reaching a decision on the outlook of a firm or security.

statement disclaiming: a choice from an accounting firm that audits financial reports of public companies disclaiming any opinion about the firm's financial condition. see also *clean opinion, except for opinion, subject to opinion.*

statement of changes in financial position: a report summarizing the flow of funds within an organization during a designated period of time. The statement should disclose aspects of the organization's financing and investing activities regardless of whether cash or other elements of working capital are directly affected.

statement of income: see *profit and loss statement.*

statement of policy (SOP): a guide issued by the SEC to assist issuers, underwriters, dealers, and salespersons in complying with statutory disclosure standards as applied to sales literature, reports to shareholders, and other communications "addressed to or intended for distribution to prospective investors."

statement savings: a savings account in which a periodic statement replaces the passbook.

statement savings account: a savings account for which the customer records his or her own balance and transactions information. A periodic balance statement is received from the bank. The balance statement is reconciled to the customer's records.

station
(1) ***general:*** a worker's assigned post or place of activity.
(2) ***investments:*** the place where a specialist on an exchange transacts orders.

statutory investment: an investment which a trustee is specifically authorized to make under the terms of the statutes of the state having jurisdiction of the trust.

statutory merger: the legal combination of two or more corporations where only one survives as a legal entity.

statutory prospectus: see *prospectus.*

statutory underwriter: an individual who performs the purchase of a security from an issuer for purpose of resale inadvertently, and subjects himself or herself to the penalties of the law for those who sell unregistered securities.

statutory voting: a stockholder voting technique where each stockholder is granted one vote for each share of security held for each director to be chosen. The shareholder can not give more than that number of votes to any one nominee. cf. *cumulative voting.*

staying power: an investor's capability for staying with (not selling) an investment that has dropped in value.

STB: special tax bond. see *bond, special tax.*

steady: showing that market prices are barely moving in any direction.

steenth: one sixteenth, as used in bids and offers quoted in 16ths.

stepped costs: costs that climb by increments with increased volumes of activity.

sterile investments: metal investments which carry no dividends, no interest, and where storage and insurance has to be paid.

sterilization: permanently attaching excess dollars to nonmarketable U.S. Treasury securities at a guaranteed market rate of interest. Under this concept, the risk will be reduced so that more dollars will be offered than purchasers are willing to buy.

sterilize: see *sterilization*

sterling bond: see *bond, sterling.*

sticky deal: a new securities issue that an underwriter believes will be difficult to sell. Consequently, the price may be lowered or the offering withdrawn from the market.

sticky prices: prices that do not change readily. The opposite is *flexible prices.*

Stk.: see *stock.*

Stk. Ex.: see *stock exchanges.*

stock: the legal capital of a corporation divided into shares. see *assented securities, authorized stock, blue chip, callable, capital stock, common stock, convertible, cumulative preferred (stock), deferred stock, face value, float, growth stock, guaranteed stock, inactive stock (bond), issue, listed securities (stocks), nonassessable stock, noncumulative, no-par-value stock, ordinary stock, outstanding, over the counter, paid-up stock, participating preferred, penny stocks, preferred stock, redeemable stock, treasury stock, unissued stock, voting right (stock), watered stock.*

stock ahead: describing a situation when an investor who has entered an order to buy or sell a stock at a certain price sees transactions at that price reported on the ticker tape before his or her own order has been executed. This may have occurred because other buy and sell orders at the same price came in to a trading specialist earlier and had priority.

stock allotment: the quantity of stock set aside by the manager of an underwriting syndicate as the portion for a member of the syndicate to distribute.

stock-appreciation rights (SARs): privileges that can be attached to a nonqualified option. With an SAR, an executive can ignore the option and take a bonus equal to the value of the stock's appreciation over a span of time. An SEC rule premits an SAR bonus to be paid in cash, rather than in company shares. The SAR can be acted on at any time during the 10-year term of the attached nonqualified stock option.

stock assessment: a levy made upon a stockholder to make up a capital deficiency created by adverse economic developments in the corporation's activities.

stock association: a savings association organized as a capital stock corporation, with investors providing operating capital by purchasing an ownership interest in the institution, represented by shares of stock. Their stock holdings entitle them to virtually the same rights as stockholders in any other corporation, including a share of the profits. Stock associations operate in 23 states.

stock-bonus trust: a trust established by a corporation to enable its employees to receive benefits in the form of the corporation's own stock as a reward for meritorious service or as a means of sharing in the profits of the enterprise.

stock borrowed: securities borrowed by one broker from another to result in delivery. These stocks are subject to going interest and premium rates. see *short sale.*

stockbroker: an individual who acts as a middleman between buyers and sellers of stock. cf. *specialist.*

stock business: in municipal bond underwriting when a dealer or a dealer bank purchases part of a municipal issue for its own account to make short-term profits by a later resale of the bonds.

stock certificate: written evidence of ownership of a company's shares, indicating the number of shares registered in the name of the owner, the corporation issuing the capital stock, and whether the stock is a par value or a non-par-value stock.

stock certificate book: a book of blank stock certificates.

stock charts: see *charting.*

stock clearing agency: an organization that periodically balances and clears accounts among trading members of an exchange, settles their debit cash balances, and aids them in distributing stocks and other securities which were bought and sold. see *Stock Clearing Corporation.*

Stock Clearing Corporation (SCC): the New York Stock Exchange's clearinghouse. Major responsibilities include the clearing and settling of money balances between members, the clearing of purchases and sales transaction, and the delivery of stock.

stock company: a company in which stockholders contribute all the capital, pay all the losses, and share in the profits.

stock dilution: see *dilution.*

stock discount: the excess of par value of a stock over the paid-in capital.

stock dividend: a portion of the net earnings of a corporation payable (in shares of fractional shares of designated stock of a given corporation) to the stockholders of record of the corporation. It is paid in securities rather than cash, and it may be additional shares of the issuing company or shares of another company held by the corporation.

stock exchanges: organizations that provide a market for the trading of bonds and stocks. Regulations for the admission of securities for trading on the stock exchanges are very stringent. see also *securities and commodities exchanges.*

stock exchange seat: a membership in a stock exchange.

stockholder (SH): the legal owner of at least one share of a security in a corporation. synonymous with *shareholder, shareowner.*

stockholder of record: a stockholder whose name is registered on the books of the issuing corporation. see *voting right (stock).*

stockholder proposal: a proposal from a shareholder, who may or may not be an officer, which is brought before other shareholders at their annual meeting.

stockholders annual report: the report compiled annually for stockholders showing financial position and progress during the fiscal year.

stockholder's equity: synonymous with *shareholder's equity.*

stockholder's ledger: a subsidiary ledger containing detailed data about the stock owned by each stockholder.

stockholders' list: a list of stockholders of a corporation entitled to vote in the affairs of the corporation. Each name appears alphabetically with corresponding address and the number of shares owned.

stockholder's meeting: synonymous with *annual meeting.*

stock indexes and averages: indicators for measuring and reporting value changes in representative stock groupings.

stock index future: a security that combines features of traditional commodity futures trading with securities trading employing composite stock indexes. Investors can speculate on general market performance or purchase an index future contract to hedge a long position or short position against a drop in value. see also *OTC stock-index futures.* cf. *stock index options.*

stock index options: similar to traditional options to buy or sell individual stocks with one exception. It is impractical for an option holder to exercise his or her right to sell or buy a whole basket of securities. Therefore, any profit or loss is settled in cash. cf. *interest rate option, stock index future.*

stock insurance company: an insurance company with stockholders who get the profit or suffer the loss of the insurance business rather than having the gain or loss distributed among the people insured.

stock-in-trade

(1) ***general:*** equipment used to carry on a trade or business; by extension, the usual activity of a trade or business.

(2) ***investments:*** the quantity of securities held.

stock jobber: an English term for commission broker. In England, the stock jobber sells to the public and buys from a floor trader.

stock jobbing: irresponsible or dishonest manipulation of the price of securities.

stock list: a responsibility of an organized exchange that is concerned with listing requirements and related investigations, the eligibility of unlisted firms for trading privileges, and the delisting of firms that have not met exchange regulations and listing requirements.

stock loan: synonymous with *securities loan.*

stock market: the buying and selling of stock for the purpose of profit for both buyers and sellers of the security. see *market.*

stock option: an arrangement for compensating top management, in addition to salary, with an opportunity to buy a certain amount of company stock, often under the market price. see *Tax Reform Act of 1976.*

stock option contract: a negotiable instrument that provides the purchaser the right to buy (call) or sell (put) the number of shares of stock designated in the contract at a fixed price within a stated period of time. synonymous with *paper.*

stock power: a power of attorney permitting a person other than the owner of stock to legally transfer the title of ownership to a third party. Stock powers are usually given when stock is pledged as collateral to loans.

stock pricing: stock prices quoted in whole digits and fractional amounts.

stock purchase plan: a company plan for the purchase of stock by employees, with or without a contribution from the employer at terms usually below the market price.

stock purchase trust: a trust under which a surviving stockholder of a closed corporation can purchase the stock of a deceased stockholder; usually, but not necessarily, as an insurance trust.

stock quotation: the price of a stock, usually given in terms of a round lot and expressed in eighths or units of $12\frac{1}{2}$ cents.

stock quotation instrument: the original name for the *stock ticker.*

stock rating: a means for evaluating the financial status and management effectiveness of a firm issuing equity stocks.

stock record: control, traditionally in the form of a ledger card or computer report, used by brokerage houses to keep track of stocks held in inventory and their exact location within the house.

stock registrar: a bank, financial institution, or person permitted to serve in a fiduciary position, to certify that a corporation's issued shares have not exceeded the approved amount.

stock repurchase agreement: an agreement by a corporation at the time the stock is issued to repurchase the stock on demand. Particularly used in the utility field for sales to employees or customers. Also used as an incentive which allows employees to own the stock during the period of employment but requires them to resell the stock to the employers upon termination of employment.

stock rights: shareholder's privileges to buy shares of a new issue of a corporation's stock at a stipulated price, in quantities limited to a proportion of their existing holdings. These rights are usually defined by an instrument known as a *stock warrant.*

stock screening: defining investment goals, such as high yields, strong earnings growth, using a computer to search through all the stocks in a database to find issues that meet the criteria.

stock split: see *split.*

stock split-down: the reverse of stock split; the total number of shares outstanding is lowered without reducing the total value of the issue, by issuing a new stock share to replace each of two or more shares presently in circulation. The motivation is to increase the market price of a stock. synonymous with *reverse stock split.*

stock subscription: an agreement to purchase the stock of a corporation from the corporation.

stock symbol: letters for identifying listed firms on the securities exchanges on which they trade. These symbols are called trading symbols, identifying trades on the consolidated tape and are used in reports.

stock tables: figures in the financial sections of papers that report market information. Usually contains high and low price for the year, high, low, and closing price for the day of trading, and change from the close of the previous day.

stock ticker: a device that was used for printing stock trading information on a continuous narrow tape within seconds following transaction on the exchange floor.

stock transfer: the act of canceling a stock certificate submitted for transfer, issuing a new certificate in the name of the designated transferee, and recording the change in ownership on the records of a corporation's stock transfer book. see *stock-transfer tax.*

stock-transfer agent: the agent of a corporation appointed for the purpose of effecting transfers of stock from one stockholder to another by the actual cancellation of the surrendered certificates and the issuance of new certificates in the name of the new stockholder.

stock transfer book: a special journal used to record transfers of securities. Its entries are posted to the stockholders' ledger.

stock-transfer tax: a tax levied by some states on the transfer of securities from one owner to another, either when purchased or given as a gift. see *stock transfer.*

stock trust certificate: issued in exchange for stock of competing firms entering the trust form of combination, deposited with trustees, who issue in exchange trust certificates under the deposit agreement, and who control the firm's activities by reason of their power. synonymous with *trust certificate.*

stock turnover: see *turnover.*

stock warrant: the document evidencing a stock right. see also *stock rights.*

stock watcher (NYSE): a computerized service for monitoring all trading and movement in NYSE listed stocks; used for identifying any unusual activity due to rumors, manipulation or other illegal practices.

stock watering: see *watered stock.*

stock yield: the rate of return on a stock based upon its market value as of a particular date and the dividend being currently paid by the company.

stop: the lowest rate the central bank charges dealers who temporarily tender their government securities for cash in these operations.

stop limit order: a stop order that becomes a limit order after the specified stop price has been reached. see *limited order, stop order.*

stop loss order
(1) ***insurance:*** a guarantee from one company (the reinsurer) to another (the reinsured) that losses over and above an agreed upon amount will be paid by the reinsuring company.
(2) ***securities:*** a client order to a broker that sets the sell price of a stock below the current market price; used to protect profits that have already been made, or to prevent further losses should the security decline. see also *stop order.*

stop order: an order to buy at a price above or sell at a price below the current market. Stop buy orders are generally used to limit loss or to protect unrealized profits on a short sale. Stop sell orders are generally used to protect unrealized profits or to limit loss on a holding. A stop order becomes a market order when the stock sells at or beyond the specified price and thus may not necessarily be executed at that price.

stop-out price: the lowest accepted price for Treasury bills at the regular weekly auction.

stopped at: a price for a security that is often guaranteed to a purchaser or a seller by the specialist in it.

stopped out: when a client's order is executed under a stop order at the price predetermined by the client.

stopped security: an order temporarily guaranteed in price to a member by a specialist. The service permits the member a short time to seek a more advantageous price, while being certain that the price quoted by the specialist will not rise. Should no better be found the member can take the guaranteed price from the specialist. synonymous with *stopping stock.*

stopping stock: synonymous with *stopped security.*

stop price: the price at which a customer's stop order to their broker becomes a market order.

story: a compelling reason for purchasing a particular security. Story securities are often from firms with a unique product or service that is difficult for competitors to copy.

straddle
(1) the purchase or sale of an equivalent number of puts and calls on a given underlying stock with the same exercise price and expiration date.
(2) an option allowing the trader to buy or sell securities at an agreed-upon price within a given period. see

also *butterfly spread, spread.* synonymous with *double option.*

straight: a bond with unquestioned right to repayment of principal at a specified future date, unquestioned right to set interest payments on given dates, and no right to any additional interest, principal, or conversion privilege.

straight investment: a preferred stock or bond, limited in interest or dividend rate, that is bought because of its income return and not for expectation of any rise in value. see *investment.*

straight life: synonymous with *ordinary life.*

straight-line depreciation: the simplest method of depreciation. Amortization of capital cost in uniform periodic amounts over the anticipated life of the asset.

straight-line interest: a method of computing interest payments which takes a straight percentage of the unpaid balance on an annual basis.

straight mortgage: a mortgage under which the borrower is obligated to pay interest during the term of the mortgage with the full amount of the principal to become due at the end of the mortgage term.

straight serial bond: see *bond, straight serial.*

straight-term mortgage loan: a mortgage loan granted for a fixed term of years, the entire loan becoming due at the end of that time.

strap: a stock option contract made up of two calls and one put. synonymous with *triple option.* see *strip.*

strategic resource monopoly: an organization having a monopoly by virtue of controlling a vital input to a production process (e.g., DeBeers of South Africa owns most of the world's diamond mines).

strategics: slang, for investments made in precious metals, including; for example, chromium, manganese, germanium, titanium, nickel, and cobalt.

Street: the New York financial community; the lower Manhattan (i.e., Wall Street) area.

street broker: an over-the-counter broker, as distinguished from a broker who is a member of an exchange.

street certificate: a stock certificate with a blank indorsement by an owner whose signature is guaranteed so that the stock can be transferred by delivery without the formality of transfer on the books of the corporation.

street name: any stock certificate in the name of a broker who trades in securities and is a member of an exchange is said to be in *street name.* This stock is never considered to be part of the broker's personal wealth.

street practice: any unwritten practice used by the financial community.

street price: in securities trading, the price for a stock delivered outside the stock exchange process.

stretching the payables: deferring payments on accounts payable beyond the due date.

strike from the list: occurs when a stock exchange prevents, by canceling, any transactions in that particular stock. The stock is suspended. see *delist.*

strike suit: in corporation finance, designating a law suit by a minority stockholder whose main purpose is to be bought out (at a high price) by the management in order to get rid of his or her objections.

striking price: synonymous with *exercise price.*

stringency: a money market condition in which it is hard to obtain credit, accompanied by an increase in the rates of interest.

strip
(1) ***options:*** a stock option contract made up of two puts and one call. see *strap.*
(2) ***bonds:*** to remove the coupons from a bond and sell the principal of the bond separately from the coupons.
(3) ***securities:*** to purchase securities with the expectation of collecting their dividends. synonymous with *dividend stripping.*

strip bond: see *bond, strip.*

stripped securities: any of Treasury bills, bonds, or notes having principal certificates and interest coupons sold separately.

stripped Treasury obligations: an artificial equivalent of zero-coupon bonds, featuring Treasury issues, with the safety of government debt. Represents a call on interest payments of U.S. government obligations, with maturities from three months to 29 years.

"strips": see *bond, strip.*

strong (or weak) hands: holders of securities held for investment purposes over a period of time are *strong hands. Weak hands* include investors who will sell at the slightest chance of profit or sell out during reactions, and include the general public, traders, and other speculators.

strong market: a greater demand for purchasing than there is for selling.

Student Loan Marketing Association (SLMA): a government-sponsored private corporation created to increase the flow of funds into student loans in the secondary market; commonly called *Sallie Mae.*

subchapter M: the sections of the Internal Revenue Code which provide special tax treatment for organizations known as *regulated investment companies.*

Subchapter S corporation: an election available to a corporation to be treated as a partnership for income tax purposes. To be eligible to make the election, a corporation must meet certain requirements as to kind and number of shareholders, classes of stock, and sources of income.

subject bid: a bid that is negotiable, rather than firm.

subject market: the quotation that a broker-dealer can not trade until he or she is able to confirm the acceptability of the bid and asked prices with the party represented.

subject offer: an offer that is not firm but instead exploratory, in the expectation that it might induce a bid permitting additional negotiation on price.

subject quote: see *subject offer.*

subject to confirmation
(1) a price quotation that is not firm.
(2) a word for potential buyers that all securities have provisionally been sold but that depending on subsequent availability, the buyer's order may be filled.

subject to opinion: an auditor's choice when auditing financial reports of public companies in which the auditor certifies that the financial statements fairly present the firm's results, but are *subject to* certain adjustments. see also *clean opinion, except for opinion, statement disclaiming.*

subject to prior sale: a condition existing when, because the market is strong and the supply of securities is limited, there may be more buy orders than stock. At times such a statement may serve as a stimulant for submitting early bids.

subject to redemption: stocks that can be called (redeemed) with advance notice to the shareholders.

subject to sale: when property has been offered for sale, a "subject to sale" stipulation provides for the automatic withdrawal of the offer if the property is sold before the party to whom the stipulation was made has accepted the offer.

submission: a mortgage banker's offering of mortgages for purchase by an investor.

submittal notice: a broker's notification to a property owner stating that the owner's property has been offered for sale; offering price and prospect's name and address are included.

submortgage: the result of a pledge by a lender of a mortgage in his or her possession as collateral to obtain a loan for himself or herself.

subordinated: a promise to pay which cannot legally be fulfilled until payments on certain other obigations have been made and any other conditions, defined in the indenture, are met.

subordinated debenture: a special debenture whose bearer has a chance for payment lower than that for other creditors. As it holds a higher yield, it is considered a risky bond.

subordinated exchangable variable-rate note: a note permitting a corporation to borrow at lower, short-term rates but guarantees access to capital for a longer period of time. The interest rate typically floats for five years, then becomes fixed for five years. At the end of any quarter in the first five years, the company can exchange the variable notes for those with a fixed rate of interest based on Treasury rates.

subordinated interest: an interest in property that is inferior to another interest (e.g., a second mortgage that is inferior to the first mortgage).

subordinated securities: securities whose asset claims are secondary to claims of specified superior securities.

subscribed capital: the total capital stock contracted for. When paid for, it becomes *paid-in capital.*

subscriber: one who agrees in writing to purchase a certain offering—for example, a certain number of shares of designated stock of a given corporation or a certain number of bonds of a given stipulated face value.

subscription: an agreement to purchase a security; a solicitation of subscribers.

subscription capital: funds received by the issuer from a public offering of stocks.

subscription cash record: a memorandum cash record of down payments and installment payments received from subscribers to capital stock.

subscription list: a subscriber signed agreement showing the amount of stock that each subscriber has agreed to buy.

subscription price: fixed asking price per share at which an issue of stocks is offered to the buying public. During the offering the price is set and will not fluctuate.

subscription privilege: a right, usually from 30 to 60 days, permitting a common shareholder to purchase, on a pro rata basis, newly issued shares at a favorable price before the shares are offered to the public. synonymous with *preemptive right.*

subscription ratio: see *subscription rights.*

subscription rights: a privilege to the stockholders of a corporation to purchase proportionate amounts of a new issue of securities, at an established price, usually below the current market price; also, the negotiable certificate evidencing such privilege.

subscriptions receivable: a current asset account showing the amount to be collected from subscribers to capital stock in a corporation.

subscription warrant: a type of stock, often issued together with a bond or preferred stock, entitling the holder to purchase a proportionate amount of common stock at a given price, usually higher than the market price at the time of issuance, for a period of years or to perpetuity.

subsidiary: any organization more than 50 percent of whose voting stock is owned by another firm. synonymous with *underlying company.*

subsidiary coins: coins with a denomination of less than one dollar, including minor coins such as pennies or cents.

subsidiary firm: a business whose activities are subject to the control of another company.

substantive: the term interest or term matter indicating a proposed corporate action that may affect stockholders or facts that will influence investor action.

substitution of collateral: exchanging or replacing one portion of collateral, such as a block of stock, with another block of stock or notes.

suitability: used when investment recommendations are appropriate and fulfills the investment goals of the customer taking into consideration the financial capability, temperament and other holdings of the customer.

suitability rules: guidelines for those selling sophisticated and risky financial products, such as limited partnerships or commodities futures contracts, must follow to ensure that investors have the financial means to assume the risks involved. These rules require that the investor have a certain level of net worth and liquid assets. A brokerage house can be sued if it permitted an unsuitable investor to purchase an investment that goes bad. see also *know your customer rule.*

summary complaint proceedings: under NASD's code of procedure, the Business Conduct Committee can allow a respondent in a trade practice complaint to plead guilty to relatively minor infractions of their rules with a resulting censure and a fine of $1000. No appeal is permitted.

sunrise industries: high-risk ventures in advanced technology with promising potential for growth and export.

super NOW account: a deregulated transaction account authorized for depository institutions in 1982. Such accounts, with a minimum balance requirement of $2500, paid an interest rate higher than on the conventional NOW accounts, but slightly less than on the money market deposit account. The super NOW minimum balance was reduced to $1000 in January 1985; on January 1, 1986 the statutory minimum disappeared.

superprime instrument: a 10-day, nonrenewable note priced only a fraction above what a bank itself pays for funds.

superrestricted account: originally applied to margin accounts that were margined at less than 30 percent of the market value of the securities in the account. Term dropped from Regulation T in 1982.

superseded suretyship rider: a continuity of coverage clause in the form of a rider attached to a new fidelity bond, taking the place of another bond and agreeing to pay the loss that would be recoverable under the first bond except that the discovery period has expired. Losses caused by dishonest employees frequently have been found to have occurred at various times stretching over a period of years. This may involve a chain of several bonds, each one superseding a prior obligation. These losses will be covered if the chain of bonds is unbroken and each has included the superseded suretyship rider.

super sinker bond: see *bond, super sinker.*

superstock: a security that will multiply at least several times in value.

super trusts: foundations which have been created regionally for the purpose of providing a conduit through which union-related employee benefit monies can be recycled to provide interim and permanent financing for construction projects, which will be built predominantly with union labor.

supervisory analyst: a member firm research analyst who has passed a NYSE examination and is now qualified to approve publicly distributed research reports.

supply: the number of shares offered for sale at a specific time.

supply and demand indicator: a market indicator purporting to measure the flow of funds into or out of the markets or groups of securities.

supply area: the price area on a security or market average chart indicating a resistance level, or a place where earlier advances have been extinguished.

supply-side economics: a concept that shifts the emphasis from aggregate demand economics (which Keynes considered the most important economic variable) to investment and production. It lays great stress on the repressive role of taxes, and it leads logically to a strong endorsement of tax cuts designed to encourage investment.

support: synonymous with *support level.*

support area: synonymous with *support level.*

supporting orders: orders entered to support the price of a specific security.

supporting schedules: additional lists of facts or financial reports used with a balance sheet or profit and loss statement as supplementary reports.

supporting the market: placing purchasing orders at or somewhat below the prevailing market level for the purpose of maintaining and balancing existing prices and to encourage a price rise.

support level: the point at which the decline in price of a specific security appears to be repeatedly arrested due to more substantial buying than selling. synonymous with *support, support area.* cf. *resistance level.*

surety

(1) ***investments:*** a bond, guaranty, or other security that protects a person, corporation, or other legal entity in cases of another's default in the payment of a given obligation, improper performance of a given contract, malfeasance of office, and so on.

(2) ***law:*** an individual who agrees, usually in writing, to be responsible for the performance of another on a contract, or for a certain debt or debts of another individual.

surplus: see *retained earnings.*

surplus equity: the amount of difference between the market value of securities and the amount required to satisfy margin requirements of a brokerage account.

surplus fund: see *guaranty fund.*

surplus reserves: an amount of surplus or net worth set up as a reserve to indicate that it is considered not available for withdrawal in dividends.

surrender value (cash surrender value): designating the amount of the total life insurance in force that will be paid to the policyholder after a certain stipulated number of premiums have been paid, if the policyholder elects to surrender the policy and receive such proportionate part. The cash surrender value of a policy is also the amount used to determine how much will be loaned against the policy.

surtax: the extra tax applied to corporations when their net taxable income has exceeded a certain amount. For example, a surtax is demanded at the rate of 26 percent for all corporate income over $25,000. see *Tax Reform Act of 1969.*

surveillance department of exchanges: a unit of any stock exchange that monitors for unusual trading activity in stocks, which may be a tipoff to an illegal activity. They work in cooperation with the SEC in investigating misconduct. see also *stock watcher.*

survivorship annuity: see *annuity, survivorship.*

suspended market order: synonymous with *buy stop order.*

suspense account: the record held by a broker-dealer for money or security balance differences until such time as they are reconciled.

suspension

(1) ***general:*** the disciplinary layoff of a worker without pay.

(2) ***general:*** a temporary closing of a bank.

(3) ***investments:*** a decision made by a stock exchange board of directors prohibiting a securities firm or broker from conducting business for a period. see *under the rule.*

swap: the simultaneous purchase and sale of a currency for different maturity dates that closes the gaps in the maturity structure of assets and liabilities in a currency.

swap fund: a fund into which many investors put their own investments and receive a share in the pooled investment portfolio. The purpose of this exchange of investments is to obtain a diversified portfolio without selling stock and paying capital gains taxes.

swap order: see *contingent order.*

swapping: involves the sale of a depressed security to register a loss, and the simultaneous purchase of a similar security to retain virtually the same market position. This paper loss is then used to shelter income from taxation.

sweep account: a central assets account feature, the transferring of available cash into interest-bearing accounts, usually some type of money-market mutual fund. synonymous with *overflow account.*

sweetener: a feature added to a security issue as an inducement to its purchase, such as the right to convert a bond issue for common-stock shares. synonymous with *kicker.*

sweetening a loan: slang, to add more securities on deposit to margin a loan following the drop in security values so as to maintain the margin or to improve the condition of the margin.

SWIFT: see *Society for Worldwide Interbank Financial Telecommunications.*

swimming market: a healthy, active market.

swindle: synonymous with *fleece.*

swindlers: unscrupulous people who distort facts and deal in worthless and doubtful securities.

swindling: the selling of worthless shares through misrepresentation.

swing: the price movement of a security, either up or down.

swingers: financial managers with considerable business transactions.

swing loan: synonymous with *bridge loan.*

switching
(1) ***securities:*** selling one security and buying another. see *switch (contingent) order.*
(2) ***mutual funds:*** shifting assets from one mutual fund to another, either within a family of funds or between different fund families; usually occurs at the shareowner's initiative, as a result of shifts in market conditions or investment goals.

switch (contingent) order: an order for the purchase (sale) of one stock and the sale (purchase) of another stock at a stipulated price difference.

symbol
(1) ***general:*** the single capital letter or combination of letters acquired by a corporation when it is to be listed on an exchange: International Business Machines is IBM; American Telephone and Telegraph is T.
(2) ***investments:*** the letters used to identify traded securities on a ticker tape, exchange board, or newspaper listing.

synchrovest: an investment strategy of choosing a stock or mutual fund and buying varying amounts of it according to how it performs. If it goes down, the investor sinks more money into the stock, if it goes up, the investor puts less in.

syndicate
(1) ***general:*** the association of two or more individuals, established to carry out a business activity. Members share in all profits or losses, in proportion to their contribution to the resources of the syndicate. cf. *joint venture, partnership.*
(2) ***investments:*** a group of investment bankers and securities dealers who, by agreement among themselves, have joined together for the purpose of distributing a new issue of securities for a corporation. cf. *underwriting group.*

syndicate account letter: synonymous with *release letter.*

syndicate agreement: a document used for joining together members of an underwriting or loan syndicate.

syndicate manager: synonymous with *managing underwriter.*

syndicate member: an investment banker, brokerage house, or bank which joins with others under the guidance of a syndicate manager in the underwriting and distribution of a security issue.

syndicate restrictions: contractual obligations placed on an underwriting group for a security relating to distribution, price limitations, and market transactions. see *syndicate termination.*

syndicate termination (release): the point when syndicate restrictions are terminated; occurs when a security involved in trading or expected to trade at or over its initial offering price. This does not necessarily apply in the Eurobond market.

synthetic put: an unregistered option that can only be purchased from or sold to a brokerage firm that created it.

systematic risk: the tendency of the asset price to move along with the market index. The measure of systematic risk is widely known as "beta." If beta is one (1.0), the asset price tends to fall in the same proportion that the market falls, other things being equal, and to rise by the same proportion that the market rises. If beta is 1.5, the asset price tends to fall (or rise) proportionally by one and one-half times as much as the market falls (or rises). see also *beta.* synonymous with *market risk.*

T

T

(1) Treasury (as in T-bill, T-bond, T-note).

(2) in newspaper statements for the Toronto Stock Exchange.

TA

(1) see *tangible assets.*

(2) see *tax abatement.*

(3) see *transfer agent.*

TAB: see *Tax Anticipation Bill.*

tables, annual investment accumulation: shows amounts to be invested yearly at a given rate of interest which will accumulate to $1000 in a given number of years.

tacking: a process of adding a junior claim to a senior one in order to create some gain. Used in a mortgage, as when a third mortgage holder adds the first mortgage and tacks them to assume a superior position over the second mortgage holder.

tag ends: indicating that only small amounts of an offering of debt securities are available from the syndicate with the remaining already sold.

tail

(1) ***underwriting:*** decimal places after the round-dollar amount of a bid by a potential underwriter in a competitive bid underwriting.

(2) ***Treasury auctions:*** the spread in price between the lowest competitive bid accepted by the U.S. Treasury for bills, bonds, and notes and the average bid by all people wishing to purchase such Treasury securities.

(3) ***insurance:*** the interval between the receipt of premium income and payment of claims.

tailgating: the practice of a broker purchasing a security for his or her own account after a customer buys the same security.

take

(1) ***general:*** to lay hold of, seize, or have in possession.

(2) ***general:*** slang, any profit from a business activity, usually one of a suspicious nature.

(3) ***securities:*** an act of accepting an offer price in a transaction between brokers or dealers.

take a bath: to have a substantial financial loss.

take a flier: purchasing securities without thought, planning, and/or advice, with the expectation of making a large profit. Of course, a significant loss may also occur.

take a position

(1) to purchase stock in a corporation with the expectation of holding it for the long term or, perhaps, even taking control of the firm.

(2) when a broker/dealer holds stocks or bonds in inventory, taking either a long or short position.

take back: the recapture of shares or bonds, by the syndicate of a new issue, that have been allotted for the retention of the selling group or the underwriters.

takedown

(1) each participating investment banker's proportionate share of the stocks to be distributed in a secondary or new offering.

(2) the price at which stocks are allocated to members of the underwriting group, especially in municipal offerings.

take it: used by brokers on the floor of an exchange to show their willingness to purchase a specific security at a stipulated price.

take on a line: purchasing a significant quantity of stock of one or more corporations over a set time period, in anticipation of climbing prices. cf. *put out a line.*

take-or-pay contract: an agreement between a buyer and a seller obligating the purchaser to pay a minimum amount of money for a product or a service, even if the product is not delivered. Such contracts are used primarily in the utility industry to back bonds to finance new power plants.

takeout

(1) ***real estate:*** a permanent loan on real property which takes out the interim, construction lender.

(2) ***securities:*** the withdrawal of cash from a brokerage account, often following a sale and purchase that has resulted in a net credit balance.

takeover: the acquisition of an ongoing organization by another through the purchase of the firm and/or exchange of capital stock. cf. *consolidation, merger.*

takeover arbitrage: buying and/or selling the stock of firms involved in takeover situations with the expectation of realizing a profit.

takeover candidate

(1) a corporation in a position for being taken over.

(2) a corporation that is presently being scrutinized as a takeover possibility by another firm.

take profits: realizing a capital gain by selling a stock.

taker: a borrower.

take-up

(1) paying for stock, originally bought on margin, in cash.

(2) an underwriters' term showing that they will handle specific securities for direct sale.

taking a bath: see *take a bath.*

taking delivery
(1) ***general:*** accepting receipt of goods from a common carrier or other shipper.
(2) ***securities:*** accepting receipt of stock or bond certificates that have been recently bought or transferred from another account.
(3) ***commodities:*** accepting physical delivery of a commodity under a futures contract or spot market contract. Requirements are set by the exchange on which the commodity is traded.

talon
(1) a special coupon (e.g., a voucher stub).
(2) that part of a debt instrument remaining on an unmatured bond after the interest coupons that were formerly attached have been presented.

TAN: see *tax-anticipation note.*

tandem option: a corporate stock option combining both qualified and nonqualified plans.

tandem plan: a method of keeping home financing active by the purchase of mortgages by GNMA for resale to FNMA at a discount.

tandem spread: a technique similar to a spread but involving the purchase of one security and the short sale of another.

tangible assets: physical and material (perceptible to touch) assets, as distinguished from intangible assets, which are imperceptible to touch. Examples of tangible assets are cash, land, and buildings.

tangible net worth
(1) ordinarily, the total capital accounts (owned capital) less miscellaneous assets (intangibles). synonymous with *total net worth.*
(2) the difference between a company's equity and the valuation of any intangible assets.

tangible property: property in physical form. It can be touched, such as a house or land.

tangible value: the difference between the striking price of a stock option contract and market price of the underlying security. see *intrinsic value.*

tap CD: a certificate of deposit issued by a bank on an as-required basis with a minimum denomination of $25,000 and for a minumum of one month in dollars.

tape
(1) any service reporting prices and size of transactions on major exchanges. synonymous with *ticker tape.*
(2) the tape of Dow Jones and other news wires. see *broad tape.*

tape price: the last sale of a stock as shown on the ticker tape.

tape racing: an unethical practice of transacting personal business in an issue with prior information of and prior to executing a client's large order in the same security.

tape reading: using only the price, volume, activity, and other factors indicated on the ticker tape to project the price movement of securities.

target company: a firm selected by another company as being attractive for takeover or acquisition.

target investments: synonymous with *socially responsible investments.*

target price
(1) ***general:*** the price at which an acquirer aims to purchase a firm in a takeover.
(2) ***options:*** the price of the underlying stock after which a certain option will become profitable for its purchaser.
(3) ***securities:*** the price that an investor is wishing that a stock he or she recently purchased will rise to within a given time period.

taux d'intérêt: French for *interest rate.*

taw: slang, sufficient funds to fully finance a business venture.

tax: a charge levied by government against the income of an individual, corporation, or other profit-making center of activity.

tax abatement: a decrease or rebate of a tax or burden improperly made. At times a tax abatement may reflect only an acknowledgment of a changed situation.

taxable distribution: in general, any distribution that is reported as taxable income to the recipient. As it relates to a generation-skipping trust, any distribution that is not out of income to a beneficiary in a generation younger than the settler's and whose generation is younger than that of any other younger-generation beneficiary.

taxable equivalent yield: the yield on a bond producing taxable income which would be required to match the yield on a tax-exempt bond.

taxable estate: as defined by a state, the gross estate of a citizen or resident less allowable administrative and funeral expenses; indebtedness; taxes; losses; transfer for public, charitable, and religious uses; transfer to a surviving spouse; and a specific exemption. see *marital deduction.*

taxable event: an economic occurrence subject to taxation.

taxable gifts: property transferred by giver to the extent that its value exceeds allowable exemptions, exclusions, and deductions.

taxable income: the amount of income remaining after all permitted deductions and exemptions have been subtracted; thus the income that is subject to taxation.

taxable value: an assessed value utilized for taxing property, items, or income.

tax act of 1981: see *Economic Recovery Tax Act of 1981.*

Tax Adjustment Act of 1966: federal legislation; restored excise tax rates on transportation equipment and telephone service to rates in effect prior to January 1966. Introduced graduated withholding on personal tax collections.

tax-advantaged investment: an investment that is tax-free, tax-favored, or has the potential for lowering personal income tax liability.

Tax Anticipation Bill (TAB): short-term debt instruments issued by the U.S. Treasury to fulfill very near term financial needs. These bills are today largely replaced with cash-management bills. see *Cash Management Bill.*

Tax Anticipation Note (TAN): short-term notes issued by municipalities to fulfill short-term requirements scheduled to mature, in anticipation of tax receipts.

tax anticipation obligation: any debt instrument issued by the U.S. government to raise funds in anticipation of tax revenue.

tax avoidance: taking advantage of deductions and other provisions of tax law to reduce one's taxes. see *tax shelter.*

tax base: the commodity, income, or service on which a tax is levied; the part of the value of an item that can be taxed.

tax-based income policy (TIP): a surcharge placed on the corporate income of a firm's tax if it grants its employees wage increases in excess of some government-set standard. Likewise, by holding their average wage increases below the standard, companies become eligible for a government tax reduction.

tax capitalization: to the extent that a tax is not shifted, it can be capitalized at an assumed rate of interest by dividing the tax (or change in tax) by the rate of interest and subtracting this amount from the value of the asset before the tax change. Most commonly done with the property tax.

tax carryback and carryover: a provision which is often in American corporation income and excess profits taxes to the effect that losses (or in the case of an excess profits tax, unused credits) can be carried over to apply against a preceding or following year's income. The effect is to level income over the years for tax purposes.

tax certificate: a certificate issued by a governmental unit as evidence of the conditional transfer of title to tax delinquent property from the original owner to the holder of the certificate. If the owner does not pay the amount of the tax arrearage and other charges required by law during the specified period of redemption, the holder can foreclose to obtain title. Also called, in some jurisdictions, *tax lien certificate.* see also *tax deed.*

tax cost: the figure used as the starting point under which gain or loss on a sale or exchange of property is determined. In the usual case, this gain or loss is simply the difference between the amount that a taxpayer paid for property (adjusted for depreciation) and the amount received when the taxpayer sells it.

Tax Court of the United States: a special federal court that hears appeals from the decisions of the Bureau of Internal Revenue about almost all federal taxes (except tariffs). Formerly called the U.S. Board of Tax

Appeals. Appeals from this court go to the U.S. Court of Appeals.

tax credit: a 100 percent offset against tax liability; a deduction provides a tax benefit equal only to the individual's tax rate times the deducted amount.

tax deed: a deed issued to the buyer of property that is sold because of nonpayment of taxes.

tax-deferred: any item, such as money contributed to an IRA, which is not taxed until it is withdrawn or distributed at an authorized time.

Tax Equity and Fiscal Responsibility Act: see *TEFRA.*

tax equivalent: the payment by a municipally (or federally) owned utility made to other units of government in lieu of taxes because of tax exemptions of the governmentally owned utility.

tax evasion: unlawful attempts to avoid payment of a tax (e.g., not properly reporting all earned income).

tax-exempt bond: see *bond, tax-exempt.*

tax exemption: a right, secured by law, permitting freedom from a charge of taxes (e.g., on income that constitutes primary support of a child).

tax-exempt securities: the interest on securities of the federal government is immune from state and local government taxation, and the interest on the securities of state and local governments is exempt from federal taxation. This immunity does not extend as between states or between the states and local governments.

tax-free instruments: debt securities issued by the federal government, state or municipal agency where the received interest is fully or partially free of federal and state income taxes.

tax-free rollover: a provision whereby an individual receiving a lump-sum distribution from a qualified pension or profit sharing plan can preserve the tax-deferred status of these funds by a "rollover" into an IRA or another qualified plan if rolled over within 60 days of receipt. see also *rollover.*

tax lease: a long-term lease issued to the buyer of tax-delinquent property when the law prevents an outright sale.

tax lien: a lien by the government against real property for unpaid taxes. see also *tax certificate.*

tax lien certificate: synonymous with *tax certificate.*

tax liens receivable: legal claims against property which have been exercised because of nonpayment of delinquent taxes, interest, and penalties. The account includes delinquent taxes, interest, and penalties receivable up to the date the lien becomes effective and the cost of holding the sale.

tax limit: a legislative decision that limits the tax ceiling that can be imposed by an appropriate authority.

tax loophole: an obvious discrimination or exemption from tax.

tax loss carryback, carryforward: a tax benefit permitting an individual or firm to apply losses to reduce tax liability.

tax-managed funds: where income from stocks in a fund's portfolio is constantly reinvested. The portfolio manager's only goal is to increase the fund's net asset value per share. Because there are no distributions to shareholders, the investor in a tax-managed fund does not pay any current taxes.

tax-managed utility mutual fund: a mutual fund that invests in utility stocks and then reinvests all dividends and capital gains as part of its policy. Shareowners do not receive any of these distributions but realize profits by selling shares in the fund.

tax note: see *Tax Anticipation Note.*

tax offset: a form of tax cancellation or exemption. A tax is levied, but it is remitted in whole or in part usually on the basis of another tax paid.

tax on net investment income: an excise tax of 4 percent imposed on the net investment income of all tax-exempt private foundations, including operating foundations, for each taxable year beginning after December 31, 1969. Net investment income is the amount by which the sum of gross investment income and the net capital gain exceeds certain allowable deductions.

taxpayer
(1) ***general:*** a small building or store.
(2) ***general:*** an owner of property who pays taxes.
(3) ***government:*** any person who pays taxes.

tax rate: the amount of tax applied per unit of tax base, expressed as a percentage; a tax of $5 on a base of $100; for example, represents a tax rate of 5 percent.

tax rate limit: the maximum rate at which a governmental unit may levy a tax. The limit may apply to taxes raised for a particular purpose, or to taxes imposed for all purposes, and may apply to a single government, to a class of governments, or to all governmental units operating in a particular area. Overall tax rate limits usually restrict levies for all purposes and of all governments, state and local, having jurisdiction in a given area.

Tax Reduction Act of 1975: federal legislation; provided for 10 percent rebate on 1974 taxes up to maximum of $200 for individuals. Provided tax cuts retroactive to January 1975 for both individuals and corporations. For individuals it was in the form of increased standard deductions, a $30 exemption credit, and an earned income credit for low-income families. Reduced corporate income tax and increased investment surtax exemption. Increased investment tax credit to 10 percent.

Tax Reduction Act Stock Ownership Plan: see *TRASOP.*

Tax Reduction and Simplification Act of 1977: legislation signed by President Carter for a $34 billion tax cut, giving credit to industry to create jobs and attempting to simplify tax-filing procedures.

Tax Reform Act of 1969: federal legislation removing major benefits from controlled corporations. Multiple surtax exemptions and multiple accumulated earnings credits were withdrawn by 1975, and the incentives for establishing additional corporations within a controlled group ceased at the end of 1974. The law provided for the accumulation of capital losses to the three preceding years prior to the loss of revenue for a corporation, with no change in the future five-year advance provision for capital losses. Restrictions are given on employee benefit plans. see *Tax Reform Act of 1976, Tax Reform Act of 1984.*

Tax Reform Act of 1976: federal legislation affecting income, estate, and gift taxes. The holding period to qualify for long-term capital gains was increased from 6 to 12 months. Also placed new restrictions on tax shelters. see also *Tax Reform Act of 1969, Tax Reform Act of 1984.*

Tax Reform Act of 1984: federal legislation enacted as part of the Deficit Reduction Act of 1984 to reduce the federal budget deficit without resorting to the repeal of across-the-board cuts in marginal tax rates adopted in the Economic Recovery Tax Act of 1981. Of the more than 100 provisions in the Act, the major provisions affecting investors were: (a) shortened the minimum holding period for assets to qualify for long-term capital gains treatment from one year to six months, for assets acquired following June 22, 1984; (b) permitted contributions to be made to an Individual Retirement Account no later than April 15 following the tax year for which an IRA benefit is sought; (c) permitted the IRS to tax the benefits of loans made on below-market, interest-free, or "gift" terms, whether the agreement is between individuals or between firms and their employees or shareowners; (d) limited golden parachute payments to executes by eliminating the corporate tax deductibility of these payments and subjecting them to a nondeductible 20 percent excise tax withheld over and above regular income taxes; (e) required registration of tax shelters with the IRS; (f) expanded rules in the Economic Recovery Tax Act of 1981 to cover additional types of stock and options transactions that make up tax straddles, thereby preventing tax deferrals and the conversion of ordinary income to long-term capital gains; (g) repeated the 30 percent withholding tax on interest, rents, dividends, and royalties paid to foreign investors by U.S. firms and government agencies, so as to encourage foreign investment in U.S. securities; (h) extended mortgage subsidy bonds through 1988; (i) altered regulations affecting taxation of stock and mutual life insurance firms; (j) disqualified from eligibility for long-term capital gains tax the appreciation of market discounts on newly issued original issue discount bonds and (k) tightened regulations for tax-shelter partnerships and persons who attempt to inflate deductions by overvaluing property donated to charity.

tax sale: a sale, often near year's end, to realize a gain or loss for tax purposes.

tax-saving retirement plan: see *Keogh Plan.*

tax search: a determination by searching official records to determine whether there are any unpaid property taxes.

tax selling: reducing or offsetting the tax liability on capital gains by selling off stocks that show a loss. It is sometimes done to realize profits.

tax shelter: a means of legal avoidance of paying a portion of one's income taxes by careful interpretation of tax regulations and adjustment of one's finances to take advantage of IRS rulings. The tax act of 1976, 1981, 1982, and 1984 placed new restrictions on tax shelters.

tax shield: the amount of depreciation charged against income, thus protecting that amount from tax; a depreciation deduction of $10,000 produces a tax shield of $3600 when the tax rate is 36 percent.

tax shifting: the process of passing the tax from the one who pays the tax to a person forward such as to the one who buys or uses the taxed article or service (e.g., adding the gasoline tax to the price of the gasoline or the admissions tax to the price of admissions). A tax may also be shifted backward to the producer of the taxed good in the form of a lower revenue after taxes for the product or service purchased.

tax straddle: a method for putting off liability for a year. An investor with a short-term capital gain takes a position in a commodities future or option to show a short-term artificial loss in the present tax year and realize a long-term gain in the following tax year.

tax swapping: an investment technique where an investor sells one stock at the end of the tax year to establish a loss for tax purposes and then reinvests the proceeds into another stock that the investor expects will show a higher potential for gain.

tax title: title to property acquired by purchasing land that was sold as the result of unpaid taxes.

tax umbrella: the current and early losses sustained by a corporation. These losses can be carried forward to shelter future profits of the firm.

tax waiver: a written consent of the state tax department permitting the withdrawal of property belonging to the estate of a decedent by the executor or administrator, in order to permit the assembling of assets and to permit distribution.

TBA: to be announced.

T bill: see *Treasury bill.*

T bond: see *bond, treasury.*

TC

(1) see *tax certificate.*
(2) see *time certificates of deposit.*

TD

(1) see *time deposit (open account).*

(2) *Department of the Treasury, U.S.*
(3) time and savings deposits of depository institutions.

TDOA: see *time deposit (open account).*

tear sheet: a sheet from one of the six loose-leaf books comprising the Standard & Poor's Corporation Records, that provide financial data and other relevant information on more than 7500 firms. These sheets are often sent by brokers to clients who make inquiries on various firms.

technical adjustment: a short-term shift in the market, either up or down. It results from investor's activities that is seen as having a short-term stabilizing effect.

technical analysis: the study and use of market prices and indexes related to the supply and demand for stocks. Used to forecast future price movements. Usually involved in near-to-intermediate-term changes. cf. *fundamental analysis.*

technical analyst: a stock analyst who studies and uses charts of stock prices and other market indicators to make forecasts based on trends and signals. see also *analyst.*

technical correction: any short-term direction shift. Occurs when fundamentals are strong or weak and still the market reverses direction for a relatively short time period. This break is looked upon as a self-adjusting market movement.

Technical Corrections Act of 1979: passed in April 1980, created a possibile refund opportunity for holders of "section 1244" stock.

technical decline (drop): the fall in price of a security or commodity resulting from market conditions and not attributed to external forces of supply and demand.

technical divergence: a part of the Dow theory; an existing condition when one of the market averages fails to follow, or confirm to, the action of the other.

technical indicator: any tool for making predictions of future price movements.

technically strong market: when markets in general increase in value on high volume.

technically weak market: when markets in general decrease in value on high volume.

technical market action: the market's overall price performance affected by technical factors, such as volume, short interest, odd-lot transactions, and the movement of individual stocks.

technical move: a short fluctuation in direction of a trend either up or down. This shift is interpreted as a self-adjusting market movement.

technical position: applied to the various internal factors affecting the market; opposed to external forces, such as earnings, dividends, and general economic conditions. Some internal factors are the size of the short-term interest, whether the market has had a sustained advance or decline without interruption, and the amount of credit in use in the market.

technical rally: the increase in the price of a security or commodity resulting from conditions within the market itself and not attributed to external supply and demand forces.

technical research: an analysis of the market and stocks based on supply and demand. The technician studies price movements, volume, and trends and patterns which are revealed by charting these factors and attempts to assess the possible effect of current market action on future supply and demand for securities and individual issues.

technical sign: a short-term trend that technical analysts identify as important in the price movement of a stock or a commodity.

technician: an individual who utilizes a technical approach to analysis, including the fundamentals of a firm, the general economy, ratios, indexes, etc.

technilist: a financial institution's publication advising subscribers not only what to sell and what to buy of securities and bonds, but also at what prices. Rates each stock simply on the basis of its price pattern, trading volume, and strength relative to the market.

TEFRA: Tax Equity and Fiscal Responsibility Act. Federal legislation of 1982 to raise tax revenue, primarily through closing various loopholes and instituting more sophisticated enforcement procedures. Some of its major components are: (a) increasing penalties for noncompliance with tax laws, (b) ten percent of interest and dividends earned was required to be withheld from bank and brokerage accounts and forwarded directly to the IRS. (Later canceled by Congress) and, (c) deduction for original issue discount bonds were limited to the amount the issuer would deduct as interest if it issued bonds with a face amount equal to the actual proceeds and paying the market rate of interest.

telegraphic transfer (T/T): the use of cable or telegraph to remit funds. Physicial money does not move, but instead the order is wired to the cashier of a firm to make payment to an identified person or firm.

telephone booth: communication facilities maintained by member firms of the exchange.

telephone switching

(1) a method to hold on to the money being withdrawn from stock funds, managers allow investors to transfer the money to a money-market fund organized by the fund family.

(2) the procedure of shifting assets from one mutual fund to another by telephone.

temporary bond: see *bond, temporary.*

temporary receipt: the printed or lithographed acknowledgment used until the engraved certificate is ready to be released and which is then exchanged for the definitive security by the holder of the temporary receipt.

temporary specialist: an exchange member appointment for a short time period to carry out the responsibilities of a specialist, with the same obligations of the regular specialist.

tenancy: the holding of real property by any form of title.

tenancy at sufferance: a tenancy in which the tenant comes into possession of real property under a lawful title or interest and continues to hold the property even after his or her title or interest has terminated.

tenancy at will: that estate which may be terminated by either the lessor or the lessee at any time.

tenancy by the entirety: tenancy by a husband and wife in such a manner that, except in concert with the other, neither husband nor wife has a disposable interest in the property during the lifetime of the other. Upon the death of either, the property goes to the survivor. To be distinguished from *joint tenancy* and *tenancy in common.*

tenancy for years: a tenancy for a definite period of time—for example, a year or 99 years. It cannot be terminated by either party alone except at the expiration of the time agreed upon.

tenancy in common: ownership of property by two or more persons, each holding a separate interest. No right of survivorship exists. see *undivided right.*

tenancy in common account
(1) a savings account that is owned by two or more persons, each of whom has a separate interest; when one owner dies, his or her shares passes to his or her heirs, not to the remaining owner(s).
(2) a type of checking account, often requiring that both parties sign checks, notes, and so on; in other words, one individual cannot act independently of the other.
(3) stock certificates that are issued to "tenants in common." see also *tenants in common.*

tenant
(1) ***general:*** one who holds or possesses real property.
(2) ***securities:*** the part owner of a security.

tenants by the entireties (ATBE): in some states, the same as joint tenants with the right of survivorship. Abbreviated on registered securities and brokerage account documents.

tenants in common (TEN COM) (TIC): joint ownership of property whereby that portion owned by a decedent passes to his or her estate for probate instead of the possession of the other party to the account. Abbreviated on registered security certificates and brokerage account documents.

TEN COM: see *tenants in common.*

tendency: the inclination for a stock or market average to shift in a specific direction, either up, down, or sideways over a period of time.

tender
(1) ***investments:*** a corporation's offer of securities by asking for bids for them, at prices above a minimum.
(2) ***law:*** the offering of money in satisfaction of a debt by producing

the money and stating to the creditor a desire to pay.

tenderable: a commodity fulfilling the standard of quality set by the commodity exchange or exchanges as well as the requirements as to time and place of delivery.

tender offer
(1) a bid by an outsider to purchase some or all of a firm's outstanding shares, usually for the purpose of obtaining effective control.
(2) an offer by a company to purchase its own shares or other types of securities such as bonds or debentures.

ten-forty: a U.S. bond that is redeemable after 10 years, and due and payable after 40 years.

10-K report: a version of an annual report that all U.S. corporations must file with the Securities and Exchange Commission. Since 1974, it has also been required that this report, which generally contains more information than the annual report to stockholders, be made available to any interested stockholders.

1099: the Internal Revenue Service form for reporting the payment of interest, dividends, and miscellaneous fees to individuals.

ten percent guideline: a municipal bond analysts' guideline that funded debt over 10 percent of the assessed valuation of taxable property in a municipality is excessive.

ten-year trust: synonymous with *Clifford trust.*

term bond: see *bond, term.*

term bonds payable: a liability account which records the face value of general obligation term bonds issued and outstanding.

term certificate: a certificate of deposit with a longer-term maturity date.

terminable bond: see *bond, terminable.*

terminal bond: see *bond, terminal.*

terminal market: a market (i.e., a commodity market) that deals in futures.

terminal reserve: the reserve of an insurance policy at the end of the policy year.

termination claim: an agreement fixing the pre-determined level for shareholders in any appreciation of their stake in shares. Dividends and voting rights are not affected.

termination of offer: an offer can be ended by acceptance, counteroffer, expiration of time, insanity, or death of the offeror or offeree, refusal to accept, or revocation of the offer.

term issue: a bond issue maturing as a whole in a single future year.

term life insurance: life insurance protection during a certain number of years, but usually expiring without policy cash value if the insured survives the stated period. see *family income rider.*

term mortgage: a mortgage with a fixed time period, usually less than five years, in which only interest is paid. Following termination of the mortgage, the total principal is demanded.

term plan: a life insurance policy where the company agrees to pay a stipulated sum of money upon the death of the insured if death occurs within the term fixed by the policy, usually 5 or 10 years.

term rider: term life insurance added to a "whole life" policy when purchased or at a later date.

territorial bond: see *bond, insular.*

tertiary movement: insignificant daily shifts in price caused by trifling developments; part of Dow theory.

test

(1) ***general:*** the criterion for measuring compliance with financial ratio requirements of indentures and other loan agreements.

(2) ***securities:*** a price shift that approaches a support level or a resistance level, established earlier by a security, commodity future, or market. A test is passed if the levels are not penetrated and is failed should prices go on to new lows or highs.

testamentary account: a category of savings accounts recognized by the Federal Savings and Loan Insurance Corporation as separately insurable, and including funds owned by an individual and invested in a revocable trust account, tentative or Totten trust account, payable-on-death account, or similar account evidencing an intention that on his or her death the funds shall belong to a specified member of the owner's family. see *Totten trust.*

testamentary disposition: the disposition of property by deed, will, or otherwise in such a manner that it shall not take effect unless or until the grantor dies.

testamentary guardian: a guardian of a minor or an incompetent person named in the decendent's will.

testing: a market price that challenges the support or resistance levels with the anticipation that the price will not drop below the support level or climb above the resistance level.

theoretical value (of a right): a mathematical ratio of market value of a subscription right following the announcement of an offering but before the stock goes ex-rights. The formula is:

$$\frac{\text{market value of common stock} - \text{subscription price per share}}{\text{number of rights needed to buy 1 share} + 1}$$

theory of contrary opinion: a market concept that the majority is usually wrong when there is no real difference of opinion.

thin corporation: a corporation owing a large number of debts relative to its equity position.

thinly held security: shares of a specific stock owned by relatively few individuals or institutions. Usually results in wide price swings on small volume.

thin margin: a condition where the owner of an item, such as a security, commodity, or other property, has a very small equity. Consequently, any small drop in the price or value of the item will result in a condition in which the debtor owes more than the value of the collateral put up for the loan.

thin market: a market in which there are comparatively few bids to buy or offers to sell or both. The phrase may apply to a single security or to the entire stock market. In a thin market, price fluctuations between transactions are usually larger than they are when the market is liquid. A thin market in a particular stock may reflect lack of interest or a lack of demand for stock.

third market: see *over the counter.*

third mortgage: a mortgage that is junior to both the first and second mortgages.

third-party account: a brokerage account carried and operated in the name of an individual other than the owner.

third-party brokers: akin to the discounters on the retail side, who offer to perform routine institutional trades at essentially rock-bottom prices. They get the same eight cents a share from an institution to execute a stock trade, but the broker returns a portion of this fee, perhaps half, either as a cash rebate to a pension fund or in the form of goods and services to a pension fund's money manager.

third-party check: a check payable to another person other than the current holder.

13-D reports: see *schedule 13-D.*

thirty-day visible supply: the total dollar volume of new municipal bonds holding maturities of 13 months or more that are scheduled to reach the market within 30 days. see also *pipeline, in the.*

thirty-day wash rule: an IRS ruling that losses on a sale of stock cannot be used as losses for tax purposes if equivalent stock is bought within 30 days before or 30 days following the date of sale.

Threadneedle Street: the financial area of London.

three against one ratio writing: a stock option ratio-writing technique involving the sale of three calls for every 100 shares held of the underlying security.

3-5-10 rule: see *ACRS.*

three-handed deal: in municipal security underwriting, the issue will combine serial maturities with two term maturities.

threshold companies: companies on the threshold of corporate maturity in that they are not yet managed by professionals but are run intuitively by a handful of entrepreneurs. This concept was developed by Donald Clifford, Jr.

threshold issuing rate: see *bogey.*

thrift account: synonymous with *savings account, special interest account.*

thrift institution: the general term for mutual savings banks, savings and loan associations, and credit unions. see *thrifts.*

thrifts: there are two types of thrifts, the savings banks and savings and loan industries. Today they are both engaged in basically the same business—taking in consumer deposits and reinvesting them in mortgages. Together they hold almost $800 billion (1981) in assets, more than any financial industry except commercial banks, whose assets amount to $1.5 trillion (1981). Savings banks, which theoretically are owned by their depositors, were established by philanthropists to promote savings among the poor. The founders gave ultimate power to self-perpetuating boards of trustees. Thus, unlike depositors in S&Ls, savings bank depositors do not have the right to elect their trustees. Several savings banks are trying to convert to federal from state charters. Under federal rules, their depositors would gain voting rights within their respective organizations. Savings and loans originally were formed by community members to finance housing, not to promote savings. Initially, they existed for limited periods, long enough for each member to buy a home. The members chipped in to raise enough money to finance home construction. Lots were drawn to determine which member would be the first to get a house. The modern version of the savings and loan association got its start in the early 1930s. The industry boomed after World War II, when 11 million returning veterans needed housing.

through the market: a situation when a new bond offering has come to market and the yield to maturity is lower than comparable bonds outstanding.

throwaway offer: an offer or bid that is nominal only and not intended to give a price at which transactions can occur.

TIC: see *tenants in common.*

tick: the minimum price movement in the trading in securities; it is one-eighth of a point, or 12½ cents, in securities transactions.

ticker: the instrument that prints prices and volume of security transactions in cities and towns throughout the United States and Canada within minutes of each trade on any listed exchange.

ticker symbol: letters identifying a stock for trading purposes on a consolidated tape.

ticker tape: synonymous with *tape.*

tick index: the net tick volume determined by substracting total downtick volume from total uptick volume on a specific exchange for one trading session.

tickler: an index for maturity dates of notes, bonds, acceptances, and so on, serving as a reminder to banks and financial institutions that these instruments will at some future time period be approaching maturity.

tick volume: the total downtick volume versus total uptick volume for a specific stock for one trading session.

tier: any class or group of securities.

Tiffany list: issuers of the highest-quality commercial paper.

TIGER: see *Treasury Investors Growth Receipt.*

tight market: the market for a specific stock, or the market in general, marked by active trading and narrow bid-offer price spreads.

TIGR: see *Treasury Investors Growth Receipt.*

time bargain: struck when a seller and a purchaser of securities consent to exchange a specific stock at a stated price at a stated future time.

time bill: a bill of exchange having a fixed or determinable date of payment.

time certificates of deposit: a time deposit evidenced by a negotiable or nonnegotiable instrument specifying an amount and a maturity. Savings bonds and savings certificates are merely forms of nonnegotiable time certificates of deposits.

time deposit: a deposit from which a customer has the right to withdraw funds at a specified date 30 or more days following the date of deposit, or from which, if the bank requires, the customer can withdraw funds only by giving the bank written notice 30 days or more in advance of the planned withdrawal.

time deposit (open account) (TDOA) (golden passbook): funds deposited under agreement. They bear interest from the date of deposit, although the agreement usually requires that such funds remain on deposit for at least 30 days. The agreement stipulates a fixed maturity date or number of days after which payment will be made, or it is stipulated that payment will be made after a given period following notice by the depositor of intention to withdraw.

time draft: a draft payable a specified number of days (30, 60, or 90 days, for example) after its date of issuance or acceptance.

time earnings: see *price/earnings ratio.*

time order: an order that becomes a market or limited price order at a specified time.

time policy: an insurance policy valid for a specified time period.

times fixed charges: see *fixed-charge coverage.*

times interest and preferred dividend earned: a common measure of the "earnings protection" which a preferred stock has. The figure is computed by dividing the net earnings per year (after taxes) by the sum of the interest and preferred dividend requirements.

times interest earned: a common measure of the "earnings protection" of a bond. The figure is computed by dividing the net earnings per year (without deducting the interest of the specific issues but after taxes) by the interest requirements of the specific issue for that year.

time spread: synonymous with *horizontal spread.*

times preferred dividend earned: a common measure of "earnings protection" of a preferred stock. The figure is computed by dividing the net earnings per year (after taxes, interest, and any prior dividends) by the preferred dividend requirements of that issue for that year.

time value

(1) ***investments:*** the price placed on the time an investor has to wait until an investment matures.

(2) ***securities:*** the difference between the price at which a corporation is taken over and the stock price prior to the takeover.

(3) ***options:*** that portion of a stock option premium reflecting the time remaining on an option contract prior to expiration. The premium is composed of this time value and the intrinsic value of the option.

time warrant: a negotiable obligation of a governmental unit having a term shorter than bonds and frequently tendered to individuals and firms in exchange for contractual services, capital acquisitions, or equipment purchases.

time warrants payable: the amount of time warrants outstanding and unpaid.

time-weighted rate of return: one method of computing rates of return. It is the investment performance of a unit of assets held continuously for the entire time period measured. This rate provides an effective standard for comparing the performance of different funds, in which cash flow could vary considerably. The money manager usually cannot control the timing or the amount of contributions to the fund. Because the time-weighted rate reduces impact of money flows into or out of the fund, it is a fairer means of appraising the fund manager's ability to make the fund assets perform.

timing: a judgment as to the preferred moment to make additions or deletions from an investor's portfolio of holdings. Usually, based on various trends.

TIMS: trusts for investments in mortgages. Gives mortgage-backed securities bond-like characteristics, including semi-annual, rather than monthly, payments and prepayment protection.

TIP: to insure promptness.

tippee: the receiver of inside information.

tips

(1) ***general:*** monies offered to encourage or ensure promptness; monies given for services rendered (e.g., 15 percent of a restaurant bill constitutes the waiter's tip).

(2) ***investments:*** supposedly *inside information* on corporation affairs; a subjective recommendation to buy or sell a particular stock. see *inside information.*

tipster: people who say that they have inside information on where you should invest your money.

tipster sheet: an unofficial list of stocks that are recommended to customers.

title: in an auction, ownership passes with the fall of the hammer—provided payment is made or credit is arranged—to the winning bidder. If the auctioner has advanced money before the sale, he has a lien on the item, but this is not construed as ownership and is not disclosed.

title company: see *title guaranty company.*

title deed: a legal document indicating proof of an individual's ownership of a piece of land.

title defect: a fact or circumstance that challenges property ownership. see *cloud on title.*

title exception: a specified item appearing in a title policy against which the title company does not insure.

title guaranty company: a business firm created to examine real estate files (i.e., to conduct title searches) to determine the legal status of the property and to find any evidence of encumbrances, faults, or other title defects. Once a search has been completed and the property found sound, the company receives a fee from the property purchaser who needs to determine that his or her title was clear and good. The property purchaser receives an abstract of the prepared title, and the title is verified by an attorney of the company who gives an opinion but does not guarantee the accuracy of the title. The company agrees to indemnify the owner against any loss that may be experienced resulting from a subsequent defect. A title guaranty policy is evidence of the title insurance, with costs based on the value of the property and the risk involved as determined by the condition of the title. see also *title insurance.*

title guaranty policy: title insurance furnished by the owner, provided as an alternative for an abstract of title. synonymous with *Torrens certificate.* see also *title guaranty company.*

title insurance: an insurance contract from a title guaranty company presented to owners of property, indemnifying them against having a defective or unsalable title while they possess the property. This contract is considered to be a true indemnity for loss actually sustained by reason of the defects or encumbrances against which the insurer agrees to indemnify. Title insurance includes a thorough examination of the evidences of title by the insurer. see *title guaranty company.*

title insurance company: see *title guaranty company.*

TL

(1) trade-last.
(2) see *trading limit.*

TLI: see *term life insurance.*

TM: see *third market.*

T note: see *Treasury note.*

To.: see *turnover.*

TO: see *Treasury obligations.*

to come—to go: the exact number of shares in a transaction which are to be sold but still remain (to go); or the number in a buying transaction yet to be purchased (to come).

today only order: see *day order.*

toehold purchase: the accumulation by an acquirer of less than 5 percent of the shares of a target firm. Following the acquisition 5 percent of the shares, the acquirer is required to file with the SEC, the appropriate exchange, and the target firm, detailing objectives and what has occured.

toll revenue bond: see *bond, toll revenue.*

tombstone: an advertisement placed by an underwriting syndicate outlining a public sale. A listing of the syndicate members is given.

tom/next: from tomorrow to the next business day.

ton: slang, bond traders' term for $100 million.

top: the highest price that a security has maintained during any state time frame. Used in the past sense, and is followed by a drop in market price. synonymous with *peak.*

top-down approach to investing: a technique where an investor initially studies patterns in the general economy, and then chooses industries and firms that would benefit from these trends. cf. *bottom-up approach to investing.*

top-down investment manager: a common stock manager who develops a portfolio with a primary emphasis on the economy and industries, as opposed to one who places his or her selection emphasis on recognizing favorable characteristics of individual companies.

topheavy: the condition of a price series such as one of securities or commodities in which the series, while being high compared with some other period, is considered to be vulnerable for a reaction downward.

topheavy market: technical conditions showing that the market appears too high and is likely to fall.

top or bottom: see *head and shoulders.*

topping a bid: improving the market; when an individual makes a bid higher than the existing prevailing bid.

topping out: employed to denote loss of upside energy at the top after a long price run-up.

toppy: slang, topheaviness in a market, or stock, indicating a possible decline.

Torrens certificate: a document, issued by the proper public authority called a *registrar* acting under the provision of the Torrens law, indicating in whom title resides. see also *registrar.*

total assets: all money, machinery, other equipment, real estate, and credits owned by a business.

total asset turnover: the ratio obtained by dividing total assets into sales but more correctly, dividing total operating assets into sales since funds devoted to outside investments do not affect sales but produce an independent income.

total capitalization: the capital structure of a firm, including long-term debt and all forms of equity.

total cost

(1) ***general:*** the sum of a firm's total fixed costs and total variable costs.

(2) ***investments:*** the contract price paid for a stock plus the brokerage commission plus any accrued interest due the seller.

total debt: all long-term obligations of the government and its agencies and all interest-bearing short-term credit obligations. Long-term obligations are those repayable more than one year after issue.

total debt to tangible net worth: obtained by dividing total current plus long-term debts by tangible net worth. When this relationship exceeds 100 percent, the equity of creditors in the assets of the business exceeds that of owners.

total fixed costs: the costs that do not change with an organization's output (e.g., payments on rent, property taxes).

total net worth: synonymous with *tangible net worth.*

total of payments: the total of all installments scheduled to be made in the repayment of a loan or sales contract; face of note; the sum of the amount financed and the finance charges.

total return: the return on an investment, accounting for capital appreciation, dividends, interest, and individual tax factors adjusted for present value and expressed on a yearly basis. For bonds, the computation used for yield to maturity adjusted for tax factors. For stocks, future capital appreciation is projected on the basis of the current price/earnings ratio. see also *performance index.*

total return investment: an investment offering a combination of income and growth with lessened capital risk.

total volume: the total number of shares or contracts traded in a stock, bond, commodity future, or option on a given day. For stocks and bonds, the total number of trades on national exchanges. For commodities futures and options, the volume of trades throughout the world on a given day. For over-the-counter securities, total volume is measured by the NASDAQ index.

to the buck: in U.S. government securities, the offer side of a quotation when the bid side is close to the offer and the offer is a round point.

Totten trust: a trust created by the deposit of one's own money in their own name as trustee for another. Title is vested in the record owner (trustee), who during his or her life holds it on a revocable trust for the named beneficiary. At the death of the depositor, a presumption arises that an absolute trust was created as to the balance on hand at the death of the depositor. see *testamentary account.*

touch off the stops: when stop orders become market orders because the price at which the stop orders were placed has been attained. A situation described as *snowballing* results should prices continue to drop and successive stop orders are hit or touched off (i.e., become market orders and creating even more selling pressure). see also *snowballing.*

tout: slang, biased recommendations to purchase a security.

TR

(1) see *tax rate.*

(2) see *Treasury Receipt.*

TRA: see *Tax Reform Act of 1969, Tax Reform Act of 1976, Tax Reform Act of 1984.*

trade

(1) ***general:*** buying or selling of goods and services.

(2) ***securities:*** carrying out a transaction of buying or selling a security, a bond, or a commodity futures contract.

trade date: the day when a stock or a commodity future trade actually occurs. The settlement date usually follows the trade date by five business days, but may vary based on the transaction and means of delivery used.

trade house: a firm that buys and sells futures and actuals for the accounts of customers as well as for its own account.

trademark: a distinctive identification of a manufactured product or of a service taking the form of a name, logo, motto, and so on; a trademarked brand has legal protection and only the owner can use the mark. Organizations that file an application at the U.S. Patent Office and use the brand for five years may be granted a trademark. A firm may lose a trademark that has become generic. Generic names are those which consumers use to identify the product, rather than to specify a particular brand (e.g., escalator, aspirin, and nylon).

trader

(1) ***general:*** anyone who is engaged in trade or commerce.

(2) ***investments:*** one who buys and sells for his or her own account for short-term profit.

traders' market: the general market situation where it is possible to make short-term trades with the expectation of making profits.

trade support system (TSS): developed in 1973 to process and transmit quote and price information at the Chicago Board Options Exchange. cf. *order support system.*

trade through: an unethical practice, when an exchange member executes a transaction on the floor when a better price is indicated on the Intermarket Trading System.

trading: purchasing and selling stocks with the expectation of making a short-term profit. Less risky than speculation, but does involve more risk than long-term investing.

trading authorization: a document providing a brokerage house employee serving as broker the power of attorney in buy-sell transactions for a client.

trading crowd: the number of members of an exchange brought together at a trading post to transact buy and sell orders.

trading days: days that exchanges are open; usually Monday through Friday, except for some holidays.

trading difference: a difference of a fraction of a point in the charged price for securities bought and sold in an odd-lot transaction, which is in excess of the price at which the security would be traded in traditional round lots.

trading dividends: a method of purchasing and selling securities in other firms by a corporation so as to maximize the number of dividends it can collect.

trading flat: see *flat.*

trading floor: see *floor.*

trading hours: hours during which trading occurs on the floor of an exchange. Effective 1985, between 9:30 A.M. and 4:00 P.M.

trading index: a market ratio that indicates advances versus declines to upside versus downside voume. see *short-term trading index.*

trading instructions: an investor's instructions to a broker that in some fashion modifies the standard buy or sell order.

trading limit
(1) the price limit above or below which trading in commodities is not allowed during a given day.
(2) as specified by the Commodity Exchange Act, the number of contracts a person may legally retain.

trading market: a condition where the primary volume of transactions is attributed to professional traders as contrasted from transactions attributed to the general public. As a result, volume is down and off with only narrow fluctuations in prices.

trading on the equity: the issuance of a funded debt by a firm. Such trading may increase the risk of bankruptcy since the fixed-interest charges on debt can exceed the return on total capital.

trading paper: highly negotiable, short-term certificates of deposit.

trading pattern: the long-range direction of a stock or commodity future price.

trading post: one of many trading locations on the floor of stock exchanges at which stocks assigned to that location are bought and sold. see *floor, specialist.*

trading profits: profits made in the course of a trade; profits made by a securities dealers from buying and selling securities.

trading range
(1) ***securities:*** the range between the highest and lowest prices at which a stock or a market has traded.
(2) ***commodities:*** the trading limit established by a commodities futures exchange for a specific commodity. The price of a commodity futures contract cannot go higher or lower than that limit during one day's trading.

trading ring: the area on the NYSE where exchange-completed trades in listed bond occurs.

trading rotation: the strategy for opening trading in the various series of options for specific stocks and for the months in commodity futures contracts. Following completion of the rotation, trading in the individual contracts resume.

trading through the fund's rate: a major indicator of a shift in the Federal Reserve monetary policy, when a debt security's yield to maturity is less than the federal fund's rate.

trading unit: the unit adopted by an association or exchange where transactions are regularly expressed. The unit varies with the exchange and can vary between the spot or futures market, as well as by the commodity.

trading variation: fractions to which securities transaction prices are rounded.

trading volume: the volume of shares traded for a specific stock, exchange, average, or index for a given time period. Usually, volume is quoted for a single day of trading.

transaction

(1) ***general:*** any agreement between two or more parties, establishing a legal obligation.

(2) ***general:*** a condition recognized by an entry in the books of account.

(3) ***securities:*** the execution of an order to purchase or sell a stock or commodity futures contract.

transaction slip: synonymous with *confirmation slip.*

transfer

(1) the legal conveyance of ownership from a seller to a buyer.

(2) a record of change in ownership in the books of a corporation.

transferable notice: a written announcement issued by a seller signifying their intention of making delivery in fulfillment of a futures contract. The recipient of the notice may make a sale of the futures contract and transfer the notice within a specified time to another party, on some exchanges directly, and on others through the clearing association. The last recipient takes delivery of the commodity tendered. Notices on some exchanges are not transferable.

transfer agent: a transfer agent keeps a record of the name of each registered shareowner, his or her address, and the number of shares owned; it is the agent's responsibility to see that certificates presented to the office for transfer are properly canceled and that new certificates are issued correctly in the name of the transferee.

transfer and ship: when the owner of a security informs the brokerage house holding the security to have it registered in his or her name and to send it to his or her address on the broker's new account form.

transfer journal: a book kept by a corporation to show stock certificates issued, transferred, and canceled.

transfer of title: the change of property title from one person to another. synonymous with *voluntary alienation.*

transfer tax: a tax imposed by the federal or some state governments when a security is sold or transferred from one person to another. The tax is paid by the seller. There is no tax on transfers of bonds. The transfer tax is usually collected as a stamp tax.

trans-lux: an electrical unit used to project the quotations of a commodity or security exchange on a screen in a board room of a brokerage house.

transmittal letter: a letter accompanying a shipment of securities, documents, or other property usually containing a brief description of the securities, documents, or property being forwarded and an explanation of the transaction.

transportation index: see *Dow Jones Transportation Average.*

TRASOP: Tax Reduction Act Stock Ownership Plan. Created by the Tax Reduction Act of 1975, phased out by the Economic Recovery Tax Act of 1981. Allowed a tax credit of 1 percent of a capital investment if an employer contributed that much to ESOP. see *PAYSOP.*

treasureship: the functions of management holding responsibility for the custody and investment of money, the granting of credit and collection of accounts, capital provision, maintenance of a market for the firm's securities, and so on.

Treasuries: negotiable debt obligations of the U.S. government, secured by its full faith and credit and issued at various schedules and maturities. Income from Treasury securities is exempt from state and local, but not federal, taxes. see *bond, Treasury, Treasury bill, Treasury certificates, Treasury note.* see also *Treasury securities.*

Treasury bill: a U.S. government short-term security sold to the public each week, maturing in 91 to 182 days.

Treasury Bill auction: a weekly U.S. Treasury auction for individuals wishing to purchase more than $500,000 of short-term government obligations may enter competitive bids at a discount from the face value. Noncompetitive bidders, $500,000 or less, are awarded bills at the average discount paid by competitive bidders.

Treasury bond: see *bond, Treasury.*

Treasury bonds and notes: interest-bearing certificates showing indebtedness of the U.S. government. Notes have maturities of between one and seven years, whereas bonds are longer term.

Treasury certificates: U.S. government short-term securities, sold to the public and maturing in one year.

Treasury Investors Growth Receipt (TIGER) (TIGR): a zero-coupon security. U.S. government-backed bonds that have been stripped of their coupons. The principal and the individual coupons are sold separately at a deep discount from their face value. Investors receive face value when the bonds mature but do not receive periodic interest payments. IRS regulation require that TIGER holders must pay income taxes on the imputed interest they would have earned had the bond been a full coupon bond.

Treasury note: a U.S. government long-term security, sold to the public and having a maturity of one to five years.

Treasury obligations: see *bond, Treasury; Treasury bill; Treasury certificates; Treasury note.*

Treasury Receipt (TR): zero-coupon bonds of U.S. Treasury-backed certificates available from brokerage and investment banking concerns.

Treasury securities: interest-bearing obligations of the U.S. government issued by the Treasury as a means of borrowing money to meet government expenditures not covered by tax revenues. Marketable Treasury securities fall into three categories: bills, notes, and bonds. The Federal Reserve System holds more than $100 billion of these obligations, acquired through open market operations.

treasury stock: the title to previously issued stock of a corporation that has been reacquired by that corporation by purchase, gift, donation, inheritance, or other means. The value of such stock should be considered to be a deduction from the value of outstanding stock of similar type rather than as an asset of the issuing corporation.

trend
(1) ***general:*** the direction that prices are taking.
(2) ***general:*** the direction that interest rates and yields are taking.
(3) ***securities:*** long-term price or trading volume movements either up, down, or sideways, characterizing a particular market, commodity or security.

trendless: without any definite direction in the upward or downward movement for a security or in the stock market.

trendline: a line going upward or downward on a chart showing movements of average prices, as of stocks, over a period of time from which future patterns are interpreted.

triangle: a chart pattern having two base points and a top point, formed by connecting a stock's price shifts with a line.

triangular arbitrage: arbitrage between the exchange rates of three foreign currencies. see *arbitrage.*

trick: a special low coupon at a high yield on a long maturity of a municipal bond issue, which enables a bidder to lower the net interest cost (NIC) to the issuer in the hopes of making a winning bid on the bonds.

TRIN: see *short-term trading index.*

triple option: synonymous with *strap.*

triple tax exempt: a characteristic of municipal bonds in which interest is exempt from federal, state, and local taxation for state residents and localities that issue them.

triple tax free: see *triple tax exempt.*

triple (bottom) top: the point, high or low, reached by the market or a particular security, duplicating a level attained on two earlier occasions. To the market specialist, the three levels establish a triple top (bottom) and show that a major wall of price support (overhead resistance) has been established.

triple witching hour: slang, the final trading hour of the third Friday of each month. The third Fridays of June, September, December and March are when the index futures expire. cf. *double witching hour.*

TRSA: see *Tax Reduction and Simplification Act of 1977.*

trust

(1) ***general:*** a fiduciary relationship between persons: one holds property for the benefit and use of another.

(2) ***investments:*** a combination of corporations, usually in the same industry; stockholders relinquish their stock to a board of trustees, who then issue certificates and dividends. The purposes of creating a trust include controlling costs of production, increasing profits, and reducing competition.

trust certificate: synonymous with *stock trust certificate.*

trusteed fund: any accumulation of capital held in trust for retirement, religious, educational, research, profit-sharing, or other purposes.

trusteed pension plan: a pension plan in which the corporation's contributions to the plan are placed in a trust for investment and reinvestment, as distinguished from a plan in which the benefits are secured by life insurance.

trustee shares: in an investment company formed under the business organization form of a Massachusetts trust, the certificates of beneficial interest.

trusteeship: the status of a carrier's property while in the charge of trustees appointed under Section 77 of the Bankruptcy Act, approved March 3, 1933. A reorganization proceeding under trustees differs from a receivership equity proceeding chiefly in the fact that the former may be instituted by a railroad as well as by creditors and must follow a detailed prescribed procedure in regard to the presentation, consideration, and adoption of plans of reorganization, involving participation by the Interstate Commerce Commission as well as by the court.

trust estate: an estate held in trust by one individual for the welfare of another.

Trust Indenture Act: federal legislation of 1939 requiring all corporate bonds and other debt securities to be issued under an indenture agreement approved by the SEC that provides for the appointment of a qualified trustee free of conflict of interest with the issuer. The Act also provides that indenture contain protective statements for bondholders, that such holders receive semiannual financial reports, that filings be made with the SEC, and that the issuer be liable for misleading statements.

trust institution: a trust company, state bank, national bank, or other corporation engaged in the trust business under authority of law. A corporation is a trust institution if any of its department is engaged in trust business, although other departments may be engaged otherwise.

trust instrument committee: a committee of directors or officers (or both) of a trust institution charged with specific duties relating to trust investments; duties other than those relating to investments may be imposed by the board of directors.

trust investments: the property in which trust funds are invested; a broad term that includes all kinds of property, not securities alone.

trust officer: the administrative officer of a trust company, or of the trust department of a bank. He or she is responsible for the proper administration of trusts, the investment of trust funds, and the administration of agencies for trust clients.

trustor: an individual who establishes a trust. synonymous with *settlor*.

trusts for investments in mortgages: see *TIMS*.

Truth in Securities Act: federal legislation requiring full disclosure of all material information relating to the public issuance of stocks. see *Securities Act of 1934*.

TS
(1) see *tax shelter*.
(2) see *treasury stock*.

TSS: see *trade support system*.

T/T: see *telegraphic transfer*.

turkey
(1) ***general:*** any poor or unprofitable venture.
(2) ***investments:*** any investment that initially appeared attractive but suddenly became unattractive.
(3) ***investments:*** a stock that suddenly, without reason, drops in value.

turn: a description of the full cycle in the buying and selling of a security or a commodity.

turnaround situation: the condition when a firm moves from an unprofitable to a profitable situation by resolving its problems relating to internal financial, manufacturing, processing, management, marketing, etc.

turnover
(1) ***general:*** the rate at which workers move into and out of employment, usually expressed as the number of accessions and separations during a fixed period for every 100 employees. The Bureau of Labor Statistics computes turnover rates by industry on a monthly basis.
(2) ***investments:*** the volume of business in a security or the entire market. If turnover on the exchange is reported at 15 million shares on a particular day, this means that 15,000,000 shares changed hands. Odd-lot turnover is tabulated separately and ordinarily is not included in reported volume. synonymous with *overturn, volume*.

turnover ratio: a measure of capital activity, or another factor of business (e.g., where the portfolio of securities is altered, or turned over, within one year). see *operating profit ratio*.

turtle-blood: slang, securities of low volatility, which are not expected to advance rapidly.

12B-1 mutual fund: a mutual fund that assesses shareowners for some of its promotional expenses. These funds traditionally rely on advertising and build their assets. A 12B-1 fund must be registered as such with the SEC.

twenty-day period: the period mandated by the SEC following filing of the registration statement and preliminary prospectus in a new issue or secondary distribution during which they are studied, and when deemed necessary, revised. The termination of the 20-day period indicates the effective date when the issue can be offered to the public.

twenty-five percent rule: a municipal bond analyst's guideline that bonded debt over 25 percent of a municipality's yearly budget is excessive.

twisting: synonymous with *switching.*

two against one ratio writing: a stock option ratio-writing technique involving the sale of two calls for each 100 shares held of the underlying security.

two-dollar brokers: members on the floor of the exchange who execute orders for other brokers having more business at that time than they can handle themselves, or for firms who do not have their exchange members on the floor. The term recalls the time when these independent brokers received $2 per hundred shares for executing such orders. see *give-up.*

twofer: synonymous with *neutral spread.*

200-day moving average: a technical indicator that shifts over time with wide market daily, weekly, or monthly swings.

two-sided market: a market in which both the bid and asked sides are firm, such as that which a specialist and other who make a market are required to maintain. In such a market, both buyers and sellers are guaranteed of their ability to complete transactions. synonymous with *two-way market.*

two-way market: synonymous with *two-sided market.*

two-way trade: simultaneously selling out of one stock and purchasing another so that the investment dollars are not left idle.

type of option: in option transactions, indicating either a call option contract or a put option contract.

U

u: in newspaper reports of transactions, indicates that the intraday high is a new high for the last 52 weeks.

UCC: see *Uniform Commercial Code.*

U-5: a notification form completed by securities industry employers for notifying exchanges, the NASD and the states to terminate registration of agents, representatives, and principals no longer associated with them. see also *U-4.*

U-4: the application form for registering agents, representatives, and principals. Provides exchanges, the NASD, and states with data on the history of applicants for registration. see also *U-5.*

UCC: see *Uniform Commercial Code.*

UGMA: see *Uniform Gift to Minors Act.*

UIT: see *unit investment trust.*

ultimate beneficiary: a beneficiary of a trust who is entitled to receive the principal of the trust property in final distribution; synonymous with *principal beneficiary.* opposed to *income beneficiary.*

ultimo: the month prior to the existing one.

unaccrued: income resulting when payments are received but not yet due, as in the case of one receiving a rent payment before the due date.

unadjusted rate of return: an expression of the utility of a given project as the ratio of the increase in future average annual net income to the initial increase in needed investment.

unallotted balance of appropriation: an appropriation balance available for allotment.

unamortized bond discount: the portion of the original bond discount that has not been charged off against earnings.

unamortized discounts on bonds sold: that portion of the excess of the face value of bonds over the amount received from their sale which remains to be written off periodically over the life of the bonds.

unamortized discounts on investments (credit): that portion of the excess of the face value of securities over the amount paid for them which has not yet been written off.

unamortized premiums on bonds sold: an account which represents that portion of the excess of bond proceeds over par value and which remains to be amortized over the remaining life of such bonds.

unamortized premiums on investments: that portion of the excess of the amount paid for securities over their face value which has not yet been amortized.

unappropriated profits: that portion of a firm's profit which has not been paid out in dividends or allocated for any special purpose.

unappropriated retained earnings: see *retained earnings, unappropriated.*

unassented securities: those stocks or bonds which a corporation wishes to alter but which have not been approved of for change by the stockholders.

unauthorized growth: capital investment that grows at different rates in different areas of an economy.

unauthorized investment: a trust investment that is not authorized by the trust instrument; to be distinguished from a *nonlegal investment.*

uncalled capital: that portion of the issued share capital of a corporation which has not yet been called up.

uncertified shares: the ownership of fund shares credited to a stockholder's account without the issuance of stock certificates. see also *book shares.*

uncovered: a short option position where the writer does not hold an offsetting, hedged position in the underlying security. synonymous with *naked.*

uncovered call writer: a writer of a call stock option contract who does not hold a hedged position in the underlying security. cf. *covered call writer.*

uncovered writer: a writer of a stock option contract who does not own shares of the underlying stock. synonymous with *naked option writer.*

uncover the stops: depressing the price of a security to a point where many stop orders are created. synonymous with *gather in the stops.*

underbanked: a new issue underwriting, when the originating investment banker has trouble finding other companies to become members of the underwriting group, or syndicate.

underbooked: a new issue of securities during the preoffering registration period when brokers searching lists of potential buyers state a limited indication of interest.

undercapitalization: a condition where a firm does not have adequate capital to discharge its normal business activities. see also *capitalization, working capital.*

undercutting an offering: trying to sell securities at a price lower than the best prevailing offer.

underlying bond: see *bond, underlying.*

underlying company: synonymous with *subsidiary.*

underlying debt: in municipal bond purchases, the debt of government entities within the jurisdiction of larger government entities where the larger entity has partial credit responsibility.

underlying futures contract: a futures contract that underlies an option on that future.

underlying mortgage: a mortgage senior to a larger one (e.g., a building first mortgage of $100,000 that has a prior claim over a second one of $200,000).

underlying movement: synonymous with *primary movement.*

underlying security
(1) ***options:*** a stock subject to purchase upon exercise of the option.
(2) ***securities:*** common stock that underlies certain types of securities issued by a corporation. This stock must be delivered if a subscription warrant or subscription right has been exercised, should a convertible bond or preferred stock be converted into common shares, or when an incentive stock option is exercised.

underlying syndicate: the original members of the underwriters of a new issue of securities as distinguished from a distributing syndicate which can include some members of the underlying syndicate and also additional brokerage houses.

undermargined account: a margin account having dropped below margin requirements or minimum maintenance requirements. Consequently, the broker must make a margin call to his or her client.

under review: see *UR.*

under the rule: an action of selling or buying by stock exchange officers to complete a transaction entered into by a delinquent member of the exchange, who is charged with any difference in price that occurs.

undertone: the technical basis of the market—strong or weak.

undervalued: an investment situation occuring when a specific stock is depressed in its price and justifies a higher current market value and price/earnings ratio. cf. *overvalued.*

underweighting: de-emphasizing a particular industry in stock selection.

underwrite
(1) ***general:*** the designing, preparing, bringing forth, and guaranteeing the sale of a new issue of stock. see *investment banker, syndicate.*
(2) ***insurance:*** assuming risk in exchange for a premium.
(3) ***investments:*** assuming the risk of purchasing a new issue of securities from an issuing firm or government entity and later reselling them to the public, either through dealers or directly. see also *underwriter.*

underwriter
(1) ***general:*** an individual or organization that assumes a risk for a fee.
(2) ***insurance:*** a firm that assumes the cost risk of death, fire, theft, illness, etc., in exchange for payments.
(3) ***securities:*** an investment banker, acting alone or as part of an underwriting group or syndicate, agrees to buy a new issue of securities from an issuer and distribute it to investors, making a profit on the underwriting spread. see *underwriting spread.* cf. *sponsor.*

underwriter's spread: compensation to investment bankers for helping the firm issue securities; expressed as the difference between gross and net security sales as a percent of gross sales.

underwriting
(1) the assumption of a risk, particularly an investment or insurance risk. Insurance underwriting involves guaranteeing a cash payment. Investment underwriting involves guaranteeing the sale of a securities issue.
(2) the analysis of risk and the settling of an appropriate rate and term for a mortgage on a given property for given borrowers.

underwriting agreement: an agreement between a corporation issuing new securities to be sold to the public and the managing underwriter as agent for the underwriting group. synonymous with *purchase agreement, purchase contract.*

underwriting fee: a percentage of the spread that accrues only to members of the syndicate, in proportion to the amount of the issue underwritten.

underwriting group: a temporary association of investment bankers, formed by the originating investment banker in a new issue of securities. synonymous with *distributing syndicate, investment banking group, purchase group.* cf. *syndicate.* see also *underwriting syndicate.*

underwriting recapture: prohibited by the NASD, a broker-dealer who is a syndicate member or selling group who sells part of the underwriting to an institutional portfolio that it either manages or controls. Should the broker-dealer pass the securities to the institution at its cost, the institution recaptures the underwriting compensation by acquiring the securities below the public offering price.

underwriting spread: the dollar difference between proceeds from the actual issuer in the public offering and the public offering price.

underwriting syndicate: a combination of underwriters joined together in a joint venture to undertake the resale of securities which are to be purchased from the corporation issuing the securities (or from an intermediary). The syndicate operates under a contract setting out the terms of their responsibilities.

undigested securities: securities that are issued beyond the need for or ability of the public to absorb them. see *overissue.* cf. *float, oversubscribed.*

undiluted stock: securities not having undergone a reduction of earnings per share, as by the potential exchange of securities.

undisclosed earnings: synonymous with *equity earnings.*

undistributed profit: the profit of a partnership, syndicate, or joint venture prior to division among the individuals concerned.

undistributed profits tax: a tax designed to supplement the income tax. By holding profits in a corporation and not paying dividends, stockholders can delay the income tax that would personally be due if dividends were paid. Letting such earnings accrue, stockholders can get the earnings out by selling part of their stock and paying only a capital gains tax. Section 102 of the Internal Revenue Code imposes a heavy tax on earnings kept in a corporation without a good business reason.

undivided account: a type of municipal securities underwriting where each member of the syndicate has undivided selling and underwriting liability. synonymous with *Eastern account.* cf. *Western account.*

undivided interests: see *joint tenancy, tenancy by the entirety, tenancy in common.*

undivided profits: undistributed earnings available for dividends and for the writing off of bad debts or special losses.

undivided right: a part owner's right that cannot be excluded from the other owner's rights. This right exists in tenancy in common and in joint tenancy.

undo: to reverse a transaction.

undue influence: the influence that one person exerts over another person to the point where the latter is prevented from exercising his or her own free will.

unearned discount: interest received but not yet earned.

unearned income: income that has been collected in advance of the performance of a contract; income derived from investment dividends, property rentals, and other sources not involving the individual's personal efforts.

unearned increment: the increase in the value of property that can be attributed to changing social or economic conditions beyond the control of the title holder, as distinguished from an increase in value that can be attributed to the improvements made or additions made by the labor or investment of the title holder.

unearned interest: interest on a loan that has already been collected but has not yet been earned because the principal has not been outstanding long enough.

unencumbered property: real estate free and clear of any mortgages, liens, or debts of any type. see *perfect title.*

uneven lot: synonymous with *odd lot.*

uneven market: a market with widely fluctuating prices.

unexpired cost: any asset.

unfunded debt: any short-term or floating debt; any indebtedness not covered by a bond.

unfunded insurance trust: an insurance trust in which the premiums on the policies are to be paid by the insured or by some third person and not by the trustee.

unified bond: see *bond, consolidated.*

unified credit: the once-in-a-lifetime credit applied against an individual's gift or estate taxes.

Uniform Commercial Code (UCC): a set of statutes purporting to provide some consistency among states' commercial laws. It includes uniform laws dealing with bills of lading, negotiable instruments, sales, stock transfers, trust receipts, and warehouse receipts.

Uniform Gift to Minors Act (UGMA): a law adopted by most states establishing regulations for the distribution and administration of assets in the name of a child. The Act provides for a custodian of the assets, often the parents, but sometimes an independent trustee. Stocks are transferred to a UGMA account from a parent's account, which is usually taxed at higher rates.

uniform practice code: regulations of the National Association of Securities Dealers for the handling of over-the-counter securities transactions, such as delivery, settlement date, ex-dividend date, and other ex-dates. Arbitration of disputes are handled by the uniform practice committees.

uniform securities agent state law examination: a test prepared for potential registered representative in many states. Prospective representatives must also pass the General Securities Representative Examination administered by the National Association of Securities Dealers prior to be permitted to trade with customers.

unissued stock: a part of the authorized capital stock of a corporation that is not issued or outstanding. It is not part of the corporation's capital stock and receives no dividends, although it must be shown on the firm's balance sheet even though it is neither an asset nor a liability. see *when issued.*

unit

(1) securities sold as a package.

(2) a group of exchange specialists responsible for maintaining a fair market in a particular number of securities.

unitary investment fund: a mutual fund that does away with both directors and shareholder voting.

unitary tax: a state tax method that calculates a local company's tax as a percentage of its total, worldwide profits, not simply on the profits of the subsidiary situated within the state.

United States: see entries under *U.S.*

unit investment trust (UIT): an investment vehicle, registered with the SEC under the Investment Company Act of 1940, that buys a fixed portfolio of income-producing securities, such as corporate, municipal, or government bonds, mortgage-backed securities, or preferred stock. Unit holders receive an undivided interest in both the principal and the income portion of the portfolio in proportion to the amount of capital they have invested. see also *USIT.*

unit of trading: the lowest amount established by a stock exchange in which the market in a specific security may be made. see *odd lot, round lot.*

unitrust: synonymous with *unit trust.*

unit share investment trust: see *USIT.*

unit trust: an investment firm that has a fixed portfolio of securities, usually of a single type, such as municipal bonds, which are held to maturity. Each investor receives a share in the amount proportionate to his or her holding. synonymous with *fixed investment trust, fixed trust, participating investment trust, participating trust, unitrust.*

universal account: see *cash management account.*

universal life policies: a variation of whole life, appears to offer excellent interest rates on the savings portion; provides greater variation of premium payment and amount of insurance to meet changing needs. Premiums are put to work in money markets or other high-yielding investments. In addition, the policyholder is regularly notified about the gross rate of return on the investment, management costs, and other fees.

unleveraged program: a limited partnership that invests in real estate, gas and oil, equipment, or other property and whose use of borrowed funds to finance the acquisition of properties is 50 percent or less of the purchase price.

unlimited mortgage: any open-end mortgage; a mortgage not limited to a fixed amount.

unlimited tax bond: see *bond, unlimited tax.*

unlisted: synonymous with *over the counter.*

unlisted market: a market created by person-to-person transactions, usually between brokers, for stocks not listed on an organized stock exchange.

unlisted option: a stock option contract that is not issued by the OCC and not traded on an organized options exchange, but is instead negotiated between the purchaser and seller.

unlisted security: any security not admitted to trading privileges on an exchange.

unlisted trading privileges: on some exchanges a stock may be traded at the request of a member without any prior application by the company itself. The company has no agreement to conform with standards of the exchange. Companies admitted to unlisted trading privileges prior to enactment of the Securities Exchange Act of 1934 are not subject to the rules and regulations under that act. Today, admission of a stock to unlisted trading privileges requires SEC approval of an application filed by the exchange. The information in the application must be made available by the exchange to the public. No unlisted stocks are traded on the New York Stock Exchange. see *listed securities (stocks).*

unloading
(1) ***general:*** selling goods at a relatively low price.
(2) ***investments:*** the sale of stocks and commodities to avoid a loss during a period of a falling market. cf. *profit taking.*
(3) see also *dumping.*

unmarginable: that which cannot be used as margin for purchasing stocks.

unpaid dividend: a dividend declared but not yet distributed.

unparted bullion: bullion containing base metals in addition to the precious metal.

Unpd.: unpaid.

unrealized appreciation: synonymous with *unrealized profits.*

unrealized loss: the decrease in the market value of a stock from the price at which it was originally bought. It is a paper loss rather than a realized loss until sold.

unrealized profits: paper profits that are not actual until the firm's securities have been sold. synonymous with *unrealized appreciation.*

unrealized revenue: revenue that is attributed to a completed business transaction but accompanied by the receipt of a noncurrent asset (e.g., an installment sale).

unrecovered cost
(1) that portion of an original investment not amortized through depreciation or depletion.
(2) uninsured losses from extraordinary obsolescence, fire, theft, or market fluctuations.

unregistered stock: a security that is not tradable and not easily converted into a cash position. It is usually sold in private transactions that are exempt from the SEC registration requirements, often at a discounted price. synonymous with *letter stock.*

unreported earnings: synonymous with *equity earnings.*

unsecured: see *side collateral.*

unsecured bond: see *bond, unsecured.*

unsecured debt: a bond having no specific collateral backing. Only the good faith and credit rating of the issuer backs the bond.

unstable market: a market in which forces of disequilibrium are reinforced so that movements away from equilibrium are not reversible.

unsteady market: a market where prices fluctuate rapidly but no identifiable trend is noted.

unsubscribed shares: shares in a stock offering not sold by the underwriter to the public. Based on the type of offering, these shares are retained by the underwriter for later sale, or the risk of unsold shares may remain with the issuing company.

unvalued stock: stock having no par or stated value. The term is a misnomer since it must have value to be purchased and sold, but the unvalued reference is to the value at which the issuer of the stock carries it on the books; usually taxed as if it had a value of $100 par.

unwind: slang, disposing of stocks by selling or short covering.

unwind a trade: reversing a securities transaction with an offsetting transaction. see also *offset.*

UOT: see *unit of trading.*

up: slang, any potenial buyer.

UP: see *unrealized profits.*

up-and-out option: when an option holder has the right of selling a fixed number of shares at a fixed price for a fixed time. Should the underlying shares climb above a set price, the option is canceled. If the price goes up, the option is out.

update: an upward trend in stock prices.

upgrade: selling out lower quality stocks in a portfolio and replacing them with higher-rated, higher-quality stocks.

up reversal: see *reversal.*

upset price: the minimum price at which a seller of property will entertain a bid in an auction.

upside: an increase in stock prices.

upside breakeven: a maximum upside price a stock needs to increase before an investor realizes a profit.

upside/downside volume ratio: the total number of shares traded that advanced divided by those that decreased for a given trading period or on a moving average basis.

upside gap: the open space on a security chart when the highest price of one day is lower than the lowest price of the next day.

upside momentum: see *momentum.*

upside potential: the amount of upward price movement an investor or an analyst expects of a given stock, bond, or commodity.

upside trend: a period of prolonged increasing prices that last for several months.

upstairs market: transactions completed within the broker-dealer's house that bypass the stock exchange. SEC and exchange regulations ensure that such trades will not occur at prices less favorable to the client than those prevailing in the general market.

up tick: a transaction made at a price higher than the preceding transaction. A stock may be sold short only on an up tick (i.e., a transaction at the same price as the preceding trade but higher than the preceding different price.) synonymous with *plus tick.*

uptick/downtick block ratio: the number of NYSE blocks traded on upticks divided by downtick blocks. Traditionally, a reading above 1.00 indicates an overbought situation whil a reading below .40 illustrates an oversold situation.

up trend: a period when a stock's prevailing price direction is upward.

UR: under review. When one or more of the bond rating services continues to have the issue under review and withholds its bond rating.

US
(1) see *underlying security.*
(2) United States.
(3) see *unregistered stock.*

USBA: United States Bureau of Standards.

USC: United States Code.

USCC: United States Chamber of Commerce.

used mortgage: synonymous with *assumable mortgage.*

U.S. government securities: direct government obligations-debt issues of the U.S. government, such as Treasury bills, notes, savings bonds, bonds as distinguished from government-sponsored agency issues.

USIT: unit share investment trust. A specialized form of unit investment trust comprising one unit of PRIME and one unit of SCORE. see also *unit investment trust.*

U.S. rule: a method traditionally employed in first-mortgage real estate financing where payments are applied first to accrued interest and then to the reduction of principal.

U.S. Savings Bond: see *Bond, U.S. Savings.*

U.S. Treasury issues: see *treasuries.*

utility revenue bond: see *bond, utility revenue.*

UW: see *underwriter.*

V

valeurs: French for *securities.*

valid: that which is sufficient to satisfy the requirement of the law; a fact.

validation: proof or confirmation; an instrument or other evidence to confirm or give legal support to a claim or contract (e.g., factual data from an experiment).

valuation: the fixing of value to anything. synonymous with *appraising.*

value-added tax (VAT): a government tax on the value added; a tax on the selling price of manufactured items less the cost of the materials and expenses used in their production.

value asset: *per common share,* a company's net resources (after deduction of all liabilities, preferred stocks' liquidating value, and accrued dividends, if any), divided by the number of common shares outstanding; *per preferred share* (another way of showing asset coverage), a company's net resources (after deduction of all liabilities, any prior preferred stocks' liquidating value, and accrued dividends, if any), divided by the number of preferred shares outstanding.

value broker: a discount broker having rates that are based on a percentage of the dollar value for each transaction. For trades of low-priced shares or a small number of shares, placing an order with such a broker will result in lower commissions.

value change: a stock price change adjusted for the number of outstanding shares of that security, so that a group of securities adjusted in this fashion are equally weighted.

value compensated: describing a purchase or sale of foreign exchange to be executed by cable; the purchaser reimburses the seller for the earlier value of the data of actual payment abroad of the foreign currency, theoretically resulting in no loss of interest to either party.

value date
(1) ***general:*** the date on which a bank deposit becomes effective. The date is fixed based on the time required to collect a payment on the item deposited from another bank.
(2) ***investments:*** in the forward exchange market, the maturity date of the contract plus one business day for North American currencies, two business days for other currencies. On spot transactions involving North American currencies, the maturity date of the contract plus one business day and two business days for other currencies.

value fund: a mutual fund that invests primarily in securities having low price-earnings ratios.

Value Line Investment Survey: an investment advisory service that ranks hundreds of stocks for timeliness and safety. Ratings are: 1—highest, 2—above average, 3—average, 4—below average, 5—lowest.

value-oriented investing philosophy: see *Graham method.*

VA mortgage: a mortgage made in conformity with requirements of the Servicemen's Readjustment Act, and guaranteed to an amount specified in the act by the Veterans Administration.

"vanilla" transactions: where a company either sold pieces of itself as shares of stock or issued bonds to borrow money for up to 30 years at a set interest rate.

variability: the fluctuation in rates of return. These measurements frequently are used as proxies for risk management.

variable annuity: an annuity contract providing lifetime retirement payments that vary in amount with the results of investment in a separate account portfolio.

variable cost: a cost that is uniform per unit but changes in total in direct proportion to changes in the related total activity or volume.

variable hedging: see *ratio spreading.*

variable income stock: stock, usually common stock, whose dividend or yield is dependent upon the firm's skill in realizing a profit.

variable interest plus (VIP): an innovative certificate of deposit. First attempted by Western Savings Bank, the second largest in Philadelphia; under the plan, the interest rate on the six-month certificate would be tied to the prevailing rate at the weekly auction of six-month Treasury bills. The primary motivation behind this new variable interest-rate certificate was to stop the flow of funds out of the bank and into higher-yielding instruments, particularly money-market mutual funds. Under terms of the VIP, a depositor also could borrow as much as $9900 against the certificate at an interest rate of 1 percent above the weekly rate being earned. Bank regulators stopped this proposal in 1981.

variable interest rate U.S. Savings Bond: see *Bond, Savings (U.S.).*

variable life insurance: a relatively new form of coverage; the death benefit is based on the performance of the stock market, or more specifically, on the performance of stocks in the insurer's portfolio. The better the market performs over the life of the policy (i.e., a lifetime), the more cash the benefit will receive. If the market should collapse, a specified minimum death benefit will be paid nonetheless. A variable life insurance policy costs a little less than a standard whole life policy that pays dividends on its investments, but somewhat more than one that pays no dividends.

variable-rate CDs: introduced in 1975, a certificate of deposit with a normal minimum maturity of 360 days. The interest rate is pegged by an issuing bank at a specified spread over the bank's current rate on 90-day CDs and is adjusted every 90 days.

variable-rate certificate: a savings certificate on which the rate of interest payable varies, depending on the term for which the money is pledged. The interest rate is set by government regulatory agencies.

variable-rate demand note: a note representing borrowings that is payable on demand and bears interest tied to a money market rate, often the bank prime rate. The rate on the note is adjusted upward or downward each time the base rate changes.

variable-rate mortgage (VRM): a type of mortgage, initially available in California, and now authorized nationally, which permits the interest charges on the loan to rise or fall automatically in accordance with a predetermined index, for instance, an index of banks' cost-of-funds. The interest rate can fluctuate every six months, but cannot be raised by more than 2½ percentage points over the life of the mortgage. In addition, banks must offer customers a choice between variable-rate and conventional mortgages. see also *renegotiable-rate mortgage, Wachovia adjustable mortgage*.

variable-ratio plan: an investment plan under which funds are divided at a time considered normal into two equal parts: a stock fund to purchase diversified common stocks and a cash fund to be held in liquid form. When prices rise, shares are sold to maintain the ratio of the stock fund value and the cash fund, and vice versa when prices fall. This assumes fluctuations about normal which may be readjusted periodically to take a long-term trend into account.

variable ratio writing: synonymous with *ratio write*.

variable spread: a stock option spread technique involving the simultaneous purchase and sale of options on the same underlying stock where the number of contracts sold varies from the number of contracts bought. see also *ratio spreading*.

variance: a statistical measure of dispersion.

variation margin: additional margin needed on commodities resulting from variations in price.

VAT: see *value-added tax*.

VC: see *venture capital*.

VCF: see *venture capital funds.*

VD
(1) see *volume deleted.*
(2) see *volume discount.*

velocity shop: a mortgage lender technique to sell most of its mortgages it makes to secondary lending markets so that it can quickly get back funds to make even more mortgages.

venture capital
(1) funds invested in enterprises that do not usually have access to conventional sources of capital (banks, stock market, etc.).
(2) funds available from the issue of new stock.
(3) reinvested monies from stockholders.

venture capital funds: mutual funds invested in securities of firms that are little known and often not yet registered with the SEC.

venture capital limited partnership: an investment vehicle of a brokerage house or entrepreneurial firm for raising capital for start-up companies or those firms in the early process of developing products or services. Typically the partnership takes shares of stock in the company in return for capital given.

vertical line charting: technical charting where the high, low, and closing prices of a security of a market are presented on one vertical line with the closing price shown by a short horizontal mark. Each vertical line is for a different day, and the chart ultimately shows any trends over a period of time, from days to years.

vertical spread: a stock option spread technique involving the simultaneous purchase and sale of options on the same underlying stock having the same expiration months but different striking prices. synonymous with *price spread.*

vestal virgin: a term of the 1960s, referring to the favorite fifty variety of institutional darlings.

vested: giving the rights of absolute ownership, although enjoyment can be postponed.

vested estate: an interest in property holding present and future rights, but with the existing interest able to be transferred.

vested interest: an immediate, fixed interest in real or personal property although the right of possession and enjoyment may be postponed until some future date or until the happening of some event.

vested remainder: a fixed interest in real property, with the right of possession and enjoyment postponed until the termination of the prior estate; to be distinguished from a *contingent remainder.*

vested rights: provisions in a pension program ensuring that if a worker leaves the firm for any reason, he or she can retain the pension rights acquired while employed by the company offering the plan.

vesting: the right of an employee under a retirement plan to retain part or all of the annuities purchased by the employer's contributions on his or her behalf; or, in some plans, the right to receive a cash payment of equivalent value on termination of employment after certain qualifying conditions have been met.

Veterans Administration Mortgage Guarantees: home mortgage guarantees issued by the VA under the Servicemen's Readjustment Act, to eligible applicants for any of the following purposes: (1) the purchase or construction of an owner-occupied home by the veteran; (2) the construction of a farm residence on land owned by a veteran; (3) the repair, alteration, or improvement of an owner-occupied farm or home by the veteran. Interest is set by the Veterans Administration.

V formation: a technical chart forming a "V" shape. This pattern indicates that the stock, bond, or commodity being charted has bottomed out and is now in a rising trend. The upside-down "V" indicates a declining market.

VI
(1) see *vested interest.*
(2) in bankruptcy or receivership; being reorganized under the Bankruptcy Act; securities assumed by such companies (in bond and stock listings of newspapers).

VIP: see *variable interest plus.*

VL: see *Value Line Investment Survey.*

void: that which has no legal effect.

voidable contract: an agreement that can be rescinded by either of the parties in the event of fraud, incompetence, or other sufficient cause.

VOL: see *volume.*

volatile: a condition of the market, describing the size and frequency of fluctuations in the price of a given stock, bond, or commodity.

volatility: a measure of a stock's tendency to move up and down in price, based on its daily price history over the latest 12 months. Stocks with higher volatilities tend to exhibit greater price fluctuation than those with lower volatility values. A volatility of 20 percent would indicate the stock has, over the last 12 months of trading activity, fluctuated about 20 percent above and below the average price for that period.

volume: synonymous with *turnover.*

volume alert: the volume breakout occurring when a stock's volume or a market index volume exceeds it moving average for a given time period by a predetermined criteria.

volume deleted: a note appearing on the consolidated tape, frequently when the tape is running late by two or more minutes because of heavy volume, that only the stock symbol and the trading price will be displayed for transactions of less than 5000 shares.

volume discount: institutional organizations that invest heavily are often given a commission discount when the order is significant, that is, $500,000 or more.

volume of trading (or sales): represents a simple addition of successive futures transactions. It is the total of the sales (or of the purchases), and not of the sum of both.

voluntary accumulation plan: a plan subscribed to by mutual fund shareowners to accumulate shares in that fund on a regular basis over a stated time period. The amount of money placed into the fund and the intervals at which it is to be invested are at the discretion of the shareowner.

voluntary alienation: synonymous with *transfer of title.*

voluntary association: any membership organization not yet incorporated.

voluntary bankruptcy: see *bankruptcy.*

voluntary conveyance or deed: the instrument of transfer of an owner's title to property to the lien holder. Usually such conveyance serves to bypass a legal situation of a court judgment showing insufficient security to satisfy a debt, and occurs without transfer of a valuable consideration.

voluntary plan: a type of accumulation plan for investment on a regular basis but without any total time period or ultimate investment amount specified. The sales charge is applicable individually to each purchase made.

voluntary trust: established by a deed of transfer of certain property made voluntarily by an individual or other legal entity to a trustee for a specified purpose.

voluntary underwriter: a person, partnership, or corporation that purchases a security from the issuer or an affiliated person and offers the security for public sale under an effective registration statement.

voting right (stock): the stockholder's right to vote his or her stock in the affairs of the company. Most common shares have one vote each. Preferred stock usually carries the right to vote when preferred dividends are in default for a specified period. The right to vote is usually delegated by proxy of the stockholder to another person.

voting trust: an agreement whereby stockholders turn over their voting rights to a small group of people, who are called voting trustees.

voting trust certificate: the receipt for common stock deposited with a trustee in a voting trust. It carries all rights granted except the voting right.

VR: see *vested rights.*

VRM: see *variable-rate mortgage.*

VT: see *voting trust.*

VTC: see *voting trust certificate.*

vulture funds: dollars pooled by investors in search of empty office buildings, apartment complexes, and tracts of land that can be picked up at bargain-basement prices. synonymous with *funds to acquire underperforming properties.*

W

WA: see *Williams Act.*

Wachovia adjustable mortgage: a recent approach in mortgage lending, developed by this North Carolina bank. For example, a customer buys a home with a 30-year adjustable mortgage. The initial mortgage rate is tied to money market and local market rates. The interest rate is adjusted every quarter in line with bill rates. The monthly payment stays the same for five years, but the new rate determines how much will go for interest and how much for principal. Every five years the monthly payment is adjusted—up or down by up to 25 percent—so the loan will be paid off on time. After 25 years the monthly payment can be adjusted by more than 25 percent if there is a danger the loan will not be paid off on time. If after 30 years the loan has not been paid off, the borrower may refinance. see *renegotiable-rate mortgage. variable-rate mortgage.*

waiting period.

(1) ***general:*** the time between filing a claim for unemployment benefits or workmen's compensation and the beginning of such benefit payments.

(2) ***investments:*** the time, usually 20 days, that must pass between the application for listing a new security from the SEC and the date when the securities can be offered to the public.

waiver of premium: nearly all life insurance companies will add to their contracts, upon payment of a small additional premium, a clause providing that if the insured becomes totally and permanently disabled, his or her insurance policy will be continued in full force and the company will exempt the insured from paying further premiums during disability.

wallflower: a stock that falls out of favor with investors.

wallpaper
(1) slang, counterfeit paper currency.
(2) worthless stock or bond certificates.

Wall Street: the popular name for the New York City business and financial district.

Wall Street Journal: one of America's leading newspapers, noted for its coverage of financial, corporate, and market news.

wanted for cash: appearing on the ticker tape showing that an individual is interested in purchasing a given quantity of shares designated and will pay for them the same day.

war babies (brides): securities of corporations involved in manufacturing materials for the U.S. Department of Defense.

Warr.: see *warrant.*

warrant
(1) ***investments:*** a certificate giving the holder the right to purchase securities at a stipulated price within a specified time limit or at any time. Sometimes offered with securities as an inducement to buy.
(2) ***law:*** a written order in the name of the state and signed by a magistrate directing an officer to make an arrest.

warrants payable: the amount of warrants out and unpaid.

warrant value: the theoretical value of a warrant derived at by subtracting the exercise price from the market price of the common stock and multiplying the sum by the number of shares that can be bought with each warrant.

wash sale: a false transaction of security or commodity sales that are purchased and sold by the same individual so as to create the impression of activity and/or volume of the item.

wasting asset
(1) an asset whose value is depleted and will eventually be exhausted by the continued operations of an extractive business (oil wells, mining claims, etc.). see *depletion allowance.*
(2) a security with a value that expires at a specific time in the future.

wasting trust: a trust of property that is gradually being consumed.

watch filing: a procedure by which losses on small risks are referred to the underwriter for his or her attention.

watch list: a list of stocks singled out for careful monitoring by a brokerage house, exchange or self-regulatory organization to spot irregularities.

watch (watching) my number: the request by a broker on an exchange floor to another broker to watch for the firm's broker's assigned number on the annunciator board should he or she be off the floor. If a broker's number is flashed on the board, it means that he or she is requested to go to his or her firm's booth on the edge of the floor.

watered capital: see *watered stock.*

watered stock: corporate stock issued by a corporation for property at an overvaluation, or stock released for which the corporation receives nothing in payment.

WCA: working-capital account. see *Cash Management Account.*

WD: see *when distributed.*

weak: a condition of declining prices for securities or commodities.

weak hands: see *strong (or weak) hands.*

weak holdings: stocks retained on margin by speculators who will use any reason to sell them.

weak market: a situation characterized by a greater demand for selling than for purchasing.

wedge: a technical chart trend where two converging lines connect a series of peaks and troughs forming a wedge. Declining wedges are temporary interruptions of upward price rallies; rising wedges as interruptions of a falling price trend.

weekly sheets: lists released by the National Quotation Bureau giving market-makers and price quotations on over-the-counter stocks. see *pink sheets, white sheets, yellow sheets.*

week order: on the stock exchange, an order to buy or sell which automatically expires if it cannot be executed during the coming week.

weighted average cost of capital: the overall required rate of return the firm must pay to raise long-term capital from a composite of capital sources.

weighting: the specification of the relative importance of items that are combined. For example, stocks included in indexes may be equally weighted or weighted according to value.

wellhead price: the price paid for gas produced and sold from a lease.

wellhead tax: a government proposal to tax domestic oil as it leaves the well; the amount of the tax is the difference between its current controlled price and the world market price imposed by the OPEC cartel.

went to the wall: any bankrupt or failing corporation or individual.

we offer retail (WOR): at a net price to the buyer because all transaction costs are to be carried by the seller.

Western account: a syndication technique where each member of the underwriting syndicate is responsible only for its own allocation and not for any other member. synonymous with *divided account.* cf. *undivided account.*

W formation: a technical chart trend of the price of a stock, bond, or commodity showing that the price has reached a support level, two times and is moving higher. The reverse "W" indicates that the price has reached a resistance level and is headed down. see *double bottom.*

when, as, and if issued (WI): see *when issued.*

when distributed (WD): trading of a new security that is distributed subject to approval by shareholders.

when issued (WI): a short form of *when, as, and if issued.* The term indicates a conditional transaction in a security authorized for issuance but not yet actually issued. All when-issued transactions are on a conditional basis, to be settled if and when the actual security is issued and the exchange or National Association of Securities Dealers rules that the transactions are to be settled.

when-issued basis (WIB): quotations for securities that are traded before they are actually issued. The sources of this type of stock vary but usually result from corporate reorganizations, mergers, rights financing, and stock splits.

whipsawed: to have experienced a substantial loss at both ends of a securities transaction.

white elephant: property that is so costly to maintain that it is virtually impossible to operate it at a profit; also property with respect to which a loss is certain.

white knight: in order to encourage a successful company takeover by another firm, a friendly suitor is brought in to put down another bidder. cf. *gray knight, white squire.*

white sheets: the daily list released by the National Quotation Bureau that provides market-makers and price quotations for regional over-the-counter stocks traded in Chicago, Los Angeles, and San Francisco. cf. *pink sheets, yellow sheets.*

white squire: a risky antitakeover tactic calling for a takeover target to place a large block of its stock with a friendly investor, to insulate itself from a hostile attack. cf. *white knight.*

White's Rating: White's Tax-Exempt Bond Rating Service's categorization of municipal securities.

whole coverage: any type of insurance that provides for payment from all losses without any deductions.

whole life insurance: synonymous with *ordinary life.* see also *term rider.*

whole loan: in secondary mortgage markets, distinguishes an investment representing an original residential mortgage loan from a loan representing a participation with one or more lenders or a pass-through security representing a pool of mortgages.

wholesale market: synonymous with *inside market.*

wholesaler

(1) ***general:*** a middleman or distributor who sells primarily to retailers and other merchants. synonymous with *distributor.*

(2) ***securities:*** an investment banker serving as an underwriter in a new issue or as a distributor in a secondary offering of securities.

(3) ***investments:*** a sponsor of a mutual fund.

(4) ***investments:*** a broker-dealer who trades with other broker-dealers instead of with the retail investor, receiving discounts and selling commissions.

WI: see *when issued* (in stock listings of newspapers).

WIB: see *when-issued basis.*

wide market

(1) quotations are relatively far apart.

(2) a market where there are a relatively large number of investors.

wide opening: a securities situation characterized by a considerable difference in the bid and asked prices at the beginning of the market day.

widow-and-orphan stock: a high-income, noncyclical stock with security but which is in other ways unrewarding—that is, a slow market mover.

wild card: an investment instrument, especially a certificate of deposit or a savings certificate, that is legally permitted to carry the highest interest rate or sometimes no limit on the rate of the yield.

wildcat drilling: exploring for gas or oil in an unproven area.

wildcat scheme: a highly speculative venture with few signs for success.

will: a document in which an individual (the testator or testatrix) having full mental faculties sets forth his or her desires and bequests regarding the disposition of his total wealth after his death.

Williams Act: federal legislation of 1968, requiring that tender offers be made to all securities holders at the same price. see *Saturday night special.* see also *blank-check tactic.*

Wilshire index: an indicator covering 5000 securities, including a cross section of the over-the-counter market, giving more of a reflection of what the small firms are doing.

windfall: an unplanned, unexpected gain. A sudden price appreciation resulting from an unusual occurence, such as a takeover announcement.

widget

(1) a plastic tube for holding messages and other information that is moved around the NYSE floor by a system of pneumatic tubes.

(2) slang, any item manufactured by a hypothecial firm (i.e., "the XYZ company makes widgets").

windfall profit: an unexpected profit arising from causes not controlled by the recipient.

windfall profits tax: federal legislation passed in 1980; a tax designed to divert from the oil industry to the government a share of profits attributable to the president's decision to phase out price controls, earmarking the money for a variety of energy-producing and energy-saving programs. The Crude Oil Windfall Profits Tax Act increased the dividend exclusion to $200 for single taxpayers and $400 for married taxpayers and $400 for married taxpayers filing separately, and broadened exclusion to cover interest. But neither change was effective for 1980 returns. The Act also increased the renewable-source energy credit to $4000 from $2200.

winding up: the process of liquidating a company.

window

(1) the limited time when an opportunity should be moved on, or it will be lost.

(2) the cashier department of a brokerage house, where delivery and settlement of securities transactions occur.

(3) the discount window of a Federal Reserve bank.

window dressing

(1) trading activity towards the end of a quarter or fiscal year that is intended to dress up a portfolio for presentation to customers and/or shareowners.

(2) an accounting strategy for making a financial statement appear to have a more favorable condition than it deserves. May or may not be construed as fraudulent.

window settlement: the physical delivery against settlement of securities with the contra broker of the trade.

winning bid: the successful bid for a particular securities issue. This will generally be the bid that produces the lowest interest cost to a municipal borrower or the one offering the highest premium in the event of a single coupon bid.

wiped out

(1) ***general:*** the failing of a business.

(2) ***investments:*** when all available margin and cash are exhausted.

(3) ***investments:*** a considerable, irreversible investment loss.

wire and order: synonymous with *wire room.*

wire house: a member firm of an exchange maintaining a communications network either linking its own branch offices to offices of correspondent firms, or linking some combination of such offices.

wire room: the operating department of a brokerage house that receives clients' orders from the registered representative and transmits vital information to the exchange floor, where a floor ticket is prepared, or to the house's trading department for execution. synonymous with *order department, order room, wire and order.*

witching hour: see *double witching hour, triple witching hour.*

withdrawal plan: an arrangement provided by certain open-end companies by which an investor can receive monthly or quarterly payments in a designated amount that may be more or less than actual investment income.

withholding: any violation of the rules of fair practice of the National Association of Securities Dealers when a participant in a public offering fails to make a bona fide public offering at the public offering price, so as to profit from the higher market price of a hot issue.

withholding tax: federal, state, or city taxes withheld by employers from the salaries of employees and paid directly to the taxing agency.

withholding tax at the source: of domestic issuers, a requirement that they withhold a portion of dividends and interest from nonresident aliens for foreign corporations for payment as U.S. tax on these distributions.

with interest: an indication in bond transactions that the buyer must pay to the seller all accrued interest from the last interest payment date up to but not including the settlement date.

with or without: the instruction on an odd-lot limit order—use an effective sale in the round-lot market or the quote for the stock, whichever comes first, for making the transaction. The price to the client must conform to the client's limit.

without an offer: used for completing a one-side quote; for example, a dealer quotes a security as 10 bid without an offer to suggest that the dealer is willing to purchase the security at 10, but is unwilling to sell, either because the dealer does not posses the security or is unwilling to sell short.

without dividend: see *ex-dividend.*

without interest: securities and other debt instruments in default sell on a flat or without interest basis where a purchaser does not make an additional payment for the accrued interest. Income bonds, although not in default, since the interest is not required to be paid unless earned, sell on a flat or without interest basis.

without warrants: see *XW.*

with warrants: see *WW.*

wolf: an experienced and often crafty speculator.

wooden ticket: the unethical practice of confirming the execution of an order to a client without actually doing so.

WOR: see *we offer retail.*

worked off: a minute drop in the price of a security or commodity.

working asset: those assets invested in securities that can be expected to fluctuate more or less with common stock prices generally. Corrections may be made to eliminate an investment company's holdings of cash and high-grade senior securities and to give weight to holdings of junior issues.

working capital: the excess of current assets over current liabilities representing the capital immediately available for the continued operation of a business. synonymous with *floating capital.*

working-capital account (WCA): see *cash management account.*

working capital fund: see *intragovernmental service fund.*

working control: theoretically, ownership of 51 percent of a company's voting stock is necessary to exercise control. In practice—and this is particularly true in the case of a large corporation—effective (i.e., working) control sometimes can be exerted through ownership, individually or by a group acting in concert, of less than 50 percent of the stock.

working interest: an interest in a well entailing bearing the costs of development and operation. see *operating interest.*

workout market: the price stated for a stock that is not firm but rather the best estimate when given.

world reserve: in an auction, a minimum price that a consignor may set for an entire collection, giving the auctioneer leeway on individual items. Hence, if one item attracts a winning bid above the amount needed to meet the reserve, that overage or surplus, can be applied to another item, allowing it to be sold for less.

worth: the total value of something, including an investment in a business. see *net worth.*

wounded: see *shark.*

WOW: written order of withdrawal.

WP: see *windfall profit.*

WPT: see *windfall profits tax.*

wraparound annuities: tax-deferral schemes allowing an individual to shelter current interest income on a bank savings certificate or shares in a mutual fund in a tax-deferred annuity administered by an insurance company.

wraparound mortgages: involves two lenders, a mortgage originator and a wraparound lender. Rather than providing an entirely new mortgage at current market rates to a home buyer, the wraparound lender agrees to continue to pay the monthly installments on the existing mortgage on the home to be bought, at the original contract interest rate of the mortgage, and also to make any additional payments needed to meet the purchase price of the home. As a result, the terms of the original mortgage continue to be satisfied, the seller is compensated for the sale of his or her investment, and the home buyer is able to purchase a home and share in the benefits of the below-market rate paid by the wraparound lender on a portion of the money financed.

wrinkle: any imaginative characteristic that can attract a purchaser for a security.

write: in option trading, to sell a call or put by supplying it to its purchaser for a premium.

write-down: the book value to which an asset has been reduced to adjust for the capital that has been lost on the decline of the asset's value.

write-off: an asset that has been determined to be uncollectible and therefore has been charged off as a loss. Sometimes it is the debt itself. cf. *written-down value.*

write out: when a specialist chooses, within exchange regulations, to trade with an order that is on his or her book. The specialist must summon the broker who has entered the order, who then writes the order, with the specialist as the other side of the trade, allowing the broker to earn the commission for the completed trade.

writer: a seller of a stock option contract with an obligation to purchase or sell shares of the underlying stock at a preset price within a given period of time. synonymous with *option writer.*

write-up: an increase in an asset's book value not resulting from added costs or an adjustment of an asset account to correspond to an appraisal value.

writing cash-secured puts: an option technique where a trader wishing to sell put options uses, to avoid having to establish a margin account. Instead of depositing margin with a broker, a put write deposits cash equal to the option exercise price. Using this strategy, the put option writer is not subject to further margin requirements in the event of changes in the underlying stock's price, and may be earning money by investing the premium he or she receives in money market instruments.

writing naked: an option seller technique where the trader does not own the underlying stock. May lead to significant profits should the stock move in the hoped-for direction and significant losses should the stock move in the other direction since the trader will then have to go into the marketplace to purchase the stock in order to deliver it to the option buyer.

writing puts to acquire stock: a technique used by an option writer who expects the security will drop in value and that its purchase at a stated price would represent a sound investment. By writing a put option exercisable at that price the writer cannot lose. Should the security, contrary to his or her expectation, go up, the option will not be exercised and he or she is at least ahead of the amount of the premium received. Should the stock go down and the option is exercised, the purchaser has the stock at what had previously been thought of as a sound buy, and the purchaser also has the premium income.

written-down value: an accounting term for the valuation or cost of any asset minus the written-off depreciation. cf. *write-off.*

written off: see *write-off.*

Ws.: warrants, see *warrant.*

WS
(1) see *Wall Street.*
(2) see *watered stock.*

WSJ: see *Wall Street Journal.*

WT
(1) see *warrant.*
(2) see *wellhead tax.*

W/Tax: see withholding tax.

WW: with warrants. Offered to the buyer of a given stock or bond. cf. *XW.*

X

X
(1) see *ex-dividend* (of stock trading).
(2) see *ex-interest* (of bond trading).

X-C: see *ex-coupon*.

XCH: exclearing house. Any transaction between broker-dealers to be completed outside the regular clearing facilities.

X-Ch.: see *exchange*.

XD: see *ex-dividend* (in stock listings of newspapers).

X-Dis: ex-distribution, denoting that the purchaser of a given security is not entitled to the distribution of a stock dividend.

X-Div.: see *ex-dividend.*

xenocurrency: currency circulating or traded in money markets of nations outside its country of issue.

X-I: see *ex-interest*.

X-In.: see *ex-interest*.

XR: see *ex-rights* (in stock listings of newspapers).

XW
(1) see *ex-warrants* (in bond and stock listings of newspapers).
(2) without warrants. Offered to the purchaser of a given security or bond. cf. *WW*.

X-Warr.: see *ex-warrants*.

XX: without securities or warrants.

Y

Y: ex-dividend and sales in full (in stock listings of newspapers).

Yankee bond market: issues floated in the United States, in dollars, by reign governments and corporations.

Yankees: American securities on the London Stock Exchange.

year-end dividend: a special or added-on dividend declared by the board of directors of a corporation at the end of the firm's fiscal year.

Yellow Book: the British Stock Exchange's listing of requirements for a London stock market quotation.

yellow knight: the merger discussion of two firms, where initially one attempts to takeover the other. cf. *gray knight, white knight*.

yellow sheets: a daily publication of the National Quotation Bureau detailing the bid and asked prices and firms that make a market in corporate bonds traded in the over-the-counter market. cf. *pink sheets, white sheets*.

yield (YLD)

(1) ***general:*** the profit or income created through an investment in property.

(2) ***investments:*** the rate of return received from one's investment in a specific security or a specific piece of property: most commonly expressed in terms that designate the annual rate of return on the investment. synonymous with *return*. see also *return on investment*.

(3) ***bonds:*** the coupon rate of interest divided by the purchase price.

(4) ***bonds:*** the rate of return on a bond, taking into account the total of yearly interest payments, the purchase price, the redemption value, and the amount of time remaining until maturity.

(5) ***securities:*** the percentage rate of return paid on a common stock or preferred stock in dividends.

(6) ***lending:*** the total money earned on a loan.

yield advantage: the extra amount of return an investor earns should he or she buy a convertible security instead of the common stock of the same issuing corporation.

yield curve: a graph indicating the term structure of interest rates by plotting the yields of all bonds of the same quality with maturities ranging from the shortest to the longest available.

yield equivalence: the rate of interest at which a tax-exempt bond and a taxable security of similar quality provide the same return.

yield maintenance: the adjustment upon delivery of the price of a GNMA or other mortgage security purchased under a futures contract or standby commitment to provide the same yield to the purchaser as that which was specified in the original agreement.

yield spread: the difference in yields on varying stocks. A concept utilized by portfolio managers.

yield test: a measurement applied to bond investments in insurance firm portfolios. It is the relationship of the yield of bonds the insurance firm has in its portfolio individually to the yield of fully taxable U.S. government bonds of the same maturity.

yield to adjusted minimum maturity: a measure designed to give the yield to the shortest possible life of a bond.

yield to average life: the yield derived when the average maturity of a bond is substituted for the final maturity date of the issue.

yield to call: measures the return on a bond investment an individual would receive stated as an average yearly return from purchase date to call date.

yield to crash: see *yield to adjusted minimum maturity.*

yield to lessor: the internal rate of return generated from a lease transaction alone.

yield to maturity (YTM): the rate of return on an investment when it is retained until maturity, given as a percentage.

yield to put: the return a bond earns assuming that it is retained until a certain date and put (sold) to the issuing company at a specific price (the put price).

yield to worst: see *yield to adjusted minimum maturity.*

YLD: see *yield* (in stock listings of newspapers).

yo-yo option: a stock appreciation feature of a firm's option plans, where the executive's option price is lowered $1 every time the company's stock price goes up $1.

yo-yo stocks: highly volatile securities; these stocks are high-priced specialty issues that fluctuate greatly in price.

Yr.: *year.*

YS: see *yield spread.*

YTB: yield to broker.

YTC: see *yield to call.*

YTM: see *yield to maturity.*

YYS: see *yo-yo stocks.*

Z

Z
(1) zero.
(2) in stock tables next to the volume figure, indicating the total volume that should not be multiplied by 100.
(3) in the report of closing mutual fund prices in the newspaper should the fund not supply the bid-offer prices by publication time.

ZBA: see *zero bracket amount.*

ZBB: see *zero-base(d) budgeting.*

Z certificate: a certificate issued by the Bank of England to discount houses in lieu of stock certificates to facilitate their dealings in short-dated gilt-edged securities.

zerial: a serial form for zero-coupon bonds giving investors a choice of maturity dates. see *bond, zero-coupon.*

zero-base(d) budgeting (ZBB)
(1) ***general:*** a financial management technique to redirect funds from lower-priority current programs to higher ones, to pinpoint opportunities for improved efficiency and effectiveness, to reduce budgets while raising operating performance, and to improve profitability.
(2) ***government:*** the approach of justifying the budget and its program for each year or two, instead of studying funding increases or decreases in the programs separately as the need arises.

zero basis: the condition occurring when a convertible bond is valued so highly by investors that they buy it at a premium high enough that interest received is canceled out by the premium paid to purchase the bond. The bond is said to be trading on a *zero basis.*

zero bracket amount: the standard amount of income free from tax depending on a taxpayer's filing status. The tax tables already incorporate these amounts into their figures.

zero coupon: a debt security issued at a discount from its face value, that matures at face value in more than one year, and promises no other cash flow than the payment of the face value at maturity. The security can be redeemable prior to maturity, depending on the indenture. Usually zero coupon corporate bonds are purchased by investors only in tax-sheltered accounts.

zero-coupon bond: see *bond, zero-coupon.*

zero-coupon Eurobonds: American company issues that pay no interest but are sold at a steep discount.

zero-coupon security (ZR): a security making no periodic interest payment but instead is sold at a deep discount from its face value. The purchaser of this bond receives the rate of return by the gradual appreciation of the security, which is redeemed at face value on a given maturity date. see also *bond, zero-coupon.*

zero downtick: synonymous with *zero-minus tick.*

zero-minus (plus) tick: any sale that takes place at the same price of the previous sale, but at a price that is lower (higher) than the earlier, different price. see *up tick.* synonymous with *zero downtick.*

zero plus tick: synonymous with *zero uptick.*

zero-rate and low-rate mortgage: a home mortgage appearing to be completely or almost interest free. Requires a large down payment and one time finance charge, then the loan is repaid in fixed monthly payments over a short term.

zero uptick: the selling price that is the same as the last previous different price, which is higher than the earlier different price. synonymous with *zero plus tick.* cf. *down tick, up tick, zero minus tick.*

zeta: a credit scoring model developed at Wood, Struthers and Winthrop that examines seven financial variables or ratios, weighs the importance of each one and sums the weighted values. The resulting index is the zeta score which is calculated for over 1600 industrial companies.

ZR: see *zero-coupon security* (in bond listings of newspapers).